Practicing Texas Politics

2013–2014 Edition

LYLE C. BROWN

Baylor University

JOYCE A. LANGENEGGER

Blinn College-Bryan Campus

SONIA R. GARCÍA

St. Mary's University

TED A. LEWIS

Lone Star College-CyFair and Pellissippi State Community College

ROBERT E. BILES

Sam Houston State University

WADSWORTH
CENGAGE Learning

Australia • Brazil • Japan • Korea • Mexico • Singapore • Spain • U United Kingdom • United States

WADSWORTH
CENGAGE Learning™

Practicing Texas Politics, 2013–2014 Edition
Lyle C. Brown, Joyce A. Langenegger,
Sonia R. García, Ted A. Lewis, Robert E. Biles

Publisher: Suzanne Jeans

Executive Editor: Carolyn Merrill

Development Editor: Lauren Athmer, LEAP
    Publishing Services, Inc.

Assistant Editor: Scott Greenan

Editorial Assistant: Eireann Aspell

Media Editor: Laura Hildebrand

Brand Manager: Lydia LeStar

Content Project Manager: Alison Eigel Zade

Senior Art Director: Linda May

Rights Acquisition Specialist: Jennifer Meyer-Dare

Manufacturing Planner: Fola Orekoya

Production Service/Compositor: Cenveo
Publisher Services

Text Designer: Rokusek Design

Cover Designer: Rokusek Design

Cover Image: © Shutterstock

For product information and technology assistance, contact us at
Cengage Learning Customer & Sales Support, 1-800-354-9706

For permission to use material from this text or product,
submit all requests online at **www.cengage.com/permissions**.
Further permissions questions can be emailed to
permissionrequest@cengage.com.

Library of Congress Control Number: 2010940437

Student Edition:
ISBN 13: 978-1-133-94049-4
ISBN 10: 1-133-94049-8

Wadsworth
20 Channel Center Street
Boston MA 02210
USA

Cengage Learning is a leading provider of customized learning solutions with office locations around the globe, including Singapore, the United Kingdom, Australia, Mexico, Brazil and Japan. Locate your local office at **http://international.cengage.com/region**

Cengage Learning products are represented in Canada by Nelson Education, Ltd.

For your course and learning solutions, visit **www.cengage.com**.

Purchase any of our products at your local college store
or at our preferred online store **www.cengagebrain.com**.

Instructors: Please visit **login.cengage.com** and log in to access instructor-specific resources.

Printed in Canada
3 4 5 6 7 16 15 14

Contents

PREFACE XV

. . . .

1   The Environment of Texas Politics   1

Political Behavior Patterns   2
Government, Politics, and Public Policy   2
Points to Ponder   3
Political Culture   4
Texas Political Culture   5
Learning Check 1.1   8
The Land   8
How Do We Compare...in Area?   8
The Politics of Geography   9
Points to Ponder   9
Points to Ponder   11
Economic Geography   12
Learning Check 1.2   15
The People   15
How Do We Compare...in Population?   16
Demographic Features   16
Racial/Ethnic Groups   18
Learning Check 1.3   23
Searching for New Economic Directions   23
Energy   24
CourseReader Assignments   24
High Technology   25
Biotechnology   26
Services   26
Agriculture   27
Trade   28
Learning Check 1.4   29
Meeting New Challenges: Social and Economic Policy Issues 30
Immigration: Federal and State Problems   30
Students in Action   32
Water   33

Point/Counterpoint...Should Oil and Gas Drillers Use
    Hydraulic "Fracking"?   **34**
Environmental Protection   35
Education and Economic Development   36
Points to Ponder   **36**
Poverty and Social Problems   37
Learning Check 1.5   **37**

Conclusion   **38**
CHAPTER SUMMARY   38
KEY TERMS   39
LEARNING CHECK ANSWERS   39
DISCUSSION QUESTIONS   40
INTERNET RESOURCES   40
NOTES   40

Selected Reading   **46**
Minorities Drove Texas Growth, Census Figures Show
Ross Ramsey/Matt Stiles/Julián Aguilar/Ryan Murphy

2   Federalism and the Texas Constitution   **48**

The American Federal Structure   **49**
Distribution of Powers   49
Students in Action   **52**
Interstate Relations and State Immunity   53
State Powers   54
Federal-State Relations: An Evolving Process   56
Learning Check 2.1   **59**

The Texas Constitution: Politics of Policymaking   **59**
Historical Developments   59
How Do We Compare...in State Constitutions?   **60**
CourseReader Assignments   **61**
Today: After More Than a Century of Usage   65
How Do We Compare...in State Constitutional Amendments?   **67**
Learning Check 2.2   **67**

Constitutional Amendments and Revision   **68**
Points to Ponder   **69**
Points to Ponder   **71**
Constitutional Revision   71
More Revision Attempts   73
**Point/Counterpoint...Should the Texas Constitution
    Be Rewritten?**   **74**
Piecemeal Revision   74
Learning Check 2.3   **75**

The Texas Constitution: A Summary — 75

The Bill of Rights — 76
The Powers of Government and Separation of Powers — 78
Suffrage — 79
Local Governments — 79
Other Articles — 80
Learning Check 2.4 — **80**

Conclusion — 80

CHAPTER SUMMARY — 81
KEY TERMS — 81
LEARNING CHECK ANSWERS — 82
DISCUSSION QUESTIONS — 82
INTERNET RESOURCES — 82
NOTES — 83

Selected Reading — 86

The American Tradition of Language Rights: The Forgotten
Right to Government in a "Known Tongue"
José Roberto Juárez Jr.

....

3   Local Governments — 90

Local Politics in Context — 91

Local Governments and Federalism — 92
Grassroots Challenges — 92
**How Do We Compare...in Employees and Spending
at State and Local Levels?** — **93**
Learning Check 3.1 — **94**

Municipal Governments — 94

Legal Status of Municipalities — 94
Forms of Municipal Government — 95
Learning Check 3.2 — **100**
Municipal Politics — 100
Points to Ponder — **101**
**Point/Counterpoint...Should Term Limits Be Instituted
for City Council Members and the Mayor?** — **103**
Municipal Services — 104
Students in Action — **105**
Municipal Government Revenue — 106
Generating Revenue for Economic Development — 108
**How Do We Compare...in Funding Services at State
and Local Levels?** — **109**
Learning Check 3.3 — **109**

Counties — 110

Structure and Operation — 110

County Finance   115
County Government Reform   117
Border Counties   117
Learning Check 3.4   **118**

Special Districts   119

Public School Districts   119
Junior or Community College Districts   120
Points to Ponder   **122**
Noneducation Special Districts   122
Learning Check 3.5   **123**

Metropolitan Areas   123

Councils of Governments   124
Municipal Annexation   125
CourseReader Assignments   **125**
Learning Check 3.6   **126**

Conclusion   126

CHAPTER SUMMARY   126
KEY TERMS   128
LEARNING CHECK ANSWERS   128
DISCUSSION QUESTIONS   129
INTERNET RESOURCES   129
NOTES   130

Selected Reading   **132**
Laredo's Modest Advocate
Robert Green

....

4   Political Parties   133

Party Structure   134

Temporary Party Organization   136
Selection of National Convention Delegates   139
Permanent Party Organization   140
Learning Check 4.1   **142**

Political Ideology   142

Conservatism   143
Liberalism   144
Learning Check 4.2   **144**

An Overview of Texas Political History   145

1840s to 1870s: The Origin of the Party System   145
Point/Counterpoint...Positions of the Two Major
    Parties on Key Issues   **146**
1870s to 1970s: A One-Party Dominant System   148
1970s to 1990s: An Emerging Two-Party System   149

Points to Ponder — 150
2000 to 2012: Republican Dominance — 151
Students in Action — 151
Learning Check 4.3 — 156

Electoral Trends — 156
Third Parties — 157
CourseReader Assignments — 158
Independents — 159
How Do We Compare…Which Party Controls the Statehouses in 2012? — 160
Points to Ponder — 161
Learning Check 4.4 — 161

Conclusion — 162
CHAPTER SUMMARY — 162
KEY TERMS — 163
LEARNING CHECK ANSWERS — 163
DISCUSSION QUESTIONS — 163
INTERNET RESOURCES — 164
NOTES — 164

Selected Reading — 166
The Swan Song of Ron: Searching for Meaning in What Is Likely to Be the Last Campaign Ron Paul Ever Runs
Nate Blakeslee

5 Campaigns and Elections — 169

Political Campaigns — 170
Conducting Campaigns in the 21st Century — 170
CourseReader Assignments — 171
Points to Ponder — 173
Campaign Reform — 173
Campaign Finance — 174
Learning Check 5.1 — 177

Racial and Ethnic Politics — 177
Latinos — 177
African Americans — 180
Learning Check 5.2 — 181

Women in Politics — 181
Learning Check 5.3 — 182

Voting — 182
Obstacles to Voting — 182
Democratization of the Ballot — 185
Voter Turnout — 187
Administering Elections — 189

Points to Ponder   191
Point/Counterpoint...Photo Identification as
    a Requirement to Vote   193
Learning Check 5.4   197

Primary, General, and Special Elections   **197**
Primaries   197
Students in Action   198
How Do We Compare...in Types of Primaries?   200
General and Special Elections   201
Learning Check 5.5   202

Conclusion   **202**
CHAPTER SUMMARY   202
KEY TERMS   203
LEARNING CHECK ANSWERS   204
DISCUSSION QUESTIONS   204
INTERNET RESOURCES   204
NOTES   205

Selected Reading   **207**
Lots of GOP Money Flowing from the Texas Two
Wade Goodwyn

· ·

6   **The Politics of Interest Groups**   **209**

Interest Groups in the Political Process   **210**
What Is an Interest Group?   210
The Reasons for Interest Groups   211
Characteristics of Interest Groups   213
Learning Check 6.1   215

Types of Interest Groups   **215**
Economic Groups   215
Professional/Career Groups   217
Social Groups   219
Public Interest Groups   222
Texas Power Groups   222
Learning Check 6.2   223

Interest Group Activities   **224**
Lobbying   224
CourseReader Assignments   225
Points to Ponder   226
Students in Action   227
Electioneering   228
Points to Ponder   229
Point/Counterpoint...Should Campaign Contributions
    Be Limited?   230

Campaign Financing by Political Action Committees   230

How Do We Compare...in Total Contributions

     in U.S. Congressional Races?   **231**

Bribery and Unethical Practices   233

Learning Check 6.3   **234**

Power and Regulation in Interest Group Politics   234

Regulation of Interest Group Politics   235

Interest Group Power and Public Policy   238

Pinpointing Political Power   239

Learning Check 6.4   **239**

Conclusion   239

CHAPTER SUMMARY   240

KEY TERMS   241

LEARNING CHECK ANSWERS   241

DISCUSSION QUESTIONS   241

INTERNET RESOURCES   242

NOTES   242

Selected Reading   **245**

Unsung Hero of Civil Rights: "Father of LULAC" a Fading Memory
Hector Saldaña

. . . .

7   The Legislature   249

Legislative Framework   250

Points to Ponder   **251**

Election and Terms of Office   251

Sessions   252

How Do We Compare...in State Legislative Seats?   **253**

Districting   253

Learning Check 7.1   **258**

Legislators   259

Qualifications and Characteristics   259

Compensation   265

How Do We Compare...in Salary of Legislators?   **266**

Learning Check 7.2   **266**

Legislative Organization   267

Presiding Officers   267

CourseReader Assignments   **269**

Committee System   270

Points to Ponder   **272**

Legislative Caucus System   272

Learning Check 7.3   **274**

Legislative Operations   274

Powers and Immunities   275

Procedure   278
**Point/Counterpoint...Should There Be Special Sessions
    to Override Vetoes?**   **285**
Learning Check 7.4   **286**
Students in Action   **286**

Influences Within the Legislative Environment   287
The Governor   287
Judges, the Attorney General, and the Comptroller of Public
    Accounts   287
Lobbyists   288
Research Organizations   288
The Media   290
Learning Check 7.5   **290**

Conclusion   290
CHAPTER SUMMARY   291
KEY TERMS   291
LEARNING CHECK ANSWERS   292
DISCUSSION QUESTIONS   292
INTERNET RESOURCES   292
NOTES   293

Selected Reading   **295**
Recent Congressional Redistricting in Texas
Charles Jerry Wilkins/Lyle C. Brown

8   The Executive   299

Overview of the Governorship   300
Gubernatorial Politics: Money Matters   302
Election   303
**How Do We Compare...in Qualifications for the
    Office of Governor?**   **303**
Compensation and Benefits   304
Succession   305
Points to Ponder   **305**
Removal from Office   306
CourseReader Assignments   **307**
Staff   307
**How Do We Compare...in Governor's Compensation
    and Staff Size?**   **309**
Learning Check 8.1   **309**
Informal Powers of the Governor   310
Learning Check 8.2   **311**
Executive Powers of the Governor   311
Appointive Power   312

Removal Power   314
Military Power   315
Law Enforcement Power   315
Budgetary Power   316
Executive Orders and Proclamations   316
**Point/Counterpoint...Should the Governor Direct by Executive
Order the Vaccination of Girls Against HPV?**   **317**
Economic Development   318
Learning Check 8.3   **319**

Legislative Powers of the Governor   **319**
Message Power   320
Bill-Signing Power   320
Veto Power   320
Special-Sessions Power   321
Learning Check 8.4   **321**

Judicial Powers of the Governor   **321**
Appointment and Removal of Judges and Justices   322
Acts of Executive Clemency   322
Learning Check 8.5   **323**

The Plural Executive   **324**
Points to Ponder   **324**
The Lieutenant Governor   325
The Attorney General   325
The Comptroller of Public Accounts   326
The Commissioner of the General Land Office   328
Students in Action   **329**
The Commissioner of Agriculture   329
The Secretary of State   330
Learning Check 8.6   **332**

Conclusion   **332**
CHAPTER SUMMARY   332
KEY TERMS   333
LEARNING CHECK ANSWERS   333
DISCUSSION QUESTIONS   333
INTERNET RESOURCES   334
NOTES   334

Selected Reading   **338**
The Low Politics of High Tech in the Lone Star State
Jeff Key

....

9   Public Policy and Administration   **341**

State Agencies and State Employees   **342**

State Agencies and Public Policy   342
The Institutional Context   343
State Employees and Public Policy   345
How Do We Compare...in Number of State Employees?   **348**
How Do We Compare...in State Employee Compensation?   **349**
Learning Check 9.1   **350**

Education   351
Public Schools   351
Points to Ponder   **353**
Colleges and Universities   357
CourseReader Assignments   **357**
Students in Action   **359**
Point/Counterpoint...Should Texas Continue to Use the
  "Top 10 Percent Rule"?   **362**
Learning Check 9.2   **362**

Health and Human Services   363
Human Services   365
Health and Mental Health Services   367
Employment   369
Learning Check 9.3   **370**

Economic, Environmental, and Homeland Security Policies   370
Economic Regulatory Policy   371
Business Promotion   373
Points to Ponder   **374**
Environmental Regulation   376
Learning Check 9.4   **380**

Conclusion   380
CHAPTER SUMMARY   381
KEY TERMS   382
LEARNING CHECK ANSWERS   383
DISCUSSION QUESTIONS   383
INTERNET RESOURCES   384
NOTES   384

Selected Reading   **389**
Cronies at the Capitol: Connecting the Dots at TCEQ
Eliot Shapleigh

10 Laws, Courts, and Justice   392

State Law in Texas   394
Sources of Law   394
Code Revision   395
Points to Ponder   **395**
Learning Check 10.1   **395**

Courts, Judges, Lawyers, and Juries   396
Trial and Appellate Courts   396
CourseReader Assignments   403
How Do We Compare...in Salaries of Highest Court Justices and Judges?   403
Disciplining and Removing Judges and Justices   406
Lawyers   407
Points to Ponder   408
Juries   410
Learning Check 10.2   412

Judicial Procedures   412
Civil Justice System   413
Criminal Justice System   415
Learning Check 10.3   419

Correction and Rehabilitation   420
The Texas Department of Criminal Justice   420
How Do We Compare...in Prison Incarceration Rates?   421
Local Government Jails   426
Private Prisons   427
Juvenile Justice   427
Point/Counterpoint...Should Governments Contract with Private Corporations to Operate Prisons?   428
Learning Check 10.4   430

Problems and Reforms: Implications for Public Policy   430
Coping with Crowded Dockets   430
Technology   431
Exoneration Issues   431
Students in Action   433
Racial and Ethnic Diversity   434
Learning Check 10.5   434

Conclusion   434
CHAPTER SUMMARY   435
KEY TERMS   436
LEARNING CHECK ANSWERS   436
DISCUSSION QUESTIONS   437
INTERNET RESOURCES   437
NOTES   437

Selected Reading   441
Jack County Minute Book A (1870s): The Trial of Satanta and Big Tree

11 Finance and Fiscal Policy   443
Fiscal Policies   444
Taxing Policy   446

How Do We Compare…in Taxes and Spending?   447
Points to Ponder   448
Budget Policy   448
Spending Policy   449
Learning Check 11.1   450

Revenue Sources   **450**
The Politics of Taxation   450
Revenue from Gambling   456
Nontax Revenues   458
The Public Debt   460
Learning Check 11.2   462

Budgeting and Fiscal Management   **462**
Budgeting Procedure   462
Point/Counterpoint…Should Texas Adopt Annual Budgeting?   463
Budget Expenditures   467
Budget Execution   467
Purchasing   468
Facilities   468
Accounting   468
Auditing   469
Learning Check 11.3   469

Future Demands   **470**
Public Education   470
Points to Ponder   470
Public Higher Education   474
Points to Ponder   474
CourseReader Assignments   475
How Do We Compare…in Tuition and Fees?   478
Public Assistance   478
Students in Action   479
Other Needs   480
Learning Check 11.4   482

Conclusion   **482**
CHAPTER SUMMARY   483
KEY TERMS   483
LEARNING CHECK ANSWERS   484
DISCUSSION QUESTIONS   484
INTERNET RESOURCES   484
NOTES   485

Selected Reading   **487**
Texas Parks and Wildlife Department

GLOSSARY 490

INDEX 498

Preface

This edition of *Practicing Texas Politics* describes and analyzes state and local politics as practiced within the Lone Star State. Published for college and university students, our textbook gives readers a realistic and up-to-date picture of how the state and its cities, counties, and special districts are governed. Approximately 85 percent of *Practicing Texas Politics* consists of text material written jointly by co-authors who critically examine public policymaking within Texas. Each chapter features one or more selected readings, designed to further enhance the specific chapter discussion.

About the Authors

Lyle C. Brown

Lyle C. Brown is Professor (Emeritus) of Political Science at Baylor University, where he served as his department's director of graduate studies and as director of Baylor's Foreign Service Program. Other academic experience includes teaching at Mexico City College (now University of the Americas), Texas College of Arts & Industries (now Texas A&M University-Kingsville), and Wayland Baptist College (now Wayland Baptist University). He was a postgraduate student at the Instituto Politécnico de Monterrey in Mexico and received his M.A. from the University of Oklahoma and Ph.D. from the University of Texas at Austin. He served as president of the Southwest Council of Latin American Studies, and he is co-editor of *Religion in Latin American Life and Literature* and author or co-author of articles in professional journals, anthologies, and textbooks. His personal involvement in Texas politics includes participation in precinct, county, and state conventions.

Joyce A. Langenegger

Joyce A. Langenegger teaches government at Blinn College-Bryan and facilitates youth and adult leadership programs. She received M.A. and J.D. degrees from Baylor University and an M.A. and Ph.D. from Fielding Graduate University. Dr. Langenegger is a Fellow of the Institute for Social

Innovation at Fielding. As a Fellow she pursues her research interest in the development, documentation, and dissemination of evidence-based teaching practices. She has been named to "Who's Who Among America's Teachers" three times, received a NISOD Award for Teaching Excellence, and was given a "Most Valuable Player" award from San Jacinto College for her work as a professor and administrator at that institution. She is a frequent workshop presenter on innovative teaching strategies. She practiced law for a number of years and has been involved with politics at state and local levels.

Sonia R. García

Sonia García is a Professor at St. Mary's University in San Antonio, where she serves as the graduate director for the Political Science Program, the Coordinator for the Women's Studies Program, as well as the Coordinator for the Latin American Studies Program. She has also served as Chair of the Political Science Department. A graduate from St. Mary's, Dr. García received her Master's from the University of Arizona and her Ph.D. from the University of California, Santa Barbara. Dr. García teaches courses in Texas politics, constitutional law, civil rights, and women and politics. She has published articles on Latina politics and is a co-author of a book entitled, *Mexican Americans & the Law: El Pueblo Unido Jamás Será Vencido*, released in 2004. Dr. García is also the lead author of another book, entitled *Políticas: Latina Public Officials in Texas*, published in 2007, which examines the first Mexican American women elected to public office in Texas at various levels of government.

Ted A. Lewis

Ted A. Lewis has taught government and political science at the college level for more than 27 years. He earned a B.A. from Texas Wesleyan University, an M.S. from the University of North Texas, and a doctorate from the University of Texas at Austin. Dr. Lewis has conducted workshops on Texas election procedure for the Texas Secretary of State and has served as a county party chairperson, on state political party executive committees, and on several statewide candidate campaign advisory committees. He has delivered over 30 national presentations and has published numerous articles on political science, instructional pedagogies, learning communities, active learning, and other student-oriented learning strategies in such journals as the *Community College Journal of Research and Practice*, the *Journal of the League for Innovation in the Community College*, and the *National Social Science Journal*. Dr. Lewis is listed in both "Who's Who in American Politics" and "Who's Who Among America's Teachers."

Robert E. Biles

Robert E. Biles has taught college students about Texas politics in Texas, Colombia, and Ecuador, and to students in the free world and in Texas prisons. He is a Professor Emeritus and former chair of Political Science at Sam Houston State University. He received his Ph.D. from the Johns Hopkins University School of Advanced International Studies and has published four books and 25 scholarly articles. He has served as a professional staff member for the U.S. Senate Foreign Relations Committee, member of a local school board, county political party chair, county election supervisor, state board member of a citizen's lobbying group, member of advisory committees to the Texas Commissioner of Higher Education and Texas State Board for Educator Certification, and secretary and president of the Women's Caucus of the Southwestern Social Science Association. He has received four Fulbright grants to teach and do research in Latin America. He has received his university's top award for research, his college's award for teaching, and the first university Faculty Senate award for administration.

What's New in This Edition

Practicing Texas Politics: An Integrated CourseReader Package with Printed Access Card for CourseReader (ISBN: 9781133940494).

COURSEREADER: TEXAS POLITICS is Cengage Learning's easy, affordable way to build your own online customizable reader. Through a partnership with Gale, COURSEREADER: TEXAS POLITICS searches thousands of primary and secondary sources, readings, and audio and video clips from multiple disciplines. This easy-to-use solution allows you to search for content, and to select the exact material you need for your courses. Each selection includes a descriptive introduction that provides important background context, and is further supported by critical-thinking and multiple-choice questions designed to reinforce key points. The COURSEREADER is loaded with convenient pedagogical features like highlighting, printing, note taking, and the option to download MP3 audio files for each reading. You have the freedom to easily create an affordable custom reader for your students, with all permissions cleared, which contains your notes and highlighting. COURSEREADER: TEXAS POLITICS is the perfect complement to any class and is updated throughout the year.

It can be bundled with your existing textbook, sold alone, and integrated into your learning management system. Please see your Cengage sales representative for details.

To demo COURSEREADER: TEXAS POLITICS, please visit us at: www.cengage.com/sso. Click on "Create a New Faculty Account" and fill out the registration page. Once you are in your new SSO account, search for "CourseReader" from your dashboard and select "CourseReader: Texas Politics." Then click "CourseReader 0-30: Texas Politics Instant Access Code" and click "Add to my bookshelf." To access the live CourseReader, click on "CourseReader 0-30: Texas Politics" under "Additional resources" on the right side of your dashboard.

CourseReader ASSIGNMENTS

Log in to www.cengagebrain.com and open CourseReader to access the reading:

The Texas Declaration of Independence
Delegates of the People of Texas

When the General Convention's delegates met in the town of Washington on-the-Brazos, Texas, on March 1, 1836, there was a significant amount of pressure and a limited amount of time to complete the business of independence. The declaration was submitted for consideration on the second day of official business.

1. Why did Texians and some Tejanos want to become an independent nation?

2. As described in the Declaration of Independence, how did the delegates at the convention view the Mexican government?

Updated Chapters

Practicing Texas Politics gives special attention to political developments since 2010. To include descriptions and analyses of recent political events and governmental changes, the narrative has been appropriately revised. Topics given special attention include, by chapter:

Chapter 1
- Coverage of 2010-2012 demographic changes
- Discussion of the Texas timber industry
- Analysis of impact of the 2010-2011 droughts on the Texas economy

Chapter 2
- Analysis of federal-state relations under the Obama Administration
- Coverage of 2011 Constitutional Amendment election results

Chapter 3
- Clarification and illustration of the nature of local property taxes
- Discussion of the growing controversies over poverty, immigration, violence, and the wall along the Texas-Mexico border

Chapter 4
- Coverage of 2012 Democratic and Republican Party primary results
- Discussion of the 2012 Democratic and Republican Party Platforms
- Analysis of the impact of the redistricting legal challenges on the dates and structure of the 2012 Democratic and Republican Party primaries and conventions in Texas

Chapter 5
- Coverage of the impact of the 2012 presidential race and the influence of SuperPACS in campaign finance
- Updated data on the number of elected officials in Texas by race/ethnicity and gender
- Analysis of voter ID legislation in Texas

Chapter 6
- Discussion of interest group activity during the 2011 legislative session
- Analysis of lobbying and gifts during the 2011 legislative session
- The role of interest groups in recent gubernatorial and legislative elections
- A look at influential PACs, their activities, and ethics reform during the 2011 legislative session

Chapter 7
- Legislative and congressional redistricting after the 2010 census
- Party affiliation, racial/ethnic classification, and gender for members of the 83rd Texas legislature
- Examples of bills, resolutions, and calendars in the 82nd Texas legislature

Chapter 8
- Discussion of the organization of the Office of the Governor, with the current organization chart
- Analysis of the relationship between gubernatorial appointments and campaign donations
- Update of Governor Perry's use of veto power

Chapter 9
- Examination of the continued consequences of the Great Recession and national recovery programs for Texas public policy
- Discussion of the increasing conflict between the invigorated U.S. Environmental Protection Agency and Texas agencies
- Analysis of the effects of changes in the state testing program for public schools and the top 10 percent rule for admission to the University of Texas
- A look at the 2010 BP oil spill in the Gulf of Mexico and its consequences

Chapter 10
- Coverage of the Michael Morton case and its implications for the Texas justice system
- Analysis of the use of private jails and prisons for incarceration
- A look at the results of the state's reforms in its medical malpractice laws and criminal justice system
- Examination of the creation of the Texas Juvenile Justice Department

Chapter 11
- Discussion of the state budget for the 2012–2013 fiscal years, with a special emphasis on spending cuts that directly affect students

- Discussion of the state's expanded ability to collect sales taxes on Internet sales
- Arguments for and against biennial and annual state budgeting
- Synopsis of court cases affecting public school funding in Texas
- Discussion of the budgetary implications of the state's water needs

Updated Design

To emphasize the importance and relevance of each topic discussed in *Practicing Texas Politics*, a new design was used throughout the book in the previous edition. To further improve upon these adjustments, the features that have been trusted and appreciated remain the same, but the layout and placement of the text and features has been reworked to ensure a greater ease of readability, as well as to ensure that all topics receive the attention that they deserve.

- Chapter Opener Each chapter opens with a cartoon from local newspapers, immediately calling attention to the chapter theme and conversation.
- Chapter Headings The list of main topics, as well as subsequent section headings, have been revised to ensure that appropriate consideration is given to each.
- Chapter Features All features found within the chapters have been refreshed, encouraging increased understanding of political interactions, civic responsibility, and social relevance.
- Learning Objectives This edition of *Practicing Texas Politics* includes brand new Learning Objectives based on the Academic Course Guide Manual's student learning outcomes. The Learning Objectives are featured on the chapter-opening page of each chapter, as well as called out within the margins of the corresponding text itself. These are referred to with the margin callout "LO" within the text and have the appropriate number following, providing students with a better understanding of exactly what they should be learning from the material.

Important Features of This Edition

To provide a wide range of views on current issues and relevant topics, keeping students well-informed, we have included improved features to *Practicing Texas Politics*.

New Learning Objectives

This feature is new to *Practicing Texas Politics* and provides students with a better understanding of what they will learn as they read the chapter.

Bringing these objectives to the students' attention before the chapter has begun enables students to read more closely, looking for specific topics and gaining a more detailed understanding of, and appreciation for, the topics at hand. Basing the Learning Objectives on the state-developed student learning outcomes allows for ease in creating assessments tied to these learning outcomes. The Learning Objectives are called out within the margin of the text itself, allowing students to fix their focus on the most important details within the chapter.

Students in Action

New to the previous edition of *Practicing Texas Politics*, this feature is designed to provide a personal connection for students by sharing the individual stories and experiences of actual Texas students. The feature provides current students with the incentive to play an active role in their community, participating in internships or organizations that enhance personal growth as well as political awareness. Within this edition, the feature has been condensed in order to dedicate more attention to the material at hand, while still offering a timely example of student engagement and interaction.

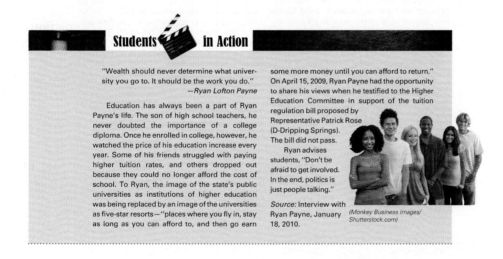

Students in Action

"Wealth should never determine what university you go to. It should be the work you do."
—*Ryan Lofton Payne*

Education has always been a part of Ryan Payne's life. The son of high school teachers, he never doubted the importance of a college diploma. Once he enrolled in college, however, he watched the price of his education increase every year. Some of his friends struggled with paying higher tuition rates, and others dropped out because they could no longer afford the cost of school. To Ryan, the image of the state's public universities as institutions of higher education was being replaced by an image of the universities as five-star resorts—"places where you fly in, stay as long as you can afford to, and then go earn some more money until you can afford to return." On April 15, 2009, Ryan Payne had the opportunity to share his views when he testified to the Higher Education Committee in support of the tuition regulation bill proposed by Representative Patrick Rose (D-Dripping Springs). The bill did not pass.

Ryan advises students, "Don't be afraid to get involved. In the end, politics is just people talking."

Source: Interview with Ryan Payne, January 18, 2010.

(Monkey Business Images/Shutterstock.com)

Selected Readings

To keep students well-informed of timely topics, one Selected Reading is found at the end of each chapter. These readings have been selected specifically to link to the chapter content, offering students further analysis and

Selected Reading

Laredo's Modest Advocate*

Robert Green

For years, Texas has had one of the largest proportions of people in poverty in the nation. Among the poorest of Texas's poor are residents of colonias, communities mostly along the border with Mexico with few basic services such as water and sewage. Most residents work, but at low-paying jobs. Yet they share the American dream of improving themselves and providing a better life for their children. This story is about a long-term advocate for these communities, and it reminds us of the force for change that a single dedicated person can be.

Along the U.S.-Mexico border, hundreds of thousands of people live without running water, sewage service, or electricity in unincorporated subdivisions known as "colonias." Texas has the largest number of colonias—an estimated 400,000 Texans live in more than 2,200 of them. The average yearly income of colonia residents is less than $10,000, and unemployment is more than eight times the state average. Texas's political leaders have done little in recent years to aid colonias. The "About" page of the Texas secretary of state's "Colonias Ombudsman Program" is blank save for a quote from Gov. Rick Perry. One person who's helped improve conditions in colonias is Israel Reyna, though you'll never hear him take credit for it. Reyna runs the Laredo office of Texas Rio Grande Legal Aid, a nonprofit that provides free representation to impoverished residents of South Texas. Reyna and his staff work to ensure that workers receive workers' compensation and overtime pay, that day laborers aren't arrested and

harassed by police merely for looking for work, and that water and sewage providers offer service to the colonias that dot the border region. Reyna joined the nonprofit straight out of law school in 1980. He's one of the rare advocates who knows how to needle political leaders into action—then step back and let them take the credit. "He is not someone that has ever been in the limelight or sought the limelight," says Jose "Chito" Vela, who work[ed] in the office of [then] State Rep. Solomon Ortiz, a Corpus Christi Democrat. Before joining Ortiz's staff, Vela served as the city manager of El Cenizo, a colonia south of Laredo that was incorporated under Reyna's guidance. Since El Cenizo incorporated, the community has levied taxes and now provides residents with some basic services. Under Reyna, the legal aid group also serves as what staff attorney Fabiola Flores calls a "baby lawyer factory." Reyna recruits law-student interns and entry-level attorneys from across the nation and puts them to work on pro bono cases. He enlists them in the cause, as he puts it, "to get things right. To move mountains ... for little people." He's reluctant to take the credit, "I am the messenger, not the messiah," Reyna says. "The heroes are the clients—the people who stick their necks out and expose themselves to the risk of litigation." Says Vela, "If you're promoting democracy, you can't come in from above and lift up these people—they have to lift themselves. At some point, you're going to go away, and the people are still going to be there. So they have to be able to organize and lead and fight for themselves."

For further resources, please visit **www.cengagebrain.com**.

application of the material learned within the chapter. Every reading has a brief introduction to prepare readers for what follows.

Point/Counterpoint

This feature examines a key controversial issue in Texas politics from both sides of the debate.

Point/Counterpoint

THE ISSUE Across the United States, approximately 130,000 inmates are incarcerated in prison facilities operated by private corporations. The percentage of Texas prisoners held in private prisons is almost twice the national average: 11 percent in Texas versus 6 percent for all states. A number of questions surround governments' contracting with private companies to incarcerate people. Considered a panacea to the prison population explosion that began in the 1980s, this same practice is undergoing renewed scrutiny as the source of revenue (inmates) continues to decline.

Should Governments Contract with Private Corporations to Operate Prisons?

Arguments For Using Private Contractors

- Contracting with private companies allows for greater flexibility. When prison populations climb rapidly, the private sector offers an immediate solution without requiring substantial, long-term investments by government in the construction of facilities. As inmate populations decline, these contracts can be renegotiated or canceled.
- Contracts are awarded to those who offer the most cost-efficient proposal; thus, the per prisoner cost of incarceration will decline.
- Private contractors will be more innovative and responsive than government in responding to and resolving problems. Competition with other service providers will force innovation and responsiveness.

[T]he existence of competition, even potential competition, will make the public less tolerant of facilities that are crowded, costly, dirty, dangerous, inhumane, ineffective, and prone to riots and lawsuits. Indeed, the fact that these conditions have existed for so long in monopolistic state prisons is a big part of what makes private prisons seem attractive.

—Charles H. Logan, *Private Prisons: Cons and Pros* (New York: Oxford, 1990).

Arguments Against Using Private Contractors

- Private contractors enjoy the benefits when business is good and step away when business is bad because the inmate population has declined. In recent years, private contractors have abandoned several privately managed, but publicly financed, jails in Texas. Without sufficient numbers of prisoners to continue profitable operations, private contractors cancelled their contracts to manage the facilities. Local taxpayers, however, were left to repay any money borrowed to build or maintain the facilities.
- Private prisons provide no cost savings to state governments, as suggested by recent studies. Further, their executives are criticized for influencing policymakers to increase incarceration.
- Contracting for incarceration services is an improper delegation of government's power. Physical freedom is one of our most cherished liberties. Allowing private contractors to enforce that loss of liberty violates our fundamental rights.

When private prison companies are successful at the game of political influence, their profits rise, benefitting their stockholders and top management…. [T]he biggest losers in this political game are the people who are taken away from their families and communities due to the policies private prison companies promote to increase the number of people going into prisons and the length of time they spend behind bars.

—Paul Ashton, *Gaming the System: How the Political Strategies of Private Prison Companies Promote Ineffective Incarceration Policies* (Washington, D.C.: Justice Policy Institute, June 2011)

Learning Checks

These features are found at the end of most sections in each chapter, consist of a few factual questions designed to test students' grasp of the major points that were just presented, and supply answers to the questions provided at the end of the chapter. "Learning Checks" offer a quick way for students to confirm that they are attending properly to each section; students who want more test practice can then go online.

☑ Learning Check 5.2 (Answers on p. 206)

1. Which party have Latinos traditionally supported?
2. True or False: In 2010, no African Americans were holding statewide elected office.

Points to Ponder

These boxed features provide interesting (and sometimes little-known) facts about Texas to stimulate student curiosity about the state.

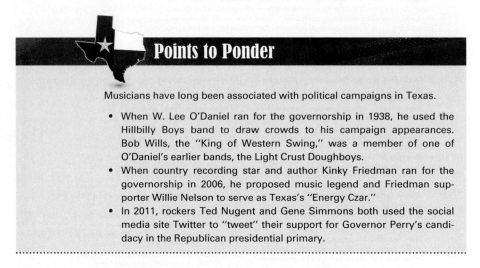

Points to Ponder

Musicians have long been associated with political campaigns in Texas.

- When W. Lee O'Daniel ran for the governorship in 1938, he used the Hillbilly Boys band to draw crowds to his campaign appearances. Bob Wills, the "King of Western Swing," was a member of one of O'Daniel's earlier bands, the Light Crust Doughboys.
- When country recording star and author Kinky Friedman ran for the governorship in 2006, he proposed music legend and Friedman supporter Willie Nelson to serve as Texas's "Energy Czar."
- In 2011, rockers Ted Nugent and Gene Simmons both used the social media site Twitter to "tweet" their support for Governor Perry's candidacy in the Republican presidential primary.

How Do We Compare

This boxed feature compares Texas with the three other most populous U.S. states (California, Florida, and New York); with the four U.S. states bordering Texas (Arkansas, Louisiana, New Mexico, and Oklahoma); and, for some subjects, with the four Mexican states bordering Texas (Chihauhua, Coahuila, Nuevo León, and Tamaulipas).

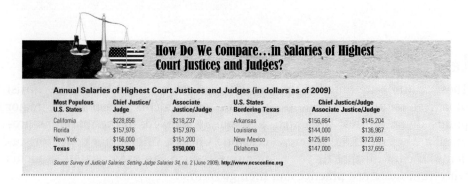

How Do We Compare...in Salaries of Highest Court Justices and Judges?

Annual Salaries of Highest Court Justices and Judges (in dollars as of 2009)

Most Populous U.S. States	Chief Justice/ Judge	Associate Justice/Judge	U.S. States Bordering Texas	Chief Justice/Judge	Associate Justice/Judge
California	$228,856	$218,237	Arkansas	$156,864	$145,204
Florida	$157,976	$157,976	Louisiana	$144,000	$136,967
New York	$156,000	$151,200	New Mexico	$125,691	$123,691
Texas	**$152,500**	**$150,000**	Oklahoma	$147,000	$137,655

Source: Survey of Judicial Salaries: Setting Judge Salaries 34, no. 2 (June 2009), http://www.ncsconline.org

End of Chapter Material

As in previous editions, each chapter includes the following features, which are designed to provide students with the most thorough study resources possible:

- Conclusion New to this edition, each chapter provides a brief conclusion before beginning the end-of-chapter material. This feature is designed to offer a concise understanding of the topics addressed within the chapter, before students continue on to the next chapter and its topics.
- Chapter Summary Bulleted key points provide students a more detailed, thorough review of the chapter.

- Key Terms Students have immediate access to key terms and their definitions as they are presented in the text. Additionally, a list of key terms follows each chapter. The glossary, at the end of the text, includes definitions arranged alphabetically.
- Learning Check Answers As mentioned previously, the Learning Check feature is found throughout the chapters—this answer portion concludes the feature by offering a quick way for students to confirm that they are attending properly to each section.
- Discussion Questions To supply students with more in-depth questions and talking points, this resource encourages dialogue by providing thought-provoking questions to be covered in class or considered on one's own.
- Internet Resources URLs are provided for agencies and organizations relevant to the chapter.
- Notes Endnotes document information provided in the text and suggest additional reading for further study.

Instructor Ancillary Package

Practicing Texas Politics offers an extensive package of supplementary materials for instructors:

- Aplia™ for Brown/Langenegger/Garcia/Lewis/Biles *Practicing Texas Politics*, 2013–2014 Edition
  - IAC: 9781285075181 (Instant Access Code)
  - PAC: 9781285075204 (Printed Access Card)
  - Book with bundle: 9781285488295
  - Easy to use, affordable, and effective, Aplia helps students learn and saves you time. It's like a virtual teaching assistant! Aplia helps you have more productive classes by providing assignments that get students thinking critically, reading assigned material, and reinforcing basic concepts—all before coming to class. The interactive questions also help students better understand the relevance of what they're learning and how to apply those concepts to the world around them. Visually engaging videos, graphs, and political cartoons help capture students' attention and imagination, and an automatically-included eBook provides convenient access. Aplia is instantly accessible via Cengage Brain or through the bookstore via printed access code. Please contact your local Cengage sales representative for more information, and go to www.aplia.com/politicalscience to view a demo.

- Political Science CourseMate for Brown/Langenegger/Garcia/Lewis/ Biles *Practicing Texas Politics*, 2013–2014 Edition
  - IAC: 9781285419480 (Instant Access Code)
  - PAC: 9781285419473 (Printed Access Card)
  - Book with Bundle: 9781285488288
  - Cengage Learning's Political Science CourseMate brings course concepts to life with interactive learning, study tools, and exam preparation tools that support the printed textbook. Use Engagement Tracker to assess student preparation and engagement in the course, and watch student comprehension soar as your class works with the textbook-specific website. An interactive eBook allows students to take notes, highlight, search, and interact with

embedded media. Other resources include video activities, animated learning modules, simulations, case studies, interactive quizzes, and timelines. The American Government NewsWatch is a real-time news and information resource, updated daily, that includes interactive maps, videos, podcasts, and hundreds of articles from leading journals, magazines, and newspapers from the United States and the world. Also included is the KnowNow! American Government Blog, which highlights three current events stories per week and consists of a succinct analysis of the story, multimedia, and discussion-starter questions. Access your course via www.cengage.com/login.

- CourseReader Texas Politics: 0–30
  - IAC: 9781133350279 (Instant Access Code)
  - PAC: 9781133350286 (Printed Access Card)
  - CourseReader: Texas Politics allows you to create your reader, your way, in just minutes. This affordable, fully customizable online reader provides access to thousands of permissions-cleared readings, articles, primary sources, and audio and video selections from the regularly-updated Gale research library database. This easy-to-use solution allows you to search for and select just the material you want for your courses. Each selection opens with a descriptive introduction to provide context, and concludes with critical-thinking and multiple-choice questions to reinforce key points. CourseReader is loaded with convenient tools like highlighting, printing, note-taking, and downloadable MP3 audio files for each reading. CourseReader is the perfect complement to any Political Science course. It can be bundled with your current textbook, sold alone, or integrated into your learning management system. CourseReader 0-30 allows access to up to 30 selections in the reader. Please contact your Cengage sales representative for details.
- PowerLecture DVD with ExamView® for Brown/Langenegger/Garcia/Lewis/Biles *Practicing Texas Politics*, 2013–2014 Edition
  - ISBN: 9781133939665
  - An all-in-one multimedia resource for class preparation, presentation, and testing, this DVD includes **Microsoft® PowerPoint® slides**, a **Test Bank** in both Microsoft® Word and **ExamView®** formats, an **Instructor Manual**, and a **Resource Integration Guide**. The book-specific slides of lecture outlines, as well as photos, figures, and tables from the text, make it easy for you to assemble lectures for your course, while the media-enhanced slides help bring your lecture to life with audio and video clips, animated learning modules illustrating key concepts, tables, statistical charts, graphs, and photos from the book as well as outside sources. The test bank, offered in Microsoft Word® and ExamView® formats, includes 60+ multiple-choice questions with answers and page references along with 10 essay questions for each chapter. ExamView® features a user-friendly testing environment that allows you to not only publish traditional paper and computer based tests, but also Web-deliverable exams. The Instructor's Manual includes learning objectives, chapter outlines, summaries, discussion questions, class activities, and suggested readings and Web resources. A Resource Integration Guide provides a chapter-by-chapter

outline of all available resources to supplement and optimize learning. Contact your Cengage representative to receive a copy upon adoption.

- Free Companion Website for Brown/Langenegger/García/Lewis/Biles *Practicing Texas Politics*, 2013–2014 Edition
  - ISBN: 9781133938729
  - This password-protected website for instructors features all of the free student assets plus an instructor's manual, book-specific PowerPoint® presentations, Resource Integration Guide, and a test bank. Access your resources by logging into your account at www.cengagebrain.com.
- Latino American Politics
  - ISBN: 9781285184296
  - This 32-page custom supplement uses real examples to detail politics related to Latino Americans. This supplement can be added to your book via our custom publishing program.

Student Ancillary Package

The text's free companion website, accessible at **www.cengagebrain.com**, contains a wealth of study aids and resources for students. Students will find open access to learning objectives, tutorial quizzes, chapter glossaries, flashcards, and crossword puzzles, all correlated by chapter. At the CengageBrain.-com home page, search for the ISBN of your title (from the back cover of your book) using the search box at the top of the page. This will take you to the product page where these resources can be found.

If Required by your Instructor . . .

- Aplia™ for Brown/Langenegger/García/Lewis/Biles *Practicing Texas Politics*, 2013–2014 Edition
  - Easy to use, affordable, and convenient, Aplia helps you learn more and improve your grade in the course. Through interactive assignments, including videos, graphs, and political cartoons, you can better understand the essential concepts of American government and how they apply to real life. Aplia helps prepare you to be more involved in class by strengthening your critical-thinking skills, reinforcing what you need to know, and helping you understand why it all matters. For your studying convenience, Aplia includes an eBook, accessible right next to your assignments. Purchase instant access via CengageBrain or via a printed access card in your bookstore. Visit www.cengagebrain.com for more information. Aplia should be purchased only when assigned by your instructor as part of your course.
- Political Science CourseMate for Brown/Langenegger/García/Lewis/Biles *Practicing Texas Politics*, 2013–2014 Edition
  - The more you study, the better the results. Make the most of your study time by accessing everything you need to succeed in one place. Read your textbook, take notes, watch videos, read case studies, take practice quizzes, and more–online with CourseMate. CourseMate also gives you access to the American Government NewsWatch website–a real-time news and information resource updated daily, and KnowNow!–the go-to blog about current events in American Government. Purchase instant access via CengageBrain or via a printed access card in your bookstore. Visit

www.cengagebrain.com for more information. CourseMate should be purchased only when assigned by your instructor as part of your course.

Acknowledgments

We are indebted to many political scientists as well as scholars in other disciplines. They have shared generously the results of their research and have stimulated our effort to produce a better textbook for classroom use. In particular, we thank the following scholars who served as reviewers for this edition of our textbook. They provided many useful comments and suggestions for which we are grateful:

- Mario Marcel Salas, Northwest Vista College
- Brian R. Farmer, Amarillo College
- Billy Hathorn, Laredo Community College
- Amy S. Glenn, Northeast Lakeview
- Jim Startin, University of Texas at San Antonio

   Reviewers of the previous edition:

- Valentine Belfiglio, Texas Woman's University
- Nancy Bond, Tarleton State University
- William E. Carroll, Sam Houston State University
- Jim Enelow, University of Texas at Austin
- Laura De La Cruz, El Paso Community College
- Yolanda Garza Hake, South Texas College
- Franklin Jones, Texas Southern University
- James Norris, Texas A&M International University
- John David Rausch, Jr., West Texas A&M University

   We would like to thank the authors of the Test Bank, Tracy Cook (Central Texas College) and Albert Waite (Central Texas College), and the author of the Instructor's Manual, Joan Johnson (Tarrant County College).

   We are also indebted to many personal friends, government officials and their staffs, political activists, lawyers, and journalists who have stimulated our thinking. Likewise, we owe much to librarians and archivists who located hard-to-obtain facts, photos, and new readings. We also appreciate the professional assistance rendered by the editorial, production, and marketing staff of Cengage Learning. Without the benefit of their publishing experience, this textbook and its ancillaries would be of much less value to students and instructors.

   Of course, expressions of appreciation are due to spouses, family members, and many others who helped to produce this new edition of our book and have learned to cope with the irregular working hours of authors struggling to meet deadlines. Last and most important, we dedicate this book to Texas students and political science instructors who, we hope, will continue to be the chief beneficiaries of our efforts to describe and analyze the practice of Texas politics.

Lyle C. Brown

Joyce A. Langenegger

Sonia R. García

Ted A. Lewis

Robert E. Biles

The Environment of Texas Politics

(anchtoon.com)

Learning Objectives

1. Evaluate the meaning of power, politics, and public policy in the role of government.
2. Describe the basic character of political culture and identify the two dominant political cultures in Texas.
3. Explain how the geography of Texas has fostered the development and growth of four land-based industries and trace the development of each industry.
4. Analyze the impact of the 2011 drought on the Texas economy.
5. Compare the major racial and ethnic groups in Texas and the opportunities and challenges presented by their growth rates.
6. Identify the major challenges Texas faces in more effectively addressing immigration, protecting the environment, developing educational programs, and formulating policies for combating poverty and social problems.

From Dalhart to Del Rio and out El Paso way,
I'll be doing fine on Houston time, and when the sun sets on the Compano Bay,
from way up where the Red River flows, on down to the Rio Grande,
I was born a native Texican, and I'm proud to say that I am.[1]

Texas is a big state, in both area and population. The 2010 census ranked Texas second largest among the 50 states, with a population of more than 25 million, up from nearly 17 million in 1990 and almost 21 million in 2000. California ranked first with more than 37 million residents; New York was third with fewer than 20 million. This increased population for the Lone Star State included more than 18 million men and women of voting age (18 years or older). Although some of them could not legally cast ballots because they lacked qualifications concerning residence, registration, or U.S. citizenship, most Texans are involved in political activities, even if they limit their actions to talking about politics with family or friends or merely listening while others talk. Everyone is affected by the words and deeds of politicians, government officials, and public employees.

Legislative actions, executive decisions, and court proceedings, as well as popular elections and lobbying activities, are parts of what political scientist Karen J. O'Conner and others refer to as the process by which policy decisions are made.[2] **Politics** involves conflict between political parties and other groups that seek to elect government officials or to influence those officials when they make public policy, such as enacting and interpreting Texas laws. As the opening illustration depicts, in 2011 Texas experienced several catastrophic wildfires. Six of the 10 largest wildfires in Texas history occurred that year, causing more than $250 million in damages. This marked the Lone Star State's third, and most severe, year-long wildfire season since 2005. These wildfires tested Texas politics, as citizens and legislators from across the state were required to work together in hopes of overcoming the extensive damage and financial demands.

politics
The process of policymaking that involves conflict between political parties and other groups that seek to elect government officials, or to influence those officials when they make public policy, such as enacting and interpreting laws.

LO1

★ Political Behavior Patterns

This book focuses on politics as practiced within Texas and on the Lone Star State's diverse and rich cultural heritage. Our analysis of the politics of Texas's current state and local governments is intended to help readers understand political action and prepare them for informed participation in the political affairs of the state and its counties, cities, and special districts. In addition, we will introduce readers to important political actors—party activists or government officials who have been elected or appointed to public office. In politics, as in sports, people need to be able to identify the players to understand the game.

Government, Politics, and Public Policy

government
A public institution with authority to allocate values by formulating, adopting, and implementing public policies.

Government may be defined as a public institution with the authority to allocate values in a society. In practice, values are allocated when a state or local government formulates, adopts, and implements a public policy, such as raising taxes to pay for more police protection or better streets and

Points to Ponder

Texans have had a large impact on national politics during the latter part of the 20th century and today. Consider the following:

- Three men who have claimed Texas as their residence have occupied the Oval Office within the past 50 years: Lyndon B. Johnson (1963–1969), George H. W. Bush (1989–1993), and George W. Bush (2001–2009).
- Texans have served in key positions as cabinet secretaries, advisers, and diplomats.
- Texans have served in the federal judicial branch as district judges and appellate judges, and one has served as a Supreme Court justice (Tom C. Clark, 1949–1967).
- Key positions in Congress held by Texans include senate majority leader (Lyndon B. Johnson, 1953–1961), speaker of the U.S. House of Representatives (John Nance Garner, D-Uvalde, 1931–1933; Sam Rayburn, D-Bonham, 1940–1947, 1949–1953, and 1955–1961; and Jim Wright, D-Fort Worth, 1987–1989), as well as numerous party leaders, whips (assistant leaders), and key committee chairs.
- When Tom DeLay (R-Sugar Land) was forced to resign his position as House majority leader in early 2006 after an indictment for criminal conspiracy and increasing ethical questions, it marked the first time since 1925 that Texas did not have a member in a key leadership position in either house of Congress.

highways. At the state level, each **public policy** is a product of political activity that may involve both conflict and cooperation among legislators; between legislators and the governor; within the courts; and among various governmental agencies, citizens, and **aliens** (persons who lack U.S. citizenship, including undocumented people who entered legally but have stayed after their authorized visa has expired).

Policymaking involves political action intended to meet particular needs or achieve specific objectives. For example, a legislator might receive a proposal to promote public health by reducing or eliminating the use of pesticides alleged to cause cancer. This proposal could come from the governor or another government official, from a nongovernmental organization such as the environmentalist Sierra Club, or from any interested person. Next, the proposal would be incorporated into a bill and submitted to the Texas legislature by a state senator or representative favoring a new policy. Then, in committee hearings and on the floor of the Senate and the House of Representatives, the bill would be discussed and debated in the presence of lobbyists representing interest groups, journalists reporting the news, and concerned citizens. When the bill is passed by the legislature and signed by

public policy
Government action designed to meet a public need or goal as determined by a legislative body or other authorized officials.

alien
A person who is neither a national nor a citizen of the country where he or she is living.

Texas State Capitol Building.

(Courtesy of the Texas House of Representatives)

the governor, the pesticide proposal would become law. Next, the new public policy must be implemented, or put into operation. That responsibility might be assigned by law to the Texas Department of Agriculture or another governmental agency. The policy measure could also be challenged in court. Judges might uphold all, or part, of the legislation or nullify it entirely if it violates a provision of the Texas Constitution or the U.S. Constitution. In sum, politics is the moving force that produces public policy, which in turn determines what government does and who is affected.

Political Culture

Politics is influenced by **political culture**, which consists of the values, attitudes, traditions, habits, and general behavioral patterns that develop over time and shape the politics of a particular region. Political culture is the result of both remote and recent political experiences. According to political scientist Daniel Elazar, "Culture patterns give each state its particular character and help determine the tone of its fundamental relationship, as a state, to the nation."[3] Professor Elazar identified three distinct cultures that exist in the United States: moralistic, individualistic, and traditionalistic.

The **moralistic culture** originated in New England with Puritanism. In the moralistic culture, the people view government as a public service. The role of government is to improve conditions for the people and to create a just society. The people expect government to provide goods and services that advance the public good. Citizens play an important role in politics in the moralistic culture. They see it as their duty to become active in governmental decision making through participation in town councils and other representative bodies or by closely monitoring the actions of their leaders. Government is viewed as a participatory endeavor in which people generally have high

political culture
Attitudes, habits, and general behavior patterns that develop over time and affect the political life of a state or region.

moralistic culture
This culture influences people to view political participation as their duty and to expect that government will be used to advance the public good.

expectations of their government and hold it accountable. Today, this culture has spread across the northern states and to the Pacific Northwest.

The **individualistic culture**, which was the second culture to emerge, grew out of westward expansion throughout the 19th century. Originally, many people migrated west to pursue economic opportunities not available to them in the east. The frontier areas in which they settled had no government to provide goods and services for the new settlers. They became more self-reliant, and the notion of the "rugged individualist" emerged. The business community also advanced the individualistic culture. Many business owners viewed government as an adversary that taxed and regulated them; therefore, they wanted to limit its size and scope. In contrast to the moralistic culture, individualistic culture does not consider government a vehicle for creating a just society and believes government intervention into private life should be limited. Today, the individualistic culture is found in a majority of the midwestern and western states.

The **traditionalistic culture**, the third culture to emerge, developed at about the same time as the individualistic culture. The traditionalistic culture, however, grew out of the Old South and is rooted in feudal-like notions of society and government that developed in the context of the agrarian plantation economy. Economically, the south differed from the north and the west in that it was based primarily on agriculture and, to a large extent, on the labor of African American slaves. As a result, property and income were unequally dispersed. Governmental policymaking fell to a few elite citizens who belonged to established families or influential social groups. Policies were designed to preserve the social order, and a one-party system developed. The poor and minorities were often disenfranchised. Even in the early 21st century, those in lower socioeconomic categories show a high degree of perceived **political inefficacy**, or belief in their inability to influence elections and political decision making. This perception has resulted in lower voter turnout for these groups. In the traditionalistic culture, government is a vehicle to maintain the status quo and its hierarchy. Today the traditionalistic culture remains dominant throughout the south.

Texas Political Culture

The foundations of Texas's political culture were laid and developed under the flags of six national governments: Spain, France, Mexico, the Republic of Texas, the Confederate States of America, and the United States. Unlike most of the other 49 states, Texas was not a U.S. territory before statehood. As an independent republic (1836–1845), Texas was given diplomatic recognition by the governments of the United States, England, France, Holland, and Belgium. With a popularly elected president and congress, the republic maintained its own army and navy, operated a postal system, printed paper money, administered justice through its courts, and provided other governmental services.

Texas Individualism Daniel Elazar asserts that the political culture of Texas is strongly individualistic in that government is supposed to maintain a stable society, but intervene as little as possible in the lives of the people.

individualistic culture
This culture looks to government to maintain a stable society but with minimum intervention in the lives of the people.

traditionalistic culture
A product of the Old South, this culture uses government as a means of preserving the status quo and its leadership.

political inefficacy
The inability to influence the nomination and election of candidates and the decision making of governing bodies. In Texas, this has been a major problem for minorities and low-income groups.

He identifies the state's politics with economic and social conservatism, strong support of personal politics, distrust of political parties, and minimization of the latter's importance.

An important source of Texas's conservatism is the 19th century **frontier experience**. In the early 19th century, a growing number of settlers from the United States entered Texas in search of cheap or free land. Some came individually; others were recruited by *empresarios*, such as Stephen F. Austin. These empresarios received large grants of land from the Spanish government initially, and subsequently the Mexican government, as compensation for colonization efforts. After securing independence from Mexico in 1836, the Republic of Texas developed its own economic, military, and education systems. The Texas republic's main success was its endurance. Texans, unlike other Americans who received military help from the federal government, had displaced Native Americans from a large region by themselves, established farms and communities, and persevered through extreme economic hardships.[4] These actions have been enlarged over time by historians and fiction writers who emphasized the violent aspects of Texans' struggle for independence from Mexico and their clashes with Native Americans who unsuccessfully resisted the westward movement of Anglo settlers. Thousands of Native Americans and settlers—men, women, and children—were slain on the Texas frontier from the 1820s to the mid-1870s. This period of frontier warfare lasted longer in Texas than in other states.

After the Texas frontier was secured, there remained the task of bringing law and order to the land. In some areas, range wars, cattle rustling, and other forms of violence continued to menace law-abiding citizens into the 20th century. As a result of these experiences, many Texans grew accustomed to the use of force in settling disputes and struggling for survival. In 1995, when the legislature legalized the carrying of concealed handguns by licensed owners, some people interpreted the action as another influence of frontier days, when many Texans carried concealed weapons or bore pistols openly in holsters. Two assumptions underlie the concealed weapons law: first, that Texans do not need to rely on law enforcement for protection; second, that citizens of the Lone Star State have a right to possess and carry weapons. Gun-rights groups have helped advance these presumptions. Today, shootings and other violence may be as common in Texas's inner cities and elsewhere as they were on the state's frontier in the 19th century.

Elements of the individualistic culture persist in other examples as well. Compared with other heavily populated states, Texas has a limited government with restricted powers: a legislature that meets biennially, with salaries that can be increased only after approval by Texas voters; a governor who has limited budgetary, appointment, and removal powers; and an elected judiciary with multiple levels of courts. Texas has a climate favorable to business. It remains one of the few states without a personal or corporate income tax. Government spending for social services on a per capita basis is consistently among the lowest in the nation. Public education in Texas is poorly funded and has remained a source of court battles and legislative conflicts for several decades. Including independent school districts, Texas has more than 3,000 special districts that perform a single service or groups of related services not

frontier experience
Coping with danger, physical hardships, and economic challenges tested the endurance of 19th-century Texans and contributed to the development of individualism.

performed by city or county governments. Participation in politics and voter turnout remain low. Turnout of the voting age population falls to less than 50 percent for presidential elections and is consistently less than 30 percent for gubernatorial elections. The public perception of government and elected officials remains negative. In 1998, George W. Bush became the first Texas governor elected to a second consecutive four-year term (although he resigned two years into his second term, following his election as U.S. president in 2000). In 2010, however, Rick Perry was elected to an unprecedented third four-year term, making him the longest serving governor in Texas history.

Texas Traditionalism The traditionalistic culture of Texas also can be traced to the early 19th century. The plantation system thrived in the rich, fertile soil of East Texas, and cotton was by far the state's largest money crop. Before Texas's entry into the Confederacy, much of its wealth was concentrated in a few families. Although only a quarter of the state's population and one-third of the farmers owned slaves, slave owners held 60 to 70 percent of the wealth and controlled state politics.[5] After the Civil War (1861–1865), **"Jim Crow" laws** limited African Americans' access to public services. In the late 19th and early 20th centuries, poll taxes and all-white primaries further restricted voting rights.

Today, many Texans are the descendants of migrants from traditionalistic states of the Old South, where conservatism, elitism (upper-class rule), and one-party politics were long entrenched. Although urbanization and industrialization, together with an influx of people from other states and countries, are changing the cultural patterns of Texas's population, Elazar insists that the traditionalistic influence of the Old South still lingers. He notes that many Texans have inherited southern racist attitudes, which for decades were reflected in state laws that discriminated against African Americans and other minority groups. It was not until 2000 that two Civil War plaques were removed from the Texas Supreme Court building, as demanded by the National Association for the Advancement of Colored People (NAACP). One plaque bore a likeness of the Confederate battle flag, and the other displayed the official Confederate seal. Similar symbols of Texas's role in the Confederacy remain in public places throughout the state and are a source of continuing controversy.

The traditionalistic influence of Mexico is discernible among Mexican American Texans, who were affected by a political culture featuring the elitist *patrón* (protective political boss) **system** that dominates certain areas of South Texas. For more than four decades, however, the old political order of that region has been challenged—and, in many instances, defeated—by new generations of Mexican Americans.[6] Compared with other areas of the state, however, voter turnout remains much lower in counties along the Mexican border.

The traditionalistic culture can also be seen in the state's social and economic conservatism. Religious groups have influenced government policies on matters such as blue (Sunday closing) laws, liquor laws, pari-mutuel betting, and the state lottery. City councils have drawn public criticism for publicly financing corporate ventures or providing certain businesses with

"Jim Crow" laws
These were ethnically discriminatory laws that segregated African Americans and denied them access to public services for many decades after the Civil War.

patrón system
A type of boss rule that has dominated areas of South Texas.

property tax abatements. Powerful families continue to play an important role in state politics and influence public policies.

A Changing Culture? Beginning in the mid-1970s, Texas experienced a large population influx from other areas of the nation and, more recently, from other countries. With regard to Elazar's appraisal of Texas's conservative political culture, important questions arise: How long will particular sociocultural influences last? Aren't past cultural influences being replaced by new ones? Will Texas's cultural identities, inherited largely from the 19th century, survive indefinitely in the face of widespread urbanization, industrialization, education, communication, and population change? With a large migration of people from northern states, will a moralistic culture ever take root and flourish in the Lone Star State?

✓ Learning Check 1.1   (Answers on p. 39)

1. True or False: Texas's population of more than 25 million ranks it third among the 50 states, behind California and New York.
2. What two types of political culture are commonly found in Texas?

....

★ The Land

LO3   Like people everywhere, Texans are influenced by their geography as well as by their history. Thus, Texas's mountains, plains, seacoasts, climate, mineral deposits, and other geographic features affect the state's economy, its political culture, and Texas's role in national and international affairs. By the 21st century, Texans had cleared the land to establish and operate thousands

How Do We Compare...in Area?

Throughout the book, we use this feature to compare Texas with the other three most populous U.S. states, as well as with Texas's four neighboring U.S. states. Some "How Do We Compare" boxes also include information about the Mexican states bordering Texas: Chihuahua, Coahuila, Nuevo León, and Tamaulipas.

Land and Inland Water Area Combined

Most Populous U.S. States	Area (sq. miles)	U.S. States Bordering Texas	Area (sq. miles)	Mexican States Bordering Texas	Area (sq. miles)
California	163,707	Arkansas	53,182	Chihuahua	95,400
Florida	65,758	Louisiana	54,813	Coahuila	58,522
New York	54,475	New Mexico	121,593	Nuevo León	25,126
Texas	**267,339**	Oklahoma	69,903	Tamaulipas	30,734

of farms and ranches; built hundreds of towns and cities; organized many banks and businesses; and produced much of the nation's oil and natural gas, cotton and mohair, fish and meat, wheat and sorghum, fruits and vegetables, and computers and computer chips.

The Politics of Geography

From the start, Texas's politics and public policy have been molded in part by the state's size. Its large area and diverse physical geography create strong regional interests. Regardless of where they live, however, most citizens of the Lone Star State strongly identify with their state and are proud to be called Texans.

Size With more than 267,000 square miles of territory, Texas is second only to Alaska (570,640 square miles) in area. The Lone Star State is as large as the combined areas of Florida, Georgia, Alabama, Mississippi, and Tennessee. Bounded by New Mexico to the west; Oklahoma to the north; Arkansas, Louisiana, and the Gulf of Mexico to the east, the state borders Mexico to its south. This international boundary follows the Rio Grande in its southeastern course from El Paso to Brownsville and the Gulf of Mexico. (Mexicans call this international stream the Rio Bravo, which means "brave river" or "fierce river.")

It is an 800-mile trip flying south in a straight line from the northwestern corner of the Texas Panhandle to the state's southern tip on the Rio Grande near Brownsville. Almost equally long is the distance from Newton County's Louisiana border to the New Mexico border near El Paso. Such great size requires approximately 222,000 miles of roadways in the state, including more than 80,000 miles of major highways constructed and maintained under the supervision of the Texas Department of Transportation. No other state has so many miles of roadways.

Points to Ponder

- The longest highway in Texas is US 83. It extends from the Oklahoma state line in the Panhandle to the border with Mexico at Brownsville. It is 899 miles long.
- The shortest highway in Texas is Loop 168 in downtown Tenaha in Shelby County. This road is 0.074 mile long, or about 391 feet.

Because of the state's vast size and geographic diversity, Texas developed a concept of five areas—North, South, East, West, and Central Texas—as five potentially separate states. In fact, the United States congressional resolution by which Texas was admitted to the Union in 1845 specifies that up to four states "in addition to said state of Texas" may be formed out of its territory and that each "shall be entitled to admission to the Union." Various plans for carving Texas into five states have been proposed to the Texas legislature. Few Texans have taken those plans seriously.

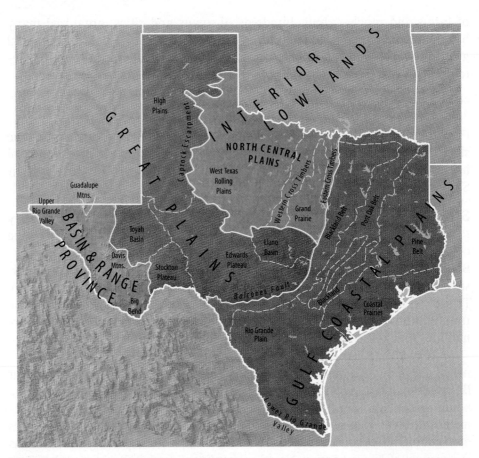

Figure 1.1 Texas Geographic Regions

Texas Almanac 2010-2011. Reprinted by permission of the *Texas Almanac,* published by *The Texas State Historical Association.*

Regions Geographically, Texas is at the confluence of several major physiographic regions of North America. The four principal **physical regions** of the state are the Gulf Coastal Plains, the Interior Lowlands, the Great Plains, and the Basin and Range Province. (For a map showing these regions, see Figure 1.1.)

The **Gulf Coastal Plains** region in East Texas is an extension of the Gulf Coastal Plains of the United States, a region that stretches westward from the Atlantic Coast and then southward into Mexico. The internal boundary of the Gulf Coastal Plains follows the Balcones Fault, so named by Spanish explorers because the westward-rising hills resemble a line of balconies. Immediately east of the fault line is the Blackland Belt. Fifteen to 70 miles in width, this strip of black soil stretches southward from the Red River, which marks the eastern half of the Oklahoma border, to the Mexican border. Within the Gulf Coastal Plains region lies the Coastal Prairies area. Bordering the Gulf of Mexico, between the Piney Woods of East Texas and the Rio Grande Plain of South Texas, this flat area has been the scene of great industrial growth since World War II, particularly in the section between Beaumont and Houston. Here are the state's chief petrochemical industries, based on oil and natural

physical region
An area identified by unique geographic features, such as the Gulf Coastal Plains and the Great Plains.

Gulf Coastal Plains
Stretching from the Louisiana border to the Rio Grande, this area is an extension of the Gulf Coastal Plains of the United States.

gas. In contrast to the arid plains of West Texas, this is the greenest region of the state, with certain areas receiving more than 50 inches of rain annually.

The **Interior Lowlands** region encompasses the North Central Plains of Texas. This territory is bounded by the Blackland Belt to the east, the Caprock Escarpment to the west, the Red River to the north, and the Colorado River to the south. Farming and ranching are important activities within this largely prairie domain. The major cities in the region are Abilene, Dallas, Fort Worth, and Wichita Falls.

In 1999, after more than a century of controversy and negotiation stemming from the 1819 Adams-Onís Treaty between the United States and Spain, the state governments of Texas and Oklahoma entered into the Red River Boundary Compact. It established the south bank of the river where vegetation begins as the boundary between the two states.

Immediately west of the Interior Lowlands and rising to higher altitudes, the Texas **Great Plains** area is a southern extension of the Great High Plains of the United States. From Oklahoma at the northern boundary of the Panhandle, this area extends southward to the Rio Grande. The Panhandle–South Plains portion of the region is known principally for its large-scale production of cotton and grain sorghum. These irrigated crops draw water from the Ogallala Aquifer, formed thousands of years ago by runoff from the Rocky Mountains. This underground, water-bearing rock formation extends northward from Texas to North Dakota, underlying parts of eight states. The chief cities of the Panhandle–South Plains are Lubbock and Amarillo.

Centered in Nevada, the **Basin and Range Province** region of the United States enters western Texas from southern New Mexico. The only part of the Lone Star State classified as mountainous, this rugged triangle provides Texans and many non-Texans with a popular vacation area that includes the Davis Mountains and Big Bend National Park. The state's highest mountains, Guadalupe Peak (8,749 feet) and El Capitán (8,085 feet), are located here. Among the few cities in this large area are the small city of Alpine (site of Sul Ross State University) and the big city of El Paso (on the north bank of the Rio Grande, just across the border from Mexico's more populous Ciudad Juárez).

Points to Ponder

- Brownsville is closer to Mexico City than to the Panhandle town of Texline.
- Texarkana is closer to Chicago, Illinois, than to El Paso.
- El Paso is closer to Los Angeles, California, on the Pacific Coast than to Port Arthur on the Gulf Coast of Texas.
- Port Arthur is closer to Jacksonville, Florida, on the Atlantic Coast than to El Paso.

Interior Lowlands
This region covers the North Central Plains of Texas, extending from the Dallas–Fort Worth metroplex westward to the Abilene area and northward to the Wichita Falls area.

Great Plains
A large area in West Texas extending from Oklahoma to Mexico, this region is an extension of the Great High Plains of the United States.

Basin and Range Province
An arid region in West Texas that includes the Davis Mountains, Big Bend National Park, and El Paso.

Economic Geography

LO4   Although geographic factors do not directly determine political differences, geography greatly influences the economic pursuits of a region's inhabitants, which in turn shape political interests and attitudes. Geography has encouraged rapid population growth, urbanization, and industrialization in East Texas; in arid West Texas, it has produced a sparsely populated rural and agricultural environment. In the course of its economic and political development, the Lone Star State has been influenced greatly by four land-based industries: cattle, cotton, timber, and hydrocarbons (including both oil and natural gas).

Cattle The origin of Texas's cattle ranching may be traced to Gregorio de Villalobos, who transported Spanish-Moorish cattle from Spain to Mexico in the early years of the conquest. Subsequently, Francisco Vásquez de Coronado and other Spanish explorers and settlers brought livestock into Texas. Later, cattle from Mexico interbred with cattle brought by Anglo settlers to produce the hardy Texas longhorn that thrives on the open range. Although "Mexican" cattle of the long-horned variety provided the basic strain, folklorist J. Frank Dobie explained that an infiltration of cattle of mongrel American blood contributed to the evolution of the Texas longhorn. Dobie estimated that the Texas longhorn evolved as the result of 80 percent Spanish influence and 20 percent mongrel influence.[7]

Plentiful land and minimal government interference encouraged huge cattle empires, established by determined entrepreneurs such as Richard King and Mifflin Kenedy. Today the famous King Ranch is composed of four separate units that total more than 825,000 acres, or almost 1,300 square miles, in Kleberg County (with the county seat at Kingsville, near the ranch headquarters) and five other South Texas counties.[8]

In 1865, an estimated five million cattle ranged over Texas's nearly 168 million acres of land. During the 25 years after the Civil War, approximately 35,000 men drove nearly 10 million cattle and one million horses north along the Chisholm and Goodnight-Loving Trails to Kansas railheads. By the late 1880s, when the railroads were built closer to Texas ranches, the cattle drives ended, and large ranches developed. In time, the political and economic impact of the beef business leveled off in the wake of newly emerging industries. Although cattle production in Texas has declined in the 21st century, Texas leads the nation in cattle production with an inventory of approximately 11 million cattle, which is more than twice as many as the next largest producer. Cattle production accounts for more than 70 percent of livestock cash receipts and approximately one-half the total for all agricultural products in the state. Texas also leads the nation in the production of sheep, goats, wool, and mohair.

In 2011, Texas experienced its most severe drought since the National Weather Service started monitoring drought conditions in 1895. As a result, the Texas AgriLife Extension Service reported a record $7.62 billion in agricultural losses, including $3.23 billion in livestock.[9] This figure represented a 20 percent decline in beef production from the previous year.

Cotton Although popular culture romanticizes the 19th-century cowboys and cattle drives, cotton formed the backbone of the state's economy in that era.

Before Spaniards brought cattle into Texas, cotton was already growing wild in the region. The rich, fertile soil led to the crop's easy cultivation, begun by Spanish missionaries. In the 1820s, the first hybrid, or improved, cotton was introduced into Texas by Colonel Jared Groce, known as the founder of the Texas cotton industry. Groce and other Anglo Texans first cultivated cotton in East and Central Texas, where crop conditions most closely resembled those in the Old South. Before the Civil War, when slaves performed much of the field labor, cotton production spread. During that war, revenue from the sale of Texas cotton to European buyers aided the Confederacy. As more frontier land was settled, cotton production moved westward and increased in volume.

Darren Hudson, director of the Cotton Economics Research Institute at Texas Tech University, estimates that the Lone Star State produces about 50 percent of U.S. cotton and approximately 10 percent of the world's cotton. In fact, Texas produces so much cotton that if you lined up all the cotton bales produced in the past 10 years end-to-end, they would circle the earth two-and-a-half times!

Although cotton is grown in each of the four principal regions across the state, the High Plains region of West Texas accounts for approximately 60 percent (more than three million bales) of the state's annual cotton yield. As a result of the 2011 drought, it was projected that cotton production in West Texas fell from a 10-year average of about 4.5 million bales per year to fewer than 1.5 million bales. This represents a loss of more than one-third of the U.S. cotton crop ($2.2 billion).[10]

In addition to cotton's contribution to the Texas economy, other important cash crops today include corn, grain sorghum, hay, rice, cottonseed, peanuts, soybeans, and pecans. Texas is also among the leading states in the production of fresh market vegetables and citrus. All of these industries were affected by the economic loss of more than $600 million from the 2011 drought.

Timber The wooded areas of the Gulf Coastal Plains region include the Piney Woods of East Texas and the Big Thicket, a densely wooded area that was largely uninhabited until the 1800s.[11] Following Texas's independence in 1836, waves of immigrants built new communities, and a construction industry was created in which timber was needed. By the mid-1800s, more than 200 sawmills were in operation from East Texas to Central Texas, employing in excess of 1,200 workers and generating more than $1.75 million dollars annually.[12] As the population of Texas grew, so did the impact of the timber industry on the Texas economy. Along with the creation of new towns throughout the state, the laying of track for new railroad lines brought increased demands for timber. This "bonanza era" in the timber industry continued well into the 20th century. By the early 1900s, the timber industry was the state's largest employer, manufacturer, and revenue generator. It has been estimated that over a 50-year period (from the 1880s until the 1930s), about 18 million acres of pine timber had been logged in Texas, producing more than 59 billion board feet of lumber.[13]

The impact of the timber industry on the state and national economies declined by the 1920s, as the practice of clear-cutting by some logging companies had depleted the availability of timber in many parts of East Texas. Hundreds of thousands of acres of woodlands had also been cleared for exploration following the discovery of oil in this region. By the late 1920s, in an effort to preserve the wooded areas of this region, several reforestation initiatives were created; and in 1933, the Texas legislature authorized the purchase of more than 600,000 acres to be used by the federal government for creation of four national forests (Angelina, Davy Crockett, Sabine, and Sam Houston). In addition, the timber industry began to implement reseeding and sustainable logging practices. In the 1940s, the Texas Forest Service, the East Texas Chamber of Commerce, the Texas Forestry Association, and the Southern Pine Association established a tree farm program for East Texas. At the end of the 20th century, Texas was the nation's tenth largest timber producer, generating more than 12.9 billion dollars annually.[14]

By 2012, the effects of the 2011 drought had resulted in the loss of between 100 and 500 million trees throughout the state. Texas Forest Service officials estimated that more than 166,000 acres of trees in East Texas would need to be replanted, at an estimated cost of $57 million.[15] An additional 1.5 million trees on more than 16,200 acres were destroyed in a catastrophic wildfire in Bastrop County in late 2011, leading one Texas Parks and Wildlife Department official to predict that it would take more than half a century to fully recover from the loss.[16]

Oil Long before Europeans arrived, Native Americans used oil seeping from the Texas soil for medicinal purposes. Early Spanish explorers in the 16th and 17th centuries used it to caulk their boats. In the late 19th century, thousands of barrels had been produced from crudely dug wells in different areas of the state. Before the 20th century, however, Texas petroleum was an unknown quantity of limited commercial value. Not until 1901, when the **Spindletop Field** was developed near Beaumont, did petroleum usher in the industry that dominated the state's economy for nearly a century. After the Spindletop boom, other wells were drilled across Texas. During the next 50 years, Texas evolved from a predominantly agricultural culture into an industrial society. Oil brought industrial employment on a grand scale to rural Texas. It offered tens of thousands of Texans an immediate and attractive alternative to life down on the farm or ranch. Many of the major oil companies, such as Gulf Oil Corporation, Humble (later ExxonMobil Corporation), Magnolia Petroleum Company, Sun Oil Company, and the Texas Company (later Texaco and more recently ChevronTexaco), were created. In 1919, the Texas legislature gave the **Railroad Commission of Texas** limited regulatory jurisdiction over the state's oil and natural gas industry.[17]

At its peak in the early 1980s, the Texas oil and gas industry employed half a million workers, who earned more than $11 billion annually. Oil and natural gas production and related industries accounted for almost one-third of the state's economy. From the mid-1980s until 1999, cheap oil and falling production plagued Texas's petroleum industry, reducing revenues for state and local governments. As a result, the Texas economy diversified and became less dependent on oil as a major revenue source. Because petroleum prices began rising sharply in 1999, Texas has been spared the economic slowdown facing most of the rest of the nation. The discovery of major natural gas deposits in South, Central, and North Texas in the early

Spindletop Field
Located near Beaumont, this oil field sparked a boom in 1901 that made Texas a leading petroleum producer.

Railroad Commission of Texas (RRC)
A popularly elected, three member commission primarily engaged in regulating natural gas and petroleum production.

21st century, along with the advent of new recovery methods such as hydraulic fracking, further insulated the state's economy. With increased economic diversification and oil prices under $100 per barrel in 2012, however, oil is not expected to regain its former level of influence.

Texas has four of the 10 largest U.S. oil fields in terms of production, but today the oil and gas industry accounts for less than 6 percent of the state's economy. About 250,000 Texans worked in this industry in 2012, and even more Texans depended on energy-related industries for their employment. Most oil and gas jobs (including those in refineries and other petrochemical plants) pay relatively high wages and salaries. Meanwhile, awareness is growing that oil-based fuels burned in automobiles, trucks, buses, and airplanes are the world's principal source of air pollution. In addition, immeasurable harm to the world's oceans has resulted from oil spills in the Gulf of Mexico and other waters around the globe. In April 2010, when the BP oil rig *Deepwater Horizon* exploded, an estimated 206 million gallons of oil were released into the Gulf of Mexico. This was the largest oil spill in the history of the petroleum industry and had an $8.7 billion impact on the economy of the Gulf of Mexico, including losses in revenue, profit, and wages, and close to 22,000 jobs.

 Learning Check 1.2   (Answers on p. 39)

1. What are the four principal physical regions located in Texas?
2. In 1901, which oil field ushered in the oil industry that would dominate Texas's economy for nearly a century?

★ The People

Texas has a large, ethnically diverse population. In every decade since 1850, Texas's population has grown more rapidly than the overall population of the United States. Like the population of the nation, Texas's population is aging as the post–World War II baby-boom generation (persons born between 1946 and 1964) nears retirement age. The Bureau of the Census estimates that the population of Texans older than the age of 64 will exceed five million by 2030. More than one-half of all Texans are either African Americans or Latinos (also called Hispanics).[18] The remainder are predominantly Anglos (non-Hispanic whites), with a small but rapidly growing number of Asians and approximately 170,000 Native Americans (also called American Indians). A study released by Rice University's Kinder Institute of Urban Research and Hobby Center for the Study of Texas in 2012 found that the Houston metropolitan area replaced New York City as the most ethnically diverse large metropolitan area in the country.[19] (For a discussion about the impact of the minority population on Texas's growth in the most recent census, see this chapter's Selected Reading, "Minorities Drove Texas Growth, Census Figures Show.")

How Do We Compare...in Population?

2011 Population Estimates as Reported by the U.S. Bureau of the Census

Most Populous U.S. States	Population	U.S. States Bordering Texas	Population
California	37,691,912	Arkansas	2,937,979
Florida	19,057,542	Louisiana	4,574,836
New York	19,465,197	New Mexico	2,082,224
Texas	**25,674,681**	Oklahoma	3,791,508

Demographic Features

According to the federal census estimate of 2011, Texas's population totaled 25,674,681—an increase of 23 percent from 2000. (At the national level, the total population estimate in 2011 was 311,591,917—an increase of nearly 11 percent from 2000.) Texas also had five of the fastest-growing metropolitan areas in the nation between 2000 and 2010. Austin–Round Rock–San Marcos grew by 37 percent; McAllen–Edinburg–Mission grew by 36 percent; Laredo grew by more than 29 percent; Houston–Sugar Land–Bay Town grew by 26 percent; and Dallas–Fort Worth–Arlington grew by more than 23 percent. By contrast, only one metropolitan area (Wichita Falls, −0.1) actually experienced a decrease in population during that period.

Population Distribution Just as Texas's physical geography makes the state a land of great contrasts, so does the distribution of its inhabitants. Densely populated, humid eastern areas contrast with sparsely populated arid regions in the west. At one extreme is Harris County (containing Houston and most of its suburbs). Located in the southeastern part of the state, Harris has approximately four million inhabitants. At the other extreme is Loving County, on the New Mexico border, where the 2010 census counted only 82 people. Today, Texas's four most populous counties (Harris, Dallas, Bexar, and Tarrant) have a combined population of more than 10 million people. These four urban counties (along with Travis County) are located within the Texas Triangle, which is roughly outlined by segments of interstate highways 35, 45, and 10.

In the 1980s and 1990s, **population shifts** within Texas matched the national pattern: movement from rural to urban areas and from large cities to suburbs. Regions in which the economy depended largely on oil and agriculture either decreased in total population or grew more slowly than the state as a whole. Although the movement from rural to urban areas and the growth of exurbs (extra-urban areas beyond suburbs) has continued into the 21st century, there has also been a repopulation of inner cities. Houston, Dallas, Fort Worth, and Austin have revitalized their downtowns and attracted new urban residents.

population shifts
Within Texas, changes in population density have featured demographic movements from rural to urban areas and from large cities to the suburbs and back.

By 2012, many rural areas in The Lone Star State experienced rapid population growth as a result of resurgence in oil and natural gas production.[20]

Urbanization Migration of people from rural regions to cities results in **urbanization**. Urban areas are composed of one or more large cities and their surrounding suburban communities. A suburb is a relatively small town or city, usually outside the boundary limits of a central city. For a century after statehood, Texas remained primarily rural. Texas was 80 percent rural at the beginning of the 20th century, but by 1970, it was 80 percent urban. Today, Texans living in metropolitan areas constitute more than 85 percent of the state's population. Suburbs adjoining or near central cities spread into rural areas and surrounding counties.

Metropolitanization Suburbanization on a large scale creates a metropolitan area, or a core city surrounded by a sprawl of smaller cities and towns. Like most states, Texas is experiencing suburbanization on a very large scale. Between 1980 and 2010, Texas suburbs experienced explosive growth. **Metropolitanization** concentrates large numbers of people in urban centers, which become linked in a single geographic entity. Although socially and economically integrated, a metropolitan area is composed of separate units of local government, which include counties, cities, and special districts.

Since 1910, federal agencies have defined metropolitan areas for census purposes. In general, a metropolitan area is a core area containing a large population nucleus together with adjacent communities economically and socially integrated with that core. The term *core-based statistical area* (CBSA) was coined in 2000 and refers collectively to metropolitan and micropolitan statistical areas. Each CBSA must contain at least one urban area with a population of 10,000 or more. Effective June 6, 2003, the U. S. Office of Management and Budget established new sets of statistical areas. Today, criteria for these designations are as follows:

- **Micropolitan statistical area:** has at least one urban cluster with a population of at least 10,000, but less than 50,000
- **Metropolitan statistical area:** the basic unit, comprising a freestanding urbanized area with a total population of at least 50,000
- **Combined statistical area:** a geographic entity consisting of two or more adjacent CBSAs
- **Metropolitan division:** a county or group of counties within a CBSA that contains a core with a population of at least 2.5 million

By 2010, the United States (including Puerto Rico) had 581 micropolitan statistical areas (42 in Texas), 374 metropolitan statistical areas (44 in Texas), 128 combined statistical areas (9 in Texas), and 29 metropolitan divisions (2 in Texas; one consisting of Dallas–Plano–Irving and the other consisting of Fort Worth–Arlington).

Cities are eager to obtain the highest possible statistical designation because many congressional appropriations are made accordingly. For example, to qualify for mass transit funds, an area must be a Metropolitan Statistical Area (MSA). The business community also uses data on population concentrations for market analysis and advertising.

urbanization
Migration of people from rural areas to cities.

suburbanization
Growth of relatively small towns and cities, usually incorporated but outside the corporate limits of a central city.

metropolitanization
Concentration of people in urban centers that become linked.

micropolitan statistical area (mSA)
An area that has at least one urban cluster with a population of at least 10,000, but less than 50,000.

metropolitan statistical area (MSA)
A freestanding urban area with a minimum total population of 50,000.

combined statistical area (CSA)
A geographic entity consisting of two or more adjacent core-based statistical areas.

metropolitan division
County or group of counties within a core based statistical area that contains a core with a population of at least 2.5 million.

Texas's rate of population growth is consistently greater in the MSAs than throughout the state as a whole. Most of these population concentrations are in the eastern part of the state and in South Texas's Rio Grande. The Lone Star State's MSAs contain more than 80 percent of the state's population but fewer than 20 percent of the state's 254 counties. It is politically significant that these 48 counties potentially account for about four of every five votes cast in state-wide elections. Thus, governmental decision makers are answerable primarily to people living in one-fifth of the state's counties. The remaining four-fifths, constituting the bulk of the state's area, have one-fifth of the people. Urban voters, however, are rarely of one mind at the polls; they do not tend to overwhelm rural voters by taking opposing positions on all policy issues.

Racial/Ethnic Groups

In 2010, the U.S. Census Bureau reported racial categories in Texas at the following percentages:

White/Anglo:	45.3
Hispanic/Latino:	37.6
Black/African American:	11.5
Asian:	3.8
American Indian or Alaskan Native:	0.3
Native Hawaiian or other Pacific Islander:	0.1
Other or two or more races:	1.3

In 1980, two-thirds of all Texans were called Anglos (that is, white people not identified as Hispanics or Latinos). By 2004, less than one-half of the Texas population could be classified as Anglo. In 2010, more than 60 percent of births in the state were non-Anglo births, with Latino births accounting for more than one-half of all newborns. Based on current population trends, some demographers suggest that by 2040, Latinos will comprise 58 percent of the state's population.[21]

Anglos As commonly used in Texas, the term *Anglo* is not restricted to persons of Anglo-Saxon lineage. Traditionally, the term applies to all whites except Latinos. By 1800, Anglo settlements began to appear in East Texas. Before the Civil War, more than one-half of the state's Anglo residents had migrated from Alabama, Arkansas, Georgia, Kentucky, Louisiana, Mississippi, Missouri, and Tennessee.[22] Most remained in the eastern half of the state as farmers. Although the first non–Spanish-speaking immigrants to Texas were largely of English ancestry, some were of Scottish, Irish, or Welsh ancestry. Additional European settlers included French, Scandinavian, and Eastern European peoples, together with a scattering of Italians, Greeks, and others.

A significant number of German immigrants established settlements in the Hill Country west and north of San Antonio before the Civil War. It has been estimated that as many as 24,000 German immigrants and descendants were settled in the Hill Country by 1860. Most opposed slavery on principle, whereas others simply had no need for slaves. As a result, 14 counties in Central Texas voted 40 percent or greater against secession in 1861. The area was scarred by

Anglo
A term commonly used in Texas to identify non–Latino white people.

what a historian called "a civil war within a Civil War,"[23] as hundreds of Union and Confederate sympathizers were killed in armed confrontations. Although Anglo migration into the state declined during the Civil War and Reconstruction, it resumed by the 1870s. By the turn of the 20th century, the largest migration came from the border states, the Northeast, and the Midwest.

According to the 2000 census, more than 52 percent of Texas's population was composed of "non–Hispanic whites." However, that percentage dropped to less than 50 percent in 2004, when Texas joined Hawaii, New Mexico, California, and the District of Columbia as majority-minority states. By 2010, the percent of Anglos dropped to around 45 percent. Population projections show that the percentage of Anglos in the state will continue to decrease and the percentage of other racial/ethnic groups will continue to increase.

Latinos Until 1836, Texas history was part of the history of Spain and Mexico. From 1836, when Texas gained independence from Mexico, until 1900, immigration from Mexico all but ceased. **Latinos** remained concentrated in settlements such as Goliad, Laredo, and San Antonio, which were founded during the 18th century. Most of the Latino population, however, was located within the regions of Central and South Texas. In South Texas, they composed a majority of the population despite the increased number of Anglo arrivals after the Mexican War of 1846–1848 (which followed admission of Texas into the Union). In the years after the Civil War, Latinos moved west, migrating along with Anglo settlers to displace Native Americans from their lands and to convert the prairies into cattle and sheep ranches.

Early in the 20th century, the rise of commercial agriculture created the need for seasonal laborers. Consequently, many Latinos picked cotton, fruits, and vegetables. Others found work as day laborers or used their skills as ranch hands or shepherds. Although Texas became more urbanized after World War I, Latinos remained mostly an agrarian people. After World War II, however, increased numbers of Latinos left agricultural work and sought employment opportunities in the industrializing cities. Most of them experienced improvements in wages and working conditions in unskilled or semiskilled positions, although a growing number of Latinos entered managerial, sales, and clerical professions.[24] In the second half of the 20th century, Texas's Latino population was enlarged by a relatively high birth rate and a surge of both legal and illegal immigration from Mexico and other countries in the Western Hemisphere. In the 1980s, Texas's Latino population became more diverse in terms of country of origin, following an increase in immigrants from Central America, South America, and the islands of the Caribbean.

By 2010, Texas Latinos numbered about 9.5 million, approximately 37 percent of the state's population. More than 84 percent of Texas Latinos are of Mexican origin. Texas ranks second in the nation in the number of Latino residents; only California, with about 14 million in 2010, has more. The majority of the population in 50 Texas counties is Latino. In seven counties in the Rio Grande Valley and along the border (Brooks, Hildago, Jim Hogg, Maverick, Starr, Zapata, and Zavala), more than 90 percent of the population is Latino. Texas's Spanish-surnamed citizens are gaining economic

Latino
This is an ethnic classification of Mexican Americans and others of Latin American origin. When applied to females, the term is *Latina*.

strength. Latinos typically have larger families and are younger than the Anglo population. Immigration from Mexico and other Spanish-speaking countries is expected to continue throughout the 21st century.

Latino political influence is also increasing. Between 1846 and 1961, only 19 Latino politicians were elected to seats in the Texas legislature. Since 1961, however, Latinos have won elections to local, statewide, and national positions. In 1984, with the election of Raul Gonzalez to the Texas Supreme Court, the first Latino won a statewide office. By 2010, Texas had more than 2,300 Latino elected officials, the largest number of any state in the United States. This figure represents more than 40 percent of all Latino elected officials in the country. Organizations such as the League of United Latin American Citizens and the Southwest Voter Registration Education Project have worked to increase voter registration and turnout among Latinos in recent years. In November 2012, one Texas Latino (Ted Cruz) was elected to the U.S. Senate and six Texas Latinos were elected to the U.S. House of Representatives. At the same time, 40 Latinos were elected to the Texas legislature: seven in the Senate and 33 in the House of Representatives. Although he died three weeks before the election, Senator Mario Gallegos's name remained on the ballot and he was re-elected to the Texas Senate. A special election was called to replace him in the Senate. A year earlier, Rebecca Forest, a co-founder of the Immigration Reform Coalition of Texas and a leader in the Tea Party movement publicly announced, "If you want to know why we can't pass legislation in Texas, it's because we have 37, no, 36 Hispanics in the legislature. So, that's part of our problem, and we need to change those numbers. We need to do something about that in fact."[25] Her remarks drew criticism from several Republican state officials.

African Americans The first **African Americans** entered Texas as slaves of Spanish explorers in the 16th century. By 1792, it was reported that Spanish Texans included 34 blacks and 414 mulattos.[26] Some of them were free men and women. About the time slavery was abolished in Mexico (1831), Anglo settlers brought larger numbers of black slaves from the United States to Texas. In addition, a few free African Americans came from northern states before the Civil War. By 1847, African Americans accounted for one-fourth of the state's population. During Reconstruction, there was a small wave of freemen migration into Texas. Many African Americans also moved from the state's rural areas to large cities. They often resided in "freedmantowns," which became the distinct black neighborhoods on the outskirts of these cities. Some of these freedmantowns have been preserved by various historical associations. Black labor also contributed substantially to the economic development of Texas cities and helped the state's transition from its agrarian roots to an increasingly industrialized society. In 1880, the African American population in Texas numbered approximately 400,000.

By 2010, Texas had 2.8 million African Americans, more than 11 percent of the state's population. Although the African American population has continued to grow, it is moving at a much slower rate than other ethnic groups. Today, Texas has the third-largest number of African Americans in the nation after New York and California. Most reside in southeast, north central, and

African American
A racial classification indicating African ancestry.

northeast Texas, concentrated in large cities. In recent years, a significant number of Africans have immigrated to the United States and settled in Texas. Their search for employment and their desire for a higher standard of living have prompted this migration. More than one-half of the state's African Americans reside in and around Houston (approximately 754,000), Dallas (518,000), Fort Worth (262,000), San Antonio (118,000), Beaumont (84,000), and Austin (83,000). Although African Americans do not constitute a majority in any Texas county, according to the 2010 census, Jefferson County had the greatest percentage of African Americans at 33.5 percent.

Like Latinos, as the African American population in Texas increased, so did its political influence. From the years following Reconstruction until 1958 (when Hattie White was elected to the Houston Independent School District Board of Trustees), no African American had held elective office in the state. In 1972, Barbara Jordan became the first African American since the Reconstruction era to represent Texas in Congress, and in 1992, Morris Overstreet became the first African American to win a statewide office when he was elected to the Texas Court of Criminal Appeals. Although his bid was ultimately unsuccessful, Ron Kirk became the first African American Texan to be nominated by a major party (Democratic) for a U.S. Senate seat in 2002. Today African Americans from Texas hold local, statewide, and national offices. Four African Americans were elected to the U.S. House of Representatives in November 2012, and 20 African Americans were elected to the Texas legislature: two in the Senate and 18 in the House of Representatives.

Asian Americans Few members of Texas's three largest ethnic populations (Anglo, Latino, and African American) are aware that the Lone Star State is home to one of the largest **Asian American** populations (nearly 1 million) in the nation. Most of Texas's Asian American families immigrated to the United States from Southeast Asia (Cambodia, Laos, and Vietnam in particular), but a growing percentage are American born. Compared with Latinos and African Americans, however, Asian Americans are newcomers to Texas. When Vietnamese-born Hubert Vo (D-Houston) defeated 11-term incumbent representative Talmadge Heflin (R-Houston) in the 2004 general election, he became the first Vietnamese American to be elected to the Texas House of Representatives. Vo was reelected in 2006, 2008, 2010 and 2012.

Most Asian Americans live in the state's largest urban centers—Houston and the Dallas–Fort Worth metroplex. Asians do not constitute a majority in any Texas county, according to the 2010 census. Fort Bend near Houston had the greatest percentage of Asian Americans at 17 percent. Although many are unskilled laborers, approximately one-half of Texas's first-generation Asian Americans entered this country with college degrees or completed degrees once they arrived. The intensity with which the state's young Asian Americans focus on education is revealed by enrollment data for the University of Texas at Austin. Although Asian Americans account for less than 4 percent of the total population of the state, they comprised 17.8 percent of the undergraduate enrollment at the University of Texas at Austin and 22.7 percent of the enrollment at the University of Texas at Dallas in the fall 2011 semester.

Asian American
A term used to identify people of Asian ancestry (such as Chinese, Vietnamese, Korean).

State Representative Hubert Vo on the House floor.

(AP Photo/Harry Cabluck)

Native Americans The Lone Star State owes part of its cultural heritage to Native Americans, who were called *indios* by Spanish explorers and American Indians by Anglo settlers. Today, relatively few Texans are identified as Native Americans, but some counties (Cherokee, Comanche, Nacogdoches, Panola, Wichita), cities and towns (Caddo Mills, Lipan, Nocona, Quanah, Watauga, Waxahachie), and other places have names that remind us that Native Americans were here first. In fact, the state's name comes from the word *tejas,* meaning "friendly," which was also the tribal name for a group of Indians within the Caddo Confederacy.

Before 1900, members of more than 50 Native American tribes or nations roamed the prairies or had permanent settlements within the territory that became Texas. The Comanches, who displaced the Lipan Apaches, were the most important tribe in shaping Texas history. Excellent horsemen, they were an obstacle to the northward expansion of Spaniards and the westward expansion of Anglos. By contrast, the Tonkawa were a peaceful tribe who lived in Central Texas and often allied with the Anglos against the Comanches and the Wichitas, another important South Plains tribe. In East Texas, the Caddo lived in organized villages that had a complex and sophisticated political system.

Estimates of the number of Native Americans in Texas when the first Spaniards arrived range from 30,000 to 150,000. Traveling in the Lone Star State in 1856, after three decades of Anglo-Indian warfare, one observer estimated the state's Native American population at about 12,000.[27] By 2010, Texas Native Americans numbered around 170,000. Most reside in towns and cities, where they work in a variety of jobs and professions.

Only a few Native Americans live on Texas reservations. Approximately 1,100 members of the Alabama and Coushatta tribes reside on a 4,351-acre reservation in Polk County in the Big Thicket region of East Texas. Far across the state, near Eagle Pass on the U.S.–Mexican border, live a few

Native American
A descendent of the first Americans, who were called *indios* by Spanish explorers and Indians by Anglo settlers who arrived later.

hundred members of another Indian nation, the Kickapoo tribe. The governments of Mexico and the United States allow them to move back and forth between Texas and the Mexican state of Coahuila. A third Native American group, the 1,700-member Tigua tribe, inhabits a 100-acre reservation near El Paso.

☑ Learning Check 1.3   (Answers on p. 39)

1. Which four counties have a combined population of more than 40 percent of the state's population?
2. True or False: The fastest-growing ethnic group in Texas is Latinos.

★ Searching for New Economic Directions

Once identified in the popular mind with cattle barons, cotton kings, and oil millionaires, the image of the Lone Star State is changing. Even though increased oil and gas production provided some protection from the full effect of the economic downturn that began in 2007, the hydrocarbon industry is still not expected to gain its former leading role in Texas business. Therefore, restructuring the state's economy has been vigorously pursued since the 1980s. In so doing, business and government leaders have launched new industrial programs within the context of rapid national and international change. Today, Texas is part of middle-class America, with its share of professionals and businesspeople employed by varied enterprises: law firms; universities; federal, state, and local government bureaucracies; real estate and insurance companies; wholesale and retail sales firms; and manufacturing, communications, and transportation industries. A continuing struggle to provide jobs and market goods and services, however, requires effective public policies, an educated and productive labor force, an adequate supply of capital, and sound management practices.

For more than half a century, petroleum production and related enterprises led Texas's industrial development. Then, devastated by plunging oil prices in the mid-1980s, the entire Texas petroleum industry decreased sharply. Even by the 1990s, with the price of oil on the rebound, Texans understood the danger of being overly reliant on one industry and recognized the need to develop an economically diverse economy. New industries have quickly spread across the state, affecting the Texas economy and playing an important role in the national economy. In 2006, for the first time, more *Fortune* 500 companies were headquartered in Texas than in any other state. By 2010, however, California tied Texas with 57 of the 500 largest corporations at the top of *Fortune*'s annual listing. In 2012, California ranked first with 53 and Texas was second with 52.[28]

Energy

A natural offspring of the state's expansive oil and gas industries, three of the four largest corporations headquartered in Texas in 2012 were energy and energy related (the other [AT&T] was communications related). These three Texas oil and gas companies were ranked within the top twelve corporations in the United States: ExxonMobil, first; ConocoPhillips, fourth; and Valero, twelfth.

Another energy-related corporation that was headquartered in Texas before its collapse, the Enron Corporation, consistently placed high on the *Fortune* list throughout the 1990s. The corporation, however, declared bankruptcy in 2001, after a series of disclosures about executives having reported inflated profits and reduced debt and having misled their employees, investors, and the general public regarding the company's financial condition. Several top Enron officials were later found guilty of charges including securities fraud; conspiracy to commit wire fraud; insider trading; and conspiracy to falsify books, records, and accounts.[29]

The process of hydraulic fracturing of underground rock formations to release the flow of natural gas is also known as "fracking." Although the natural gas and oil industry has been using this process since the 1940s, recent advancements in equipment and technology have made fracking a common practice. By 2012, there were more than 216,000 of these active injection wells in Texas. In fracking, chemicals are mixed with sand and water. Then the mixture is injected under high pressure into an underground

 CourseReader ASSIGNMENTS

Log in to www.cengagebrain.com and open CourseReader to access the reading:

Texas Wind Industry's Rapid Growth Creates New Challenges
Will Furgeson

The state of Texas has taken the lead in the development of alternative energy generation and transmission. This often comes as a surprise to those expecting the state to resist alternative sources of energy given the large oil and gas deposits with which geography and geology have blessed the state. Whether the state can maintain this initial interest in the benefits (financial and environmental) of wind power will depend on a number of very important factors, as this article shows. Some of these are within the power of the state to control, but others place Texas in an uncomfortable position of wait-and-see.

1. Trace the growth of the wind energy industry in Texas. What factors have led to the development of this industry, and how have public policies facilitated or limited its growth?

2. What political, economic, and environmental challenges face the continued growth of the wind energy industry in Texas? How might these challenges be addressed?

shale formation to force out oil and gas. This process has raised concerns by the U.S. Environmental Protection Agency (EPA) and environmental groups about depletion of water, contamination of drinking water, and induction of earthquakes. As a result of a bill passed in 2011 by the 82nd legislature, Texas became the first state in the nation to require drillers to publicly disclose chemicals used in the fracking process.

With environmental concerns about the oil and gas industry, many Texans, including members of groups such as the Sustainable Energy and Economic Development (SEED) Coalition, the Lone Star Chapter of the Sierra Club, the Texas Campaign on the Environment, and the Texas Clean Air Working Group (a project of the Texas Conference of Urban Counties), have identified alternative fuel strategies for the Lone Star State. In 2010, Texas experienced a 30 percent increase in renewable sources over 2009, with the overwhelming share being wind power.[30] Wind generated 8 percent of the state's electricity and more than 26 million (of 28 million) renewable megawatt-hours. Most of Texas's wind farms are located in West Texas. Although the Texas legislature has twice refused to create financial incentives to encourage the solar industry in Texas, it was announced in 2011 that one of the nation's largest solar photovoltaic generation farms would be erected east of Austin, near Webberville, to generate power for Austin Energy, the nation's ninth largest community-owned electric utility.[31]

Anticipating the need to train workers in alternative energy technologies, several institutions of higher education in the state (including Texas Tech, Texas A&M, West Texas A&M, the University of Texas at Austin, the University of Houston, and Texas State Technical College in Sweetwater) offer renewable energy programs and classes in wind and solar power.

High Technology

The term *high technology* applies to research, development, manufacturing, and marketing of a seemingly endless line of electronic products. Among these are computers, calculators, digital watches, microwave ovens, telecommunications devices, automatic bank tellers, aerospace guidance systems, medical instruments, and assembly-line robots. Although high-technology businesses employ less than 6 percent of Texas's labor force, these enterprises contribute about 10 percent of all wages paid to private-sector employees. Most "high-tech" jobs are in manufacturing. Approximately 85 percent of all high-tech employment in Texas is centered in Austin, Dallas, El Paso, Fort Worth, Houston, and San Antonio. Major high-tech manufacturers include Motorola, Dell, Hewlett-Packard, Texas Instruments, and Applied Materials (which produces machinery for manufacturing semiconductors).

The occupational structure of many high-tech companies differs from those of most other industrial firms. High-tech enterprises employ larger percentages of professional, technical, and managerial personnel. More than one-third of all high-tech jobs are in these categories, and wages and salaries are nearly twice as much as the average for other private-sector positions. At the request of Governor Rick Perry and other leaders in government

high technology
Technology that applies to research, development, manufacturing, and marketing of computers and other electronic products.

and business, the 79th Texas legislature created the Texas Emerging Technology Fund in 2005, providing $200 million for research and development activities in emerging technology industries. The Texas Emerging Technology Fund is designed to expand the state's high-tech industry, to encourage relocation of high-tech companies from other states (especially California), and to challenge Texas's community colleges and universities to educate more students for high-tech careers. (For more information on the Texas Emerging Technology Fund, see Jeff Key, "The Low Politics of High Tech in the Lone Star State," the Selected Reading in Chapter 8.) During the first decade of the 21st century, however, in cities such as Houston, Dallas, and Austin, jobs in semiconductor, computer, and circuit board manufacturing actually declined. Several high-tech companies relocated to other states and countries in pursuit of lower labor costs, predictable regulations, access to markets, incentives, and a skilled workforce.[32] Despite this trend, by 2012, approximately 450,000 Texans held high-tech jobs, and Texas has continued to rank second only to California in the size of its high-tech workforce.

Biotechnology

The history of biotechnology dates back more than 6,000 years, when the Egyptians began using ycast to leaven bread, brew beer, produce wine, and make cheese. Today biotechnology ("biotech") exerts a growing influence on the state's economy. This multibillion-dollar industry produces many new medicines and vaccines, exotic chemicals, and other products designed to benefit medical science, human health, and agricultural production. In the past two decades, biotech-related jobs have increased four times faster than the overall increase in employment in Texas. As home to more than 4,500 biotechnology firms, manufacturing companies, industry consortia, and research university facilities, Texas employs more than 100,000 workers in the biotech sector at an average annual salary of over $74,800.[33]

Texas A&M University, which has become a recognized national leader in the biotechnology revolution in agriculture, hosts an annual conference for biotechnology educators each fall. Supported by Monsanto and other biotech companies, scientists at Texas A&M University have played an important role in research leading to the production of genetically modified organism (GMO) crops, such as corn, soybeans, and cotton. Greenpeace and other environmental groups, however, have opposed the marketing of gene-altered products without long-term safety tests and have called for labeling of all foods containing GMOs.[34] The Center for Innovation in Advanced Development and Manufacturing is likely worth $1.5 to $2 billion. This is the largest sum of federal money to come to Texas since NASA.

Services

One of the fastest-growing economic sectors in Texas is the service industry. Employing one-fourth of all Texas workers, service industries continue to provide new jobs more rapidly than all other sectors. Service businesses include health-care providers (hospitals and nursing homes); personal services (hotels, restaurants, and recreational enterprises such as bowling alleys and video arcades); and commercial services (printers, advertising agencies, data-processing companies, equipment rental companies, and management consultants). Other service providers include education, investment brokers, insurance and real estate agencies, banks and credit unions, and numerous merchandising enterprises.

Influenced by an aging population and the availability and use of new medical procedures, health services employment has steadily increased. According to the Texas Workforce Commission, private and public health-care services employ about 1.1 million workers (including 624,000 in ambulatory health care services, 297,000 in hospitals, and about 174,000 in nursing and residential care).[35] It is projected that these positions will be among the fastest growing occupations over the next several years.[36]

Most service jobs pay lower wages and salaries than manufacturing firms that produce goods. Thus, the late journalist Molly Ivins warned that "the dream that we can transform ourselves into a service economy and let all the widget-makers go to hell or Taiwan is bullstuff. The service sector creates jobs all right, but they're the lowest paying jobs in the system. You can't afford a house frying burgers at McDonald's, even if you're a two-fryer family."[37]

Agriculture

Endowed with a wide range of climates, as well as adequate transportation and harbor facilities, Texas ranks second in the nation in agricultural production. It leads the country in total acreage of agricultural land and numbers of farms and ranches, as well as in production of beef, grain sorghum, cotton, wool, and mohair (from Angora goats).

Gross income from the products of Texas agriculture amounts to about $22 billion annually, making agriculture the second largest industry in Texas. The nation's second largest exporter of agricultural products (behind California), the Lone Star State leads the country in exported cotton, much of which goes to South Korea and Taiwan. Mexico is the largest purchaser of Texas's farm and ranch products, and Japan is a major consumer of Texas-grown wheat and corn. Beef is the state's most important meat export.

Despite these impressive statistics, however, farming and ranching provide less than 2 percent of the state's jobs and total income. Furthermore, most agricultural commodities are shipped abroad or to other parts of the United States without being processed in Texas by Texans. Consequently, Texas needs industrial development for the processing of food and fiber to derive maximum economic benefit from the products of its farms and ranches.

The number and size of Texas farms and ranches have changed greatly during the past eight decades. These developments largely reflect the availability of labor-saving farm machinery and the use of chemicals to kill weeds, defoliate cotton before harvesting, and protect crops from insects and diseases. In the 1930s, Texas had more than 500,000 farms and ranches, with an average size of 300 acres. By 2010, the number of farms and ranches had decreased to less than 250,000 and the average size had grown to approximately 527 acres.[38]

Most small farms are operated by part-time farmers, many of whom can farm only because a spouse has nonfarm employment. When farm commodity prices are low (because of overproduction and weak market demand) or when crops are poor (as a result of drought), many farmers end the year deeply in debt. Some are forced to sell their land—usually to larger farm operators and sometimes to corporations. But some rich corporate executives, professional people, and politicians purchase agricultural property (especially ranchland) because such ownership is a status symbol they can afford—even though their land generates little or no income. Some use their agricultural property ownership to qualify for various exemptions and reductions for state or local sales and property taxes and for federal income tax deductions. In addition, economic pressures have led to the loss of much farm and ranchland near expanding cities to urban sprawl. According to the U.S. Department of Agriculture, every minute, a half-acre of Texas farmland is converted into part of a road, shopping mall, or subdivision.

In late 2011, the Texas drought was the worst single-year Texas drought since recordkeeping began. It may also prove to be one of most devastating economic events in the history of the Lone Star State. Texas AgriLife Extension Service reported a record $7.62 billion in agricultural losses in 2011 as a result of the record drought.[39]

Trade

In 1993, the U.S. Congress approved the **North American Free Trade Agreement (NAFTA),** to which the United States, Canada, and Mexico are parties. By reducing and then eliminating tariffs during a 15-year period, the agreement stimulated U.S. trade with both Canada and Mexico. Because more than 60 percent of U.S. exports to Mexico are produced in Texas or transported through the Lone Star State from other states, expanding foreign trade produces more jobs for Texans, more profits for the state's businesses, and more revenue for state and local governments.

Maquiladoras (partner plants) on the Mexican side of the border typically use cheap labor to assemble imported parts for a wide range of consumer goods and then export these goods back to the United States. Under NAFTA, these exports are subject to reduced or no taxation by Mexican and U.S. governments. Consequently, Texas border cities (especially Brownsville, McAllen, Laredo, and El Paso) attract many manufacturers who set up supply and distribution facilities in Texas that serve the maquiladoras in Mexico.[40] A report by the director of the United Nations Development Fund for Women revealed that labor policies at maquiladora assembly plants, including late shifts and turning away employees for tardiness, endanger women in Ciudad Juárez, a Mexican city across the border from El Paso, where hundreds of women and girls have disappeared or have been raped and murdered in recent years.[41]

NAFTA is not without its critics. Texas's garment industry has been adversely affected, especially in border counties. Most clothing manufacturers have closed their plants and moved to Mexico, Central America, the Caribbean islands, or Asia. Likewise, some Texas fruit and vegetable producers have been hurt by Mexican competition. In addition, increased trucking on highways

North American Free Trade Agreement (NAFTA)
An agreement among the United States, Mexico, and Canada designed to expand trade among the three countries by reducing and then eliminating tariffs over a 15-year period.

maquiladora
An assembly plant that uses cheap labor and is located on the Mexican side of the U.S.–Mexican border.

between Mexico and Canada has contributed to air pollution in Texas and causes serious traffic problems that make travel more dangerous for all drivers and passengers and that slow transportation of goods.

Since 1995, a succession of political and economic crises in Mexico has raised serious questions concerning NAFTA's future. In fact, the survival of Mexico's political system has been jeopardized by assassinations of public figures, kidnappings of wealthy businesspeople, drug-related corruption of government officials, attacks on tourists, widespread unemployment and hunger in both urban and rural areas, and acts of armed rebellion (especially in the southern states of Chiapas, Oaxaca, and Guerrero).[42]

The election of President Vincente Fox in 2000 raised hopes for expanding political democracy, reducing poverty, and suppressing crime and corruption in Mexico.[43] After dominating Mexican politics for 71 years, the Institutional Revolutionary Party (PRI) lost the presidency to Fox and his National Action Party (PAN). Although Fox's victory demonstrated Mexico's capacity for peaceful political change, his country's serious economic and social problems were not easily solved. By the end of his six-year term, President Fox had experienced only limited economic success.

Slow growth of the Mexican economy and increased violence has led many Mexican citizens to migrate. A more prosperous and stable Mexico would help reduce the flow of jobless workers to Texas and other parts of the United States, while increasing the volume of trade between the two countries.[44] In 2006, Mexico's voters selected PAN candidate Felipe Calderón to succeed Fox. Despite the Mexican government's efforts to disrupt drug-trafficking operations, a report issued by the U.S. General Accounting Office in December 2009 highlighted a record-breaking escalation of drug-related assassinations, kidnappings, and other violent crimes.[45] In January 2012, the Mexican government reported that 47,515 people had been killed in drug-related violence since President Felipe Calderón began a military assault on criminal cartels soon after taking office in late 2006. Although drug-related killings in 2011 increased by 11 percent (to 12,903) from the previous year, violence and homicides along the border (including Ciudad Juárez, the bloodiest city) had actually declined.[46] In July 2012, PRI candidate Enrique Peña Nieto was elected to serve as president until November 30, 2018.

Several Texas politicians, including Agriculture Commissioner Todd Staples and U.S. Senator John Cornyn have advocated for increasing trade with Cuba. Although Cuba has been designated as a sponsor of terrorism, Texas agriculture exports to the island continue to grow.[47]

☑ Learning Check 1.4   (Answers on p. 39)

1. True or False: The five largest private corporations in Texas are in the high-tech industry.
2. What is the term for "partner plants" on the Mexican side of the border that use cheap labor to assemble imported parts for a variety of consumer goods and then export these goods back to the United States?

Meeting New Challenges: Social and Economic Policy Issues

LO6   Social and economic influences on government, politics, and policymaking are evident as we continue to move deeper into the 21st century. Texas has experienced a wave of uncontrolled immigration and rapid economic change, and Texans are greatly affected by public policy decisions concerning the state's economy and its entire social order. The most important of these decisions relate to immigration and Texas's workforce, protection of the ecological system, job-creating economic development, technological changes in communications and industry, and restructuring and financing of the state's public schools and institutions of higher education.[48]

Immigration: Federal and State Problems

Since Texas became part of the United States, the meandering Rio Grande boundary with Mexico has been the source of many controversies. Controlling the flow of aliens across the river, deciding how long they may remain within U.S. territory, determining what labor (if any) they may perform, and other immigration policy matters are issues that affect state, national, and international politics. Persons who enter the United States in violation of federal immigration laws are called **undocumented aliens**. Although they supply Texas employers with cheap labor, some compete with U.S. citizens for jobs and require costly social services for themselves or for their children who come into this country or are born here. As with immigration issues involving other racial and ethnic groups today and in earlier periods of American history, passions and prejudices produce explosive politics.

In response to heavy political pressure and 14 years of debate and political maneuvering, the U.S. Congress enacted into law the Immigration Reform and Control Act of 1986. This federal statute was designed to restrain the flow of illegal immigrants into the United States by penalizing employers who knowingly hire undocumented aliens and by appropriating funds to provide more enforcement personnel for the Naturalization Service, the agency then in charge of controlling immigration and the nation's borders, especially border patrol officers, called *la migra* by many Latinos immigrating into the country. Despite this act, hundreds of thousands of undocumented aliens continue to enter Texas each year. Many are arrested, detained, and subsequently expelled from the country. Others have voluntarily returned home after earning money to support their families. Thousands of undocumented aliens, however, remain in Texas and often arrange for family members to join them. Some undocumented aliens are exploited by employers, merchants, and landlords. Others receive fair wages and humane treatment. Even today, all live and work in fear of arrest and deportation.

In the 1990s, an anti-immigration groundswell developed throughout most parts of the United States. Central to the controversy was the issue of costs and benefits resulting from both legal and illegal immigration. In

undocumented alien
A person who enters the United States in violation of federal immigration laws.

1994, Texas joined other states in suing the federal government to recover various costs (for example, for health, welfare, education, and law enforcement) incurred from illegal immigration. Meanwhile, immigration issues continued to attract the attention of social scientists, special-interest groups, politicians, the general public, and policymaking officials at all levels of government in Texas and throughout the country.

With the approach of congressional and presidential elections in 1996, the matter of undocumented aliens became a "hot button" issue that some politicians exploited. Before the November election of that year, the U.S. Congress enacted the Immigration Control and Financial Responsibility Act of 1996, which was cosponsored by Representative Lamar Smith, a Republican from San Antonio. In addition to increasing the number of border patrol officers, the law increased penalties for immigrant smuggling and sped up the deportation of illegal immigrants who used false documents or committed other crimes while in the United States.

In the wake of the terrorist attacks of September 11, 2001, the U.S. Congress passed the Enhanced Border Security and Visa Entry Reform Act of 2002, which President George W. Bush signed into law. The act concerns the tracking of international students who are studying at U.S. educational institutions, the issuance of visas, and other details regarding foreign nationals. In October 2006, President Bush signed the Secure Fence Act authorizing, among other barriers, more than 700 additional miles of fencing along the U.S.–Mexico border from California to Texas to combat illegal immigration. As originally planned, part of the fence would have cut across the joint campus of the University of Texas at Brownsville and Texas Southmost College. Parts of the campus are immediately adjacent to the Mexican border. After a long legal battle, an agreement was reached to avoid splitting the campus. University officials agreed to increase the height of an existing campus perimeter fence. The Border Patrol agreed to install and maintain related surveillance equipment. In 2003, the Border Patrol was transferred to the the U.S. Department of Homeland Security's new Customs and Border Protection (CBP) and the Immigration and Naturalization Service was folded into the U.S. Department of Homeland Security's new Bureau of Immigration and Customs Enforcement (ICE).

Despite legal obstacles to immigration, low wages, unemployment, and drug-related violence in Mexico continue to motivate masses of Mexican workers to cross the border in search of jobs. At the same time, many businesspeople, farmers, and ranchers in Texas and elsewhere are willing to violate U.S. law (and

An estimated crowd of 25,000 march through downtown Dallas to City Hall in support of immigration reform, summer 2010.

(Rodger Mallison/MCT/Landov)

run the risk of incurring fines) by hiring undocumented aliens. They do so because other labor is unavailable or because illegal immigrants will work harder for lower wages.

Texas (and national) politicians often face the difficult task of balancing constituents' demands for increased border security against the demands of a growing Latino constituency pushing for immigration reforms. More than

Students in Action

One Family's Story of Immigration

"Being involved in the political process lets us express our voices and opinions regarding immigration reform."

Kathy Casares

Kathy's Family's Journey to America
Kathy considers Texas her home, but she is a part of a very unique Mexican heritage. Her maternal great grandparents were raised on a farm outside of San Luis Potosí. Both had little formal education and married very young. They later moved to Monterrey, where they started their family. After divorcing, Kathy's grandmother made the tough decision to come to the United States and leave her teenage children with her sister. She came legally with a worker's visa, but she overstayed her allotted time and remained in Houston to work and send her family money so that they could come to the United States. She worked in housekeeping and other odd jobs with no real skills or degree. Several years later, her eldest daughter and Kathy's mom came to Houston with student visas, and both began working in the food service industry. Her sons travelled to the United States illegally. One raised $400 to pay a "coyote" to help him cross the Laredo

(Monkey Business Images/Shutterstock.com)

border. The trip was made smoothly, and, with very little border patrol in the late 1980s, he crossed the Rio Grande and bought a bus ticket to Houston. The youngest son was caught by the border police and put on a bus back to Monterrey. On his second attempt, he successfully crossed the border and made it to Houston.

Kathy's Reflections on Her Family's Journey
Their family history was difficult to tell, but it is one of many stories of the families that live here in the United States. It is realizing this struggle that pushes Kathy to want to further her education and take advantage of the opportunities available … here. Her mother did not have the chance to go to college and follow her dreams because of many factors, but she encourages Kathy to do so every day. Kathy's family had to deal with many problems in their pursuit of happiness, but understanding all their sacrifices allows her to also understand why they are the way they are. Being involved in the political process lets us express our voices and opinion regarding immigration reform, and her father has always actively participated in the political process to voice his. This is something he has instilled in Kathy and her siblings. Kathy want to go to law school after she completes her undergraduate work at St. Mary's and maybe one day work as an immigration lawyer to help people and families like hers.

30 bills addressing the rights of immigrants were filed in the regular session of the Texas legislature in 2011. Most of these bills were labeled as anti-immigration by civil rights groups, including one bill that would remove the right of U.S. citizenship to children born in this country whose parents immigrated here and another that would allow law enforcement to ask about immigration status when in contact with a person they suspect to be undocumented. The latter is the so-called "sanctuary cities" bill.[49] Although these bills received considerable support from Texas Tea Party activists, after months of intense debate, none passed. The sanctuary cities bill was placed on the agenda of the 2011 special legislative session by Governor Perry as an "emergency item," but again it failed to pass. Although this move earned Perry criticism from immigration rights groups, his defense of Texas's policy of granting in-state tuition for undocumented students drew criticism from many conservative groups during his campaign for the Republican presidential nomination in 2012.

Water

With the state's population expected to double by the middle of the 21st century, Texas faces a formidable challenge in meeting the water needs of its citizens. In 2012, the Office of the Comptroller of Public Accounts issued a report, "The Impact of the 2011 Drought and Beyond," that projected that demand for water will rise by 22 percent by 2060, and the state's current dependable water supply will meet only about 65 percent of that projected demand. Texas comptroller of public accounts Susan Combs declared that "planning for and managing our water use is perhaps the most important task facing Texas policymakers in the 21st century."[50] As the population continues to shift from rural to urban areas, and as people from other states migrate to Texas cities, urban communities will increasingly compete with rural communities and agricultural interests for the same water. This population change and related water-supply problems are especially visible along the Interstate 35 corridor and around fast-growing cities such as Dallas, Fort Worth, Austin, and San Antonio.[51]

The process of fracking has also placed increased demands on water consumption. The amount of water required to frack a well is between 50,000 gallons and 4 million gallons, depending on the nature of the rock penetrated. In 2010, the total amount of water used for fracking purposes was 13.5 billion gallons. That amount is likely to more than double by 2020.[52] To meet the increased demands for water and to provide necessary flows of water for maintaining the environment, Texas will need to rely on water conservation and alternative water management strategies.[53]

After a devastating drought in the 1950s, the Texas legislature created the **Texas Water Development Board (TWDB)** in 1957 and mandated statewide water planning. Since then, the TWDB and the Texas Board of Water Engineers have prepared and adopted nine state water plans, including *Water for Texas–2012*. This plan makes several recommendations for the development, management, and conservation of water resources and for the preparation and response to drought conditions so that sufficient water may be available for the foreseeable future.[54]

Texas Water Development Board (TWDB)
A board that conducts statewide water planning as mandated by state law.

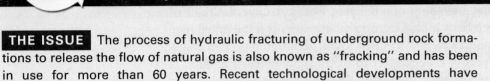

Point/Counterpoint

Should Oil and Gas Drillers Use Hydraulic "Fracking"?

THE ISSUE The process of hydraulic fracturing of underground rock formations to release the flow of natural gas is also known as "fracking" and has been in use for more than 60 years. Recent technological developments have increased the use of this practice, leading to both increased criticism of fracking and support for this process.

Arguments For Fracking

1. The oil and gas industry in the Lone Star State is experiencing large profits at a time when other sectors have not performed as well. This has created an economic boom in many parts of the state, contributing to a state economy that is stronger than the national economy. Unemployment is low, and taxes are generated from increased revenue as a result of fracking.

2. As conventional supplies of oil and gas have dwindled in Texas, the process of fracking has allowed industry to unlock large reserves of gas found in shale and other rock formations. Releasing gas though fracking provides another valuable energy resource, reducing Texas's (and the country's) dependence on oil.

3. There is no conclusive proof that fracking causes earthquakes. A report released by the National Research Council in mid-2012 revealed that fracking does not pose a high risk for triggering earthquakes large enough to feel. There are conflicting studies regarding links between earthquakes and fracking.

Arguments Against Fracking

1. Fracking poses higher environmental risks than does conventional drilling. The equipment used in fracking emits pollutants into the air. Fracking fluid contains hazardous chemicals and will ultimately return to the surface. Pipes may leak, causing groundwater contamination. Texas already leads the nation in recognized cancer-causing carcinogens released into the air and toxic chemicals released into its ground water. Fracking adds to these pollutants.

2. Fracking requires between 50,000 gallons and 4 million gallons of water to fracture a single well. This resource is too valuable to use in such quantities at this time. The agriculture and timber industries have been gravely affected by record drought conditions and need available water.

3. Fracturing rock may cause geological instability, leading to earthquakes. Geologists have made direct links between fracking and earthquakes in Ohio and Oklahoma in 2011. As the petroleum industry continues to expand the process of fracking, more earthquakes may be expected.

This "Point/Counterpoint" is based on Debra Black, "Fracking Fracas: Pros and Cons of Controversial Gas Extraction Process," *The Toronto Star,* February 5, 2012; *Induced Seismicity Potential in Energy Technologies,* Report of the National Research Council, June 15, 2012.

In 2011, the Lone Star State's water supply was severely depleted by the hottest and driest 21-month period in Texas history. As a result, the nine major and 21 minor aquifers, which supply about 60 percent of the state's water supply, declined to levels predating the levels of the 1950s' drought. Scientists project that it could take years to recover from this low level.[55] TWDB chair Edward Vaughn explained that the message of *Water for Texas—2012* is simple: "During serious drought conditions, Texas does not and will not have enough water to meet the needs of its people, its businesses, and its agricultural enterprises."[56]

Despite continued warnings about the insufficient supply of water to meet the future needs of the Lone Star State, the 82nd Texas legislature failed to pass legislation that would create the first permanent funding source for the state's water plan in 2011. The legislature proposed a constitutional amendment, however, ratified by the voters in the November 2011 election, authorizing the issuance of up to $6 billion in general obligation bonds to make loans to local governments for water, wastewater, and flood control projects.[57] The voters rejected another amendment that would have provided tax breaks for water conservation on agricultural lands.

Environmental Protection

Poor air quality and impure water are causing serious health problems for many Texans. The Lone Star State leads the nation in the amount of hazardous waste generated; carbon dioxide emissions; volatile organic compounds, which are recognized cancer-causing carcinogens; toxic chemicals released into the air; and toxic chemicals released into the ground water.[58] Coal-fired power plants and oil refineries in Texas generate approximately 294 million tons of carbon dioxide and heat-trapping gases, which is more than the next two states (Pennsylvania and Florida) combined.

In 2010, the Environmental Protection Agency (EPA) rejected the Texas Commission on Environmental Quality's (TCEQ's) "flexible permit program," which allowed facilities more flexibility in managing operations by staying under an overall emissions cap or individual emission limitation. The EPA determined that this program did not meet several national Clean Air Act requirements that help to ensure the protection of health and the environment.[59] In 2011, the EPA issued a ruling that required coal-fired power plants in Texas and 26 other states to be upgraded with modern equipment to reduce toxic emissions. Texas has led several other states in a legal challenge to EPA regulations. Governor Rick Perry has frequently criticized EPA mandates as "overreaching regulation," stating that they have led to a loss of more than 500 jobs in the Lone Star State.

Some effects of environmental pollution are revealed in observations concerning fish and wildlife populations. For example, Texas (along with California, Hawaii, and Florida) leads all other states in the number of endangered fish and wildlife species. Bordered by Florida, Alabama, Mississippi, Louisiana, and Texas, the Gulf of Mexico covers nearly 700,000 square miles, or seven times as much area as the Great Lakes. Industries in each of these states and Mexico release toxic chemicals directly into the gulf or into rivers that flow into it. Also contributing greatly to the gulf's environmental problems is the continuing flow of nitrate-laden rivers that draw their water from the chemically fertilized farms of rural areas, as well as from the lawns and gardens of cities large and small. With declining catches of fish, shrimp, and oysters from gulf waters, Texans must do with less seafood or import it from abroad at high prices. Of course, an obvious solution to the problem would be environmental protection measures designed to clean up the Gulf of Mexico and restore its productivity.[60]

Education and Economic Development

Along with a poor record of environmental protection, Texas gets low marks in other critical areas that affect its residents' quality of life and economic welfare. More well-paying jobs, along with increasing productivity, depend largely on a well-educated Texas workforce. Teachers are the key element in any educational system; but from year to year, the Lone Star State confronts shortages of certified personnel to instruct its four million elementary and secondary school students. Included within this total are more than a half million students with limited English proficiency.

Although estimates of the teacher shortage vary, the Texas Education Agency reports that approximately one-fifth of the state's 250,000 teachers quit teaching each year. Some retire, but most of them leave their profession for reasons that include inadequate pay and benefits, low prestige, and time-consuming chores, such as grading, that often must be done at night and on weekends. Contributing to their decision to seek other careers is stress over student performance on standardized tests and classroom problems affected by the poverty and troubled home lives of many students. Although the public tends to overlook the needs of teachers, many Texans complain about students' high dropout rates, low levels of academic achievement, and inadequate preparation for work or college.

Success in addressing educational needs will be especially important in determining Texas's ability to compete nationally and internationally in business, as well as in science and technology. The urgency of this matter is suggested in studies that rank Texas near the bottom of the nation in the literacy of its residents. Employers are particularly concerned that one of every three Texans cannot read and write well enough to fill out a simple job application. Moreover, the state loses many billions of dollars annually because most illiterate Texans are doomed to unemployment or low-paying jobs and thus generate little or no tax revenue.

Points to Ponder

Texas ranks second in public school enrollment, yet it is only:

- #44 in state and local expenditures per pupil in public shools
- #47 in state aid per pupil in average daily attendance
- #43 in high school graduation rate
- #50 in percentage of population 25 and older with a high school diploma

Source: Texas on the Brink: A Report from the Texas Legislative Study Group on the State of Our State (February 2011), **http://texaslsg.org/texasonthebrink/texasonthebrink.pdf.**

Early in 2010, Governor Perry announced that Texas would not compete for a federal education grant that could have provided as much as $700 million for the state. Criticizing a goal of the Race to the Top grant in establishing national curriculum standards for math and English as a "federal takeover of public schools," Perry rejected the program, leaving Texas as one of only two states (the other is Alaska) in the nation not to participate in the common standards effort.[61] Despite voicing support for education, the state's elected officials cut funding for both public education and higher education in 2011.

Poverty and Social Problems

Although many of America's public figures stress the importance of family values, serious social and economic problems affect homes throughout the country. The Lone Star State has alarming numbers of children living in poverty and in single-parent homes, births to unwed teenagers, juvenile arrests, and violent acts committed by teenagers and preadolescents. More than one of every five Texas children lives in poverty, and many children at all levels of society suffer from abuse and neglect. Estimates of the number of homeless people (including many children) vary widely, but at least 100,000—and perhaps more than 200,000—Texans cannot provide themselves with shelter in a house or apartment. In 2010, more than one-third of all Texas workers were earning less than $22,113 a year, which was below the federal poverty level for food stamps for a family of four.

Texas's limited response to its residents' social and economic needs continues to excite debate. Some Texans argue that any public assistance for the poor is too much. They believe government assistance encourages dependence and discourages self-reliance, personal initiative, and desire to work. Other Texans advocate for greatly increased government spending to help people who are unable to care for themselves and their families because of mental or physical health problems, lack of job opportunities, or age. Between these extremes are Texans who support a limited role for government in meeting human needs but who call for churches and other nongovernmental organizations to play a more active role in dealing with social problems. Texas voters, however, tend to support candidates for public office who promise lower taxes, tighter government budgets, fewer public employees, and a reduction or elimination of social services. As a result, the Lone Star State continues to rank near the bottom of the 50 states in governmental responses to poverty and social problems.

☑ Learning Check 1.5   (Answers on p. 39)

1. True or False: Demand for water will rise by 10 percent by 2060, and the state's current dependable water supply will meet that projected demand.
2. True or False: More than one-third of Texas workers are earning below the federal poverty level.

★ Conclusion

With changing demographic, economic, social, and environmental conditions in the Lone Star State, Texas policymakers face several challenges. Both ordinary citizens and public officials must realize that their ability to cope with public problems now and in the years ahead depends largely on how well homes and schools prepare young Texans to meet the crises and demands of an ever-changing state, nation, and world.

Chapter Summary

- The political culture of Texas is both individualistic and traditionalistic. The individualistic culture is rooted in the state's frontier experience and includes economic and social conservatism, strong support of personal politics, distrust of political parties, and minimization of political parties' importance. The traditionalistic culture grew out of the Old South, where a one-party system developed, policies were designed to preserve the social order, and the poor and minorities were often disenfranchised (not allowed to vote). Today, these two cultures can still be found in the values, attitudes, traditions, habits, and general behavior patterns of Texans and in the governmental policies of the Lone Star State.

- With more than 267,000 square miles of territory, Texas ranks second in size to Alaska among the 50 states. Cattle, cotton, timber, and hydrocarbons have at different times dominated the Texas economy and influenced the state's politics. Today, Texas is a highly industrialized state in which high-tech products are of increasing importance.

- Texas has a population of over 25 million. More than 80 percent of all Texans live in the state's most highly urbanized counties. The three largest groups are Anglos, Latinos (mostly Mexican Americans), and African Americans. Latinos are the fastest growing racial/ethnic group in the Lone Star State. Texas has a small but growing population of Asian Americans, and fewer than 170,000 Native Americans.

- Although the state's energy industry has decreased in importance, Texas has become a leading manufacturer of computers and other high-tech products. Agriculture continues to be important in the state's economy, though it employs relatively few Texans. Service businesses provide many low-paying jobs.

- Challenges that face Texas include the need to more effectively address immigration, protect the environment, develop educational programs to meet the demands of an industrial society, and formulate policies for combating poverty and social problems.

Key Terms

politics, p. 2
government, p. 2
public policy, p. 3
alien, p. 3
political culture, p. 4
moralistic culture, p. 4
individualistic culture, p. 5
traditionalistic culture, p. 5
political inefficacy, p. 5
frontier experience, p. 6
"Jim Crow" laws, p. 7
patrón system, p. 7
physical region, p. 10
Gulf Coastal Plains, p. 10
Interior Lowlands, p. 11
Great Plains, p. 11
Basin and Range Province, p. 11
Spindletop Field, p. 14
Railroad Commission of Texas (RRC), p. 14
population shifts, p. 16
urbanization, p. 17
suburbanization, p. 17
metropolitanization, p. 17
micropolitan statistical area (mSA), p. 17
metropolitan statistical area (MSA), p. 17
combined statistical area (CSA), p. 17
metropolitan division, p. 17
Anglo, p. 18
Latino, p. 19
African American, p. 20
Asian American, p. 21
Native American, p. 22
high technology, p. 25
North American Free Trade Agreement
  (NAFTA), p. 28
maquiladora, p. 28
undocumented alien, p. 30
Texas Water Development Board (TWDB),
  p. 33

Learning Check Answers

1.1
1. False. Only California, with an estimated population of more than 37 million, is more populous than Texas.
2. Texas has elements of the individualistic culture and the traditionalistic culture.

1.2
1. The four principal physical regions of the state are the Gulf Coastal Plains, the Interior Lowlands, the Great Plains, and the Basin and Range Province.
2. In 1901, the Spindletop Field near Beaumont ushered in the Texas oil industry.

1.3
1. Harris, Dallas, Bexar, and Tarrant counties have a combined population of more than 10 million, which is more than 40 percent of all Texans.
2. True. The fastest-growing ethnic group in Texas is Latinos. More than 60 percent of births in the state are minority births, with Latino births accounting for half of all newborns. In addition, with migration trends, it is estimated that Latinos could constitute a majority within 35 years.

1.4
1. False. Only one of the five largest private corporations in Texas, as identified by *Fortune*'s 2009 listing, was technology related. The others were energy and energy related.
2. "Partner plants" on the Mexican side of the border that use cheap labor to assemble goods and then export these goods back to the United States are called maquiladoras.

1.5
1. False. Demand for water will rise by 22 percent by 2060, and the state's current dependable water supply will meet only about 65 percent of that projected demand.
2. True. In 2010, more than one-third of Texas workers were earning less than $20,000 a year, which was below the federal poverty level for food stamps for a family of four.

Discussion Questions

1. In what ways is Texas's political culture (individualism and traditionalism) reflected in politics, policies, and the people's attitudes about, and expectations of, government today?
2. What political advantages accompany Texas's rank as second most populous state in the nation?
3. What challenges does Texas government face in the state's growing urban population in cities such as Houston, San Antonio, Dallas, and Fort Worth? How can government respond to these challenges?
4. What challenges does Texas government face with the state's shrinking rural population? How can government respond to these challenges?
5. How have various ethnic and racial groups contributed to the state's culture and economic development?
6. What challenges does Texas government face with the state's racial and ethnic diversity? How can government respond to these challenges?
7. What industries are essential to sustain and continue to develop the Texas economy in the 21st century?
8. What impact did the drought of 2011 have on the Texas economy?
9. What social services are essential to sustain and continue to develop the Texas economy in the 21st century?

Internet Resources

Free Trade Area of the Americas:
http://www.ftaa-alca.org

The Handbook of Texas Online:
http://www.tshaonline.org/handbook

Hobby Center for the Study of Texas:
http://hobbycenter.rice.edu/

North American Free Trade Agreement:
http://www.nafta-sec-alena.org

Texas Department of Agriculture:
http://www.agr.state.tx.us

Texas Railroad Commission:
http://www.rrc.state.tx.us

Texas State Comptroller:
http://www.window.state.tx.us

Texas State Data Center:
http://txsdc.utsa.edu

Texas State Library and Archives Commission:
http://www.tsl.state.tx.us/

Texas Water Matters:
http://www.texaswatermatters.org/

United States Census Bureau:
http://www.census.gov

Notes

1. Pat Green, "I Like Texas," from *Here We Go* (Dead Horse Music, 1995). Lyrics by Pat Green. Copyright © Dead Horse Music (BMI). Reprinted by permission.
2. Karen J. O'Connor. Larry J. Sabato, and Alexandra B. Yanus, *American Government: Roots and Reform*, 11th ed. (New York: Longman, 2011).
3. Daniel Elazar, *American Federalism: A View from the States*, 3d ed. (New York: Harper & Row, 1984), 84–126, 134. For a different view of political culture, see Dante Chinni and James Gimpel, *Our Patchwork Nation: The Surprising Truth about the "Real" America* (New York: Penguin Group, 2010) and its web site at

http://www.patchworknation.org/. This view identifies 12 political cultures nationally, of which nine are present in Texas.

4. See Mike Kingston, "A Brief Sketch of Texas History," edited and expanded by Robert Plocheck, *Texas Almanac 2012–2013* (Denton, TX: Texas State Historical Association, 2012), 45–50. For a description of events that led up to Texas's war for independence from Mexico and the battle at the Alamo, see James Donovan, *The Blood of Heroes: The 13-day Struggle for the Alamo—and the Sacrifice That Forged a Nation* (New York: Little Brown, 2012).

5. Kingston, "A Brief Sketch of Texas History," 53; and Rupert N. Richardson, Adrian Anderson, Cary D. Wintz, and Ernest Wallace, *Texas: The Lone Star State*, 10th ed. (Upper Saddle River, NJ: Prentice Hall, 2010), 151–154.

6. For a case study of the *patrón* system, see J. Gilberto Quezada, *Border Boss: Manuel B. Bravo and Zapata County* (College Station: Texas A&M University Press, 1999).

7. For more on Texas longhorns, see J. Frank Dobie, *Longhorns* (Austin: University of Texas Press, 1980). Results of the most recent research on the origin of longhorn cattle are found in T. J. Barragy, *Gathering Texas Gold: J. Frank Dobie and the Men Who Saved the Longhorn* (Corpus Christi, TX: Cayo de Grullo Press, 2003). Barragy disputes assertions in Don Worcester's popular *The Texas Longhorn: Relic of the Past, Asset for the Future* (College Station: Texas A&M University Press, 1987) that English Bakewell longhorns and other British breeds played a significant role in the genetic makeup of Texas longhorns.

8. See Don Graham, *Kings of Texas: The 150-Year Saga of an American Empire* (Hoboken, NJ: John Wiley & Sons, 2003); Jane Clements Monday and Betty Bailey Colley, *Voices from the Wild Horse Desert: The Vaquero Families of the King and Kenedy Ranches* (Austin: University of Texas Press, 1997); Armando C. Alonzo, *Tejano Legacy: Rancheros and Settlers in South Texas, 1734–1900* (Albuquerque: University of New Mexico Press, 1998); Andrés Tijerina, *Tejano Empire: Life on the South Texas Ranchos* (College Station: Texas A&M University Press, 1998); and Daniel D. Arreola, *Tejano South Texas: A Mexican American Cultural Province* (Austin: University of Texas Press, 2002).

9. Blair Fannin, "Updated 2011 Texas Agricultural Drought Losses Total $7.62 Billion," *TexasAgriLife Today,* March 21, 2012, http://today.agrilife.org/2012/03/21/updated-2011-texas-agricultural-drought-losses-total-7-62-billion/.

10. See Kate Galbraith, "Catastrophic Drought in Texas Causes Global Economic Ripples," *New York Times*, October 30, 2011; and Elizabeth Campbell, "'White Gold' Withers in Texas Cotton Fields," *Bloomberg Business Week,* September 15, 2011; Mindy Riffle, "Cotton Crop: Future of Cotton Is Questionable," Country World Online Edition, May 29, 2012; and Blair Fannin, "Updated 2011 Texas Agricultural Drought Losses Total $7.62 Billion," *TexasAgriLife Today,* March 21, 2012, http://today.agrilife.org/2012/03/21/updated-2011-texas-agricultural-drought-losses-total-7-62-billion/.

11. James Cozine, *Saving the Big Thicket: From Exploration to Preservation, 1685–2003* (Denton: University of North Texas, 2004).

12. Robert S. Maxwell. "Lumber Industry," *Handbook of Texas Online*, http://www.tshaonline.org/handbook/online/articles/drl02.

13. Ronald H. Hufford, "Tree Farming," *Handbook of Texas Online*, http://www.tshaonline.org/handbook/online/articles/drt04.

14. Texas Comptroller of Public Accounts, "Texas Timber Grows Up," *Fiscal Notes*, October 1999, http://www.window.state.tx.us/comptrol/fnotes/fn9910/fn.html.

15. Nathan Koppel and Daniel Gilbert, "Even after Rain, Texas Drought Persists," *Wall Street Journal,* February 6, 2012.
16. Ricardo Gandera, "Bastrop Park Won't Be Back to Full Glory for Decades, Official Says," *Austin American Statesman*, October 13, 2011.
17. For an account of the history of the early years of the oil industry in Texas, see Roger M. Olien and Diana Davids Olien, *Oil in Texas: The Gusher Age, 1895–1945* (Austin: University of Texas Press, 2002).
18. For a personal view of Hispanic (or Latino) culture, see Richard Rodriguez, "What Is a Hispanic?" *Texas Journal of Ideas, History and Culture* 22 (Summer 2000): 32–41.
19. Michael O. Emerson, Jenifer Bratter, Junia Howell, P. Wilner Jeanty, and Mike Cline, *Houston Region Grows More Racially/Ethnically Diverse, With Small Declines in Segregation: A Joint Report Analyzing Census Data from 1990, 2000, and 2010* (March 2012), http://kinder.rice.edu/uploadedFiles/Urban_Research_Center/Media/Houston%20Region%20Grows%20More%20Ethnically%20Diverse%202-13.pdf.
20. Mitchell Schnurman, "Oil Boom 2.0 Pumps Up West Texas Economy," *Fort Worth Star Telegram*, May 23, 2012.
21. Paul Burka, "The Party Never Ends," *Texas Monthly,* June 2012, 16, 18, 20.
22. Terry G. Jordan, "The Imprint of Upper and Lower South on Mid-Nineteenth Century Texas," *Annals of the American Association of Geographers* 57 (December 1967): 667–690.
23. Kent Biffle, "If at First You Don't Secede," *Dallas Morning News*, November 3, 2002.
24. Arnoldo De León, "Mexican Americans," in *The Handbook of Texas Online* (2002), http://www.tsha.utexas.edu/handbook/online/articles/view/MM/pqmue.html.
25. Patricia Kilday Hart, "Senate Committee OKs Sanctuary Cities Bill," *Houston Chronicle,* June 13, 2011.
26. Alwyn Barr, *Black Texans: A History of Negroes in Texas, 1528–1971* (Austin: Jenkins, 1973).
27. Frederick Law Olmsted, *A Journey through Texas* (New York: Dix, Edwards, 1857; reprint, Burt Franklin, 1969), 296. For more information on Texas Indian tribes, see Richard L. Schott, "Contemporary Indian Reservations in Texas: Tribal Paths to the Present," *Public Affairs Comment* (Austin: Lyndon B. Johnson School of Public Affairs, University of Texas at Austin) 39 (1993): 1–9; and David LaVere, *The Texas Indians* (College Station: Texas A&M University Press, 2004).
28. *Fortune*, May 3, 2012, http://money.cnn.com/magazines/fortune/fortune500/2012/states/TX.html.
29. Carol J. Loomis, "Got Energy Trading Contracts?" *Fortune*, April 15, 2002, 190. Several Texas politicians were tied to Enron through campaign contributions, and Enron's lobbyists were active in Austin and Washington, DC. Dozens of books concerning Enron have been published. For example, see Robert Bryce and Molly Ivins, *Pipe Dreams: Greed, Ego, and the Death of Enron* (New York: Public Affairs Press, 2002); Brian Cruver, *Anatomy of Greed: The Unshredded Truth from an Enron Insider* (New York: Avalon, 2002); Loren Fox, *Enron: The Rise and Fall* (Hoboken, NJ: Wiley, 2002); Mimi Swartz and Sherron Watkins, *Power Failure: The Inside Story of the Collapse of Enron* (New York: Doubleday, 2003); Bethany MacLean and Peter Elkind, *The Smartest Guys in the Room: The Amazing Rise and Scandalous Fall of Enron* (New York: Penguin, 2003); and

Kurt Eichenwald, *Conspiracy of Fools: A True Story* (New York: Broadway Books, 2005).

30. Tom Fowler, "State Getting by with a Little Help from the Winds," *Houston Chronicle*, August 11, 2011.

31. Laylan Copelin, "Moving ahead on Solar," *Austin American-Statesman*, June 26, 2011.

32. Laylan Copelin, "Austin, State Urged to Improve Job Growth in Tech Sector," *Austin American-Statesman*, January 13, 2012.

33. Office of the Governor, *Texas Biotechnology Industry Report*, http://www.governor.state.tx.us/files/ecodev/Biotech_Report.pdf.

34. For criticism and questions concerning genetic engineering for food production, see Nate Blakeslee, "Banking on Biotech: Is the Latest Food Science from Aggieland a Lemon?" *Texas Observer*, March 30, 2001, 6–9, 14; Sandra Kill Leber, "Biotechnology: Curse or Cure?" *State Government News*, January 2000, 23–26; and Ronnie Cummins, "Exposing Biotech's Big Lies," *BioDemocracy News* 39 (May 2002), http://www.organicconsumer.org/newsletter/blod39.cfm. Concerning the use of GMOs to reduce risks of chronic diseases, see Edward A. Hiler, "Houston Has a Stake in High-Tech Agriculture, Too," *Houston Chronicle,* June 18, 2001.

35. These statistics were provided by the Texas Workforce Commission, 2012, http://www.tracer2.com/admin/uploadedPublications/2056_TLMR-May12.pdf.

36. These statistics were provided by Texas Workforce Commission, Labor Market & Career Information Department, http://www.careerinfonet.org.

37. Molly Ivins, "Top to Bottom Reform of Financial Structures Essential," *Dallas Times Herald,* June 3, 1990.

38. These statistics were provided by the Texas AgriLife Extension Service, Texas Department of Agriculture. http://agrilifeextension.tamu.edu/.

39. Blair Fannin, "Updated 2011 Texas Agricultural Drought Losses Total $7.62 Billion," *TexasAgriLife Today,* March 21, 2012, http://today.agrilife.org/2012/03/21/updated-2011-texas-agricultural-drought-losses-total-7-62-billion/.

40. For a case study of an assembly-line manufacturing job that passed (with big pay cuts) from Paterson, New Jersey, to Blytheville, Arkansas, to the Mexican border city of Matamoros (across the Rio Grande from Brownsville, Texas), see William M. Adler, *Mollie's Job: A Story of Life and Work on the Global Assembly Line* (New York: Scribner, 2000).

41. "UNIFEM Head Decries Feminization of Poverty," *UN Wire*, December 3, 2002, http://www.unwire.org/UNWire/20021203/30674_story.asp; and Amnesty International, "Demand Justice for the Women and Girls of Ciudad Juárez and Chihuahua, Mexico," February 20, 2006, http://www.amnestyusa.org/women/juarez/.

42. See Denise Dresser, "Mexico: Uneasy, Uncertain, Unpredictable," *Current History* 96 (February 1997): 51–54.

43. See Lucy Conger, "Mexico's Long March to Democracy," *Current History* 100 (February 2001): 58–64; Carlos E. Casasillas and Alejandro Mújica, "Mexico: New Democracy with Old Parties?" *Politics* 23 (September 2003): 172–180; Julia Preston and Samuel Dillon, *Opening Mexico: The Making of a Democracy* (New York: Farrar, Straus and Giroux, 2004); and Jeffrey Davidow, *The U.S. and Mexico: The Bear and the Porcupine* (Princeton, N.J.: Marcus Weiner Publishers, 2004). Davidow was the U.S. ambassador to Mexico from 1998–2002.

44. Guillermina Guillén, "Political Decisions Stopped Development of Mexico," *The Universal*, September 7, 2005. See also Peter Andreas, "Politics on the Edge:

Managing the U.S.-Mexican Border," *Current History* 105 (February 2006): 64–68; Jorge G. Casteneda, "NAFTA at 10: A Plus or a Minus?" *Current History* 103 (February 2004): 51–55; and Sidney Weintraub, "Scoring Free Trade: A Critique of the Critics," *Current History* 103 (February 2004): 56–60.

45. GAO-10-253R Mérida Initiative Funding.

46. Damien Cave, "Mexico Updates Death Toll in Drug War to 47,515, but Critics Dispute the Data," *New York Times*, January 11, 2012. For additional information about the drug war in Mexico and violence along the border, see George W. Grayson, *Mexico: Narco-Violence in a Failed State* (Piscataway, NJ: Transaction Publishers, 2009); Teresa Rodriguez and Diana Fontane with Lisa Pulitzer, *The Daughters of Juarez: A True Story of Serial Murder South of the Border* (New York: Atria Books, 2007); Howard Campbell, *Drug War Zone: Frontline Dispatches from the Streets of El Paso and Juarez* (Austin: University of Texas Press, 2009); and Charles Bowden, *Murder City: Ciudad Juarez and the Global Economy, New Killing Fields* (New York: Nation Books, 2011).

47. Julian Aguilar, "Is the Border Vulnerable to Terrorists?" *The Texas Tribune*, March 17, 2011; Blair Fannin, "Texas Agricultural Exports to Cuba Continue to Grow," *Agrilife Today*, February 6, 2012, http://today.agrilife.org/2012/02/06/texas-agricultural-exports-to-cuba-continue-growth/.

48. For indicators assessing Texas's environment, education, economy, human services, public safety, and democracy, see *Texas on the Brink: A Report from the Texas Legislative Study Group on the State of Our State* (February 2011), http://texaslsg.org/texasonthebrink/texasonthebrink.pdf.

49. Tim Eaton, "Not Many Immigration Bills Likely to Make It Through Legislature," *Austin American Statesman,* May 10, 2011.

50. Office of the Comptroller of Public Accounts, "The Impact of the 2011 Drought and Beyond" (February 2012), http://www.window.state.tx.us/specialrpt/drought/Texas.

51. Kiah Collier, "Water—and Lots of It—Is the Key to West Texas' Second Oil Boom," *Abilene Reporter News*, July 3, 2011.

52. Steve Campbell, "Drought Is Taking Toll on Texas Aquifers," *Fort Worth Star Telegram*, July 24, 2011.

53. For an excellent overview of the state's water problems, see Ted Holladay, *Groundwater Management Issues in Texas,* Focus Report No. 79-4 (Austin: House Research Organization, Texas House of Representatives, June 6, 2006); Andrew Samson, *Water in Texas: An Introduction* (Austin: University of Texas Press, 2008); Lawrence Ernest Estaville, Richard Allen Earl, and Andrew Sansom, *Texas Water Atlas* (College Station: Texas A&M University Press, 2008); Ken Kramer and Charles Kruvand, *The Living Waters of Texas* (College Station: Texas A&M University Press, 2008); and Special Report on "Water: The Last Drop: Everything You Ever Wanted To Know About Water and Drought in Texas But Were Too Freaked Out, Discouraged, or Too Parched to Ask," *Texas Monthly*, July, 2012.

54. Texas Water Development Board, *Water for Texas: 2012 State Water Plan* (2012), http://www.twdb.state.tx.us/publications/state_water_plan/2012/2012_SWP.pdf.

55. Ramit Plushnick-Masti, "It Could Take Years for State's Aquifers to Fill," *San Antonio Express-News*, December 1, 2011.

56. Texas Water Development Board, *Water for Texas: 2012 State Water Plan.*

57. For more information about the effect of this amendment, see Texas Water Development Board, "Proposed Constitutional Amendment for Water Financial Assistance Bonds," http://www.twdb.state.tx.us/newsmedia/constitutional/doc/Const_Amend_Fact.pdf; Texas Water Resources Institute, "Propositions Up for Vote in November Could Affect Texas' Water Future," http://twri.tamu.edu/publications/new-waves/2011/october/propositions-up-for-vote-in-november.

58. *Texas on the Brink: A Report from the Texas Legislative Study Group on the State of Our State.*

59. Environmental Protection Agency, "EPA Disapproves Texas Flexible Air Permit Program," (news release), June 30, 2010, http://yosemite.epa.gov/opa/admpress.nsf/0/1D91BF2747C5682B8525775200626AA6.

60. For information on all aspects of Texas's environmental problems, see Mary Sanger and Cyrus Reed, comps., *Texas Environmental Almanac*, 2d ed. (Austin: University of Texas Press, 2000); and Texas Center for Policy Studies, http://www.TexasCenter.org.

61. Kate Alexander, "Texas Will not Compete for Federal Education Grant," *Austin American-Statesman*, January 13, 2010.

Minorities Drove Texas Growth, Census Figures Show

Ross Ramsey, Matt Stiles, Julián Aguilar, and Ryan Murphy

This reading appeared in the February 18, 2011, edition of the Texas Tribune *and discusses the role that minority groups played in Texas's population growth as reported in the 2010 census. The full story may be accessed at http:// www.texastribune.org/texas-counties-and-demo graphics/census/minorities-drove-texas-growth-census-figures-show/.*

The state's explosive growth during the past decade was fueled by a boom in its minority population, which accounted for 89 percent of the total increase in population, according to the U.S. Census Bureau. Hispanics alone accounted for 65 percent of the state's growth over the last 10 years.

Census officials said late last year (2010) that Texas grew 20.6 percent during the last decade, to 25,145,561. The new numbers released Thursday include data for counties and cities, all the way down to the city block level. The widely anticipated decennial population numbers will be used to determine several key issues from federal funding for state projects to business decisions based on populations and demographics.

The state's Hispanic population grew 42 percent over the decade. The black population was up 22 percent. Both outgrew the white population in percentage terms and in raw numbers. The white population grew by 4.2 percent. And while Texas added 464,032 whites over the decade, it added 522,570 blacks and 2.8 million Hispanics. In 17 counties, the Hispanic population grew by more than 100 percent.

The white population in Texas now accounts for 45.3 percent of the total. Hispanics make up 37.6 percent of the population, blacks 11.8 percent and Asians 3.8 percent. The voting age population is a little different: 49.6 percent Anglo, 33.6 percent Hispanic, 11.4 percent black and 3.9 percent Asian.

It's not just the trend in Texas, but nationwide, according to Steve Murdock, a former U.S. census director and Texas state demographer who's now at Rice University. Six of the first 11 states to receive data saw a decline in the white populations and an increase in their Hispanic populations. The shift in demographics signals what he says is a necessary cooperation between the two groups.

"You have this aging set of Anglos, literally aging off the end of their life chart who are going to need assistance in terms of Social Security, Medicare and in terms of direct care. At the same time, you have a young population that is overwhelmingly minority that needs the financial assistance through taxes and other factors of the older Anglo population to help get the education it needs to be competitive," he said.

Don't be surprised to see Texas experience growing pains, he said. The state recorded about a quarter of the nation's overall growth, about 4.3 million of the country's 17 million.

"We've had phenomenal rates of growth and we in Texas generally like that growth but we also have to prepare to pay for the implications," he said. "It means more infrastructure, more educational services. I worry a great deal, if we forget with our older Anglo population that younger population, because that younger population is the future of Texas," he said.

Where Texas grew, Houston, with just under 2.1 million people, remains the biggest city in the state, followed by San Antonio, Dallas, Austin, and Fort Worth, which leap-frogged El Paso.

Harris County, with 4.1 million residents, remains the state's largest, followed by Dallas, Tarrant, Bexar and Travis.

Most of the state's largest counties kept pace with the statewide population growth rate of 20.6 percent, but Dallas County's population only increased by 6 percent, from 2.21 million to 2.36 million residents. The city of Dallas' population increased less than 1 percent, a fact that's likely to have implications for redistricting of urban seats in the Texas House.

Suburban and exurban areas around Dallas County, however, showed strong growth, following a trend seen throughout the last decade in the rolling census sampling known as the American Community Survey. Both Collin and Denton counties grew by more than 50 percent, and Rockwall County led all counties in the rate of growth (81 percent).

A similar phenomenon occurred in Houston, where the city population grew by just over 7 percent, despite the influx of Hurricane Katrina evacuees who fled southern Louisiana in the summer of 2005. The city's current population is less than estimates from a few years ago, when suspected population increase once sparked a fight over whether City Council districts should be redrawn because of charter provisions. Then-Mayor Bill White fought the effort, saying he preferred to wait for the official hard count released after the 2010 census.

But all around Houston, population spiked since 2000. Montgomery County to the north saw its population increase by more than 60 percent, while Fort Bend County to the southeast grew by more than 50 percent.

Seventy-nine of the state's 254 counties lost population during the decade, most of them clustered in West Texas. Another 97 counties grew less than 10 percent, and another 41 grew between 10 and 20 percent. The fastest growth, on a percentage basis, was in 37 counties that grew between 20 and 82 percent during the decade. Those are clustered in the Hill Country, the Metroplex, the Valley and around Houston.

....

Federalism and the Texas Constitution

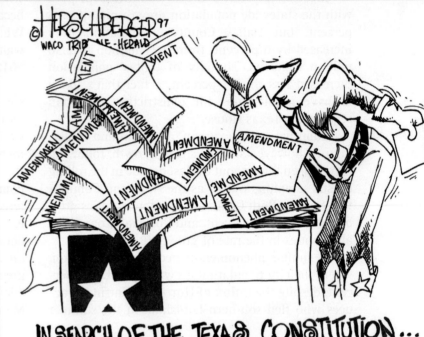

IN SEARCH OF THE TEXAS CONSTITUTION...

(Waco/Tribune-Herald/Herschberger/Herschberger Cartoon Service)

Learning Objectives

1. Summarize the constitutional powers of the federal government, as well as the constitutional guarantees for (and limitations on) the states.
2. Analyze the constitutional powers affecting federal-state relations, as well as the state's powers.
3. Evaluate the evolving nature of the balance of power between the federal and state governments.
4. Summarize the characteristics of the present-day Texas Constitution and how each of the state's previous constitutions shaped its content.
5. Analyze the amendment process, focusing on recent constitutional amendment elections as well as attempts to revise the constitution.
6. Explain the basic sections of the Texas Constitution.

The Texas Constitution, adopted in 1876, serves as the Lone Star State's fundamental law. This document outlines the structure of Texas's state government, authorizes the creation of counties and cities, and establishes basic rules for governing. It has been amended frequently over the course of nearly 14 decades (as illustrated by the cartoon at the beginning of this chapter). Lawyers, newspaper editors, political scientists, government officials, and others who consult the state constitution tend to criticize it for being too long and for lacking organization. Yet despite criticism, Texans have expressed strong opposition to, or complete lack of interest in, proposals for wholesale constitutional revision.

The Texas Constitution is the primary source of the state government's policymaking power. The other major source of its power is membership in the federal Union. Within the federal system, state constitutions are subject to the U.S. Constitution.

The American Federal Structure

Federalism can be defined as a structure of government characterized by the division of powers between a national government and associated regional governments. The heart of the American federal system lies in the relationship between the U.S. government (with Washington, D.C., as the national capital) and the governments of the 50 states. Since 1789, the U.S. Constitution has prescribed a federal system of government for the nation, and since 1846, the state of Texas has been a part of that system.

Political scientist David Walker emphasizes the important role that states play in federalism: "The states' strategically crucial role in the administration, financing, and planning of intergovernmental programs and regulations—both federal and their own—and their perennial key position in practically all areas of local governance have made them the pivotal middlemen in the realm of functional federalism."[1]

Described by North Carolina's former governor Terry Sanford as "a system of states within a state," American federalism has survived more than two centuries of stresses and strains. Among the most serious threats were the Civil War from 1861 to 1865, which almost destroyed the Union, and economic crises such as the Great Depression, which followed the stock market crash of 1929.

Distribution of Powers

Division of powers and functions between the national government and the state governments was originally accomplished by listing the powers of the national government in the U.S. Constitution and by adding the **Tenth Amendment**. The latter asserts that "the powers not delegated to the United States by the Constitution, nor prohibited by it to the States, are reserved to the States, respectively, or to the People." Although the Tenth Amendment may seem to endow the states with powers comparable to those delegated

Tenth Amendment
The Tenth Amendment of the U.S. Constitution declares that "the powers not delegated by the Constitution, nor prohibited by it to the States, are reserved to the States, respectively, or to the people."

national supremacy clause
Article VI of the U.S. Constitution states, "This Constitution, and the Laws of the United States which shall be made in Pursuance thereof; and all Treaties made, or which shall be made, under the Authority of the United States, shall be the supreme Law of the Land."

LO1

delegated powers
Specific powers entrusted to the national government by Article I, Section 8, of the U.S. Constitution (e.g., regulate interstate commerce, borrow money, and declare war).

implied powers
Powers inferred by the constitutional authority of the U.S. Congress "to make all laws which shall be necessary and proper for carrying into execution the foregoing [delegated] powers, and all other powers vested by this Constitution in the government of the United States, or in any department or officer thereof."

constitutional guarantees
Included among the U.S. Constitution's guarantees to members of the Union are protection against invasion and domestic uprisings, territorial integrity, a republican form of government, representation by two senators and at least one representative in the U.S. Congress, and equitable participation in the constitutional amendment process.

to the national government, Article VI of the U.S. Constitution contains the following clarification: "This Constitution, and the laws of the United States which shall be made in pursuance thereof; and all treaties made, or which shall be made, under the authority of the United States, shall be the supreme law of the land; and the judges in every State shall be bound thereby, anything in the Constitution or laws of any State to the contrary notwithstanding." Referred to as the **national supremacy clause**, this article emphasizes that the U.S. Constitution and acts of Congress, as well as U.S. treaties, must prevail over state constitutions and laws enacted by state legislatures.

Constitutional Powers of the National Government Article I, Section 8, of the U.S. Constitution lists powers that are specifically delegated to the national government. Included are powers to regulate interstate and foreign commerce, borrow and coin money, establish post offices and post roads, declare war, raise and support armies, provide and maintain a navy, levy and collect taxes, and establish uniform rules of naturalization. Added to these **delegated powers** is a clause that gives the national government the power "to make all laws which shall be necessary and proper for carrying into execution the foregoing powers, and all other powers vested by this Constitution in the government of the United States, or in any department or officer thereof." Since 1789, Congress and the federal courts have used this grant of **implied powers** to expand the national government's authority. For instance, the U.S. Supreme Court, in a case originating in Texas, gave significant leeway to Congress under the commerce clause to legislate in matters traditionally reserved for the states. In this case, the Court allowed Congress to set a minimum wage for employees of local governments.[2]

Constitutional Guarantees to the States The U.S. Constitution provides all states with an imposing list of **constitutional guarantees**, which include the following:

- States may be neither divided nor combined with another state without the consent of Congress and the state legislatures involved. (Texas, however, did retain power to divide itself into as many as five states under the terms of its annexation to the United States.)
- Each state is guaranteed a republican form of government (that is, a representative government with elected lawmakers).
- To serve the ends of federalism, the framers of the U.S. Constitution gave states an important role in the central government's affairs. Accordingly, each state is guaranteed that it will have two senators in the U.S. Senate and at least one member in the U.S. House of Representatives.
- As provided by the U.S. Constitution, Texas and the other states participate in presidential elections through the electoral college. Each state has electoral college votes equal to the number of U.S. senators and U.S. representatives from that state. (As of 2012, Texas has 38 electoral college votes).

- All states participate equally in approving or rejecting proposed amendments to the U.S. Constitution. Approval requires ratification by either three-fourths of the state legislatures (used for all but the Twenty-First Amendment, which repealed Prohibition) or by conventions called in three-fourths of the states.
- Each state is entitled to protection by the U.S. government against invasion and domestic violence, although Texas may also have its own militia (Army National Guard, Air National Guard, and State Guard units).
- Finally, Texas is assured that trials by federal courts for crimes committed in Texas will be conducted in Texas.

Constitutional Limitations on the States As members of the federal Union, Texas and other states are constrained by limitations imposed by Article I, Section 10, of the U.S. Constitution. For example, they may not enter into treaties, alliances, confederations, or, without the consent of Congress, make compacts or agreements with other state or foreign governments. Furthermore, they are forbidden to levy import duties on another state's products. From the outcome of the Civil War and the U.S. Supreme Court's landmark ruling in *Texas v. White* (1869), Texans learned that states cannot secede from the Union. In the *White* case, the Court ruled that the national Constitution "looks to an indestructible union, composed of indestructible states." States also learned that state legislatures cannot limit the number of terms for members of the state's congressional delegation. The U.S. Supreme Court held that term limits for members of Congress could be constitutionally imposed only if authorized by an amendment to the U.S. Constitution.[3]

Other provisions in the U.S. Constitution prohibit states from denying anyone the right to vote because of race, gender, failure to pay a poll tax, or age (if the person is 18 years of age or older). The Fourteenth Amendment forbids states from denying citizens the privileges and immunities of U.S. citizenship. For example, in a 1950 Supreme Court case (prior to the Thelma White case highlighted in the "Students in Action" segment), segregation on the basis of race at the University of Texas law school was held to be in violation of the Fourteenth Amendment's equal protection clause.

The Fourteenth Amendment also provides that no state may deprive persons of life, liberty, or property without due process of law. These protections include those rights covered in the U.S. Constitution's Bill of Rights. This expansion of the U.S. Constitution's Bill of Rights to the states has occurred primarily through a series of constitutional law cases heard by the U.S. Supreme Court. In a principle known as the *incorporation theory,* courts have applied portions of the Bill of Rights to the states by virtue of the Fourteenth Amendment's due process clause. In effect, states are obligated to protect the provisions covered in the Bill of Rights. To ensure these protections, Congress has enforcement powers under the Fourteenth Amendment.

Students in Action

Thelma White Case Forced College Integration

''In his court order no. 1616 issued July 25, 1955, Judge Robert E. Thomason prohibited Texas Western College from denying Thelma White or any member of the class of persons she represents, the right or privilege of matriculating or registering ... because of their race or color.''

—Veronica Herrera and Alan A. Johnson

How It All Began

On March 30, 1955, Thelma White filed suit in the U.S. District Court challenging the denial of her admission to Texas Western College (TWC; now University of Texas at El Paso [UTEP]). When she applied at TWC, officials rejected her application because of her race. The college was forced to obey the state's segregation law. Black students could attend only two public colleges in Texas: Prairie View A&M or Texas Southern University, both considerable distances from El Paso.

Winning Her Case

While waiting for her lawsuit to go to court, White enrolled at New Mexico A&M (later New Mexico State University), where she continued her education. Before the case went to judgment, the University of Texas System decided that TWC could admit black students. Judge R. E. Thomason ruled that the state laws requiring segregation were invalid, that White must be admitted, and that the entire University of

(Monkey Business Images/Shutterstock.com)

Texas System must admit black students to its undergraduate programs. Before this case, the law and medical schools as well as several graduate programs had been opened to blacks, but all undergraduate schools had remained closed.

Fighting for Educational Rights

White felt that she and other black students were being denied their educational rights. TWC admitted White and 12 other black students for the 1955 fall semester. White's victory opened the door for the students, although she remained at New Mexico A&M. The next year several more black students came to TWC.

Leaving a Legacy

White's legacy lives on at UTEP to this day. In her memory, UTEP founded the Thelma White Network for Community and Academic Development. The network's single purpose is to assist black students with social and academic development at UTEP. Today, African American students are enrolled in virtually every academic program at UTEP, a fact made possible by White and her pioneering efforts to change the educational system in El Paso.

Edited excerpt from Veronica Herrera and Alan A. Johnson, ''Thelma White Case Forced College Integration,'' *Borderlands* 14 (Spring 1996); abridged and reprinted by permission of the authors. *Borderlands* is a collection of student-written articles on the history and culture of the El Paso–Juárez–Las Cruces border region, comprising the states of Texas, New Mexico, and the Mexican state of Chihuahua. It is published annually by El Paso Community College. The website for this publication can be found at **http://epcc.libguides.com/borderlands**.

Interstate Relations and State Immunity

Two provisions of the U.S. Constitution specifically affect relations between the states and between citizens of one state and another state. These provisions are Article IV and the Eleventh Amendment. Article IV of the U.S. Constitution provides that "citizens of each state shall be entitled to all privileges and immunities of citizens in the several states." This means that citizens of Texas who visit another state are entitled to all the **privileges and immunities** of citizens of that state. It does not mean, however, that such visiting Texans are entitled to all the privileges and immunities to which they are entitled in their home state. More than 200 years ago, the U.S. Supreme Court broadly defined "privileges and immunities" as follows: protection by government, enjoyment of life and liberty, right to acquire and possess property, right to leave and enter any state, and right to the use of courts.

Article IV also states that "full faith and credit shall be given in each State to the public acts, records, and judicial proceedings of every other State." The **full faith and credit clause** means that any legislative enactment, state constitution, deed, will, marriage, divorce, or civil court judgment of one state must be officially recognized and honored in every other state. This clause does not apply to criminal cases. For example, a person convicted in Texas for a crime committed in Texas is not punished in another state to which he or she has fled. Instead, such cases are handled through extradition, whereby the fugitive would be returned to the Lone Star State at the request of the governor of Texas. Furthermore, for some felonies, the U.S. Congress has made it a federal offense to flee from one state to another for the purpose of avoiding arrest.

A continuing controversy regarding the full faith and credit clause revolves around whether states must recognize same-sex marriages. In 1996, during President Bill Clinton's administration, Congress passed the Defense of Marriage Act. This law allows states or political subdivisions (such as cities) to deny any marriage between persons of the same sex recognized in another state. Although several challenges to the law's constitutionality have been presented to the U.S. Supreme Court, the court has declined to review any such cases, and all lower court rulings have upheld the law's constitutionality.

In 2003, the Texas legislature passed a law prohibiting the state or any agency or political subdivision (such as a county or city) from recognizing a same-sex marriage or civil union formed in Texas or elsewhere. In February 2004, the leadership of the state legislature, as well as Governor Rick Perry, expressed support of President George W. Bush's call for a proposed U.S. constitutional amendment that would ban gay marriage. Then, in November 2005, Texas joined 15 other states by passing a constitutional amendment banning same-sex marriage.[4] According to the National Conference of State Legislatures, as of 2012, a total of 38 states have similar bans, either in their constitutions or by statutory law. Although Texas became the 16th state to approve the ban, it was among the first to define marriage as "the union of one woman and one man." Many opponents believe the constitutional

LO2

privileges and immunities
Article IV of the U.S. Constitution guarantees that "citizens of each state shall be entitled to the privileges and immunities of citizens of the several states." According to the U.S. Supreme Court, this means that citizens are guaranteed protection by government, enjoyment of life and liberty, the right to acquire and possess property, the right to leave and enter any state, and the right to use state courts.

full faith and credit clause
Most government actions of another state must be officially recognized by public officials in Texas.

amendment was unnecessary, given the existing state law. In contrast, supporters of the amendment contend that it was necessary to amend the constitution to preempt any constitutional challenges to the state law.

The Eleventh Amendment also affects relations between citizens of one state and another state. It provides that "The Judicial power of the United States shall not be construed to extend to any suit in law or equity, commenced or prosecuted against one of the United States by citizens of another state." U.S. Supreme Court rulings have ensured that a state may not be sued by its own citizens, or those of another state, without the defendant state's consent, nor can state employees sue the state for violating federal law.[5] This law, otherwise known as sovereign immunity, gives a tremendous shield to the government. Yet, this power is not absolute. For example, when Texas was sued in federal courts on behalf of several families for the state's failure to provide federally required Medicaid programs, the lower federal courts ordered the state to correct the problem after the plaintiffs and state officials agreed to a consent decree (an agreement of both parties to avoid further litigation). Texas appealed to the U.S. Supreme Court, arguing that sovereign immunity did not allow federal courts to enforce the consent decree. The Supreme Court ultimately held that this was not a sovereign immunity case, because the suit was not against the state but was against state officials who had acted in violation of federal law. The Eleventh Amendment does not prohibit enforcement of a consent decree; enforcement by the federal courts is permitted to ensure observance of federal law.[6]

State Powers

LO3 Nowhere in the U.S. Constitution is there a list of state powers. As mentioned, the Tenth Amendment simply states that all powers not specifically delegated to the national government, nor prohibited to the states, are reserved to the states or to the people. The **reserved powers** of the states are, therefore, undefined and often very difficult to specify, especially when the powers are concurrent with those of the national government, such as the taxing power. Political scientists, however, view reserved powers in broad categories:

- Police power: protection of the health, morals, safety, and convenience of citizens, and provision for the general welfare
- Taxing power: raising revenue to pay salaries of state employees, meet other costs of government, and repay borrowed money
- Proprietary power: public ownership of property, such as airports, energy-producing utilities, and parks
- Power of eminent domain: taking private property at a fair price for various kinds of public projects, such as highway construction

Needless to say, states today have broad powers, responsibilities, and duties. They are, for example, responsible for the nation's public elections—national, state, and local—because there are no nationally operated election facilities. State courts conduct most trials (both criminal and civil). States

reserved powers
Reserved powers are derived from the Tenth Amendment of the U.S. Constitution. Although not spelled out in the U.S. Constitution, these reserved powers to the states include police power, taxing power, proprietary power, and power of eminent domain.

operate public schools (elementary and secondary) and public institutions of higher education (colleges and universities), and they maintain most of the country's prisons.

One broad state power that has raised controversy is the power of eminent domain. Customarily, government entities have used the power of eminent domain to appropriate private property for public projects, such as highways, parks, and schools, as long as the property owners are paid a just compensation. In 2005, the U.S. Supreme Court expanded this power under the Fifth Amendment, allowing local governments to seize private homes for private development; the Supreme Court, however, left the door open for states to set their own rules.[7] Governor Rick Perry responded by calling a special legislative session in the summer of that year. As a result, statutory limits were imposed on government entities condemning private property where the primary purpose is for economic development. Exceptions, however, were made for public projects and to protect Arlington's plan for building the Cowboys Stadium, home of the Dallas Cowboys National Football League team. To ensure constitutional protection of private property rights against abuses of this power, an amendment to the Texas Constitution was proposed and adopted in 2009.

Although most state powers are recognizable, identifying a clear boundary line between state and national powers often remains complicated. Once again, the U.S. Supreme Court has played a critical role in defining this balance of power. Take, for example, the constitutional provision of interstate commerce in the U.S. Constitution. Not until *United States v. Lopez* (1999), a case that originated in Texas, did the U.S. Supreme Court indicate that the U.S. Congress had exceeded its powers to regulate interstate commerce when it attempted to ban guns in public schools. Operation of public schools has traditionally been considered a power of state and local governments, and the Supreme Court used the *Lopez* case, as well as other recent rulings, to rein in the federal government's power.[8] States have also become more willing to make claims of state sovereignty over federal authority in these cases. In 2005, however, in another interstate commerce case, the Supreme Court drew a line on state sovereignty when it came to regulating the use of a class of products—specifically, marijuana for medical treatment of terminally ill patients. In *Gonzales v. Raich*, the court struck down a California initiative that made an exception to the illegalization of marijuana. It ruled that Congress has the sole power to regulate local and state activities that substantially affect interstate commerce.[9] Although the California measure would have protected noncommercial cultivation and use of marijuana that did not cross state lines, the federal government contended that it would handicap enforcement of federal drug laws. In this regard, the court ruled that the federal government is primarily responsible for regulating narcotics and other controlled substances. Nevertheless, federal officers have not fully enforced the U.S. restriction on marijuana in California. As of May 2012, fifteen other states and the District of Columbia had legalized its use for medical purposes. In effect, these states have nullified a limited area of national law.

As of May 2012, Texas had 17 lawsuits against the federal government in its continuing fight for states' rights and a broad interpretation of state power under the Tenth Amendment. The suits covered a variety of issues, including environmental standards, funding for women's health programs, and health-care reform. Texas was one of 26 states led by Republican attorneys general and governors to challenge the constitutionality of the Patient Protection and Affordable Care Act of 2010 (federal health-care reform). The contested provisions included congressional mandates requiring states to expand coverage and eligibility for Medicaid programs, as well as requiring that individuals purchase health insurance or face a penalty. Relying on the same interpretation of the interstate commerce clause as the *Gonzales v. Raich* decision discussed above, the national government argued Congress had the authority to require citizens to purchase health insurance because the failure to do so affected commerce. The states maintained the mandates exceeded congressional authority.[10]

Federal-State Relations: An Evolving Process

Since the establishment of the American federal system, states have operated within a constitutional context modified to meet changing conditions. At the same time, the framers of the U.S. Constitution sought to provide a workable balance of power between national and state governments that would sustain the nation indefinitely. This balance of power between federal and state governments has evolved over the years, with certain periods reflecting an expansion or decline of the federal government, while also reflecting Texas's resistance of national control over state power.

Beginning in 1865 until about 1930, Congress acted vigorously to regulate railroads and interstate commerce within and among states. In addition, with the onset of the Great Depression of the 1930s, the federal government extended its jurisdiction to areas traditionally within the realm of state and local governments, such as regulating the workplace. For example, expansion of federal law extended to worker safety, minimum wages, and maximum hours. This expansion occurred principally through broad interpretation of the interstate commerce clause by the U.S. Supreme Court, which, in a series of cases, expanded the national government's power to include these matters.

Grants of money to the states from the federal government have also been used to influence state policymaking. The number and size of **federal grants-in-aid** grew concurrently as Congress gave states more financial assistance. As federally initiated programs multiplied, the national government's influence on state policymaking widened, and the states' control lessened in many areas. However, beginning in the 1980s, and continuing through the administration of George W. Bush, state and local governments gained more freedom to spend federal funds as they chose. In some areas, however, such as public assistance programs, they were granted less money to spend.

federal grants-in-aid
Money appropriated by the U.S. Congress to help states and local governments provide needed facilities and services.

The decline in national control over state governments has often been identified as another development—called *devolution*—in federal-state relations. The underlying concept of devolution is to bring about a reduction in the size and influence of the national government by reducing federal taxes and expenditures and by shifting many federal responsibilities to the states. Because one feature of devolution involves sharp reductions in federal aid, states are compelled to assume important new responsibilities with substantially less revenue to finance them. Texas and other states have been forced to assume more responsibility for formulating and funding their own programs in education, highways, mental health, public assistance (welfare), and other areas. In some cases, federal programs are shared, whereby the states must match federal monies in order to benefit from a program, such as the Children's Health Insurance Program (CHIP), or risk losing the funds. (See Chapter 11, "Finance and Fiscal Policy," for a discussion of CHIP funding.)

An important feature of devolution is Congress's use of **block grants** to distribute money to state and local governments. Block grants are fixed sums of money awarded according to an automatic formula determined by Congress. Thus, states that receive block grants have greater flexibility in spending. Welfare policy is an excellent case. Welfare programs became primarily a federal responsibility during Franklin D. Roosevelt's administration's (1933–1945). Federal response to widespread unemployment and poverty of the Great Depression included newly enacted programs such as food stamps and medical assistance for the poor as part of President Lyndon B. Johnson's Great Society. The Clinton administration (1993–2001) and a Republican-controlled Congress, however, eventually forced states to assume more responsibility to provide welfare programs and supplied federal funding in the form of block grants.[11] President George W. Bush continued these trends and added a new twist to devolution by giving federal financial assistance to faith-based organizations that provide social services to the poor.

Despite the focus on devolution from 2001 to 2009, federal laws such as the No Child Left Behind Act of 2001 suggest that the George W. Bush administration aggressively pursued policies that once again expanded the federal government's role. No Child Left Behind, which among other things requires participating states to administer an accountability test (selected by the state) in public schools, expands the national government's reach into a traditional area of state and local responsibility. In response to compliance pressures, the National Education Association and various school districts from three states, including Texas, sued the U.S. Department of Education for failing to provide adequate money to comply with the initiative and for forcing states and local school districts to incur the unfunded costs. A federal judge dismissed the suit, stating that Congress had allocated significant funding and that the federal government had the power to require states to meet educational standards in exchange for funds.[12]

Under President Obama's administration, federal-state relations evolved once again. Responding to the economic downturn that began in 2008, the Obama administration (in 2009) poured billions of dollars into state and

block grant
Congressional grant of money that allows the state considerable flexibility in spending for a program, such as providing welfare services.

local governments to stimulate the economy. For some observers, this action indicated another wave of national authority. In response, during the 2009 session of the Texas legislature, Representative Brandon Creighton (R-Conroe) introduced House Concurrent Resolution (H.C.R) 50, which demanded that the federal government cease and desist mandates beyond constitutionally delegated powers. A concurrent resolution requires passage in both the House and Senate, along with the signature of the governor. Creighton's resolution was similar to legislative actions that are part of the State Sovereignty Movement. In the end, the House adopted the resolution but time did not permit action in the Senate.

State legislators challenged federal law more directly in the 82nd legislative session with the passage of Senate Bill 7, a law that prohibited spending state money "to contract with entities . . . that affiliate with entities that perform or promote elective abortions." This provision targeted Planned Parenthood, an organization that offers family planning and other women's health care services. Some, though not all, Planned Parenthood clinics provide abortion services and do not receive any taxpayer funding. They operate as separate corporations from health care clinics. Nonetheless, because they are both affiliates of the Planned Parenthood Federation of America, they are affiliates with each other. In February 2012, the Texas Department of Health and Human Services adopted a rule, consistent with SB 7, that made Planned Parenthood health clinics ineligible for further funding by the state. More than 60,000 low-income Texas women use the health care services offered by Planned Parenthood. The Medicaid Women's Health Care Program is jointly financed by the federal government, which provides 90 percent of funding, and the State of Texas, which provides the remaining 10 percent of funding. In response to Texas's decision, the federal government announced that Texas was ineligible for further funding if it denied payment to Planned Parenthood because to do so interfered with a patient's ability to select a health care provider. Planned Parenthood sued the state arguing the state's rule violated Planned Parenthood's federal constitutional rights. The state sued the federal government, arguing that the national government was interfering with state's rights.

Governor Perry also received national attention when, in 2009, he hinted at the possibility of secession and his willingness to initially refuse federal stimulus funds because he was concerned there would be too many strings attached. Under tremendous criticism, Perry ultimately accepted these monies with the exception of funds for the state's unemployment insurance program. During his 2012 presidential bid, Governor Perry positioned himself as a champion of states' rights and described the fight to defend the Tenth Amendment as the "battle for the soul of America." In his 2010 book, *Fed Up! Our Fight to Save America from Washington*, he stated that "the spirit and intent of the Tenth Amendment . . . is under assault and has been for some time. The result is that today we face unprecedented federal intrusion into numerous facets of our lives."[13] Talk of secession was even more pertinent in 2011 during the 150th anniversary of Texas seceding from the Union after the outbreak of the Civil War.

Learning Check 2.1   **(Answers on p. 82)**

1. True or False: The Tenth Amendment specifically identifies states' powers.
2. Does devolution give states more or less freedom to make decisions?

★ The Texas Constitution: Politics of Policymaking

As already mentioned, the current Texas Constitution is the main source of
power for the Texas state government. Surviving for close to 140 years, this
constitution establishes the state's government, defines governing powers
and imposes limitations thereon, and identifies Texans' civil liberties and
civil rights. Political scientists and legal scholars generally believe that a
constitution should indicate the process by which problems will be solved,
both in the present and in the future, and should not attempt to solve specific problems. Presumably, if this principle is followed, later generations
will not need to adopt numerous amendments. In many areas, however, the
Texas Constitution mandates specific policies in great detail, which has
required frequent amendments.

LO4

The preamble to the Texas Constitution states, "Humbly invoking the
blessings of Almighty God, the people of the state of Texas do ordain and
establish this Constitution." These words begin the 28,600-word document
that became Texas's seventh constitution in 1876. By the end of 2012, that
same document had been changed by no fewer than 474 amendments and
contained more than 87,000 words.

The constitution's unwieldy length has grown by amendments, chiefly
because the framers spelled out policymaking powers and limitations in
minute detail. This specificity, in turn, made frequent amendments inevitable, as constitutional provisions were altered to fit changing times and conditions. For more than a century, the length of the Texas Constitution has
increased through an accumulation of amendments, most of which are
essentially statutory (resembling a law made by the legislature). The resulting document more closely resembles a code of laws than a fundamental
instrument of government. To fully understand the present-day Texas Constitution, we will examine the historical factors surrounding its adoption, as
well as previous historical periods and constitutions.

Historical Developments

The Texas Constitution provides the legal basis on which the state functions
as an integral part of the federal Union. In addition, the document is a product of history and an expression of the dominant political philosophy of
Texans living at the time of its adoption.

In general, constitution drafters have been pragmatic people performing an important task. Despite the idealistic sentiment commonly attached to constitutions in the United States, however, the art of drafting and amending them is essentially political in nature. In other words, these documents reflect the drafters' views and political interests, as well as the political environment of their time. With the passing of years, the Texas Constitution reflects the political ideas of new generations of people who amend or change it.

The **constitutional history of Texas** began more than two centuries ago, when Texas was a part of Mexico. Each of its seven constitutions has reflected the political situation that existed when the specific document was drafted.[14] In this section, we will see the political process at work as we examine the origins of these constitutions and note the efforts to revise and amend the current Texas Constitution.

The First Six Texas Constitutions In 1824, three years after Mexico gained independence from Spain, Mexican liberals established a republic with a federal constitution. Within that federal system, the former Spanish provinces of Tejas and Coahuila became a single Mexican state that adopted its own constitution. Thus, the Constitution of Coahuila y Tejas, promulgated in 1827, marked Texas's first experience with a state constitution.

Political unrest among Anglo Texans, who had settled in Mexico's northeastern area, arose almost immediately. Factors that led Texians (as Texans identified themselves at the time) to declare independence from Mexico included their desire for unrestricted trade with the United States, Anglo attitudes of racial superiority, anger over Mexico's abolition of slavery, increasing numbers of immigrant settlers, and insufficient Anglo representation in the 12-member Texas-Coahuila legislature.[15] (Selected Reading "The American Tradition of Language Rights: The Forgotten Right to Government in a 'Known Tongue'" is a perspective on the new Texian settlers and the role of language.)

constitutional history of Texas
Texas's constitutional history began with promulgation of the Constitution of Coahuila y Tejas within the Mexican federal system in 1827 and the Constitution of the Texas Republic in 1836. Texas has since been governed under its state constitutions of 1845, 1861, 1866, 1869, and 1876.

How Do We Compare. . .in State Constitutions?

Year of Adoption and Length of State Constitutions in Various U.S. States

Most Populous U.S. States	Year of Adoption	Approximate No. of Words	U.S. States Bordering Texas	Year of Adoption	Approximate No. of Words
California	1879	67,000	Arkansas	1874	59,000
Florida	1968	57,000	Louisiana	1974	70,000
New York	1894	44,000	New Mexico	1911	33,000
Texas	**1876**	**87,000**	Oklahoma	1907	81,000

Source: The Book of States, 2012 ed., vol. 44 (Lexington, KY: Council of State Governments, 2012), 11.
The website can be found at **http://knowledgecenter.csg.org/drupal/system/files/1.1_2012.pdf**

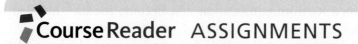

CourseReader ASSIGNMENTS

Log in to www.cengagebrain.com and open CourseReader to access the reading:

The Texas Declaration of Independence
Delegates of the People of Texas

When the General Convention's delegates met in the town of Washington-on-the-Brazos, Texas, on March 1, 1836, there was a significant amount of pressure and a limited amount of time to complete the business of independence. The declaration was submitted for consideration on the second day of official business.

1. Why did Texians and some Tejanos want to become an independent nation?

2. As described in the Declaration of Independence, how did the delegates at the convention view the Mexican government?

On March 2, 1836, at Washington-on-the-Brazos (between present-day Brenham and Navasota), a delegate convention of 59 Texians and some Tejanos issued a declaration of independence from Mexico. Tejanos were Mexicans in Texas who also wanted independence and who fought for a free Texas state. As mentioned in the Selected Reading, three Tejanos in particular served as delegates at the convention: Lorenzo de Zavala (representing Harrisburg), Francisco Ruiz, and Jose Antonio Navarro (both representing Béxar). The delegates drafted the Constitution of the Republic of Texas, modeled largely after the U.S. Constitution.

During this same period, in an effort to retain Mexican sovereignty, General Antonio López de Santa Anna defeated the Texians (many of whom were not even from Texas) and some Tejanos in San Antonio in the siege of the Alamo, which ended on March 6, 1836. Shortly afterward, Sam Houston's troops, including a company of Tejanos who were recruited by Captain Juan N. Seguín, crushed the Mexican forces in the Battle of San Jacinto on April 21, 1836. Part of Texas's unique history in the United States is its existence as an independent nation for close to 10 years.

After Houston's victory over Santa Anna, Texas voters elected Houston as president of their new republic; they also voted to seek admission to the Union. Not until 1845, however, was annexation authorized by a joint resolution of the U.S. Congress. Earlier attempts to become part of the United States by treaty had failed. Admitting Texas as another slave state in the Union, as well as concerns that annexation would lead to war with Mexico, stalled the earlier efforts. Texas president Anson Jones ultimately called a constitutional convention, whose delegates drew up a new state constitution and agreed to accept the invitation to join the Union. In February

1845, after Texas voters ratified both actions of the constitutional convention, Texas obtained its third constitution and became the 28th member of the United States.

These events, however, set the stage for war between Mexico and the United States (1846–1848), especially with regard to where the boundary lines would be drawn. Historians argue that U.S. expansionist politicians and business interests actively sought this war. When the Treaty of Guadalupe Hidalgo between Mexico and the United States was signed in 1848, Mexico lost more than half its territory and recognized the Rio Grande as Texas's southern boundary. Negotiations also addressed the rights of Mexicans left behind in Texas, many of whom owned land in the region. Under the treaty, Mexicans had one year to choose to return to Mexico or to remain in the newly annexed part of the United States; it also guaranteed Mexicans all the rights of citizenship. For all intents and purposes, these residents became the first Mexican Americans of Texas and the United States. Mexican Americans, however, were soon deprived of most of their rights, especially their property rights.

The Texas Constitution of 1845 lasted until the Civil War began. When Texas voted to secede from the Union in 1861, it functioned with other southern states as a member of the Confederate States of America. At the time, secessionists argued that the U.S. Constitution created a compact among the states, and that each state had a right to secede. During this period, Texas adopted its Constitution of 1861, with the aim of making as few changes as possible in government structure and powers. The new constitution included changes necessary to equip the government for separation from the United States, as well as the maintenance of slavery. After the Confederacy's defeat, however, the Constitution of 1866 was drafted amid a different set of conditions during Reconstruction. For this constitution, the framers sought to restore Texas to the Union with minimal changes in existing social, economic, and political institutions. Although the Constitution of 1866 was based on the Constitution of 1845, it nevertheless recognized the right of former slaves to sue in the state's courts, to enter into contracts, to obtain and transfer property, and to testify in court actions involving black citizens (but not in court actions involving white citizens). Although the Constitution of 1866 protected the personal property of African American Texans, it did not permit them to vote, hold public office, or serve as jurors.

The relatively uncomplicated reinstatement of Texas into the Union ended abruptly when the Radical Republicans gained control of U.S. Congress after the election of November 1866. Refusing to seat Texas's two senators and three representatives, Congress set aside the state's reconstructed government, enfranchised former slaves, disenfranchised prominent whites, and imposed military rule across the state. U.S. Army officers replaced civil authorities. As in other southern states, Texas functioned under a military government.

Under these conditions, delegates to a constitutional convention met in intermittent sessions from June 1868 to February 1869 and drafted yet another state constitution. Among other provisions, the new constitution

E. J. Davis and some of the Constitutional Convention delegates of 1875

(Left: The State Preservation Board, Austin, Texas; Right: Texas State Library and Archives Commission)

centralized more power in state government, provided compulsory school attendance, and guaranteed a full range of rights for former slaves. This document was ratified in 1869. Then, with elections supervised by federal soldiers, Radical Republicans gained control of the Texas legislature. At the same time, Edmund Jackson Davis (commonly identified as E. J. Davis), a former Union army general, was elected as the first Republican governor of Texas. Some historians (such as Charles William Ramsdell and T. R. Fehrenbach) described the Davis administration (January 1870–January 1874) as one of the most corrupt in Texas history.[16] In recent years, however, revisionist historians (such as Patrick G. Williams, Carl H. Moneyhon, and Barry A. Crouch) have made more positive assessments of Davis and his administration.[17]

White Texans during the Davis Administration tended to react negatively and with hostility to the freedom of former black slaves and to the political influence, albeit quite limited, that these freedmen exercised when they became voters. Violence and lawlessness were serious problems at the time. Thus, Governor Davis imposed martial law in some places and used police methods to enforce his decrees. Opponents of the Davis administration claimed that it was characterized by extravagant public spending, property tax increases to the point of confiscation, gifts of public funds to private interests, intimidation of newspaper editors, and control of voter registration by the military. In addition, hundreds of appointments to various state and local offices were filled with Davis' supporters.

Although the Constitution of 1869 is associated with the Reconstruction era and the unpopular (with most whites) administration of Governor Davis, the machinery of government created by this document was quite modern. The new fundamental law called for annual sessions of the legislature, a four-year term for the governor and other executive officers, and gubernatorial appointment (rather than popular election) of judges. It abolished county courts and raised the salaries of government officials. These changes centralized more governmental power in Austin and weakened local government.

During the Davis administration, Democrats gained control of the legislature in 1872. In December 1873, Governor Davis (with 42,633 votes) was badly defeated by Democrat Richard Coke from Waco (with 85,549 votes). When Davis refused to leave his office on the ground floor of the Capitol, Democratic lawmakers and Governor-elect Coke are reported to have climbed ladders to the Capitol's second story where the legislature convened. When President Ulysses S. Grant refused to send troops to protect him, Davis left the Capitol under protest in January 1874. In that same year, Democrats wrested control of the state courts from Republicans. The next step was to rewrite the Texas Constitution.

Drafting the Constitution of 1876 In the summer of 1875, Texans elected 75 Democrats and 15 Republicans (six of whom were African Americans) as delegates to a constitutional convention; however, only 83 attended the gathering in Austin. The majority of the delegates were not native Texans. More than 40 percent of the delegates were members of the **Texas Grange** (the Patrons of Husbandry), a farmers' organization committed to strict economy in government (reduced spending) and limited governmental powers. Its slogan of "retrenchment and reform" became a major goal of the convention.[18] So strong was the spirit of strict economy among delegates that they refused to hire a stenographer or to allow publication of the convention proceedings. As a result, no official record was ever made of the convention that gave Texas its most enduring constitution.

In their zeal to undo the policies of the Davis administration, the delegates on occasion overreacted. Striking at Reconstruction measures that had given Governor Davis control over voter registration, the overwrought delegates inserted a statement providing that "no law shall ever be enacted requiring a registration of voters of this state." Within two decades, however, the statement had been amended to permit voter registration laws.

As they continued to dismantle the machinery of the Davis administration, the delegates restricted the powers of the three branches of state government. They reduced the governor's salary, powers, and term (from four to two years); made all executive offices (except that of secretary of state) elective for two-year terms; and tied the hands of legislators with biennial (once every two years) sessions, low salaries, and limited legislative powers. All judgeships became popularly elected for relatively short terms of office. Justice of the peace courts, county courts, and district courts—all with popularly elected judges—were established. In addition, public services were trimmed to the bone. The framers of the new constitution limited the public debt and severely curbed the legislature's taxing and spending powers. They also inserted specific policy provisions. For example, they reinstated racially segregated public education and repealed the compulsory school attendance law, restored precinct elections, and allowed only taxpayers to vote on local bond issues.

Texas's proposed constitution was put to a popular vote in 1876 and was approved by a more than two-to-one majority. Although Texans in the state's largest cities—Houston, Dallas, San Antonio, and Galveston—voted against it, the much larger rural population voted for approval.

Texas Grange
Known as the Patrons of Husbandry, this farmers' organization was well represented in the constitutional convention that produced the Constitution of 1876.

Distrust of Government and Its Legacy Sharing in the prevailing popular distrust of, and hostility toward, government, the framers of the **Texas Constitution of 1876** sought with a vengeance to limit, and thus control, policymaking by placing many restrictions in the state's fundamental law. The general consensus of the time held that a state government could exercise only those powers listed in the state constitution. Therefore, instead of being permitted to exercise powers not denied by the U.S. Constitution, Texas lawmakers are limited to powers spelled out in the state's constitution. In addition, the 19th-century Texas Constitution (even with amendments) provides only limited powers for the governor's office in the 21st century. It is considered one of the weakest gubernatorial offices in the nation. (See Chapter 8, "The Executive," for a discussion of the governor's office.)

Today: After More Than a Century of Usage

The structural disarray and confusion of the Constitution of 1876 compound the disadvantages of its excessive length and detail. Unlike the Texas Constitution, the U.S. Constitution has only 4,400 words and merely 27 constitutional amendments. Yet with all its shortcomings, the Texas Constitution of 1876 has lasted for more than 135 years. For one observer, the virtues of the constitution are "its democratic impulses of restraining power and empowering voters." It is a "document of history as much as it is a charter of governance."[19]

Yet, it was inevitable that filling the Texas Constitution with many details and creating a state government with restricted powers would soon lead to constitutional amendments. In fact, many substantive changes in Texas government require an amendment. For example, an amendment is needed to change the way the state pays bills, to abolish certain unneeded state and county offices, or to authorize a bond issue pledging state revenues. Urbanization, industrialization, technological innovations, population growth, demands for programs and services, and countless social changes contribute to pressures for frequent constitutional change.

Most amendments apply to matters that should be resolved by statutes enacted by the Texas legislature. Instead, an often uninformed and usually apathetic electorate must decide the fate of many frequently complex policy issues. In this context, special interests represented by well-financed lobbyists and the media often play influential roles in constitutional policymaking. They are also likely to influence the success or defeat of constitutional amendments.

Governor Rick Perry, for instance, has played a pivotal role in advocating for specific constitutional amendment proposals. As the most visible policymaker in Texas, his public support or nonsupport of key propositions can sway voters. In 2005, for example, Governor Perry supported Proposition 2, which signified a new direction in the substantive nature of constitutional amendment proposals on the ballot. The controversial nature of Proposition 2, which sought to ban same-sex marriages, produced unprecedented media coverage and interest group activity. As mentioned

Texas Constitution of 1876
Texas's lengthy, much-amended constitution is a product of the post-Reconstruction era.

previously, the amendment proposal defined marriage as the "union of one man and one woman." It also prohibited the state and all political subdivisions from "creating or recognizing any legal status identical or similar to marriage."

Nevertheless, the proposed amendment contained language allowing the appointment of guardians, rights to property, hospital visitation, and the designation of life insurance beneficiaries without the necessity of legal marriage. Despite opposition from most of Texas's leading newspapers (in cities such as Austin, Houston, Dallas, Fort Worth, El Paso, and San Antonio), the measure overwhelmingly passed with 76 percent of the voters (more than 1.7 million) supporting it and 24 percent (more than 500,000) opposing it. Although the vote margin varied from county to county, only one county disapproved the constitutional amendment—Travis County (Austin) opposed the measure by a margin of close to 27,000 votes (81,170 in opposition to 54,246 in support).[20]

Often, Texas voters are expected to evaluate numerous constitutional amendments. (Table 2.1 provides data on amendments proposed and adopted from 1879 through 2012.) Along with Proposition 2, eight other proposals were submitted to voters in 2005. The 80th Legislature submitted only one constitutional amendment proposal to voters in May 2007 and 16 in November 2007. A proposal of particular interest for the Texas news media in 2007 was Proposition 11, which required state House and Senate members to cast a record vote on final passage of all bills and resolutions, other than resolutions of a purely honorary or ceremonial nature. The proposed amendment was approved by voters.[21]

In 2009, voters were presented with 11 constitutional proposals, all of which passed with comfortable majorities. Among the subjects were veterans' affairs, use of and access to public beaches, and the power of eminent domain. One proposal that received special attention by graduate students and faculty at four-year universities was Proposition 4. It allowed Texas's seven public "emerging research universities," such as the University of Houston, University of Texas at El Paso, and Texas Tech, to compete for research money from the state's National Research University Fund. The objective was to raise the status of these schools to what are referred to as "Tier One" research institutions. As of 2012, there are only three institutions ranked as Tier One by all ranking groups: the University of Texas at Austin, Texas A&M University, and Rice University. Tier One status by a university benefits the institution and enables the state to attract more research funding and to educate a globally competitive workforce required for economic development.[22] (See Chapter 9, "Public Policy and Administration," for discussion of higher education.)

In 2011, voters considered 10 constitutional amendment proposals. Seven of the 10 proposals passed with comfortable margins. These proposals included a property tax exemption for survivors of disabled veterans, bonds to finance water conservation, pardoning power of the governor, and distribution of the Permanent School Funds. One proposal in particular that affected college students dealt with authorizing the Texas Higher Education

How Do We Compare....in State Constitutional Amendments?

Comparison of Number and Frequency of State Constitutional Amendments, 2011

Most Populous U.S. States	No. of Amendments Added Since Adoption of Current Constitution	Average No. of Amendments Approved Annually by Voters Through 2011	U.S. States Bordering Texas	No. of Amendments Added Since Adoption of Current Constitution	Average No. of Amendments Approved Annually by Voters Through 2011
California	525	4.0	Arkansas	98	0.7
Florida	118	2.7	Louisiana	168	4.4
New York	220	1.8	New Mexico	160	1.6
Texas	**474**	**3.5**	Oklahoma	187	1.8

Source: The Book of States, 2012 ed., vol. 44 (Lexington, KY: Council of State Governments, 2012) at, **http://knowledgecenter.csg.org/drupal/system/files/1.1_2012.pdf**.

Coordinating Board to expand the state's ability to create bonds for the College Access Loan program. This program provides low-interest loans to college students, irrespective of financial need. Private colleges and universities strongly supported this proposal, because of the high costs of tuition. The proposition came as lawmakers were making cuts in educational funding sources for students, specifically the Texas Grants Program and the Texas Equalization Program. (See Chapter 11, "Finance and Fiscal Policy," for a discussion of higher education funding.) In addition, three constitutional proposals were defeated. Two addressed the powers of county governments: one would have allowed them to use bonds to finance redevelopment projects, especially in deteriorating areas; and the other would have allowed El Paso County to create conservation districts to develop and finance parks and recreation areas. Although the second measure was approved by voters in El Paso County, the vote in other areas of the state was sufficient to defeat it. The third proposal would have provided additional tax breaks to landowners who use their property for agriculture or the protection of wildlife, if they also practice water conservation.[23]

☑ Learning Check 2.2   (Answers on p. 82)

1. How many different constitutions has Texas had throughout its history?
2. True or False: Texas's present-day constitution has been amended just under 100 times.

Constitutional Amendments and Revision

LO5

Each of the 50 American state constitutions provides the means for changing the powers and functions of government. Without a provision for change, few constitutions would survive long. A revision may produce a totally new constitution to replace an old one. Courts may alter constitutions by interpreting the wording of these documents in new and different ways. Finally, constitutions may be changed by formal amendment, which is the chief method by which the Texas Constitution has been altered.

Because Texas's registered voters have an opportunity to vote on one or more proposed amendments every two years—and sometimes each year—an understanding of the steps in the **constitutional amendment process** is important. Article XVII, Section 1, provides a relatively simple procedure for amending the Texas Constitution. The basic steps in that process are as follows:

constitutional amendment process Article XVII, Section 1, of the Texas Constitution stipulates that an amendment must be proposed by a two-thirds vote of members in each chamber of the legislature and approved by a simple majority of voters in a general or special election.

- A joint resolution proposing an amendment is introduced in the House or in the Senate during a regular session or during a special session called by the governor.
- Two-thirds of the members in each chamber must adopt the resolution.
- The secretary of state prepares an explanatory statement that briefly describes the proposed amendment, and the attorney general approves this statement.

After the U.S. Supreme Court's ruling that expanded the power of eminent domain for local governments (*Kelo v. New London*), U.S. Senator Kay Bailey Hutchison (1993–2013) advocated for a state constitutional amendment providing stronger protection of private property rights.

(AP Photo/Donna McWilliam)

- The explanatory statement is published twice in Texas newspapers that print official state notices.
- A copy of the proposed amendment is posted in each county courthouse at least 30 days before the election.
- The voters must approve the proposed amendment by a simple majority vote in a regular or special election.
- The governor, who has no veto power in the process, proclaims the amendment.

Points to Ponder

For a proposed constitutional amendment to be considered by Texas voters, the legislature must adopt a joint resolution by a two-thirds vote in each chamber. The following were among some of the joint resolutions introduced, but *not* adopted, by the 82nd legislature's regular session in 2011:

- Repealing the state constitutional provision defining marriage
- Restricting government from burdening a religious organization's conduct
- Authorizing a state video lottery system
- Authorizing certain persons younger than the age of 18 to vote in a primary election
- Prohibiting a state income tax unless there is a two-thirds vote in the legislature and it is submitted to voters for approval
- Changing Senate terms of office to six years and House terms to four years
- Abolishing the State Board of Education
- Increasing the number of state senators from 31 to 41

The Texas legislature decides whether a proposed amendment will be submitted to the voters in the November general election of an even-numbered year or in a special election scheduled for an earlier date. For instance, among the 17 amendments proposed in 2007, only one was presented to voters in May; the other proposals were presented in November of that year.

Part of the problem with frequent **constitutional amendment elections** relates to the typically low voter turnout in odd-numbered years. In 2002, given the gubernatorial contest and other competitive races, turnout was relatively high (36 percent), but only a single amendment was on the ballot. A year later, despite the controversy surrounding some of the proposed amendments, voter turnout in this special election was low (12 percent). In 2005, however, given the controversial amendment to ban same-sex marriages, turnout increased (close to 18 percent). By contrast, however, turnout was low in 2007 and 2009 (roughly 8 percent each year). Turnout in 2011 was at an all-time low (less than 5 percent).

constitutional amendment election
Takes place in a regular election in even-numbered years or in a special election. Voters must approve proposed constitutional amendments with a simple majority.

Table 2.1 Texas Constitution of 1876: Amendments Proposed and Adopted, 1879–2012

Year Proposed	Number Proposed	Number Adopted	Year Proposed	Number Proposed	Number Adopted
1879	1	1	1951	7	3
1881	2	0	1953	11	11
1883	5	5	1955	9	9
1887	6	0	1957	12	10
1889	2	2	1959	4	4
1891	5	5	1961	14	10
1893	2	2	1963	7	4
1895	2	1	1965	27	20
1897	5	1	1967	20	13
1899	1	0	1969	16	9
1901	1	1	1971	18	12
1903	3	3	1973	9	6
1905	3	2	1975	12	3
1907	9	1	1977	15	11
1909	4	4	1978	1	1
1911	5	4	1979	12	9
1913	8	0	1981	10	8
1915	7	0	1982	3	3
1917	3	3	1983	19	16
1919	13	3	1985	17	17
1921	5	1	1986	1	1
1923	2	1	1987	28	20
1925	4	4	1989	21	19
1927	8	4	1990	1	1
1929	7	5	1991	15	12
1931	9	9	1993	19	14
1933	12	4	1995	14	11
1935	13	10	1997	15	13
1937	7	6	1999	17	13
1939	4	3	2001	20	20
1941	5	1	2003	22	22
1943	3	3	2005	9	7
1945	8	7	2007	17	17
1947	9	9	2009	11	11
1949	10	2	2011	10	7
			Totals	663	474

Source: Research Division, Texas Legislative Council, Amendments to the Texas Constitution Since 1876, **http//www.tlc.state.tx.us/pubsconamend/constamend1876.pdf**.

Points to Ponder

- State law, as well as federal law, requires explanatory statements for each proposed constitutional amendment to be published in both English and Spanish in Texas newspapers.
- Typically, in the past, these notices were published in both languages in the English-language press.
- In 2003, the U.S. Department of Justice and the Texas secretary of state entered into an agreement whereby only a Spanish-language version of the explanatory notice would be mailed to each registered voter with a Hispanic surname, instead of publishing the notice in Spanish in the newspapers. Their aim was to provide an efficient and economical method of reaching monolingual Spanish speakers.
- Many bilingual Texans with Hispanic surnames were upset when they received this communication. They believed that government officials should not infer or assume that people with Hispanic surnames are unable to read English or, for that matter, are fluent in Spanish.

Unlike voters in other states, Texans do not have the power of **initiative** at the state level; however, this power is exercised under some local governments. (See Chapter 3, "Local Governments," for a discussion of how these powers work locally.) If adopted, the initiative process would bypass the legislature and allow individual Texans or interest groups to gather signatures required for submitting proposed constitutional amendments and statutes (ordinary laws) to direct the popular vote. According to the *Book of States*, 18 states have some form of constitutional amendment procedure by initiative.[24] In recent years, no serious legislative efforts to amend the Texas Constitution to authorize the initiative process at the state level have emerged.

Constitutional Revision

Attempts to revise Texas's Constitution of 1876 began soon after its adoption. A legislative resolution calling for a constitutional revision convention was introduced in 1887 and was followed by others. Limited success came in 1969, when an amendment removed 56 obsolete constitutional provisions.

The most comprehensive movement to achieve wholesale **constitutional revision** began in 1971. In that year, the 62nd Legislature adopted a joint resolution proposing an amendment authorizing the appointment of a study commission and naming the members of the 63rd Legislature as delegates to a constitutional convention. Except for the state Bill of Rights, any part of the Texas Constitution of 1876 could be changed or deleted. Submitted to the voters in 1972 as a proposed constitutional amendment, the resolution

initiative
A citizen-drafted measure proposed by a specific number or percentage of qualified voters, which becomes law if approved by popular vote. In Texas, this process occurs only at the local level, not at the state level.

constitutional revision
Extensive or complete rewriting of a constitution.

was approved by a comfortable margin of more than half a million votes (1,549,982 for to 985,282 against).

A six-member committee (composed of the governor, the lieutenant governor, the speaker of the House, the attorney general, the chief justice of the Texas Supreme Court, and the presiding judge of the Court of Criminal Appeals) selected 37 persons to serve as members of the Constitutional Revision Commission. The commission prepared a draft constitution on the basis of opinions and information gathered at public hearings conducted throughout the state and from various authorities on constitutional revision. One-fourth the length of the present constitution, the completed draft was submitted to the legislature on November 1, 1973.

On January 8, 1974, all 181 members of both chambers of the Texas legislature met in Austin at a **constitutional revision convention**. Previous Texas constitutions had been drafted by convention delegates popularly elected for that purpose. When the finished document was put to a vote, the result was 118 for and 62 against, three votes short of the two-thirds majority of the total membership needed for final approval. (Approval required a total of at least 121 votes.) Attempts to reach compromises on controversial issues proved futile.

The Constitutional Convention of 1974 provided perhaps the best demonstration of the politics surrounding Texas's constitution making. First, the convention was hampered by a lack of positive political leadership. Governor Dolph Briscoe maintained a hands-off policy throughout the convention. Lieutenant Governor Bill Hobby similarly failed to provide needed political leadership, and the retiring speaker of the House, Price Daniel Jr., pursued a nonintervention course. Other members of the legislature were distracted by their need to campaign for reelection.

The primary reason that the convention failed to agree on a proposed constitution was the phantom "nonissue" of a right-to-work provision. A statutory ban on union shop labor contracts was already in effect. Adding this prohibition to the constitution would not have strengthened the legal hand of employers to any significant degree. Nevertheless, conservative, anti-labor forces insisted on this provision, and a pro-labor minority vigorously opposed it. The controversy aroused much emotion and at times produced loud and bitter name-calling among delegates on the floor and spectators in the galleries.[25]

Stung by widespread public criticism of the 1974 convention's failure to produce a proposed constitution for public approval or rejection, the 64th legislature resolved to submit a proposal to Texas voters. In 1975, both houses of the legislature agreed on a constitutional revision resolution comprising 10 articles in eight sections to be submitted to the Texas electorate in November of that year. The content of the articles was essentially the same as that of the final resolution of the unsuccessful 1974 convention.

The revision proposed in 1975 represented years of work by men and women well informed about constitution making. Recognized constitutional authorities evaluated the concise and orderly document as one of the best-drafted state constitutions ever submitted to American voters. Although new

constitutional revision convention
A body of delegates who meet to make extensive changes in a constitution or to draft a new constitution.

and innovative in many respects, the proposal did not discard all of the old provisions. In addition to retaining the Bill of Rights, the proposed constitution incorporated such basic principles as limited government, separation of powers, and bicameralism (a two-house legislature).

Nevertheless, Texas voters demonstrated a strong preference for the status quo by rejecting each proposition. Voters in 250 of the state's 254 counties rejected all eight proposals. A mere 23 percent of the estimated 5.9 million registered voters cast ballots, meaning that only about 10 percent of the state's voting-age population participated in this important referendum. When asked to explain the resounding defeat of the eight propositions, Bill Hobby, then lieutenant governor, responded, "There's not enough of the body left for an autopsy."

More Revision Attempts

After the revision debacle of 1975, two decades passed before the next attempt to revise the constitution. In 1995, Senator John Montford (D-Lubbock) drafted a streamlined constitution that incorporated many of the concepts contained in the failed 1975 proposal. Montford's plan also called for a voter referendum every 30 years (without legislative approval) on the question of calling a constitutional revision convention. But Montford resigned from the Texas Senate to become chancellor of the Texas Tech University system in 1996. With such issues as tax changes, welfare reform, and educational finance pressing for attention, the 75th Legislature did not seriously consider constitutional revision in 1997.

In 1998, Senator Bill Ratliff (R-Mount Pleasant) and Representative Rob Junell (D-San Angelo) launched another attempt to revise the constitution.[26] With assistance from San Angelo State University students and others, they prepared a complete rewrite of the much-amended 1876 document. Subsequently, Ratliff and Junell introduced another draft for consideration by the 76th Legislature in 1999. It failed to muster enough support for serious consideration in committee and never received a floor vote in either legislative chamber.[27] This proposal would have cut the then 80,000-word document to approximately 19,000 words. Significant changes included expanding powers of the governor, repealing the current partisan election method of selecting state judges, and increasing salaries of the House speaker and the lieutenant governor.

One proposal that the legislature may consider in the future was created by a bipartisan team led by Roy Walthall (a semiretired instructor at McLennan Community College in Waco). In 2010, the team set out to reorganize the constitution. Rather than make substantive changes, which would provoke political opposition, their proposal included changes that would make it more readable and usable. The team claims that they did not change the content or legal meaning. According to Walthall, the bulk of their work was in rearranging many of the existing provisions to more logical sections. The governor would have to appoint a commission to study the reorganized constitution, and it could take several legislative sessions before the constitutional proposal would be presented to the state's voters. If approved, a

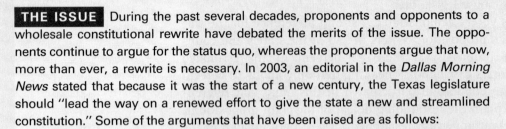

Point/Counterpoint

THE ISSUE During the past several decades, proponents and opponents to a wholesale constitutional rewrite have debated the merits of the issue. The opponents continue to argue for the status quo, whereas the proponents argue that now, more than ever, a rewrite is necessary. In 2003, an editorial in the *Dallas Morning News* stated that because it was the start of a new century, the Texas legislature should "lead the way on a renewed effort to give the state a new and streamlined constitution." Some of the arguments that have been raised are as follows:

Should the Texas Constitution Be Rewritten?

Arguments For Rewriting the Constitution

1. It is excessively long and outdated.
2. Voter turnout for constitutional amendment elections tends to be very low.
3. Voters are asked to decide on complex proposals that are not (or cannot be) adequately summarized in brief explanatory statements.
4. Expanding the powers of the government would better serve the needs of Texans.

Arguments Against Rewriting the Constitution

1. Despite its flaws, the Texas Constitution remains a functioning document.
2. The amendment process allows changes when needed.
3. Special interests would, in all likelihood, control constitutional revision.
4. A comparison of state constitutional revision attempts suggests that constitutional revision can be a high-risk endeavour that does not ensure success.

new state constitution would cause Texas to join the other 49 states that have updated their constitutions since the beginning of the 20th century.[28]

During the 21st century, the legislature has ignored or delayed the issue of constitutional revision. A series of budget crises, redistricting issues, and school funding has dominated the legislative agenda. As a result, large-scale constitutional reform remains an unaddressed problem. However, certain individuals in the legislature want to keep the subject on the agenda. At the end of the regular legislative session in 2011, Representative Charles Anderson (R-Waco) introduced a resolution asking the leadership in the legislature to create a joint study committee to examine a reorganization of the state constitution, similar to Walthall's proposal, prior to the 2013 session. The request, however, was never brought up for a vote in the legislature.

Piecemeal Revision

Because extensive constitutional reform has proved futile, Texas legislators have sought to achieve some measure of government reform by other means, including legislative enactments and piecemeal constitutional amendments. In 1977, for example, the 65th legislature enacted into law two parts of the 1975 propositions defeated at the polls. One established a procedure for reviewing state administrative agencies; the other created a planning agency within the Office of the Governor. In 1979, the 66th legislature proposed six amendments designed to implement parts of the constitutional revision package rejected in 1975. Three were adopted by the voters and added to the Texas Constitution. They accomplished the following:

- Established a single property tax appraisal district in each county (discussed in Chapter 3, "Local Governments")
- Gave criminal appellate jurisdiction to 14 courts of appeals that formerly had exercised civil jurisdiction only
- Allowed the governor restricted removal power over appointed statewide officials[29]

Proposals for important constitutional changes have been unsuccessful in the House and the Senate. For example, during the regular session of the 77th Legislature in 2001, Representative Rob Junell (D-San Angelo) submitted a proposal that was considered and approved by the House Select Committee on Constitutional Revision. Among other items, the proposal would have changed the terms of office for state senators and House members. It also would have created a Texas Salary Commission to set salaries for elected and appointed officials of the executive, judicial, and legislative branches. This proposal, however, was never brought up for a floor vote in the legislature.[30]

To modernize the Texas Constitution, one constitutional amendment (adopted in 1999) authorized elimination of certain "duplicative, executed, obsolete, archaic and ineffective provisions of the Texas Constitution." Among resulting deletions were references to the abolished poll tax and the governor's authority "to protect the frontier from hostile incursions by Indians." In November 2007, voters also eliminated the constitutional county office of inspector of hides and animals, which had been created in the 1880s. Nevertheless, the Texas Constitution still has problems.

☑ Learning Check 2.3 (Answers on p. 82)

1. When was the last time voters were presented with a wholesale constitutional revision proposal from the state legislature?
2. True or False: Amending the Texas Constitution requires two-thirds of the members of each chamber of the state legislature voting for a proposed amendment and three-fourths of the voters approving it in a constitutional amendment election.

★ The Texas Constitution: A Summary

Chiefly because of its length, complete printed copies of the Texas Constitution are not readily available to the public. Until publication of its Millennium Edition (2000–2001), the *Texas Almanac* was the most widely used source for the text of this document. That edition and subsequent editions,

LO6

however, now refer persons seeking the text of the Texas Constitution to the Internet. (See this chapter's "Internet Resources.")

Although *Practicing Texas Politics* does not include the entire text of the Texas Constitution, each chapter looks to Texas's basic law for its content. The rest of this chapter presents a brief synopsis of the document's 17 articles.[31]

The Bill of Rights

We begin by examining Article I, the Texas Constitution's Bill of Rights. The **Bill of Rights** is made up of 30 sections that cover a multitude of topics, including protection against arbitrary governmental actions, the rights of accused and convicted criminals and victims of crime, and equal rights for women. Article I also includes philosophical observations that have no direct force of law.

Constitutional Rights against Arbitrary Governmental Actions Eleven of Article I's sections provide protections for people and property against arbitrary governmental actions. Guarantees such as freedom of speech, press, religion, assembly, and petition are included. The right to keep and bear arms, prohibitions against the taking of property by government action without just compensation, and protection of contracts are also incorporated. Most of these rights found in the Texas Constitution are also protected under the U.S. Constitution. Thus, with their basic rights guaranteed in both national and state constitutions, Texans, like people in other states, have a double safeguard against arbitrary governmental actions.

One of these constitutional rights, protected for Texans by both state and federal constitutions, centers on freedom of religion. A constitutional right to freedom of religion is essentially the same in both the Texas Constitution and the U.S. Constitution. Yet, when one examines the actual wording, it is different. The Texas Bill of Rights, Section 6, states, "All men have a natural and indefeasible right to worship Almighty God according to the dictates of their own conscience. No man shall be compelled to attend, erect or support any place of worship, or to maintain any ministry against his consent . . . and no preference shall ever be given to any religious society or mode of worship." Under the U.S. Constitution, the First Amendment (as applied to the states under the Fourteenth Amendment) provides that states "shall make no law respecting an establishment of religion, or prohibiting the free exercise thereof."

Cases on religious freedom have gone from Texas all the way to the U.S. Supreme Court. Included among these are two cases that yielded different results—one centered on student-led prayer before a school football game, while another involved a Ten Commandments monument placed on the Texas state Capitol grounds. The U.S. Supreme Court interpreted the establishment clause of the U.S. Constitution to require a separation of church and state, and thus struck down school prayer before football games, contending that the message conveyed amounted to an endorsement of religion on the school grounds.[32] In contrast, the U.S. Supreme Court upheld the Ten Commandments display, concluding that it is a historical monument among other historical monuments on the state grounds.[33]

Bill of Rights
Composed of 30 sections in Article I of the Texas Constitution, it guarantees protections for people and their property against arbitrary actions by state and local governments. Included among these rights are freedom of speech, press, religion, assembly, and petition. The Texas Bill of Rights is similar to the one found in the U.S. Constitution.

Rights of Criminals and Victims Thirteen sections of the Texas Constitution's Bill of Rights relate to the rights of persons accused of crimes and to the rights of individuals who have been convicted of crimes. For example, one section concerns the right to release on bail; another prohibits unreasonable searches and seizures; and a third declares that "the right to trial by jury shall remain inviolate." These provisions relate closely to similar language in the national Bill of Rights.

The Texas Constitution is even more protective of certain rights than the U.S. Constitution is. An additional set of rights added by constitutional amendment in 1989 protects crime victims. This provision was developed in the early 1980s in the early 1980s in response to findings of a presidential task force which explored the inequality of rights for crime victims. In general, the state constitution now gives victims rights to restitution, information about the accused (conviction, sentence, release, etc.), protection from the accused throughout the criminal justice process, and respect for the victim's privacy.

Equal Rights for Women Another example of the Texas Constitution's providing more protection than the U.S. Constitution relates to equal rights for women. Attempts nationwide to add the proposed Equal Rights Amendment (ERA) to the U.S. Constitution failed between 1972 and 1982 (even though the amendment was approved by the Texas legislature). Nevertheless, the **Texas Equal Legal Rights Amendment (ELRA)** was added to Article I, Section 3, of the Texas Constitution in 1972. It states: "Equality under the law shall not be denied or abridged because of sex, race, color, creed, or national origin." This constitutional amendment was proposed and adopted after several unsuccessful attempts dating back to the 1950s.[34] Interestingly, the Texas Constitution still has a provision that states, "All free men have equal rights."

Additional Protections Additional protections in the Texas Constitution include prohibitions against imprisonment for debt, outlawry (the process of putting a convicted person outside of the protection of the law), and transportation (punishing a convicted citizen by banishment from the state). Monopolies are prohibited by a provision of the Texas Bill of Rights, but not by the U.S. Constitution.

Interpretation of the Texas Constitution by the Texas Supreme Court has also provided additional rights, such as the court's interpretation of Article VII, Section 1, which requires the state legislature to provide support and maintenance for an efficient system of free public schools. In 1989, the high court first held that the state legislature had a constitutional requirement to create a more equitable public school finance system. The Texas Supreme Court revisited school finance in 2005 and declared the school finance system unconstitutional. Rather than focusing on the system's continued and persistent inequities, however, the court focused on whether the state-imposed property tax cap amounted to a statewide property tax, which the Texas Constitution forbids. (Property taxes can be collected only at the local level.) Because more than 80 percent of all school districts had reached this cap, and state funding had continued to decline, the court held that school boards had

Texas Equal Legal Rights Amendment (ELRA)
Added to Article I, Section 3, of the Texas Constitution, it guarantees that "equality under the law shall not be denied or abridged because of sex, race, color, creed, or national origin."

effectively lost control of tax rates. Equally important, the court rejected district court judge John Dietz's 2004 ruling that more money in the system was necessary to comply with the Texas Constitution's requirement to provide the "general diffusion of knowledge."[35] Challenges to school funding in the courts continued in 2011 and 2012. (For more on school finance, see Chapter 11, "Finance and Fiscal Policy.")

Philosophical Observations Three sections of the Texas Bill of Rights contain philosophical observations that have no direct force of law. Still stinging from what they saw as the "bondage" years of Reconstruction, the angry delegates to the constitutional convention of 1875 began their work by inserting this statement: "Texas is a free and independent state, subject only to the Constitution of the United States." They also asserted that all political power resides with the people and is legitimately exercised only on their behalf and that the people may at any time "alter, reform, or abolish their government." To guard against the possibility that any of the rights guaranteed in the other 28 sections would be eliminated or altered by the government, Section 29 proclaims that "everything in this 'Bill of Rights' is excepted out of the general powers of government, and shall forever remain inviolate."

The Powers of Government and Separation of Powers

Holding fast to the principle of limited government and a balance of power, the framers of the Constitution of 1876 firmly embedded in the state's fundamental law the familiar doctrine of separation of powers. In Article II, they assigned the lawmaking, law-enforcing, and law-adjudicating powers of government to three separate branches, identified as the legislative, executive, and judicial departments, respectively.

Article III is titled "Legislative Department." Legislative powers are vested in the bicameral legislature, composed of the House of Representatives with 150 members and the Senate with 31 members. A patchwork of more than 60 sections, this article provides vivid testimony to many decades of amendments directly affecting the legislative branch. For example, in 1936, an amendment added a section granting the Texas legislature the authority to levy taxes to fund a retirement system for public school, college, and university teachers. Today, public school teachers and personnel employed by public universities and community colleges benefit from pension programs provided by the state.

Article IV, "Executive Department," states unequivocally that the governor "shall be the Chief Executive Officer of the State" but then shares executive power with four other popularly elected officers independent of the governor: the lieutenant governor, the attorney general, the comptroller of public accounts, and the commissioner of the General Land Office. (A state treasurer was originally included in this list, but a constitutional amendment abolished the office.) With this and other provisions for division of executive power, some observers consider the Texas governor no more than first among equals in the executive branch of state government.

separation of powers
The assignment of lawmaking, law-enforcing, and law-interpreting functions to separate branches of government.

Through Article V, "Judicial Department," Texas joins Oklahoma as the only two states in the country with a bifurcated court system that includes two courts of final appeal: one for civil cases (the Supreme Court of Texas) and one for criminal cases (the Court of Criminal Appeals). Below these two supreme appellate courts are the courts authorized by the Texas Constitution and created by the legislature: the intermediate appellate courts (14 courts of appeals) and thousands of courts of original jurisdiction (district courts, county courts, and justice of the peace courts).

Suffrage

Article VI, titled "**Suffrage**" (the right to vote), is one of the shortest articles in the Texas Constitution. Before 1870, states had the definitive power to conduct elections. Since that time, amendments to the U.S. Constitution, acts of Congress such as the Voting Rights Act of 1965, and U.S. Supreme Court rulings have vastly diminished this power. In addition, amendments to the Voting Rights Act of 1975 require Texas to provide bilingual ballots. The act also added Texas, among other states, under federal preclearance, which means that any changes to voting laws at the state level and within certain jurisdictions of Texas must be cleared by the U.S. Department of Justice. Within the scope of current federal regulations, the Texas Constitution establishes qualifications for voters, provides for citizen voter registration, and governs the conduct of elections. In response to federal-level changes, this article has been amended to abolish the payment of a poll tax or any form of property qualification for voting in the state's elections and to change the minimum voting age from 21 to 18.

Local Governments

The most disorganized part of the Texas Constitution concerns units of **local government**: counties, municipalities (cities), school districts, and other special districts. Although Article IX is titled "Counties," the provisions concerning county government are scattered through four other articles. Moreover, the basic structure of county government is defined not in Article IX on counties but in Article V on the judiciary. Article XI on municipalities is equally disorganized and inadequate. Only four of the sections of this article relate exclusively to municipal government. Other sections concern county government, taxation, public indebtedness, and forced sale of public property.

Along with counties and municipalities, the original text of the Constitution of 1876 referred to school districts but not to other types of special-district governments. Authorization for special districts, however, crept into the Texas Constitution with a 1904 amendment that authorizes the borrowing of money for water development and road construction by a county "or any defined district." Since then, special districts have been created to provide myriad services, such as drainage, conservation, urban renewal, public housing, hospitals, and airports.

suffrage
The right to vote.

local government
The Texas Constitution authorizes these units of local government: counties, municipalities, school districts, and other special districts. These "grassroots governments" provide a range of services that include rural roads, protection of persons and property, city streets, and public education.

The 1853 Capitol of Texas. Construction was completed on this building in Austin in 1853, but it was destroyed by fire in 1881.

(PICA 16340, Austin History Center, Austin Public Library)

Other Articles

The nine remaining articles also reflect a strong devotion to constitutional minutiae: Education, Taxation and Revenue, Railroads, Private Corporations, Spanish and Mexican Land Titles, Public Lands and Land Office, Impeachment, General Provisions, and Mode of Amendment. The shortest is Article XIII, "Spanish and Mexican Land Titles." The entire text was deleted by amendment in 1969 because its provisions were deemed obsolete. The longest article is Article XVI, "General Provisions." Among other provisions, it prohibits bribing of public officials and authorizes the legislature to regulate the manufacture and sale of intoxicants.

 Learning Check 2.4   (Answers on p. 82)

1. True or False: The Texas Constitution contains constitutional rights not found in the U.S. Constitution.
2. Article II of the Texas Constitution assigns powers to which branches of government?

★ Conclusion

As a member of the United States, Texas is provided with certain constitutional guarantees as well as limitations on its powers. The U.S. Constitution plays a significant role in defining federal-state relations. As we have learned, this balance of power between the federal government and the state government is constantly evolving. The Texas government derives most of its powers from the Texas Constitution. Understanding Texas's constitutional history explains to a large degree the characteristics of its present-day constitution. As we have discovered, amending the Texas Constitution occurs frequently through constitutional amendment elections, but any recent attempts to revise the constitution have not been successful. So, the Constitution of 1876 remains essentially unchanged.

Chapter Summary

- The American federal system features a division of powers between a national government and 50 state governments. Powers not delegated (nor implied, as interpreted by federal courts) to the federal government are reserved to the states or to the people under the Tenth Amendment. A balance of power between the national and state governments has evolved over time.
- The Texas Constitution is the fundamental law that sets forth the powers and limitations of the state's government. Texas has had seven constitutions, each reflecting the political situation that existed when the specific document was drafted. The Constitution of 1876 has endured, despite its excessive length, confusion, and statutory detail.
- Today's Texas Constitution is the country's second longest and, at the end of 2012, had 474 amendments. Most amendments are statutory in nature, so the document resembles a code of laws.
- Changing the Texas Constitution requires an amendment proposed by a two-thirds majority vote of the members in each legislative chamber and approved by a simple majority of the state's voters in a general or special election. Despite several efforts to revise the Texas Constitution, only piecemeal revisions have occurred.
- The Texas Constitution is composed of 17 articles. Included are the Bill of Rights, an article on suffrage, articles on the three branches of state government, and provisions concerning the powers of state and local governments.

Key Terms

Tenth Amendment, p. 49
national supremacy clause, p. 50
delegated powers, p. 50
implied powers, p. 50
constitutional guarantees, p. 50
privileges and immunities, p. 53
full faith and credit clause, p. 53

reserved powers, p. 54
federal grants-in-aid, p. 56
block grant, p. 57
constitutional history of Texas, p. 60
Texas Grange, p. 64
Texas Constitution of 1876, p. 65
constitutional amendment process, p. 68

constitutional amendment election, p. 69
initiative, p. 71
constitutional revision, p. 71
constitutional revision convention, p. 72
Bill of Rights, p. 76
Texas Equal Legal Rights Amendment
   (ELRA), p. 77
separation of powers, p. 78
suffrage, p. 79
local government, p. 79

Learning Check Answers

2.1
1. False. The Tenth Amendment does not specifically identify the powers of the states.
2. Devolution gives the states more freedom to make decisions.

2.2
1. Texas has had seven constitutions throughout its history.
2. False. Our present-day Texas Constitution has been amended more than 400 times.

2.3
1. November 1975 was the last time that voters were presented with a constitutional revision proposal from the state legislature; recent attempts have failed.
2. False. Amending the Texas Constitution requires two-thirds of the members of each chamber of the state legislature to vote for a proposed amendment, and only a simple majority of the voters to approve it in a constitutional amendment election.

2.4
1. True. The Texas Constitution does contain additional constitutional rights, such as the Equal Legal Rights Amendment, not found in the U.S. Constitution.
2. The Texas Constitution assigns power to the legislative, executive, and judicial branches.

Discussion Questions

1. What recent examples reflect an evolving nature of federalism?
2. Given the state's police power, how does government protect the health, morals, and safety of its citizens? Can you think of specific policies?
3. How does Texas's constitutional history continue to influence the state's present-day constitution and government?
4. What were your initial impressions of some of the constitutional amendments considered or proposed by the Texas legislature? Are these the kinds of issues that should be placed in the Texas Constitution?
5. In your opinion, should the Texas Constitution be rewritten?
6. What recommendations would you offer for revision of the Texas Constitution?

Internet Resources

FindLaw: U.S. Constitution:
http://www.findlaw.com/casecode/constitution

National Governors Association:
http://www.nga.org

Texas Constitution:
http://www.constitution.legis.state.tx.us/

Texas Legislature Online:
http://www.capitol.state.tx.us

Texas Office of State-Federal Relations:
http://www.osfr.state.tx.us

Texas Office of the Secretary of State:
http://www.sos.state.tx.us

Texas State Historical Association Online:
http://www.tshaonline.org

Notes

1. David B. Walker, *The Rebirth of Federalism: Slouching Toward Washington,* 2nd ed. (New York: Chatham House, 2000).
2. *Garcia v. San Antonio Metropolitan Transit Authority,* 469 U.S. 528 (1985).
3. *U.S. Term Limits v. Thornton,* 514 U.S. 115 (1995).
4. Paul Burka, "The M Word," *Texas Monthly,* January 2006, 14–16.
5. *Kimel v. Florida Board of Regents,* 528 U.S. 62 (2000); *Alden v. Maine,* 527 U.S. 706 (1999); and *Seminole Tribe v. Florida,* 517 U.S. 44 (1996).
6. *Frew v. Hawkins,* 540 U.S. 431 (2004). See also Carlos Guerra, "High Court Orders Texas to Honor Its Word—and Pay Up," *San Antonio Express-News,* January 15, 2004.
7. *Kelo v. New London,* 545 U.S. 469 (2005).
8. *United States v. Lopez,* 514 U.S. 549 (1995).
9. *Gonzales v. Raich,* 545 U.S. 1 (2005).
10. Becca Aaronson, Chris Chang, Ben Hasson, and Todd Wiseman, "Interactive: Texas v. the Federal Government," *Texas Tribune,* February 15, 2012.
11. Sanford F. Schram, "Welfare Reform: A Race to the Bottom?" *Publius: The Journal of Federalism* 28 (Summer 1998): 1–8. (Special issue: "Welfare Reform in the United States: A Race to the Bottom?" edited by Sanford F. Schram and Samuel H. Beer.)
12. For a concise study examining the influence of this important law, see Frederick M. Hess and Michael J. Petrilli, *No Child Left Behind* (New York: Peter Lang, 2007). For more information regarding the law, see the National Education Association at http://www.nea.org/esea/more.html. See also Toni Locy, "Judge Dismisses Suit Against No Child Left Behind Law," *Houston Chronicle,* November 24, 2005.
13. Manny Fernandez and Emily Ramshaw, "As States-Rights Stalwart, Perry Draws Doubts," *San Antonio Express-News,* August 29, 2011. See also, Rick Perry, *Fed Up! Our Fight to Save America from Washington* (New York: Little, Brown & Company, 2010), 187–188.
14. For a more detailed account of early Texas constitutions, see John Cornyn, "The Roots of the Texas Constitution: Settlement to Statehood," *Texas Tech Law Review* 26, 4 (1995): 1089–1218. The author served as a member of the Texas Supreme Court and as the state's attorney general before being elected to the U.S. Senate in 2002.
15. Leobardo F. Estrada, F. Chris Garcia, Reynaldo Flores Macias, and Lionel Maldonado, "Chicanos in the United States: A History of Exploitation and Resistance," in *Latinos and the Political System,* ed. F. Chris Garcia (Notre Dame, Ind.: University of Notre Dame Press, 1988), 28–64.
16. Charles William Ramsdell, *Reconstruction in Texas* (New York: Columbia University Press, 1910); and T. R. Fehrenbach, *Lone Star: A History of Texas and the Texans* (New York: Macmillan, 1968), especially Chapter 22, "The Carpetbaggers."
17. Patrick G. Williams, *Beyond Redemption: Texas Democrats after Reconstruction* (Austin: University of Texas Press, 2007); Carl H. Moneyhon, *Edmund J. Davis of Texas: Civil War General, Republican Leader, Reconstruction Governor* (Fort Worth: TCU Press, 2010); and Barry A. Crouch, *The Dance of Freedom: Texas*

African Americans During Reconstruction, edited by Larry Madaras (Austin: University of Texas Press, 2007).

18. New light on writing Texas's seventh constitution is presented in Patrick G. Williams, "Of Rutabagas and Redeemers: Rethinking the Texas Constitution of 187," *Southwestern Historical Quarterly* 106, 2 (2002): 230–253.

19. Roy Walthall, "Celebrate Texas's Anniversary with a Reorganized Constitution," *Waco Tribune-Herald*, March 5, 2011.

20. Jane Elliott, "Gay Marriage Ban Put in Texas Constitution," *Houston Chronicle,* November 9, 2005. See also *Summary Report of the 2005 Constitutional Election Results* at http://www.sos.state.tx.us.

21. See "Constitutional Amendments Proposed for November 2007 Ballot," *Focus Report*, No. 80-8 (House Research Organization, Texas House of Representatives, August 24, 2007), at http://www.hro.house.state.tx.us/focus/amend80.pdf.

22. Ralph Haurwitz, "From College to Beach, All Amendments Pass," *Austin American-Statesman,* November 4, 2009; Holly Hacker, "Prop. 4 Would Let Colleges Tap Fund," *Dallas Morning News,* October 4, 2009; and "Constitutional Amendments Proposed for November 2009 Ballot," *Focus Report* No. 81-8 (House Research Organization, Texas House of Representatives, August 20, 2009) at http://www.hro.house.state.tx.us/focus/amend81.pdf.

23. See "Constitutional Amendments Proposed for November 2011 Ballot," *Focus Report,* No. 82-6 (House Research Organization, Texas House of Representatives, July 20, 2011) at http://www.hro.house.state.tx.us/pdf/focus/amend82.pdf. See also, Ralph Haurwitz, "Voters to Consider Boosting College Loan Program," *Austin American-Statesman*, October 17, 2011.

24. *The Book of States,* 2012 ed., vol 44 (Lexington, KY: Council of State Governments, 2012), 15; and the Institute of Initiatives and Referendums at http://www.iandrinstitute.org/.

25. Texas's right-to-work law was enacted in 1947 by the 50th Legislature. The law bans the union shop arrangement whereby newly hired workers must join a union after employment.

26. Jim Lewis, "Getting Around to a New Constitution," *County* (January/ February 1999): 11–13. For a profile of Representative Rob Junell and his collaboration with Senator Bill Ratliff, see Janet Elliott, "Maverick in the Middle," *Texas Lawyer* (January 1999): 19–20.

27. For the text of the Ratliff-Junell draft constitution, refer to *Texas Legislature Online* at http://www.capitol.state.tx.us and search by bill number for the 76th Regular Session, HJR1 or SJR1.

28. The proposed constitution can be found at http://www.reorgtexascon.com/2011_Proposed_Constitution.html. See also, Roy Walthall, "Waco Group Reorganizes Texas Constitution," *Waco Tribune-Herald*, November 15, 2010; and Roy Walthall, "Texas Constitution Needs Makeover," *Amarillo Globe-News*, October 23, 2011.

29. For an analysis of amendments proposed between 1976 and 1989, see James G. Dickson, "Erratic Continuity: Some Patterns of Constitutional Change in Texas Since 1975," *Texas Journal of Political Studies* 14 (Fall–Winter 1991–1992): 41–56.

30. For the text of Junell's constitutional proposal, refer to *Texas Legislature Online* at http://www.capitol.state.tx.us and search by bill for the 77th Legislature, HJR 69.

31. For detailed analyses of the contents of the Texas Constitution, see Janice C. May, *The Texas State Constitution: A Reference Guide* (Westport, Conn.: Greenwood Press, 1996); and George D. Braden, *Citizen's Guide to the Texas Constitution* (Austin: Texas Advisory Commission on Intergovernmental Relations, 1972).

32. *Santa Fe v. Doe,* 530 U.S. 290 (2000).

33. *Van Orden v. Perry,* 545 U.S. 677 (2005).

34. For details concerning the struggle for equal legal rights, see Rob Fink, "Hermine Tobolowsky, the Texas ELRA, and the Political Struggle for Women's Equal Rights," *Journal of the West* 42 (Summer 2003): 52–57; and Tai Kreidler, "Hermine Tobolowsky: Mother of Texas Equal Rights Amendment," in *The Human Tradition in Texas,* edited by Ty Cashion and Jesûs de la Teja (Wilmington, Del.: SR Books, 2001), 209–220.

35. Jason Embry, "School Tax System Unconstitutional: State Supreme Court Wants a Fix by June 1," *Austin American-Statesman,* November 23, 2005. See also Gary Scharrer, "Justices Warn that Changes Will Have to Be Significant," *San Antonio Express-News,* November 23, 2005.

Selected Reading

The American Tradition of Language Rights: The Forgotten Right to Government in a "Known Tongue"*

José Roberto Juarez, Jr.**

Scholars have long debated the various factors leading Texians to declare independence from Mexico. One factor not adequately explored is the role of language. This reading sheds light on the importance of language rights for the early Anglo American settlers of Texas.

Language Rights and the Struggle for Independence from Mexico: The Multiple Causes of Independence

The reasons that led some of the Anglo American immigrants and native Tejanos to declare their independence from Mexico were many and varied. Among the reasons cited in the Texas Declaration of Independence were military abuses, the inadequacies of the Mexican justice system, the failure of the Mexican Republic to abide by the federalist guarantees of the Mexican Constitution of 1824, and the failure of the Mexican government to make Texas its own separate state. Other reasons not cited by the Texians included a desire to protect their purported "right" to own slaves, and Manifest Destiny, the belief held by many Americans in the 19th century that the United States was destined to extend from the Atlantic Ocean to the Pacific Ocean. Others have attributed the

break to "differences in folkways and mores, in the culture patterns of the two groups." Like most historical phenomena, there is no single cause that explains why a group of immigrants who had entered a foreign country less than 15 years before felt compelled to declare their independence. In the rush to consider other explanations, however, the role that language played in this effort has been minimized....

Before proceeding, the limits of my argument should be noted. I do not claim that language discrimination was the principal motive leading the Texians to declare their independence from Mexico. Given the interplay among Texians and Tejanos, and the wide variety of motivations among the players, any attempt to identify one motive as *the* motive is ludicrous. Nonetheless, Mexico's failure to provide even greater access to government in the English language did play a significant role in motivating many Anglo American immigrants to seek independence from Mexico. Notwithstanding the fact that these Anglo Americans were recent immigrants to a foreign country, they believed they had a fundamental right of access to governmental services in a language they could understand.

This belief was manifested before any attempt to declare independence from Mexico. In 1832, the Texians pledged their support to Antonio Lopez de Santa Anna in his struggle for the presidency of Mexico. In return for this pledge of support, the immigrants asked for reforms. At a convention held at San Felipe de Austin in October, 1832, a committee was appointed to petition the state government "to pass a law authorizing the people of Texas (whose native language is English) to have all their transactions, and obligations, written in the English

*Edited excerpt from José Roberto Juarez, Jr., "The American Tradition of Language Rights: The Forgotten Right to Government in a 'Known Tongue,'" *Law & Inequality: A Journal of Theory and Practice* 13, no. 2 (1995): 495–518. Abridged and reprinted by permission of the author. (Note: Readers should refer to the original source for all the footnotes and references.)

**José Roberto Juarez, Jr. was a professor at St. Mary's University School of Law, San Antonio, and is currently the dean of the Sturm College of Law at the University of Denver.

language, except those which have an immediate connection with Government." Two days later, the Anglo American immigrants requested bilingual education.... The proposal authorizing government in English was ultimately rejected by the Convention. Instead, the Convention sought to organize a state government separate from Coahuila. This was the first of several attempts to establish Texas as a state separate from Coahuila; one of the reasons the immigrants sought a separate state government was to obtain more multilingual governmental services. Ultimately, not one of the Convention's proposals was ever presented to the Mexican government.

Dissatisfied with the outcome of the 1832 Convention, some of the Anglo American immigrants soon called for another convention. The circular calling for the convention at San Felipe de Austin asserted a right of access to the Mexican justice system in English:

> The laws which ought to be info reed [sic], if any such there be, are locked up in a language known to a few only, and, therefore, for all practical purposes, [are] utterly beyond our reach....
>
> The accurate observer, on taking a survey of our situation, must pronounce the decisive opinion, that we are without *remedy* for wrongs; that we are without *redress* for grievances; and that we must remain without them, until they are provided by the deliberate, and *declared will* of a majority of the people, assembled by delegation, in Public Convention.

Stephen F. Austin prepared an address for the Central Committee which was presented to the convention in April, 1833. Austin began by noting the fundamental right of the Anglo American immigrants to present their petitions to the government:

> The people of Texas ought therefore to rely with confidence on the government for protection, and to expect that an adequate remedy will be applied to the many evils that are afflicting them.
>
> [T]he *right* of the people of Texas to represent their wants to the government, and to explain in a respectfull [sic] manner the remedies that will relieve them cannot therefore be doubted or questioned. It is not merely a right, it is also a sacred and bounden duty which they owe to themselves and to the whole Mexican nation....

One could conclude from Austin's remarks that if individuals have a fundamental right to address the government, that right is meaningless if they do not have access to the government in a language they speak. But reliance on implication for an understanding of the role of language at the 1833 Convention is unnecessary, for the participants explicitly stated the importance of communication with the government in their own language:

> The unnatural annexation of what was formerly the province of Texas to Coahuila by the constituent congress of the Mexican nation, has forced upon the people of Texas *a system of laws which they do not understand....*
>
> A total disregard of the laws has become so prevalent, both amongst the officers of justice, and the people at large, that reverence for laws or for those who administer them has almost intirely [sic] disappeared and contempt is fast assuming its place, so that the protection of our property[,] our persons and lives is circumscribed almost exclusively to the moral honesty or virtue of our neighbor....

The Texians in 1833 did not yet seek independence; they claimed they wished to remain a part of the Mexican nation. But they also claimed the fundamental right to communicate with their government in their own language....

Language Rights as a Factor in the Attempt to Make Texas a Separate State of Mexico

The Texas Declaration of Independence asserted that the failure of the Mexican government to establish Texas as a separate state had deprived the Texians of their right to government in a "known tongue"....

In considering the problems the framers of the Texas Bill of Rights were attempting to remedy, the Texas courts must consider the failure of the Mexican government to establish Texas as a separate state. The analysis cannot end there, however. The reasons the Anglo American immigrants gave for seeking a separate state must also be considered. One of the most important forces behind the move for statehood was the failure of the Mexican state of Coahuila and Texas to address the needs of immigrants who did not speak the national language....

While the Anglo Americans insisted on the right to communicate with the government in their own language, the assertion of this right did not mean that government should be conducted *only* in English. Austin believed Texas would be made a separate state only if the native Tejano population supported the move. Tejanos would not have supported an effort by recently-arrived immigrants to condemn natives to government in a language they did not understand. The efforts of the Texians were bilingual....

While Mexico did not agree to make Texas a separate state, further concessions were made to address the needs of monolingual English-speaking immigrants. Stephen F. Austin had asserted that "[w]ith only two measures Texas would be happy-judges who understand English even if only in provisional cases and the trial by jury." In May, 1833, the state legislature responded to these requests. Judges were required to provide interpreters in civil and criminal cases "commenced or contested in the state by persons unacquainted with the language of the country."

In 1834, a Department of Brazos was established. Article 11 of the decree establishing the new Department gave English full equality with Spanish in local government in Texas: "The Castilian and English shall be lawful languages in Texas; both may be used in the acts of the public administration as the case may require, except in communications with the supreme power, which shall be made expressly in Castilian."

One month later, the state legislature responded to the immigrants' continuing complaints about the judicial system by establishing a bilingual court system for Texas. Judges who were not "acquainted with both the legal idioms of Texas" were required to appoint an interpreter at a salary of $1000 per year. Criminal trials were required to be conducted in the language of the accused party, so long as the accused spoke either English or Spanish. If jurors who spoke the language of the accused could not be found in that district, the case had to be transferred to the nearest district where such jurors could be found. A party appealing a case to the state supreme court with a written record in English was given the right to have the record translated into Spanish at his own cost by a translator appointed by the judge. The law was ordered published in both English and Spanish.

Mexico attempted to respond to the needs of her new monolingual English-speaking immigrants by providing for bilingual services far greater than any provided by the State of Texas or by the United States today....

The Declaration of Independence

On December 11, 1835, the General Council called for an election on February 1, 1836, to elect delegates to a convention at Washington-on-the-Brazos. Consistent with Stephen F. Austin's earlier guarantee that the rights of Tejanos would be protected, the elections for delegates in Béxar to the convention at Washington-on-the-Brazos were held in Spanish. Three Tejanos were elected as delegates: Lorenzo de Zavala (representing Harrisburg), and Francisco Ruiz and Antonio Navarro (representing Béxar).

The Convention at Washington-on-the-Brazos began on March 1, 1836. On the second day of the convention, a Declaration of Independence was adopted by the delegates. The Texas Declaration of Independence began with a list of the circumstances that had driven the Texians to declare independence from Mexico: "When a government has ceased to protect the lives, liberty, and property of the people, from whom its legitimate powers are derived, and for the advancement of whose happiness it was instituted...." Language is not explicitly cited in this introduction, but in fact it was one of the principal complaints the Texians had about the Mexican justice system. The Texians had complained about the inability to enforce laws published in Spanish, and how this had created an atmosphere of lawlessness. Thus this complaint regarding the lack of protection of Texian lives, liberty, and property must be read in the context of the complaints that had previously been presented to the Mexican government. Inaccessibility to the Mexican judicial and legal system because of language problems was a perennial complaint of the Texians. Later in the Declaration of Independence, the Texians directly asserted the right to communicate with their government in their own language.... The Mexican government's refusal to establish Texas as a separate state from Coahuila has been well-recognized as a cause of the independence movement. But often overlooked is the role that language played in this desire to establish a separate state. It was not language differences alone which were complained of; rather, it is that the Coahuila-dominated state government was unwilling to address the needs of the English-speaking immigrants in Texas by expanding multilingual governmental services. This is one of the principal complaints registered in the text of the Texas Declaration of Independence....

The Texas Declaration of Independence did not merely assert these complaints as grievances. It asserted a fundamental right to have these grievances remedied.... The Texians practiced what they preached. Immediately after the draft of the Constitution for the Republic of Texas was presented to the Convention, de Zavala moved to appoint an interpreter to translate "the constitution and laws of this government into the Spanish language." The motion was approved on March 10, 1836.

By 1836, the influx of Anglo American immigrants had made Tejanos a minority in their own land. One might expect that the Texians would ignore the Tejano minority and conduct government in English, the language of the majority of the population.

But such was not the case. The government of the Republic of Texas recognized the Tejanos as citizens, and respected the language rights of the Tejano minority. The Texians who, when they had been the minority had asserted a right to communicate with the Mexican government in English, now provided opportunities for the Tejanos to communicate with the government of the Republic of Texas in Spanish.

For further resources, please visit **www.cengagebrain.com**.

Local Governments

(© Nick Anderson of the Houston Chronicle, *dist. by The Washington Post Writers Group. Reprinted with Permission.*)

Learning Objectives

1. Explain the relationships that exist between local governments, as well as the relationships between local government and the state and national governments.
2. Describe the importance of municipal governments and their forms of organization.
3. Identify the forces that shape local government outcomes.
4. Analyze the structure and responsibilities of counties.
5. Examine the importance of special districts and how they function within the greater community.
6. Discuss ways that local governments deal with metropolitan-wide and regional issues.

When most Texans think about government, they think about the national government. Yet of all three levels of government, local government has the greatest effect on citizens' daily lives. Most people drive every day on city streets or county roads, drink water provided by the city or a special district, attend schools run by the local school district, play in the city or county park, eat in restaurants inspected by city health officials, and live in houses or apartments that required city permits and inspections to build.

Many citizens' contacts with local government are positive—potholes are filled, trash is picked up regularly, baseball fields are groomed for games—but other experiences are less positive. Streets and freeways are increasingly congested, many schools are overcrowded, and the property taxes to support them seem high. The cartoon that begins this chapter illustrates the complexity of local politics. With very limited resources, local governments must choose from among competing interests—most of them good causes. For many years, local governments in Texas have felt the need to build (or help build) sports arenas to attract and keep professional teams. Putting together a sports deal usually involves several local governments (from neighboring cities or counties) and affects many other local government programs across the area that are competing for funds. Such cooperation and conflicts were the case with the attempt in 2010 to finance a stadium for the Houston Dynamo professional soccer team. In May 2012, after two months on the road, Dynamo played (and won) its first home game in the $95 million stadium. To confront problems and make local governments more responsive to citizens' needs and wishes, people have to understand how those governments are organized and what they do.

Local government comes in many forms. Texas has municipalities (approximately 1,200 city and town governments), counties (254), and special districts (more than 3,000). The special district that most students know best is the school district, but there are also special districts for water, hospitals, conservation, housing, and a multitude of other services. Each local government covers a certain geographical area and has legal authority to carry out one or more government functions. Most collect revenue such as taxes or fees, spend money while providing services, and are controlled by officials ultimately responsible to voters. These local, or **grassroots**, governments affect our lives directly.

 # Local Politics in Context

Who are the policymakers for grassroots governments? How do they make decisions? What challenges do they face daily? Putting local politics in context first requires an understanding of the place of local government in American federalism.

LO1

grassroots
Local (as in grassroots government or grassroots politics).

Local Governments and Federalism

In the 19th century, two opposing views emerged concerning the powers of local governments. **Dillon's Rule**, which is still followed in the majority of states today, dictates that local governments have only those powers granted by the state government, those powers implied in the state grant, and those powers indispensable to their functioning.[1] The opposing Cooley Doctrine, which is followed in ten states, says "Local Government is a matter of absolute right; and the state may not take it away."[2]

Texas's local governments, like those of other states, are at the bottom rung of the governmental ladder, which makes them politically and legally weaker than the state and federal governments. In addition, Texas is among those states that more strictly follow Dillon's Rule.[3] Cities, counties, and special-district governments are creatures of the state of Texas. They are created through state laws and the Texas Constitution, and they make decisions permitted or required by the state. Local governments may receive part of their money from the state or national government, and they must obey the laws and constitutions of both. States often complain about unfunded mandates (requirements placed on states by the federal government without federal money to pay the costs). Local governments face mandates from both the national and state governments. Some of these mandates are funded by the higher level of government, but some are not. Examples of mandates at the local level are as diverse as improving the quality of the air, meeting state jail standards, providing access for the disabled, and meeting both federal and state educational standards.

At the local level, federalism is more than just dealing with the state and national governments. Local governments have to deal with each other as well. Texas has almost 5,000 local governments. Bexar County (home of San Antonio) has 62 local governments, Dallas County has 61, and Travis County (Austin) has 119. The territories of local governments often overlap. Your home, for example, may be in a county, a municipality, a school district, a community college district, and a hospital district—all of which collect taxes, provide services, and hold elections. Local governments generally treat each other as friends but occasionally behave as adversaries. For example, the City of Houston and Harris County worked with each other, as well as with state and national officials, to coordinate the response to Hurricanes Katrina, Rita, and Ike. On the other hand, a smaller city sued a water district over the size of water pipes serving areas that the city hoped to annex. Clearly, federalism, and the resulting relationships between and among governments or **intergovernmental relations**, are important to how local governments work. (For more on federalism, see Chapter 2, "Federalism and the Texas Constitution.")

Grassroots Challenges

When studying local governments, it is important to keep in mind the challenges these governments face daily. More than 80 percent of all Texans

Dillon's Rule
A legal principle that local governments have only those powers granted by their state government. Still followed in the majority of states, including Texas.

intergovernmental relations
Relationships between and among different governments that are on the same or different levels.

How Do We Compare...in Employees and Spending at State and Local Levels?

In this chapter's "How Do We Compare?" features, rather than compare Texas with other large and neighboring states, we compare Texas state government with Texas local governments.

	State Government		Local Governments	
	Number	**Texas's Rank Among the 50 States**	**Number**	**Texas's Rank Among the 50 States**
Government employees*	318,000	2	1,134,000	2
Government employees per 10,000 population	126	44	451	7
Average annual earning of full-time employee	$ 50,139	27	$ 42,489	35
Per capita government expenditure	$ 4,411	50	$ 4,827	21
Per capita government debt	$ 1,210	48	$ 7,868	3

*Full-time equivalent.

Source: Calculations by author based on U.S. Census Bureau, *Annual Survey of Public Employment and Payroll, 2010* (revised January 2012); and *Annual Survey of State and Local Government Finances, 2009* (tabulated 2011), **http://www.census.gov**.

reside in cities, and residents have immediate concerns they want addressed: fear of crime; decaying infrastructures, such as streets, roads, and bridges; controversies over public schools; and, since September 11, 2001, the threat of terrorism.

Texas cities are also becoming increasingly diverse, with many African American and Latino Texans seeking access to public services and local power structures long dominated by Anglos. Making sure that all communities receive equal access to public services is a key challenge for grassroots-level policymakers, community activists, and political scientists.

Grassroots government also faces the challenge of widespread voter apathy. Many times, fewer than 10 percent of a community's qualified voters participate in a local election. The good news is that voter interest increases when people understand that they can solve grassroots problems in Texas through political participation. Opportunities to participate in local politics begin with registering and then voting in local elections. (See Chapter 5, "Campaigns and Elections," for voter qualifications and registration requirements under Texas law.) Some citizens may even seek election to a city council, county commissioners court, school board, or other policymaking body. Other opportunities to be politically active include homeowners' associations, neighborhood associations, community or issue-oriented organizations, voter registration drives, and election campaigns of candidates seeking local offices. By gaining influence in city halls, county courthouses, and special-district offices, individuals and groups may address grassroots problems through the democratic process.

Learning Check 3.1   (Answers on p. 128)

1. Do local governments have more flexibility to make their own decisions under Dillon's Rule or the Cooley Doctrine? Which one does Texas follow?
2. Are federal (or intergovernmental) relations marked by conflict, cooperation, or both?

★ Municipal Governments

LO2

Perhaps no level of government influences the daily lives of citizens more than **municipal (city) government**. Whether taxing residents, arresting criminals, collecting garbage, providing public libraries, or repairing streets, municipalities determine how millions of Texans live. Knowing how and why public policies are made at city hall requires an understanding of the organizational and legal framework within which municipalities function.

Legal Status of Municipalities

municipal (city) government
A local government for an incorporated community established by law as a city.

general-law city
A municipality with a charter prescribed by the legislature.

home-rule city
A municipality with a locally drafted charter.

ordinance
A local law enacted by a city council or approved by popular vote in a referendum election.

recall
A process for removing elected officials through a popular vote. In Texas, this power is available only at the local level, not at the state level.

City government powers are outlined and restricted by municipal charters, state and national constitutions, and statutes (laws). Texas has two legal classifications of cities: **general-law cities** and **home-rule cities**. A community with a population of 201 or more may become a general-law city by adopting a charter prescribed by a general law enacted by the Texas legislature.[4] A city of more than 5,000 people may be incorporated as a home-rule city, with a locally drafted charter adopted, amended, or repealed by majority vote in a citywide election. Once chartered, a general-law city does not automatically become a home-rule city just because its population increases to greater than 5,000 people, nor does home-rule status change when a municipality's population decreases to 5,000 or fewer people. At that point, local voters must decide the legal designation of their city.

Texas has almost 900 general-law cities, most of which are fairly small in population. Although some of the more than 350 home-rule cities are small, larger cities tend to have home-rule charters. The principal advantage of home-rule cities is greater flexibility in determining their organization and how they operate. Citizens draft, adopt, and revise their city's charter through citywide elections. The charter establishes powers of municipal officers; sets salaries and terms of offices for council members and mayors; and spells out procedures for passing, repealing, or amending **ordinances** (city laws). Home-rule cities may exercise three powers not held by the state government or general-law cities: recall, initiative, and referendum. **Recall** provides a process for removing elected officials through a popular vote. In 2011–12, for example, voters in such diverse cities as El Paso, Killeen (next to Fort Hood), Jasper (in East Texas), and College Station petitioned for recall elections. An **initiative** is a citizen-drafted measure proposed by a specified number or percentage of qualified voters. If approved by popular vote, an initiative becomes law without city council approval, whereas a **referendum** approves or repeals an existing ordinance. Ballot referenda and initiatives require voter approval and, depending on city charter provisions, may be binding or nonbinding on municipal governments. Initiatives and referenda can be contentious, as in 2000, when San Antonio voters approved an initiative allowing fluoridation of their drinking water, or in 2007, when voters in Farmers Branch (near Dallas) approved an ordinance that attempted to prevent undocumented immigrants from renting housing in the city. On occasion, implementation of voters' decisions may be slow or blocked. Enforcement of the Farmers Branch ordinance was blocked by federal courts in 2008 and 2010 and remained under appeal in 2012. Red-light cameras installed by various cities to reduce the number of accidents (and, according to critics, produce more revenue for the city) brought popular votes over repeal in a number of communities. In College Station and Baytown, city councils responded to the citizens' rejection of the cameras by turning them off fairly promptly. Voters in Houston rejected the cameras in 2010, but because of legal issues the cameras were not turned off definitively until well into 2011. A suit by the company administering the program for the city was not settled until 2012.

Forms of Municipal Government

The four principal forms of municipal government used in the United States and Texas—strong mayor-council, weak mayor-council, council-manager, and commission—have many variations. The council-manager form prevails in almost 90 percent of Texas's home-rule cities, and variations of the two mayor-council systems operate in many general-law cities.

Citizens often ask, "How do you explain the structure of municipal government in my town? None of the four models accurately depicts our government." The answer lies in home-rule flexibility. Various combinations of the forms discussed in the following sections are permissible under a home-rule charter, depending on community preference, as long as they do not conflict with state law. Informal practice also may make it hard to define a city's form. For example, the council-manager form may work like a strong mayor-council form if the mayor has a strong personality and the city manager is timid.

Strong Mayor-Council Among larger American cities, the **strong mayor-council form** continues as the predominant governmental structure. Among the nation's 10 largest cities, only Dallas, San Antonio, and San Jose, California, operate with a structure (council-manager) other than some variation of the strong mayor-council system. In New York City, Los Angeles, Chicago, and Philadelphia, the mayor is the chief administrator and the political head of the city. Of Texas's 25 largest cities, however, only Houston and Pasadena still have the strong mayor-council form of government. Many

initiative
A citizen-drafted measure proposed by a specific number or percentage of qualified voters, which becomes law if approved by popular vote. In Texas, this process occurs only at the local level, not at the state level.

referendum
A process by which issues are referred to the voters to accept or reject. Voters may also petition for a vote to repeal an existing ordinance. In Texas, this process occurs at the local level in home rule cities. At the state level, bonds secured by taxes and state constitutional amendments must be approved by the voters.

strong mayor-council form
A type of municipal government with a separately elected legislative body (council) and an executive head (mayor) elected in a citywide election with veto, appointment, and removal powers.

people see the strong mayor-council system as the best form for large cities because it provides strong leadership and is more likely than the council-manager form to be responsive to the full range of the community. In the early 20th century, however, the strong mayor-council form began to fall out of favor in many places, including Texas, because of its association with the corrupt political party machines that once dominated many cities. Now, most of Texas's home-rule cities have chosen the council-manager form.

In Texas, cities operating with the strong mayor-council form have the following characteristics:

- A council traditionally elected from single-member districts, although many now have a mix of at-large and single-member district election
- A mayor elected at large (by the whole city), with the power to appoint and remove department heads
- Budgetary power (for example, preparation and execution of a plan for raising and spending city money) exercised by the mayor, subject to council approval before the budget may be implemented
- A mayor with the power to veto council actions

Houston's variation of the strong mayor-council form features a powerful mayor aided by a strong appointed chief of staff and an elected controller with budgetary powers (see Figure 3.1). Most Houston mayors delegate administrative details to the chief of staff, leaving the mayor free to focus on the larger picture. Duties of the chief of staff, however, vary widely depending on the mayor currently in office.

Weak Mayor-Council As the term **weak mayor-council form** implies, this model of local government gives the mayor limited administrative powers. The mayor's position is weak because the office shares appointive and removal powers over municipal government personnel with the city council. Instead of being a chief executive, the mayor is merely one of several elected officials responsible to the electorate. Popular elections choose members of the city council, some department heads, and other municipal officials. A city council has the power to override the mayor's veto.

The current trend is away from this form. None of the largest cities in Texas has the weak mayor-council form, though some small general-law and home-rule cities in Texas and other parts of the country use it. For example, Conroe, a city with a population of more than 55,000 in Montgomery County (north of Houston), describes itself on its website as having a mayor-council form of government. The mayor's powers are limited, and the city administrator manages city departments on a day-to-day basis. The mayor, however, maintains enough status to serve as a political leader.

Council-Manager When the cities of Amarillo and Terrell adopted the council-manager form in 1913, a new era in Texas municipal administration began. Today, most of Texas's almost 350 home-rule cities follow the **council-manager form** (sometimes termed the commission-manager form).

weak mayor-council form
A type of municipal government with a separately elected mayor and council, but the mayor shares appointive and removal powers with the council, which can override the mayor's veto.

council-manager form
A system of municipal government in which an elected city council hires a manager to coordinate budgetary matters and supervise administrative departments.

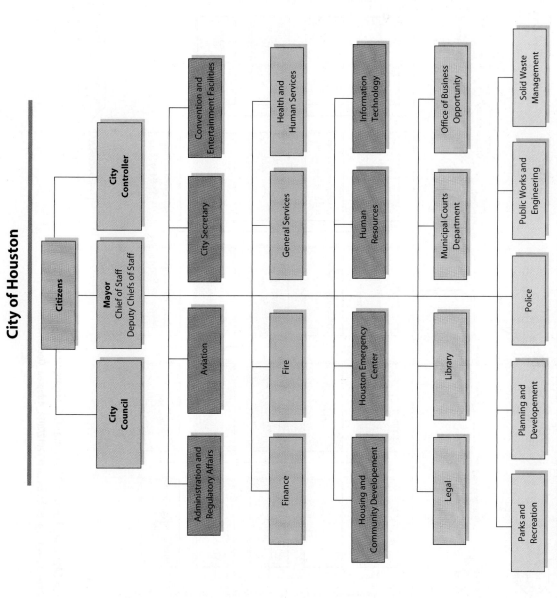

Figure 3.1   Strong Mayor-Council Form of Municipal Government: City of Houston

Source: http://www.houstontx.gov/budget/11budadopt/orgchrt.pdf.

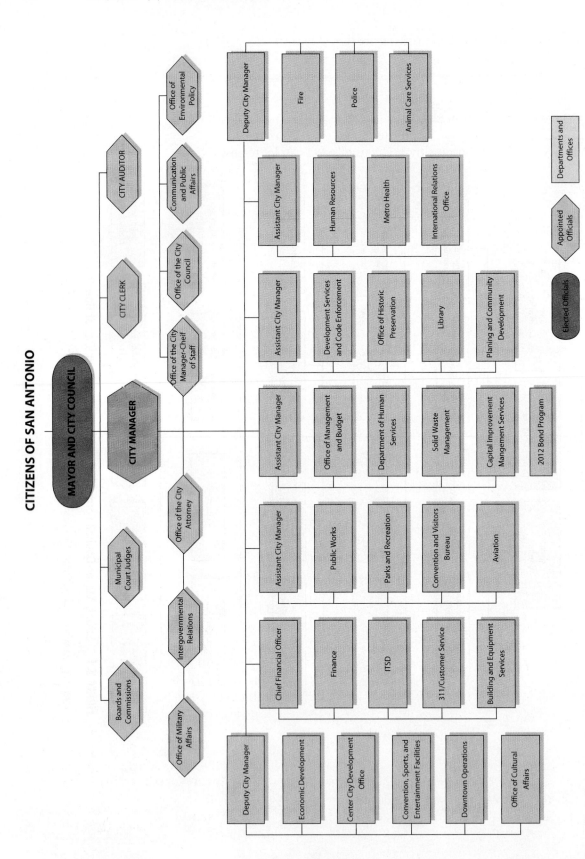

Figure 3.2 Council-Manager Form of Municipal Government: City of San Antonio

Source: **http://www.sanantonio.gov/budget/documents/FY2012/2012_Adopted_Document.pdf.**

Figure 3.2 illustrates how this form is used in San Antonio. The council-manager form has the following characteristics:

- A mayor, elected at large, who is the presiding member of the council but who generally has few formal administrative powers
- City council or commission members elected at large or in single-member districts to make general policy for the city
- A city manager who is appointed by the council (and can be removed by the council) and who is responsible for carrying out council decisions and managing the city's departments

Under the council-manager form, the mayor and city council make decisions after debate on policy issues, such as taxation, budgeting, annexation, and services. The city manager's actual role varies considerably; however, most city managers exert strong influence. City councils generally rely on their managers for the preparation of annual budgets and policy recommendations. Once a policy is made, the city manager's office directs an appropriate department to implement it. Typically, city councils hire professionally trained managers. Successful applicants usually possess graduate degrees in public administration and can earn competitive salaries. In 2012, city managers for Texas's five largest cities earned $227,000 to $355,000 annually, plus bonuses.[5]

Obviously, a delicate relationship exists between appointed managers and elected council members. In theory, the council-manager system has a weak mayor and attempts to separate policymaking from administration. Councils and mayors are not supposed to "micromanage" departments. However, in practice, elected leaders experience difficulties in determining where to draw the line between administrative oversight and meddling in departmental affairs.

A common major weakness of the council-manager form of government is the lack of a leader to whom citizens can bring demands and concerns. The mayor is weak; the city council is composed of a number of members (anywhere from four to 16 individuals, with an average of seven, among the 25 largest cities); and the city manager is supposed to "stay out of politics." Thus, council-manager cities tend to respond more to elite and **middle-class** concerns than to those of the **working class** and ethnic minorities. (The business elite and the middle class have more organizations and leaders who have access to city government and know how to work the system.) Only a minority of council-manager cities have mayors who regularly provide strong political and policy leadership. One of these exceptions is San Antonio, where mayors generally are strong leaders. The council-manager form seems to work well in cities where most people are of the same ethnic group and social class and, thus, share many common goals. Obviously, few central cities fit this description, but many suburbs do.

Commission Today, none of Texas's cities operates under a pure **commission form** of municipal government. First approved by the Texas legislature for Galveston after a hurricane demolished the city in 1900, this form lacks a single executive, relying instead on elected commissioners that form a policymaking board.

middle class
Social scientists identify the middle class as those people with white-collar occupations (such as professionals and small business workers).

working class
Social scientists identify the working class as those people with blue-collar (manual) occupations.

commission form
A type of municipal government in which each elected commissioner is a member of the city's policymaking body, but also heads an administrative department (e.g., public safety with police and fire divisions).

In the commission form, each department (for example, public safety, finance, public works, welfare, or legal) is the responsibility of a single commissioner. Most students of municipal government criticize this form's dispersed administrative structure and lack of a chief executive. The few Texas municipalities that have a variation of the commission form operate more like the mayor-council form and designate a city secretary or another official to coordinate departmental work.

☑ Learning Check 3.2   (Answers on p. 128)

1. Name the two legal classifications of cities in Texas and indicate which has more flexibility in deciding its form and the way it operates.
2. Which form of municipal government is most common in Texas's larger home-rule cities? In smaller cities?

Municipal Politics

LO3   Election rules and socioeconomic change make a difference in who wins and what policies are more likely to be adopted. This section examines several election rules that affect local politics. It then looks at social changes that affect the nature of local politics in Texas.

Rules Make a Difference All city and special district elections in Texas are **nonpartisan elections**. That is, candidates are listed on the ballot without party labels in order to reduce the role of political parties in local politics. This system succeeded for a long time. However, party politics is again becoming important in some city elections, such as those in the Houston and Dallas metropolitan areas. Nonpartisan elections have at least two negative consequences. First, without political parties to stir up excitement, voter turnout tends to be low compared with state and national elections. Those who do vote are more likely to be Anglos and middle class, which reduces the representation of ethnic minorities and the working class. San Antonio, for example, has a majority Latino population, but the greater Anglo voter turnout has meant that most San Antonio mayors have been Anglo. The three recent exceptions have been Mexican Americans who appeal to both Anglos and Latinos (Henry Cisneros, Edward Garza, and Julián Castro). A second problem is that nonpartisan elections tend to be more personal and less issue oriented. Thus, voters tend to vote for personalities, not issues. In smaller cities and towns, local elections are often decided by who has more friends and neighbors.

Throughout the country, representative bodies whose members are elected from districts (such as the state legislature and city councils) must **redistrict** (redraw their districts) after every 10-year census. (As we will see later, this also applies to county commissioners courts and some school boards.) After the 2010 census, Texas's city council districts had to be redrawn because of

nonpartisan election
An election in which candidates are not identified on the ballot by party label.

redistricting
Redrawing of boundaries after the federal decennial census to create districts with approximately equal population (e.g., legislative, congressional, commissioners court districts, and city council districts in Texas).

shifts in population within cities and between districts. Under federal law, all of a city's council districts must have approximately the same population, and any changes in districting in Texas must be approved by the U.S. Department of Justice. (In 1975, because of its history of racial discrimination, Texas was placed under a provision of the Federal Voting Rights Act that requires governments to receive clearance from the U.S. Attorney General or the Federal District Court for the District of Columbia for rule changes.)

In recent decades, the major controversy within redistricting at the local level has been the issue of the representation of Texas's major ethnic groups—particularly Latinos, who were the main source of the state's population growth in the 2010 census. The expansion of the Latino population in urban areas has increased the number of districts in which Latino candidates have a better chance of winning. Low Latino turnout, however, has limited the number of Latino council members who are actually elected. In 2011, Houston had a hard fight over increasing Latino representation while also providing representation of African and Asian Americans and Anglos. The final 2011 redistricting included four majority Hispanic districts, two majority Black districts, three majority Anglo districts, and two without a majority of one group. Asian Americans were 18 percent of one of the districts with no single ethnic majority. (There were also five at-large positions elected by the whole city.) In the elections that year, two of the Hispanic-majority districts were won by Hispanics, two by Anglos. Blacks won the two Black-majority districts and one in which there was no ethnic majority. An Asian American won the other district without an ethnic majority. Anglos won all three Anglo-majority districts. In that same year, Dallas saw conflict between Latinos and African Americans over the number of

Points to Ponder

- In 1999, Houston voters defeated an initiative that would have repealed the city's affirmative action rules for hiring women and minorities.
- In 2001, Houston voters approved a city charter amendment banning the city council from offering benefits, such as health insurance, to same-sex domestic partners of city workers.
- In 2003, in the case of *Lawrence v. Texas*, the U.S. Supreme Court threw out the Texas law criminalizing gay sex. The case began with a 1998 arrest of two men by Harris County sheriff's deputies just outside of Houston.
- In 2009, Houston elected Annise Parker, the first openly gay mayor of a major U.S. city. Having been elected previously as city councilwoman and controller for a total of 12 years, this was her seventh straight city election victory. She was reelected in 2011.

seats that they would have the opportunity to win. The map drawn by Dallas and approved by the U.S. Justice Department provided six Anglo, four Black, and four Latino opportunity districts. (A *Latino opportunity district*, for example, is one in which there is a large enough population of Latinos to give a Latino candidate a good chance of winning.)[6]

The two most common ways of organizing municipal elections are the **at-large election**, in which council members are elected on a citywide basis, and the **single-member district election**, in which voters cast a ballot only for a candidate who resides within their district. Texas long used at-large elections. However, these were challenged because they tended to overrepresent the majority Anglo population and underrepresent ethnic minorities. In at-large elections, the city's majority ethnic group tends to be the majority in each electoral contest. This works to the disadvantage of ethnic minorities, because voting remains racially polarized (that is, people tend to vote for candidates of their own race or ethnicity).

On the other hand, dividing a city into single-member districts creates some districts with a majority of historically excluded ethnic minorities, thereby increasing the chance of electing a Latino, African American, or Asian American candidate to the city council. Prompted by lawsuits and ethnic conflict, 20 of Texas's 25 largest cities have adopted single-member districts or a mixed system of at-large and single-member districts. Houston, for example, has five council members elected at-large (citywide) and 11 elected from single-member districts. Increased use of single-member districts has led to more ethnically and racially diverse city councils.[7] Low voter turnout by an ethnic group, however, can reduce the effect of single-member districts, as happened in Houston in 2011.

Approximately 50 Texas local governments (including 40 school districts) use **cumulative voting** to increase minority representation. In this election system, voters cast a number of votes equal to the positions available and may cast them for one or more candidates in any combination. For example, if eight candidates vie for four positions on the city council, a voter may cast two votes for Candidate A, two votes for Candidate B, and no votes for the other candidates. By the same token, a voter may cast all four votes for Candidate A. In the end, the candidates with the most votes are elected to fill the four positions. Where racial minority voters are a numerical minority, this system increases the chances that they will have some representation. The largest government entity in the country to use cumulative voting is the Amarillo Independent School District, which adopted the system in 1999 in response to a federal Voting Rights Act lawsuit. The district was 30 percent minority, but had no minority board members for two decades. With the adoption of cumulative voting, African American and Latino board members were elected.

Home-rule cities may also determine whether to institute **term limits** for their elected officials. Beginning in the 1990s, many cities, including San Antonio and Houston, amended their charters to institute term limits for their mayor and city council members. Houston has a limit of three 2-year terms for its mayor. Although Houston's popular mayor, Bill White, won election in 2003 with 63 percent of the vote and was reelected twice with 91

at-large election
Members of a policymaking body, such as some city councils, are elected on a citywide basis rather than from single-member districts.

single-member district election
Voters in an area (commonly called a district, ward, or precinct) elect one representative to serve on a policymaking body (e.g., city council, county commissioners court, state House and Senate).

cumulative voting
When multiple seats are contested in an at-large election, voters cast one or more of the specified number of votes for one or more candidates in any combination. It is designed to increase representation of historically underrepresented ethnic minority groups.

term limit
A restriction on the number of terms officials can serve in a public office.

Point/Counterpoint

THE ISSUE Municipal term limits are increasingly common. Currently, there are approximately 70 cities in Texas that limit the number of terms an elected official may serve. Critics raise strong arguments for and against term limits. The following are examples of the more common arguments on both sides.

Should Term Limits Be Instituted for City Council Members and the Mayor?

Arguments For Instituting Term Limits

1. Long tenure tends to encourage corruption and complacency.
2. Term limits facilitate new approaches to solving public problems.
3. Turnover ensures election of citizen public officials instead of professional office-seekers.

"Local limits transform political culture from one of entrenched careers to one of progression and citizen representation."

—Danielle Fagre, former research director for the U.S. Term Limits Foundation

Arguments Against Instituting Term Limits

1. Turnover does not guarantee better or more honest leaders.
2. Turnover produces amateurs easily outwitted by experienced lobbyists and bureaucrats.
3. By the time officeholders learn their job, they have to leave.

"As an organization dedicated to protecting and enhancing the role of citizens in our representative democracy, the League strongly opposes term limits."

—Becky Cain, former president of the National League of Women Voters

and 86 percent of the vote, he could not run again in 2009. (In 2010, he was the unsuccessful Democratic nominee for governor.) In 2008, San Antonio changed its limits from two to four 2-year terms for its mayor and city council members, a move expected to make it easier for Latino city council members to build the support necessary to run for mayor. Both supporters and opponents feel strongly about term limits.

Socioeconomic Changes It should be clear, then, that election rules make a difference in who is elected. Historical, social, and economic factors make a difference as well. Texas's increasing levels of urbanization, education, and economic development have made the state more economically, culturally, and politically diverse (or more *pluralist,* in political science terminology). Local politics reflect these changes. Many Texas city governments were long dominated by elite business organizations, such as the Dallas Citizens Council and the San Antonio Good Government League. But greater pluralism and changes in election rules have given a say to a wider range of Texans in how their local governments are run. Racial and ethnic conflict remains a problem in Texas, but communities are working to resolve their issues, albeit in differing ways and to different degrees. Growth in the population's size, amount of citizen organization, and income tends to increase the demands on local government and produce higher public spending.

Houston has long been Texas's most diverse local political system. It has a strong business community, many labor union members, an African American community with more than 80 years' experience in fighting for its views and interests, a growing and increasingly organized Latino community, a growing Asian American community that is becoming more active, and an activist gay community. Multiethnic coalitions have been the norm in Houston's mayoral races for decades, and nonbusiness interests have significant, if variable, access to city hall. Dallas has long had serious black-white racial tensions. Although these have not been resolved, election rules have been changed to increase the number of minorities on the city council. In 1995, Dallas's Ron Kirk became the first African American in modern times elected mayor of a major Texas city. In 1998, Laredo elected its first Latina mayor, Betty Flores; in 1991, Austin elected its first Latino mayor, Gus Garcia; and in 2009, San Antonio elected Julián Castro, the youngest mayor (at age 34) of a major U.S. city. Castro was reelected in 2011. Today, there are more Latino elected officials in Texas than in any other state, with most of them serving at the local level.[8]

Since the 1970s, South Texas's majority Latino population has elected Latino (and some non-Latino) leaders at all levels. In the rest of the state, central cities and some near-in suburbs tend to have a majority of Latinos, African Americans, and Asian Americans, which gives these groups more electoral clout. Suburbs further from the center tend to be heavily Anglo and often heavily middle class, which produces more middle-class Anglo leaders. Texas, however, is following the national trend of growing ethnic minority populations in the suburbs.

Clearly, increased use of single-member districts; greater pluralism in the state; and the growing number, organization, and political activity of minority Texans are all changing the face of local government.

Municipal Services

In the eyes of most citizens and city officials, city government's major job is to provide basic services that affect people's day-to-day lives: police and fire protection, streets, water, sewer and sanitation, and perhaps parks and recreation. These basic services tend to be cities' largest expenditures, though the amounts spent vary from city to city. Municipalities also regulate important aspects of Texans' lives, notably zoning, construction, food service, and sanitation. Zoning ordinances regulate the use of land, for instance, by separating commercial and residential zones, because bringing businesses into residential areas often increases traffic and crime. Zoning has received more

Students in Action

Win-Win: A Tale of Two Internships

"The experience helped me see what a community is and how it can work together rather than everyone just going their separate ways."

—Megan Bryant

As a paid intern with the city of Huntsville in the spring of 2008, Megan Bryant (not an artist herself) was asked to organize art classes to be held in the Wynne Home, the city's arts center. She recruited instructors, scheduled the program, marketed the classes to local schools and organizations, purchased supplies, and handled administrative problems for the classes. In addition to assisting with tours and gallery openings, she also organized and marketed a free concert for a local musical group at the center.

That fall, Megan received an internship with the City Recreation Department. Her major job was to revise an old project—the city's "Winter in the Park," which took place in one of the city parks with recreational activities, food, and games. Under her guidance, the project drew two and a half times more participants than before and was widely praised for its quality. In her first internship, she had learned that the city government had many fine departments but that they tended to do their own thing. For the festival, she involved other departments, such as the Wynne Home and the library, as well as community organizations such as the Boys and Girls Club and the YMCA.

When asked what advice she would share with students, she replied, "Go for it! You can build your own skills and have a lot of fun while helping to bring the community together."

Source: Interviews with Megan Bryant and R. Mike Yawn.

(Monkey Business Images/Shutterstock.com)

---

opposition in Texas than in most other states, although its use is growing. Among Texas's 10 largest municipalities, only Houston has no zoning authority, though the city does help enforce deed restrictions that protect neighborhoods and uses its control of access to utilities to control and direct growth.

Over time, many Texas cities have added libraries, airports, hospitals, community development, and housing to their list of services. Scarce resources (particularly money) of local governments increase competition between traditional services and newer services demanded by citizens or the state and national governments, such as protection of the homeless, elderly services, job training, fighting air pollution, and delinquency prevention. These competing demands for municipal spending often result in controversy, thus requiring city councils to make difficult decisions.

The San Antonio City Council conducts a meeting.

(© Marjorie Cotera/Bob Daemmrich Photography, Inc.)

Municipal Government Revenue

Most city governments in Texas and the nation face a serious financial dilemma: they barely have enough money to provide basic services and thus must reject or shortchange new services. Cities' two largest tax sources—sales and property taxes—are limited by state law. These taxes produce inadequate increases in revenue as the economy grows, and they are regressive (that is, they put a heavier burden on those who make less money). Moreover, Texas voters are increasingly hostile toward higher property taxes. Adding to the problem are low levels of state assistance to Texas cities as compared with the pattern exhibited in many other states. As a result, Texas cities are relying more heavily on fees (such as liquor licenses, franchise fees for cable television companies, and water rates) and are going more heavily into debt. Per capita local government debt in Texas, for example, is more than six times greater than state government debt (see "How Do We Compare" on page 93). Local governments have also been hurt by the recent "Great Recession," particularly the decrease in property values (which are the basis of property taxes) and the slowing of sales tax receipts. The 2009 federal stimulus bill provided $16.8 billion to Texas, but most of that money went to the state rather than to local governments. Even as the state's economy has begun to improve, the major revenue sources for local government—property and sales tax receipts—have been slow to recover.

Taxes The state of Texas allows municipalities to levy taxes based on the value of property (**property tax**). The tax rate is generally expressed in terms of the amount of tax per $100 of the property's value. This rate varies greatly from one city to another. In 2008 (the most recent year for comprehensive data), rates varied from 2 cents per $100 valuation to $1.34, with an average of 49 cents.[9] A problem with property taxes is that poorer cities with low property values must charge a high rate to provide minimum services. In the

property tax
A tax that property owners pay according to the value of their homes and businesses. At the local level, property owners pay this tax to the city, the county, the school district, and often other special districts.

Dallas area, for example, Highland Park, which has a median family income of $228,000 a year, set a property tax rate of 22 cents in 2011, whereas Wylie, which has a $72,000 median annual family income, set its rate at 90 cents.

The other major source of city tax revenue is the optional 1¼–2 percent sales tax, which is collected with the state sales tax. Local governments are in competition for sales tax dollars. The sum of city, county, and special-district government sales taxes cannot exceed 2 percent. So, for example, a city might assess 1 percent; the county, 0.5 percent; and a special district, 0.5 percent. An additional problem is that sales tax revenues fluctuate with the local economy, making it difficult to plan how much money will be available. The hotel occupancy tax has become particularly important for cities with tourism or major sports events, such as the NFL Super Bowl or the NCAA Final Four.

Fees Lacking adequate tax revenues to meet the demands placed on them, Texas municipalities have come to rely more heavily on fees (charges for services and payments required by an agency upon those subject to its regulation). Cities levy fees for such things as beer and liquor licenses and building permits. They collect traffic fines and may charge franchise fees based on gross receipts of public utilities (for example, telephone and cable television companies). Texas municipalities are authorized to own and operate water, electric, and gas utility systems, which may generate a profit for the city. Charges also are levied for such services as sewage treatment, garbage collection, hospital care, and use of city recreation facilities. User fees may allow a city to provide certain services with only a small subsidy from its general revenue fund or perhaps no subsidy at all.

Bonds Taxes and fees normally produce enough revenue to allow Texas cities to cover day-to-day operating expenses. Money for capital improvements (such as construction of city buildings or parks) and emergencies (such as flood or hurricane damage) often must be obtained through the sale of **municipal bonds**. The Texas Constitution allows cities to issue bonds, but any bond issue to be repaid from taxes must be approved by the voters. During the recent recession, local governments have made more use of certificates of obligation, which do not require voter approval. The certificates traditionally have been used for smaller amounts and short-term financing.

Property Taxes and Tax Exemptions Property owners pay taxes on the value of their homes and businesses not just to the city but also to the county, the school district, and often other special districts. When property values or tax rates go up, the total tax bill goes up as well. To help offset the burden of higher taxes resulting from reappraisals of property values, local governments (including cities) may grant homeowners up to a 20 percent homestead exemption on the assessed value of their homes. Cities may also provide an additional homestead exemption for disabled veterans and their surviving spouses, for homeowners 65 years of age or older, or for other reasons such as adding pollution controls.

Cities, counties, and community college districts may also freeze property taxes for senior citizens and the disabled. Property tax caps (or ceilings) can

municipal bond
A mechanism by which cities borrow money. General obligation bonds (redeemed from city tax revenue) and revenue bonds (redeemed from revenue obtained from the property or activity financed by the sale of the bonds) are authorized under Texas law.

Table 3.1   One Home but Property Taxes from Four Governments (An Example from Walker County on a Home with an Appraised Value of $120,220; Taxes Paid in January 2012)

Taxing Unit	Exemption Amount* Homestead	Exemption Amount* Over Age 65	Taxable Value	Tax Rate Per $100 of Taxable Value	Nominal Tax**	Ceiling***	Actual Tax***
Huntsville ISD	$15,000	$16,000	$ 89,220	$1.2100	$1,080	$595	$ 595
Walker County	0	$12,000	$108,220	$0.5536	$ 599	$455	$ 455
City of Huntsville	0	$12,000	$108,220	$0.3915	$ 424	$319	$ 319
Walker County Hospital District	0	$12,000	$108,220	$0.1568	$ 170	—	$ 170
Total					$2,273		$1,539

Explanation: A county appraisal district decides the value of each property, and each local government sets its tax rate and the amount of the exemption it will give for special circumstances, such as living in a home the taxpayer owns (homestead exemption), being 65 or older, or being disabled all within the limits of state law. The local government does not collect taxes on the exemption amount. Sales tax revenue also reduces the amount of property tax paid in this case, $234 in city taxes and $139 in county taxes. The property owner in this case pays a total of $1,539 in property taxes to four different local governments.

*The Exemption Amount is deducted from the Appraised Value ($120,220 for each government entity).
**The Nominal Tax is the Taxable Value multiplied by the Tax Rate.
***The Actual Tax may be less than the Nominal Tax because an entity may place a "ceiling" on the taxes of those 65 and over and the disabled. As long as the person owns and lives in the residence, the tax from that entity will not go up. Note that three of the four entities use the ceiling, saving this taxpayer $734.

Sources: Calculated by the author from data and rules provided by Walker County Appraisal District, **http://www.walkercounty appraisal.com**, and Texas Comptroller, **http://www.window.state.tx.us/taxes.**

be implemented by city council action or by voter approval. The dilemma is that cities can help their disadvantaged citizens, but doing so costs the city revenue. In 2008, exemptions cost Texas cities $122 billion in revenue. As baby boomers reach retirement age, exemptions and property tax caps will reduce revenue even further. Table 3.1 illustrates property taxes from different local governments and the consequences of exemptions and caps.

The Bottom Line Because of pressure against increasing property tax rates, municipal governments sometimes refrain from increased spending, cut services or programs, or find new revenue sources. Typically, city councils are forced to opt for one or more of the following actions:

- Create new fees or raise fees on services such as garbage collection
- Impose hiring and wage freezes for municipal employees
- Cut services (such as emergency rooms) that are especially important for inner-city populations
- Contract with private firms for service delivery
- Improve productivity, especially by investing in technology

Generating Revenue for Economic Development

State and federal appropriations to assist cities are shrinking, especially for economic development. Inner cities face the challenge of dilapidated housing, abandoned buildings, and poorly maintained infrastructure (such as sewers

How Do We Compare…in Funding Services at State and Local Levels?

Expenditures (in millions of dollars)

Type of Government	Number	Total Spent	Hospitals	Public Education	Highways	Police and Corrections
State	1	$ 90,853	$3,353	$14,634	$7,979	$3,783
County	254	$ 14,494	$4,262	$ 51	$1,337	$2,660
Municipality	1,215	$ 30,914	$ 39	$ 48	$2,115	$3,522
School district	1,081	$ 47,863		$44,245		
Other special districts	2,291	$ 10,861	$1,892		$ 241	$ 4
Total for all local governments	**4,841**	**$103,719**	**$6,193**	**$44,344**	**$3,693**	**$6,186**

Source: U.S. Census of Governments, 2007, Revised October 24, 2011, **http://www.census.gov**. The next Census of Governments is in 2012, with results released over several years. More recent total expenditure data are available for the state and all local governments taken together, but the Census of Governments provides the breakdown for each form of local government. Expenditures are Direct General Expenditures for the function. Totals may vary because of rounding.

and streets). This neglect blights neighborhoods and contributes to social problems such as crime and strained racial relations. Texas cities do have the local option of a half-cent sales tax for infrastructure upgrades, such as repaving streets and improving sewage disposal. The increased sales tax, however, must stay within the two percent limit the state imposes on local governments.

Following a national trend, some Texas cities are trying to spur development by attracting businesses through tax incentives. The Texas legislature authorizes municipalities to create **tax reinvestment zones (TRZs)** to use innovative tax breaks to attract investment in blighted inner cities and other areas needing development. Major cities using TRZs include Houston, Dallas, Fort Worth, Austin, San Antonio, and El Paso. Smaller cities also have used TRZs. Whether such plans work is controversial. Many observers of similar plans argue that companies attracted by tax breaks often make minimal actual investments and leave as soon as they have realized a profit from the tax subsidies. Yet, because TRZs sometimes work, many cities starved for the monetary resources to combat decay are willing to take the gamble.

✓ Learning Check 3.3 (Answers on p. 128)

1. Which of the following election forms tend to increase the representation of minorities in local government: nonpartisan elections, redistricting, at-large elections, single-member district elections, or cumulative voting?
2. What are the two largest tax sources that provide revenue to local governments? Do these taxes usually provide enough revenue for local governments to meet the demands placed on them?

tax reinvestment zone (TRZ)
An area in which municipal tax incentives are offered to encourage businesses to locate in and contribute to the development of a blighted urban area. Commercial and residential property taxes may be frozen.

Counties

LO4

Texas **counties** are an interesting set of contradictions. They are technically an arm of the state, created to serve its needs, but both county officials and county residents see them as local governments and resent any state "interference." Counties collect taxes on both urban and rural property, but focus more on the needs of rural residents and people living in unincorporated suburbs, who do not have city governments to provide services. The form of county governments is out of the 19th century, but they serve 21st-century Texans.

Texas is divided into 254 counties, the most for any state in the nation. The basic form of Texas counties is set by the state constitution, though their activities are heavily shaped by whether they are in rural or metropolitan areas. As an agent of the state, each county issues state automobile licenses, enforces state laws, registers voters, conducts elections, collects certain state taxes, and helps administer justice. In conjunction with state and federal governments, the county conducts health and welfare programs, maintains records of vital statistics (such as births and deaths), issues various licenses, collects fees, and provides a host of other public services. Yet, state supervision of county operations is minimal.

Rural counties generally try to keep taxes low and provide minimal services. They are reluctant to take on new jobs, such as regulating septic systems and residential development. In metropolitan areas, however, counties have been forced by citizen demands and sometimes the state to take on varied urban tasks such as providing ballparks and recreation centers, hospitals, libraries, airports, and museums.[10]

Structure and Operation

As required by the state constitution, all Texas counties have the same basic governmental structure, despite wide demographic and economic differences between rural and urban counties. (Figures 3.3 and 3.4 contrast Harris County, the most populous Texas county with more than four million residents in 2010, and Loving County, the least populous with 82 residents in that year.)

The Texas Constitution provides for the election of four county commissioners, county and district attorneys, a county sheriff, a county clerk, a district clerk, a county tax assessor-collector, a county treasurer, and constables, as well as judicial officers, including justices of the peace and a county judge. All elected county officials are chosen in partisan elections and serve four-year terms. In practice, Texas counties are usually highly decentralized, or fragmented. No one person has formal authority to supervise or coordinate the county's elected officials, who tend to think of their office as their personal fiefdom and to resent interference by other officials. Sometimes, however, the political leadership of the county judge produces cooperation.

county
Texas is divided into 254 counties that serve as an administrative arm of the state and that provide important services at the local level, especially within rural areas.

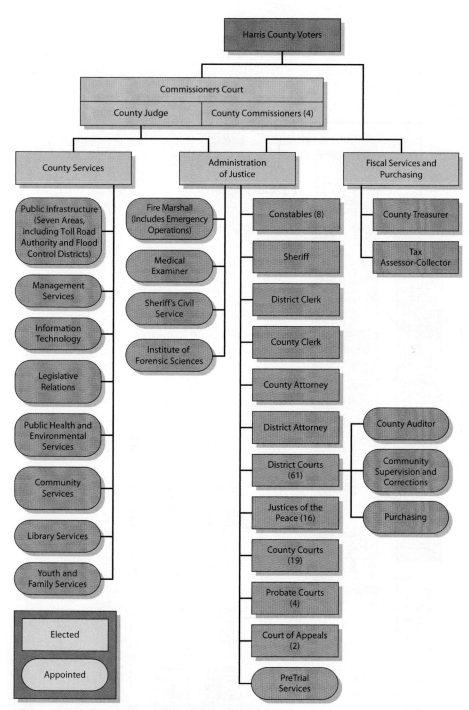

Figure 3.3   Harris County Government (County Seat: Houston)

Source: Compiled by author using FY2011–2012 Approved Budget, http://www.hctx.net/budget.

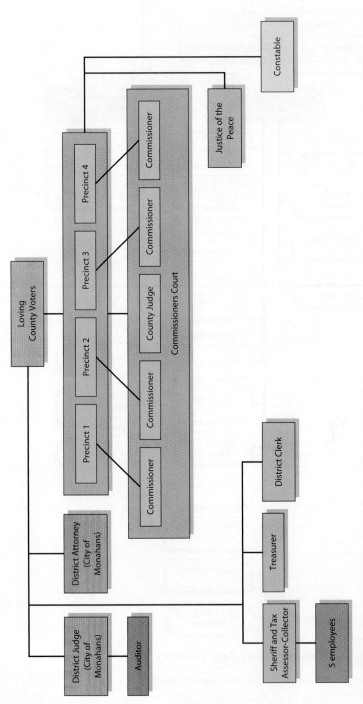

Figure 3.4   Loving County Government (County Seat: Mentone)

Commissioners Court All elected county officials make policies for their area of responsibility, but the major policymaking body is called the **commissioners court**. Its members are the county judge, who presides, and four elected commissioners. The latter serve staggered four-year terms, so that two commissioners are elected every two years. Each commissioner is elected by voters residing in a commissioner precinct. Boundary lines for a county's four commissioner precincts are set by its commissioners court. Precincts must be of substantially equal population as mandated by the "one-person, one-vote" ruling of the U.S. Supreme Court in *Avery v. Midland County* 390 U.S. 474 (1968). Like cities, counties must redistrict every 10 years, following the federal census. After the 2010 census, county redistricting battles centered on political party power in Dallas County, while racial and ethnic representation were major sources of conflict in Harris County (Houston), Galveston County, and Travis County (Austin). In Dallas County, the democratically controlled commissioners court added another Democratic seat, while the Republican majority on Harris County's commissioners court was sued over slight dilution of Latino votes. The Galveston County plan was rejected by the U.S. Department of Justice for diluting minority votes. Bexar County's (San Antonio) redistricting was less controversial than usual and was overshadowed by the battle over congressional redistricting.

The term *commissioners court* is actually a misnomer, because its functions are administrative and legislative rather than judicial. The court's major functions include the following:

- Adopting the county budget and setting tax rates, which are the commissioners court's greatest sources of power and influence over other county officials
- Providing a courthouse, jails, and other buildings
- Maintaining county roads and bridges, which is often viewed by rural residents as *the* major county function
- Administering county health and welfare programs
- Administering and financing elections (general and special elections for the nation, state, and county)

Beyond these functions, a county is free to decide whether to take on other programs authorized, but not required, by the state. In metropolitan areas, large numbers of people live in unincorporated communities with no city government to provide services such as police protection and water. In those communities, the county takes on a multitude of functions. In rural areas, counties take on few new tasks, and residents are generally happy not to be "hassled" by too much

commissioners court
A Texas county's policymaking body, with five members: the county judge, who presides, and four commissioners representing single-member precincts.

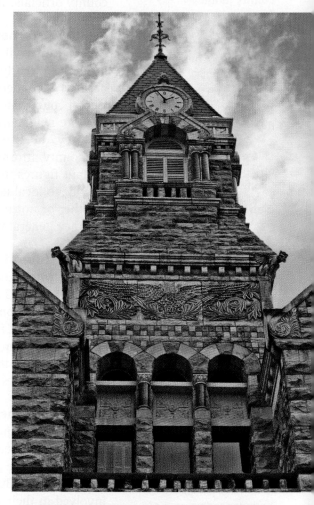

Fayette County Courthouse, built in 1891 and restored to its historic appearance in 2005. Its Romanesque Revival style uses four kinds of native stone to detail the exterior. Located in La Grange, between Houston and Austin.

(Kushal Bose/Shutterstock.com)

government. In addition to their collective responsibilities, county commissioners may have individual duties. In rural counties, for example, they are commonly responsible for the roads and bridges in their respective precincts.

County Judge The **county judge**, who holds the most prominent job in county government and usually has a higher-status background, generally is the most influential county leader. The judge presides over the commissioners court, has administrative responsibility for most county agencies not headed by another elected official, and, in some counties, presides over court cases. Much of the judge's power or influence comes from his or her leadership skills and from playing a lead role in the commissioners court's budget decisions. The judge has essentially no formal authority over other elected county officials. The county judge need not be a lawyer.

County Attorney and District Attorney The county attorney represents the state in civil and criminal cases and advises county officials on legal questions. Nearly 50 counties in Texas do not elect a county attorney because a resident **district attorney** performs those duties. Other counties elect a county attorney but share the services of a district attorney with two or more neighboring counties. Where there are both a county and a district attorney, the district attorney generally specializes in the district court, while the county attorney handles lesser matters. District attorneys tend to be important figures in the criminal justice system because of the leadership they provide to local law enforcement and the discretion they exercise in deciding whether or not to prosecute cases. The legal advice of the county or district attorney generally carries considerable weight with other county officials.

County Sheriff The **county sheriff**, as chief law enforcement officer, is charged with keeping the peace in the county. In this capacity, the sheriff appoints deputies and oversees the county jail and its prisoners. In practice, the sheriff's office commonly focuses on crime in unincorporated areas and leaves law enforcement in cities primarily to the municipal police. In a county with a population of fewer than 10,000, the sheriff may also serve as tax assessor-collector, unless that county's electorate votes to separate the two offices. In a few rural counties, the sheriff may be the county's most influential leader.

Law Enforcement and Judges Counties have a number of officials associated with the justice system. The judicial role of the constitutional **county judge** varies. In counties with a small population, the county judge may exercise considerable judicial role, handling probate, small civil cases, and serious misdemeanors. But in counties with a large population, county judges are so involved in their political, administrative, and legislative roles that they have little time for judicial functions. Instead, there are often **statutory county courts** that have lawyers for judges and tend to operate in a more formal manner. In addition to the sheriff and county and district attorneys discussed above, there are the district court clerk, justices of the peace, and constables. The **district court clerk** maintains records for the county and district courts.

county judge
A citizen popularly elected to preside over the county commissioners court and, in smaller counties, to hear civil and criminal cases.

county attorney
A citizen elected to represent the county in civil and criminal cases, unless a resident district attorney performs these functions.

district attorney
A citizen elected to serve one or more counties who prosecutes cases, gives advisory opinions, and represents the county in civil cases.

county sheriff
A citizen popularly elected as the county's chief law enforcement officer; the sheriff is also responsible for maintaining the county jail.

statutory county court
Courts created by the legislature at the request of a county; may have civil or criminal jurisdiction or both depending on the legislation creating them.

district court clerk
A citizen elected to maintain records for the county and district courts.

Each county has from one to eight justice of the peace precincts. The number is decided by the commissioners court. **Justices of the peace** (commonly called JPs) handle minor civil and criminal cases, including small claims court cases. Statewide, JPs hear a large volume of legal action, with traffic cases representing a substantial part of their work. Other duties vary. In most counties, they also serve as coroner (to determine cause of death in certain cases) and as a magistrate (to fix bail for arrested persons). Similar to the constitutional county judge, they do not have to be lawyers but are required to take some training. The quality of the justice they dispense varies greatly, and they tend to be viewed negatively by the public. **Constables** assist the justice court by serving papers. They and their deputies are peace officers and may carry out security and investigative responsibilities. In some counties, they are an important part of law enforcement, particularly for unincorporated areas of the county. Like other county officials, the judges, justices of the peace, district court clerk, and constables are elected in partisan elections. Their judicial function is covered in Chapter 10, "Laws, Courts, and Justice."

County Clerk and County Tax Assessor-Collector A county clerk keeps records and handles various paperwork chores for both the county court and the commissioners court. In addition, the county clerk files legal documents (such as deeds, mortgages, and contracts) in the county's public records and maintains the county's vital statistics (birth, death, and marriage records). The county clerk may also administer elections, though counties with larger populations often have an administrator of elections.

A county office that has seen its role decrease over time is the **county tax assessor-collector**. The title is partially a misnomer. Since 1982, the **county tax appraisal district** assesses property values in the county. The tax assessor-collector, on the other hand, collects county taxes and fees and certain state fees, including the license tag fees for motor vehicles. The office also commonly handles voter registration, although some counties have an elections administrator.

Treasurer and Auditor The **county treasurer** receives and pays out all county funds authorized by the commissioners court. If the office is eliminated by constitutional amendment (as in Tarrant and Bexar counties), the county commissioners assign treasurer duties to another county office. A county of 10,000 or more people must have a **county auditor**, appointed by the county's district court judges. The auditing function involves checking the account books and records of officials who handle county funds.

County Finance

Increasing citizen demands for services and programs impose on most counties an ever-expanding need for money. Just as the structure of county governments is frozen in the Texas Constitution, so is the county's power to tax and, to a lesser extent, its power to spend. Financial problems became even more serious for most counties during the recent Great Recession.

justice of the peace
A judge elected from a justice of the peace precinct who handles minor civil and criminal cases, including small claims court.

constable
A citizen elected to assist the justice of the peace by serving papers and in some cases carrying out security and investigative responsibilities.

county clerk
A citizen elected to perform clerical chores for the county court and commissioners court, keep public records, maintain vital statistics, and administer pubic elections, if the county does not have an administrator of elections.

county tax assessor-collector
This elected official no longer assesses property for taxation but does collect taxes and fees and commonly handles voter registration.

county tax appraisal district
The district appraises all real estate and commercial property for taxation by units of local government within a county.

county treasurer
An elected official who receives and pays out county money as directed by the commissioners court.

county auditor
A person appointed by the district judge or judges to check the financial books and records of other officials who handle county money.

Taxation The Texas Constitution authorizes county governments to collect taxes on property, and that is usually their most important revenue source. Although occupations may also be taxed, none of the counties implements that provision. The commissioners court may impose higher property taxes that would generate up to 8 percent more than the previous year's revenues. If the court opts for a higher rate, citizens may circulate a petition for an election to roll back (limit) the higher rate. (The other local governments face similar limitations.) Counties may also add 0.5 to 1.5 cents onto the state sales tax, which is 6.25 cents on the dollar. (Remember, however, that the add-on by all local governments may not exceed 2 cents.) Less than half of Texas counties (primarily smaller counties) impose a sales tax, and most set the rate at 0.5 cents.

Revenues from Nontax Sources Counties receive small amounts of money from various sources that add up to an important part of their total revenue. Counties may impose fees on the sale of liquor, and they share in state revenue from liquor sales, various motor vehicle taxes and fees, and traffic fines. Like other local governments, counties receive federal grants-in-aid; but over the long term, this source continues to shrink. The 2009 federal stimulus bill provided aid primarily to the state government. Although local governments were eligible for assistance, the grants available benefitted cities and school districts more than county governments. With voter approval, a county may borrow money through **bonds** to pay for capital projects such as a new courthouse or jail. The Texas Constitution limits county indebtedness to 35 percent of a county's total assessed property value.

Tax Incentives and Subsidies Like cities, a commissioners court may grant tax abatements (reductions or suspensions) on taxable property, reimbursements (return of taxes paid), or tax increment financing (TIF; the use of future gains in property value to finance current development projects) to attract or retain businesses. For instance, in 2003, Bexar County offered a $22 million tax abatement for a Toyota factory to be built to produce pickup trucks in San Antonio. The offer was part of a complex incentive package put together by state, county, city, and other officials that totaled an estimated $133 million in tax breaks and infrastructure spending. The plant went into operation in 2006, creating more than 2,000 high-paying jobs and contributing to economic development in the region. From 2008 to 2010, the plant suffered from the national economic downturn, but had returned to full production by 2011.[11]

The Bottom Line Despite various revenue sources, Texas counties, like other units of local government, are pressured to increase property taxes or to balance their budgets by eliminating or reducing programs and services. Although administrative costs and demands for expanded public services continue to increase, sources of county revenue are not expanding as quickly as demand.

bond
A certificate of indebtedness issued by a borrower to a lender that constitutes a legal obligation to repay the principal of a loan plus accrued interest. In Texas, both state and local governments issue bonds under restrictions imposed by state law.

Expenditures The state restricts county expenditures in certain areas and mandates spending in others. Yet patterns of spending vary considerably from county to county. The biggest variation is between rural and metropolitan counties. The table "How Do We Compare ... In Funding Services at State and Local Levels?" (page 109) shows that hospitals and health care, public safety, and roads are the largest expenditures for Texas counties overall. This holds for Texas's largest counties, which also spend smaller but still significant amounts on urban amenities (such as parks) and social services (such as housing and welfare). Rural counties tend to spend a large portion of their budget on public safety and roads and little on social services and urban amenities. Many counties spend little on health and hospitals because they have shifted the costs to a hospital district. (See "How Do We Compare" on page 109.)

Although the county judge, auditor, or budget officer prepares the budget, the commissioners court is responsible for final adoption of an annual spending plan. Preparation of the budget generally enhances the commissioners court's power within county government. Counties do not have complete control over their spending, because state and federal rules mandate certain county services and regulatory activities. Examples include social services, legal assistance and medical care for poor people, and mental health programs. Since 2004, counties have made a major effort to pressure the legislature to limit unfunded mandates. Almost all counties have passed resolutions calling for a state constitutional amendment to ban mandates.

County Government Reform

Texas counties experience various problems: rigid structure and duties fixed in the state constitution and statutes, inefficiency related to too many elected officials and the lack of merit systems for hiring employees, and too little money. Counties with larger populations may establish merit systems, and half of those eligible have done so. One often-suggested reform is county home rule to give counties more ability to organize and operate in accordance with local needs and wishes. Research suggests that although county home rule better meets community demands, it also tends to expand county spending.

Different states allow varying degrees of county home rule. Texas is among the states that are most strongly against home rule.[12] Until 1969, Texas actually had a home-rule provision in the constitution, but it was too difficult to implement. Reviving a workable version today would be hard to achieve. Many (probably most) county officials prefer the present system, as do many people served by counties outside of the metropolitan areas.

Border Counties

In recent years, there has been unprecedented population growth in Texas's counties near the Rio Grande because of the North American Free Trade

Agreement (NAFTA) and immigration. Unfortunately, the population growth has outstripped the substantial economic growth, and the traditionally poor border region now has even more poor people. The counties in the Mexican border area between El Paso and Brownsville are among the most impoverished places in the country. Many of the poor live in **colonias** (depressed housing settlements often without running water or sewage systems). It is estimated that there are currently about 2,300 colonias in Texas, and as many as 400,000 Texans live in substandard conditions in these settlements.[13]

Minimal efforts have been made to deal with problems of the colonias. Counties were given planning and inspection powers; the Texas secretary of state created a plan to provide water and sewage to 32 (of 2,300) colonias; voters approved a constitutional amendment for bonds to fund roads and streets within the colonias; and the federal government provided some aid. However, the state legislature's antitax attitude in recent years has caused actual funding to lag. Advocates for the border counties fear that the area's serious infrastructure, educational, and medical needs will continue to be neglected.

In recent years, the flow across the border of undocumented immigrants–including refugees from drug-related violence–combined with the sharp increase in drug-gangs on the Mexican side of the border, has created great concern and controversy. Sheriffs and police departments have sought and obtained federal and state money to increase their law enforcement efforts. The state spent $400 million on border security between 2005 and 2011, while the federal government provided $18 million in aid in 2011 alone. The national government's decision to build a physical wall along major portions of the border has created great controversies in the communities affected because of the divisions the wall creates in the communities, the damage to the relationships with family and friends in Mexico, and the environmental dislocation. Yet, although the conflict in Mexico occasionally spills over the Rio Grande, the Texas side of the border remains relatively safe. In spite of great growth in population (usually associated with higher crime rates), border cities have lower crime rates than Houston, San Antonio, and Austin. Anecdotal evidence suggests, however, that safety in some rural areas has significantly declined.[14]

☑ Learning Check 3.4   (Answers on p. 128)

colonia
A low-income community, typically located in South Texas and especially in counties bordering Mexico, that lacks running water, sewer lines, and other essentials.

1. True or False: Local residents of each county can determine the structure of their own county government.
2. What is the major policymaking body in each Texas county?
3. What is usually the most important source of revenue for county governments?

Special Districts

Among local governmental units, the least known and least understood are special-district governments yet they represent the fastest-growing form of government. They fall into two categories: school districts and noneducation special districts. Created by an act of the legislature or, in some cases, by local ordinance (for example, establishing a public housing authority), a **special district** usually has one function and serves a specific group of people in a particular geographic area.

Public School Districts

Citizen concerns over public education cause local school systems to occupy center stage among special-district governments. More than 1,000 Texas **independent school districts (ISDs)**, created by the legislature, are governed by popularly elected, nonsalaried boards of trustees. The school board selects the superintendent, who by law and practice makes most major decisions about the district's educational programs and who tends to influence other decisions as well. The board members, generally made up of local business-people and professionals, tend to focus on things they know—particularly money issues, such as taxes and budgets. School board elections are generally low-turnout friends-and-neighbors affairs. When these elections become heated, it is generally because of sharp divisions within the community over volatile cultural issues, like sex education or prayer in the schools, racial and ethnic conflict, or differences over taxing and spending.

Texas has traditionally had a highly centralized educational system in which the Texas Education Agency significantly limited local district decisions. Since 1995, however, school boards have been given increased local autonomy over some decisions. National influence has been far more limited and targeted than that of the state. Federal involvement has focused on improving the situation of groups historically neglected or discriminated against in Texas education. Districts must comply with federal regulations in areas such as racial and gender nondiscrimination and treatment of students with disabilities. Money is also a source of influence. In the six school years from fall 2005 through spring 2011, local districts raised an average of 50 percent of their revenue locally (primarily from property taxes), the state contributed 40 percent, and the federal government added 11 percent.[15] Federal aid has particularly targeted the children of the poor and language minorities. Thus, school districts make local educational policy in the context of substantial limits, mandates, and influences from the state and federal governments.

This shared control of public education has been highlighted in recent years by increased state, and now federal, requirements for testing students. Districts have been forced to spend more time and money on preparing for tests. Supporters say that testing has improved student performance and made local schools more accountable. Critics charge that although students are now better at taking tests, they learn less in other areas.

LO5

special district
A unit of local government that performs a particular service, such as providing schools, hospitals, or housing, for a particular geographic area.

independent school district (ISD)
Created by the legislature, an independent school district raises tax revenue to support its public schools. Voters within the district elect a board that hires a superintendent, determines salary schedules, selects textbooks, and sets the district's property tax rate.

A second challenge for local education is the increasing ethnic and economic diversity of Texas's school children. For two decades, traditional minorities have been a majority in Texas schools, and for a decade a majority of Texas students have come from economically disadvantaged families. Meeting their needs is important not only for the children but for the economic health of the entire state.

A third challenge facing Texas education is school finance, which actually has two faces: equity and how much should be spent. In 1987, a state district court (later affirmed by the Texas Supreme Court) held that the state's system for school finance violated the Texas Constitution. The basic problem was that poor districts, relying on property taxes, had to tax at a high rate to provide minimum expenditures per pupil. Wealthier districts, on the other hand, could spend considerably more with significantly lower tax rates. The other school finance issue is the conflict between the increased need for services and the slow growth of funding. Clearly, demands on the schools to do more (and therefore to spend more) have increased. Yet the two major sources of funding for the school districts (state appropriations and the property tax) have expanded more slowly than demand. The proportion of education funding provided by the state has remained under 50 percent, and property tax revenue tends to grow slowly and to fluctuate. In the face of the Great Recession, the 2011 legislature (for the first time in 60 years) reduced the actual amount appropriated for schools. The result was 11,000 teacher layoffs, larger classes, and cuts in programs such as arts and athletics, field trips, support staff, and custodians.

The property tax is the only local source of tax revenue for Texas public schools. Unlike other local governments, schools cannot use the sales tax for revenue. Not surprisingly, school districts receive more than 50 percent of property taxes collected in the state. As schools have increased property taxes to pay their bills, many property owners have objected. In response, the legislature required that if a school district increases its tax rate by more than 4 cents per $100 of property value over the previous year's revenue, the district must hold a rollback election, in which voters can decide to keep or roll back the increase. (In the case of other local governments, the increase must exceed 8 percent, and citizens must collect signatures on a petition to force a rollback election.) In 2009, 48 school districts held elections, and in 24 cases, voters disapproved the increase.[16]

For more detailed discussions of education policy and finance, see Chapter 9, "Public Policy and Administration" and Chapter 11, "Finance and Fiscal Policy."

Junior or Community College Districts

junior college or community college district
Establishes one or more two-year colleges that offer both academic and vocational programs.

Another example of a special district is the **junior college or community college district**, which offers two-year academic programs beyond high school, as well as various technical and vocational programs. The latter two may be part of the regular degree and certificate programs or special non-degree training programs to meet local worker and employer needs. Each district is governed by an elected board that has the power to set property tax rates, within limits established by the state; issue bonds (subject to voter approval); and adopt an annual budget. There are 50 districts, and many have two or more campuses. In addition to the community college districts, Lamar University has three 2-year units, and the Texas State Technical College System has four campuses. Together, Texas's two-year schools enroll almost 790,000 students, which is more than the enrollment of the state's four-year universities. (See Figure 3.5 for the locations of these districts.)

Community colleges, like state universities and technical colleges, are funded by state appropriations, student tuition and fees, and small amounts of federal aid and private donations. Where they differ from public universities is the support that community colleges receive from property taxes raised by the local district. Because of these funds, community colleges were traditionally able to charge lower tuition rates than four-year schools. As a result of the Great Recession, however, community college enrollment has increased markedly, while revenues from taxes and the state have slowed. Schools have been forced to make cuts, enforce class size minimums,

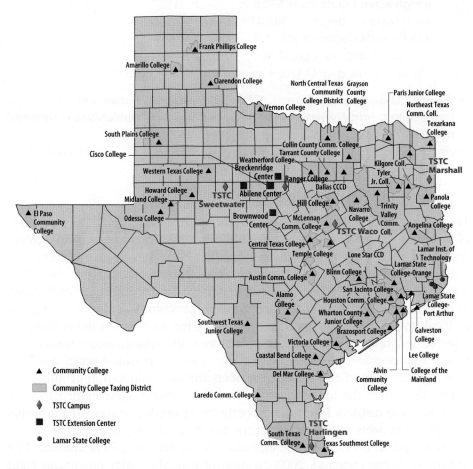

Figure 3.5 Texas Community, Technical, and State Colleges

Source: Reprinted by permission of the Texas Association of Community Colleges.

increase tuition, and consider limiting enrollment. By 2012, recovery was under way, but budgets remained difficult.

Studies by both the state comptroller and a scholar commissioned by the Texas Association of Community Colleges have found that community colleges stimulate the local economy and are critical to a region's economic development. The study also found that community colleges help the state improve the health of Texans and reduce crime, welfare costs, and unemployment.[17]

Points to Ponder

Going to college pays off financially. Income goes up for every year of college completed and even for every hour of college credit. Nationwide, average (median) annual income for people with

- a high school diploma is $35,035.
- an associate's degree is $42,419.
- a bachelor's degree is $55,864.
- a master's degree is $68,879.
- a professional degree (such as law or medicine) is $101,737.

Source: U.S. Census Bureau, CPS 2011 Annual Social and Economic Supplement, **http://www.census.gov/hhes/www/cpstables/032011/perinc/new03_028.htm**.

Noneducation Special Districts

Texas has almost 2,300 **noneducation special districts** handling a multitude of problems—water supply, sewage, parks, housing, irrigation, and fire protection, to name a few. Of the many reasons that Texas has so many special districts, three stand out. First, many local needs—such as mass transit, hospitals, and flood protection—cut across the boundaries of cities and counties. Second, in other cases, restrictive state constitutional provisions or the unwillingness of local government leaders make it difficult for an existing government to take on new tasks. And finally, in some cases, individuals create special districts to make money for themselves. For example, personal profit has long been a motivation of real estate developers for the proliferation of municipal utility districts in the unincorporated Houston suburbs. New homeowners in some of these districts face high property taxes needed to pay off municipal utility district debts accumulated for the benefit of the developer.

How special districts can be manipulated for private gain is illustrated by oilman T. Boone Pickens's 2007 creation of a public water district on eight acres outside of Amarillo. Pickens sold the land at the back of his ranch to five employees. Two of them, the couple who managed his ranch (and the only residents of the eight acres), voted approval of the district, which is trying to use

noneducation special districts
Special districts, other than school districts or community college districts, such as fire prevention or water districts, that are units of local government and may cover part of a county, a whole county, or areas in two or more counties.

the government power of eminent domain to acquire right of way and issue tax-exempt bonds to finance a $2.2 billion pipeline to transport water to Dallas or San Antonio. The right of way also would serve to transport power generated by the wind farm Pickens was developing in the area. The Great Recession and other problems put the wind farm on hold. In addition, the district is meeting serious legal and political challenges, because it will be using a public entity for private gain, promoting the unpopular taking of land for right of way, and potentially extracting huge amounts of water from the already troubled Ogallala Aquifer, on which Panhandle agriculture and cities depend.

The structure and powers of special districts vary. Most are governed by a board, collect property taxes and fees, can issue bonds, and spend money to provide one or more services. Mass transit authorities, such as Houston's Metro or Dallas's DART, rely on a 1 percent sales tax. Depending on the board, members may be elected or appointed, or they may automatically sit on the board because of another position they hold. Most special districts are small and hardly noticed by the general public. Only a few, such as the mass transit authorities in the state's largest metropolitan areas, receive continuing public attention.

Special districts will remain an important part of Texas government because they provide so many necessary services. But because they are so invisible to most voters, they are the form of government most subject to corruption and abuse of power.

 Learning Check 3.5   **(Answers on p. 129)**

1. What are the two categories of special districts in Texas?
2. Why are special districts so important?

 # Metropolitan Areas

About 88 percent of Texans live in metropolitan areas, mostly central cities surrounded by growing suburbs. People living in a metropolitan area share many problems, such as traffic congestion, crime, pollution, and lack of access to health care. Yet, having so many different governments makes it difficult to effectively address problems affecting the whole area. The situation is made worse by differences between central city residents and suburbanites. Many who live in central cities need and use public facilities, such as public transportation, parks, and medical care, whereas many suburban residents have less interest in public services, particularly public transportation. Class and ethnic differences also divide metropolitan communities, particularly the central city from the suburbs.

One way to deal with areawide problems would be **metro government** (consolidation of local governments into one "umbrella" government for the entire metropolitan area). Examples include Miami-Dade County, Florida; Louisville-Jefferson County, Kentucky; and Nashville-Davidson County, Tennessee. Given the divisions within Texas metropolitan areas and the

LO6

metro government
Consolidation of units of local government within an urban area under a single authority.

opposition of local officials, observers do not see this solution as probable in Texas in the foreseeable future. Instead, Texans are likely to continue to rely on councils of governments and annexation.

Councils of Governments

Looking beyond city limits, county lines, and special-district boundaries requires expertise from planners who think regionally. In the 1960s, the Texas Legislature created the first of 24 regional planning bodies known as **councils of governments (COGs)** or, in some areas, planning/development commissions/councils. (See Figure 3.6.)

COGs are voluntary associations of local governments. Their members perform regional planning activities and provide services requested by

council of government (COG)

A regional planning body composed of governmental units (e.g., cities, counties, special districts); functions include review and comment on proposals by local governments for obtaining state and federal grants.

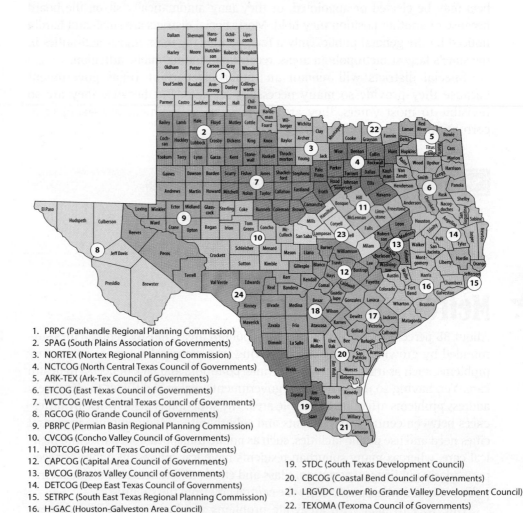

1. PRPC (Panhandle Regional Planning Commission)
2. SPAG (South Plains Association of Governments)
3. NORTEX (Nortex Regional Planning Commission)
4. NCTCOG (North Central Texas Council of Governments)
5. ARK-TEX (Ark-Tex Council of Governments)
6. ETCOG (East Texas Council of Governments)
7. WCTCOG (West Central Texas Council of Governments)
8. RGCOG (Rio Grande Council of Governments)
9. PBRPC (Permian Basin Regional Planning Commission)
10. CVCOG (Concho Valley Council of Governments)
11. HOTCOG (Heart of Texas Council of Governments)
12. CAPCOG (Capital Area Council of Governments)
13. BVCOG (Brazos Valley Council of Governments)
14. DETCOG (Deep East Texas Council of Governments)
15. SETRPC (South East Texas Regional Planning Commission)
16. H-GAC (Houston-Galveston Area Council)
17. GCRPC (Golden Crescent Regional Planning Commission)
18. AACOG (Alamo Area Council of Governments)
19. STDC (South Texas Development Council)
20. CBCOG (Coastal Bend Council of Governments)
21. LRGVDC (Lower Rio Grande Valley Development Council)
22. TEXOMA (Texoma Council of Governments)
23. CTCOG (Central Texas Council of Governments)
24. MRGDC (Middle Rio Grande Development Council)

Figure 3.6 Texas Councils of Texas Government, http://www.txregionalcouncil.org

Source: Reprinted by permission of the Texas Association of Regional Councils.

member governments or directed by federal and state mandates. Their expertise is particularly useful in implementing state and federally funded programs. Membership may be necessary or helpful in obtaining state or federal grants. COGs also provide a forum where local government leaders can share information with each other and coordinate their efforts.

Municipal Annexation

In an attempt to provide statewide guidelines for home-rule cities grappling with suburban sprawl, the Texas Legislature enacted a municipal annexation law in 1963. Under the law, cities have **extraterritorial jurisdiction (ETJ)**, or limited authority outside their city boundaries. Within the ETJ, the city can regulate some aspects of development and **annex** (make an area a part of the city) contiguous unincorporated areas without a vote by those who live in that area. How far out an ETJ goes (from ½ mile to five miles) increases with the city's population size, which thus gives central cities an advantage over the suburbs. In most other states, central cities are surrounded by incorporated suburbs and cannot expand. Because of ETJ, however, Texas central cities tend to be much larger in physical size than cities in other states.

The idea of ETJ is to improve order and planning in metropolitan growth. The timing for annexation varies. Houston tends to wait until

extraterritorial jurisdiction (ETJ)
The limited authority a city has outside its boundaries. The larger the city's population size, the larger the reach of its ETJ.

annex
To make an outlying area part of a city. Within a city's extraterritorial jurisdiction, the city can annex unincorporated areas without a vote by those who live there.

CourseReader ASSIGNMENTS

Log in to www.cengagebrain.com and open CourseReader to access the reading:

Bryan Woman Loses Property Fight
April Avison

Municipalities may annex land to expand. When the municipality annexes land, it also brings more residents into the municipality. According to Texas state law, cities must develop service plans to provide full services to the residents of newly annexed areas within 4.5 years. The law is silent on who pays for expanding those services—the residents of the annexed area or the municiplaity.

This article examines a legal challenge to the city of Bryan, which annexed an area near the city limits, but only provided minimal city services because the newly annexed residents did not pay for additional services. Some of the residents of the annexed area chose to petition to be disannexed from Bryan, an effort the Texas Supreme Court denied.

1. Drawing on the description of annexation in the text and this article, what would it have taken to reconcile the two sides?

2. Sometimes citizens and citizen groups can change public policy. What factors led to failure in this case?

areas have developed and will provide tax revenue, whereas cities in the Dallas–Fort Worth area tend to annex undeveloped areas and oversee their development. Some areas with few urban services (such as police, fire, and sewer) are happy to be annexed. But, not surprisingly, established suburban communities generally object strenuously to being "gobbled up" without their permission. Examples from the Houston area include Clear Lake City (home of the Johnson Space Center) and Kingwood. In 2006–2007, The Woodlands, a planned community between Houston and Conroe, worked out financial settlements with both cities to avoid annexation. A widespread complaint is that while the annexing city is required by law to provide the same level of service to annexed areas, this is often slow in happening.

 Learning Check 3.6   (Answers on p. 129)

1. What are the two primary ways that Texas deals with problems in metropolitan areas?
2. Which groups want to be annexed? Which do not?

★ Conclusion

Local governments deliver a substantial amount of government services directly to their residents. The success of these governments depends heavily on the actions and cooperation of other local governments and the two levels above them. What local governments do is heavily shaped by three forces: formal rules (such as laws, the way governments are organized, and election rules), socioeconomic forces (such as economic power and ethnic/racial cooperation and conflict), and the efforts of individuals and groups. Texas has four kinds of local government with differences in structure and behavior both within each kind and between kinds. Understanding the basic forces at work in local government helps those who want to make a difference apply the general principles of government organization and citizen participation to the issues affecting their own community.

Chapter Summary

- Local governments are part of the federal system and thus are affected by decisions made by governments above them (state and national) and other local governments.
- Under Texas law and its constitution, local governments are largely limited to what is required or permitted by the state.

- Although local governments provide the most direct contact between residents and their government, voter apathy at this level of government remains a problem.
- Local government is important to most Texans' day-to-day lives.
- Election rules and the way local governments are organized make a major difference in who is elected and who benefits from government.
- Texas has two legal classifications of municipalities: general-law cities and home-rule cities. Large municipalities have home-rule charters that spell out the structures and powers of individual cities.
- Four principal forms of municipal government operate in Texas: strong mayor-council, weak mayor-council, council-manager, and commission.
- Elections for cities and special districts are nonpartisan, and most are organized as at-large or single-member districts.
- Increased use of single-member districts; greater pluralism; and the growing number, organization, and political activity of minority Texans are all changing the face of local government. Said another way, both formal rules and socioeconomic change shape the way government works, including who wins and who loses.
- City governments focus primarily on delivering basic services—police and fire protection, streets, water, sewer and sanitation, and perhaps parks and recreation. They also regulate important aspects of our lives, such as construction and food service sanitation.
- The two major sources of revenue for cities are property taxes and the sales tax. For counties, it is the property tax. Both cities and counties are making more use of fees and debt.
- Local governments have a difficult time because they face increasing demands for services from their residents and from the state and national government but have limited revenue sources.
- County governments have fragmented organizational structures and powers restricted by the Texas Constitution. Counties provide an array of services, conduct elections, and enforce state laws. Actual county activities vary greatly between metropolitan and rural counties.
- Various county officials are policymakers, but the major policymaker is the commissioners court, comprised of the county judge and four elected commissioners.
- The many special-district governments are separate legal entities providing services that include public schools, community colleges, and mass transit systems. Although they are important for the multitude of services they provide, the smaller and more obscure districts are more subject to fraud and manipulation.
- Dealing with metropolitanwide problems is a difficult task. To do so, Texas relies heavily on councils of government to increase cooperation and on annexation, a controversial process.

Key Terms

grassroots, p. 91
Dillon's Rule, p. 92
intergovernmental relations, p. 92
municipal (city) government, p. 94
general-law city, p. 94
home-rule city, p. 94
ordinance, p. 94
recall, p. 94
initiative, p. 95
referendum, p. 95
strong mayor-council form, p. 95
weak mayor-council form, p. 96
council-manager form, p. 96
middle-class, p. 99
working class, p. 99
commission form, p. 99
nonpartisan election, p. 100
redistricting, p. 100
at-large election, p. 102
single-member district election, p. 102
cumulative voting, p. 102
term limit, p. 102
property tax, p. 106
municipal bond, p. 107
tax reinvestment zone (TRZ), p. 109
county, p. 110
commissioners court, p. 113
county judge, p. 114
county attorney, p. 114
district attorney, p. 114
county sheriff, p. 114
statutory county court, p. 114
district court clerk, p. 114
justice of the peace, p. 115
constable, p. 115
county clerk, p. 115
county tax assessor-collector, p. 115
county tax appraisal district, p. 115
county treasurer, p. 115
county auditor, p. 115
bond, p. 116
colonia, p. 118
special district, p. 119
independent school district (ISD), p. 119
junior college or community college district, p. 120
noneducation special districts, p. 122
metro government, p. 123
council of government (COG), p. 124
extraterritorial jurisdiction (ETJ), p. 125
annex, p. 125

Learning Check Answers

3.1

1. Local governments have the greatest flexibility under the Cooley Doctrine. Under Dillon's Rule, which is followed closely in Texas, local governments can do only those things permitted by the state.
2. The relations among the three levels of government and among the various local governments are marked by both cooperation and conflict.

3.2

1. The two legal classifications of cities in Texas are general-law and home-rule cities. A home-rule city has more flexibility because it establishes its own charter, which specifies its form and operation. A general-law city adopts a charter set in law by the Texas legislature.
2. The council-manager form is most common in larger home-rule cities, whereas smaller cities are more likely to have a weak mayor-council form of municipal government.

3.3

1. Single-member districts and cumulative voting are most likely to increase the representation of minorities in government. Redistricting may help or hurt, depending on how lines are drawn.
2. Most revenue of local governments comes from property tax and sales tax, but these two sources are frequently inadequate to meet the demands.

3.4

1. False. The structure of county governments is determined by the state constitution.
2. The major policymaking body in each Texas county is the commissioners court.
3. In most cases, the most important source of revenue for county governments is property taxes.

3.5

1. The two categories of special districts in Texas are school districts and noneducational districts.
2. Many local needs cut across boundaries of cities and counties; limitations in the state constitution and the unwillingness of some officials to act make it difficult to take on new tasks; and special districts are an important source of abuse of the public interest.

3.6

1. The two primary ways Texas deals with problems in metropolitan areas are through councils of government and annexation.
2. Unincorporated communities lacking services such as police and sewers often want to be annexed. Established communities with existing services generally oppose annexation.

Discussion Questions

1. What is the form of municipal government for your hometown?
2. What are the advantages or disadvantages of one form of municipal government over another?
3. What are some different election rules and ways to organize government at the local level, and why do they make a difference in who is elected and which groups have more influence?
4. What are some changes taking place in urban Texas that are putting pressure on local governments?
5. County activities vary between metropolitan and rural areas. What are some differences, and why do they exist?
6. What recommendations would you offer to the state legislature to ensure equal funding for students attending Texas's public schools?
7. Give the arguments supporting and opposing term limits. What is your position on this issue?
8. What is the most important local issue facing your community? How is it being handled? What could be done better?

Internet Resources

Austin city government:
http://www.austintexas.gov/

Dallas city government:
http://www.dallascityhall.com

El Paso city government:
http://home.elpasotexas.gov/

Fort Worth city government:
http://fortworthtexas.gov/

Houston city government:
http://www.houstontx.gov

Houston Independent School District:
http://www.houstonisd.org

Kinder Institute for Urban Research, Rice University: **http://kinder.rice.edu**

San Antonio city government:
http://www.ci.sat.tx.us

State attorney general site on colonias:
http://www.oag.state.tx.us/consumer/border/colonias.shtml

Texas Association of Counties:
http://www.county.org

Texas Association of Regional Councils:
http://www.txregionalcouncil.org

Texas Municipal League: **http://www.tml.org**

Texas State Data Center:
http://www.txsdc.utsa.edu

U.S. Census Bureau: **http://www.census.gov**

Notes

1. *Clinton v. Cedar Rapids and the Missouri River Railroad,* 24 Iowa 455 (1868).
2. *People v. Hurlbut,* 24 Mich 44, 95 (1871).
3. Jesse J. Richardson, Jr., Meghan Zimmerman Gough, and Robert Puentes, "Is Home Rule the Answer? Clarifying the Influence of Dillon's Rule on Growth Management," Brookings Institute, http://www.brookings.edu/reports/2003/01metropolitanpolicy_richardson.aspx.
4. See "Local Government Code," http://www.statutes.legis.state.tx.us. A good description of local governments is "Local Governments in Texas" by the Texas Municipal League, http://www.tml.org/Jan2009TTC/LocalGovernmentsinTexas.pdf. The less common but real issue of ending a city government is discussed in Michelle Wilde Anderson, "Dissolving Cities," *Yale Law Journal,* 2012, http://blogs.law.stanford.edu/mlisymposium2012/files/2012/01/MLISymposiumAnderson.pdf.
5. "City Manager Salaries," *Texas Tribune,* March 11, 2012, http://www.texastribune.org/library/data/government-employee-salaries/titles/city-manager/3651/.
6. The definition of a minority opportunity district varies by source and situation. It is particularly affected by the degree of ethnic polarization in voting. Commonly, it would require that a group be 50 percent of the citizens of voting age, but for Latinos, the percentage may be as high as 65 percent. Rudolph Bush, "Justice Department Approves Dallas Redistricting Plan," *DallasNews.com,* December 21, 2011, and City of Houston, "Approved City Council Redistricting Plan and Documents," http://www.houstontx.gov/planning/2011/index.html.
7. See Robert Bezdek, David Billeaux, and Juan Carlos Huerta, "Latinos, At-Large Elections, and Political Change: Evidence from the Transition Zone," *Social Science Quarterly* 81 (March 2000): 207–225. Data collected from city websites by author, March 2012.
8. *Directory of Latino Elected Officials* (Los Angeles: NALEO Educational Fund, 2011). Sonia R. Garcia, Valerie Martinez-Ebers, Irasema Coronado, Sharon Navarro, and Patricia Jaramillo, *Politicas: Latina Trailblazers in the Texas Political Arena* (Austin: University of Texas Press, 2008) provides biographical essays on the first Latina elected public officials in Texas; and *The Houston Area Survey,* http://has.rice.edu, details changes in the attitudes of Houstonians each year from 1982 to 2012 and beyond.
9. Texas Comptroller, *Annual Property Tax Report, Tax Year 2008,* rev. ed., issued February 2010, http://www.window.state.tx.us/taxinfo/proptax/annual0896-318-09.pdf. The next report should be issued in December 2012.
10. An interesting account of the problems facing a rural county undergoing population change is Dave Mann, "The Battle for San Jacinto," *Texas Observer,* February 10, 2006.
11. Tom Bower, "Toyota Incentives Gets County's OK," *San Antonio Express-News,* May 21, 2003; Jack Dennis, "San Antonio Toyota Plant Ceasing Production of Tundras," *San Antonio Headlines Examiner,* January 26, 2010; and Vicki Vaughan, "Toyota Factories Back in High Gear," MySanAntonio.Com,

September 14, 2011, http://www.mysanantonio.com/business/article/Toyota-factoriesback-in-high-gear-2170706.php.

12. Gyusuck Geon and Geoffrey K. Turnbull, "The Effect of Home Rule on Local Government Behavior: Is There No Rule Like Home Rule?" Georgia State University, September 2004, http://aysps.gsu.edu/sites/default/files/documents/urag_0405.pdf.

13. Estimates of the number of colonias and of their residents vary. However, as of 2012, the Texas attorney general's website has an interactive list with maps (https://maps.oag.state.tx.us/colgeog/colgeog_online.html#). Likewise, other state agencies keep updated websites (http://www.sos.state.tx.us/border/colonias/index.shtml; and http://www.hhsc.state.tx.us/hhsc_projects/oba/index.shtml).

14. Jason Buch and Lynn Brezosky, "The Texas Border May Not be Safe, But It's Safer than Houston, Austin, or San Antonio," September 19, 2011, http://blog.chron.com/rickperry/2011/09/the-texas-border-may-not-be-safe-but-it-is-safer-than-houston-austin-or-san-antonio/.

15. Texas Education Agency, *Snapshot: School District Profiles, 2006* to *2011,* http://ritter.tea.state.tx.us/perfreport/snapshot.

16. "Texas Taxes," Window on State Government (Texas Comptroller), http://www.window.state.tx.us/taxinfo/proptax/.

17. Reeve Hamilton, "Study: Texas Economy Benefits from Community Colleges," *Texas Tribune*, November 26, 2010, http://www.texastribune.org/texas-education/higher-education/study-tx-economy-benefits from-community-colleges/; and "The Economic Impact of Community Colleges," Window on State Government, n.d., http://www.window.state.tx.us/specialrpt/workforce/colleges.php.

Laredo's Modest Advocate*

Robert Green

For years, Texas has had one of the largest proportions of people in poverty in the nation. Among the poorest of Texas's poor are residents of colonias, communities mostly along the border with Mexico with few basic services such as water and sewage. Most residents work, but at low-paying jobs. Yet they share the American dream of improving themselves and providing a better life for their children. This story is about a long-term advocate for these communities, and it reminds us of the force for change that a single dedicated person can be.

Along the U.S.-Mexico border, hundreds of thousands of people live without running water, sewage service, or electricity in unincorporated subdivisions known as "colonias." Texas has the largest number of colonias—an estimated 400,000 Texans live in more than 2,200 of them. The average yearly income of colonia residents is less than $10,000, and unemployment is more than eight times the state average. Texas's political leaders have done little in recent years to aid colonias. The "About" page of the Texas secretary of state's "Colonias Ombudsman Program" is blank save for a quote from Gov. Rick Perry.** One person who's helped improve conditions in colonias is Israel Reyna, though you'll never hear him take credit for it. Reyna runs the Laredo office of Texas Rio Grande Legal Aid, a nonprofit that provides free representation to impoverished residents of South Texas. Reyna and his staff work to ensure that workers receive workers' compensation and overtime pay, that day laborers aren't arrested and harassed by police merely for looking for work, and that water and sewage providers offer service to the colonias that dot the border region. Reyna joined the nonprofit straight out of law school in 1980. He's one of the rare advocates who knows how to needle political leaders into action—then step back and let them take the credit. "He is not someone that has ever been in the limelight or sought the limelight," says Jose "Chito" Vela, who work[ed] in the office of [then] State Rep. Solomon Ortiz, a Corpus Christi Democrat. Before joining Ortiz's staff, Vela served as the city manager of El Cenizo, a colonia south of Laredo that was incorporated under Reyna's guidance. Since El Cenizo incorporated, the community has levied taxes and now provides residents with some basic services. Under Reyna, the legal aid group also serves as what staff attorney Fabiola Flores calls a "baby lawyer factory." Reyna recruits law-student interns and entry-level attorneys from across the nation and puts them to work on pro bono cases. He enlists them in the cause, as be puts it, "to get things right. To move mountains ... for little people." He's reluctant to take the credit, "I am the messenger, not the messiah," Reyna says. "The heroes are the clients—the people who stick their necks out and expose themselves to the risk of litigation." Says Vela, "If you're promoting democracy, you can't come in from above and lift up these people—they have to lift themselves. At some point, you're going to go away, and the people are still going to be there. So they have to be able to organize and lead and fight for themselves."

*Robert Green, "Laredo's Modest Advocate"; Texas Observer, March 19, 2010. http://www.texasobserver.org/cover-story/laredos-modest-advocate. Reprinted by permission.

**While true in 2010, there is more information today.

For further resources, please visit **www.cengagebrain.com**.

Political Parties

4

(ck Anderson of the Houston Chronicle, *dist. by The Washington Post Writers Group. Reprinted with Permission.)*

Learning Objectives

1. Describe the structure of political parties in Texas, distinguishing between the temporary party structure and the permanent party structure.
2. Compare and contrast the different political ideologies found in the Lone Star State.
3. Trace the history of political parties in Texas.
4. Identify the roles that minor parties and independents have played in Texas.

As the Nick Anderson cartoon illustrates, political parties' delegate-selection methods are complex. Some commentators call the process that the Texas Democratic Party uses the "Texas Two-Step," because of the two ways delegates are selected. The results of the presidential preference primary are one way in which Democratic candidates win delegates. Another group of delegates is chosen by those who attend precinct conventions held in the evening after the voting polls close on Election Day. In 2012, this intricate procedure was even more convoluted. Legal challenges to district boundaries drawn for seats in the U.S. House of Representatives forced a rescheduling of elections from March to May. Changing the election day eliminated Democratic and Republican party precinct conventions, altered the dates and procedures for delegate selection, and mandated conventions. Delegates to the state and national Democratic Party conventions were selected without consideration of the presidential preference primary results. This chapter examines the structure of political parties in Texas, their history, recent electoral trends, voting coalitions, and the effect of the redistricting dilemma on the political parties in 2012.

★ Party Structure

LO1

Although neither the U.S. Constitution nor the Texas Constitution mentions political parties, these organizations are an integral part of the American governmental process. A **political party** can be defined as a combination of people and interests whose primary purpose is to gain control of government by winning elections. Whereas interest groups tend to focus on influencing governmental policies, political parties are chiefly concerned with the recruitment, nomination, and election of citizens to governmental office. (For a discussion of interest groups, see Chapter 6, "The Politics of Interest Groups.") In Texas, as throughout the United States, the Democratic and Republican parties are the two leading political parties. State election laws have contributed to the continuity of the two-party system. These laws specify that the general election, held in November of even-numbered years, is won by the candidate who receives the largest number of votes (a plurality) without a runoff. Third-party candidates have little chance of winning an election by defeating the two major-party nominees.

American political parties exist on four levels: national, state, county, and precinct. In part, these levels correspond to the organization of the U.S. federal system of government. Whereas a corporation is organized as a hierarchy, with a chain of command that makes each level directly accountable to the level above it, a political party is organized as a **stratarchy**, in which power is diffused among and within levels of the party organization.[1] Each major party is loosely organized so that state and local party organizations are free to decide their positions on party issues. State- and local-level organizations operate within their own spheres of influence, separate from one another. Although these levels of the two major parties are encouraged

political party
An organization influenced by political ideology whose primary interest is to gain control of government by winning elections.

stratarchy
A political system wherein power is diffused among and within levels of party organization.

to support national party policies, this effort is not always successful. As mandated by the Texas Election Code, Texas's two major parties are alike in structure. Each has permanent and temporary organizational structures (see Figure 4.1).

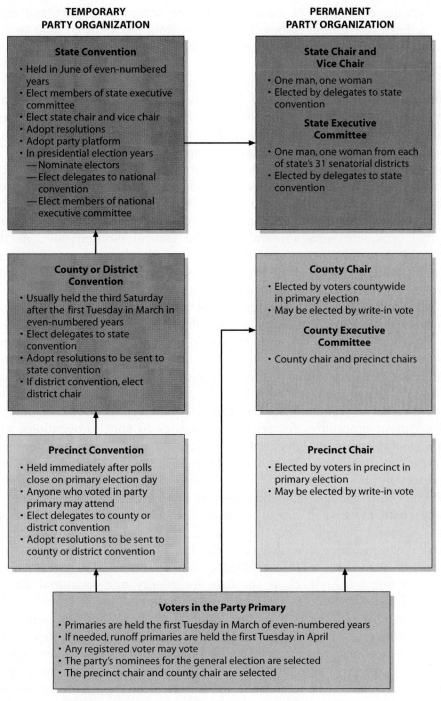

TEMPORARY PARTY ORGANIZATION

State Convention
- Held in June of even-numbered years
- Elect members of state executive committee
- Elect state chair and vice chair
- Adopt resolutions
- Adopt party platform
- In presidential election years
  — Nominate electors
  — Elect delegates to national convention
  — Elect members of national executive committee

County or District Convention
- Usually held the third Saturday after the first Tuesday in March in even-numbered years
- Elect delegates to state convention
- Adopt resolutions to be sent to state convention
- If district convention, elect district chair

Precinct Convention
- Held immediately after polls close on primary election day
- Anyone who voted in party primary may attend
- Elect delegates to county or district convention
- Adopt resolutions to be sent to county or district convention

PERMANENT PARTY ORGANIZATION

State Chair and Vice Chair
- One man, one woman
- Elected by delegates to state convention

State Executive Committee
- One man, one woman from each of state's 31 senatorial districts
- Elected by delegates to state convention

County Chair
- Elected by voters countywide in primary election
- May be elected by write-in vote

County Executive Committee
- County chair and precinct chairs

Precinct Chair
- Elected by voters in precinct in primary election
- May be elected by write-in vote

Voters in the Party Primary
- Primaries are held the first Tuesday in March of even-numbered years
- If needed, runoff primaries are held the first Tuesday in April
- Any registered voter may vote
- The party's nominees for the general election are selected
- The precinct chair and county chair are selected

Figure 4.1 Texas Political Party Organization

Temporary Party Organization

The **temporary party organization** consists of primaries and conventions in which members of the major political parties participate in elections to select candidates for public office. Primary election voting may involve a second, or runoff, primary. Conventions elect state-level party officers and are scheduled at precinct, county, and state senatorial district and state levels. Each convention lasts a limited time, from less than an hour to one or two days. These events are temporary because they are not ongoing party activities.

At the state level, conventions select party leaders chosen by delegates elected at the local level. Rules of the Texas Democratic and Republican parties mandate that party policy be determined at their conventions. These policy decisions are evidenced by resolutions, passed in both local and state conventions, and by party platforms adopted at the state conventions. A party's **platform** is a document that sets forth the party's position on current issues. In presidential election years, state-level conventions select delegates who attend a party's national convention. Additionally, state delegates nominate a slate of electors to vote in the electoral college if their party's presidential candidate wins a plurality of the general election vote. At the national party convention, candidates are officially chosen to run for president and vice president of the United States. All Texas political conventions must be open to the media, according to state law.

In March 2012, a three-judge federal panel in San Antonio issued an order setting a May 29 primary election date for the Lone Star State—nine days before the Republican state convention and 10 days before the Democratic state convention. The new primary election date significantly affected the Texas Democratic and Republican parties' temporary party organizations and altered their processes for delegate selection. The political parties were unable to accommodate the May 29 primary election date, comply with current procedures for selecting delegates to state conventions, and hold their state conventions the first weekend of June. Due to the necessity of selecting convention sites (Fort Worth for the Republican Party and Houston for the Democratic Party), lining up convention facilities, and securing hotel rooms well in advance of the actual conventions, neither party could move their already-scheduled convention dates. As a result, both parties held emergency sessions of their respective state executive committees to adopt new delegate-selection plans. The State Democratic Executive Committee (SDEC) adopted a plan that eliminated precinct conventions and set April 21 as the date for county and senatorial district conventions.[2] The State Republican Executive Committee (SREC) adopted a plan that also set April 21 as the date for their county and senatorial district conventions (April 14 for some counties). Under the Republican delegate-selection plan, precinct conventions were optional as determined by county executive committees. For counties that wanted to conduct precinct conventions, those conventions occurred on the morning of the county and senatorial district conventions.[3]

temporary party organization
Primaries and conventions that function briefly to nominate candidates, pass resolutions, adopt a party platform, and select delegates to party conventions at higher levels.

platform
A document that sets forth a political party's position on issues such as income tax, school vouchers, or public utility regulation.

Precinct Conventions In contrast to the changes in party rules for 2012, **precinct conventions** in Texas traditionally occur every even-numbered year on the first Tuesday in March, which is the day of the first primary. At the lowest level of the temporary party organization, these conventions (both Democratic and Republican) assemble in almost all of the state's voting precincts. Precinct conventions start immediately after the polls close that evening and last approximately 30 minutes to two hours. Usually, precinct conventions are sparsely attended. Because Texas remained important to the selection of the Democratic presidential nominee in 2008, attendance at precinct conventions soared, with reports of as many as one million people in attendance throughout the state. That number represented a 10-fold increase in delegates over previous years and resulted in long registration lines and overpacked facilities.[4]

By state law, any citizen who voted in the party primary is permitted to attend and participate in that party's precinct convention as a delegate. Delegates elect a chairperson to preside over the convention and a secretary to record the proceedings. The main business of the precinct convention is to elect delegates to the county or district convention. Under long-standing rules of both the Democratic and Republican parties, precinct conventions have been authorized to elect one delegate to the county (or district) convention for every 25 votes cast in the precinct for the party's gubernatorial nominee in the previous general election. Delegates to a party's precinct convention are allowed to submit and debate resolutions. These resolutions express the positions of precinct convention participants on any number of issues, ranging from immigration, to abortion, to the national debt. If adopted, a resolution will be submitted to a county or district convention for consideration.

In addition to introducing and voting on resolutions at precinct conventions, the Republican Party usually places several nonbinding resolutions on the primary ballot for voters to decide upon. In 2010, the SREC selected five propositions for the primary ballot to assess primary voters' opinions and intensity on the issues. Two of these five propositions (requiring voters to provide valid photo identification to vote and mandating a sonogram be performed and shown to each woman about to undergo an elective abortion procedure) were later passed into law by the Republican-dominated Texas legislature.

In 2012, the SREC placed five propositions on the Texas Republican primary ballot, each of which was approved by the percentage of voters indicated below:

- **Requiring the state to fund** private schools based on parental choice (85 percent)
- **Directing the U.S.** Congress to immediately repeal the Patient Protection and Affordable Care Act (93 percent)
- Prohibiting government from restricting the content of public prayer (91 percent)
- **Requiring voter approval, through constitutional amendment, of increased government spending beyond the** combined increase of population and inflation (94 percent)

precinct convention
At the lowest level of political party organization, voters convene in March of even-numbered years to adopt resolutions and to name delegates to a county (or district) convention.

- Allowing the Texas Legislature to redraw court-imposed lines for national and state legislative districts in its upcoming session (76 percent)

The following three propositions appeared on the 2012 Democratic ballot and were approved by percentages indicated:

- Making all Texas high school graduates eligible for in-state college/university tuition (85 percent)
- Calling on the legislature to fund colleges with affordable tuition and fees (93 percent)
- Advocating legalized casino gambling with all revenue dedicated to education (74 percent)[5]

County and District Conventions State law requires that both **county conventions** and **district conventions** occur the third Saturday after the precinct conventions, which is normally 11 days after the primary election. If that Saturday is during Passover or Easter weekend, however, the conventions are held the next Saturday in which neither religious holiday occurs. District conventions, rather than a single-county convention, are held in heavily populated counties (such as Harris, Dallas, and Bexar) that have more than one state senatorial district. Delegates to a party's county or district convention elect a chairperson to preside over the convention and a secretary to record the proceedings. The main business of county and district conventions is to elect delegates to the state convention.

Under the rules for each party, county and district conventions may select one delegate to the state convention for every 300 votes cast in the county or district for the party's gubernatorial nominee in the most recent general election. Under Republican Party rules, all delegate candidates are submitted by the county or district convention's committee on nominations for approval by convention participants. Rules of the Democratic Party allow state delegates to be selected by precinct delegations. If not all state delegate positions are filled in this manner, the county or district convention's nominations committee proposes the remaining state delegates in proportion to the percentage of women, young people, and minorities present in the county or district and subject to approval by the county or district convention delegates. Even though precinct conventions were not held in 2012, delegates to Democratic county or district conventions caucused (or met) within their precinct delegations. Delegates attending the state or district convention also consider resolutions. These resolutions then go to the party's state convention for consideration.

State Conventions In accordance with the Texas Election Code, in June of even-numbered years, each political party must hold a biennial **state convention** to conduct party business. State conventions occur during a two-day period. Delegates to a party's state convention elect a chairperson to preside over the convention and a secretary to record the proceedings. In addition, delegates conduct the following tasks:

county convention
A party meeting of precinct delegates held on the second Saturday after precinct conventions; it elects delegates and alternates to the state convention.

district convention
Held on the second Saturday after the first primary in counties that have more than one state senatorial district. Participants elect delegates to the party's state convention.

state convention
Convenes every even-numbered year to make rules for a political party, adopt a party platform and resolutions, and select members of the state executive committee; in a presidential election year, it elects delegates to the national convention, names members to serve on the national committee, and elects potential electors to vote if the party's presidential candidate receives the plurality of the popular vote in the general election.

- Certify to the secretary of state the names of party members nominated in the March and April primaries for Texas elective offices (or by convention if no primary was held)[6]
- Write the rules that will govern the party
- Draft and adopt a party platform
- Adopt resolutions regarding issues too specific to be included in the party platform
- Select members of the party's state executive committee

In presidential election years, state convention delegates also perform the following three functions:

- Elect delegates to the national presidential nominating convention (the total number for Texas is calculated under national party rules)
- Elect members from Texas to serve on the party's national committee
- Elect a slate of potential presidential electors to cast Texas's electoral votes if the party's ticket wins a plurality of the state's popular presidential vote

Texas casts 38 electoral votes. A state's electoral vote equals the number of its members in the U.S. Congress (for Texas, two senators and 36 representatives, based on the state's population according to the 2010 census).

Selection of National Convention Delegates

Selection of delegates to a national party convention depends on the delegates' support of particular candidates for the party's presidential nomination. In a **presidential preference primary**, rank-and-file party members can vote directly for the presidential candidates of their choice. Primary voting is by precinct. Delegates to the party's national convention are usually chosen according to the results of the primary vote; however, the situation in 2012 altered the Democrats' national delegate selection process. Republicans continued to rely on presidential preference primary results for selection of national delegates. The respective national conventions nominate the parties' candidates for president and vice president.

In many states, parties select delegates to a national convention in **caucuses**. Party members assemble in caucuses at the respective precinct, county, and state levels. Here, they choose national convention delegates who either are pledged to support a particular presidential candidate or are uncommitted.

Democratic Selection In recent years, Texas Democrats have combined the two delegate-selection plans into a primary-caucus described as the "Texas Two-Step." In presidential election years, participants are asked to identify their presidential preferences at each convention. However, individuals may choose not to pledge their support to any candidate. Instead, they may indicate that they are uncommitted. Presidential candidates are awarded delegates to local and state conventions in proportion to the number of their supporters in attendance. National delegates include those selected by state senatorial districts, those selected on an at-large basis, and **superdelegates** (unpledged

presidential preference primary
A primary in which the voters indicate their preference for a person seeking nomination as the party's presidential candidate.

caucus
A meeting at which members of a political party assemble to select delegates and make other policy recommendations at the precinct, county or state senatorial district and state levels.

superdelegate
An unpledged party official or elected official who serves as a delegate to a party's national convention.

Images from Barack Obama's and Mitt Romney's 2012 presidential campaigns in Texas.

(left: Jewel Samad/AFP/Getty images; right: AP Photo/Evan Vucci)

party and elected officials). In 2012, Texas sent 288 (out of a total of 5,555) delegates to the Democratic National Convention. Pledged delegates were chosen proportionally based on the number of delegates to county and senate district conventions who signed in favoring a particular candidate.

Republican Selection The Republican Party selects national delegates from the results of the presidential preference primary. Some Republican delegates are chosen by congressional district caucuses (at least one was chosen from each district in 2012). Others are chosen on an at-large basis by the entire convention. A nominating committee selects all at-large delegates. State convention delegates approve all national delegates. In 2012, Texas sent 155 (out of a total of 2,286) delegates to the Republican National Convention.

Permanent Party Organization

Each major political party in the United States consists of thousands of virtually autonomous executive committees at the local, state, and national levels. These committees are given great latitude in their operating structures. For Democrats and Republicans alike, the executive committees across the nation are linked only nominally. At the highest level, each party has a national committee. In Texas, the precinct chairs, together with the county, district, and state executive committees, make up the permanent organization of the state parties. The role of the **permanent party organization** is to recruit candidates, devise strategies, raise funds, distribute candidate literature and information, register voters, and turn out voters on Election Day.

Precinct Chair In Texas, the basic party official in both the temporary and the permanent party structures is the **precinct chair**, who is elected to a

permanent party organization
In Texas, the precinct chairs, county and district executive committees, and the state executive committee form the permanent organization of a political party.

precinct chair
The party official responsible for the interests and activities of a political party in a voting district; typical duties include encouraging voter registration, distributing campaign literature, operating phone banks, and getting out the vote on Election Day.

two-year term by precinct voters in the party primaries. A party precinct chair's duties and responsibilities include registering and persuading voters within the precinct, distributing candidate literature and information, operating phone banks within the precinct on behalf of the party and its candidates, and getting people to the polls. If both parties are evenly matched in strength at the polls, the precinct chairs become more vital in getting people out to vote. A precinct chair is an unpaid party official who also arranges for the precinct convention and serves on the county executive committee. Many of these positions go unfilled in more populous counties (those that have 100 or more precincts) and in counties where one party dominates the other in numbers of voters. In 2012, for instance, out of approximately 700 precincts in Dallas County, neither Democrats nor Republicans filled chairs in more than 400 precincts. Likewise, Democrats and Republicans each filled chairs in only slightly more than half of the 1,000 precincts in Harris County that year.

County and District Executive Committees A county executive committee comprises all the precinct chairs and the county chair, who are elected by county party members in the primaries. The county chair heads the party's countywide organization. County executive committees conduct primaries and arrange for county conventions. At the local level, the **county chair** is the key party official and serves as the party's chief strategist within that county. Duties of the county chair include recruiting local candidates for office, raising funds, establishing and staffing the party's campaign headquarters within the county, and serving as the local spokesperson for the party. The Texas Election Code also provides for a **district executive committee**, which is composed of the county chairs from each county in a given district (senatorial, representative, or judicial). District executive committees rarely meet except to nominate candidates to fill a district vacancy, when one occurs.

State Executive Committee For each major political party, the highest permanent party organization in the state is the **state executive committee**. As mandated by state law, an executive committee is composed of one man and one woman from each of the 31 state senatorial districts, plus a chair and a vice chair, one of whom must be a woman. For both the Democratic and Republican parties, a state executive committee with 64 members is elected at the party's state convention. On that occasion, delegates from each of the 31 senatorial districts choose two members from their district and place these names before the convention for its approval. At the same time, convention delegates choose the chair and vice chair at-large. The party's state chair serves as its key strategist and chief spokesperson. The role of vice chair has traditionally been more honorary in nature. In addition to the 64 statutory members of the party's state executive committee, party rules may allow "add-on" members. An add-on member may represent recognized statewide auxiliary organizations that have voting power within the party, such as women's groups (e.g., Texas Democratic Women, Texas Federation of Republican

county executive committee
Composed of a party's precinct chairs and the elected county chair, the county executive committee conducts primaries and makes arrangements for holding county conventions.

county chair
Elected by county party members in the primaries, this key party official heads the county executive committee.

district executive committee
Composed of county chairs within a district that elects a state senator, U.S. or state representative, or district judge, this body fills a vacancy created by the death, resignation, or disqualification of a nominated candidate.

state executive committee
Composed of a chair, vice chair, and two members from each senatorial district, this body is part of a party's permanent organization.

Women), racial groups (Texas Coalition of Black Democrats, Hispanic Caucus, Republican National Hispanic Assembly), House and Senate caucus chairs, youth groups (Texas Young Democrats, Texas College Republicans), and county chairs associations (e.g., Texas Democratic County Chairs Association and the Texas Republican County Chairmen's Association).

The party's state chair works with the party's state executive committee to recruit candidates for statewide and district offices, plan statewide strategies, and raise funds for the party at the state level. The importance of the state party chair's role as chief fundraiser was emphasized in the 2010 ouster of the incumbent chair of the Republican Party of Texas. Steve Munisteri, a retired Houston attorney, argued that then-chair Cathie Adams lacked both administrative skills and fundraising abilities in his successful attempt to unseat her. Noting that the state party's debts exceeded its assets by more than $300,000 and that the party continued to lose money every month, Munisteri vowed that he would not take a break "until the debt [was] 100 percent retired."[7] Munisteri was reelected state party chair in 2012 at the Republican state convention in Forth Worth in June. At its 2012 state convention, the Democratic Party chose the first Latino chair of a major political party in Texas when it selected Rio Grande Valley native and former court of appeals judge Gilberto Hinojosa as its state chair. The state executive committee of each party must also canvass (or count) statewide primary returns and certify the nomination of party candidates. It also conducts the state convention, promotes party unity and strength, maintains relations with the party's national committee, and raises some campaign money for party candidates (though most campaign funds are raised by the candidates themselves).

☑ Learning Check 4.1   (Answers on p. 163)

1. What is the difference between a party's permanent organization and its temporary organization?
2. True or False: A political party's state chair is chosen by the temporary organization.

★ Political Ideology

LO2

Today's politics in the Lone Star State reflect Texas's political history. Traditions that have been determined by centuries of political experience and culture influence current attitudes toward parties, candidates, and issues. Nevertheless, Texans' changing demands and expectations have forced revisions in party platforms and have affected the campaigns of candidates for public office. Political parties cannot remain static and survive, nor can politicians win elections unless they are in step with the opinions of a large percentage of voters.

Since the 1930s, the terms *liberal* and *conservative* have meant more to many Texas voters than the actual names of political parties have. In view of long-standing ideological differences between liberals and conservatives, this terminology must be explained. These ideological labels almost defy definition, however, because meanings change with time and circumstances. Furthermore, each label has varying shades of meaning for different people. In Texas, because of the influences of the individualistic and traditionalistic political cultures, both Democrats and Republicans tend to be conservative. The Republican Party tends to be dominated by right-wing social conservatives, whereas the Democratic Party is influenced (but not dominated) by left-wing liberals.

The origins of the terms *left* and *right* to refer to political affiliation can be traced back to the time of the French Revolution, when monarchists sat to the right side of the president in the French National Assembly and supporters of a republic sat to his left. The assignment of seats in legislative bodies determined by political affiliation or ideology continues in many countries today. Despite the use of right-left terminology throughout the United States, the Texas legislature has not traditionally used partisan or ideological criteria for assigning floor seats on the right and left sides of House and Senate chambers.

Conservatism

In its purest form, modern conservative doctrine envisions ideal social and economic orders that would be largely untouched by government. According to this philosophy, if all individuals were left alone (the doctrine of laissez-faire) to pursue their self-interests, both social and economic systems would benefit, and the cost of government would be low. **Conservatives**, therefore, are generally opposed to government-managed or government-subsidized programs, such as assistance to poor families with dependent children, unemployment insurance, and federal price-support programs for the benefit of farmers producing commodities such as cotton and wheat. Conservatives are further divided between fiscal conservatives and social conservatives. Today's fiscal conservatives give the highest priority to reduced taxing and spending; whereas social conservatives (such as those associated with the Christian Coalition) stress the importance of their family values, including opposition to abortion and homosexuality. Social conservatives support school vouchers that would provide government-funded assistance to parents who choose to send their children to private schools, especially church-affiliated schools.[8] Texas governor Rick Perry identifies himself as a social conservative. In a television ad aired in Iowa during his unsuccessful presidential campaign in 2012, he proclaimed, "I'm not ashamed to admit that I am a Christian. But you don't need to be in the pew every Sunday to know there's something wrong in this country when gays can openly serve in the military, but our kids can't openly celebrate Christmas or pray in school."[9]

Attempting to distance himself from more extreme conservative Republicans, President George W. Bush used the phrase "compassionate conservatism" to describe his political philosophy when he ran for governor of Texas in 1998 and for the presidency in 2000 and 2004. Bush insisted that he was "a conservative who puts a compassionate face on a conservative philosophy."[10]

conservative
A person who advocates minimal intervention by government in social and economic matters and who gives a high priority to reducing taxes and curbing public spending.

Chapter 4 ★ Political Parties

His ideology is sometimes described as **neoconservatism**, in part, because it is fiscally conservative while also allowing for a limited governmental role in solving social problems.

In 2009, several conservatives formed the Tea Party movement. Taking their name from the Boston Tea Party, an event that led to the American Revolution, Tea Party activists have argued that the size and scope of government has grown out of control. Although the Tea Party actually consists of thousands of separate, autonomous groups, the "Tea Party Patriots" is a national umbrella group that is affiliated with more than 3,500 local organizations. Governor Perry has actively courted the support of Tea Party sympathizers, stating that he does not regard Tea Party activists as extremists and then adding "but if you are, I'm with you."[11] Drawing on the support of Tea Party activists, Perry was considered by many to be an early front-runner for the Republican nomination for president, before a series of poor debate performances and a fifth-place finish in the Iowa caucus forced him to end his presidential campaign. In the 2012 Republican Primary Run-off, Ted Cruz defeated David Dewhurst for the U.S. Senate nomination due in large part to his support from members of the Tea Party.

Liberalism

Liberals favor government regulation of the economy to achieve a more equitable distribution of wealth. Only government, liberals insist, is capable of guarding against air, water, and soil pollution by corporations and individuals. Liberals claim that government is obligated to aid the unemployed, alleviate poverty (especially for the benefit of children), and guarantee equal rights for minorities and women. Liberalism seeks a limited role for government involvement with regard to other social issues, especially those related to morality or religion. Liberals are more likely to oppose prayer in public schools, government subsidies for religious institutions, and any church involvement in secular politics. Many Texas Democrats have a **neoliberal** ideology. This position incorporates a philosophy of less government regulation of business and the economy, while adopting a more liberal view of greater government involvement in social programs.

Both Texas liberals and conservatives are often ideologically inconsistent. A conservative may oppose government subsidies, such as welfare assistance for citizens, but support similar payments to corporations. Liberals may support pollution control laws for corporations but oppose antipollution measures that require installation of emission control devices for their own automobiles. Frequently, individuals who have extreme conservative or liberal ideologies accuse individuals with more moderate views of being ideologically inconsistent.

neoconservatism
A political ideology that reflects fiscal conservatism, but accepts a limited governmental role in solving social problems.

liberal
A person who advocates for government support in social and economic matters and who favors political reforms that extend democracy, achieve a more equitable distribution of wealth, and protect individual freedoms and rights.

neoliberal
A political ideology that advocates less government regulation of business but supports more governmental involvement in social matters.

✓ **Learning Check 4.2** (Answers on p. 163)

1. What is the primary difference between conservatives and neoconservatives?
2. True or False: Texas Democrats generally have a liberal political ideology.

An Overview of Texas Political History

LO3

From the time political parties developed in Texas until the 1960s, the Lone Star State was dominated primarily by one political party: the Democratic Party. In the 1970s and 1980s, Texas moved toward a competitive two-party structure. By the 1990s and into the 21st century, however, the state had seemingly become a one-party state with the Republican Party in control. Changing demographics, in particular a rapidly growing Latino population have given Democrats hope that they will be competitive and regain a majority status.

1840s to 1870s: The Origin of the Party System

Before Texas's admission into the Union in 1845, its political parties had not fully developed. Political factions during the years that Texas was an independent republic tended to coalesce around personalities. The two dominant factions were the pro-(Sam) Houston and the anti-Houston groups. Even after the Lone Star State's admission into the Union, these two factions remained. By the 1850s, the pro-Houston faction began referring to itself as the Jackson Democrats (Unionists), whereas the anti-Houston faction called themselves the Calhoun Democrats (after South Carolina senator John C. Calhoun, a states' rights and proslavery advocate). In the course of the Civil War, Texas politics became firmly aligned with the Democratic Party.

During the period of Reconstruction (1865–1873) that followed the Civil War, the Republican Party controlled Texas politics. The Reconstruction acts passed by the U.S. Congress purged all officeholders with a Confederate past. Congress also disenfranchised all Southerners who had ever held a state or federal office before secession and who later supported the Confederacy. In Texas, any man who had ever been a mayor, a school trustee, a clerk, or even a public weigher (a position originally created to weigh all cotton, wool, hides, and other staples offered for sale, but today a position whose functions are largely obsolete) was denied the right to vote.[12] Republican governor Edmund J. Davis, a former Union army general, was elected in 1869 during this period of radical Reconstruction. The Davis administration quickly became unpopular with Texas's Anglo majority. During his tenure in office, Davis took control of voter registration and appointed more than 8,000 public officials. From the Texas Supreme Court justices to the state police to city officials, Davis placed Republicans (including some African Americans) in office throughout the state. Opposed by former Confederates, Davis's administration was condemned by most Anglo Texans for corruption, graft, and high taxation.[13] After Davis's defeat for reelection in 1873 by a newly enfranchised electorate, Texas voters did not elect another Republican governor for more than 100 years.

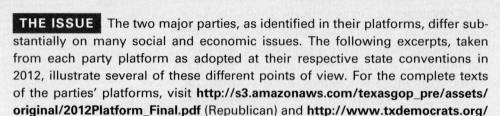

Point/Counterpoint

THE ISSUE The two major parties, as identified in their platforms, differ substantially on many social and economic issues. The following excerpts, taken from each party platform as adopted at their respective state conventions in 2012, illustrate several of these different points of view. For the complete texts of the parties' platforms, visit **http://s3.amazonaws.com/texasgop_pre/assets/original/2012Platform_Final.pdf** (Republican) and **http://www.txdemocrats.org/2012/platform.pdf** (Democratic).

Positions of the Two Major Parties on Key Issues

The Texas Republican Party

Abortion
- Believes the unborn child has a fundamental individual right to life that cannot be infringed.
- Supports a human life amendment to the U.S. Constitution.
- Urges the reversal of *Roe v. Wade.*

Education
- Supports reducing taxpayer funding to all levels of educational institutions.
- Believes the Department of Education (DOE) should be abolished.
- Believes theories such as life origins and environmental change should be taught as challengeable scientific theories subject to change as new data is produced.
- Encourages non-English speaking students to transition to English within three years.
- Urges Congress to repeal government-sponsored programs that deal with early childhood development.
- Opposes the teaching of Higher Order Thinking Skills (HOTS) (values clarification), critical thinking skills, and similar programs that are simply a relabeling of Outcome-Based Education (OBE) (mastery learning), which focus on behavior modification and have the purpose of challenging the student's fixed beliefs and undermining parental authority.
- Opposes any sex education other than abstinence until marriage.

Capital Punishment
- Believes that properly applied capital punishment is a legitimate and effective

The Texas Democratic Party

Abortion
- Trusts women to make personal and responsible decisions about when and whether to bear children, in consultation with their family, their physician, and their God, rather than having these personal decisions made by politicians.
- Supports prevention measures which have proven effective at reducing unintended pregnancies.

Education
- Believes the state should establish a 100% equitable school finance system with sufficient state revenue to allow every district to offer an exemplary program.
- Believes the state should provide environmental education programs for children and adults.
- Rejects efforts to destroy bilingual education. Believes the state should promote multilanguage instruction, beginning in elementary school, to make all students fluent in English and at least one other language.
- Believes the state should support expanded access to early childhood education, targeting at-risk students.
- Believes all children should have access to an exemplary educational program that values and encourages critical thinking and creativity.

Capital Punishment
- Calls for the passage of legislation that would abolish the death penalty in Texas and replace it with the punishment of life in prison without parole.

Energy
- Supports increased development of renewable-energy technologies that spur the economy, protect

The Texas Republican Party

deterrent and that it should be swift and unencumbered.

Energy

- Encourages a comprehensive energy policy that allows more development of domestic energy sources and reduces the need for foreign energy.
- Opposes government restrictions on drilling and production operations on public and private lands and waters, refineries, electric power generation and distribution, and federal gas mileage standards and fuel blends.
- Supports the immediate approval and construction of the Keystone XL and other pipelines that will reduce reliance on imported oil and natural gas from unstable or unfriendly countries.

Environment

- Opposes all efforts of the extreme environmental groups that stymie legitimate business interests.
- Strongly opposes efforts that attempt to use environmental causes to purposefully disrupt and stop those interests within the oil and gas industry.
- Strongly supports the immediate repeal of the Endangered Species Act.
- Believes the Environmental Protection Agency should be abolished.
- Believes in the right to own property without governmental interference.

Health Care

- Believes health care decisions should be between a patient and health care professional and should be protected from government intrusion.
- Demands the immediate repeal of the Patient Protection and Affordable Care Act.

School Vouchers

- Encourages the Texas governor and legislature to enact child-centered school funding options to allow maximum freedom of

The Texas Democratic Party

the environment, create high-paying jobs, and reduce reliance and dependence on foreign oil.

- Supports a transportation policy that encourages the development of affordable, fuel-efficient vehicles that can run on alternative fuels.
- Supports tax incentives for both homeowners and landlords to invest in conservation and energy efficiency.

Environment

- Believes that environmental protection, regulation, and enforcement are essential to preserve the health of people, the quality of life, and to secure long-term economic growth.
- Supports the enactment of state policy that allows local governments to protect air and water quality, public safety, historical sites, and health from actions that adversely affect communities.
- Supports open space acquisition to protect Texas aquifers and watersheds that provide the sole source of drinking water for millions of Texans.
- Supports the adoption, immediate implementation, and strong enforcement of clean air plans by state officials.

Health Care

- Supports guaranteed access to affordable, comprehensive, single-payer health care for all U.S. citizens and legal residents.
- Supports creation of a Texas universal health-care plan, as permitted under the Affordable Care Act, to ensure that every Texas resident has health insurance that covers medical, vision, and dental care, full reproductive health services, preventive services, prescription drugs, and mental health counseling and treatment.

School Vouchers

- Opposes private school vouchers in all forms, including tax breaks for people or corporations.

Social Security

- Believes Social Security should continue to be the foundation of income security for working Americans and that Social Security is an insurance program placed in the trust of the federal government and not a public welfare cost of government.

The Texas Republican Party

choice in public, private, or parochial education for all children.

Social Security

- Supports an immediate and orderly transition to a system of private pensions based on the concept of individual retirement accounts, and gradually phasing out the Social Security tax.

Voter Registration

- Supports the repeal of all motor-voter laws.
- Supports re-registering voters every four years.
- Supports requiring photo identification of all registrants.
- Supports proof of residency and citizenship as part of the voter registration application.

The Texas Democratic Party

- Opposes privatization of the Social Security program as fiscally irresponsible, and considers the use of tax dollars as capital to invest in the stock market as a threat to the income security of working Americans.

Voter Registration

- Believes voter registration should be a lifetime status for all qualified, non-felon Texas citizens, requiring only change of address documentation in person or online.
- Supports efforts to defeat restrictive voter identification and proof of citizenship legislation that would serve only to reduce turnout among the elderly, poor, and people of color.
- Supports expansion of the types of legal identification that can be used to verify residence when a voter does not have a voter registration card at the polling place.
- Supports stronger penalties and stricter enforcement to prevent vote suppression.

1870s to 1970s: A One-Party Dominant System

From the end of Reconstruction until the 1970s, Texas and other former Confederate states had a one-party identity in which the Democratic Party was strong and the Republican Party weak. During those years (when a gubernatorial term in Texas was two years), Democratic candidates won 52 consecutive gubernatorial elections, and Democratic presidential nominees carried the state in all but three of the 25 presidential elections.

In the latter part of the 19th century, Democrats faced a greater challenge from the Populist Party than they did from Republicans. The Populist (or People's) Party formed in Texas as an agrarian-based party, winning local elections throughout the state. From 1892 to 1898, their gubernatorial nominees received more votes than did Republicans. Although its ideas remained influential in Texas (for example, protection of common people by government regulation of railroads and banks), the Populist Party became less important after 1898. Rural Texans continued to be active in politics, but most farmers and others who had been Populists shifted their support to Democratic candidates. In large measure, the Populist Party declined because the Democratic Party adopted Populist issues, such as government regulation of railroads.[14]

In the early 20th century, the Democratic Party strengthened its control over state politics. Having adopted Populist issues, Democratic candidates faced no opposition from Populist candidates. During the next five decades, two factions emerged within the Democratic Party: conservatives and liberals. Fighting between these two factions was often as fierce as between two separate political parties. By the late 1940s and early 1950s, Republican presidential candidates began enjoying greater support from the Texas electorate. With the backing of conservative Democratic governor Alan Shivers, Republican presidential nominee Dwight D. Eisenhower successfully carried Texas in 1952 and 1956. Evidence of the growing strength of the Texas GOP (Grand Old Party, a nickname that the Republican Party adopted in the 1870s) was sharply revealed in 1961, with the election to the U.S. Senate of Texas Republican John Tower, a political science professor at Midwestern State University in Wichita Falls. Originally elected to fill the vacancy created when Lyndon Johnson left the Senate to become vice president, Tower was the first Republican to win statewide office in Texas since 1869; he won successive elections until his retirement in 1984.

1970s to 1990s: An Emerging Two-Party System

Beginning in the late 1940s, a majority of conservative Democrats began to support the national Republican ticket. At the state and local levels, however, the Democratic Party remained firmly in control. Three decades later, however, the Republican Party enjoyed greater electoral support in Texas. No longer was the winner in a Democratic primary assured of victory in the general election contest in November. When Bill Clements was elected governor of the Lone Star State in 1978, he became the first Republican to hold that office since Reconstruction. In the 1980s, GOP voters elected growing numbers of candidates to the U.S. Congress, the Texas legislature, and county courthouse offices. Moreover, GOP elected officials began to dominate local politics in suburban areas around the state.

The Republican Party continued to make substantial gains throughout the 1990s. In 1992, Bill Clinton became the first Democratic president elected without carrying Texas. In 1993, Lloyd Bentsen resigned from the U.S. Senate after his appointment as Treasury Secretary by President Clinton. With the Republican victory of U.S. senatorial candidate Kay Bailey Hutchison in the 1993 special election to fill that seat, the Texas GOP began a series of "firsts." Hutchison's victory included two firsts: she was the first woman to represent Texas in the U.S. Senate, and, for the first time in modern history, Texas was represented by two Republican senators.

The elections of 1994 were a preview of future elections. Elected governor in 1990, Democrat Ann Richards failed to win reelection, despite her personal popularity. Republican George W. Bush beat Richards in the 1994 gubernatorial race. At the same time, Senator Hutchison easily defeated her Democratic opponent. Democrats holding four executive offices (lieutenant governor, attorney general, comptroller of public accounts, and commissioner of the general land office) defeated their Republican challengers. Republican incumbent agriculture commissioner Rick Perry, however, had a one-million-vote margin of victory over his Democratic opponent, and all six Republican statewide candidates below him on the ballot won. These victories gave Republicans two railroad commission members, two more Supreme Court justices, and two more Court of Criminal Appeals judges. Republicans also won many lower-level judgeships. For the first time, Republicans also gained control of the 15-member State Board of Education. Active support by members of the Christian Coalition resulted in Republican victories in three of the six contested races for seats on this board.

In 1996, for the first time since the primary system was established, Republican primaries were conducted in all 254 Texas counties. More of the Lone Star State's voters participated in the Republican primary than in the Democratic primary. In addition, Republican victories continued in the general election of that year, as all statewide Republican candidates won. Republicans now held all three positions on the Texas Railroad Commission and gained three more Court of Criminal Appeals judgeships and four more positions on the Texas Supreme Court. In that year, Republican presidential candidate Bob Dole carried the state over President Bill Clinton. By 1996, Clinton was certain that he could be elected without Texas's electoral votes, so his campaign effort focused on closely contested states where he was more likely to win. This decision demonstrated the acceptance by national Democratic candidates that Texas was a Republican state and that its electoral votes were not needed for a Democratic presidential victory.

The 1998 elections gave Republicans control of all statewide offices but one. Texas Supreme Court Justice Raul Gonzalez was the lone Democrat in statewide office when he announced his retirement in December 1998. The GOP sweep was complete when Governor George W. Bush appointed a Republican to replace Gonzalez. In 1998, Bush was so popular that he received endorsements from more than 100 elected Democratic officials and almost 70 percent of the vote in the gubernatorial election. With the prospect of a Bush presidential bid in 2000 likely, Republican lieutenant gubernatorial nominee Rick Perry campaigned on the issue that a Republican should succeed Governor Bush if he resigned to become president. The 1998 elections allowed Republicans to retain control of the Texas Senate and to increase their representation in the state House of Representatives, although they did not gain control of the latter chamber. After the dismal performance of Democratic candidates, then-chair of the Republican Party, Susan Weddington, advised Democrats to "turn out the lights, [because] the Democratic party [was] definitely over."

Points to Ponder

- In the election of 1956, incumbent Texas governor Alan Shivers secured both the Democratic and the Republican nominations for governor.
- Supporters of Governor Shivers began referring to themselves as "Shivercrats."
- Shivers, the Democrat, beat Shivers, the Republican, by a three-to-one margin.

2000 to 2012: Republican Dominance

After their party's statewide success in 1998, Texas Republicans focused attention on the 2000 national elections. Governor Bush's candidacy for the presidency was enhanced by his ability to maintain the backing of social conservatives within his party, while gaining support from minority voters, women, and some Democrats. National Republican leaders seeking an electable candidate found Bush's 1998 gubernatorial victory and his inclusive strategy appealing. Although Bush did not announce that he would seek the Republican presidential nomination until after the Texas legislature completed its 1999 regular session, Republican leaders streamed to Austin during the session. More than one-fourth of Texas Democrats told pollsters they would vote for Bush for president.

Students in Action

"I only hope that the Republican Party is up to the challenge and will make a serious investment in reaching out to Latinos, specifically young Latinos, who are ready to hear something new and positive about our future."

—Fernando Trevino, Jr.

About Fernando Trevino

Fernando Trevino Jr. attended the Mays School of Business at Texas A&M University. He was born in Del Rio, Texas, and later moved to Brownsville. Fernando's interest in politics and public service began very early in life, but was not fully realized until the 2008 Democratic presidential primary. Before this time, he considered himself a "liberal" Democrat. However, it was at this point that he realized the correlations between Latino beliefs and the principles of conservatism and the Republican Party.

What Is It About the Republican Party That Attracted Him to It?

Fernando's parents raised him very conservatively, teaching him never to abandon faith and to be fiscally responsible. He was also always taught that we must cherish and respect our differences. These are traits that he feels make up the essence of the Republican Party: faith, fiscal responsibility, and the power of the individual.

What Is He Doing Now to Share His Beliefs and Encourage Action?

Fernando began his involvement as a congressional intern at the district office of U.S. Congressman Solomon P. Ortiz (D-Corpus Chris). After leaving the office, Fernando cofounded a Republican club at his high school as well as a political blog: Write for the Right. He then went on to co-organize a Tea Party protest in Brownsville. Fernando has been on talk radio shows in the Rio Grande Valley and on "Canto Talk" on Blog Talk Radio. In 2011, Governor Rick Perry appointed Fernando to a one-year term as a student regent of the Texas A&M University System. Although no longer a regent because his term expired, he has now been appointed to the Texas Guaranteed Student Loan Corporation's Board of Directors.

(Monkey Business Images/Shutterstock.com)

In the closest presidential election of modern times, Governor Bush defeated Democratic nominee Al Gore by four electoral votes (271 to 267) in 2000. After controversial recounts and protracted court battles over Florida's 25 electoral votes, George W. Bush was ultimately declared the victor in mid-December 2000 after a 5–4 ruling by the U.S. Supreme Court, a decision that fell along ideological lines. In the Lone Star State, Bush received 3,795,262 popular votes (59 percent) to Gore's 2,428,187 (38 percent), giving Bush Texas's 32 electoral votes. (Bush's election made lieutenant governor Rick Perry governor.) For the third straight election, all statewide Republican candidates won, including U.S. Senator Kay Bailey Hutchison, who became the first candidate in Texas history to receive more than four million votes. Democrats did not even have candidates in most statewide contests or in many local races. In fact, in 2000, the Libertarian Party and Green Party, minor parties with limited support among voters, each had more candidates for statewide office than did the Democratic Party. Of the nine statewide offices up for election in that year, the Democratic Party fielded candidates in only three contests. By contrast, the Libertarian Party ran candidates in seven of the nine races, and the Green Party had candidates in five.

As early as 2000, potential gubernatorial candidates began to solicit campaign contributions for the 2002 election. Governor Perry established the Century Council, whose members pledged to donate or raise $100,000 each for Perry's 2002 campaign.[15] Meanwhile, some Democrats encouraged Tony Sanchez, a Laredo businessman with a fortune of more than $600 million who had previously been a strong supporter of George W. Bush, to seek the office. Sanchez, a political newcomer, brought two major assets to the campaign: a Latino surname and an ability to fund more than $50 million from his own resources for the gubernatorial campaign.

Dallas mayor Ron Kirk, an African American, emerged as the Democratic Party's nominee for the U.S. Senate. To complete the Democratic lineup of candidates for the top three state offices, former comptroller John Sharp, an Anglo, was nominated for lieutenant governor.

Sanchez, Kirk, and Sharp were dubbed the "dream team," because of their expected appeal to Latino, African American, and Anglo voters. Texas Democrats ran with a full slate of candidates for other statewide offices and presented their strongest field of candidates in 20 years. Many political analysts believed that the multiracial Democratic ticket would significantly increase minority voter turnout and help Democrats reclaim several statewide offices. On election night, however, the dream quickly turned into a nightmare as the GOP swept all statewide races, including contests for seats on the state's highest courts. The anticipated increase in voter turnout to support Tony Sanchez, Ron Kirk, John Sharp, and other Democratic candidates never materialized. The 2002 election increased Republican control over the Texas Senate from a one-seat majority to a seven-seat majority (19 to 12). For the first time since Reconstruction, the GOP gained control of the Texas House of Representatives, winning 88 of 150 seats. The stage was set to elect a Republican speaker of the Texas House in the 78th regular legislative session in January 2003.

| **Table 4.1** | Number of Selected Republican Officeholders, 1974–2012 |

Year	U.S. Senate	Other Statewide Offices	U.S. House	Texas Senate	Texas House	S.B.O.E.*	Total
1974	1	0	2	3	16	—	22
1976	1	0	2	3	19	—	25
1978	1	1	4	4	22	—	32
1980	1	1	5	7	35	—	49
1982	1	0	5	5	36	—	47
1984	1	0	10	6	52	—	69
1986	1	1	10	6	56	—	74
1988	1	5	8	8	57	5	84
1990	1	6	8	8	57	5	85
1992	1	8	9	13	58	5	94
1994	2	13	11	14	61	8	109
1996	2	18	13	17	68	9	127
1998	2	27	13	16	72	9	137
2000	2	27	13	16	72	10	140
2002	2	27	15	19	88	10	161
2004	2	27	21	19	87	10	166**
2006	2	27	21	20	79	10	159***
2008	2	27	20	19	77	10	155***
2010	2	27	20	19	77	10	155***
2012	2	27	23	19	101	10	182***

*State Board of Education.
**Data for 1974–2004 reprinted by permission of the Republican Party of Texas.
***Data for 2006–2012 were compiled by the authors.

Because of redistricting efforts orchestrated by then-majority leader of the U.S. House of Representatives, Tom DeLay, the Texas congressional delegation has been majority Republican since 2004. In addition to gaining a majority of Texas congressional seats in the 2004 general election (21 of 32 positions), Republicans won all statewide elections, maintained control of the Texas Senate and the Texas House, and picked up approximately 200 more county- and district-level offices. Benefiting many of the Republican candidates was the fact that at the top of the ballot, President Bush carried the state with more than 61 percent of the popular vote, compared with Senator John Kerry's 38 percent. Inevitably, Republican candidates down the ballot were assisted by the president's coattails.

In 2006, Democrats fielded candidates in only nine of 15 statewide races. All lost; however, Democrats won all countywide races in Dallas County (a Republican stronghold throughout the 1980s and 1990s) and narrowed the margin of Republican control in Harris County. In the gubernatorial election, Republican incumbent Rick Perry defeated Democratic challenger Chris Bell by 1,716,792 votes to 1,310,337 votes. Due, in part, to the strength of independent candidates Carole Keeton Strayhorn and Richard S. "Kinky" Friedman, Perry became the first gubernatorial candidate of a political party to be elected with less than 40 percent of the vote (39.02 percent). In 1861, following Texas' secession from the union, F. R. Lubbock, was elected governor with 38.05 percent of the vote.

In the presidential election of 2008, Barack Obama became the second Democratic presidential candidate in history to be elected without carrying Texas. Republican nominee John McCain carried the state with almost one million more popular votes than Obama (4,479,328 to 3,528,633). Although Obama did not carry the state, Democrats could point to gains in several areas. The 2008 election marked the first presidential election in more than a quarter of a century in which the Democratic nominee carried at least four of the state's five most populous counties (see Figure 4.2). One reason Obama fared so well in these counties was the support he received from Latino and African American voters. Democratic candidates also won a majority of countywide offices in Harris County for the first time in more than 20 years. In addition, for the third straight general election cycle, Democrats gained seats in the Texas House of Representatives. In 2012, Obama was reelected president without carrying Texas. Challenger Mitt Romney defeated Barack Obama by more than one million popular votes in the Lone Star State (4,555,857 to 3,294,482). However, again Democrats could point to gains in the Texas legislature having picked up seven seats in the Texas House of Representatives.

In the 2010 Republican primary, U.S. Senator Kay Bailey Hutchison challenged incumbent Rick Perry for the gubernatorial nomination. In her two most recent contests (2000 and 2006), she had led all candidates on the ballot

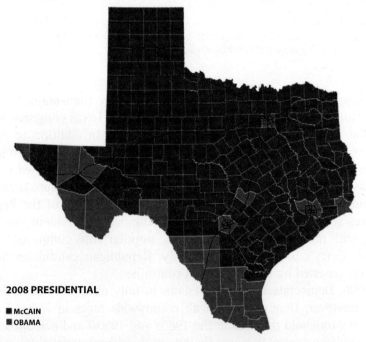

2008 PRESIDENTIAL

■ McCAIN
■ OBAMA

Figure 4.2   Texas counties that Obama won in 2008 presidential election

© The Texas Tribune

in votes received. Several polls in 2009 showed Hutchison with a 20-point lead over Perry. During an often bitter and contentious primary campaign, however, Perry effectively portrayed her as a "Washington insider" on the basis of her 17 years of experience in the U.S. Senate. Drawing upon the anti-Washington sentiment that was pervasive among Republican voters that year, Perry erased any lead that Hutchison had held in the polls and surged ahead of her by Election Day. Hutchison also failed to secure the support of the Republican base of voters needed to unseat the incumbent governor in the primary.

Another factor benefiting Perry was the candidacy of a former Republican county chairperson and a Tea Party activist, Debra Medina. Although several political observers expected Medina's presence to force a runoff between Perry and Hutchison, it had the unanticipated effect of allowing the governor to portray himself as a centrist candidate. In the Republican primary, Perry received 51 percent, Hutchison received 30 percent, and Medina received 19 percent. The primary results confirmed Perry's presence as a national figure in Republican politics. In the weeks immediately after his primary victory, he made speeches to national gatherings of Republicans. This activity fueled speculation that Perry aspired to be the Republican nominee for the presidency in 2012, a goal he initially denied.[16] Hutchison chose to remain in the U.S. Senate after losing the gubernatorial primary contest; but in January 2012 she announced that she would not seek reelection in November of that year.

Perry's victory in the 2010 Republican primary set up a showdown with popular three-term Houston mayor and former Texas Democratic Party chair, Bill White. Many believed White to be the most viable Democratic gubernatorial nominee since Ann Richards in 1990. In the general election, however, White lost to Perry, receiving 42 percent of the vote to Perry's 55 percent of the vote. Following his reelection to an unprecedented third term, Perry embarked on a national tour promoting his book, *Fed Up! Our Fight to Save America from Washington*, further confirming the belief that he intended to seek higher office.

Texas GOP gubernatorial candidates Texas governor Rick Perry, U.S. senator Kay Bailey Hutchison, and Debra Medina are seen during a debate at the WFAA Channel 8 studios in downtown Dallas in January 2010.

(AP Photo/Louis DeLuca, Pool)

In 2010, Republican candidates were once again elected to all statewide offices and gained three additional seats in the Texas delegation to the U.S. House of Representatives, with 23 Republicans and nine Democrats elected. The Republican Party continued to maintain its majority in the Texas Senate (19 Republicans to 12 Democrats) and extended its majority in the Texas House of Representatives, winning 99 seats (to the Democrats' 51 seats). The Republican Party increased its membership in the Texas House of Representatives to 101 when Democratic state representatives Allan Ritter (Nederland) and Aaron Peña (Edinburg) switched to the Republican Party in late 2010, after the November election. With more than two-thirds of the membership in the Texas House of Representatives, Republicans enjoyed a "supermajority" for the first time since Reconstruction. Supermajority status allowed the Republican Party to regularly suspend the rules of the Texas House of Representatives and push a legislative agenda though the 2011 session, with limited opposition from the Democratic Party.

Following the 2012 general election, the Republican Party remained firmly in control of all three branches of government. Although it lost its "supermajority" status in the Texas House of Representatives, providing Democrats with more input on proposed legislation, the Republican Party still held 95 (out of 150) seats in the House, 19 (out of 31) seats in the Senate, and all statewide offices.

 Learning Check 4.3 (Answers on p. 163)

1. True or False: In 2008, Democratic presidential candidate Barack Obama received the majority of popular votes in four of Texas's five largest (or urban) counties.
2. What has been the impact of Latino and African American support in urban counties?

★ # Electoral Trends

LO4

During the past 30 years, competition between Texas's Democratic and Republican parties has brought more women, Latinos, and African Americans into the state's political system. As a result, party politics has become more competitive and more nationalized. Compared with the politics of earlier years, Texas politics today is more partisan (party centered). However, both the Democratic and the Republican parties experience internal feuding (factionalism) among competing groups.

Some political scientists interpret recent polling and election results as evidence of a **dealignment** of Texas voters. These scholars explain that the large percentage of Texans who claim to be independent voters have no allegiance to a political party. Nonetheless, many self-identified independent voters tend to vote for Republican candidates. Other political scientists assert that the rising tide of Republican electoral victories throughout the 1990s and into the 21ˢᵗ century demonstrates that many Texans, who were

dealignment
Occurs when citizens have no allegiance to a political party and become independent voters.

previously Democrats, have switched their political affiliation and loyalty to the Republican Party in a **realignment** of voters.

Republican candidates carried Texas in 12 of the 16 presidential elections between 1952 and 2012, including the last nine elections in that period. Republican candidates also won seven of nine gubernatorial elections between 1978 and 2010. As the GOP's dominance of statewide elections increased, so did intraparty competition, just as occurred for the Democrats before them. Texas GOP strongholds are in West Texas; the Panhandle–South Plains; some small towns and rural areas in East Texas; and the suburbs of Dallas, Fort Worth, Houston, San Antonio, and Austin. With the exception of Democratic El Paso, West Texas Republicanism is predominant from the Permian Basin (Midland–Odessa) through the Davis Mountains and the German Hill Country. This West Texas region, like the Panhandle–South Plains area to the north, is populated primarily by conservative farmers and ranchers, as well as people connected with the oil and gas industry in Midland–Odessa and other parts of the Permian Basin.

Although the Democratic Party has been unsuccessful in statewide election contests in recent years, it still controls many county offices. Democratic voting strength is concentrated in El Paso, South Texas, parts of East Texas, the Golden Triangle (Beaumont, Port Arthur, and Orange), portions of the diverse Central Texas region, and the lower-income neighborhoods of larger cities. **Straight-ticket voting** for all Democratic candidates on the general election ballot has declined, however, as fewer Texans (especially those in rural East Texas) choose to remain "yellow-dog Democrats." This term has been applied to people whose party loyalty is said to be so strong that they would vote for a yellow dog if it were a Democratic candidate for public office. Due to changing demographic patterns in the urban areas, Democrats remain optimistic about their long-term chances of regaining a position of prominence in Texas politics. As discussed in Chapter 1 ("The Environment of Texas Politics"), Latinos are increasing in population and, as a result, political influence. A poll conducted by Univision/ABC/Latino Decisions in December of 2011 showed that 64 percent of the Latino voters in Texas believed that Republicans "don't care" about them or are "hostile" toward them. This figure, however, was lower than the national average of 73 percent Latinos who expressed this view. Republican platform positions on such issues as immigration and bilingual education, as well as primary losses by incumbents Texas Railroad Commissioner Victor Carrillo and State District Judge Rueben Gonzalez, Jr. in 2010, have in large part fueled this view.

Republican expansion has diminished the intensity of factional politics within the Democratic Party. Nevertheless, Democrats are divided by many interests and issues, and factionalism within Republican ranks has increased.

Third Parties

Americans commonly apply the term **third party** (or minor party) to any political party other than the Democratic or Republican party. Both in the United States and in Texas, third parties have never enjoyed the same

realignment
Occurs when members of one party shift their affiliation to another party.

straight-ticket voting
Voting for all the candidates of one party.

third party
A party other than the Democratic Party or the Republican Party. Sometimes called a "minor party" because of limited membership and voter support.

CourseReader ASSIGNMENTS

Log in to www.cengagebrain.com and open CourseReader to access the reading:

Democrats Messing with Texas
Reid Wilson

At one time, the Democratic Party was the dominant party in the state of Texas. From Reconstruction until the 1980s, the Republican Party struggled to make inroads in a system that was rigged in the ruling party's favor. The white primary and poll taxes were used to effectively bar opposition at the ballot box. That same party, however, has now been tossed from power; they play little if any significant role in the state's legislative process and have been unable to muster enough votes to win a single statewide office since the election of Ann Richards in 1990. The rapidly increasing Latino population, combined with increasing levels of turnout among registered Latino voters, presents challenges for both the current Republican majorities in both legislative chambers and the Democratic Party organizations that are working to guarantee that those new voters go blue. For both parties, the opportunities are ignored at their peril, as this article shows.

1. How has the Texas Democratic Party fared over the last 30 years in electing candidates to office?

2. What demographic changes does the Texas Democratic Party point to as a sign of hope for future electoral success? What challenges does this changing demographic pose to electoral success?

success as the two principal parties. A major party's success is measured by its ability to win elections. By this measure, minor parties are unsuccessful. Instead, third parties' successes can be better measured by their ability to make the public aware of their issues, persuade the major parties to adopt those issues, and/or force the major parties to bring those issues into a coalition. When judged by these measures, third parties in Texas have enjoyed modest success.

During the 1890s, the Populist Party successfully promoted agricultural issues and displaced the Republicans as the "second" party in Texas.[17] In the 1970s, La Raza Unida elected a few candidates to local offices in South Texas (principally Crystal City, Zavala County, and school board offices) and forced the Democratic Party to begin to address Latino concerns. In the 1990s, Ross Perot's Reform Party had organizations in many areas in the state. During the past 30 years, the Libertarian Party (a party that advocates minimizing government involvement at all levels, while maximizing individual freedom and rights) has nominated candidates for national, state, and local offices throughout Texas. In 1988, the Libertarian Party nominated Texas congressman and long-time advocate of limited government Ron Paul for president. When Paul ran for president in 2008 and 2012, he maintained his advocacy of limited government. In his past two presidential campaigns,

Texas governor Rick Perry and U.S. congressman Ron Paul of Texas are shown participating in CNBC's "Your Money, Your Vote" Republican presidential debate in November 2011. The two candidates vowed to reduce the size and scope of government, if elected. When Perry couldn't recall the third of three agencies that he would abolish as president, Paul told him that it should be five.

(AP Photo/Paul Sancya, File)

however, he did so as a candidate for the Republican nomination. (For a detailed discussion of Ron Paul's political career and ideological views, see this chapter's selected reading, "The Swan Song of Ron"). As of mid-2012, eight Libertarians held local elective offices in the Lone Star State.

Other parties have nominated candidates and increased public awareness of their issues: the Greenback Party (late 19th century), the Prohibition Party (late 19th and early 20th centuries), the Socialist and Socialist Labor parties (early 20th century), the Progressive Party (early to mid-20th century), and the Green Party (late 20th century to early 21st century). The Green Party has advocated environmental protection and government reform policies. In 2000, Green Party presidential candidate Ralph Nader received 2.2 percent of the popular vote in Texas. In 2002, the Green Party fielded candidates for U.S. senator, governor, lieutenant governor, attorney general, comptroller, land commissioner, agriculture commissioner, railroad commissioner, and several statewide judgeships and congressional seats. However, Green candidates (like Libertarians) won no elections and rarely received more than 3 percent of the vote. In 2010, with a gubernatorial nominee for the first time in eight years, a Green Party candidate was on the general election ballot in Texas. The Green Party candidate for governor, however, received less than 0.4 percent of the vote.

Independents

The term **independent** applies to candidates who have no party affiliation. Their success is less likely, because they usually lack a ready-made campaign organization and fundraising abilities. In addition, they have difficulty in gaining ballot access. For instance, the Texas Election Code

independent candidate
A candidate who runs in a general election without party endorsement or selection.

requires independent candidates to file by gathering signatures on a petition. The number of signatures required for a statewide office is "one percent of the total vote received by all candidates for governor in the most recent gubernatorial general election."[18] Based on this criteria, to qualify for statewide ballot access in 2012, an independent candidate was required to gather 49,798 signatures from registered voters who had not voted in either the Democratic or Republican primary elections or the primary runoff elections and who had not signed another candidate's petition for that office that year.

In 2006, two candidates declared themselves independents and "threw their hats into the ring" for governor: Carole Keeton Strayhorn and Richard S. "Kinky" Friedman. Strayhorn had long been active in leadership roles in Republican politics. An extremely popular politician, Strayhorn capitalized on her self-promoted reputation as "one tough grandma." With almost 10 years of experience in statewide elected offices, she emerged as a competitor with Governor Rick Perry for the Republican gubernatorial nomination in 2006. Strayhorn positioned herself as a leading critic of the governor within his party. However, after internal polls showed that Strayhorn would be competitive with Perry in a general election but not in the Republican primary, Strayhorn announced in early January 2006 that she would seek the office of governor as an independent. In her announcement, she invoked the rugged individualism of Sam Houston, the last independent candidate to be elected governor of Texas. Strayhorn's image, political organization, and ability to raise funds provided her with resources most independent candidates lack. Even with these resources, her election experience was the same as most independent candidates: she lost.

How Do We Compare...Which Party Controls the Statehouses in 2013?

Most Populous U.S. States	Governor/Senate/House	U.S. States Bordering Texas	Governor/Senate/House
California	Democrat/Democrat/Democrat	Arkansas	Democrat/Republican/Republican
Florida	Republican/Republican/Republican	Louisiana	Republican/Republican/Republican
New York	Democrat/Democrat/Democrat	New Mexico	Republican/Democrat/Democrat
Texas	**Republican/Republican/Republican**	Oklahoma	Republican/Republican/Republican

Source: **http://www.ncsl.org/legislatures-elections/elections/statevote-2012-election-night-results-map.aspx.**

Points to Ponder

- The origin of the phrase "to throw one's hat into the ring" is from an English idiom. In the days of fairground boxing competitions (when most men wore hats), the public was invited to try their skills against resident boxers. Those wishing to participate would throw their hats into the ring for all to see their willingness to compete. Since the competitor was without a hat, he could easily be identified as he made his way to the ring.
- The term was later adapted to those declaring their political candidacy when former president Theodore Roosevelt entered the presidential campaign of 1912 as an independent.

In 2005 songwriter, author, and humorist Richard S. "Kinky" Friedman ran for governor as an independent. Since the 1970s, Friedman, best known for his band, Kinky Friedman and the Texas Jewboys, and songs like "They Ain't Makin' Jews Like Jesus Anymore," had developed a cult following. After declaring his candidacy, he was profiled nationally on programs such as *60 Minutes* and *CBS Sunday Morning,* and he frequently appeared as a guest on national political talk shows, such as *Imus in the Morning* and *Real Time with Bill Maher.* Friedman's unorthodox campaign included selling Kinky Friedman action figures as a fundraiser and the announcement that musician Willie Nelson would serve as his "Texas Energy Czar." Nelson—an advocate of biodiesel, a diesel fuel substitute made from soybean oil and other natural fats and vegetable oils had established several BioWillie stations to sell clean-burning, American-made fuel.

In the general election, Strayhorn received slightly more than 18 percent of the vote, and Friedman garnered a little more than 14 percent. In 2010, Friedman ran for the position of Texas Agriculture Commissioner; this time he filed as a candidate in the Democratic primary. He received less than 48 percent of the vote, however, and lost the nomination to Hank Gilbert.

☑ Learning Check 4.4 (Answers on p. 163)

1. Who was the last independent candidate to be elected governor of Texas?
2. True or False: Third parties' success comes more often in the form of their ability to make the public aware of the issues than in the number of their candidates elected to office.

Conclusion

Historically, Texas politics has been characterized by prolonged periods of one-party domination—first the Democrats and later the Republicans. With changing demographic patterns, however, the nature of partisan politics in Texas and the struggle for control of public office by political parties continue to evolve. Shifts in voting alignments will change how both parties develop campaign strategies and target groups of voters.

Chapter Summary

- Political parties perform two functions: administering party primaries and conducting party conventions. These are activities of a party's temporary organization. The permanent party organization includes autonomous executive committees at the local, state, and national levels that direct party activities.
- Texas voters and political parties represent various political ideologies, including conservatism and liberalism. The two major political parties are Republican and Democratic. Minor, or third, parties also often appear on general election ballots.
- Historically, Texas was a one-party state, dominated by the Democratic Party following Reconstruction through the 1960s. Beginning in the 1970s and 1980s, the state moved toward a competitive two-party structure. In the 1990s and into the 21st century, however, it appears that the state has become a one-party state again, with the Republican Party in control.
- A shift in the Lone Star State's demographics may likewise be reflected in a strengthening of the Democratic Party.
- Recent elections reflect two major trends: the Republican Party now dominates statewide electoral contests, and Democratic Party candidates are successful only in some district and local races.

Key Terms

political party, p. 134
stratarchy, p. 134
temporary party organization, p. 136
platform, p. 136
precinct convention, p. 137
county convention, p. 138
district convention, p. 138
state convention, p. 138
presidential preference primary, p. 139
caucus, p. 139
superdelegate, p. 139
permanent party organization, p. 140
precinct chair, p. 140
county executive committee, p. 141
county chair, p. 141
district executive committee, p. 141
state executive committee, p. 141
conservative, p. 143
neoconservatism, p. 144
liberal, p. 144
neoliberal, p. 144
dealignment, p. 156
realignment, p. 157
straight-ticket voting, p. 157
third party, p. 157
independent candidate, p. 159

Learning Check Answers

4.1

1. The role of the permanent party organization is to recruit candidates, devise strategies, raise funds, distribute candidate literature and information, register voters, and turn out voters on Election Day. The temporary party organization consists of primaries and conventions in which members of the major political parties select candidates for public office.
2. True. Although the state chair presides over the party's permanent organization at the state level, he or she is selected by delegates to the party's state convention, which is its temporary organization at the state level.

4.2

1. Conservatives are generally opposed to government-managed or government-subsidized programs, whereas neoconservatives allow for a limited governmental role in solving social problems.
2. False. Many Texas Democrats have a neoliberal ideology that incorporates a philosophy of less government regulation of business and the economy, while adopting a more liberal view of greater government involvement in social programs.

4.3

1. True. In 2008, Obama won the majority of the popular vote in Bexar (San Antonio), Dallas (Dallas), Harris (Houston), and Travis (Austin) counties.
2. One reason Democratic candidates are faring better, especially in urban counties, is the support received from Latino and African American voters.

4.4

1. Sam Houston was the last independent candidate to be elected governor of Texas.
2. True. Rather than judging their success on the basis of elections won, third parties' success can be better measured by their ability to make the public aware of the issues, persuade the major parties to adopt those issues, and/or force the major parties to bring those issues into a coalition.

Discussion Questions

1. How has Texas's political culture in the past been reflected in the development of the state's political parties? How is it reflected today?
2. In what ways does the structure of political parties in Texas encourage participation in partisan politics? In what ways does it discourage participation?
3. What challenges face the Democratic Party in Texas in the 21st century? What challenges face the state's Republican Party in the 21st century?
4. Can third parties be successful in Texas? How?

Internet Resources

Green Party of Texas:
http://www.txgreens.org

Independent Conservative Republicans of
Texas: **http://www.icrepublicans.com**

Independent Texans:
http://www.independenttexans.org

Texas Democratic Party:
http://www.txdemocrats.org

Texas Libertarian Party:
http://lptexas.org

Texas Reform Party:
http://www.texasreformparty.org

Texas Republican Party:
http://www.texasgop.org

Texas Tea Party Patriots:
**http://teapartypatriots.org/
groups?escape=LOCAL&s=TEXAS**

Texas Young Republican Federation:
http://texasyoungrepublicans.com

Texas Young Democrats:
http://www.texasyds.com

Notes

1. Samuel J. Eldersveld and Hanes Walton Jr., *Political Parties in American Society,* 2nd ed. (New York: Palgrave Macmillan, 2000), 125–126.
2. "Texas Delegate Selection Plan: For the 2012 Democratic National Convention," Texas Democratic Party, February 2012, http://www.dallasdemocrats.org/sites/default/files/TX_Delegate_Selection_Plan_%28Revised%29.pdf.
3. "Proposed Temporary and Emergency Changes to RPT [Republican Party of Texas] Rules," Texas Republican Party," adopted February 29, 2012, http://s3.amazonaws.com/texasgop_pre/assets/original/2012-Rules-FINAL.pdf.
4. "Fact Sheet: Texas County/Senate District Conventions," http://lonestarproject.net/Permalink/2008-04-09.html.
5. For 2012 ballot propositions and voting data, see Office of the Secretary of State, "Election Night Returns" at http://elections.sos.state.tx.us/elchist.exe.
6. For example, in June 2010, almost 200 members of the Libertarian Party of Texas met to nominate Houston attorney Kathie Glass as their gubernatorial candidate. "Libertarian Party of Texas Holds Convention, Nominates Glass for Governor," *Independent Political Report,* June 15, 2010, http://www.independentpoliticalreport.com/2010/06/libertarian-party-of-texas-holds-convention/.
7. Joe Holley, "State GOP Chief Tackles Party's Big Debt," *Houston Chronicle,* June 20, 2010.
8. For discussions of contemporary Texas conservatism, see Karl Rove, *Courage and Consequence: My Life as a Conservative in the Fight* (New York: Threshold, 2010); and Tom Pauken, *Bringing America Home* (Rockford, IL: Chronicles Press, 2010).
9. Quoted by W. Gardner Selby, "Rick Perry Says Kids Can't Openly Celebrate Christmas or Pray in School," *Austin American Statesman,* December 11, 2011.

10. Paul A. Gigot, "GOP's Clinton? George W. Bush Says No Way," *Wall Street Journal,* October 30, 1998.
11. Quoted by Evan Thomas and Arian Campo-Flores, "Don't Mess with Texas," *Newsweek,* April 28, 2010, 30.
12. For different views on Reconstruction in Texas, see Patrick G. Williams, *Beyond Redemption: Texas Democrats After Reconstruction* (College Station: Texas A&M University Press, 2007); Carl H. Moneyhon, *Texas After the Civil War: The Struggle of Reconstruction* (College Station: Texas A&M University Press, 2004); T. R. Fehrenbach, *Lone Star: A History of Texas and Texans* (New York: Macmillan, 1999); and Alwyn Barr, *Reconstruction to Reform: Texas Politics, 1876–1906* (Dallas: Southern Methodist University Press, 2000).
13. For an alternate view, see Carl Moneyhon, *Edmund J. Davis of Texas: Civil War General, Republican Leader, Reconstruction Governor* (Fort Worth: TCU Press, 2010).
14. See Gregg Cantrell, "A Host of Sturdy Patriots: The Texas Populists," in *The Texas Left: The Radical Roots of Lone Star Liberalism,* ed. David O'Donald Cullen and Kyle G. Wilkison (College Station: Texas A&M University Press, 2010), 53–73.
15. Wayne Slater, "Governor Lines Up Millions in Pledges," *Dallas Morning News,* February 25, 2001.
16. Evan Smith, "The Perry Doctrine," *Newsweek,* April 26, 2010, 31–32.
17. For more information on the Populist Party in Texas, see Alwyn Barr, *Reconstruction to Reform: Texas Politics, 1876–1906* (Dallas: Southern Methodist University Press, 2000).
18. Tex. Elec. Code Ann. §141.007 (2012).

The Swan Song of Ron: Searching for Meaning in What Is Likely to Be the Last Campaign Ron Paul Ever Runs

Nate Blakeslee

The 2012 Republican primary will most likely be Ron Paul's final run for office. This article, which appeared in the February 2012 issue of Texas Monthly Magazine, *explores Paul's campaign, his political views, and his long-term impact on politics. The full article may be accessed at http://www.texasmonthly.com/preview/2012-02-01/letterfromiowa.*

At 10:40 on the morning of the Iowa caucuses, Ron Paul entered the brightly lit gymnasium of Valley High School in West Des Moines surrounded by so many reporters thrusting so many recording devices into the airspace around his head that neither he nor his son Rand, the junior U.S. senator from Kentucky, could see the stage in the center of the gym's sparkling parquet floor. As the cluster gradually advanced, amoeba-like, the director of MTV's Rock the Vote, which was hosting the event, introduced Paul to an audience of perhaps five hundred juniors and seniors, which is to say all of Valley High's new or soon-to-be-eligible voters. It was a good crowd. Michele Bachmann, who opened the morning's program, had been greeted enthusiastically ("Who here wants to make a lot of money?" she shouted), while Mitt Romney's four tall, handsome sons garnered polite attention. But when Paul finally reached the microphone, the applause was thunderous and sustained.

Paul, who is 76 and finally beginning to look a bit frail after some 35 years as a standard-bearer for the libertarian wing of the Republican Party,

quickly turned philosophical, musing about his recent surge in popularity with the millennial generation. "I don't know the exact reason for it," he told the students. "I defend the Constitution constantly in Washington, and that's very appealing to young people. Sometimes the two parties mesh together, and it's not too infrequent that I feel obligated to vote by myself. And when [young people] see that, they say, 'He won't go back and forth and will always stick to principle.'"

Paul has run for president twice before and has given a version of this same speech hundreds of times in his career, but he had never enjoyed a moment quite like this crisp January morning in West Des Moines. After decades spent in the political wilderness, he was polling dead even with fellow front-runners Romney and Rick Santorum in the first nominating contest of a wide-open Republican primary season. He was far ahead of his much-better-known fellow Texan, Rick Perry, despite the millions the governor had spent in Iowa, and was also sure to beat a resurgent Newt Gingrich. Even if he didn't win the caucus outright, Paul had a top-three spot locked up, which meant that the media, never quite sure what to make of Paul, were finally treating him with respect. A growing chorus of pundits on the cable news channels praised his prolific grassroots fundraising, his strong organization, and the loyalty and energy of his supporters, which he seems to have in abundance in every state.

Having never truly ended his last campaign, and having clung tenaciously to the same contrarian ideas for decades, Paul has emerged as perhaps the most steadfast candidate in a field of constant flux. No moment was more emblematic of Paul's new stature than the spectacle of the former pariah taking pity on Perry during the governor's own debate nightmare, in November, when he inexplicably forgot the name of one of the three federal bureaucracies he had just promised to shutter if he reached the Oval Office. As Perry flailed and floundered, Paul, standing just to Perry's left, gamely tried to fill the awkward silence. "It's not three, it's five," he quipped, referring to his own plan to cut $1 trillion from the federal budget. Alas, there was no saving Perry, nor was there any escaping the takeaway from his disastrous evening: the ideas underlying his campaign would be much easier for him to remember if they were his own.

This is a problem that Ron Paul has never had to worry about. His political philosophy has not changed since his first term in Congress, in 1976. In fact, many of the ideas in Perry's anti-government manifesto *Fed Up!*—such as the possibility of eliminating huge portions of the federal government—seem to have been cribbed from Paul's voluminous writings. When Perry questions the constitutionality of Social Security and the federal income tax, he is channeling vintage Paul. That Perry would embrace such radical notions speaks volumes about how Paul has managed to climb up from the lower rungs of the conservative caste system over the past four years. There is no question that independent voters and more and more Republicans have moved closer to his position on the wars in Iraq and Afghanistan. A profound global recession, meanwhile, has put the nation's precarious balance sheet at the top of the agenda, making Paul seem like a prophet to his longtime followers, and to those new to his message, someone worth at least a listen. Ron Paul's moment, it seems, has finally arrived. The mountain has come to Mohammed.

Or so it seemed on the morning of the Iowa caucuses. Paul remains, and likely will remain, an outlier in the GOP field, but his idiosyncrasies have become strengths. A good part of his appeal is that he is so fundamentally unlike any of his fellow aspirants. This is why Paul's negative ad castigating Gingrich as an unprincipled opportunist was so devastatingly effective and did so much to take the wind out of the onetime front-runner's sails in Iowa. It had the obvious advantage of being true, but it would have rung hollow coming from a more polished figure like Romney, who can pander with the best of them. Likewise, there was something poetic about Paul's dismissal of Donald Trump's preposterous effort to host his own primary debate. "I don't understand the marching to his office," Paul told CNN. "I didn't know that he had the ability to lay on hands." Everyone knows that Trump is a pompous ass, but this sounds a lot better coming from somebody who looks like Jack Sprat, sounds like Jimmy Stewart, and publishes a combination cookbook and family album as campaign literature.

Truth be told, Paul is not a very good politician—not if your definition of political success includes realizing your public policy goals. Nothing about Paul suggests that he would, if he did somehow win the nomination, become another Ronald Reagan, the beneficiary of the last wave of right-wing populist anger that swept the country, in the late seventies. Paul doesn't have the natural leadership skills to take the reins of government and steer the nation in a new direction. But his hard-core backers don't want another Reagan, who, for all his talk about the perils of "big government," oversaw enormous increases in deficit spending, mostly for the military, and added more layers of federal bureaucracy than he cut. Paul occupies that space where the libertarian right curves around and meets the anti-corporate, anti-authoritarian left. The "liberty" movement is a diffuse one, and Paul is not always careful about whom he associates with or what causes he lends his name to—a shortcoming that cost him votes when a batch of offensive quotes from his old newsletters, apparently ghost-written by someone else, resurfaced yet again during the stretch run in Iowa. But Paul's apparent inclusiveness is also his strength. His people are just as likely to be found at Tea Party events as they are at Occupy Wall Street encampments, and their loyalty to his ideas may be Paul's lasting contribution to the politics of the moment.

His long-term impact is hard to judge. Paul's moment in the sun has coincided with a time of national crisis, and a crisis—so long as it lasts—is a great time to be a demagogue. Ron Paul is not that, exactly, but he is undeniably a fundamentalist: a man who sees every question in black and white, with little room for nuance and compromise. His bible is a doctrine laid down more than sixty years ago by an Austrian economist named Ludwig von Mises, who argued, in essence, that every government intervention in the market is bad and that more government inevitably means less freedom. This philosophy underlies every decision Paul makes. It is the source of his breathtaking adherence to principle, but it is also the reason his legacy as a lawmaker will be so limited. Policymaking is a messy process, especially in tumultuous times, and often requires even principled public officials to choose between two undesirable alternatives. Paul decided a long time ago that this was not his way.

But as a catalyst for change, Paul's legacy may be more lasting. His willingness to gore the sacred cows of the Republican Party, while managing to grow his base of support, has demonstrated that there is room for change in some of the party's hidebound positions. And he also has lessons for Democrats, if they're willing to listen, about the power of ideas and principles in organizing young people. Of course, Paul has another, much more tangible legacy, as a supporter I talked to on caucus day reminded me. Nick Sinclair, just sixteen, told me his biggest regret was that he'd never get a chance to vote for Ron Paul for president. But then he brightened. "Rand Paul," he said. "Rand Paul will pick up where he left off."

For further resources, please visit **www.cengagebrain.com**.

Campaigns and Elections

Most powerful person in the Free World...

VOTER

ick Anderson of the Houston Chronicle, dist. by The Washington Post Writers Group. Reprinted with Permission.)

Learning Objectives

1. Analyze the components of a political campaign, specifically how the process of running and financing a campaign has changed over the years.
2. Describe the role that race and ethnicity play in politics, focusing on the importance of minority voters.
3. Explain the complexities of voting and how the voting process promotes, and inhibits, voter participation.
4. Identify the differences between primary, general, and special elections.

The fundamental principle on which every representative democracy is based is citizen participation in the political process. As Nick Anderson's cartoon depicts, voters are considered to be the most powerful people in the free world. Yet, in Texas, even as the right to vote was extended to almost every citizen 18 years of age or older, participation declined throughout the 20th century's final decades and into the 21st century. This chapter focuses on campaigns and the role that media and money play in our electoral system. Citizen participation through elections and the impact of that participation are additional subjects of our study.

Political Campaigns

LO1 Elections in Texas allow voters to choose officials to fill national, state, county, city, and special-district offices. With so many electoral contests, citizens are frequently besieged by candidates seeking votes and asking for money to finance election campaigns. The democratic election process, however, gives Texans an opportunity to influence public policymaking by expressing preferences for candidates and issues when they vote.

Conducting Campaigns in the 21st Century

Campaigns are no longer limited to speeches by candidates on a courthouse lawn or from the rear platform of a campaign train. Today, prospective voters are more likely to be harried by a barrage of campaign publicity involving television and radio broadcasting, newspapers, billboards, yard signs, and bumper stickers. Moreover, voters will probably encounter door-to-door canvassers, receive political information in the mail, be asked to answer telephone inquiries from professional pollsters or locally hired telephone-bank callers, receive campaign information by electronic mail, and be solicited for donations to pay for campaign expenses. In recent years, the Internet and the array of available social media tools have altered political campaigns in the state. Politicians set up Facebook pages inviting voters to befriend them. Other campaigners "tweet" their supporters on Twitter to announce important events and decisions. To the dismay of some politicians, YouTube videos provide a permanent record of misstatements and misdeeds. The private and public lives of candidates remain open 24/7 for review and comment.

Despite increasing technological access to information about candidates and issues, a minority of Texans, and indeed other Americans, are actively concerned with politics. To most voters, however, character and political style have become more important than issues. A candidate's physical appearance and personality are increasingly important, because television has become the primary mode of campaign communication.

Importance of the Media Since the days of W. Lee "Pappy" O'Daniel, the media have played an important role in Texas politics. In the 1930s, O'Daniel gained fame as a radio host for Light Crust Flour and later his own Hillbilly

CourseReader ASSIGNMENTS

Log in to www.cengagebrain.com and open CourseReader to access the reading:

Barnstorming for a More Constructive Brand of Politics
Jeanne Claire van Ryzin

Politics is a difficult game. There are winners and losers, but the process is not pretty: lying, cheating, smoke and mirrors, not to mention the occasional legal violation. We are witnessing a decline in the public discourse about the often messy process of governing. It is important to differentiate between the words that the public uses to discuss the issues of the day and the process of developing policy to meet the demands of the public. In addition, a high level of discourse in the public domain holds the system to a higher, if seldom supervised, standard.

1. According to Congressman Leach, how has the media contributed to political incivility?

2. According to Congressman Leach, is there a generational aspect to the disintegrating civility in public discourse?

Flour Company. On his weekly broadcast show, the slogan "Pass the biscuits, Pappy" made O'Daniel a household name throughout the state. In 1938, urged by his radio fans, O'Daniel ran for governor and attracted huge crowds. With a platform featuring the Ten Commandments and the Golden Rule, he won the election by a landslide.[1] In an attempt to duplicate O'Daniel's feat, Kinky Friedman, a singer, author, and humorist with a cult following, ran unsuccessfully as an independent candidate for governor in 2006.

By the 1970s, television and radio ads had become a regular part of every gubernatorial and U.S. senatorial candidate's campaign budget. By the 1980s, candidates from the top of the ballot to the local city council and school board used radio to reach potential voters. Many "middle of the ballot" candidates have found television time to be cost-prohibitive, with the exception of smaller media markets and local cable providers. Today, with more than 13 million potential voters in 254 counties, Texas is, by necessity, a media state for political campaigning. To visit every county personally during a primary campaign, a candidate would need to go into four counties per day, five days a week, from the filing deadline in January to the March primary date (the usual date for party primaries). Such extensive travel would leave little time for speechmaking, fundraising, and other campaign activities. Although some candidates for statewide office in recent years have traveled to each county in the state, none won an election. Therefore, Texas campaigners must rely more heavily on television and radio exposure than do candidates in other states.

Most Texas voters learn about candidates through television commercials that range in length from 10 seconds for a **sound bite** (a brief statement

sound bite
A brief statement of a candidate's theme communicated by radio or television in a few seconds.

of a candidate's campaign theme) to a full minute. Television advertisements allow candidates to structure their messages carefully and avoid the risk of a possible misstatement that might occur in a political debate. Therefore, the more money a candidate's campaign has, the less interest the candidate has in debating an opponent. Usually, the candidate who is the underdog (the one who is behind in the polls) wants to debate.

Candidates also rely increasingly on the Internet to communicate with voters. The benefit of low cost must be balanced against problems unique to the medium of websites and email. Issues with using the Internet include limited access to and limited use of computers by the older voting population (over 60 years of age), consumer resistance to "spam" (electronic junk mail), "blogging" (creating web logs), hyperlinks to inappropriate websites, and "cybersquatting" (individuals other than the candidate purchasing domain names similar to the candidate's name and then selling the domain name to the highest bidder). In his 2010 general election campaign, Jim Prindle, a Libertarian, purchased rights to RalphHall.org in his bid to defeat U.S. representative Ralph Hall (R-Rockwall). This site rerouted viewers to Prindle's campaign site. Although he was unsuccessful in his bid to unseat the 15-term incumbent, Prindle said that he had "explored many strategies in marketing and campaigning to help bridge the advantage that incumbents share."[2]

Mudslide Campaigns Following gubernatorial candidate Ann Richards's victory over Jim Mattox in the Democratic runoff primary of April 1990, one journalist reported that Richards had "won by a mudslide." This expression suggests the reaction of many citizens who were disappointed, if not infuriated, by the candidates' generally low ethical level of campaigning and by their avoidance of critical public issues. Nevertheless, as character became more important as a voting consideration in the 1990s and early 21st century, negative campaigning became even more prominent.

The 2010 Republican gubernatorial primary became particularly acrimonious. Drawing upon anti-Washington sentiments within the Republican Party, governor Rick Perry ran the "bailout" commercial. The ad showed a clip of U.S. senator Kay Bailey Hutchison saying, "I could not give a blank check of $700 billion to anyone," followed by the narration, "Just one day later, Senator Hutchison bailed on Texans and voted for the $700 billion Wall Street bailout." The commercial ended with the narrator saying, "No surprise. For 17 years, she voted for billions in earmarks, spending, and more debt. Senator Hutchison: voting with Washington since 1993." Many Perry campaign staff members publicly referred to Hutchison as Kay "Bailout" Hutchison. Her campaign countered with the "cha-ching" ad, featuring Texas Department of Transportation (TxDOT) electronic billboards reading, "This is not a European road, yet Rick Perry tried to seize private land and toll existing roads so a foreign company could collect tolls too. A top Perry aide was the company's lobbyist before Perry gave them billions in TxDOT contracts. Cha-ching, cha-ching, cha-ching. Rick Perry: slippery conditions ahead."[3]

Points to Ponder

Musicians have long been associated with political campaigns in Texas.

- When W. Lee O'Daniel ran for the governorship in 1938, he used the Hillbilly Boys band to draw crowds to his campaign appearances. Bob Wills, the "King of Western Swing," was a member of one of O'Daniel's earlier bands, the Light Crust Doughboys.
- When country recording star and author Kinky Friedman ran for the governorship in 2006, he proposed music legend and Friedman supporter Willie Nelson to serve as Texas's "Energy Czar."
- In 2011, rockers Ted Nugent and Gene Simmons both used the social media site Twitter to "tweet" their support for Governor Perry's candidacy in the Republican presidential primary.

Campaign Reform

Concern over the shortcomings of American election campaigns has given rise to organized efforts toward improvement at all levels of government. Reformers range from single citizens to members of the U.S. Congress and large lobby groups. Reform issues include eliminating negative campaigning, increasing free media access for candidates, and regulating campaign finance.

Eliminating Negative Campaigning The Markle Commission on the Media and the Electorate has concluded that candidates, the media, consultants, and the electorate are all blameworthy for the increase in negative campaigns. Candidates and consultants, wishing to win at any cost, employ negative advertising and make exaggerated claims. The media emphasize poll results and the horserace appearance of a contest, rather than basic issues and candidate personalities that relate to leadership potential. Thus, voters must be the corrective force for reform. Because the bottom line of campaign reform involves educating citizens, however, little can be achieved quickly. In 2010, one study tested the effectiveness of "comparative" ads run during the Texas governor's race to see if they persuaded voters. The results showed that negative commercials influenced voters (especially undecided voters), drawing their preference away from the candidate being attacked.[4]

Increasing Free Media Access Certainly a candidate for statewide office in Texas cannot win without first communicating with a large percentage of the state's voting population. As noted previously, television is the most important, and the most expensive, communication tool. One group supporting media access reform is the Campaign Legal Center (http://www.campaignlegalcenter.org/). As long as paid media advertising is a necessary part of political campaigns and media outlets generate a significant source of revenue from political campaigns, fundraising will remain important in electoral success.

By the early 21st century, many political campaigns had begun using social networking resources to get their message out to a larger voter base. Twitter, Facebook, and MySpace became commonly used tools for candidates to reach potential voters. In 2008, Barack Obama used cell phone text messaging as one means of announcing his vice presidential selection (U.S. senator Joe Biden). That year, Obama also became the first presidential candidate to provide a free iPhone application (Obama '08). Users could get current updates about the campaign and network with other users. Using cell phones to relay campaign information also provided the Obama campaign with millions of cell phone numbers. These strategies became common practice in both the Obama and Romney presidential campaigns in 2012.

Campaign Finance

On more than one occasion, president Lyndon Johnson bluntly summarized the relationship between politics and finance: "Money makes the mare go." Although most political scientists would state this fact differently, it is obvious that candidates need money to pay the expenses of election campaigns. Texas's 1990 gubernatorial campaign established a record of $45 million spent on the primary and general election races combined, including more than $22 million by Midland oilman Clayton Williams. He narrowly lost to Ann Richards, who spent $12 million. The 1990 record, however, was shattered by the 2002 gubernatorial election. Tony Sanchez's and Rick Perry's campaigns spent a combined record of more than $95 million. Sanchez outspent Perry by more than two to one ($67 million to $28 million) in the race for governor. Despite his big spending, however, Sanchez lost by 20 percent.[5] Even though $95 million set a new record for spending in a Texas race, it ranks as only the fifth most expensive gubernatorial race. California's 2010 gubernatorial contest, which cost an estimated $250 million, ranks first, followed by New York's gubernatorial race in 2002 ($148 million) and California's gubernatorial races in 1998 ($130 million) and 2002 ($110 million).

Many Texans are qualified to hold public office, but relatively few can afford to pay their own campaign expenses (as gubernatorial candidates Clayton Williams and Tony Sanchez and lieutenant gubernatorial candidate David Dewhurst did). Others are unwilling to undertake fundraising drives designed to attract significant campaign contributions (unlike the fundraising appeals of George W. Bush in his gubernatorial and presidential campaigns and Rick Perry in his campaigns for lieutenant governor and governor).

Candidates need to raise large amounts of cash at local, state, and national levels. Successful Houston City Council candidates often require from $150,000 (for district races) to $250,000 (for at-large races), and mayoral candidates may need $2 million or more. In 2003, Houston businessman Bill White spent a record $8.6 million on his mayoral election, including

$2.2 million of his own money. Some individuals and **political action committees (PACs)**, or organizations created to collect and distribute contributions to political campaigns, donate because they agree with a candidate's position on the issues. The motivations of others, however, may be questionable. In return for their contributions, some donors receive access to elected officials. Many politicians and donors assert that access does not mean that donors gain control of officials' policymaking decisions. Yet others, such as former Texas House Speaker Pete Laney, attribute the decline in voter participation to a growing sense that average citizens have no voice in the political process because they cannot afford to make large financial donations to candidates.

Both federal and state laws have been enacted to regulate various aspects of campaign financing. Texas laws on the subject, however, are relatively weak and tend to emphasize reporting of contributions. Federal laws are more restrictive, featuring both reporting requirements and limits on contributions to a candidate's political campaign by individuals and PACs. In 1989, chicken magnate Lonnie "Bo" Pilgrim handed out $10,000 checks on the Texas Senate floor, leaving the "payable to" lines blank, as legislators debated reforming the state's workers' compensation laws. Many were surprised to find that Texas had no laws prohibiting such an action. Two years later, the Texas legislature passed laws prohibiting political contributions to members of the legislature while they are in session; and in 1993 Texas voters approved a constitutional amendment establishing the **Texas Ethics Commission**. Among its constitutional duties, this commission requires financial disclosure from public officials. Unlike the Federal Election Campaign Act, however, Texas has no laws that limit political contributions.

Further restricting the amount of money that can be contributed to campaigns is another area of possible reform. Efforts in this area, however, have been unsuccessful. In 2002, the U.S. Congress passed the long-awaited **Campaign Reform Act**, signed into law by President Bush. This federal law includes the following reforms:

- The prohibition of **soft money**
- An increase in the limits of individual **hard money** (or direct) contributions
- A restriction on corporations' and labor unions' ability to run "electioneering" ads that feature the names or likenesses of candidates close to election day[6]

Plaintiffs such as former Texas congressman Ron Paul (R-Clute) and others challenged the constitutionality of this act, claiming it was an unconstitutional restraint on freedom of speech. In a sharply divided decision, the U.S. Supreme Court upheld the constitutionality of the "soft money" ban in *McConnell v. FEC* 540 U.S. 93 (2003). Seven years later, however, in a 5–4 decision, the U.S. Supreme Court in *Citizens United v. Federal Election Commission* 558 U.S. 50 (2010) overturned a provision of the act that banned unlimited independent expenditures made by corporations, unions, and nonprofit organizations in federal elections. This decision was widely

political action committee (PAC)
An organizational device used by corporations, labor unions, and other organizations to raise money for campaign contributions.

Texas Ethics Commission
A state agency that enforces state standards for lobbyists and public officials, including registration of lobbyists and reporting of political campaign contributions.

Campaign Reform Act
Enacted by the U.S. Congress and signed by President George W. Bush in 2002, this law restricts donations of "soft money" and "hard money" for election campaigns, but its effect has been limited by federal court decisions.

soft money
Donations made to national political parties for federal election purposes.

hard money
Campaign money donated directly to candidates or political parties and restricted in amount by federal law.

criticized by Democrats and by some members of the Republican Party as judicial activism that would give corporations and unions unlimited power in federal elections. In his 2010 State of the Union address, President Obama admonished the Supreme Court, stating, "Last week, the Supreme Court reversed a century of law to open the floodgates for special interests, including foreign corporations, to spend without limit in our elections. Well, I don't think American elections should be bankrolled by America's most powerful interests, or worse, by foreign entities."

That same year, a nine-judge federal appeals court unanimously ruled in *SpeechNow.org v. Federal Election Commission* 599 F. 3rd 686 (2010) that campaign contribution limits by independent organizations that use the funds only for independent expenditures are unconstitutional. The U.S. Supreme Court refused to hear this case on appeal, upholding the lower court's decision. The decisions in these cases led to the creation of **super PACs**, which are independent expenditure-only committees that may raise unlimited sums of money from corporations, unions, nonprofit organizations, and individuals. They are then able to spend unlimited sums to openly support or oppose political candidates. Although they had been in existence for fewer than two years by mid-2012, 590 super PACs reported having raised more than $220 million, as well as spending more than $121 million on the 2012 presidential candidates. Some of the better-known, better-funded super PACs of the 2012 presidential election included "Priorities USA Action" (supporting Barack Obama), "Restore Our Future" (supporting Mitt Romney), "American Crossroads" (headed by Republican strategist Karl Rove), and "Make Us Great Again" (supporting Rick Perry). Founded by Perry's former chief of staff, Mike Toomey, "Make Us Great Again" contributors included Dallas businessman Harold Simmons, Dallas tax consultant Brint Ryan, Houston attorney Tony Buzbee, Dallas energy executive Kelcy Warren, and Midland energy executive Javaid Anwar. "Make Us Great Again" spent approximately $4 million on Perry's behalf. In a parody of campaign finance rules, comedian Stephen Colbert formed his own super PAC—"Americans for a Better Tomorrow, Tomorrow," also known as "Stephen Colbert's Super PAC."

The state's campaign finance laws have focused on making contributor information more easily available to citizens. Restrictions on the amount of donations apply only to some judicial candidates. Treasurers of campaign committees and candidates are required to file periodically with the Texas Ethics Commission. With limited exceptions, these reports must be filed electronically. Sworn statements list all contributions received and expenditures made during designated reporting intervals. Candidates who fail to file these reports are subject to a fine.

During the 78th regular session in 2003, the Texas legislature passed House Bill 1606, which Governor Perry later signed into law. Supported by such public interest groups as Common Cause Texas, Public Citizen, and Campaigns for People, this statute strengthens the Texas Ethics Commission, curbs conflicts of interest, and requires greater disclosure of campaign contributions. Specifically, the law requires officials of cities with a population of more than 100,000 and trustees of school districts with enrollments of

super PAC
Independent expenditure-only committees that may raise unlimited sums of money from corporations, unions, nonprofit organizations, and individuals.

5,000 or more to disclose the sources of their income, as well as the value of their stocks and their real estate holdings. In addition, candidates for state political offices must identify employers and occupations of people contributing $500 or more to their campaigns and publicly report "cash on hand." The measure also prohibits lawmakers from lobbying for clients before state agencies. "This bill eliminates several chronic ethics loopholes and gives the Ethics Commission some teeth," said Tom "Smitty" Smith, Texas director of Public Citizen, a government watchdog group. "It's a big step forward."[7]

In practice, however, both federal and state campaign finance laws have largely failed to cope with buying influence through transfers of money in the form of campaign contributions. It may well be that as long as campaigns are funded by private sources, they will remain inadequately regulated.

 Learning Check 5.1   (Answers on p. 204)

1. True or False: Most Texas voters learn about candidates through newspaper editorials.
2. Which state commission requires financial disclosure from public officials?

★ Racial and Ethnic Politics

Racial and ethnic factors are strong influences on Texas politics, and they shape political campaigns. Slightly more than half of Texas's total population is composed of Latinos (chiefly Mexican Americans) and African Americans. Politically, the state's historical ethnic and racial minorities wield enough voting strength to decide any statewide election and determine the outcomes of local contests in areas where their numbers are concentrated. Large majorities of Texas's African American and Latino voters participate in Democratic primaries and vote for Democratic candidates in general elections. However, increasing numbers of African Americans and Latinos claim to be politically independent and do not identify with either the Republican or the Democratic Party.

LO2

Latinos

Early in the 21st century, candidates for elective office in Texas, and most other parts of the United States, recognized the potential of the Latino vote. Most Anglo candidates use Spanish phrases in their speeches, advertise in Spanish-language media (television, radio, and newspapers), and voice their concern for issues important to the Latino community (such as bilingual education and immigration). In each presidential election since 2000, candidates from both major political parties included appearances in Latino communities and before national Latino organizations, such as the League of

United Latin American Citizens (LULAC) and the National Council of La Raza, as a part of their campaign strategy. Such appearances recognize the political clout of Latinos in the Republican and Democratic presidential primaries, as well as in the general election.

Although Mexican Americans played an important role in South Texas politics throughout the 20th century, not until the 1960s and early 1970s did they begin to have a major political impact at the state level. A central turning point was during the late 1960s with the creation of a third-party movement, La Raza Unida Party. Founded in 1969 by José Ángel Gutiérrez of Crystal City and others, La Raza Unida fielded numerous candidates at the local and state level and mobilized many Mexican Americans who had been politically inactive. It also attracted others who had identified with the Democratic Party but who had grown weary of the party's unresponsiveness to the needs and concerns of the Mexican American community. By the end of the 1970s, however, Raza Unida had disintegrated. According to Ruben Bonilla, former president of LULAC, the main reason Raza Unida did not survive as a meaningful voice for Texas's Mexican American population was "the maturity of the Democratic Party to accept Hispanics."

In the 1980s, Mexican American election strategy became more sophisticated as a new generation of college-educated Latinos sought public office and assumed leadership roles in political organizations. Among Latinos elected to statewide office over the past 30 years were Democrat Raul Gonzalez, Jr. (the first Latino elected to statewide office in Texas), who served on the Texas Supreme Court from 1984 until 1999; Democrat Dan Morales, the state's attorney general for two terms from 1991 through 1998; Republican Tony Garza, elected to the Texas Railroad Commission in 1998; and Republican David Medina, elected to the Texas Supreme Court in 2004. Although Latinos are more likely to vote for Democratic candidates, Republican candidates such as George W. Bush have succeeded in winning the support of many Latino voters. Successful GOP candidates emphasize family issues and target heavily Latino areas for campaign appearances and media advertising. Bush selected several Latinos for high-profile positions, most notably Texas secretary of state (Tony Garza) and Texas Supreme Court justice (Alberto Gonzales). Gonzales resigned from the supreme court in 2001 to become White House counsel to President Bush and then U.S. attorney general.

During his years as governor, Rick Perry has also appointed several Latinos to statewide office. In 2003, Governor Perry appointed Victor Carrillo to the Texas Railroad Commission. When Carrillo lost his bid for reelection in the 2010 Republican primary, he blamed his defeat by an unknown and underfinanced candidate on his Hispanic surname and its inability to attract support among Republican voters. Governor Perry has also appointed two Latino secretaries of state (Henry Cuellar in 2001, and Esperanza "Hope" Andrade in 2008), one Texas Supreme Court justice (Eva Guzman in 2009), and one judge to the Texas Court of Criminal Appeals (Elsa Alcala in 2011). Justice Guzman became the first Latina to win a statewide election in 2010.

Many members of the Democratic Party believe it is important to have Latino nominees for high-level statewide offices in order to attract Latino voters to the polls. They argue that since the majority of Latinos are more likely to support Democratic candidates, a higher voter turnout will elect more Democrats to office. In 2002, Laredo businessman Tony Sanchez, Jr. became the first Latino candidate nominated for governor by a major party in Texas. Challenged for the Democratic nomination by former Texas attorney general Dan Morales, on March 1, 2002, the two men held the first Spanish-language gubernatorial debate in U.S. history. Underscoring its strategy to attract more Latino voters, in 2012 the Democratic Party selected the first Latino chair of a major political party in Texas when it chose Gilberto Hinojosa to be its state chair. By early 2013, a substantial number of Latinos held elected office, including the following:

- Two statewide positions (one supreme court justice and one judge on the Court of Criminal Appeals)
- One U.S. senator
- Six U.S. representative seats in Texas's congressional delegation
- 40 legislative seats in the Texas legislature
- More than 2,100 of the remaining 5,200 elected positions in the state

Among the many issues, such as bilingual education and political representation, affecting the Latino community, none is more relevant than immigration reform. The Latino community's political impact was clear in the debate over immigration laws, when millions of Latinos in Texas took part in demonstrations or boycotts in early 2006. In addition, on May 1, 2010, an estimated 28,000 people participated in a May Day demonstration outside of Dallas City Hall, protesting Arizona's controversial immigration law that provides law enforcement with broad authority to inquire about the immigration status of anyone who is detained. A similar bill was defeated in the Texas legislature in 2011. Another piece of legislation, however, that would require people to prove U.S. citizenship or legal residence before they could get or renew their Texas driver's license passed and took effect in 2011.[8] As the Latino population continues to grow, how each party addresses the immigration issue will in large part determine the future of that party's support among Latino voters.

Unlike in the past, Democratic candidates can no longer assume they have Latino voter support in statewide electoral contests. Latinos' voting behavior indicates that they respond to candidates and issues, not to a particular political party. Although both national and state Republican Party platforms discourage bilingual education and urge stricter immigration controls, Republican candidates frequently do not endorse these positions. Often, successful Republican candidates actually distance themselves from their party, especially in the Latino community. For instance, during a Republican presidential candidate debate in 2011, Governor Perry drew criticism from his opponents by defending his support for a state law that allows some undocumented students, who graduated from a high school in Texas and are working toward legal status, to qualify for in-state tuition at Texas state colleges.[9]

The sheer size of the Latino population causes politicians to solicit their support, because Latino voters can represent the margin of victory for a successful candidate. Lower levels of political activity than the population at

Dallas City Hall protest against Arizona's new crackdown on illegal immigrants.

(© Michael Ainsworth/ DMN)

large, however, both in registering to vote and in voting, limit an even greater impact of the Latino electorate.

African Americans

In April 1990, the Texas State Democratic Executive Committee filled a candidate vacancy by nominating Potter County court-at-law judge Morris Overstreet, an African American Democrat, for a seat on the Texas Court of Criminal Appeals. Because the Republican candidate, Louis Sturns, was also African American, this historic action guaranteed the state's voters would elect the first African American to statewide office in Texas. Overstreet won in 1990 and again in 1994. He served until 1998, when he ran unsuccessfully for Texas attorney general. Governor George W. Bush appointed Republican Michael Williams to the Texas Railroad Commission in 1999. This African American commissioner was elected to a six-year term in 2002 and again in 2008. Williams stepped down from the Texas Railroad Commission in 2011 to make an unsuccessful run for Congress, but in August 2012 he was appointed by Governor Perry as commissioner of education.

The appointment of Justice Wallace Bernard Jefferson to the Texas Supreme Court in 2001 made him the first African American to serve on the court. He and another African American, Dale Wainwright, were elected in 2002 and again in 2008 to that court. Jefferson made history in 2004 when Governor Perry appointed him as chief justice. In 2002, former Dallas mayor Ron Kirk became the first African American nominated by either major party in Texas as its candidate for U.S. senator. Although unsuccessful in the general election, Kirk's candidacy appeared to many political observers as an important breakthrough for African American politicians.

Since the 1930s, African American Texans have tended to identify with the Democratic Party. With a voting-age population in excess of one million, they constitute roughly 10 percent of the state's potential voters. As demonstrated in recent electoral contests, approximately 80 percent of Texas's African American citizens say they are Democrats, and only 5 percent are declared Republicans. The remainder are independents. In recent years, African American support for the Democratic Party and its candidates has declined slightly. By early 2013, a number of African Americans held elected office, including the following:

- One statewide position (chief justice on the Texas Supreme Court)
- Four U.S. representative seats in Texas's congressional delegation
- 20 seats in the Texas legislature
- More than 500 of the remaining 5,200 elected positions in the state

☑ Learning Check 5.2   (Answers on p. 204)

1. Which party have Latinos traditionally supported?
2. True or False: In 2013, no African Americans were holding statewide elected office.

★ Women in Politics

Texas women did not begin to vote and hold public office for three-quarters of a century after Texas joined the Union. Until 1990, however, only four women had won a statewide office in Texas, including two-term governor Miriam A. ("Ma") Ferguson (1925–1927 and 1933–1935). Ferguson owed her office to supporters of her husband, Jim, who had been impeached and removed from the governorship in 1917. Nevertheless, in 1990, Texas female voters outnumbered male voters, and Ann Richards was elected governor. After 1990, the number of women elected to statewide office increased dramatically.

In the early 1990s, Texas women served as mayors in about 150 of the state's towns and cities, including the top four in terms of population (Houston, Dallas, San Antonio, and El Paso). Mayor of Dallas Annette Strauss (1988–1991) was fond of greeting out-of-state visitors with this message: "Welcome to Texas, where men are men and women are mayors."

In 2010, when Annise Parker was sworn in as mayor of Houston, she made history as the first openly gay mayor of a major U.S. city. Although Parker had been open about her sexual orientation during her previous elections as the city's comptroller and, before that, as a city council member, her November 2009 election as mayor of the nation's fourth-largest city received national media attention. The impact of women's voting power was also evident in 2000, 2002, and 2006, when women led all candidates on either ticket in votes received. With her reelection to the U.S. Senate in 2000, Republican Kay Bailey Hutchison became the first person to receive more than four million votes. In 2002, Carole Keeton Rylander received more than 2.8 million votes in her reelection as state comptroller. (Rylander changed her name to Strayhorn following her marriage in early January 2003.) In 2006, when Hutchison was reelected to the U.S. Senate, she again led all candidates on the ballot with more than 2.6 million votes received.

Female candidates also succeeded in winning an increasing number of seats in legislative bodies. In 1971, no women served in Texas's congressional delegation, and only two served in the Texas legislature. As a result of the 2012 election, in 2013 the number had increased to three women in Texas's congressional delegation (Senator Hutchison did not seek reelection in 2012) and 37 in the Texas legislature (six in the Senate and 31 in the House of Representatives). The expanded presence of women in public office is changing public policy. For example, increased punishment for family violence and sexual abuse of children, together with a renewed focus on public education, can be attributed in large part to the presence of women in policymaking positions.

Despite their electoral victories in Texas and elsewhere across the nation, fewer women than men seek elective public office. Several reasons account for this situation, chief of which is difficulty in raising money to pay campaign expenses. Other reasons also discourage women from seeking public office. Although women enjoy increasing freedom, they still shoulder more responsibilities for family and home than men do (even in two-career families). Some mothers feel obliged to care for children in the home until the children finish high school. Such parental obligations, together with age-old prejudices, deny women their rightful place in government. Yet as customs, habits, and attitudes change, new opportunities for women in public service are expanding.

☑ Learning Check 5.3 (Answers on p. 204)

1. True or False: Women candidates received the most votes for a single office in the elections of 2000, 2002, and 2006.
2. By 2013, how many women had served as governor of Texas?

★ Voting

LO3

The U.S. Supreme Court has declared the right to vote the "preservative" of all other rights.[10] For most Texans, voting is their principal political activity. For many, it is their only exercise in practicing Texas politics. Casting a ballot brings individuals and their government together for a moment and reminds people anew that they are part of a political system.

Obstacles to Voting

universal suffrage
Voting is open for virtually all persons 18 years of age or older.

The right to vote has not always been as widespread in the United States as it is today. **Universal suffrage,** by which almost all citizens 18 years of age and older can vote, did not become a reality in Texas until the mid-1960s. Although most devices to prevent people from voting have been abolished, their legacy remains.

Adopted after the Civil War (1861–1865), the Fourteenth and Fifteenth Amendments to the U.S. Constitution were intended to prevent denial of the right to vote based on race. But for the next 100 years, African American citizens in Texas and other states of the former Confederacy, as well as many Latinos, were prevented from voting by one barrier after another—legal or otherwise. For example, the white-robed Ku Klux Klan and other lawless groups used terrorist tactics to keep African Americans from voting. Northeast Texas was the focus of the Klan's operations in the Lone Star State.[11]

Literacy Tests Beginning in the 1870s, as a means to prevent minority people from voting, some southern states began requiring prospective voters to take a screening test that conditioned **voter registration** on a person's literacy. Individuals who could not pass these **literacy tests** were prohibited from registering. Some states required constitutional-interpretation or citizenship-knowledge tests to deny voting rights. These tests usually consisted of difficult and abstract questions concerning a person's knowledge of the U.S. Constitution or understanding of issues supposedly related to citizenship. In no way, however, did these questions measure a citizen's ability to cast an informed vote.

Grandfather Clause Another device, not used in Texas, but enacted by other southern states to deny suffrage to minorities was the **grandfather clause**. Laws with this clause provided that persons who could exercise the right to vote before 1867, or their descendants, would be exempt from educational, property, or tax requirements for voting. Because African Americans had not been allowed to vote before adoption of the Fifteenth Amendment in 1870, grandfather clauses were used, along with literacy tests, to prevent African Americans from voting, while assuring this right to many impoverished and illiterate whites. The U.S. Supreme Court, in *Guinn v. United States* (1915), declared the grandfather clause unconstitutional because it violated equal voting rights guaranteed by the Fifteenth Amendment.

Poll Tax Beginning in 1902, Texas required that citizens pay a special tax, called the **poll tax**, to become eligible to vote. The cost was $1.75 ($1.50, plus $0.25 that was optional with each county). For the next 62 years, many Texans—especially low-income persons, including disproportionately large numbers of African Americans and Mexican Americans—frequently failed to pay their poll tax during the designated four-month period from October 1 to January 31. This, in turn, disqualified them from voting during the following 12 months in party primaries and in any general or special election. As a result, African American voter participation declined from approximately 100,000 in the 1890s to about 5,000 in 1906. With ratification of the Twenty-Fourth Amendment to the U.S. Constitution in January 1964, the poll tax was abolished as a prerequisite for voting in national elections. Then, in *Harper v. Virginia State Board of Elections* 383 U.S. 663 (1966), the U.S. Supreme Court invalidated all state laws that made payment of a poll tax a prerequisite for voting in state elections.

All-White Primaries The so-called **white primary**, a product of political and legal maneuvering within the southern states, was designed to deny

voter registration
A qualified voter must register with the county voting registrar, who compiles lists of qualified voters residing in each voting precinct.

literacy test
Although not used in Texas as a prerequisite for voter registration, this test was designed and administered in ways intended to prevent African Americans and Latinos from voting.

grandfather clause
Although not used in Texas, exempted people from educational, property, or tax requirements for voting if they were qualified to vote before 1867 or were descendents of such persons.

poll tax
A tax levied in Texas from 1902 until a similar Virginia tax was declared unconstitutional in 1962; failure to pay the annual tax (usually $1.75) made a citizen ineligible to vote in party primaries or in special and general elections.

white primary
A nominating system designed to prevent African Americans and some Mexican Americans from participating in Democratic primaries from 1923 to 1944.

African Americans and some Latinos access to the Democratic primary.[12] Following Reconstruction, Texas, like most of the south, was predominantly a one-party (Democratic) state. Between 1876 and 1926, the Republican Party held only one statewide primary in Texas. By contrast, the Democratic primary was the main election in every even-numbered year.

White Democrats nominated white candidates, who almost always won the general elections. The U.S. Supreme Court had long held that the Fourteenth and Fifteenth Amendments, as well as successive civil rights laws, provided protection against public acts of discrimination; but they did not protect against private acts of discrimination. In 1923, the Texas legislature passed a law explicitly prohibiting African Americans from voting in Democratic primaries. When the U.S. Supreme Court declared this law unconstitutional, the Texas legislature enacted another law giving the executive committee of each party the power to decide who could participate in its primaries. The State Democratic Executive Committee immediately adopted a resolution that limited party membership to whites only, which in effect allowed only whites to vote in Democratic primaries. This practice lasted from 1923 to 1944, when the U.S. Supreme Court declared it unconstitutional in *Smith v. Allwright* 321 U.S. 649 (1944).[13]

Racial Gerrymandering Gerrymandering is the practice of manipulating legislative district lines to underrepresent persons of a political party or group. "Packing" black voters into a given district or "cracking" them to make black voters a minority in all districts both illustrate **racial gerrymandering**. Although racial gerrymandering that discriminates against minority voters is disallowed, federal law allows **affirmative racial gerrymandering** that results in the creation of "majority-minority" districts that favor the election of more racial and ethnic minority candidates. These districts as well must be reasonable in their configuration and cannot be based solely on race. In *Shaw v. Reno* 509 U.S. 630 (1993), the U.S. Supreme Court condemned two extremely odd-shaped, African American–majority districts in North Carolina.

A controversial redistricting plan adopted by the Texas legislature in 2003 to draw new U.S. congressional districts was challenged both by the Texas Democratic Party and by minority groups, contending it diluted minority voting strength. Although the primary purpose of the plan, as crafted by U.S. House majority leader Tom DeLay, was to increase the number of Republican representatives in the Congress, an internal memo from the U.S. Justice Department revealed that all of the attorneys in the department's voting section believed that the plan "illegally diluted black and Hispanic voting power in two congressional districts."[14] Despite these conclusions, senior-level administrators at the Justice Department approved the redistricting plan. Shortly after the plan was passed, it was challenged in court. The U.S. Supreme Court, however, upheld most of the plan by a 5–4 margin, which altered the Texas congressional delegation from a 17–15 Democratic majority to a 21–11 Republican majority for the remainder of the decade. But the Court invalidated one GOP-held district in South Texas on the grounds that it violated the Voting Rights Act by removing approximately 100,000 Democrats of Latino origin.[15]

affirmative racial gerrymandering
Drawing districts designed to affect representation of a racial group (e.g., African Americans) in a legislative chamber, city council, commissioners court, or other representative body.

In 2011, the Texas legislature passed controversial redistricting plans designed to increase the number of Republicans in the state's congressional delegation and both chambers of the Texas legislature. This time, Texas was allowed four additional seats in the U.S. House of Representatives as a result of its population growth in relation to that of other states between 2000 and 2010. African American and Latino groups argued that growth in minority populations accounted for 89 percent of the state's population increase over that period. The congressional redistricting plan passed by the Republican-controlled state legislature, however, did not reflect the growth in these populations. Several minority groups, including the Mexican American Legal Defense and Educational Fund; the League of United Latin American Citizens; the Southwest Voter Registration Education Project; and the Texas NAACP, the state branch of the National Association for the Advancement of Colored People, brought suit against this plan because it diluted minority representation. In February 2012, the U.S. District Court for the Western District of Texas drew interim congressional district maps that included two new districts with Latino majorities and two new districts with Anglo majorities. (For details on this subject, see the Chapter 7 reading, "Recent Congressional Redistricting in Texas.") In early March of that year, the district court also ordered a revised election schedule that moved the primary election date to late May.[16] In August, a three-judge federal district court in Washington ruled that the intent of the Texas legislature was to illegally discriminate against minorities; but the congressional and legislative redistricting plans were retained for the November general election.

Diluting Minority Votes Creating **at-large majority districts** (each electing two or more representatives) for state legislatures and city councils can prevent an area with a significant minority population from electing a representative of its choice. Under this scenario, the votes of a minority group can be diluted when combined with the votes of a majority group. Federal courts have declared this practice unconstitutional where representation of ethnic or racial minorities is diminished.[17] In 2009, a U.S. District Court judge ruled that the city of Irving's method of choosing council members through citywide at-large elections diluted the influence of Latinos and violated the 1965 Voting Rights Act.

Democratization of the Ballot

In America, successive waves of democratization have removed obstacles to voting. In the latter half of the 20th century, the U.S. Congress enacted important voting rights laws to promote and protect voting nationwide.

Federal Voting Rights Legislation The Voting Rights Act of 1965 expanded the electorate and encouraged voting. This act has been renewed and amended by Congress four times, including in 2006, when it was extended until 2031. The law (together with federal court rulings) now does the following:

- Abolishes the use of all literacy tests in voter registrations
- Prohibits residency requirements of more than 30 days for voting in presidential elections

at-large majority district
A district that elects two or more representatives.

- Requires states to provide some form of absentee or early voting
- Allows individuals (as well as the U.S. Department of Justice) to sue in federal court to request that voting examiners be sent to a particular area
- Requires states and jurisdictions within a state with a significant percentage of residents whose primary language is one other than English to use bilingual ballots and other written election materials as well as provide bilingual oral assistance. In Texas, this information must be provided in Spanish throughout the state and in Vietnamese and Chinese in Harris County and Houston
- Requires some states, such as Texas, to obtain preclearance from the U.S. Department of Justice before changing any voting qualifications or prerequisites to voting standards, practices, or procedures with respect to voting within certain jurisdictions

A bill passed by the Texas legislature in 2011 that required voters to provide a photo identification to cast a ballot failed to obtain Department of Justice preclearance in August 2012. (For a detailed discussion about the photo identification requirement, see this chapter's Point/Counterpoint feature.)

In 1993, Congress passed the National Voter Registration Act, or **motor-voter law**, which simplified voter registration by permitting registration by mail; at welfare, disability assistance, and motor vehicle licensing agencies; or at military recruitment centers. The new procedures allowed people to register to vote when they apply for, or renew, driver's licenses or when they visit a public assistance office. By mail, using an appropriate state or federal voter registration form, Texas citizens can also apply for voter registration or update their voter registration data. In addition to registration by mail, motor vehicle offices and voter registration agencies are required to provide voter registration services to applicants. If citizens believe their voting rights have been violated in any way, federal administrative and judicial agencies, such as the U.S. Department of Justice, are available for assistance.

Amendments to the U.S. Constitution have also expanded the American electorate. The Fifteenth Amendment prohibits the denial of voting rights because of race; the Nineteenth Amendment precludes denial of suffrage on the basis of gender; the Twenty-Fourth Amendment prohibits states from requiring payment of a poll tax or any other tax as a condition for voting; and the Twenty-Sixth Amendment forbids setting the minimum voting age above 18 years.

Motor-voter law
Legislation requiring certain government offices (e.g., motor vehicle licensing agencies) to offer voter registration applications to clients.

Two Trends in Suffrage From our overview of suffrage in Texas, two trends emerge. First, voting rights have steadily expanded to include virtually all persons, of both genders, who are 18 years of age or older. Second, there has been a movement toward uniformity of voting policies among the 50 states. However, democratization of the ballot has been pressed on the states largely by the U.S. Congress, by federal judges, and by presidents who have enforced voting laws and judicial orders.

Voter Turnout

Now that nearly all legal barriers to the ballot have been swept away, the road to the voting booth seems clear for rich and poor alike; for historical minority groups, as well as for the historical majority; and for individuals of all races, colors, and creeds. But universal suffrage has not resulted in a corresponding increase in voter turnout, either nationally or in Texas.

Voter turnout is the percentage of the voting-age population casting ballots. In Texas, turnout is higher in presidential elections than in nonpresidential elections. Although this pattern reflects the national trend, electoral turnout in Texas tends to be significantly lower than in the nation as a whole. Even with George W. Bush running for reelection in the 2004 presidential election, Texas ranked below the national average in voter turnout of the voting-age population at 46 percent, compared with the 55 percent national average. According to the Center for the Study of the American Electorate national turnout was much lower in 2012. Texas had the fifth worst turnout in the nation.

Texas's lower voter turnout rates can be explained in part by the lower percentage of eligible voters in the state. Researchers at the U.S. Election Project at George Mason University estimated that 14 percent of the Lone Star State's population was ineligible to vote in 2008 because of citizenship status. Another 0.2 percent of Texas's population was ineligible to vote due to their status as convicted felons who had not completed serving their sentences. Therefore, voter turnout in Texas fares better when the voting-eligible population (rather than voting-age population) is considered, reflecting a 2008 statewide turnout of almost 55 percent compared with a national turnout rate of 62 percent.[18]

In part, due to less media attention, voter turnout in state and local elections in Texas is usually lower than turnout in presidential elections. For instance, the 2010 gubernatorial election yielded only a 27 percent turnout in Texas. Although few citizens believe their vote will determine an election outcome, some races have actually been won by a single vote. In local elections at the city or school district level, a turnout of 20 percent is relatively high. Among the five largest cities conducting city council elections in Texas in 2011, none yielded a turnout greater than 20 percent. These figures illustrate one of the greatest ironies in politics: People are less likely to participate at the level of government where they can potentially have the greatest influence.

Low citizen participation in elections has been attributed to the influence of pollsters and media consultants, voter fatigue resulting from too many elections, negative campaigning by candidates, lack of information about candidates and issues, and feelings of isolation from government. Members of the Texas legislature determined that low voter turnout was caused by governmental entities holding too many elections. To cure "turnout burnout," the legislature passed a law that limits elections to two uniform election dates each year: the second Saturday in May and the first Tuesday after the first

voter turnout
The percentage of the voting-age population casting ballots in an election.

Monday in November. However, the effects of this change have failed to yield a higher voter turnout as anticipated. For instance, in 2011, less than 5 percent of the voting-age population participated in the state's constitutional amendment election. Elections specifically exempted by statute that can be held on nonuniform dates include the following:

- Runoff elections
- Local option elections under the Alcoholic Beverage Code
- Bond or tax levy elections for school districts or community college districts
- Emergency elections called for or approved by the governor
- Elections to fill vacancies in the two chambers of the Texas legislature
- Elections to fill vacancies in the Texas delegation to the U.S. House of Representatives
- Recall elections as authorized by city charters[19]

People decide to vote or not to vote in the same way they make most other decisions: on the basis of anticipated consequences. A strong impulse to vote may stem from peer pressure; self-interest; or a sense of duty toward country, state, local community, political party, or interest group. People also decide whether to vote based on costs measured in time, money, experience, information, job, and other resources.

Cultural, socioeconomic, and ethnic or racial factors also contribute to the low voter turnout in the Lone Star State. As identified in Chapter 1, some elements of Texas's political culture place little emphasis on the importance of voting.

Of all the socioeconomic influences on voting, education is by far the strongest. Statistics clearly indicate that as educational level rises, people are more likely to vote, assuming all other socioeconomic factors remain constant. Educated people usually have more income and leisure time for voting; moreover, education enhances one's ability to learn about political parties, candidates, and issues. As discussed in Chapter 1, education strengthens voter efficacy (the belief that one's vote makes a difference). In addition, income strongly affects voter turnout. Texas ranks fourth in the nation in the percentage of its population living in poverty. People of lower income often lack access to the polls, information about the candidates, or opportunities to learn about the system. Income levels and their impact on electoral turnout can be seen in the 2008 general election. For example, Starr County, with a median household income of less than $24,000, had a turnout of slightly over 35 percent of its registered voters. By contrast, Collin County, with a median income of more than $81,000, experienced a turnout of almost 70 percent of its registered voters.

Although far less important than education and income, gender and age also affect voting behavior. In the United States, women are slightly more likely to vote than men. Young people (ages 18–25) have the lowest voter turnout of any age group. Nevertheless, participation by young people increased in the 2004 and 2008 presidential elections. The highest voter turnout is among middle-aged Americans (ages 40–64).

Race and ethnicity also influence voting behavior. Historically, the turnout rate for African Americans has remained substantially below that for Anglos. African Americans tend to be younger, less educated, and poorer than Anglos. In 2008, however, perhaps because of President Obama's candidacy, the percentage of African Americans who registered to vote and voted exceeded the state average for all races. Although Latino voter turnout rates in Texas are slightly below the state average in primaries and general elections, findings by scholars indicate that the gap is narrowing. Latino voter registration rates for eligible voters in 2008 was more than 10 percent below other groups, and their voting rate remained approximately two-thirds of the state average.[20]

Administering Elections

In Texas, as in other states, determining voting procedures is essentially a state responsibility. The Texas Constitution authorizes the legislature to provide for the administration of elections. State lawmakers, in turn, have made the secretary of state the chief elections officer for Texas, but have left most details of administering elections to county officials.

All election laws currently in effect in the Lone Star State are compiled into one body of law, the **Texas Election Code**.[21] In administering this legal code, however, state and party officials must protect voting rights guaranteed by federal law.

Qualifications for Voting To be eligible to vote in Texas, a person must meet the following qualifications:

- Be a native-born or naturalized citizen of the United States
- Be at least 18 years of age on Election Day
- Be a resident of the state and county for at least 30 days immediately preceding Election Day
- Be a resident of the area covered by the election on Election Day
- Be a registered voter for at least 30 days immediately preceding Election Day
- Not be a convicted felon (unless sentence, probation, and parole are completed)
- Not be declared mentally incompetent by a court of law[22]

Most adults who live in Texas meet the first four qualifications for voting, but registration is required before a person can vote. Anyone serving a jail sentence as a result of a misdemeanor conviction or not finally convicted of a felony is not disqualified from voting. The Texas Constitution, however, bars from voting anyone who is incarcerated, on parole, or on probation as a result of a felony conviction and anyone who is "mentally incompetent as determined by a court." A convicted felon may vote immediately after completing a sentence or following a full pardon. (For examples of misdemeanors and felonies, see Table 10.3 on page 416.) Voter registration is intended to determine in advance whether prospective voters meet all the qualifications prescribed by law.

Texas Election Code
The body of state law concerning parties, primaries, and elections.

Most states, including Texas, use a permanent registration system. Under this plan, voters register once and remain registered unless they change their mailing address and fail to notify the voting registrar within three years or lose their eligibility to register in some other way. However, a story published in the *Houston Chronicle* in 2012 revealed that, as a result of outdated computer programs and faulty procedures, over 1.5 million voters in Texas could have their registrations cancelled for failure to vote or update their records for two consecutive federal elections. It was reported that one out of every 10 Texas voters' registration was currently suspended (one out of every five Texas voters' under 30). In Collin County, 70 percent of the voters who were removed from voter registration rolls were actually able to prove their eligibility.[23] Because the requirement of voter registration may deter voting, the Texas Election Code provides for voter registration centers in addition to those sites authorized by Congress under the motor-voter law. Thus, Texans may also register at local marriage license offices, in public high schools, with any volunteer deputy registrar, or in person at the office of the county voting registrar. Students away at college may choose to re-register using their college address as their residence if they want to vote locally. Otherwise, they must request an absentee ballot or be in their hometown during early voting or on Election Day if they wish to cast a ballot.

Between November 1 and November 15 of each odd-numbered year, the registrar mails a registration certificate that is effective for the succeeding two voting years to every registered voter in the county. Postal authorities may not forward a certificate mailed to the address indicated on the voter's application form if the applicant has moved to another address; instead, the certificate must be returned to the registrar. This enables the county voting registrar to maintain an accurate list of names and mailing addresses of persons to whom voting certificates have been issued. Registration files are open for public inspection in the voting registrar's office, and a statewide registration file is available in Austin at the Elections Division of the Office of the Secretary of State. Although normally issued in early November, the issuance of new voter registration certificates in 2011 was delayed due to legal battles surrounding redistricting. In early 2012, an order by the U.S. District Court for the Western District of Texas instructed counties to issue the new certificates no later than April 25 of that year.

The color of voter registration certificates mailed to eligible voters differs from the color of the cards sent two years earlier to distinguish the new cards from the old. The Office of the Secretary of State determines the color of voter registration certificates. In 2012, new voter registration certificates were issued in yellow and white. Although voter registration certificates are issued after a person registers to vote, one can legally cast a ballot without a certificate by providing some form of identification (such as a driver's license) and signing an affidavit of registration at the polls.

Voting Early Opportunities to vote early in Texas are limited to in-person **early voting**, voting by mail, and facsimile machine voting (for military personnel and their dependents in hostile fire or combat zones). Texas law allows voters to vote "early"—that is, during a 17-day period preceding a scheduled election or first primary and for 10 days preceding a runoff

early voting
Conducted at the county courthouse and selected polling places before the designated primary, special, or general election day.

primary. Early voting ends, however, four days before any election or primary. In less-populated rural counties, early voting occurs at the courthouse. In more populous urban areas, the county clerk's office accommodates voters by maintaining branch offices for early voting, including malls, schools, college campuses, and mobile units. Polling places are generally open for early voting on weekdays during the regular business hours of the official responsible for conducting the election. If requested by 15 registered voters within the county, polling places must also be opened on Saturday or Sunday.

Registered voters who qualify may vote by mail during an early voting period. Voting by mail has been available for decades to elderly Texans and those with physical disabilities. Today, anyone meeting the following qualifications can vote by mail-in ballot:

- Will not be in his or her county of residence during the entire early-voting period and on Election Day
- Is at least age 65
- Is, or will be, physically disabled on Election Day, including those who expect to be confined for childbirth on Election Day
- Is in jail (but not a convicted felon) during the early-voting period and on Election Day
- Is in the military or is a dependent of military personnel and has resided in Texas[24]

Since early voting was first used in 1998, the percentage of early voters has consistently been about 20 percent in the general elections. In 2008, however, the Texas secretary of state reported that some counties (Collin and Fort Bend) had early voter turnout in excess of 50 percent of registered voters. Although such measures make voting easier, at least one study indicates that states with longer early-voting periods have experienced a greater decline in voter turnout than states with more restrictive election laws.[25]

Points to Ponder

In 1997, the Texas legislature enacted a provision allowing people on space flights to vote electronically from space on Election Day.

- Six astronauts have cast ballots from space (three of those in presidential elections).
- The county clerk of the astronaut's home county sends an electronic ballot to the astronaut-voter through NASA; the astronaut votes; and someone in the county clerk's office then decrypts the ballot, so it can be counted.

Source: Tariq Malik, "Astronauts to Cast Votes from Space Station," November 3, 2008, http://www.msnbc.msn.com/id/27518943/.

NASA astronaut Michael Fincke, Expedition 18 commander, sent a message from the International Space Station urging all citizens to vote.

(NASA)

Voting Precincts The basic geographic area for conducting national, state, district, and county elections is the **voting precinct**. Each precinct usually contains between 100 and approximately 2,000 registered voters. Texas has more than 8,500 voting precincts, drawn by the 254 county commissioners courts (a county judge and four commissioners). When a precinct's population exceeds a number prescribed by the Texas Election Code (3,000; 4,000; or 5,000, depending on the county's population), the commissioners court must draw new boundaries.[26] Citizens vote at polling places within their voting precincts or, if voting precincts have been combined for an election, at a polling place convenient to voters in each of the combined voting precincts. Municipal precincts must follow the boundary lines of county-designed voting precincts adjusted to city boundaries. Subject to this restriction, municipal and special-district voting precincts are designated by the governing body of each city and special district, respectively.

Election Officials Various county and political party officials administer federal, state, and county elections. Municipal elections and special district elections are the responsibility of their respective jurisdictions (see Chapter 3, "Local Government"), although they may contract with the county to administer elections. Whereas party officials conduct primary elections, the county clerk or elections administrator prepares general- and special-election ballots based on certification of candidates by the appropriate authority (that is, the secretary of state for state and district candidates and the county clerk or elections administrator for county candidates). Some counties have officials whose sole responsibility is election administration. In other counties, election administration is one of many responsibilities of the tax assessor-collector or (if designated by the county commissioners

voting precinct
The basic geographic area for conducting primaries and elections; Texas is divided into more than 8,500 voting precincts.

court) the county clerk. In 2012, fewer than 30 percent of the counties in Texas employed a full-time **elections administrator**. There is also a county election commission, which consists of the county judge, county clerk or elections administrator, sheriff, and the chairs of the two major political parties. Commission responsibilities include selecting polling places, printing ballots, and providing supplies and voting equipment.

elections administrator
Person appointed to supervise voter registration and voting.

Point/Counterpoint

Photo Identification as a Requirement to Vote

THE ISSUE In 2011, the Texas legislature passed a law requiring voters to present one form of photo identification in order to vote. This law enhances the penalties for illegal voting from a third-degree felony to a second-degree felony (two to 20 years in prison and an optional fine of up to $10,000). Attempted illegal voting is a state-jail felony (180 days to two years in a state jail and an optional fine of up to $10,000) instead of a class A misdemeanor. Acceptable forms of photo identification include a driver's license, passport, military ID card, concealed handgun license, or state-issued ID card from the Department of Motor Vehicles. Although this law was scheduled to take effect January 1, 2012, litigation prevented implementation for the 2012 primaries. Then in August of that year the U.S. District Court for the District of Columbia struck down the law because it disproportionately affected the poor and minorities. Texas Attorney General Greg Abbott appealed to the U.S. Supreme Court.

Arguments For Requiring Photo Identification to Vote

- *The election process is strengthened.* Requiring a photo ID deters voter fraud and keeps ineligible voters from voting, while restoring and enhancing public confidence in elections. When deceased or other unqualified individuals are on the voter rolls, illegal votes may be cast, canceling out legitimate votes. Since voters do not need to prove their identities at the polls, anyone can vote with anyone else's voter certificate because these documents include no photo. This lax screening process makes it impossible to know how many ineligible voters slip through the system. Voter fraud drives honest citizens out of the democratic process and breeds distrust of government. Requiring a photo ID boosts confidence in the election process and may promote higher voter turnout.

- *The integrity of elections is secured.* Requiring voters to show a government-issued photo ID and increasing the criminal penalty for voter fraud helps ensure the integrity of elections.

Arguments Against Requiring Photo Identification to Vote

- *Voters are disenfranchised and election procedures become increasingly complicated.* Eligible voters should not be needlessly hassled by the state and discouraged or intimidated from exercising their fundamental right to vote without legitimate justification. There is no proof that this extra requirement to vote is needed at all. This bill would be an extreme, costly solution in search of a problem not proven to exist. Almost all evidence of voter fraud involves mail-in ballots. This requirement, however, addresses only voter impersonation at the polls, not mail-in balloting.

- *Voting among eligible voters is suppressed.* The process of obtaining a photo ID is cumbersome and cost prohibitive for some citizens, even if the state photo ID cards are free. Requiring a photo ID inhibits voting in rural areas, where citizens may have to travel more than 100 miles to a Department of Public Safety (DPS) office. There is no DPS office in 77 of Texas's 254 counties. According to the D.C. Court's opinion in *Texas v.*

Arguments For Requiring Photo Identification to Vote

It guarantees continued access to the polls by providing exceptions for certain disabled voters and by authorizing free election ID certificates for eligible voters lacking a photo ID.

- *No additional burden is placed on citizens.* Currently, photo identification is commonly required to open bank accounts, board airlines, or purchase some items (alcohol, tobacco, or medications). Such safeguards benefit our society and enhance our security. Furthermore, requiring a photo ID to vote is a common practice throughout the United States. By 2012, some form of photo ID was required by 30 states at the polls to vote.

Arguments Against Requiring Photo Identification to Vote

Holder (2012), the time and money required to obtain proper documentation would have a disproportionate effect on members of historical minority groups because they have a higher poverty rate. The court described this result as a "retrogressive effect" on minority voting rights, a violation of the Voting Rights Act. Although the Texas law provided that the election ID certificate could be issued without cost, the documentation required to obtain such a certificate was not cost-free.

- *A substantial obstacle to the right to vote is created.* Although citizens must show proof of their identity when boarding an airplane or renting movies, these activities are not constitutional rights. Although other states have voter ID laws, this requirement gives Texas one of the most restrictive voter ID laws in the nation. States such as Indiana, Michigan, and Georgia have less stringent voter ID laws that contain photo ID alternatives, such as student IDs, expired driver's licenses, or valid employee ID cards with photographs.

Source: This Point/Counterpoint is abridged and adapted from Rita Barr, "Requiring Voters to Present Voter ID," in *Major Issues of the 82nd Legislature, Regular Session and First Called Session*, Focus Report No. 82-7 (Austin: House Research Organization, Texas House of Representatives, September 30, 2011), 55–56; Mike Ward, "Top 10 Reasons, Pro and Con, on Voter ID," *Austin American Statesman* January 25, 2011; and Sari Horwitz, "Texas Voter-ID Law is Blocked," *Washington Post* August 30, 2012. Reprinted by permission.

County commissioners courts appoint one **election judge** and one alternate judge, each from different political parties, to administer elections in each precinct for a maximum term of two years. Furthermore, each county's commissioners court canvasses and certifies election results. The election judge selects as many clerks as will be needed to assist in conducting general and special elections in a precinct. Clerks must be selected from different political parties. In city elections, the city secretary appoints election judges. In special district elections, election judges are appointed by the district's governing body

Voting Systems In general elections, Texas uses three voting systems: paper ballot, optical scan (similar to a Scantron), and Direct-Record Electronic (DRE) also known as a touch screen. In every county, the county commissioners court determines which system will be used. Each system has advantages and disadvantages in such matters as ballot and equipment costs, ease of use by voters, accuracy of counting, labor cost, and time

election judge
Appointed by the county commissioners court to administer an election in a voting precinct.

A voter uses a new electronic voting system.

(AP Photo/Timothy Jacobsen)

required to count the votes. For example, paper ballots are relatively cheap and easy to use, but counting is a slow, laborious, and error-prone process. Some sparsely populated counties continue to use paper ballots, which must be counted by hand. Some optical scan and DRE systems automatically count each vote as the ballot is cast. Optical scan and DRE systems require mechanical and electronic voting equipment which is expensive to purchase and store but can reduce election costs when many voters are involved.

After the controversial 2000 presidential election, in which the state of Florida and the U.S. Supreme Court questioned the accuracy of punch-card ballots, both federal and state elected officials evaluated various voting systems. A study conducted by the Office of the Secretary of State of Texas revealed that the 14 Texas counties that used punch-card ballots (including Harris County [Houston]) had many more overvotes (in which voters selected more than one candidate for the same office) than counties using any other balloting method. Punch-card ballot systems were discontinued in Texas elections by 2006.[27]

On ballot forms, a list of parties for straight-party-ticket voting appears first, followed by lists of candidates for national, state, district, and local offices, in that order. (Figure 5.1 shows a sample ballot used in a recent general election.) A list of all write-in candidates who have filed an appropriate declaration is posted in each polling place on the day of election. The name of one of these candidates may be written in to indicate the voter's selection in the appropriate contest.

In some instances, candidates for nomination or election to an office may request a recount of ballots if they believe vote tabulations are inaccurate. The Texas Election Code also provides detailed procedures for settling disputed elections. Since the 1960s, several changes in voting procedures have been made to encourage full, informed participation in elections.

As a result of the 1975 extension of the federal Voting Rights Act, registration and election materials used in all Texas counties must be printed in both English and Spanish. As noted above in Harris County and the City of Houston, materials in Chinese and Vietnamese must also be provided. Texas

Vote Both Sides   *Vote en Ambos Lados de la Página*

Sample Ballot *Boleta Muestra*   Tarrant County   *Condado de Tarrant*
Joint General and Special Elections
Elecciones Generales y Especiales Conjuntas
November 06, 2012 - *06 de Noviembre de 2012*   Precinct   *Precinto*   Sample

Instruction Note:
Please use a black or blue ink pen to mark your choices on the ballot. To vote for your choice in each contest, fill in the box provided to the left of your choice. To vote for a write-in candidate, completely fill in the box provided to the left of the words "Write-in" and write in the name of the candidate on the line provided. To enter a straight-party vote (that is, a vote for all the nominees of one party), completely fill in the box to the left of the name of that party. Selecting a party automatically selects all candidates associated with that party. If you select a candidate associated with a party other than the straight-party selection, your vote for that candidate will be counted in that particular contest.

Nota de Instruccion:
Favor de usar una pluma de tinta negra o azul para marcar su boleta. Para votar por su selección en cada carrera, llene el espacio cuadrado a la izquierda de su selección. Para votar por voto escrito, llene completamente el espacio cuadrado a la izquierda de las palabras "Voto Escrito" y escriba el nombre del candidato en la línea provista. Para escoger un voto de partido completo (es decir, un voto por todos los candidatos nombrados del mismo partido político), llene completamente el espacio cuadrado a la izquierda del nombre de ese partido. Seleccionar un partido automáticamente escogerá todos los candidatos asociados con ese partido. Si selecciona un candidato asociado con un partido distinto a su selección de partido completo, su voto por ese candidato se computará en esa carrera.

Straight Party
Partido Completo
- [ ] Republican Party (REP) *Partido Republicano (REP)*
- [ ] Democratic Party (DEM) *Partido Democratico (DEM)*
- [ ] Libertarian Party (LIB) *Partido Libertario (LIB)*
- [ ] Green Party (GRN) *Partido Verde (GRN)*

President and Vice-President of the United States
Presidente Y Vice-Presidente de los Estados Unidos
- [ ] Mitt Romney / Paul Ryan   REP
- [ ] Barack Obama / Joe Biden   DEM
- [ ] Gary Johnson / Jim Gray   LIB
- [ ] Jill Stein / Cheri Honkala   GRN
- [ ] Write-in   *Voto Escrito*

United States Senator
Senador de los Estados Unidos
- [ ] Ted Cruz   REP
- [ ] Paul Sadler   DEM
- [ ] John Jay Myers   LIB
- [ ] David B. Collins   GRN

United States Representative, District 6
Representante de los Estados Unidos, Distrito 6
- [ ] Joe L. Barton   REP
- [ ] Kenneth Sanders   DEM
- [ ] Hugh Chauvin   LIB
- [ ] Brandon Parmer   GRN

United States Representative, District 12
Representante de los Estados Unidos, Distrito 12
- [ ] Kay Granger   REP
- [ ] Dave Robinson   DEM
- [ ] Matthew Solodow   LIB

United States Representative, District 24
Representante de los Estados Unidos, Distrito 24
- [ ] Kenny E. Marchant   REP
- [ ] Tim Rusk   DEM
- [ ] John Stathas   LIB

United States Representative, District 25
Representante de los Estados Unidos, Distrito 25
- [ ] Roger Williams   REP
- [ ] Elaine M. Henderson   DEM
- [ ] Betsy Dewey   LIB

United States Representative, District 26
Representante de los Estados Unidos, Distrito 26
- [ ] Michael Burgess   REP
- [ ] David Sanchez   DEM
- [ ] Mark Boler   LIB

United States Representative, District 33
Representante de los Estados Unidos, Distrito 33
- [ ] Chuck Bradley   REP
- [ ] Marc Veasey   DEM
- [ ] Ed Lindsay   GRN

Railroad Commissioner
Comisionado de Ferrocarriles
- [ ] Christi Craddick   REP
- [ ] Dale Henry   DEM
- [ ] Vivekananda (Vik) Wall   LIB
- [ ] Chris Kennedy   GRN

Railroad Commissioner (Unexpired Term)
Comisionado de Ferrocarriles (Duración Restante del Cargo)
- [ ] Barry Smitherman   REP
- [ ] Jaime O. Perez   LIB
- [ ] Josh Wendel   GRN

Justice, Texas Supreme Court, Place 2
Juez, Corte Suprema, Lugar Núm 2
- [ ] Don Willett   REP
- [ ] RS Roberto Koelsch   LIB

Justice, Texas Supreme Court, Place 4
Juez, Corte Suprema, Lugar Núm 4
- [ ] John Devine   REP
- [ ] Tom Oxford   LIB
- [ ] Charles E. Waterbury   GRN

Justice, Texas Supreme Court, Place 6
Juez, Corte Suprema, Lugar Núm 6
- [ ] Nathan Hecht   REP
- [ ] Michele Petty   DEM
- [ ] Mark Ash   LIB
- [ ] Jim Chisholm   GRN

Presiding Judge, Court of Criminal Appeals
Juez Presidente, Corte de Apelaciones Criminales
- [ ] Sharon Keller   REP
- [ ] Keith Hampton   DEM
- [ ] Lance Stott   LIB

Judge, Court of Criminal Appeals, Place 7
Juez, Corte de Apelaciones Criminales, Lugar Núm. 7
- [ ] Barbara Parker Hervey   REP
- [ ] Mark W. Bennett   LIB

Judge, Court of Criminal Appeals, Place 8
Juez, Corte de Apelaciones Criminales, Lugar Núm. 8
- [ ] Elsa Alcala   REP
- [ ] William Bryan Strange, III   LIB

Member, State Board of Education, District 11
Miembro de la Junta Estatal de Educación Pública, Distrito 11
- [ ] Patricia "Pat" Hardy   REP
- [ ] Jason Darr   LIB

Member, State Board of Education, District 13
Miembro de la Junta Estatal de Educación Pública, Distrito 13
- [ ] S.T. Russell   REP
- [ ] Mavis Best Knight   DEM

State Senator, District 9
Senador Estatal, Distrito Núm. 9
- [ ] Kelly Hancock   REP
- [ ] Pete Martinez   DEM
- [ ] Dave (Mac) McElwee   LIB

State Senator, District 10
Senador Estatal, Distrito Núm. 10
- [ ] Mark M. Shelton   REP
- [ ] Wendy R. Davis   DEM

State Senator, District 12
Senador Estatal, Distrito Núm. 12
- [ ] Jane Nelson   REP
- [ ] John A. Betz, Jr.   LIB

State Senator, District 22
Senador Estatal, Distrito Núm. 22
- [ ] Brian Birdwell   REP
- [ ] Tom Kilbride   LIB

State Representative, District 90
Representante Estatal, Distrito 90
- [ ] Lon Burnam   DEM

State Representative, District 91
Representante Estatal, Distrito 91
- [ ] Stephanie Klick   REP

State Representative, District 92
Representante Estatal, Distrito 92
- [ ] Jonathan Stickland   REP
- [ ] Sean Fatzinger   LIB

State Representative, District 93
Representante Estatal, Distrito 93
- [ ] Matt Krause   REP
- [ ] Shane Hardin   DEM
- [ ] Bruce Beckman   LIB

State Representative, District 94
Representante Estatal, Distrito 94
- [ ] Diane Patrick   REP
- [ ] David Eyerly   LIB

State Representative, District 95
Representante Estatal, Distrito 95
- [ ] Monte Mitchell   REP
- [ ] Nicole Collier   DEM

State Representative, District 96
Representante Estatal, Distrito 96
- [ ] Bill Zedler   REP
- [ ] Max W. Koch III   LIB

Sample Ballot   Sample Ballot

Vote Both Sides   *Vote en Ambos Lados de la Página*

Figure 5.1   Sample Portion of Election Ballot for Travis County, Texas

Source: Travis County, Texas, ballot from The Hart Intercivic eSlate Voting System.

voters can also take voting guides, newspaper endorsements, and other printed material into the voting booth. In 1999, the Texas legislature passed a series of laws ensuring disabled voters access to polling places and the opportunity to cast a secret ballot. The legislature established the same accessibility requirement for all local elections as well, effective January 1, 2006.

 Learning Check 5.4   (Answers on p. 204)

1. Identify four traditional obstacles used in Texas to limit people's right to vote.
2. True or False: The only people who can vote early are those who will be away from their regular polling place on Election Day.

★ # Primary, General, and Special Elections

The electoral process includes the nomination and election of candidates through primary, general, and special elections. A clear distinction must be made between party primaries and general elections. Primaries are party functions that allow party members to select nominees to run against the candidates of opposing parties in a general election. General elections determine which candidates will fill government offices. These electoral contests are public and are conducted, financed, and administered by state, county, and municipal governments as well as by special districts. This distinction between party primaries and general elections is valid, even though the U.S. Supreme Court has ruled that primaries are of such importance in the selection of general election candidates that they are subject to government regulation.

Thus, even though the state regulates and largely finances primaries, they serve only as a means for political parties to nominate candidates. The general election ballot also includes the names of **independent candidates**, space for write-in candidates, and names of candidates nominated by party convention because the law does not require nomination by direct primary.

Primaries

Political parties conduct **primaries** to select their nominees for public office. Among the states, party primaries are held every two years. Presidential primaries occur every four years and provide a means for Democrats and Republicans to select delegates to their parties' national conventions, where candidates for president and vice president are nominated. Other primaries occur every two years, when party members go to the polls to choose candidates for the U.S. Congress and for many state, district, and county offices.

Development of Direct Primaries A unique product of American political ingenuity, the **direct primary** was designed to provide a nominating method

LO4

independent candidate
A candidate who runs in a general election without party endorsement or selection.

primary
A preliminary election conducted within the party to select candidates who will run for public office in a subsequent general election.

direct primary
A nominating system that allows voters to participate directly in the selection of candidates for public office.

general election
Held in November of even-numbered years to elect county and state officials from among candidates nominated in primaries or (for small parties) in nominating conventions.

Students in Action

Kolby Flowers, Candidate, Board of Trustees, Little Cypress-Mauriceville (LCM) Consolidated Independent School District (CISD)

Most seniors in high school spend the year applying for scholarships, completing college admission applications, and working through the week at their jobs. Kolby Flowers focused on other goals as well. On January 19, 2010, he announced his campaign for a seat on the LCM CISD's board of trustees.

Flowers decided to pursue this position because he saw a lot of the problems associated with the district that cannot be seen from other than a student's perspective.

"I feel that LCM has given me a great experience," Flowers said. "My time as a student in the district provides me a fresh perspective of the issues that our students and teachers face on a daily basis. Typical school board members graduated at a time when issues today weren't a problem."

In 2009, Flowers created KolbyFlowers.com as a public forum for students, teachers, and

(Monkey Business Images/Shutterstock.com)

parents to communicate with him about problems they faced at an individual level at school. The site spawned from a petition to change the high school's dress code policy regarding shaving. While a student in the LCM district, Flowers served as student council president for two years. His role as president helped him realize his goal in this campaign, helping out his peers and future students.

"It's a wonderful feeling when you know you've helped impact someone's life," Flowers said. "It is the job of the district to prepare its children for challenges they will face beyond the classroom, and that's what I want to do. I want that ability to say 'I helped them get the best education they could receive.'"

"I now want to be a part of improving the district for the benefit of the students and the community," Flowers said. "My time in school was great, but the underlying issues need to be addressed to create a more creative and productive learning experience for every student who walks through our hallways."

Flowers was unsuccessful in his election bid.

---

runoff primary
Held a month after the first primary to allow party members to choose a candidate from the first primary's top two vote-getters.

closed primary
A primary in which voters must declare their support for the party before they are permitted to participate in the selection of its candidates.

that would avoid domination by party bosses and allow wider participation by party members. This form of nomination permits party members to choose their candidates directly at the polls. For each office (except president and vice president of the United States and some local officials), party members select by popular vote the person they wish to be their party's candidate in the **general election**, in which candidates of all parties compete. An absolute majority of the vote (more than 50 percent) is required for nomination. If the primary fails to produce such a majority, a **runoff primary** is held a month after the first primary to allow party members to choose a candidate from the first primary's top two vote-getters.

Four basic forms of the direct primary have evolved in America. Most states use some form of **closed primary**, which requires voters to declare a party affiliation when registering to vote. They must show party identification when voting in a primary election and can vote only in the party primary for which they are registered. Other states use an **open primary**, which does not require party identification of voters. At the polls, voters in an open primary can choose a ballot for any party, regardless of their party affiliation.

Some states use a variation of the open primary, called the top-two primary (California, Washington) or **jungle primary** (Louisiana). Here all voters receive the same ballot, on which are printed the names of all candidates. Candidates from all parties run in a single election. If a candidate receives more than 50 percent of the vote, he or she is declared the winner. If no candidate receives more than 50 percent, the top two vote-getters will participate in a run-off election. A criticism of the open primary is that it gives voters of one party an opportunity to sabotage the primary of another party. This can occur when voters who normally affiliate with one party try to nominate a "fringe" candidate from the other who has little chance of victory in the general election. A criticism of top-two and jungle primaries is that they may produce two candidates from the same party competing for the same office in the general election.

Texas Primaries Before 1905, various practices had been used to select a party's nominees for public office. With the enactment of the Terrell Election Law in 1905, however, Texas political parties gained the opportunity to conduct primaries. The Texas Democratic Party has held primaries since 1905. The Republican Party did not begin conducting primaries until 1926. In 1996, for the first time in Texas history, the Republican Party held primaries in all 254 counties of the state. (If there are no locally contested races, a political party has the option of not conducting a primary election within its county.) In 2012, the Republican Party conducted primaries in 248 (out of 254) counties whereas the Democratic Party conducted primaries in 241 counties.

In Texas, bonds of party loyalty loosen at general election time. Beginning in the early 1950s, it became common practice for Texans to participate in the primaries of the Democratic Party and then legally cross over to vote for Republican candidates in the general election. **Crossover voting** is evidence of a long-term trend toward voter independence of traditional party ties. Historically, Texas Republicans were more likely to engage in crossover voting. As the number of Republican candidates increased, however, the number of crossover Republican voters correspondingly declined. Today, Democrats in Republican-dominated counties (such as Collin, Denton, Midland, Montgomery, and Williamson) are likely to participate in crossover voting.

The Texas Election Code requires voters to identify their party affiliation at the time of voting, making Texas a combination of a closed primary state and an open primary state. Voter registration certificates are stamped with the party name when voters participate in a primary. Qualified voters may vote in the primary of any party, as long as they have not already voted in another party's primary or convention in the same year. The primary ballot contains the following restriction: "I am a Republican (Democrat) and understand that I am ineligible to vote or participate in another political party's primary election or convention during this voting

open primary
A primary in which voters are not required to declare party identification.

jungle primary
A nominating process whereby voters indicate their preferences by using a single ballot on which are printed the names and respective party labels of all persons seeking nomination. California and Louisiana conduct a jungle primary in which candidates from all parties compete in a single election. A candidate who receives 50 percent or more of the vote is elected; otherwise, a runoff between the top two candidates must be held.

crossover voting
A practice whereby a person participates in the primary of one party, then votes for one or more candidates of another party in the general election.

How Do We Compare...in Types of Primaries?

Most Populous U.S. States	Primary Type	U.S. States Bordering Texas	Primary Type
California	Jungle	Arkansas	Open
Florida	Closed	Louisiana	Jungle
New York	Closed	New Mexico	Closed
Texas	**Combination (open/closed)**	Oklahoma	Closed

Source: Pew Center on the States (http://www.pewstates.org/projects/stateline).

year."[28] Violation of a party pledge is a misdemeanor offense punishable by a fine of $500.

Administering Primaries In most states, political parties sponsor and administer their own primaries. The Texas Election Code allocates this responsibility to each party's county executive committee. Political parties whose gubernatorial candidate received 20 percent or more of the vote in the preceding general election must nominate all of their candidates in direct primaries conducted in even-numbered years.

A law passed in 2003 by the 78th Texas legislature requires that Texas's first primary must be conducted a week earlier than under previous law. As a result of this legislation, the first primary normally occurs the first Tuesday of March. In 2012, however, legal battles regarding redistricting delayed primary elections. The U.S. District Court for the Western District of Texas, in ordering new legislative districts, also set primary election dates for that year. The first primary election was conducted the last Tuesday in May (which occurred on May 29), and the runoff (second) primary was conducted the last Tuesday in July (which occurred on July 31). By May 29, 2012, 44 states, five territories (U.S. Virgin Islands, Guam, Northern Mariana Islands, American Samoa, Puerto Rico), and the District of Columbia (D.C.) had already conducted presidential primaries earlier than Texas.

Individuals who want to run in a direct primary for their party's nomination for a multicounty district office or a statewide office must file the necessary papers with their party's state chair. This party official certifies the names of these persons to each county chair in counties in which the election is administered. Prospective candidates who want their names placed on the primary ballot for a county or precinct office must file with their party's county chair. County executive committees for each political party supervise the printing of primary ballots. If the parties conduct a joint primary, the county elections administrator or the county clerk administers the election. If each party conducts its own primaries, county chairs arrange for voting equipment and polling places in the precincts. With the approval of the county executive committee, the county chair obtains supplies and appoints a presiding judge of elections in each precinct. Together with the state executive committee, the county executive committee determines the order of names of candidates on the ballot and **canvasses** (that is, confirms and certifies) the vote tally for each candidate.

Financing Primaries Major expenses for administering party primaries include renting facilities for polls (the places where voting is conducted), printing ballots and other election materials, and paying election judges and clerks. In recent years, approximately 30 percent of the cost of holding Texas primaries has come from filing fees paid by candidates. The balance of these expenses is usually paid by the State of Texas. For example, candidates for the office of U.S. senator pay $5,000, and candidates for governor and all other statewide offices pay $3,750. Candidates for the Texas Senate and the Texas House of Representatives pay $1,250 and $750, respectively.[29]

In lieu of paying a fee, a candidate may file a nominating petition containing a specified number of signatures of people eligible to vote for the office for which that candidate is running. A candidate for statewide office must obtain 5,000 signatures. Candidates for district, county, or precinct office, and for offices of other political subdivisions, must obtain either 500 signatures or the equivalent of 2 percent of the area's votes for all candidates for governor in the last general election, whichever is less. Although second (or runoff) primaries are usually less expensive, the average expenditure per voter is greater because voter turnout tends to be lower.

General and Special Elections

Throughout the United States, the date prescribed by federal law for congressional elections is the first Tuesday following the first Monday in November of even-numbered years (for example, November 6, 2012, and November 4, 2014). Presidential elections take place on the same day in November every four years (for example, November 6, 2012, and November 8, 2016).

In Texas's general elections involving candidates for state, district, and county offices, the candidate who receives a plurality (the largest number of votes) in a contest is the winner. Even if no candidate wins a majority, because of votes received by third-party or independent candidates, the state does not hold a runoff election. Thus, Governor Perry was reelected in 2008 after receiving only 39 percent of the total vote. Elections for governor and other statewide officers serving terms of four years are scheduled in the off year. These **off-year or midterm elections** are held in November of the even-numbered years between presidential elections (for example, November 4, 2014 and November 6, 2018). Along with most other states, Texas follows this schedule to minimize the influence of presidential campaigns on the election of state and local officials. Elections to fill offices for two-year or six-year terms must be conducted in both off years and presidential years.

canvass
To scrutinize the results of an election and then confirm and certify the vote tally for each candidate.

off-year or midterm election
A general election held in the even-numbered year following a presidential election.

special election
An election called by the governor to fill a vacancy (e.g., U.S. congressional or state legislative office) or to vote on a proposed state constitutional amendment or local bond issue.

In addition, **special elections** are called to fill interim vacancies in legislative and congressional districts. If no candidate obtains a majority in a special election, a runoff contest between the top two contenders must be conducted to obtain a winner. For example, on November 8, 2011, voters participated in a special election to replace District 14 Representative Fred Brown (R-Bryan) following his resignation from the Texas House of Representatives to manage a car dealership in Temple outside of his district. Because no candidate received a majority of votes in the special election, a special runoff election was held on December 13, 2011, in which Republican John Raney defeated Republican Bob Yancey for the vacant seat. Raney won election to a full term in November 2012. In addition to participating in special elections to fill vacancies in U.S. congressional and state legislative offices, Texans vote in special elections to act on local bond issues and, occasionally, to elect members of city councils and special-district boards. Vacancies in state judicial and executive offices are filled by gubernatorial appointment until the next general election and do not require special elections.

Learning Check 5.5   (Answers on p. 204)

1. True or False: Political parties are responsible for conducting primary elections.
2. On which day are general elections held?

Conclusion

Although most obstacles to voting have been abolished and Texas election laws have extended voting periods and simplified the elections process, many Texans do not exercise their right to vote. In national, state, and local elections, Texans vote at or below the national average. In addition, because education, income, and race are critical factors affecting voter turnout, concern is increasing that decisions are being made by an "elite" minority.

Chapter Summary

- Political campaigns reflect the influence of the media (especially television), mudslide (negative) campaigning, and money. Both federal and state laws regulate election campaigns, with federal law requiring disclosure of donor information and limiting contributions. State law establishes reporting requirements. A possible solution to money's influence on Texas politics is public funding of campaigns.
- An increasing number of African Americans and Latinos have won office in recent years at both the state and local levels of government.

African American voters consistently favor Democratic candidates. Latino voters, though tending to favor Democratic candidates, have given strong support to some Republican candidates.

- Gender-based politics grew in importance during the final decades of the past century, as women became more politically active and had a direct influence on public policy decisions.
- Historically, obstacles to voting included poll taxes, all-white primaries, racial gerrymandering, and diluting minority votes. Today, most of those restrictions have been removed.
- Nearly every citizen over the age of 18 can vote. One area of concern is how few eligible voters choose to exercise this right.
- Factors that affect voter turnout include education, income, gender, age, race, and ethnicity.
- Low citizen participation in elections has been attributed to the influence of pollsters and media consultants, voter fatigue resulting from too many elections, negative campaigning by candidates, lack of information about candidates and issues, and feelings of isolation from government.
- Primaries and state and county elections are administered by state, local, and party officials as prescribed by the Texas Election Code.
- There are three types of elections: party primaries, general elections, and special elections. In primaries, political parties select their nominees for public office. General elections are conducted by state and local officials. Special elections serve to fill vacancies in public office.

Key Terms

sound bite, p. 171
political action committee (PAC), p. 175
Texas Ethics Commission, p. 175
Campaign Reform Act, p. 175
soft money, p. 175
hard money, p. 175
super PAC, p. 176
universal suffrage, p. 182
voter registration, p. 183
literacy test, p. 183
grandfather clause, p. 183
poll tax, p. 183
white primary, p. 183
affirmative racial gerrymandering, p. 184
at-large majority district, p. 185
motor-voter law, p. 186
voter turnout, p. 187

Texas Election Code, p. 189
early voting, p. 190
voting precinct, p. 192
elections administrator, p. 193
election judge, p. 194
independent candidate, p. 197
primary, p. 197
direct primary, p. 197
general election, p. 198
runoff primary, p. 198
closed primary, p. 198
open primary, p. 199
jungle primary, p. 199
crossover voting, p. 199
canvass, p. 201
off-year or midterm election, p. 201
special election, p. 202

Learning Check Answers

5.1

1. False. Most Texas voters learn about candidates through television commercials.
2. The Texas Ethics Commission; unlike the Federal Election Campaign Act, however, Texas has no laws to limit political contributions, except for some judicial positions.

5.2

1. Although more Latinos today are likely to split their tickets, traditionally they have supported the Democratic Party.
2. False. In 2013, two African Americans were holding statewide elected positions: Texas Supreme Court justices Wallace Bernard Jefferson and Dale Washington.

5.3

1. True. With her reelection to the U.S. Senate in 2000, Republican Kay Bailey Hutchison became the first person to receive more than four million votes. In 2002, Carole Keeton Rylander (later Strayhorn) received more than 2.8 million votes in her reelection as state comptroller. Hutchison led all candidates on the ticket in 2006 with over 2.6 million votes received.
2. Two: Miriam A. ("Ma") Ferguson (1925–1927 and 1933–1935) and Ann Richards (1991–1995)

5.4

1. Historically, obstacles to voting in Texas included poll taxes, all-white primaries, racial gerrymandering, and diluting minority votes.
2. False. Texas law allows any qualified voter to vote "early" during a 17-day period preceding a scheduled election or first primary and for 10 days preceding a runoff primary.

5.5

1. True. Primary elections are party functions in which party members select nominees to run against the candidates of opposing parties in a general election.
2. General elections are held on the first Tuesday following the first Monday in November of even-numbered years.

Discussion Questions

1. With the increasing political importance of women and of racial and ethnic minorities, how has Texas politics changed? What changes can we anticipate in the future?
2. What electoral reforms are suggested to improve all levels of government? Which of these reforms have the best chance of succeeding?
3. Is Texas's low voter turnout a problem? If so, how can this issue be addressed to increase voter participation?
4. What obstacles exist today that prevent people from voting?
5. What are the differences among primary, general, and special elections?
6. Besides voting, in what other ways can a person effectively participate in the election process?

Internet Resources

William C. Velasquez Institute:
http://www.wcvi.org

Elections Division, Texas Secretary of State:
http://www.sos.state.tx.us/elections/index.shtml

Texas Election Code:
http://www.statutes.legis.state.tx.us/?link=EL

Texas Ethics Commission:
http://www.ethics.state.tx.us

Vote Texas: **http://votexas.org**

Notes

1. George N. Green, "O'Daniel, Wilbert Lee [Pappy]," *The Handbook of Texas Online,* http://www.tshaonline.org/handbook/online/articles/OO/fod11.html.

2. Marc Lacey, "Clicking Candidate.com, Landing at Opponent.com," *The New York Times*, September 14, 2010, http://www.nytimes.com/2010/09/15/us /politics/15squatters.html.

3. Reeve Hamilton, "Ads Infinitum: Hutchison's Cha-Ching," *The Texas Tribune*, January 15, 2010.

4. Ross Ramsey. "Do Negative Campaign Ads Work?" *Texas Tribune,* February 18, 2010, http://www.texastribune.org/texas-politics/2010-texas-governors-race /do-negative-campaign-ads-work/.

5. W. Gardner Selby, "Sanchez Campaign Fueled Record," *San Antonio Express-News*, January 15, 2002.

6. Bipartisan Campaign Reform Act of 2002, 2 U.S.C. § 431 (2002).

7. Quoted in "House Panel OK's Disclosure Rules," *Waco Tribune-Herald*, April 17, 2003.

8. Tim Eaton, "ID Measure Passed Quietly, While Sanctuary Cities Bill Died Noisily" *Austin American Statesman*, June 29, 2011.

9. Quoted by Trip Gabriel, "Stance on Immigration May Hurt Perry Early On," *The New York Times*, September 23, 2011.

10. *Yick Wo v. Hopkins,* 118 U.S. 356, 370 (1886).

11. Christopher Long, "Ku Klux Klan," *The Handbook of Texas Online,* http://www.tshaonline.org/handbook/online/articles/KK/vek2_print.html.

12. David Montejano, *Anglos and Mexicans in the Making of Texas, 1836–1986* (Austin: University of Texas Press, 1987), 143.

13. Other U.S. Supreme Court cases involving the Texas white primary are *Nixon v. Herndon* 273 U.S. 536 (1927), *Nixon v. Condon* 286 U.S. 73 (1932), and *Grovey v. Townsend* 295 U.S. 45 (1936). For more information on the history of the white primary in Texas, see Darlene Clark Hine, *Black Victory: The Rise and Fall of the White Primary in Texas* (Millwood, NY: KTO Press, 1979).

14. Dan Eggen, "Justice Staff Saw Texas Districting Plan as Illegal," *Washington Post*, December 2, 2005.

15. *League of United Latin American Citizens v. Perry*, 548 U.S. 399 (2006).

16. For more information about the 2011 redistricting process in the Lone Star State, see Texas Legislative Council, "Texas Redistricting," http://www.tlc .state.tx.us/redist/redist.htm; and Michael Li, "Texas Redistricting," http://txredistricting.org/.

17. For more information on racial gerrymandering and the use of at-large districts to disenfranchise minorities, see Christopher M. Burke, *The Appearance of Equality: Racial Gerrymandering, Redistricting, and the Supreme Court* (Westport, CT: Greenwood Press, 1999).

18. This information is available at Michael McDonald, "United States Election Project," George Mason University, http://elections.gmu.edu/voter_turnout.htm.

19. Tex. Elec. Code Ann. §41.001 (2012).

20. "Texas Latino Voter Statistics," William C. Velasquez Institute, http://www.wcvi.org/latino_voter_research/latino_voter_statistics/tx_lv.html.

21. The Texas Election Code is a compilation of state laws that govern voter qualifications, procedures for nominating and electing party and government officials, and other matters related to suffrage and elections.

22. Tex. Elec. Code Ann. §11.001 and §11.002 (2012).

23. Lise Olsen, "Watch Out for Voter Registration Cancellations," *Houston Chronicle*, June 4, 2012.

24. Tex. Elec. Code Ann. Chapter 82, "Eligibility for Early Voting" (2012).

25. Sam Attlesey, "Fewer Elections, More Votes?" *Dallas Morning News*, May 17, 1999.

26. Tex. Elec. Code Ann. §42.006 (2012).

27. Office of the Secretary of State, "Amended Texas State Plan Pursuant to the Help America Vote Act of 2002 (HAVA)," January 2005, http://www.sos.state.tx.us/elections/forms/stateplan0105.pdf

28. Tex. Elec. Code Ann. §172.086 (2012)

29. Tex. Elec. Code Ann. §172.024 (2012).

Lots of GOP Money Flowing from the Texas Two

Wade Goodwyn

Among the largest fundraisers and donors to Republican candidates and the National Republican Party are two Texas businessmen: Harold Simmons and Bob Perry (no relation to Governor Rick Perry). This story, which was broadcast March 2, 2012, on National Public Radio's "All Things Considered," explores the motivations behind and the strategies used by these two individuals in their political donations. The full transcripts may be accessed at http://www.npr.org/templates/transcript/transcript.php?storyId=149070080

The latest reports from the Federal Election Commission shed new light on the political largesse of two Texas businessmen who have become common names in the world of Republican fundraising. With a $1 million check in February (2012) to the superPAC backing Rick Santorum, Dallas nuclear waste dump owner Harold Simmons and his wife, Annette, have now contributed to groups supporting all three of the top GOP candidates. And Houston home builder Bob Perry tripled his 2011 investment in the superPAC supporting Mitt Romney: His $3 million donation made up nearly half of Restore Our Future's total take in February [2012], according to FEC figures released Tuesday.

Republican political consultant Bill Miller says that over the last 30 years, [Bob] Perry has used his money to build the Texas Republican Party. He's been the single largest donor at the national level, too. According to figures compiled by the Center for Responsive Politics, the National Institute for Money in State Politics and Texans for Public Justice, during the last decade Perry has donated $79,944,942 to various campaigns. "He's been generous and he's been the go-to guy," Miller says. "The first and last to ask, for Republicans, as long as I can remember."

Simmons has not been donating as long as Perry. But in the last eight years he's made a big impact as well, donating more than $20 million to the GOP. "They both play big. They're very generous and their checks are large," Miller says, "and when they step in you know that they're there."

Consistent Conservative Donations

In the past, Simmons has been drawn to what some might say is the seedier side of presidential campaigns. He gave $3 million to the Swift Boat Veterans for Truth to torpedo Sen. John Kerry's Vietnam War record during the 2004 presidential race. To help Sen. John McCain in 2008, Simmons gave nearly $3 million more to help pay for an ad that linked Barack Obama to a 1970's radical left-wing group called the Weathermen. The attack strategy, which attempted to link Obama to the militant group's leader Bill Ayres, didn't get much traction, perhaps because Obama was in elementary school in 1970. But the Swift Boat ads did do meaningful damage to Kerry.

This election cycle, Simmons and his wife have been spreading his money around, with donations to support Romney, Santorum and Newt Gingrich. Simmons gave another $14 million to Karl Rove's superPAC, American Crossroads – the Supreme Court's Citizens United ruling's effect clearly on display here.

Paying For Influence?

Political observers in Austin, Texas, speculate this spreading of the wealth has to do with Simmons' main business, a nuclear waste dump in West Texas. "His motive these days is to expand as much as he can the volume of waste that comes into the dump," says Craig McDonald, who heads Texans for Public Justice, which tracks campaign contributions in Texas. Simmons' dump takes low-level nuclear waste, McDonald says, but it could be the long-term storage solution for high-level nuclear waste. This material is usually stored on site at the reactor and is a security and environmental threat.

Given how politically charged the subject is, Simmons is going to need political allies at both the state and federal levels. "We've also noticed the last couple of years, he not only has been moving money to federal candidates, but he's also been moving a lot of campaign money to state leaders in states that, right now, don't have a location to place their own low-level [nuclear] waste, so he's out there shopping," McDonald says.

"There's an old joke that a taxidermist and a veterinarian go into business together and the sign says, 'Either Way You Get Your Dog Back,'" says Ross Ramsey, who has been covering Texas politics for more than 30 years and is the editor of the online journal *The Texas Tribune.* "Simmons is playing this so that however it lands, he's got a winner."

"Establishment" Republicans

Ramsey says Simmons and Perry, while pretty conservative, are nevertheless considered mainstream Republicans. In fact, Perry, who relies on immigrant laborers to staff his construction crews, successfully blocked the most severe immigration reform measures that Tea Party supporters wanted to pass in Texas. "I think this is the establishment. Perry is more of, you know, what might be called a movement conservative. He's supported socially conservative and fiscally conservative Republicans," Ramsey says. "I think Simmons is more of a classic establishment Republican. He's supported, you know, business-friendly conservatives."

Learning Objectives

1. Explain what interest groups are, why they form, and what their essential characteristics are.
2. Describe the types of interest groups and analyze the qualities of a powerful interest group.
3. Evaluate the kinds of activities that interest groups use to influence Texas government.
4. Analyze how interest groups are regulated and evaluate the effectiveness of these laws.

T he typical focus of politics is on the nomination and election of citizens to public office. There is, however, much more to politics than that. Politics is perhaps best understood as the process of influencing public policy decisions to protect and preserve a group, to achieve the group's goals, and to distribute benefits to the group's members. Organized citizens demand policies that promote their financial security, education, health, welfare, and protection.

Because government makes and enforces public policy decisions, it is not surprising that people try to influence officials who make and apply society's rules or policies, nor is it surprising that one important approach is through group action. History shows that people who organize for political action tend to be more effective in achieving their goals than persons acting alone. This principle is particularly true if a group is well financed. Money plays a big role in state government and state elections, and groups that help politicians finance their campaigns often achieve their goals.

Interest Groups in the Political Process

When people attempt to influence political decisions or the selection of the men and women who make such decisions, they usually turn either to political parties (examined in Chapter 4, "Political Parties") or to interest groups (the subject of this chapter).

What Is an Interest Group?

LO1

An **interest group** may be identified as a pressure group, a special interest group, or a lobby. It is an organization whose members share common views and objectives. To promote their interests, such groups participate in activities designed to influence government officials and policy decisions. During every regular legislative session, one of the interest groups in action includes the Independent Colleges and Universities of Texas, which lobbies the legislature against cuts to the Texas Equalization Grants (TEG), a student aid program that provides financial assistance to students who attend private colleges and universities. Another interest group is the Texas Coalition to Abolish the Death Penalty, which continues to lobby actively for a moratorium on the death penalty. Parent groups, teacher organizations, and school board associations all actively lobby for more state money for the state's public schools.

Although political parties and interest groups both attempt to influence policy decisions by government officials, they differ in their methods. The principal purpose of party activity is to increase the number of its members who are elected or appointed to public offices, in order to gain control of government and achieve party goals. In contrast, an interest group seeks to influence government officials (regardless of their party affiliation) to the

interest group
An organization that seeks to influence government officials and their policies on behalf of members sharing common views and objectives (e.g., labor union or trade association).

advantage of the group. In general, an interest group wants government to create and implement policies that benefit the group, without necessarily placing its own members in public office.

Part of the purpose of economic groups (for example, the Texas Association of Business) and professional groups (such as the Texas Trial Lawyers Association) is to make their policy preferences known to government officials. Interest groups act as intermediaries for people who share common interests but reside throughout the state; in this way, interest groups add to the formal system of geographic representation used for electing many officeholders. In essence, such organizations serve the interests of their members by providing functional representation within the political system. They offer a form of protection by voicing the interests of such groups as businesspeople, laborers, farmers, religious groups, Latinos, teachers, physicians, and college students across the state. These groups are composed of people who have similar interests but who may not constitute a majority in any city, county, legislative district, or state.

The Reasons for Interest Groups

The growth and diversity of interest groups in the United States continue unabated. An increasingly complex society has much to do with the rate of growth of interest groups in the country and within states. Political scientists Allan Cigler and Burnett Loomis contend that these growing numbers, plus high levels of activity, distinguish contemporary interest group politics from previous eras.[1] Interest groups proliferate in Texas and throughout the country for several reasons.

Legal and Cultural Reasons In *NAACP v. Alabama* 357 U.S. 449 (1958), the U.S. Supreme Court recognized the **right of association** as part of the right of assembly granted by the First Amendment of the U.S. Constitution. This decision greatly facilitated the development of interest groups, ensuring the right of citizens to organize for political, economic, religious, and social purposes.

The nation's political culture has traditionally encouraged citizens to organize themselves into a bewildering array of associations—religious, fraternal, professional, and recreational, among others. Americans have responded by creating literally thousands of such groups. In the 1960s and 1970s, for example, social movements sparked interest group activities on issues involving civil rights, women's rights, student rights, and opposition to the Vietnam War. More recently, in Texas, controversies over social issues (e.g., the ban on same-sex marriage) and education policy issues (e.g., school finance) have sparked new groups and revitalized existing interest groups. For instance, in 2012, Texans for Real Efficiency and Equity in Education, a new education group, formed to intervene in the latest round of public school financing lawsuits, claiming that the current school financing system is not efficient as required by the Texas Constitution.

right of association
The U.S. Supreme Court has ruled that this right is part of the right of assembly guaranteed by the First Amendment of the U.S. Constitution and that it protects the right of people to organize into groups for political purposes.

Decentralized Government In a decentralized government, power is not concentrated at the highest level. Decentralization is achieved in two principal ways. First, the federal system divides power between the national government and the 50 state governments (as explained in Chapter 2, "Federalism and the Texas Constitution"). In turn, each state shares its power with a variety of local governments, including counties, cities, and special districts. Second, within each level of government, power is separated into three branches, or departments: legislative, executive, and judicial. This separation of powers is especially apparent at the national and state levels.

A decentralized structure increases the opportunities for interest groups to form and influence government. This structure provides different access points for groups to fight their battles at different levels of government and within different branches at each level. For instance, in 2009, the Texas Bicycle Coalition was unsuccessful in obtaining legislation at the state level to protect bicyclists on Texas roads. Nevertheless, the organization pressed successfully for protective city ordinances, such as in Austin and San Antonio. More recently, with the governor's veto of a legislative bill banning texting while driving in 2011, many cities, such as San Antonio, have passed city ordinances banning texting while driving, especially in school zones. Thus, dispersal of power within branches of government enhances an interest group's chance of success.

The Strength of the Party System and Political Ideologies Two other factors have precipitated the influence of interest groups: the strength (or weakness) of the party system and political ideologies. First, the absence of unified and responsible political parties magnifies opportunities for interest group action. A lack of strong, organized political parties can particularly affect policymakers (both state and local). In such cases, public officials are less likely to vote along party lines and therefore be more susceptible to pressure from well-organized interest groups, particularly if those candidates rely on interest group campaign contributions. In recent years, Texas has arguably experienced party competition between Republicans and Democrats, which has produced a degree of party unity for each. Many believe that a strong party system is still lacking in Texas. For instance, in 2009 and in early 2010, the Texas Tea Party emerged as part of the larger national Tea Party movement. It formed in reaction to the perceived failure of the Republican Party to mobilize right-wing opposition against the Obama administration's expanding role of the federal government regarding issues affecting the federal debt and taxation.

Second, ideologies, or developed systems of political, social, and economic beliefs, have not been strong factors in Texas politics. Instead, public officials rely more on their constituents or on the issues and less on ideology. Yet, while public officials are more likely to have a stronger commitment to ideological beliefs than most voters, they remain susceptible to the pressures of interest groups.

decentralized government
Decentralization is achieved by dividing power between national and state governments and separating legislative, executive, and judicial branches at both levels.

Characteristics of Interest Groups

Citizens may join an interest group for a variety of reasons, whether financial, professional, or social. Students who graduate from college often find themselves joining a professional or occupational group (see Table 6.1).

Table 6.1   Texas Professional and Occupational Associations*
Health Related
Texas Dental Association
Texas Health Care Association
Texas Hospital Association
Texas Medical Association
Texas Ophthalmological Association
Texas Nurses Association
Texas Physical Therapy Association
Texas Counseling Association
Law Related
Texas Criminal Defense Lawyers Association
Texans for Lawsuit Reform
Texas Civil Justice League
Texas Trial Lawyers Association
Mexican American Bar Association
Texas Women Lawyers
Texas Young Lawyers Association
Education Related
Texas Federation of Teachers
Texas Association of College Teachers
Texas Classroom Teachers Association
Texas PTA
Texas Community College Teachers Association
Texas State Teachers Association
Texas Library Association
Texas Association of College and University Student Personnel
Texas Faculty Association
Texas School Counselor Association
Texas Association of School Administrators
Miscellaneous
Association of Environmental and Engineering Geologists (AEG) Texas
Texas Society of Architects
Texas Society of Certified Public Accountants
Intelligent Transportation Society (ITS) Texas

*All organizations listed can be found on the Internet.

In some cases, people join an interest group simply because they want to be part of a network of like-minded individuals working for a cause. The interest group often provides members with information and benefits and usually tries to involve them in the political process. Such a description suggests that any organization becomes an interest group when it influences or attempts to influence governmental decisions.

There are almost as many **organizational patterns** as there are interest groups. This variety arises from the fact that in addition to lobbying, most interest groups perform nonpolitical functions that are of paramount importance to their members. A religious organization, for example, emphasizes charitable and spiritual activities, but it may also undertake political activity.

Some interest groups are highly centralized organizations that take the form of a single controlling body without affiliated local or regional units. An example of such a centralized group currently operating in Texas is the National Rifle Association. Other groups are decentralized, consisting of loose alliances of local and regional subgroups. Their activities may be directed at either the local, state, or national level. Many trade associations (such as the Texas Mid-Continent Oil and Gas Association) and labor unions (such as those affiliated with the American Federation of Labor–Congress of Industrial Organizations [AFL-CIO]) are examples of decentralized organizations active in Texas politics. Groups with national organizations, including the National Women's Political Caucus and Common Cause, usually have both state and local chapters in Texas.

Interest groups are composed chiefly of persons from professional and managerial occupations. Members of interest groups tend to have greater resources than most people possess. For instance, members are more likely to be homeowners, with high levels of income and formal education, who enjoy a high standard of living. Participation in interest groups, especially active participation, varies. Many citizens are not affiliated with any group, whereas others are members of several. Although recent technology provides individuals easier access to interest group membership, many will not join an organization—especially when they believe that they still benefit without the costs of membership.[2]

An organized group of any size usually comprises an active minority and a passive majority. As a result, decisions are regularly made by relatively few members. These decision makers may range from a few elected officers to a larger body of delegates representing the entire membership. Organizations generally leave decision making and other leadership activities to a few people. Widespread apathy among rank-and-file members and the difficulty of dislodging entrenched leaders probably account for limited participation in most group decisions. Factors that influence **group leadership** include the group's financial resources (members who contribute most heavily usually have greater weight in making decisions), time-consuming leadership duties (only a few people can afford to devote much of their time without compensation), and the personality traits of leaders (some individuals have greater leadership ability and motivation than others).

organizational pattern
The structure of a special interest group. Some interest groups have a decentralized pattern of organization (e.g., the AFL-CIO, with many local unions). Others are centralized (e.g., the National Rifle Association, which is a national body without affiliated local or regional units).

group leadership
Individuals who guide the decisions of interest groups. Leaders of groups tend to have financial resources that permit them to contribute money and devote time to group affairs.

Learning Check 6.1 (Answers on p. 241)

1. True or False: Similar to political parties, interest groups are interested in shaping public policy.
2. Name five factors that motivate interest group formation.
3. True or False: Most interest groups have an active membership.

Types of Interest Groups

LO2

The increasing diversity of American interest groups at the national, state, and local levels of government permits the groups to be classified in several ways. Not only can interest groups be studied by organizational patterns (as discussed earlier), they can also be categorized according to the level or branch of government to which they direct their attention. Some groups exert influence at all levels of government and on legislative, executive (including administrative), and judicial officials. Others may try to spread their views among the general public and may best be classified according to the subject matter they represent. Some groups do not fit readily into any category, whereas others fit into more than one. In the next section, we examine various types of interest groups—from economic groups, professional and government employee groups, and social groups to public interest groups.

Economic Groups

Many interest groups exist primarily to promote their members' economic self-interest. These organizations are commonly known as **economic interest groups**. Traditionally, many people contribute significant amounts of money and time to obtain the financial benefits of group membership. Thus, some organizations exist to further the economic interests of a broad group, such as trade associations, whereas others seek to protect the interests of a single type of business, such as restaurant associations. The Texas Association of Business and Chambers of Commerce (generally known as TAB) is an example of a broader type of interest group, known as an umbrella organization. There are also individual corporations, such as communications giant AT&T, that use the political process to promote a company's particular economic interests.

Business Groups Businesspeople understand that they have common interests that may be promoted by collective action. They were among the first to organize and press national, state, and local governments to adopt favorable public policies. **Business organizations** typically advocate lower taxes, a lessening or elimination of price and quality controls by government, and

economic interest group
Trade associations and labor unions are classified as economic interest groups because they are organized to promote policies that will maximize profits and wages.

business organization
An economic interest group, such as a trade association (e.g., Texas Association of Builders), that lobbies for policies favoring Texas business.

minimal concessions to labor unions. At the state level, business organizations most often take the form of trade associations (groups that act on behalf of an industry). The Texas Gaming Association (a group that favors the creation of destination casino resorts in the state) and the Amusement and Music Operators of Texas (a trade group representing bars and taverns) are two of the interest groups that have lobbied the state legislature in recent legislative sessions in support of gambling interests. Two of the many other Texas trade associations are the Texas Association of Builders (a group that focuses on creating a positive environment for the housing industry) and the Texas Good Roads and Transportation Association (a group dedicated to ensuring efficient transportation).

In past legislative sessions, Texas businesses and their representatives succeeded in having many of their policy preferences enacted into law. Some reports indicate that the TAB, along with Texans for Lawsuit Reform, contributed more than $2.6 million to support Republican candidates in key legislative races in 2002. Subsequently, the newly GOP-controlled 78th legislature passed several "business friendly" bills. One of the more significant bills limited lawsuits against manufacturers, pharmaceutical companies, and retailers.[3] In 2005, TAB credited the Texas legislature with providing a strong probusiness climate. During the special legislative sessions of that year, business groups successfully lobbied against tax reform proposals that would shift the cost of school finance from property taxes to increased business taxes. Furthermore, the tobacco industry successfully defeated a statewide ban on smoking in public places, hiring as many as 40 lobbyists during the 2009 legislative session.[4] During the 2011 legislative session, big business (such as oil and gas, banking and finance, and insurance) was successful in defending current tax breaks and subsidies. Unlike big businesses, however, small businesses were only able to extend a business franchise tax exemption through 2013.

Labor Groups Unions representing Texas workers, though relatively active, are not as numerous or powerful as business-related groups. The state's **labor organizations** seek, among other goals, government intervention to increase wages, obtain adequate health insurance coverage, provide unemployment insurance, and promote safe working conditions.

Although Texans are traditionally sensitive to the potential political power of organized labor, certain industrial labor organizations are generally regarded as significant in Texas government. These are the Texas affiliates of the AFL-CIO (comprising 1,300 local unions and more than 200,000 members), the Communication Workers of America, and local affiliates of the International Brotherhood of Teamsters. For a highly industrialized state with a large population, union membership in Texas is small compared with that of other states. In 2010, about 545,000 union members were employed in Texas. Union membership dropped in 2011 to about 534,000 members, which is about 5.2 percent of the wage and salary workers, according to the U.S. Bureau of Labor Statistics. With the pending cuts in education, health care, and state jobs in the state legislature, the Texas State Employees Union,

labor organization
A union that supports pubic policies designed to increase wages, obtain adequate health insurance coverage, provide unemployment insurance, promote safe working conditions, and otherwise protect the interests of workers.

an affiliate of the Communication Workers of America, relied on rallies as a means of expressing opposition. This union was a lead organizer of the "Save Our State Rally," in which an estimated 6,000 to 7,000 people participated at the steps of the state capitol during the 2011 legislative session.

Professional/Career Groups

Closely related to economic interest groups are groups dedicated to furthering the interests of a profession or an occupation or career.

Professional Groups Standards of admission to a profession or an occupation, as well as the licensing of practitioners, concern **professional groups.** Examples of Texas professional and occupational associations are the State Bar of Texas (attorneys), the Texas Health Care Association, and the Texas Society of Certified Public Accountants. (See Table 6.1 for a list of some of the more important Texas professional and occupational associations.) Professionals are more effective if they organize in groups that advocate for their interests. For instance, in 1999, physicians won a significant victory in the 76th legislature when Texas became the first state to allow doctors to bargain collectively with health maintenance organizations over fees and policies. Furthermore, in 2003, the Texas Medical Association (TMA) succeeded in lobbying passage of the constitutional amendment, Proposition 12, which authorized the state legislature to impose a $250,000 cap for noneconomic damages in medical malpractice cases. In recent years, the TMA has advocated for a new medical school in the Rio Grande Valley and an increase in the state's cap on student loans for young physicians in order to increase the number of primary care doctors. In addition, TMA has sought to increase state funding for Medicare and the Children's Health Insurance Program (CHIP) to ensure that Texas receives its full share of federal matching funds.

Government Employee Groups Officers and employees of state and local governments organize to obtain better working conditions, higher wages, more fringe benefits, and better retirement packages. The Texas State Employees Union, for instance, lobbies for legislation that prevents job cuts and increases pay and health-care benefits. Teacher groups made headway in the 76th legislative session in 2001, when $2 billion was allocated to fund a $3,000 pay raise for every public school teacher, librarian, and registered school nurse in Texas. Building on that momentum, teacher groups successfully pushed a plan to fully or partially fund state-supported health insurance for public school teachers and other school employees, both active and retired. However, when the 78th legislature first faced a budget crisis in 2003, teacher groups unsuccessfully lobbied the legislature against cuts in education funding. These groups included the Texas State Teachers Association (TSTA), Texas Federation of Teachers, Texas Association of College Teachers, and Texas Community College Teachers Association. According to TSTA, however, 39 bills that the organization opposed were defeated in the

professional group
An organization of physicians, lawyers, accountants, or other professional people that lobbies for policies beneficial to members.

Participants in a Texas AFL-CIO "Health Care Can't Wait" rally, held at the capitol building in Austin.

(Courtesy of Texas AFL-CIO)

2003 legislative session. During the 2005 regular legislative session and two special sessions, as well as in a 2006 special session, teacher organizations lobbied against school finance legislation that they believed would provide inadequate new funding and would intrude on local control of school matters. TSTA, which represented at the time more than 65,000 teachers, sued the state in 2008 for funneling state dollars to nonprofit organizations, including religious ones, to educate school dropouts, claiming the arrangement constituted a private school voucher program. During the 2011 legislative session, teacher associations participated in rallies outside the state capitol to demand that the legislature use the "rainy day" fund rather than make big cuts in education. (For more on school finance, see Chapter 11, "Finance and Fiscal Policy.") They also unsuccessfully lobbied against legislative proposals authorizing school districts to furlough teachers and cut salaries as cost-saving options.

Among state government employees, the largest group is the Texas Public Employees Association with more than 17,000 members. City government groups include the Texas City Management Association and the Texas City Attorneys Association. Through their organizational activities, these **public officer and employee groups** resist efforts to reduce the size of state and local governmental bureaucracies (though not always with success). The County Judges and Commissioners Association of Texas and the Justices of the Peace and Constables Association of Texas, for example, have been instrumental in blocking measures designed to reform Texas's justice of peace courts and county courts. During the 2009 legislative session, two of the state's largest police unions, the Texas Municipal Police Association and the Combined Law Enforcement Associations of Texas, which together

public officer and employee group
An organization of city managers, county judges, or other public employees or officials that lobbies for public policies that protect group interests.

represent more than 30,000 officers, joined forces to lobby for police officer rights. Although unsuccessful, the police unions went on record in support of a legislative proposal during the 2011 legislative session that would have banned texting while driving statewide.

Social Groups

Texas also has a wide array of **social interest groups**. These include racial and ethnic organizations, civil rights organizations, gender-based organizations, religious-based organizations, and several public interest groups.

Racial and Ethnic Groups Leaders of Texas's **racial and ethnic groups** recognize that only through effective organizations can they hope to achieve their cherished goals. Examples of these goals include eliminating racial discrimination in employment, improving public schools, increasing educational opportunities, and obtaining greater representation in the state legislature, city councils, school boards, and other policymaking bodies of government.

One formidable group, the National Association for the Advancement of Colored People (NAACP), is an effective racial interest group. The organization has been successful in influencing public policies relating to school integration and local government redistricting. The NAACP also fought for hate crimes legislation that enhances penalties for crimes on the basis of race, color, disability, religion, national origin, gender, or sexual preferences.[5] The organization also continues to fight against racial profiling. Texas law defines racial profiling as an action by law enforcement personnel on the basis of an individual's race, ethnicity, or national origin as opposed to the individual's behavior or information identifying the individual as being engaged in criminal activity. In 2011, the Texas NAACP actively opposed making a Confederate battle flag image available on specialty Texas license plates. The organization successfully appealed to the Texas Department of Motor Vehicles to prevent legitimizing a symbol, which in their view, represents brutality and fear and that is used by hate groups to promote a racist ideology.[6]

In Texas, Latino groups, especially Mexican American organizations, are more numerous than African American interest groups. The oldest Latino group, the League of United Latin American Citizens (LULAC), was founded in 1929.[7] (See the Selected Reading, "Unsung Hero of Civil Rights," for information on one of LULAC's founders, Alonso S. Perales.) LULAC has worked for equal educational opportunities for Latinos, as well as for full citizenship rights. It continues to advocate for adequate public school funding and bilingual education, as well as the "Top Ten Percent Rule" and affirmative action, both of which are designed to diversify higher-education institutions. In addition, LULAC successfully pressed for state funds to open the school of pharmacy at Texas A&M-Kingsville, which was named after the late state legislator and strong advocate for higher education, Irma Rangel.[8] More recently, LULAC brought attention to the importance of the U.S. census, as well as to the State Board of Education's unwillingness to incorporate more Hispanic historical figures in public school textbooks.

social interest group
Included among groups concerned primarily with social issues are organizations devoted to civil rights, racial and ethnic matters, religion, and pubic interest protection.

racial and ethnic groups
Organizations that seek to influence governmental decisions that affect a particular racial or ethnic group, such as the National Association for the Advancement of Colored People (NAACP) and the League of United Latin American Citizens (LULAC), which seek to influence government decisions affecting African Americans and Latinos, respectively.

Another organization, the Mexican American Legal Defense and Education Fund (MALDEF), uses court action to obtain political equality, equal education, immigration rights, and representation for Latinos. Both LULAC and MALDEF have been instrumental in addressing redistricting, especially when it comes to voting rights. For instance, MALDEF filed a lawsuit challenging the 2003 redrawing of congressional districts by the Republican-controlled state legislature, specifically the congressional district affecting San Antonio and Laredo. The case, *LULAC v. Perry* 548 U.S. 399 (2006), was heard by the U.S. Supreme Court in 2006. MALDEF successfully argued that the new redistricting scheme had diluted the voting strength of Latinos in violation of the Voting Rights Act. More recently, MALDEF has continued to address redistricting issues in the courts. On behalf of a statewide coalition of Texas Latino organizations called the Texas Latino Redistricting Task Force, among other plaintiffs, MALDEF successfully challenged the redistricting plans created by the Texas legislature for Congress and the Texas House of Representatives, claiming that the plans did not provide fair representation for Latinos. A three-judge court allowed for the creation of two out of the four new congressional seats to be Latino-majority districts. The court also created an additional Latino-majority district in the Texas House of Representatives, thus increasing the number of Latino-majority districts to 34. During the 2011 legislative session, MALDEF successfully advocated against the Voter ID law, anti-immigrant legislative proposals, as well as a bill banning sanctuary cities, which would have authorized local law enforcement officers to inquire into the immigrant status of detainees and report violations to federal immigration enforcement officers.

Women's Groups The Texas Women's Political Caucus is an example of a **women's organization** that promotes equal rights and greater participation by women in the political arena. The League of Women Voters of Texas is a nonpartisan organization advocating greater political participation and public understanding of governmental issues. It also assists voters in becoming better informed by publishing *The Texas Voters Guide*, which provides information about elections, candidates, and candidates' positions on various issues.

The Texas Federation of Republican Women, a partisan interest group with more than 160 local clubs, provides resources for women to influence government actions and policies. This organization actively encourages Republican women to run for public office. Another organization that formed in 2003, in response to the dwindling number of Democratic women in the state legislature, is Annie's List. This organization recruits, trains, and supports progressive female candidates, as well as raises money for these candidates.

Other interest groups, such as the Hispanic Women's Network of Texas, focus on the concerns and needs of Hispanic women. This organization is a statewide organization dedicated to advancing the interests of Latina women in the public, corporate, and civic arenas. Another organization, Las Comadres Para Las Americas, serves as a network for Latinas and provides training for candidates and public policy advocates.

women's organization
A women's group, such as the League of Women Voters, that engages in lobbying and educational activities to promote greater political participation by women and others.

Religious-Based Groups The Christian Coalition is an example of a religious-based group. With millions of Texans identifying themselves as conservative Christians, the organization continues to be one of the state's most influential political forces, though it had more momentum in the 1990s than it does now. This interest group engages in political action, primarily within the Republican Party. Issues that have precipitated the Christian Coalition's entrance on the political scene are abortion, homosexuality, limits on prayer in public schools, and the decline of the traditional nuclear family.[9]

In 1995, Cécile Richards (daughter of former governor Ann Richards) played a leading role in organizing the Texas Freedom Network to oppose the Christian Coalition. The organization watches the activities of right-wing conservatives, musters liberal and mainstream voters, and provides an alternative voice on current political issues.[10] The Texas Faith Network, the official blog of the Texas Freedom Network, also formed in 1996, monitors religious leaders statewide who represent the religious right and who intend to influence political conservatives (usually Republicans). In recent years, the Texas Freedom Network has opposed pro–school voucher forces and supporters who promote teaching competing theories to evolution, such as intelligent design, and providing biblical study in the public schools. The organization has also opposed social conservatives on the State Board of Education who influence the public school curriculum and the content of textbooks.

Another religious-based organization, the Texas Industrial Areas Foundation, which operates in cities such as Dallas and in the Rio Grande Valley, supports increased funding for parent training, for making it easier for children to qualify for Medicaid benefits, and for increasing Children's Health Insurance Program (CHIP) eligibility to more families.[11] Valley Interfaith, made up primarily of churches and schools, has successfully lobbied the Brownsville school district to increase wages for employees and has indirectly influenced other public institutions and companies to provide a "living wage" for their workers so they can live above the poverty level. In recent legislative sessions, Valley Interfaith actively lobbied the state legislature, demanding restoration of funds cut from CHIP, increases in Medicaid funding, and increases in state funding for public schools, as well as an equitable tax system that does not burden the poor. During the 2009 legislative session, the group also lobbied for the establishment of programs to support workforce development in high-demand occupations and "green jobs" that promote protection of the environment. In addition, sister organizations in San Antonio (Metro Alliance and Communities Organized for Public Service [COPS]) successfully lobbied the 77th legislature to pass a bill that allows cities to use sales tax revenue to create job training and early childhood development programs.[12] Many religious organizations (including Texas Impact, a statewide religious grassroots network) mobilized against proposed cuts in social services, participated in rallies, and organized an all-day prayer vigil during the 2011 legislative session.

religious-based group
An interest group, such as the Texas Faith Network, that lobbies for policies promoting its religious interests.

Table 6.2	Texas Public Interest Groups*
Consumer	
Consumers Union	
Texas Consumer Rights Action League	
Environmental	
Texas Campaign for the Environment	
Texas Wildlife Association	
Environment Texas	
Sierra Club, Lone Star Chapter	
Public Participation	
Texas Association of Community Action Agencies	
Communities Organized for Public Service	
Public Citizen/Texas	
The League of Women Voters of Texas	
Public Morality	
Mothers against Drunk Driving	
Texas Right to Life Committee	
Texas Abortion and Reproductive Rights Action League	

*All organizations listed can be found on the Internet.

Public Interest Groups

Unlike most interest groups, **public interest groups** claim to promote the general interests of society, rather than narrower private or corporate interests. Environmental, consumer, political participation, and public morality (not directly associated with established religion) organizations are often identified as public interest groups.

Public interest organizations pursue diverse goals. Common Cause Texas, for example, focuses primarily on governmental and institutional reform. It advocates open-meeting laws, public financing of political campaigns, stricter financial disclosure laws, and recorded votes in legislative chambers. Texans for Public Justice supports efforts toward campaign finance reform, such as limitations on campaign contributions by political action committees and individuals. Likewise, the Texas League of Conservation Voters monitors the voting records of state legislature members who support environment-friendly "green" bills. (See Table 6.2 for a partial list of Texas public interest groups.)

Texas Power Groups

Texas legislators readily identify the types of interest groups they consider most powerful: business-oriented trade associations (representing oil, gas, tobacco, chemical manufacturers, insurance, and railroads), professional

public interest group
An organization claiming to represent a broad public interest (environmental, consumer, political participation, and public morality) rather than a narrow private interest.

associations (physicians, lawyers, and teachers), and labor unions. Other groups wielding considerable influence include brewers, truckers, automobile dealers, bankers, and realtors. Some of the most influential interest groups operating not only in Texas but also nationwide are general business organizations (e.g., chambers of commerce), schoolteacher associations, utility companies, insurance companies and associations, hospital and nursing home associations, and bar associations for attorneys.[13]

Interest groups typified as **power groups** have several common traits. For one, these groups maintain strong links with both legislators (whose policy decisions affect group interests) and bureaucrats (whose regulatory authority controls activities of group members). Power groups often are repeat players in Texas politics, meaning they have been influencing politics in consecutive legislative sessions for a long time.

Another indication of power-group influence is having headquarters in Austin. Many business-related associations, for example, own a headquarters building in the capital city. Others lease or rent buildings and office suites there. This proximity to the Texas Capitol and the main offices of state agencies provides regular contact with state officials and gives such associations a path to influence in state government.[14] In some cases, according to watchdog organizations, interest groups have received free use of meeting rooms in the Texas capitol building for receptions.

One of the most influential power groups is the Texas Medical Association (TMA), formed in 1853. With a well-organized grassroots network, a skilled lobbying team, and more than 45,000 licensed physicians and medical students in Texas, TMA is one of Texas's most powerful professional groups. According to TMA's figures, the group succeeded in passing as much as 90 percent of its agenda items in the late 1990s.[15] Later, this association claimed success in defeating most bills that it opposed during the 79th regular session of the Texas legislature. Subsequently, TMA succeeded in preserving the 2003 medical liability reforms that had been under attack in the 2009 legislative session. The organization also successfully fought for increased funding for medical schools and for creating initiatives to improve health-care access to rural and underserved areas of the state. Although TMA was not able to persuade the state legislature to restore funding cuts in Medicaid from previous legislative sessions, the organization succeeded during the 2011 legislative session in preventing severe cuts to physicians' Medicaid payments, so that doctors would continue seeing needy patients.

☑ Learning Check 6.2 (Answers on p. 241)

1. True or False: All interest groups have one objective in common: to promote their self-interest.
2. Which are generally more powerful in Texas, business interest groups or labor groups?
3. True or False: LULAC is considered to be the oldest interest group dedicated to the interests and rights of Latinos in the United States.

power group
An effective interest group strongly linked with legislators and bureaucrats for the purpose of influencing decision making and having a continuing presence in Austin as a "repeat player" from session to session.

Interest Group Activities

LO3

When interest groups urge their members and others to become actively involved, they encourage people to participate in the political process. In some cases, interest groups even encourage their members to consider running for public office. Groups benefit from having their supporters serve in decision-making positions, especially on influential boards and commissions. Local property taxpayers' associations, for example, frequently put forward candidates for public school boards and municipal offices in an effort to keep property taxes low. Likewise, when organizations of real estate agents successfully lobby for the placement of their members in appointed positions on local planning and zoning commissions, they gain a distinct advantage. Because government officials need support for their policies, interest groups seek to mobilize and build that support, particularly for policies that form part of a group's goals and interests. Having the support or opposition of certain interest groups may determine the success or failure of policy decisions.

Interest groups also serve as an outlet for discussions concerning policy issues. In doing so, they shape conflict and consensus in society. Conflict is the more usual outcome, because each group is bent on pursuing its own limited ends. This, in turn, leads to clashes with other groups seeking their own ends. Conflict is even more likely when addressing controversial issues, such as school finance, abortion, environmental protection, same-sex marriage, voter identification, redistricting, and immigration.

In some cases, however, certain issues may galvanize coalitions among various interest groups. In 2011, for instance, groups representing teachers, parents, religious organizations, and civil rights organizations rallied around the need for increased school funding. Even business organizations, such as the Texas Association of Business, joined forces. Many groups organized rallies called "Save Texas Schools," which were centered on the issue of increased school funding and the necessity to use the "rainy day" fund to cover any budgetary shortfalls. For more on the "rainy day" fund, see Chapter 11, "Finance and Fiscal Policy."

Political scientists know that interest groups use a wide range of techniques to influence policy decisions. These **interest group techniques** may be classified as lobbying, personal communication, giving favors and gifts, grassroots activities, electioneering, campaign financing by political action committees, and, in extreme instances, bribery and other illegal or unethical practices.

Lobbying

Lobbying is perhaps the oldest, and certainly the best-known, interest group tactic. According to Texans for Public Justice, special interests spent $345 million on lobbying contracts in 2011. Identifying interest groups that hire lobbyists is one way to determine which interests are being represented before the state legislature and which are not. Lobbyists are individuals who attempt to influence government decision makers on behalf of special

---

interest group technique
An action such as lobbying, personal communication, giving favors and gifts, grassroots activities, electioneering, campaign financing by political action committees, and, in extreme instances, bribery and other unethical practices intended to influence government decisions.

lobbying
Communicating with legislators or other government officials on behalf of an interest group for the purpose of influencing decision makers.

CourseReader ASSIGNMENTS

Log in to www.cengagebrain.com and open CourseReader to access the reading:

Decade of Lobbying Growth Sidetracked by Recession, but Even with a Sour Economy, Number of Lobbyists Grew to 1,690
R. G. Ratcliffe

Lobbying is big business in the state of Texas for a number of reasons, one of which is the fact that interest groups dominate the political landscape. Political parties in Texas have traditionally been weak, and interest groups fill the vacuum. As the voice of interest groups, few of which do their own lobbying, the professional lobbyist is in high demand. Of course, an economic downturn can dampen the expansion of the lobby industry. However, dampening growth is not equivalent to eliminating growth. As this article shows, the increased use of social networking technology has reduced the costs associated with group formation and increased the demand for experienced representation in the halls of the legislature.

1. How did the economic recession affect spending by lobbyists?

2. What does the article suggest about the relationship between lobbyists and the government?

interests. Lobbying is most often directed at legislators and the lawmaking process, although it is also practiced within state agencies.

Some interest groups, such as the Texas Motorcycle Rights Association, which claims to represent close to 900,000 licensed motorcycle riders in Texas, including Governor Perry, will hold a "lobby day" at the Capitol. On this day, association members talk with lawmakers about preserving bikers' rights. In 2011, several hundred bikers began the day on the steps of the state Capitol with the rally cry, "This is your house. Come on in!" As this chapter's "Students in Action" feature suggests, even "lobbyists for the day" require a lot of planning and strategy in order to be effective advocates.

Not all lobbyists are full-time professionals. Most work for businesses and only occasionally go to Austin to speak to lawmakers about their concerns. Some lobbyists represent cities and counties. Among the most successful lobbyists are former state legislators, legislative aides, and gubernatorial aides.[16] In recent years, Texas has ranked second in the country, after California, in money spent on lobbying the state government. One report indicates that lobbyists in Texas spent $12.8 million wooing legislators from 2005 to 2008, with the top lobbyists representing large electric, cable, and construction interests.[17] There were more than 1,600 registered lobbyists during the 81st regular session in 2009, outnumbering the 181 legislators by a margin of roughly nine to one.[18] By 2011, the number of registered lobbyists had increased to more than 1,800 according to the Texas Ethics Commission.

Points to Ponder

- In the past decade, gifts to lawmakers by lobbyists cost more than $1.6 million.
- Gifts range from flower bouquets to spa treatments for female lawmakers.
- For male lawmakers, gifts range from guns and knives to deer processing.
- Gifts valued at more than $250 must be reported by public officials to the Texas Ethics Commission.
- Gifts are also given to state agency employees who set rules and approve contracts after lawmakers pass legislation.

Source: Matt Stiles, "Are Gifts Used as Calling Cards or as Keys to Legislators' Offices?" *San Antonio Express-News*, February 5, 2009.

Personal Communication One of the main interest group techniques is personal communication by lobbyists. The immediate goal of lobbyists is to inform the legislators of their group's position on an issue. Because professional lobbyists are often experts in their field (and in some cases are former state officials), their tools of influence are the information and research they convey to state legislators. The first task of the lobbyist is to gain access to legislators and other government decision makers. Once the lobbyist has made personal contact with a legislator and captured the desired attention, he or she may use a variety of techniques to make the government official responsive to the group's demands, preferences, and expectations.

In addition, because the process requires careful strategy, the lobbyist chooses the most appropriate time and place to speak with an official and determines how best to phrase arguments in order to have a positive impact. For maximum effectiveness in using this technique, a lobbyist must select the proper target (e.g., a key legislative committee chair, regulatory agency administrator, county commissioner, or city zoning board member). Successful lobbyists rely heavily on computers, calculators, pagers, cellular telephones, Internet communications, and other high-tech devices to store and communicate information. In fact, an important study of interest group politics in Texas concluded that lobbying in the Lone Star State has shifted from an emphasis on personal argument to information-based communications.[19]

A former Texas legislator compared lobbyists with pharmaceutical salespeople who explain new medicines to doctors who are too busy to keep up with the latest developments. To perform their jobs effectively, successful lobbyists should clearly indicate the group they represent, define their interests, make clear what they want to do and why, answer questions readily, and provide enough information for politicians to make judgments.

Students in Action

Student Lobbyist for the Day

"There is nothing like trying to convince a decision maker about the importance of issues you feel strongly about."

David Zapata

Since 2003, at the start of every spring semester in odd-numbered calendar years, a delegation of faculty, staff, and students from St. Mary's University in San Antonio* are recruited and trained on the principles of lobbying. The lobbying team goes to the Capitol for the day to lobby targeted state legislators and senators to try to increase, or at minimum maintain, funding for Texas Equalization Grants (TEG) funding. This particular source of funding for college students was authorized first in the 1970s to provide the opportunity for low-income students to attend private colleges and universities in Texas.

In 2007, several students were selected to lobby the state legislature for a one-day event. One of these students was David Zapata, a TEG recipient and political science student who ultimately plans to pursue a career in public service.

Getting Ready

David pointed out, "We received training on campus, where faculty members held practice sessions, pairing us with other students to practice short talking points we were expected to convey during our one-on-one sessions with policymakers. We wouldn't have much time, so we needed to be quick and effective."

They had one final workshop, where a professional lobbyist taught them how real lobbying takes place. According to David, the lobbyist explained that it is better to talk to staff before talking to an assigned legislator, because the staff members inform the legislators about the main issues during each legislative session.

Lobbying at the Capitol

David indicated that there was a sense of urgency throughout the Capitol, as time is a valuable commodity when you're trying to get bills passed. David concluded that his experience at the capitol was extremely rewarding because he felt he learned how legislators conduct their business on a daily basis.

Overall, David said, "This experience taught me important real life lessons, which I hope to apply in a career in government. There are things students can't learn inside a classroom, and lobbying is one of them. There is nothing like trying to convince a decision maker about the importance of issues you feel strongly about. It showed me another important way of representing my community, since lobbyists work on behalf of various constituencies."

*Part of St. Mary's University's mission is dedicated to civic engagement and servant leadership.

Source: Interview with David Zapata, March 7, 2010.

(Monkey Business Images/Shutterstock.com)

Successful lobbyists befriend as many legislators as possible, especially influential legislative leaders, such as committee chairs, and they discover their interests and needs. These relationships are formed over time. Lobbyists also put pressure on sympathetic legislators to influence other legislators.

Favors and Gifts Another lobbying technique used by interest groups, and especially by lobbyists, involves giving favors and gifts for legislators and other government decision makers. Common favors include arranging daily or weekly luncheon and dinner gatherings; providing free liquor, wine, or beer; furnishing tickets for entertainment events, air transportation, and athletic contests; and giving miscellaneous gifts. However, there are limits on the value of "travel gifts" for public officials and soon-to-be-elected candidates, as well as for state agency employees.[20]

Grassroots Activities Yet another influential technique by interest groups is grassroots lobbying. Interest groups rely heavily on pressure from a grassroots network of organization members and sympathizers. Interest groups attempt to create an image of broad public support for a group's goals—mobilizing support when it is needed. They use such political campaign techniques as direct mailings, television and newspaper advertisements, rallies and demonstrations, and local group action. The Internet, in particular, has emerged as a forum for grassroots lobbying. Interest groups are increasingly using social media such as Facebook, Twitter, and blogs. These communication methods are designed to generate information favorable to an interest group's cause and to spread it widely among legislators, other policymakers, and the general public. For instance, the Texas State Teachers Association (TSTA) is very effective at communicating its agenda through Flickr and Facebook.

Lobbyists wait in the halls of the state Capitol in hope of speaking with state legislators.

(© Bob Daemmrich/The Image Works)

Electioneering

Participating in political campaign activities, or **electioneering**, is widespread among interest groups. These activities usually center on particular candidates, but may also revolve around issue advocacy. If a candidate who favors a group's goals can be elected, the group has a realistic expectation that its interests will be recognized and protected once the candidate takes office. Interest group participation in the election process takes various forms. Publishing or otherwise publicizing the political records of incumbent candidates is one of the simplest and most common forms of interest group participation. Providing favored candidates with group membership information and mailing lists is another valuable contribution that helps candidates solicit money and votes. In addition, groups may allow candidates to speak at their meetings, thus giving them opportunities for direct contact with voters and possible media coverage. Public endorsements can also

electioneering
Active campaigning by an interest group in support of, or opposition to, a candidate; actions urging the public to act on an issue.

Points to Ponder

- At present, no effective laws prohibit former Texas legislators (including former legislative officers) from becoming lobbyists and immediately lobbying former colleagues.
- In 2012, according to the National Conference of State Legislatures, 35 states required some kind of waiting period, ranging from the conclusion of the legislative session during which the legislator resigns to two years, before a legislator can become a lobbyist.
- Former lawmakers who become lobbyists do not have to disclose their previous public official status when registering with the Texas Ethics Commission.
- At least five former state lawmakers were registered as new lobbyists in 2010.*
- It was reported that one senator resigned in the middle of the 2011 legislative session in order to become a lobbyist.*
- Three bills that would have required a waiting period for lawmakers before becoming lobbyists were defeated during the 2011 legislative session.*

*Source: Karen Brooks, "Revolving Door Likely to Stay Open for Lawmakers." *Dallas Morning Times*, May 9, 2011.

benefit candidates, sending a cue to the group's membership and other interested voters with regard to which candidates they should support.

During the gubernatorial primary campaigns in 2010, various interest groups publicly endorsed specific candidates. For instance, Governor Perry received endorsements from such groups as the Texas Association of Manufacturers, Texas Right to Life, Texas Association of Realtors, and the National Rifle Association. His supporters also included the Business and Commerce PAC, the Texas Economic Development Council PAC, and the Texas and Southwestern Cattle Raisers Association PAC. Likewise, the leading Democratic gubernatorial candidate and former Houston mayor, Bill White, gained support from various organizations, such as the Texas State Teachers Association, the Texas League of Conservation Voters, and the AFL-CIO. Leading up to the November 2010 election, Rick Perry received additional endorsements from PACs representing several organizations, including the Texas Medical Association and Texans for Lawsuit Reform. Meanwhile, Bill White received endorsements primarily from several major newspapers, including the *Dallas Morning News* and the *Austin American-Statesman*.

Another type of group participation in electioneering involves "getting out the vote"—that is, the favorable vote. Typically, increasing favorable voter turnout entails mailing campaign propaganda, making telephone calls to members, registering voters, transporting voters to the polls, and door-to-door canvassing (soliciting votes). Group members may also volunteer their time

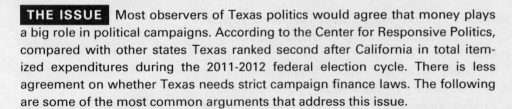

Point/Counterpoint

THE ISSUE Most observers of Texas politics would agree that money plays a big role in political campaigns. According to the Center for Responsive Politics, compared with other states Texas ranked second after California in total itemized expenditures during the 2011-2012 federal election cycle. There is less agreement on whether Texas needs strict campaign finance laws. The following are some of the most common arguments that address this issue.

Should Campaign Contributions Be Limited?

Arguments For Limiting Campaign Contributions

- Current federal law requires caps on all campaign contributions by individuals and PACs for federal elections.
- Without a cap on campaign contributions, money will control politics, and wealthy individuals and PACs will have tremendous influence in public policymaking.

"Wealthy individuals, businesses, and lobby interests write the big checks that have thrown Lone Star democracy out of balance."

— Craig McDonald, Director for Texans for Public Justice

Arguments Against Limiting Campaign Contributions

- Campaign contributions to political candidates are still considered a form of freedom of expression protected by the U.S. Constitution.
- Campaign contributions to candidates and public officials guarantee only access, not policy outcomes.

"It never ceases to amaze me that people are so cynical they want to tie money to issues, money to bills, money to amendments."

—Tom DeLay, former U.S. Representative and former member of the Texas House of Representatives

to the campaigns of sympathetic candidates. Regarding Texas's controversial constitutional amendment banning same-sex marriages, groups on both sides of the issue worked diligently in 2005 to get out the vote in their favor. The Liberty Legal Institute and the Texas Eagle Forum, for instance, supported the ban, whereas a coalition group calling themselves No Nonsense in November opposed the ban.

Campaign Financing by Political Action Committees

Because political campaigns are becoming more expensive with each election, contributions from interest group members constitute an important form of participation, especially in both federal and state level elections. Although individuals continue to make personal financial contributions to candidates, more campaign funds are coming from **political action committees.** The Texas Ethics Commission defines a PAC as "a group of persons that has a principal purpose of accepting political contributions or making political contributions."[21] Texas statutes prohibit direct political contributions by corporations and labor unions to individual candidates. These and other groups, however, may form PACs composed of their employees or members.

political action committee (PAC)
An organizational device used by corporations, labor unions, and other organizations to raise money for campaign contributions.

How Do We Compare...in Total Contributions in U.S. Congressional Races?

Most Populous U.S. States	Total Contributions	Percent Given to Democrats	Percent Given to Republicans	Ranking* to Democrats	Ranking** to Republicans
California	$191,900,752	52.30%	33.8%	10	42
Florida	$ 90,687,298	34.7%	55.1%	27	25
New York	$135,511,850	54.5%	31.0%	2	46
Texas	**$155,189,536**	**19.5%**	**51.7%**	**42**	**29**
U.S. States Bordering Texas					
Arkansas	$ 7,876,106	25.9%	56.7%	36	24
Louisiana	$14,638,500	17.0%	66.8%	43	10
New Mexico	$ 8,090,034	55.8%	41.0%	8	38
Oklahoma	$14,415,732	14.3%	62.4%	45	15

*This figure includes PAC contributions to candidates, individual contributions to candidates and parties, and soft money contributions to parties in federal elections. (Soft money contributions are unlimited funds spent independently by political parties to benefit a candidate or to educate voters.)

**Refers to how the state compares with all 50 states. For example, Texas's percentage of contributions to Republicans ranked 29th in the nation. The balance of contributions in California and other states went to other sources, such as Super PACs.

Note: Contributions continued to increase during the 2012 election cycle.

Source: Center for Responsive Politics, "Open Secrets," data reported as of June 4, 2012, **http://www.opensecrets.org/states/**.

PACs have the task of raising funds and distributing financial contributions to candidates who are sympathetic to their cause. A PAC may also influence political campaigns involving issues that affect the group's vital interests. Currently, Texas imposes no limits on what PACs (or citizens for that matter) can raise or contribute to candidates running for statewide offices or the legislature, except in judicial races. A proposed law that would have placed limits on the amounts that citizens and PACs can contribute to candidates died in committee during the 80th legislature. Although bills introduced in the 81st legislature related to the regulation and reporting of political contributions and expenditures, only one bill passed that set deadlines for when judicial candidates or officeholders may accept political contributions. No significant bills were passed that impacted PACs during the 82nd legislative session.

PAC activities and their influence continue to increase. According to the Texas Ethics Commission, more than 1,700 active PACs were registered as of 2011. (See Table 6.3 for a list of some of the top Texas PACs.) During the 2010 election cycle, Texans for Public Justice reported that a record number of 1,302 active PACs spent more than $133 million. PAC contributions were dominated by interests representing ideological and single-issue groups, lawyers and lobbyists, and energy and natural resource groups.[22] (See Table 6.4 for a list of PAC spending by sector in 2010.)

Table 6.3   Top Ten Texas PACs in Spending and by Interest Category, 2010–2011

Donor	2010–2011 Spending*	Category
Texans for Lawsuit Reform	$6,166,000	Focuses on lawsuit restrictions
Back to Basics PAC	$4,218,000	Supports Democrats
Associated Republicans of Texas Campaign	$2,981,000	Supports Republicans
Texas Democratic Trust	$3,211,000	Supports Democrats
Texans for Insurance Reform	$2,991,000	Trial lawyer group
House Democratic Campaign Committee	$2,462,000	Supports Democrats
Texas Association of Realtors	$2,253,000	Business group
Valero Energy Corp.	$1,095,000	Business group

Note: List does not include PACs that are directly tied to specific candidates or county party. Period includes January 2010 through January 2011.

*Dollar amounts have been rounded up.

Source: Texas Ethics Commission, **http://www.ethics.state.tx.us**.

Table 6.4   PAC Spending by Sector, 2010

Interest Category	Spending Total	Percentage of Total Spending
Business	$68,236,000	51.0%
Ideological/Single Issue	$57,847,000	43.0%
Labor	$ 7,032,000	5.0%
Miscellaneous	$ 331,000	1.0%

Source: Texans for Public Justice, "Texas PACs: 2010 Election Cycle Spending," **http://www.tpj.org**.

Reports made by Texans for Public Justice before the 2010 gubernatorial primaries showed that Governor Perry had raised more than $12 million from individuals and PACs and spent more than $16 million, whereas Kay Bailey Hutchison had raised more than $14 million and spent more than $19 million. Debra Medina, a newcomer, raised less than $1 million and spent more than $500,000. Democrat Bill White had collected more than $9 million in campaign contributions and spent more than $3 million. Reports prior to the November general election indicated that Governor Perry had raised and spent more than $20 million in the campaign, whereas White had collected close to $17 million and spent more than $6 million.

Perhaps the best indication of power among interest groups is the connection between the election campaign contributions of PACs and lobbying activities. It takes a coordinated effort on the part of an interest group to influence one part of the political process (the campaign), while also affecting policy decisions in another part (the legislative process). In this way, interest groups can exercise far greater control over the output of the Texas legislature than their numbers would indicate.

Bribery and Unethical Practices

Bribery and blackmail, though not common in Texas, nevertheless have taken place in state and local government. There were, for example, several well-publicized scandals in the 1950s involving Texas legislators. In the 1970s, the Sharpstown Bank scandal rocked the legislature. House Speaker Gus Mutscher (D-Brenham) and others were convicted of conspiring to accept bribes for passing deposit insurance bills as requested by Houston banker Frank Sharp. After the scandal, the state legislature passed a law prohibiting candidates for the office of Speaker of the House of Representatives from giving anything of value to a supportive legislator as a means of being elected as Speaker. The law requires separate campaign finance committees for election as a representative and for the Speaker's race.

In February 1980, as revealed by an FBI investigation, House Speaker Billy Clayton (D-Springlake) accepted (but did not spend) $5,000 intended to influence the awarding of a state employee insurance contract. Because he had not cashed the checks, a federal district court found Clayton innocent of all bribery charges. In January 1981, he was elected to a fourth term as Speaker of the House. After eight years as Speaker, Clayton left the House to become a lobbyist.

In 1991, five-time Speaker Gib Lewis (D-Fort Worth) was indicted on two misdemeanor ethics charges by a Travis County grand jury. Rather than face the possibility of a trial, subjecting him to a stiffer penalty, Lewis agreed to a plea bargain, was fined $2,000, and announced his decision not to seek reelection to the House of Representatives in 1992. He became a successful lobbyist.

Scrutiny also centered on state Representative Tom Craddick (R-Midland). Although Texas law prohibits a Speaker candidate from giving money to House candidates, in 2002, Craddick donated $20,000 from his reelection campaign to Campaign for Republican Leadership, a political action committee. In turn, the PAC gave all of its $176,500 to eight GOP House candidates. After Republicans won a majority of House seats, Craddick was elected Speaker in January 2003.[23] Another political action committee, Texans for a Republican Majority (TRMPAC), was organized under the patronage of former U.S. House member Tom DeLay (R-Sugar Land). In 2002, TRMPAC was involved in raising money for GOP candidates seeking seats in the Texas House. Later, in cooperation with DeLay, Speaker Craddick played a major role in the success of a 2003 congressional redistricting effort that resulted in the 2004 election of more Republicans in the Texas delegation to the U.S. House of Representatives.

Former House Majority leader Tom DeLay (left) waits for the start of his pretrial hearing at the 331ˢᵗ District Court of Travis County Court House in Austin on August 24, 2010.

(AP Photo/The Daily Texan, Tamir Kalifa)

Craddick was not charged with violation of any law, but DeLay and three associates involved with TRMPAC were indicted in 2005 by a Travis County grand jury for money laundering and conspiracy to launder $190,000 of campaign contributions from corporate contributors.[24] After indictment, DeLay was forced to step down as majority leader in the U.S. House of Representatives. In June 2006, while awaiting trial, DeLay resigned from his congressional seat. (Convicted and given a three-year sentence in 2011, as of September 2012 DeLay remained free on bond during his appeal.)

 Learning Check 6.3   (Answers on p. 241)

1. Name two techniques lobbyists use to influence legislators.
2. Does Texas place limits on PAC contributions, as the federal government does?
3. True or False: At present, Texas forbids corporations to contribute campaign funds directly to state candidates.

★ # Power and Regulation in Interest Group Politics

LO4   Clearly, interest groups play a significant role in Texas politics. They have access to a number of strategies and tactics to influence elections and policy decisions. So, how are interest groups regulated? Are these regulations effective? Do interest groups have too much political influence in shaping public policy?

Regulation of Interest Group Politics

Prompted by media reports of big spending by lobbyists and a grand jury investigation into influence peddling, the 72nd legislature proposed a constitutional amendment to create the eight-member **Texas Ethics Commission**, which would enforce new legal standards for lobbyists and public officials. The voters approved the amendment in November 1991, thereby allowing commission members to be appointed by the governor (four members), the lieutenant governor (two members), and the House Speaker (two members).[25] This legislation was initially designed to increase the power of public prosecutors to use evidence that contributions to lawmakers by lobbyists and other individuals are more than mere campaign donations. The legislation also expanded disclosure requirements for lobbyists and legislators, and it put a $500 annual cap on lobbyist-provided food and drink for a lawmaker. The law also bans honoraria (gratuitous payments in recognition of professional services for which there is no legally enforceable obligation to pay) and lobby-paid pleasure trips (unless a legislator makes a speech or participates in a panel discussion). Although state law also requires public officials to disclose any gifts valued greater than $250 and include a description, the Texas Ethics Commission drew criticism in 2006 when it ruled that elected officials need only disclose the existence of a monetary gift without revealing the dollar amount. In response, the 80th legislature enacted a law requiring the amount to be reported.

The ethics law defines as illegal, any campaign contribution accepted with an agreement to act in the contributor's interest. The law also prohibits a candidate or official from receiving a contribution in the Capitol building itself. The problem, however, is the difficulty in proving a candidate or public official has intentionally accepted a campaign contribution from a particular interest group in exchange for policy benefits.

Detailed records of political contributions and how this money is spent must be filed with the Texas Ethics Commission between two and seven times each year. These records are open to the public and are available on the commission's website. Candidates for legislative and statewide office are required to file electronic campaign disclosure reports, so that this information can be made instantly available. Current law requires that all candidates file semiannual reports. In contested elections, however, candidates must file itemized contribution and expenditure reports every six months, 30 days, and eight days before the election.

Contributions and expenditures in the last two days of an election campaign need not be disclosed until the next semiannual report is due. For instance, a 2002 study by Texans for Public Justice reported that 102 candidates raised $18.7 million in the primary election, with $1.7 million comprising contributions in the last two days before the election took place. Among the top donors were plaintiffs' attorneys, doctors, and the Republican National State Elections Committee.[26] At present, there are no laws in Texas preventing these last-minute contributions by interest groups. Therefore, interest groups can potentially alter the outcome of key races in the

Texas Ethics Commission A state agency that enforces state standards for lobbyists and public officials, including registration of lobbyists and reporting of political campaign contributions.

few days before the election. It is also not uncommon for special interests to make campaign contributions after the election takes place. Current law prohibits lawmakers and state officials from raising money during the regular legislative session. However, these postelection, or "late train," donations typically take place immediately following the November election until early December.

On its website, the Texas Ethics Commission lists the names of lobbyists and their clients, as well as payments received by each lobbyist. The commission's records, however, do not give a complete picture. Lobbyists do not have to report exact dollar amounts for their contracts; they only need to indicate ranges. For example, compensation from each client is reported as less than $10,000, and then in $15,000 increments up to more than $500,000. For anything over $500,000, the exact amount is required under a 2007 state law. In addition, lobbyists are required to notify their clients if they represent two or more groups with competing interests, as well as notify the Texas Ethics Commission about any possible conflicts. This information, however, is not made available to the public or lawmakers.

The Texas Ethics Commission is authorized to hear ethics complaints against state officials, candidates for office, and state employees, though its budget and staff are typically very small and allow only a limited number of reviews each year. From January 2008 to March 2010, there were 794 sworn ethics complaints.[27] Most infractions center on penalties against campaign and PAC treasurers who failed to file reports, missed filing reports deadlines, or provided faulty reports on contributions, earnings, or expenditures. Many infractions center on violations of the Texas Election Code. Fines are assessed by the Ethics Commission on any infractions. In 2011, for instance, the agency fined a political action committee $10,000 for failing to respond to an investigation into a complaint.

Reform advocates and others contend that staff members with the commission are restricted from investigating complaints because of strict confidentiality rules that expose them to possible criminal prosecution, fines, and jail time. The 2009 legislature revised the sworn complaints procedure, requiring that the complainant be a Texas resident and be able to demonstrate proof of residency. The complaint must be filed on a form provided by the commission and include information about the respondent and the complainant. The commission must immediately attempt to contact the respondent when the complaint has been filed.[28] In 2011, another law was passed that effectively weakens the ability of the agency to impose fines for some infractions. According to Texans for Public Justice, the legislature passed an ethics law, adding an amendment that orders the Texas Ethics Commission to dismiss any Election Code complaint if the defendant claims that the violation was a clerical error and corrects the mistake within two weeks. In effect, the agency would no longer levy fines for these kinds of complaints.[29]

Although some ethics laws are in place, they remain ineffective. Questionable connections between lobbyists and legislators are largely unchecked. For instance, Governor Perry drew criticism when he first took office after issuing a "strict" revolving-door lobbying policy for his staff, preventing staff members from leaving their employment to become lobbyists. Shortly thereafter, however, he hired senior staff personnel who had been registered as lobbyists during the preceding legislative session. In a report entitled *Texas Lobby Watch*, Texans for Public Justice concluded that special interests had entered the governor's office through a revolving back door.[30] During the 2010 GOP primary, challenger Kay Bailey Hutchison raised the same issue. One particular television attack focused on how Governor Perry's staff members move in and out of the lobby; some of his aides were former lobbyists or left his office to lobby. Likewise, when Tom Craddick first became Speaker, he received criticism from watchdog groups for selecting lobbyists with ties to the insurance industry as members of his transition team. A study by political watchdog group Campaigns for People highlighted the continued relationship between corporate money and politics.

Although Texas law prohibits corporations and unions to provide campaign contributions directly to candidates, "soft money" can be directed to state Republican and Democratic party coffers for the use of "administrative expenses." In 2009, in light of the U.S. Supreme Court decision *Citizens United v. Federal Election Commission*, the Texas Ethics Commission issued an advisory opinion stating that corporations and unions are allowed to make expenditures independent of a political candidate, such as paying for political advertising that calls for the election or defeat of candidates.[31] In 2011, the legislature revised the Election Code to repeal the prohibition of direct political expenditures on behalf of a political candidate and to clarify reporting requirements to the Texas Ethics Commission. In addition, the Texas Ethics Commission left it up to the legislature to determine whether the donations from a corporation or union to a PAC must be made public.

As a result of *Citizens United*, a proliferation of super PACs, especially at the federal level, took place. Unlike state law, federal law allows so-called super PACs to raise unlimited sums for independent expenditures; however, the donors must be reported and made public, unless a nonprofit organization is involved. Leading up to the 2012 presidential primary elections, Rick Perry benefited from these super PACs, especially from one called "Make Us Great Again."[32] After withdrawing from the Republican presidential nomination race, Perry received approval from the Federal Election Commission to form his own PAC or super PAC with funds remaining from his presidential campaign, or to transfer these funds to his gubernatorial campaign account.

A powerful relationship continues between campaign contributions and policy decisions. Sam Kinch (a long-time political reporter and founder of the political newsletter *Texas Weekly*) and Anne Marie Kilday (a former capitol correspondent for Texas newspapers) concluded in 2000 that little had changed since creation of the Ethics Commission, as the system was still set up to support incumbents.[33] In the past decade, all attempts to significantly reform campaign finance were defeated. Proposed reforms have included contribution limits for individuals and PACs in legislative and statewide races, as well as full disclosure laws. As the late Molly Ivins pointed out, "Texas is the Wild Frontier of campaign financing."[34]

Campaign contributions are also connected to influential political appointments. During Perry's presidential bid in 2011, media reports revealed that many of his donors received appointments to influential state boards and commissions.

After a 2002 review of the Ethics Commission by the Texas Sunset Advisory Commission, the 78th legislature passed H.B. 1606, which renewed the Texas Ethics Commission until 2015. First and foremost, the law strengthens the commission's enforcement powers. Second, the law provides stricter disclosure requirements. For example, legislators must disclose the occupation and employer of large donors. Furthermore, reports from elected officials concerning campaign cash on hand, as well as personal financial disclosure statements by municipal officers, are now required. Other features include disclosure reports of lawyer-legislators who seek trial postponements during a legislative session, along with broadened requirements for disclosing conflicts of interest.[35]

Interest Group Power and Public Policy

The **political influence of interest groups** is determined by several factors. Some observers argue that a group with a sizable membership, above-average financial resources, a knowledgeable and dedicated leadership, and a high degree of unity (agreement on and commitment to goals among the membership) will be able to exert virtually limitless pressure on governmental decision makers. Others point out that the more the aims of an interest group are consistent with broad-based public beliefs or stem from issue networks, the more likely the group is to succeed and wield significant power. They also observe that if interest groups are well represented in the structure of the government itself, their power will be enhanced materially. Also, it is noted that a structure of weak governments will ordinarily produce strong interest groups.

From a different point of view, others insist that factors external to the group are also highly relevant. Research indicates that a strong relationship exists between the larger socioeconomic conditions in a state and the power of interest groups. These findings have led some observers to conclude that states with high population levels, advanced industrialization, significant per capita wealth, and high levels of formal education are likely to produce relatively weak interest groups and strong political parties. Interestingly, despite a large population, Texas is among the states with strong interest groups and relatively weak political parties. Compared with other states, scholars rank Texas as one of 26 states where interest groups dominate or fluctuate in power over time.[36] The Center for Public Integrity, in its analysis of transparency and accountability of the 50 state governments, graded Texas a D+, ranking it 27th among all states.[37]

Three circumstances explain why states such as Texas may not fit the expected pattern. First, many Texas interest groups are readily accepted, because they identify with free enterprise, self-reliance, and other elements of the state's individualistic political culture. Most Texans are predisposed to

political influence of interest groups
A highly variable factor that depends largely on the size of a group's membership, financial resources, quality of leadership, and degree of unity to measure its effectiveness.

distrust government and its agents but to trust interest groups and their lobbyists. Second, the century-long, one-party Democratic tradition in Texas,
and the subsequent one-party Republican trend, have rendered interparty
competition negligible in many counties and districts. Low levels of political
participation, the absence of strong parties and meaningful competition
between parties has made Texas government vulnerable to the pressures of
strong interest groups and their lobbyists. Finally, the Texas Constitution of
1876 and its many amendments have created state and local governments
beset by weak, uncoordinated institutions. Faced with a government lacking
sufficient strength to offer any real opposition, interest groups often obtain
decisions favorable to their causes.

Pinpointing Political Power

Assessing the political power and influence that interest groups have in
American government is difficult, and determining the extent of their power
in Texas is especially complex. There is no simple top-down or bottom-up
arrangement. Rather, political decisions (especially policy decisions) are
made by a variety of individuals and groups. Some of these decision makers
participate in local ad hoc (specific-purpose) organizations; others wield
influence through statewide groups. Ascertaining which individuals or
groups have the greatest influence often depends on the issue or issues
involved.

The political influence of any interest group cannot be fairly calculated
by looking at the distribution of only one political asset, whether it be
money, status, knowledge, organization, or sheer numbers. Nevertheless, we
may safely conclude that organized interest groups in Texas often put the
unorganized citizenry at a great disadvantage when public issues are at
stake.

☑ Learning Check 6.4　(Answers on p. 241)

1. True or False: Texas's campaign finance laws often involve public disclosure by public officials and lobbyists.
2. True or False: The Texas Ethics Commission is the primary state agency
   regulating political contributions and expenditures by lobbyists and public officials.
3. True or False: A campaign contribution accepted by a public official with
   an agreement to act in the contributor's interest is against the law.

★ Conclusion

As we have learned, there are numerous interest groups in Texas. They exert
tremendous influence over public decisions at all levels, and in all branches,

of government. Some interest groups, however, have more influence than others. They participate in an assortment of activities and use a variety of techniques to influence government. What's more, few, if any, regulations effectively control the power of interest groups in Texas. These factors suggest that interest groups will continue to play a significant role in Texas politics for years to come.

Chapter Summary

- Interest groups act on behalf of their members to influence policy decisions made by government officials. Various factors foster interest group formation or effectiveness, such as legal and cultural reasons, a decentralized government, and the strength of the party system and political ideologies.
- Involvement in an interest group provides members with information and opportunities to become active in the political process.
- Interest groups vary by organizational pattern, membership, and leadership.
- In general, all interest groups at all levels of government can be classified according to their interests, membership, and the public policies they advocate.
- Interest groups are involved in all types and areas of political activity. They serve various functions, which include recruiting candidates for public office, shaping consensus on issues, and providing an outlet for concerned citizens.
- To influence policy decisions, interest groups use several techniques, including lobbying, personal communication, giving favors and gifts, grassroots activities, electioneering, campaign financing by political action committees (PACs), and, in extreme cases, resorting to bribery and other unethical or illegal practices.
- An eight-member Texas Ethics Commission is charged with enforcing legal standards for lobbyists and public officials. Texas's campaign finance laws are best characterized as involving public disclosure by public officials, lobbyists, and PACs.
- There are various ways to gauge an interest group's potential for political influence, such as the group's size of membership, financial resources, quality of leadership, and the degree of unity among members.
- Interest group participation influences public policy at all levels and within each branch (legislative, executive, judicial) of Texas government, and it allows all group members to become a part of the political process.

Key Terms

interest group, p. 210
right of association, p. 211
decentralized government, p. 212
organizational pattern, p. 214
group leadership, p. 214
economic interest group, p. 215
business organization, p. 215
labor organization, p. 216
professional group, p. 217
public officer and employee group, p. 218
social interest group, p. 219
racial and ethnic group, p. 219
women's organization, p. 220
religious-based group, p. 221
public interest group, p. 222
power group, p. 223
interest group technique, p. 224
lobbying, p. 224
electioneering, p. 228
political action committee (PAC), p. 230
Texas Ethics Commission, p. 235
political influence of interest group, p. 238

Learning Check Answers

6.1

1. True. Similar to political parties, interest groups are interested in shaping public policy. But, unlike political parties, interest groups do not necessarily field candidates to run for office.
2. Legal decisions, political culture, a decentralized government, the strength of the party system, and political ideologies contribute to the formation of interest groups.
3. False. Active membership will vary, depending on the organization and leadership of the organization.

6.2

1. False. Unlike most interest groups, public interest groups are interested in promoting the public interest.

2. In Texas, business groups are generally more powerful than labor groups.
3. True. LULAC was formed in 1929 and has been dedicated to improving educational opportunities and obtaining full citizenship rights for Latinos in the United States.

6.3

1. Lobbyists use personal communication as well as favors and gifts to influence legislators.
2. Unlike federal law, Texas law does not limit campaign contributions by PACs.
3. True. Texas law prohibits corporations and unions from directly contributing campaign funds to political candidates.

6.4

1. True. Texas's campaign finance laws often involve disclosure by public officials and lobbyists, though critics would argue that current disclosure requirements are not sufficient to reform the system.
2. True. The Texas Ethics Commission is the primary state agency regulating the political contributions and expenditures by lobbyists and public officials.
3. True. A campaign contribution accepted by a public official with an agreement to act in the contributor's interest is against the law; yet, it is very difficult to prove.

Discussion Questions

1. What interest groups are you familiar with? If you are not already a member of an interest group, would you consider joining one?
2. Are interest groups beneficial in Texas politics? What are the advantages and disadvantages?
3. Do you think interest groups have too much power in Texas politics?
4. Do you think Texas should have stricter campaign finance law? Or do you think the disclosure laws we currently have suffice?

5. Do you think Texas law should place caps on campaign contributions for individuals and PACS in state elections?
6. What are your recommendations for increasing or decreasing the powers of the Texas Ethics Commission?

Internet Resources

Christian Coalition of America-Texas Chapter: **http://www.ccoatx.com**

League of Women Voters of Texas: **http://www.lwvtexas.org**

Mexican American Legal Defense and Education Fund: **http://www.maldef.org**

Public Citizen/Texas: **http://www.citizen.org/texas**

Sierra Club, Lone Star Chapter: **http://texas.sierraclub.org**

Texans for Public Justice: **http://www.tpj.org**

Texas Common Cause: **http://www.commoncause.org/tx**

Texas Community College Teachers Association: **http://www.tccta.org**

Texas Ethics Commission: **http://www.ethics.state.tx.us**

Texas League of United Latin American Citizens: **http://www.tx-lulac.org**

Texas NAACP: **http://texasnaacp.org**

Texas Public Employees Association: **http://www.tpea.org**

Texas State Teachers Association: **http://www.tsta.org**

Notes

1. Allan Cigler and Burdett Loomis, *Interest Group Politics,* 8th ed. (Washington, DC: CQ Press, 2012), 2.
2. Joseph M. Bessette, John J. Pitney, Jr., Lyle C. Brown, Joyce A. Langenegger, Sonia R. García, Ted A. Lewis, and Robert E. Biles, *American Government and Politics: Deliberation, Democracy and Citizenship* (Boston: Wadsworth, 2012), 273.
3. Christy Hoppe, "Business Lobby Flexes Muscle in Legislature," *Dallas Morning News,* April 12, 2003.
4. Robert T. Garrett and Christy Hoppe, "Two Bills Down to Embers," *Dallas Morning News,* May 11, 2009.
5. Peggy Fikac, "Perry Signs Hate Crimes Legislation," *San Antonio Express-News,* May 12, 2001.
6. Gary Scharrer, "Board Rejects Rebel Plate," *San Antonio Express-News,* November 11, 2011.
7. For an examination of the origins of LULAC and its founders, Alonso S. Perales and Adela Sloss-Vento, see Cynthia Orozco, *No Mexicans, Women, or Dogs Allowed: The Rise of the Mexican American Civil Rights Movement* (Austin: University of Texas Press, 2009).
8. See Sonia R. García, Valerie Martinez-Ebers, Irasema Coronado, Sharon A. Navarro, and Patricia A. Jaramillo, *Politicas: Latina Public Officials in Texas* (Austin: University of Texas Press, 2008). Chapter 3 concerns Representative Irma Rangel.
9. For information on the role of the Christian Coalition, see James Lamare, Jerry L. Polinard, and Robert D. Wrinkle, "Texas: Religion and Politics in God's

Country," in *The Christian Right in American Politics: Marching Toward the Millennium,* ed. John C. Green, Mark J. Rozell, and Clyde Wilcox (Washington, DC: Georgetown University Press, 2003), 59–78.

10. Peggy Fikac, "Alliance Formed to Monitor Radical Right," *Houston Chronicle,* October 1, 1995.

11. See Dennis Shirley, *Valley Interfaith and School Reform: Organizing for Power in South Texas* (Austin: University of Austin Press, 2002).

12. For a history of COPS, see Mark R. Warren, *Dry Bones Rattling: Community Building to Revitalize an American Democracy* (Princeton, NJ: Princeton University Press, 2001).

13. Richard Kearney, "Political Parties, Interest Groups and Campaigns" in *State and Local Government,* 8th ed., ed. Ann O'M. Bowman and Richard Kearney (Boston: Wadsworth Cengage Learning, 2010), 150.

14. H. C. Pittman, *Inside the Third House: A Veteran Lobbyist Takes a 50-Year Frolic through Texas Politics* (Austin: Eakin Press, 1992), 219. See also John Spong, "State Bar," *Texas Monthly,* July 2003, 110–113, 148–149.

15. "Doctors' Orders: Medical Lobby Becomes a Powerhouse in Austin," *Wall Street Journal,* May 19, 1999.

16. Lisa Sanberg, "Texas Capitol's Lobby Has a Revolving Door," *San Antonio Express-News,* January 29, 2006. See also, Randy Lee Loftis, "Cashing in on Their Capital Floor Time," *Dallas Morning News,* January 6, 2009.

17. Matt Stiles, "Lobbyists Reports: $12.8 Million Spent Wooing Legislators," *San Antonio Express-News,* January 25, 2009.

18. Texas Ethics Commission, "2010 Lobby Lists and Reports" and "2011 Lobby Lists and Reports," *Search Campaign Finance and Lobby Reports,* http://www.ethics.state.tx.us.dfs/loblists.htm.

19. Keith E. Hamm and Charles W. Wiggins, "Texas: The Transformation from Personal to Informational Lobbying," in *Interest Group Politics in the Southern States,* ed. Ronald J. Hrebenar and Olive S. Thomas (Tuscaloosa: University of Alabama Press, 1992), 80.

20. Texans for Public Justice, "Making Connections: Officials and Their Special Interest Travel Agency," *Major Reports,* April 24, 2007, http://www.tpj.org.

21. Texas Ethics Commission, "Campaign Finance Reports—Political Committee Lists," *Search Campaign Finance and Lobby Reports,* http://www.ethics.state.tx.us/dfs/paclists.htm.

22. Jason Embry, "Top-Spending PACs Backed by Lawyers, Businesses, Parties," *Austin American-Statesman,* January 26, 2009. See also Texas for Public Justice, "Texas PACs: 2010 Election Cycle Spending," *Major Reports,* August 2010, http://www.tpj.org.

23. Texans for Public Justice, "Craddick-Tied PAC Cash Routed to Just 8 GOP House Candidates." *Lobby Watch,* April 2, 2004, http://www.tpj.org.

24. See Ralph Blumenthal and Carl Hulse, "Judge Lets Stand 2 of 3 Charges Faced by DeLay," *New York Times,* December 6, 2005; Gary Martin, "Texas Jury Indicts DeLay," *San Antonio Express-News,* September 29, 2005.

25. Texas Ethics Commission, "A Brief Overview of the Texas Ethics Commission and Its Duties," *Search for Publications and Guides,* September 22, 2009, http://www.ethics.state.tx.us/main/guides.htm. See also in the same website, "Campaign Finance Guide for Political Committees," revised September 28, 2011.

26. "The Morning After: Last-Minute Contributions in Texas's 2002 Primary Elections," October 2002, http://www.tpj.org/docs/2002/10/reports/morningafter.

See also Robert Garrett, "PACs Late Aid Altered Races," *Dallas Morning News*, March 10, 2006.

27. Texas Ethics Commission, "Enforcement and Sworn Complaints," http://www.ethics.state.tx.us/sworncomp/orders.html. The 2008–2010 information is based on a phone interview with Brad Johnson from the Texas Ethics Commission, April 5, 2010.

28. Dave Lieber, "Texas Ethics Laws Are Tightened, But not as Much as They Could Have Been," *Fort Worth Star-Telegram*, June 26, 2009. See also Texas Ethics Commission, "2011 Legislation," http://www.ethics.state.tx.us/whatsnew/leg2011.html.

29. Texans for Public Justice, "Ethics Commission's Teeth in Perry's Hands," *Lobby Watch*, June 16, 2011, http://www.tpj.org.

30. Texans for Public Justice, "New Governor Hires Hired Guns as He Hypes Lobby Ethics Code," *Lobby Watch*, January 5, 2001. And see Laylan Copelin, "Public Stirring Election Change," *Austin American-Statesman*, May 4, 2008; and Laylan Copelin, "Ethics Panel Works Quietly to Discipline Public Officials," *Austin American-Statesman*, July 19, 2008.

31. See Texas Ethics Commission, "U.S. Supreme Court Ruling Impacting Texas," *Research, Advisory Opinions, and Rules*, http://www.ethics.state.tx.us/whatsnew/US_Supreme_Court_Ruling.html.

32. Laylan Copelin, "State Law Holds Back Corporate Donations," *Austin American-Statesman*, January 2, 2011. See also Tom Benning, "Super PACs Pointed to Help Rick Perry's Presidential Run," *Dallas Morning News*, September 16, 2011.

33. See Sam Kinch Jr. with Anne Marie Kilday, *Too Much Money Is Not Enough: Big Money and Political Power in Texas* (Austin: Campaigns for People, 2000). See also Lisa Sandberg and Kelly Guckian, "Lobbyists' Money Talks—Softly, But It's Heard," *San Antonio-Express News*, April 12, 2006.

34. Molly Ivins, "Who Let the PACs Out? Woof, Woof!" *Fort Worth Star-Telegram*, February 18, 2001.

35. "With Perry's Signature, Texas Campaign Laws Will Get Boost They Need," *Austin American-Statesman*, June 9, 2003; Ginger Richardson, "Stronger Ethics Rules Hang on House Vote," *Fort Worth Star-Telegram*, June 2, 2003.

36. Clive S. Thomas and Ronald J. Hrebenar, "Political Parties, Interest Groups and Campaigns," in *State and Local Government*, 8th ed., ed. Ann O'M. Bowman and Richard Kearney (Boston: Wadsworth, 2010), 157.

37. See Center for Public Integrity, "Grading The Nation: How Accountable Is Your State?" *State Integrity Investigation*, March 19, 2012, http://www.iwatchnews.org/accountability/state-integrity-investigation.

Unsung Hero of Civil Rights: "Father of LULAC" a Fading Memory*†

Hector Saldaña

Mexican American civil rights leader Alonso S. Perales is all but a fading memory for most students of Texas politics. His collected papers, however, are now available to students and researchers. This reading sheds light on a Texas hero and on efforts to preserve Perales's papers for an archival collection in a university depository.

Though he was once hailed as the "Father of LULAC" and a civil rights giant, Alonso S. Perales today is a historical shadow figure, little more than a name frozen on an elementary school building on the West Side [of San Antonio]. Students pass by his portrait daily without much thought, says Perales Elementary School principal Dolores Mena. "The kids know what he looks like, but they don't know what he's done." "He was a most extraordinary man," recalls retired County Commissioner and Municipal Court Judge Albert Perla, a friend who says he is perplexed why such a historic leader is forgotten to a generation. "But he was very well known when I knew him." That was more than 40 years ago. Perales died in 1960 at the age of 61.

A self-made man, highly educated and erudite, Perales was a prolific writer of position papers and books on the second-class status of Mexican Americans, a newspaper columnist, a spokesman at rallies, a foreign diplomat and shaper of laws. He traveled the globe to promote his culture and to fight for its rights—"*En defensa de mi raza.*" "He was the great intellectual of LULAC," says Ed Peña, former LULAC national president in Washington, D.C. "He was our Thomas Jefferson."

In the late 1920s, Perales founded the League of United Latin American Citizens in his image-working alongside other activist-philosophers such as J. T. Canales, Ben Garza, M. C. González, Gus García, Carlos Castañeda, George Sánchez, and Jose Luz Sáenz to shape its goals. Perales delineated that vision in a draft of LULAC bylaws: "To develop within the members of our race the best, purest, and most perfect type of true, loyal citizen of the United States." "We are going to show the world that we have just and legitimate aspirations, that we have self-pride, dignity, and racial pride; that we have a very high concept of our American citizenship; that we have a great love of our country," Perales said in a 1943 radio address.

And as politico Romulo Munguia notes, Perales had the wisdom, guts, and skills to "fight the fight in English." Seventy-five years ago, he declared English "the official language" of LULAC and campaigned for Hispanics to be classified as "white" in the census—actions that rankle modern Latinos, many of whom accuse Perales of elitism in light of today's continuing struggle for equality. But the fiery speaker whose persuasive rhetoric often kept LULAC from splintering also considered certain Anglos the enemy, says one family member. Perales' language in 1929 is blunt: "We shall resist and attack energetically all

---

machinations tending to prevent our social and political unification." He was the voice of calm, however. "We should pity and not despise those who are yet in darkness," Perales wrote. Perales was a bridge builder who never forgot where he came from, say those who knew him. His ideas were born of early struggle and poverty.

A dark-skinned Mexican American, Perales was born in Alice in 1898. Orphaned young, he picked cotton in the fields to earn a living and enlisted in the army during World War I. Through guts and determination, and the belief that education could overcome other handicaps, he graduated with a law degree from George Washington University. He passed the Texas State Bar exam in 1925 and became an early civil rights lawyer in San Antonio.

"He was a poor kid that had nothing and it's hard to visualize how he got from this point to that point. He had a vision; he had a dream. I want to say he was like Martin Luther King—but he preceded Martin Luther King," says Carrizales. To his nephew and namesake, Alonso M. Perales, 77, his uncle was down-to-earth "and a real Tejano."

In 1931, *La Prensa* called Perales the one American [who] defends Mexicans. His early radio speeches made clear that Mexicans were "thirsty for justice" and had a rightful place in the society they labored to support. By the mid-'40s, he had documented more than 150 towns in Texas with establishments that barred service to Hispanics and wrote about it in the book, "*Are We Good Neighbors*?" Throughout the '50s, Perales fought for a living wage for braceros. He opposed restrictive covenants that kept Mexican Americans out of certain neighborhoods; he fought the poll tax. His fight against segregation and for equal rights rivals the work of Martin Luther King, say historians and admirers....

Yet for all his work on behalf of Mexican Americans, Perales has all but faded from collective memory. "We don't know how to take care of our heroes," says Dallas attorney José Ángel Gutiérrez, co-founder of La Raza Unida and a guiding light of the Chicano Movement of the '60s and '70s, about Perales' modern obscurity—

which he considers a travesty. "[Perales'] history is there for those who seek it out," Houston attorney Alfred J. Hernandez says. "This is a deep story about *nosotros.*" It's a story that can be found in a cache of Perales' personal documents—and that has yet to see the light of day.

Died Too Soon

They say that history belongs to those who write it. Perales' story rests in dozens of moldy boxes once coveted by his widow, a high-strung former opera singer who in later years vacillated between guarding that packaged legacy and threatening to burn the entire lot, says Perales' nephew. The boxes have collected dust since Perales died in 1960. When Marta Perales died a couple of years ago, heirs Raymond Perales and Martha Carrizales—Perales' adopted children—vowed to preserve their father's papers and restore his rightful image. But action has been slow. They eventually asked Henry Cisneros' politically savvy uncle, printer Ruben Munguia, to help sort mountains of pioneering material....

It was Ruben Munguia's last great undertaking, his brother says. He worked meticulously sorting the delicate treasure of documents at his draft table at his Buena Vista Street print shop "because he liked to be around all the action," says Ruben Munguia's daughter Mary Perales. Since his death, the project has languished. Brother and sister do what they can in their spare time. As Carrizales pores over reams of her father's delicate documents, she gushes, "It's like learning about a character in history." Perales' collection is voluminous.... Historian and University of Texas associate professor Emilio Zamora agrees and urged the family to deposit the papers at the Mexican American Library Program at the University of Texas because of its "unmatched historical value." In 2001, he wrote to Carrizales: "I honestly believe that Perales is the most important Mexican American leader of the 20th century." Zamora cites Perales' prominence as an author, diplomat, and LULAC officer, and his ties to Latino organizations, civic service, and civil rights activism. "Not only within the Mexican American community, but I think he's a major civil rights leader of the nation," Zamora says.

That the materials are still out of the hands of researchers is a serious issue, he says. There is also a fear that the integrity of the collection could be unintentionally undermined and lose research value. "Anyone who's involved in archival collection will tell you that a collection of that immense value has to be deposited somewhere and processed and then made available for researchers," Zamora says. His hope is that the University of Texas gets them ("It's the natural home," he says) because Perales' contemporaries are archived there....

Not Really "Radical"

"My mother was a radical and marched with César Chavez," says Carrizales. "Of course, she could afford that. She was bourgeois. My father wouldn't have agreed with the '60s." Certainly Perales' words from the late '20s—"We shall oppose any radical and violent demonstration which may tend to create conflicts and disturb the peace and tranquility of our country"—had no place in the Chicano Movement. "He was a realist," says Chicano leader Gutiérrez, who notes that the FBI's surveillance of LULAC started because of Perales' overseas activities. "It was very dangerous to be an activist Mexican at that time, very dangerous. You could lose your life, and people did. This was not a time to stand up and be radical, and what he was doing was perceived to be radical."

Zamora argues that Perales' great achievement was taking the cause of Mexican Americans to international forums. Perales spoke at international conferences; he appealed for nations to put pressure on the United States for Mexican American equal rights. Perales participated in founding meetings of the United Nations in 1945. "At that meeting, he again included the Mexican American in the deliberations of human rights," Zamora explains.

"He was an extraordinary man. If we had him today, I'm telling you, he'd be up in front.

And he'd be shaking stuff," Zamora says. "He had conservative ideas, but some of his ideas for that time were pretty radical. He had so much courage and intellect. His stamina and sense of civic responsibility was just tremendous." Many say that the true value of the Perales papers is to put his "conservative" activism in perspective. "It was a very primitive democracy for us," LULAC historian Peña adds. "He was visible when there were very few (Mexican Americans) that were visible." ...

He outlined his views in October 1931 in a position paper, "*El Mexico Americano y la Politica del Sur Texas.*" "If we want to accelerate our political evolution, it's imperative that we change the system," wrote Perales, who argued that self-education on issues was more important than party affiliation.

In his eyes, pulling a voting lever blindly was akin to a sin: "It's one thing to vote and know what you're voting for, but it's another thing to do it because someone ordered you to do it and who to vote for," he wrote in Spanish. And though he fought against the poll tax, he urged Latinos to pay it and participate. Former Houston judge Hernandez says that Perales is responsible "for Mexican Americans coming of age" because he was willing to enter *un nido de viboras* (the viper's nest) of an often-racist Texas legal system....

Lost History

It was only in the '70s that major universities became interested in collecting the papers of major Latino figures. In some cases, that was more than 50 years too late. "Man, I could tell you some stories that would make you cry about stuff we've lost," Zamora says from Austin. "We're lacking in the telling of the story because the historical record is not readily available," Zamora adds.

Sociologist and Mexican American studies expert Avelardo Valdez at the University of Houston says that Perales is "part of a constellation of lost figures" in the Mexican American experience. "It's highly significant and important that these kinds of papers are found, and that they be archived and that we have access to them," says Valdez, adding that the find will show "Perales' founding generation was much more progressive than our generation today. It took a lot of guts to be organizing political organizations in the 1920s and '30s in South Texas.

Carrizales says her ultimate dream is that researchers will restore her father's legacy. "He was an activist for human dignity—like César Chavez, like Martin Luther King," Carrizales says. "He needs to be recognized, not glorified, for his efforts. History must do him justice. People need a full cup of information."

The Legislature

(Nick Anderson of the Houston Chronicle, dist. by The Washington Post Writers Group. Reprinted with Permission.)

Learning Objectives

1. Analyze conflicts involved in districting.
2. Identify similarities and differences in the formal qualifications for a state representative and for a state senator.
3. Compare and contrast the powers of the president of the Texas Senate and the Speaker of the Texas House of Representatives.
4. Outline the steps by which a bill becomes a law according to House and Senate rules of procedure.
5. Explain the influences on voting decisions made by elected legislators.

249

In 2009, two years after the Virginia Tech shootings that killed more than 30 people, Senator Jeff Wentworth (R-San Antonio) introduced Senate Bill 1164. It would allow concealed handguns—but not openly displayed pistols, as suggested by Nick Anderson's cartoon—to be carried on Texas college and university campuses by students and employees licensed to do so. A private institution of higher education could opt out. "Guns on campus" advocates cheered when Wentworth's bill passed in the Senate, but they were disappointed when the companion bill by Representative Joe Driver (R-Garland) failed to reach the House floor for a vote. In 2011, a year after a student used an assault rifle to fire several shots and then kill himself on the campus of the University of Texas at Austin, Senator Wentworth and Representative Driver sought unsuccessfully to enact similar legislation. Of course, lawmaking by any elected representative body with many members is a slow, frustrating, and often disappointing process. Most citizens are impatient with political tactics and procedural delays, even if their policy objectives are eventually achieved. And they often dislike the inevitable compromises involved in the legislative process.

Nevertheless, our legislators perform work of vital importance. They make laws that affect the life, liberty, and property of all persons in the state. After years of research, Professor Alan Rosenthal of Rutgers University concluded: "Despite the popular perceptions that legislatures are autocratic, arbitrary, isolated, unresponsive, and up for sale, legislatures are in fact extraordinarily democratic institutions." He explained: "They have been becoming more democratic of late, so that a systematic shift from representative democracy to participatory democracy now seems to be under way."[1] Rosenthal also stated, "There is always room for improving legislatures. They are far from perfect, yet they are the best we have, and preferable to any conceivable alternative. Not only that, they actually work, albeit in rather messy and somewhat mysterious ways—representing, lawmaking, and balancing the power of the executive."[2] After reading this chapter on the Texas legislature, you can decide whether Rosenthal's conclusions apply to the Lone Star State.

★ Legislative Framework

LO1   In their Declaration of Independence dated March 2, 1836, delegates elected to the convention at Washington-on-the-Brazos complained that the Mexican government "had dissolved, by force of arms, the state Congress of Coahuila and Texas, and obliged our representatives to fly for their lives from the seat of government, thus depriving us of the fundamental right of representation." That fundamental right was subsequently established in the Constitution of the Republic of Texas and in all of Texas's four state constitutions, wherein Texans have entrusted the power to enact bills and adopt resolutions to popularly elected legislators. These powers are the essence of representative government. Other legislative functions include proposing constitutional amendments, adopting a budget for state government, levying taxes, redistricting for election

Points to Ponder

- A copy of the King James Bible (bearing desk number and state seal on its blue cover) is provided to each senator and representative. Some Texas legislators also wear official rings and official lapel pins, which they purchase at their own expense.
- Department of Public Safety troopers, accompanied by dogs trained to sniff for explosives, patrol the Capitol and surrounding grounds. Metal detectors are installed at the four entrances to the state Capitol, but persons licensed to carry concealed handguns can enter with their weapons; other eligible persons with a Capitol Access Pass costing nearly $120 can enter without going through security checkpoints.
- Hung behind the House Speaker's rostrum during legislative sessions is the original San Jacinto battle flag, on which is painted a partially bare-breasted woman clutching a sword draped with a streamer proclaiming "Liberty or Death." When legislators are not in session, a reproduction of this flag is displayed, and the original is covered by a curtain to reduce fading from exposure to light.

of Texas's state legislators and U.S. representatives, and impeaching and removing executive and judicial officials if warranted.

In Texas and 40 other states, the larger chamber of the **bicameral** (two-chamber, or two-house) legislature is called the House of Representatives. Some other states use the terms *Assembly, House of Delegates,* or *General Assembly.* Only Nebraska has a **unicameral** (one-chamber, or one-house) legislature, with 49 senators. In the 49 states with bicameral legislatures, the larger chamber ranges in size from 40 members in Alaska to 400 members in New Hampshire. Texas has 150 members in its House of Representatives. The smaller legislative chamber is called the Senate. Alaska has the smallest Senate, with 20 members; Minnesota has the largest, with 67. The Texas Senate has 31 members.

Election and Terms of Office

Voters residing in representative and senatorial districts elect Texas legislators. Representatives are elected for two years. Senators are usually elected for four years. Terms of office for members of both houses begin in January of odd-numbered years.

Legislative redistricting for both the Texas House and the Senate occurs in the first odd-numbered year in a decade (for example, 2011). Voters elect a new House of Representatives in every even-numbered year. After redistricting, a new Senate is elected in the general election of the following year (for example, November 2012). In January of the next odd-numbered year (for example, 2013), Senators draw lots by choosing from 31 numbered pieces of paper sealed in envelopes. The 16 who draw odd numbers get four-year terms, while the 15

bicameral
A legislature with two houses or chambers, such as Texas's House of Representatives and Senate.

unicameral
A one-house legislature, such as the Nebraska legislature.

Governor Rick Perry gives a "State of the State" address to a joint session of the Texas House and Senate in the Texas House of Representatives. Behind Perry (left to right) are a "tote" board for displaying votes of House members, a portrait of Governor James S. Hogg (1891–1895), the San Jacinto battle flag, and a portrait of Governor Sam Houston, president of the Texas Republic (1836–1838 and 1841–1844) and governor of the state (1859–1861).

(AP Photo/Harry Cabluck)

who draw even numbers get only two-year terms. Thus, approximately one-half of the senators (that is, 15 or 16) will be elected in each even-numbered year.

A legislator may be expelled by a two-thirds majority vote of the membership of the legislator's chamber. If a member of the legislature dies, resigns, or is expelled from office, the vacancy is filled by special election. A 2003 constitutional amendment allows a legislator called to active military duty for longer than 30 days to retain the office if he or she appoints a constitutionally qualified temporary replacement of the same political party and if the replacement is approved by the appropriate chamber. As of late 2012, three male representatives had been called to military duty. Each appointed his wife as a temporary replacement.[3]

Sessions

regular session
A session of the Texas legislature that begins on the second Tuesday in January of odd-numbered years and lasts for a maximum of 140 days.

special session
A legislative session called by the governor and limited to no more than 30 days.

A Texas law requires a **regular session** to begin on the second Tuesday in January of each odd-numbered year (for example, January 8, 2013). In practice, these regular biennial sessions always run for the full 140 days, as authorized by the Texas Constitution (for example, through May 27, 2013). Legislative sessions mean "big money" for many Austin businesses. Whenever the Texas legislature convenes for a regular session, spending by legislators and lobbyists, as well as by the people who work for them, boosts the Austin economy by many millions of dollars.

The governor may also call **special sessions**, lasting no longer than 30 days each, at any time. From 2001 through 2012, Rick Perry, governor of Texas, called nine special sessions on matters ranging from congressional redistricting to transportation funding. During a special session, the legislature

How Do We Compare...in State Legislative Seats?

Most Populous U.S. States	Senate Seats	House Seats*	U.S. States Bordering Texas	Senate Seats	House Seats	Mexican States Bordering Texas	Unicameral *Congreso* Seats
California	40	80	Arkansas	35	100	Chihuahua	35
Florida	40	120	Louisiana	39	105	Coahuila	35
New York	62	150	New Mexico	42	70	Nuevo León	42
Texas	**31**	**150**	Oklahoma	48	101	Tamaulipas	32

Source: The Book of the States, 2012 (Lexington, Ky.: Council of State Governments, 2012), 118; and Gobiernos Estatales, http://www.diputados.gob.mx/cedia/sia/dir/DIR-ISS-09-06.pdf.
*In California and New York, this chamber is called the Assembly.

may consider only those matters placed before it by the governor. Such limits on sessions indicate a deep-seated popular distrust of legislators and a fear of change. Governor Bill Clements expressed his sentiments with the statement that "all kinds of bad things can happen when the legislature is in session." This attitude further reflects the individualistic political ideology of many Texans, who believe in limiting government control.

Districting

Providing equal representation in a legislative chamber involves dividing a state into districts with approximately equal numbers of inhabitants. Population distribution changes constantly as the result of migration and different birthrates and death rates. Therefore, legislative district boundaries must be redrawn periodically to ensure equitable representation. Such **redistricting** can be politically disadvantageous to a legislator. It may take away areas of constituents who have provided strong voter support; it may add an area of constituents who produce little support and much opposition; or it may produce a new district that includes the residences of two or more representatives or senators, only one of whom can be reelected to represent the district.[4]

In Texas, the first legislative and congressional elections in districts determined by the 2010 census were conducted in November 2012 for offices filled in January 2013. For the previous ten years the 2000 census had been the basis for legislative and congressional representation.

State Legislative Districts The Texas Constitution stipulates that "the legislature shall, at its first session after the publication of each United States decennial census, apportion the State into Senatorial and Representative districts." Nevertheless, in the decades after 1876, the legislature sometimes failed to redivide the state's population and map new districts for legislators. Thus, some districts became heavily populated and greatly underrepresented; others experienced population decline or slow growth, resulting in overrepresentation.

redistricting
Redrawing of boundaries after the federal decennial census to create districts with approximately equal population (e.g., legislative, congressional, commissioners court, and city council districts in Texas).

In 1948, legislative districting inequities finally led to the adoption of a Texas state constitutional amendment designed to pressure the legislature to remedy this situation. Under the amendment, failure of the legislature to redistrict during the first regular session after a decennial (every 10 years) census brings the Legislative Redistricting Board into operation. This board consists of the following five ex officio (that is, "holding other office") members: lieutenant governor, Speaker of the House of Representatives, attorney general, comptroller of public accounts, and commissioner of the General Land Office. The board must meet within 90 days after the legislative session and redistrict the state within another 60 days.

Although the legislature drew new legislative districts after the federal censuses of 1950 and 1960, the Texas Constitution's apportionment formulas for the Texas House and Senate discriminated against heavily populated urban counties. These formulas were not changed until after the U.S. Supreme Court held in *Reynolds v. Sims*, 377 U.S. 533 (1964) that "the seats in both houses of a bicameral state legislature must be apportioned on a population basis." This "one person, one vote" principle was first applied in Texas by a federal district court in *Kilgarlin v. Martin*, 252 F. Supp. 404 (1965).

Redistricting by the Texas legislature often sparks complaints about **gerrymandering**, a practice that involves drawing legislative districts to include or exclude certain groups of voters in order to favor one group or political party. Usually, gerrymandered districts are oddly shaped rather than compact. In fact, the term *gerrymander* originated to describe irregularly shaped districts created under the guidance of Elbridge Gerry, governor of Massachusetts, in 1812. The political party holding the most positions in the legislature often benefits in elections conducted after redistricting. Many state and federal court battles have been fought over the constitutionality of Texas's legislative districting arrangements.

Members of the Texas Senate have always represented **single-member districts**—that is, the voters of each district elect one senator. Redistricting according to the 2010 federal census provided for an ideal population of 811,147 (the total state population of 25,145,561 divided by 31) in each senatorial district. Many of the 31 senatorial districts cover several counties, but a few big-city senatorial districts are formed from the territory of only part of a county (see Figure 7.1).

Until 1971, a Texas county with two or more seats in the House was a **multimember district** in which voters elected representatives at-large to represent the whole county. Thus, a voter in such a county could vote in all of the county's House races. In 1971, however, single-member districts were established in Harris, Dallas, and Bexar counties. Four years later, the single-member districting system was extended to all other counties in which voters elected more than one representative. Today, all representatives in Texas are elected on a single-member-district basis. The change to single-member districts was largely a result of court actions. Election results demonstrate that single-member districts reduce campaign costs and increase the probability that more African American and Latino candidates will be elected. As a result of the 2010 federal census, redistricting provided each state representative district with an ideal population of 167,637 (total state population divided by 150). House

gerrymandering
Drawing the boundaries of a district, such as a state senatorial or representative district, to include or exclude certain groups of voters and thus affect election outcomes.

single-member district
An area that elects only one representative to serve on a policymaking body, such as a city council, county commissioners court, state House, or state Senate.

multimember district
A district in which all voters participate in the election of two or more representatives to a policymaking body, such as a city council, a state House, or a state Senate.

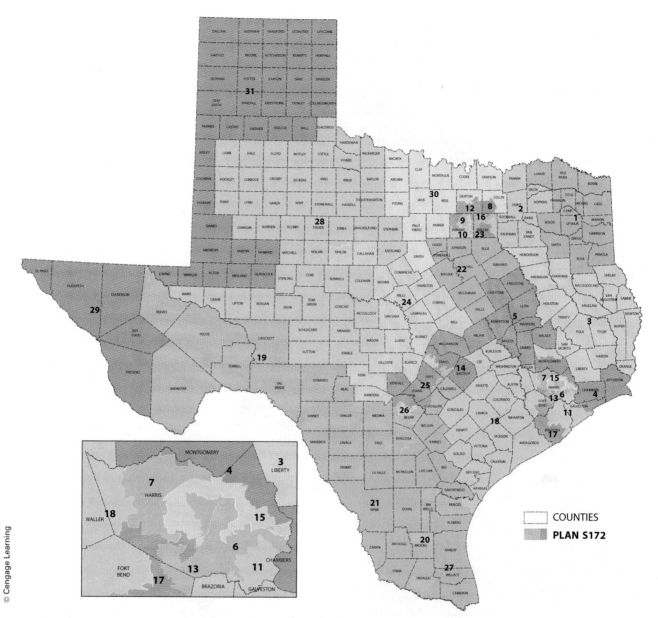

Figure 7.1   Court-ordered Interim Texas State Senate Districts (for electing state senators in 2012–2013). The accompanying map shows districts wholly or partially within Harris County.

© Cengage Learning

District 68, in the Panhandle region of West Texas, covers 22 counties, whereas densely populated Harris County is divided into 24 districts (see Figure 7.2).

In 2011, House and Senate redistricting bills were passed in the regular session of the 82nd legislature, signed by Governor Perry, and submitted by Attorney General Greg Abbott for preclearance by a three-judge panel of the U.S. District Court for the District of Columbia in Washington, D.C., as required by the federal Voting Rights Act. An alternative would have been to seek preclearance from the Civil Rights Division of the U.S. Department of Justice; however, Republican Abbott chose to avoid this Democrat-controlled

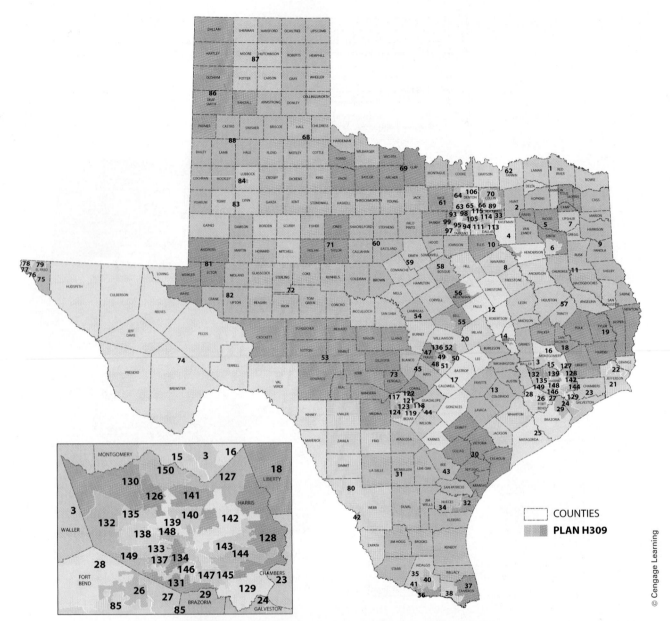

Figure 7.2   Court-ordered Texas State House Districts (for electing state representatives in 2012–2013). The accompanying map shows districts wholly or partially within Harris County.

department of President Barack Obama's administration. Under Section 5 of the Voting Rights Act, preclearance was required because of Texas's history of racial discrimination against minority voters.

Before the Washington, D.C., court considered the preclearance issue, the legislature's new maps for state House and Senate districts were challenged by historical minority groups on the grounds that they discriminated against Latinos and African Americans. The lawsuits were consolidated for trial by a three-judge panel of the U.S. District Court for the Western District of Texas in

San Antonio. Because the 2012 party primaries could not be held until district boundaries were established, that court decided to produce interim House and Senate maps to be used for primaries in that year. On November 17, 2011, the San Antonio court issued these new maps as well as new Congressional maps.

The Senate map satisfied most Democrats, because it largely restored the district of Senator Wendy Davis (D-Fort Worth) to pre-2011 boundaries. Because Republicans protested that new maps benefited Democrats, however, Attorney General Abbott appealed to the U.S. Supreme Court. In a per curiam decision (with justices ruling collectively and anonymously) dated January 20, 2012, the Supreme Court rejected the interim maps and ordered the San Antonio district court to use the legislature's maps as a "starting point" for drawing districts. After negotiations involving Attorney General Abbott, the Texas Latino Redistricting Task Force, and other groups, the district court ordered maps similar to those authorized in the regular session of the 82nd legislature in 2011. Court-ordered primaries were conducted on May 29, 2012, but on August 28 the U.S. District Court for the District of Columbia denied preclearance for the state House and Senate maps authorized by the Texas legislature in 2011 as well as the Congressional district maps. The San Antonio district court, however, ordered use of its maps for the November general elections. The League of United Latin American Citizens (LULAC) appealed this action; but on September 19, 2012, the U.S. Supreme Court denied the appeal.

U.S. Congressional Districts According to former U.S. House Speaker Jim Wright, when long-time Speaker Sam Rayburn was asked why so many Texan congressmen frequently chaired important committees in Washington, D.C., Rayburn responded: "We pick 'em young, and we pick 'em honest. We send them there, and we keep 'em there."[5] Although keeping congress members in office so that they develop seniority is important, longevity is no longer the sole determining factor in appointing U.S. House committee chairs. Reelection is influenced by redistricting that can affect election results.

In the year after a federal census, the Texas legislature is supposed to draw new boundaries for the state's U.S. congressional districts (from which representatives to the U.S. House of Representatives are elected). District lines must be drawn to make the number of people in respective districts equal. Results of the 2010 federal census indicated that each of Texas's 36 congressional districts should have an ideal population of 698,488.

In 2011, the Texas legislature failed to pass a bill that would redistrict Texas's seats in the U.S. House of Representatives. Because congressional redistricting does not fall within the jurisdiction of the Legislative Redistricting Board, Governor Perry gave this task to a special session of the Texas legislature that convened on May 31 of that year.

As the result of a large growth in Texas's population between 2000 and 2010, the number of the state's congressional districts increased from 32 to 36. (See Figure 7.3.) The legislature's redistricting effort was found in violation of the Voting Rights Act. For details concerning congressional redistricting politics in 2011 and 2012, along with the court-ordered Interim U.S. Congressional Plan for 2012-2013, see Figure 7.3 as well as this chapter's Selected Reading, "Recent Congressional Redistricting in Texas."

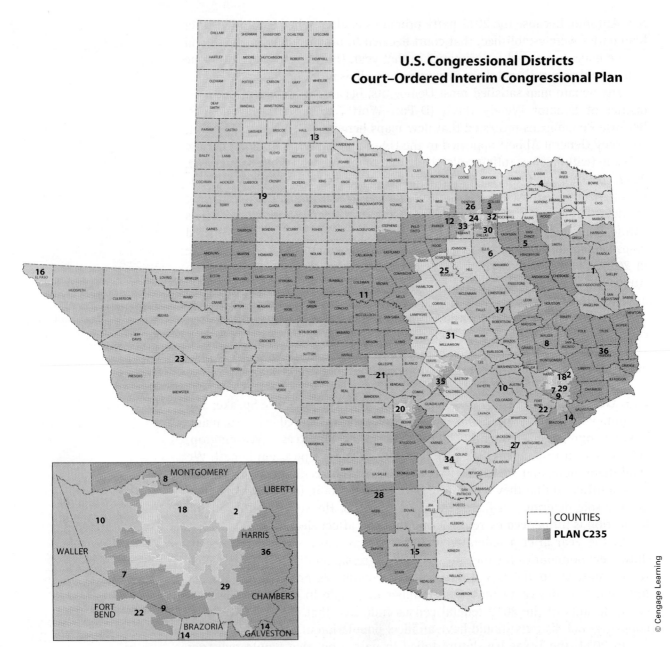

U.S. Congressional Districts
Court–Ordered Interim Congressional Plan

COUNTIES

PLAN C235

© Cengage Learning

Figure 7.3   Court-Ordered Interim U.S. Congressional Districts (for electing U.S. representatives for 2012–2013). Accompanying map shows districts wholly or partially within Harris County.

☑ Learning Check 7.1   (Answers on p. 292)

1. How many years make a full term for a member of the Texas House of Representatives?
2. True or False: Usually, gerrymandered districts are compact in shape.

Legislators

Members of the Texas legislature may not hold another government office. Furthermore, they must meet specific state constitutional qualifications concerning citizenship, voter status, state residence, district residence, and age. Despite such restrictions, millions of Texans possess all of the prescribed legal qualifications to serve in the legislature. As is true of the memberships in other state legislatures, however, the biographical data for members of recent Texas legislatures suggest the existence of informal qualifications that restrict opportunities for election to either of the two chambers.

LO2

Qualifications and Characteristics

The Texas Constitution specifies the formal qualifications for House and Senate members. All of these elected legislative officials must be U.S. citizens, qualified Texas voters, and residents of the districts they represent for one year immediately preceding a general election. In matters of state residence and age, however, qualifications differ between the two chambers (see Table 7.1).

A House candidate must have resided in Texas for two years before being elected, whereas a Senate candidate must have five years of state residence. To be eligible for House membership, a person must be at least 21 years of age; to serve in the Senate, a person must be at least 26. If a question arises concerning constitutional qualifications or if a dispute develops over election returns, each legislative chamber determines who will be seated.

The typical Texas legislator is an Anglo Protestant male between 35 and 50 years of age, a native-born Texan, and an attorney or a businessperson who has served one or more previous terms of office. Although such characteristics do not guarantee any predetermined reaction to issues and events, legislators do tend to be influenced by their experiences and environments. Because these factors can have policy consequences, any study of the legislature must account for the biographical characteristics of legislators. See Table 7.2 for data on political party affiliation, racial/ethnic classification, and gender of legislators from 1971 to 2013.

Table 7.1 Constitutional Qualifications for Membership in the Texas Legislature		
Qualification	**House**	**Senate**
Citizenship	U.S. citizen	U.S. citizen
Voter status	Qualified Texas voter	Qualified Texas voter
Residence in district to be represented	One year immediately preceding election	One year immediately preceding election
Texas residence	Two years immediately preceding election	Five years immediately preceding election
Age	21 years	26 years

Source: Constitution of Texas, Art. 3, Secs. 6 and 7.

Table 7.2 Some Characteristics of Texas Legislators at the Beginning of 22 Legislatures, 1971–2013

HOUSE OF REPRESENTATIVES

No. of regular session	Year of regular session	Total membership	POLITICAL PARTY				RACIAL/ETHNIC CLASSIFICATION								GENDER			
			Democrat		Republican		Anglo		Latino		African American		Asian American		Man		Woman	
			No.	%	No.	%	No.	%	No.	%	No.	%	No.	%	No.	%	No.	%
62nd	1971	150	140	93.33	10	6.67	137	91.33	11	7.33	2	1.33	0	00.00	149	99.33	1	0.67
63rd	1973	150	133	88.67	17	11.33	131	87.33	11	7.33	8	5.33	0	00.00	145	96.67	5	3.33
64th	1975	150	134	89.33	16	10.67	127	84.67	14	9.33	9	6.00	0	00.00	143	95.33	7	4.67
65th	1977	150	132	88.00	18	12.00	119	79.33	18	12.00	13	8.67	0	00.00	140	93.33	10	6.67
66th	1979	150	128	85.33	22	14.67	118	78.67	18	12.00	14	9.33	0	00.00	139	92.67	11	7.33
67th	1981	150	114	76.00	36	24.00	119	79.33	18	12.00	13	8.67	0	00.00	139	92.67	11	7.33
68th	1983	150	115	76.67	35	23.33	117	78.00	21	14.00	12	8.00	0	00.00	137	91.33	13	8.67
69th	1985	150	98	65.33	52	34.67	118	78.67	19	12.67	13	8.67	0	00.00	135	90.00	15	10.00
70th	1987	150	94	62.67	56	37.33	118	78.67	19	12.67	13	8.67	0	00.00	134	89.33	16	10.67
71st	1989	150	93	62.00	57	38.00	118	78.67	19	12.67	13	8.67	0	00.00	134	89.33	16	10.67
72nd	1991	150	92	61.33	58	38.67	117	78.00	20	13.33	13	8.67	0	00.00	131	87.33	19	12.67
73rd	1993	150	91	60.67	59	39.33	110	73.33	26	17.33	14	9.33	0	00.00	125	83.33	25	16.67
74th	1995	150	88	58.67	62	41.33	110	73.33	26	17.33	14	9.33	0	00.00	121	80.67	29	19.33
75th	1997	150	82	54.67	68	45.33	108	72.00	28	18.67	14	9.33	0	00.00	120	80.00	30	20.00
76th	1999	150	78	52.00	72	48.00	108	72.00	28	18.67	14	9.33	0	00.00	121	80.67	29	19.33
77th	2001	150	78	52.00	72	48.00	108	72.00	28	18.67	14	9.33	0	00.00	120	80.00	30	20.00
78th	2003	150	62	41.33	88	58.67	105	70.00	30	20.00	14	9.33	1	00.67	118	78.67	32	21.33
79th	2005	150	63	42.00	87	58.00	104	69.33	30	20.00	14	9.33	2	1.33	119	79.33	31	20.67
80th	2007	150*	69	46.00	81	54.00	104	69.33	31	20.67	14	9.33	1	00.67	118	78.67	32	21.33
81st	2009	150	74	49.33	76	50.67	103	68.67	31	20.67	14	9.33	2	1.33	112	74.67	38	25.33
82nd	2011	150	51	34.00	99	66.00	101	67.33	30	20.00	17	11.33	2	1.33	118	78.67	32	21.67
83rd	2013	150	55	36.67	95	63.33	96	64.00	33	22.00	18	12.00	3	2.00	119	79.33	31	20.67

*Includes vacancy filled by special election on January 16, 2007.

Table 7.2 (Continued)

SENATE

No. of regular session	Year of regular session	Total membership	POLITICAL PARTY				RACIAL/ETHNIC CLASSIFICATION								GENDER			
			Democrat		Republican		Anglo		Latino		African American		Asian American		Man		Woman	
			No.	%	No.	%	No.	%	No.	%	No.	%	No.	%	No.	%	No.	%
62nd	1971	31	29	93.55	2	6.45	29	93.55	1	3.23	1	3.23	0	00.00	30	96.77	1	3.23
63rd	1973	31	28	90.32	3	9.68	29	93.55	2	6.45	0	0.00	0	00.00	30	96.77	1	3.23
64th	1975	31	28	90.32	3	9.68	29	93.55	2	6.45	0	0.00	0	00.00	30	96.77	1	3.23
65th	1977	31	28	90.32	3	9.68	28	90.32	3	9.68	0	0.00	0	00.00	30	96.77	1	3.23
66th	1979	31	27	87.10	4	12.90	27	87.10	4	12.90	0	0.00	0	00.00	30	96.77	1	3.23
67th	1981	31	24	77.42	7	22.58	27	87.10	4	12.90	0	0.00	0	00.00	30	96.77	1	3.23
68th	1983	31	26	83.87	5	16.13	26	83.87	4	12.90	1	3.23	0	00.00	31	100.00	0	0.00
69th	1985	31	25	80.65	6	19.35	26	83.87	4	12.90	1	3.23	0	00.00	30	96.77	1	3.23
70th	1987	31	25	80.65	6	19.35	23	74.19	6	19.35	2	6.45	0	00.00	28	90.32	3	9.68
71st	1989	31	23	74.19	8	25.81	23	74.19	6	19.35	2	6.45	0	00.00	28	90.32	3	9.68
72nd	1991	31	23	74.19	8	25.81	24	77.42	5	16.13	2	6.45	0	00.00	27	87.10	4	12.90
73rd	1993	31	18	58.06	13	41.94	23	74.19	6	19.35	2	6.45	0	00.00	27	87.10	4	12.90
74th	1995	31	17	54.84	14	45.16	24	77.42	5	16.13	2	6.45	0	00.00	27	87.10	4	12.90
75th	1997	31	14	45.16	17	54.84	22	70.97	7	22.58	2	6.45	0	00.00	28	90.32	3	9.68
76th	1999	31	15	48.39	16	51.61	22	70.97	7	22.58	2	6.45	0	00.00	28	90.32	3	9.68
77th	2001	31	15	48.39	16	51.61	22	70.97	7	22.58	2	6.45	0	00.00	27	87.10	4	12.90
78th	2003	31	12	38.71	19	61.29	22	70.97	7	22.58	2	6.45	0	00.00	27	87.10	4	12.90
79th	2005	31	12	38.71	19	61.29	22	70.97	7	22.58	2	6.45	0	00.00	27	87.10	4	12.90
80th	2007	31	11	35.48	20	64.51	23	74.19	6	19.35	2	6.45	0	00.00	27	87.10	4	12.90
81st	2009	31	12	38.71	19	61.29	23	74.19	6	19.35	2	6.45	0	00.00	25	80.65	6	19.35
82nd	2011	31	12	38.71	19	61.29	22	70.97	7	22.58	2	6.45	0	00.00	25	80.65	6	19.35
83rd	2013	31	12*	38.71	19	61.29	22	70.97	7	22.58	2	6.45	0	00.00	25	80.65	6	19.35

*Includes Mario Gallegos (House, Dist. 6), who died October 16, 2012, but whose name remained on the November general-election ballot. His successor will be elected in a special election called by the governor.

Source: Texas Legislative Reference Library, Texas Legislative Council, and the unofficial count of the Office of the Secretary of State (November 9, 2012).

Gender and Ethnic Classifications Although Anglo men continue to dominate the Texas legislature, their number has decreased in recent years. In January 1971, the legislature's rolls included just two women, Senator Barbara Jordan (D-Houston) and Representative Frances "Sissy" Farenthold (D-Corpus Christi).[6] Forty-two years later, after the 2012 general election, 37 women (six senators and 31 representatives) held seats in the 83rd legislature. Three of the female senators were Anglo Republicans; two were Latina Democrats; and one was an Anglo Democrat. Sixteen of the female representatives were Democrats (seven Latinas, eight African Americans, and one Anglo), and 15 were Republicans (13 Anglos, one African American, and one Asian American).

Representation of members of historical racial or ethnic minorities increased substantially from the late 1960s through the early 1990s. Barbara Jordan, the first African American elected to the Texas Senate in the 20th century, served from 1967 until she was seated in the U.S. Congress in 1973. At the beginning of the regular session of the 83rd legislature in 2013, Senate seats were held by two African Americans and six Latinos. At the same time, 18 African American representatives and 33 Latino representatives served. Although both African Americans and Latinos have been underrepresented in the Texas legislature, total African American representation increased from three legislators in 1971 to 20 in 2013, and the number of Latino legislators grew from 12 to 39 during that same period. Texas's first Asian American legislator was Thomas J. Lee (D-San Antonio, January 1965–January 1967). The state's voters did not elect another Asian American for almost 40 years. Three Asian Americans served in the House of Representatives in 2013.

Some female members of the Texas House of Representatives wear red to show support for the American Heart Association.

(Texas House of Representatives Photography Department)

Political Party Affiliation In 1961, no Republican held a seat in the Texas legislature. But when the legislature convened in 1997, the GOP had a Senate majority. By January 2003, Republicans controlled both the Senate and the House. Since that year, each chamber has produced more "party line" votes—that is, all Democrats voting one way on an issue, and all Republicans voting the other way.

With the 2006 election, Democrats increased their numbers in the House from 63 to 69. By the end of 2007, Democrats held 71 of the 150 seats in the House. As a result of the general election in November 2008 and a special election in the following month, party divisions in the 81st legislature were 76 Republicans and 74 Democrats in the House and 19 Republicans and 12 Democrats in the Senate. The House division changed to 77 Republicans and 73 Democrats in November 2009, when Representative Chuck Hopson (Jacksonville) switched to the GOP. After the November 2010 election, the Senate division remained unchanged, but the original House division for the 82nd legislature was 99 Republicans and 51 Democrats. In mid-December of that year, however, Representatives Aaron Peña (Edinburg) and Allan Ritter (Nederland) announced their switch to the Republican Party; and in March 2012, Representative Jose Lozano (Kingsville) became the third Democrat to make this change of party. Following the November 2012 election, the House division was 95 Republicans and 55 Democrats. The Senate division was 19 Republicans and 11 Democrats (not counting Democrat Mario Gallegos, elected shortly after his death).

Central city residents usually elect African American and Latino Democrats, whereas Republican senators and representatives receive their strongest support from rural and suburban Anglo voters. Residents of Mexican border districts largely elect Latino Democrats.

Education and Occupation In government, as in business, most positions of leadership call for college credentials. Thus, it is not surprising to find that nearly all members of recent Texas legislatures attended one or more institutions of higher education. Most of them could claim a bachelor's degree, and many had graduate degrees or professional degrees (especially in law).

Traditionally, Texas legislators have included a large number of attorneys and business owners or managers. Lesser numbers of real estate and insurance people, as well as some farmers, ranchers, and teachers, also have served. Health-care professionals, engineers, and accountants have held few legislative seats. Laborers have held almost none.

Lawyer-legislators may receive retainers (payments) from corporations and special-interest groups, with the understanding that legal services will be performed if needed. In some cases, these retainer payments appear intended to influence legislation rather than guarantee availability of legal counsel. It is also noteworthy that lawyer-legislators, some of whom represent defendants in courts, exercise a decisive influence in amending and revising the Penal Code and the Code of Criminal Procedure. A legislator may not represent a paying client before a state agency, such as the Railroad Commission or the Alcoholic Beverage Commission.

Individuals and corporations desiring to delay justice may seek the services of lawyer-legislators because these attorneys are entitled to obtain a continuance (that is, a postponement) of any case set for trial during a period extending from 30 days before to 30 days after a legislative session. As a result of blatant abuse of this privilege, a state law now grants judges the authority to deny a continuance if a lawyer was hired to assist with a case within 10 days of trial or any related legal proceeding. A legislator is also required to disclose payment received for obtaining a continuance.

Religious Affiliation The Texas Constitution guarantees freedom of religion and prohibits use of public funds for the benefit of a sect or religious group. Since the era of the Texas Republic, Texans have tended to support separation of church and state. However, this principle has become the subject of recent controversies. Because religion may play a critical role in the formulation of public policy, political analysts must take a legislator's denominational ties and church doctrines into consideration. These factors are especially important when considering legislation involving abortion, birth control, gambling, the sale of alcoholic beverages, state aid to church-related schools, Sabbath observance, and other matters of vital concern to some religious groups. Although the religious affiliation of each legislator is not a matter of record, it does appear that in Texas, Catholic senators and representatives are most numerous, followed (in order) by Baptists, Methodists, and Episcopalians.

Legislative Experience In a legislative body, experience is measured in terms of turnover (that is, first-termers replacing experienced members who have retired or lost an election) and tenure (years served in a legislative chamber). For the 10 most recent Texas legislatures (74th–83rd), the average turnover in the House was 25.7, or about 17 percent of the membership every two years. In the Senate, it was 2.8 or about 9 percent. Turnover tends to be greater for the first legislature after redistricting. For example, in 2013 it was 43 (nearly 29 percent) in the House and 6 (slightly more than 19 percent) in the Senate.

The average length of service by legislators in the 10 most recent legislatures was more than six years in both the House and the Senate. Most senators served first as representatives. In 2013, for example, 15 of the 31 senators in the 83rd legislature had served as representatives. After a term in office, an incumbent is more likely to win an election than is an inexperienced challenger.

As a general rule, lawmakers become most effective after they have spent two or more years learning procedural rules related to enacting legislation and working with constituents, bureaucrats, lobbyists, fellow legislators, and other elected officials. Many Texans believe, however, that long legislative tenure should be discouraged, if not prohibited. To date, all efforts to propose term-limit amendments to the Texas Constitution have been unsuccessful.

Compensation

Rhode Island recently raised legislators' salaries from an average of $300 per year to more than $14,000; nearby, New Hampshire pays only $200 per year. New Mexico does not pay members of its legislative bodies any annual salary (though it does provide an allowance for expenses). In contrast, California pays legislators an annual salary of $95,291, which is more than any other state pays its legislators. Texas's state senators and representatives receive low pay, reasonable allowances, and a relatively generous retirement pension after a minimum period of service.

Pay and Per Diem Allowance Originally, Texas legislators' salaries and per diem (daily) personal allowances during a regular or special session were specified by the state constitution and could be changed only by constitutional amendment. Today, Texas voters retain the right to approve salary increases for legislators; however, as authorized by a constitutional amendment, the Texas Ethics Commission sets the per diem expense allowance. In addition, this commission may recommend salary increases for legislators and even higher salaries for the Speaker and the lieutenant governor, though the ultimate decision on a salary increase rests with voters. The $600 monthly salary ($7,200 per year) has not been increased since 1975.

For the 82nd legislature, which convened in January 2011, the per diem allowance to cover meals, lodging, and other personal expenses was $150 for senators, representatives, and the lieutenant governor. This per diem amounted to a total of $21,000 per official for the 140-day regular session.

Expense Allowances At the beginning of a session, each chamber authorizes contingent expense allowances. For example, during the 82nd regular session, the House authorized every representative's operating account to be credited monthly with $11,925. The monthly allowance for the interim was $11,500. House members could use money in this account to cover the cost of official work-related travel within Texas, postage, office operations, and staff salaries. Staff members assist legislators with office management, research, constituent service, and communication. Although assistance in responding to postal mail and email is still an important staff function, communications via social media (for example, Twitter, YouTube, and Facebook) are of increasing importance for legislators. Representatives can also use money from campaign contributions to supplement their assistants' salaries, and some legislators use political money to pay rent for living quarters in Austin. Double-billing the state and his campaign fund for the same travel expenses caused Representative Joe Driver (R-Garland) to plead guilty in 2011 to abuse of official capacity, which is a third degree felony. His punishment included a fine of $5,000, restitution of more than $63,000, and five years of deferred adjudication without time in prison. He did not seek re-election in 2012.

From January 2011 to January 2013, each senator in the 82nd legislature had a maximum monthly allowance of $35,625 for intrastate travel expenses

How Do We Compare...in Salary of Legislators?

Annual Salary of Legislators for the Year of the Last Regular Session

Most Populous U.S. States	Annual Salary	U.S. States Bordering Texas	Annual Salary
California	$95,291	Arkansas	$15,869
Florida	$29,687	Louisiana	$16,800
New York	$79,500	New Mexico	$0*
Texas	**$ 7,200**	Oklahoma	$38,400

Source: The Book of the States, 2012 (Lexington, Ky.: Council of State Governments, 2012), 130–131.
*Legislators in New Mexico receive mileage and a per diem allowance but no annual salary.

and staff salaries. Other expenses for carrying out official duties (for example, subscriptions, postage, telecommunications, and stationery) were paid from the Senate's contingent expense fund. Like representatives, Senate members can supplement staff salaries with money from campaign contributions.

Retirement Pension Under the terms of the Texas State Employees Retirement Act of 1975, legislators contribute 8 percent of their state salaries to a retirement fund. Retirement pay for senators and representatives amounts to 2.3 percent of the state-funded portion of a district judge's annual salary ($125,000 in fiscal years 2012 and 2013) for each year served. When Representative Paul Moreno (D-El Paso) retired at the beginning of 2009 after 40 years of service in the House, his annual pension amounted to $115,000, along with full health-care benefits.

As a result of an unpublicized amendment slipped into a state employee benefits bill in 1991, legislators with a minimum of 12 years of service may retire at age 50 with an annual pension of $34,500. Those with at least eight years of service may retire at age 60 with a pension of $23,000 per year. Of course, many legislators do not serve long enough to qualify for a pension, but those who do can begin collecting payments while they are still relatively young.

☑ Learning Check 7.2   (Answers on p. 292)

1. What is the minimum age for a state senator and for a state representative as specified in the Texas Constitution?
2. True or False: Salary increases for legislators must be submitted to the state's voters for approval or disapproval.

★ Legislative Organization

Merely bringing men and women together in the Capitol does not ensure the making of laws or any other governmental activity. Gathering people to transact official business requires organized effort. The formal organization of the Texas legislature features a presiding officer and several committees for each chamber. The informal organization involves various caucuses that do not have legal status.

LO3

Presiding Officers

The Texas Constitution establishes the offices of president of the Senate and Speaker of the House of Representatives. It designates the lieutenant governor as president of the Senate and provides for the election of a Speaker to preside over the House of Representatives.

President of the Senate: The Lieutenant Governor The most important function of the lieutenant governor of Texas is to serve as **president of the Senate.**[7] Just as the vice president of the United States is empowered to preside over the U.S. Senate but is not a member of that national lawmaking body, so too the lieutenant governor of Texas is not a member of the state Senate. The big difference between them is that the lieutenant governor presides over most sessions and plays a leading role in legislative matters, whereas the vice president seldom presides or becomes involved in the daily business of the U.S. Senate.

Chosen by the people of Texas in a statewide election for a four-year term, the lieutenant governor is first in line of succession in the event of the death, resignation, or removal of the governor. When the governor is absent from the state, the lieutenant governor serves as acting governor and receives the gubernatorial salary, which amounted to more than $400 per day at the beginning of 2013. Ordinarily, however, the lieutenant governor's salary is the same as those of senators and representatives: $600 per month, which amounts to about $20 per day.

As president of the Texas Senate, the lieutenant governor has the following duties:

- Appoints Senate committee and standing subcommittee chairs and vice chairs.
- Appoints Senate committee and standing subcommittee members.
- Determines the Senate committee to which a bill will be sent after introduction.
- Recognizes senators who wish to speak on the Senate floor or make a motion (for example, to take up a bill out of order of calendar listing).
- Votes only to break a tie vote in the Senate.
- Serves as joint chair, with the Speaker of the House, on the Legislative Council (a research arm of the legislature), the Legislative Budget Board, and the Legislative Audit Committee.

president of the Senate
Title of the lieutenant governor in his or her role as presiding officer for the Texas Senate.

Because of the lieutenant governor's powers (most of which have been granted by Senate rules rather than by the Texas Constitution), this official is perhaps the most powerful elected officer in the state, especially when the legislature is in session. If the lieutenant governor dies, resigns, or is elected to another office, the Senate elects one of its members to serve as acting lieutenant governor. At the beginning of each session, the Senate elects a president pro tempore, who presides when the lieutenant governor is absent or disabled.

Speaker of the House The presiding officer of the House of Representatives is the **Speaker of the House**, a representative elected to that office for a two-year term by the House in an open (that is, not secret) vote by the House membership.[8]

Like the lieutenant governor in the Senate, the Speaker controls proceedings in the House. In the dual roles of elected state representative and presiding officer of the House, the Speaker has the following responsibilities:

- Appoints all chairs and vice chairs of House substantive and procedural committees.
- Appoints all members of House procedural committees.
- Appoints House substantive committee members, within limitations of the seniority rule.
- Recognizes members who wish to speak on the House floor or to make a motion.
- Assigns bills and resolutions to House committees.
- Votes (rarely) on bills and resolutions.
- Serves as joint chair, with the lieutenant governor, on the Legislative Council, the Legislative Budget Board, and the Legislative Audit Committee.

House rules authorize the Speaker to name another representative to preside over the chamber temporarily. The Speaker may also name a member of the House to serve as permanent speaker pro tempore for as long as the Speaker desires. A speaker pro tempore performs all the duties of the Speaker when that officer is absent.[9] The Speaker occupies an apartment in the Capitol.

Because of the Speaker's power, filling this House office involves intense political activity. Lobbyists make every effort to ensure the election of a Speaker sympathetic to their respective causes, and potential candidates for the position begin to line up support several months or even years before a Speaker's race begins. Long before this election, anyone aspiring to the office of Speaker will attempt to induce House members to sign cards pledging their support. House rules, however, prohibit soliciting written pledges during a regular session. Once elected, a Speaker usually finds it easier to obtain similar pledges of support for reelection in future regular sessions.

Speaker candidates must file with the Texas Ethics Commission. A 1973 law put a $100 limit on spending by individuals to influence a Speaker's election and prohibited organizations from contributing "anything of value." In 2008, however, a federal district judge held these provisions unconstitutional, because they "significantly chill political speech protected by the First Amendment" of the U.S. Constitution.[10]

Speaker of the House
The state representative elected by House members to serve as the presiding officer for that chamber.

When 88 Republicans won House seats in November 2002, it was apparent that the GOP would capture the Texas Speaker's office for the first time in more than 130 years. On January 14, 2003, House members elected Tom Craddick (R-Midland) as presiding officer in the House by a vote of 149–1.[11] Craddick named Democrats to chair nearly one-third of all committees in the 78th legislature; however, his professed dedication to bipartisanship ended with partisan conflict over the state budget and congressional redistricting.

Party differences over school finance and other issues also caused problems for Craddick in the 79th legislature, but he controlled the House. Meanwhile, Democrat Ronnie Earle, Travis County district attorney, investigated Craddick's relations with Congressman Tom DeLay and the transmitting of questionable campaign funds to certain Republican legislative candidates.[12] After the loss of six GOP House seats in 2006, Craddick barely survived a challenge by Jim Pitts (R-Waxahachie) at the beginning of the 80th regular session in January 2007. With the help of 15 Democrats (called "Craddick Ds"), however, Craddick was elected Speaker for a third term.

At the end of the 80th regular session in May 2007, Craddick survived as Speaker by refusing to recognize representatives wanting to offer a motion for him to "vacate the chair" or give up the Speaker's office. Some Craddick supporters and some opponents were defeated in the general election of 2008.[13] A few days before the 81st Texas legislature convened on January 13, 2009, a House majority (mostly Democrats, but some Republicans) staged an uprising and elected Joe Straus (R-San Antonio) to replace Craddick as Speaker.

In 2011, Straus won a second term as Speaker, but not without opposition from right-wing Republicans. Nevertheless, he gained support of the House Republican Caucus by a vote of 70–30, and House members elected him as Speaker by a vote of 132–15.[14] Straus's opponents contended that he was not sufficiently conservative. Early in 2012, conservative activists

CourseReader ASSIGNMENTS

Log in to www.cengagebrain.com and open CourseReader to access the reading:

Texas House Speaker Becomes Target for not Being Christian

Politicians are no strangers to having their personal lives and belief systems examined and their religious convictions carefully scrutinized. The Texas House Speaker is facing an examination of his religious beliefs and a challenge for his office because he is not a Christian.

1. Why do some religious Right activists believe that Joe Straus should be replaced as Speaker?

2. How did Speaker Straus and Republican State Executive Committee member Rebecca Williamson respond to attacks on Straus by religious Right activists?

and Tea Party–backed organizations campaigned to remove him from the office of Speaker by supporting an opponent, San Antonio businessman Matt Beebe, in the Republican primary; but Straus won the contest.[15]

Committee System

Presiding officers appoint committee chairs and vice chairs and determine the committees to which bills will be referred. (See Table 7.3 for committee titles and the numbers of members for House and Senate committees in the 82nd legislature.) Because both House and Senate committees play important roles in the fate or fortune of all bills and resolutions, selection of committee members goes a long way toward determining the amount and type of legislative output during a session. Permanent staff members are available to assist legislators with committee work on a continuing basis. Usually, these staff members also work on interim study committees created to examine legislative issues between regular sessions.

House Committees In the Texas House of Representatives, **substantive committees** consider bills and resolutions relating to the subject identified by a committee's name (for example, elections or transportation). Seniority, based on years of service in the House of Representatives, determines a maximum of one-half the membership for substantive committees, excluding the chair and the vice chair. When a regular session begins, each representative, in order of seniority, designates three committees in order of preference. A representative is entitled to become a member of the committee of highest preference that has a vacant seniority position. The Speaker appoints other committee members.

Seniority does not apply to membership on **procedural committees**, each of which considers bills and resolutions relating primarily to an internal legislative matter (for example, the Calendars Committee, which determines when a bill will be considered by the full House). The Speaker appoints all members of procedural committees.

Although substantive and procedural committees are established under House rules adopted in each regular session, the Speaker independently creates select committees and appoints all members. A Speaker usually creates select committees during a session to consider legislation that crosses committee jurisdictional lines or during an interim to conduct special studies. In the 82nd legislature, for example, Speaker Straus created three select committees (see Table 7.3.)

Senate Committees Senate rules provide for **standing committees** (though the rules do not identify them as substantive or procedural committees), **select committees**, and **special interim committees** (for studying important policy issues between sessions). As president of the Senate, the lieutenant governor appoints all committee members and designates the chair and vice chair of each committee. This power of appointment also extends to one subcommittee with three members: Flooding and Evacuations.

---

substantive committee
Appointed by the House Speaker, this committee considers bills and resolutions related to the subject identified by its name (such as the House Agriculture Committee) and may recommend passage of proposed legislation to the appropriate calendars committee.

procedural committee
These House committees (such as the Calendars Committee and House Administration Committee) consider bills and resolutions relating primarily to procedural legislative matters.

standing committee
A Senate committee appointed by the lieutenant governor for the purpose of considering proposed bills and resolutions before possible floor debate and voting by senators.

select committee
This committee, created independently by the House Speaker, may consider legislation that crosses committee jurisdictional lines or may conduct special studies.

special interim committee
A Senate committee appointed by the lieutenant governor to study an important policy issue between regular sessions.

Table 7.3 Texas House and Senate Committees, 82nd Legislature, January 2011–January 2013

House Committee (number of members)
30 Substantive Committees

Agriculture and Livestock (9)
Appropriations (27)
Border and International Affairs (9)
Business and Industry (9)
Corrections (9)
County Affairs (9)
Criminal Jurisprudence (9)
Culture, Recreation, and Tourism (9)
Defense and Veterans' Affairs (9)
Economic and Small Business
   Development (7)
Elections (9)
Energy Resources (9)
Environmental Regulation (9)
Government Efficiency and Reform (7)
Higher Education (9)
Homeland Security and Public Safety (9)
Human Services (9)
Insurance (9)
Judiciary and Civil Jurisprudence (11)
Land and Resource Management (9)
Licensing and Administrative Procedures
   (9)
Natural Resources (11)
Pensions, Investments, and Financial
   Services (9)
Public Education (11)
Public Health (11)
State Affairs (13)
Technology (5)
Transportation (11)
Urban Affairs (19)
Ways and Means (11)

House Committee (number of members)
6 Procedural Committees

Calendars (15)
General Investigating and Ethics (5)
House Administration (11)
Local and Consent Calendars (11)
Redistricting (17)
Rules and Resolutions (11)

3 House Select Committees

Election Contest (7)
State Sovereignty (9)
Voter Identification and Voting Fraud (9)

Senate Committee (number of members)
18 Standing Committees

Administration (7)
Agriculture and Rural Affairs (5)
Business and Commerce (9)
Criminal Justice (7)
Economic Development (7)
Education (9)
Finance (15)
Government Organization (7)
Health and Human Services (9)
Higher Education (7)
Intergovernmental Relations (5)
International Relations and Trade (7)
Jurisprudence (7)
Natural Resources (11)
Nominations (7)
State Affairs (9)
Transportation and Homeland Security (9)
Veterans Affairs and Military Installations (6)

2 Senate Select Committees

Open Government (5)
Redistricting (15)

Source: Texas State Directory, 2011, 54th ed. (Austin: Texas State Directory Press, 2011); and websites for the House (http://www.house.state.tx.us) and Senate (http://www.senate.state.tx.us).

Points to Ponder

- For nearly a century after Texas became part of the federal Union (1846–1931), Speakers of the state House of Representatives were elected for a single two-year term (with only three exceptions, and none held this office for consecutive terms).
- In the 40 years from 1933 to 1973, 10 Speakers were elected for one term, and five were elected for two consecutive terms.
- In the 34 years from 1975 to 2009, only four representatives were elected as Speaker: Bill Clayton (four terms, 1975–1983), Gib Lewis (five terms, 1983–1993), Pete Laney (five terms, 1993–2003), and Tom Craddick (three terms, 2003–2009).
- Joe Straus was elected in 2009 and 2011. Did he retain the speakership in 2013?

Legislative Caucus System

With the House and Senate firmly controlled for several years by Speaker Gib Lewis (1983–1993) and Lieutenant Governor Bill Hobby (1973–1991), respectively, caucuses of like-minded members exercised limited influence on the Texas legislature. **Legislative caucuses** are legislative organizations determined on the basis of partisan, philosophical, racial, ethnic, or other special interests. Both Speaker Lewis and Lieutenant Governor Hobby sought to absorb potential opponents within their teams and to discourage caucuses. Although increasingly important for legislators and interest groups, legislative caucuses are prohibited from receiving public money.

Party Caucuses In the 1980s and 1990s, the growing importance of party caucuses in each chamber of the Texas legislature was one indication that Texas was becoming a two-party state. The House Democratic Caucus was organized in 1981. In recent years, all Democratic legislators have been reported as belonging to their party's House or Senate caucuses. Under the leadership of Tom Craddick, the House Republican Caucus was organized in 1989. Although they have no formal organizational role in either chamber, party caucuses take policy positions on some issues and promote unity among their members.

Racial/Ethnic Caucuses In the U.S. Congress and in many state legislatures, racial and ethnic groups organize and form voting blocs to maximize their power. Because African Americans and Latinos constitute significant minorities in the Texas legislature, it is not surprising that they have formed caucuses for this purpose. Composed of African American senators and representatives, the Legislative Black Caucus concentrates on issues affecting

legislative caucus
An organization of legislators who seek to maximize their influence over issues in which they have a special interest.

African American Texans, such as the 2001 hate crimes law that increased punishment for violent acts committed against individuals based on the victim's race, ethnicity, or sexual orientation.

In the 1980s, the House-based Mexican American Legislative Caucus successfully pushed legislation placing farmworkers under state workers' compensation, unemployment compensation, and minimum wage protection. Since the 1990s, pressure from this caucus has produced larger appropriations for state universities in South Texas and along the Mexican border area from El Paso to Brownsville and north to Corpus Christi and San Antonio. In recent years, the caucus has been instrumental in creating and funding the Irma Lerma Rangel College of Pharmacy in Kingsville, the Regional Academic Health Center to serve the Lower Rio Grande Valley, and the Paul L. Foster School of Medicine in El Paso. In 2009, its members supported Senate bill (S.B.) 957, which authorized a state law school in Dallas (a high-priority matter for the Legislative Black Caucus) and that required the Texas Higher Education Coordinating Board to evaluate the feasibility of locating another law school "in the Texas-Mexico region of the state." Both the Mexican American Legislative Caucus and the Senate Hispanic Caucus include a few Anglo and African American members who have large numbers of Latino voters in their districts. In January 2011, a Hispanic Republican caucus was formed with six Latino representatives and three Anglos representing districts with 30 percent or more Latino residents.

Ideological Caucuses House-based ideological caucuses have also emerged. The Texas Conservative Coalition attracts Republicans and conservative Democrats, whereas the liberal Legislative Study Group appeals to many Democrats (including several who are also members of the Legislative Black Caucus and the Mexican American Legislative Caucus). As might be expected, the conservative and liberal caucuses reflect opposing views on taxing and spending, as well as on public interest issues such as environmental protection. A few representatives, however, belong to both caucuses.

Organized in 1985, the Texas Conservative Coalition owes its creation to an increased number of Republican legislators elected in the early 1980s and to dissatisfaction with education reforms and tax increases enacted during a special session in 1984. Although not a typical caucus, the Independent Conservative Republicans of Texas (ICRT) counts nearly all Republican legislators as its "founding members." Launched by Senator Dan Patrick (R-Houston) early in 2010, the ICRT offers an ideological "Contract for Texas," combats the influence of GOP moderates, and reaches out to the Tea Party movement. In December 2010, shortly before the beginning of the 82nd regular legislative session, the Tea Party Caucus was formed with 49 members. The initial membership included Senator Patrick as chairman, Senator Brian Birdwell (R-Granbury), and 47 Republican representatives. Working with the caucus is an advisory council composed of Tea Party organizers from across Texas.[16]

Established in November 1993, the Legislative Study Group represents the liberal Democrats' response to the Texas Conservative Coalition. The

State Senator Leticia Van de Putte, mother of six children and a pharmacist, waves to the crowd before giving remarks at a Planned Parenthood rally at the state Capitol on March 8, 2011. Supporters of Planned Parenthood rallied on the south steps of the Capitol before going inside to visit legislative offices.

(Austin American-Statesman/ World Picture Network LLC)

liberal caucus has called for ethical conduct throughout state government, campaign finance reform, consumer and environmental protection, long-term solutions to problems involving public safety, and various changes in Texas's public education, health and human services, and criminal justice systems.

☑ Learning Check 7.3   (Answers on p. 292)

1. True or False: The Speaker of the House of Representatives presides over that body but cannot vote on a bill or resolution.
2. True or False: The president of the Senate determines the Senate committee to which a bill will be sent after introduction.

★ Legislative Operations

LO4   As the chief agent in making public policy in Texas state government, the legislature must have powers to function, and legislators need immunity from interference while performing their official duties. Thus, lawmaking is governed by detailed rules of procedure for each legislative chamber.

Powers and Immunities

Although bound by restrictions found in few state constitutions, the legislature is the dominant branch of Texas government and the chief agent in making public policy. Legislators, for example, control government spending, which makes state agencies and personnel—and, to some extent, units of local government—dependent upon them. Composed of one or more appropriation bills, the biennial state budget authorizes state spending. Thus, it is the most important legislation for regular (and, sometimes, special) sessions. To become law, an appropriation bill must pass in both legislative chambers, but it is subject to the governor's veto power (see Chapter 8, "The Executive"). Although appropriation bills may originate in either the House or the Senate, all revenue-producing bills, such as a bill that imposes a state tax, must originate in the House. (For more on taxing and spending, see Chapter 11, "Finance and Fiscal Policy.") In addition to their powers, lawmakers enjoy certain immunities designed to allow them to function freely.

Making Public Policy The most typical exercise of legislative power involves making public policy by passing bills and adopting resolutions. As explained in this section, each bill or resolution has a distinctive abbreviation that indicates the chamber of origin, and every legislative proposal is given a number indicating the order of introduction. The history of each bill or resolution introduced since 1989 is found online at **http://www.capitol.state.tx.us/**. Included for each legislative proposal is the bill or resolution text, as well as a fiscal note (if appropriate) and an analysis.

A **simple resolution**, abbreviated H.R. (House Resolution) if introduced in the House and S.R. (Senate Resolution) if introduced in the Senate, involves action by one chamber only and is not sent to the governor. Adoption requires a simple majority vote (more than one-half) of members present. Matters dealt with by simple resolution affect only the chamber that is voting on the resolution and include rules of the House or Senate, procedures for House or Senate operations, and invitations extended to nonmembers to address a particular chamber.

After adoption by simple majority votes of members present in both the House and the Senate, a **concurrent resolution** (H.C.R. or S.C.R.) is sent to the governor, who has two options: sign it or veto it. Typical examples are resolutions that request action by the U.S. Congress, demand information from state agencies, establish joint study committees composed of senators and representatives, or grant permission to sue the state. In addition, the chambers adopt a concurrent resolution to adjourn at the end of any legislative session—a measure that does not require approval by the governor.

Adoption of a **joint resolution** (H.J.R. or S.J.R.) requires approval by both houses but no action by the governor. The nature of a joint resolution determines whether a simple majority or a two-thirds vote is required. Proposed amendments to the Texas Constitution are examples of joint resolutions requiring a two-thirds majority vote of the membership of each house.

simple resolution
A resolution that requires action by one legislative chamber only and is not acted on by the governor.

concurrent resolution
A resolution adopted by House and Senate majorities and then approved by the governor (for example, a request for action by Congress or authorization for someone to sue the state).

joint resolution
A resolution that must pass by a majority vote in each house when used to ratify an amendment to the U.S. Constitution. As a proposal for an amendment to the Texas Constitution, a joint resolution requires a two-thirds majority vote in each house.

To date, all proposed amendments to the U.S. Constitution initiated by Congress, with the exception of the Twenty-First Amendment, have been submitted to state legislatures for ratification. The Texas legislature ratifies a proposed U.S. constitutional amendment with a joint resolution adopted by simple majority votes of members present in both houses.

Before enactment, a proposed law is known as a **bill** (House bill [H.B.] or Senate bill [S.B.]). Each regular session brings forth an avalanche of bills, but fewer than 25 percent became law in 2011. In that year's regular session of the 82nd legislature, 3,865 bills were introduced in the House and 1,931 in the Senate. Together, both chambers enacted 797 House bills and 582 Senate bills. The governor vetoed 17 House bills and seven Senate bills.[17]

For purposes of classification, bills fall into three categories: special, general, and local. A special bill makes an exception to general laws for the benefit of a specific individual, class, or corporation. Of greater importance are general bills, which apply to all people or property in all parts of Texas. To become law, a bill must pass by a simple majority of votes of members present in both the House and the Senate, but a two-thirds majority vote of the membership in each chamber is required to pass an emergency measure that will take effect as soon as the governor signs it. A local bill creates or affects a single unit of local government (for example, a city, county, or special district). Such bills usually pass without opposition if sponsored by all legislators representing the affected area.

Constitutional Amendment Power In addition to exercising their principal powers by passing bills and adopting resolutions, the House and Senate have other important powers. Members of either chamber may introduce a joint resolution to amend the Texas Constitution. A proposal is officially made when the joint resolution is approved by a two-thirds majority vote of the *total* membership of each house. (The constitutional amendment process is covered in detail in Chapter 2, "Federalism and the Texas Constitution.")

Administrative and Investigative Powers The legislature also defines the responsibilities of state agencies and imposes restrictions on them through appropriation of money for operations and through **oversight** of activities. One form of oversight involves requiring state agencies to make both periodic and special reports to the legislature.

Both the House and the Senate receive information from the state auditor concerning irregular or inefficient use of state funds by administrative agencies. The auditor is appointed by (and serves at the will of) the Legislative Audit Committee. This six-member committee is composed of the Speaker, the chair of the House Appropriations Committee, the chair of the House Ways and Means Committee, the lieutenant governor, the chair of the Senate Finance Committee, and a senator appointed by the lieutenant governor.

Another important instrument of control over state agencies is the legislature's Sunset Advisory Commission, which makes recommendations to the House and Senate concerning the continuation, merger, division, or abolition

bill
A proposed law or statute.

oversight
A legislative function that requires reports from state agencies concerning their operations; the state auditor provides information on agencies' use of state funds.

of nearly every state agency. Affected agencies are reviewed every 12 years (see Chapter 9, "Public Policy and Administration").

Most of the governor's board and commission appointments to head state agencies must be submitted to the Senate and approved by at least two-thirds of the senators present. Thus, the Senate is in a position to influence the selection of many important officials. The unwritten rule of **senatorial courtesy** requires that the Senate "bust" (reject) an appointment if the appointee is declared "personally objectionable" by the senator representing the district in which the appointee resides. Consequently, a governor will privately seek prior approval by that senator before announcing a selection.

To support its power to exercise oversight of administrative agencies and to investigate problems that may require legislation, the legislature has the authority to subpoena witnesses to testify, administer oaths, and compel submission of records and documents. Such action may be taken jointly by the two houses as a body, by one house, or by a committee of either house. Refusal to obey a subpoena may result in prosecution for contempt of the legislature, which is a misdemeanor offense punishable by a jail sentence of from 30 days to a year and a fine ranging from $100 to $1,000.

Impeachment and Removal Powers The House of Representatives has the power to impeach judges of hundreds of district courts, justices of the 14 state courts of appeals and the Supreme Court of Texas, and judges of the Texas Court of Criminal Appeals. The House may also impeach executive officers, such as the governor, the lieutenant governor, the attorney general, the comptroller of public accounts, and the commissioner of the General Land Office. Impeachment power is rarely used, however.

Impeachment involves bringing charges by a simple majority vote of House members present. It resembles the indictment process of a grand jury (see Chapter 10, "Law, Courts, and Justice"). Following impeachment, the Senate conducts a proceeding with the Chief Justice of the Supreme Court presiding, after which it renders judgment. Conviction requires a two-thirds majority vote of the Senate membership. The only punishment that the Senate may impose is removal from office and disqualification from holding any other public office under the Texas Constitution. If a crime has been committed, the deposed official may also be prosecuted before an appropriate court like any other person.

Immunities In addition to their constitutional powers, state senators and representatives enjoy legislative immunities conferred by the Texas Constitution. First, they may not be sued for slander or otherwise held accountable for any statements made in a speech or debate during the course of a legislative proceeding. This protection does not extend to remarks made under other circumstances. Second, they may not be arrested while attending a legislative session or while traveling to or from the legislature's meeting place for the purpose of attending, unless charged with "treason, felony, or breach of the peace."

senatorial courtesy
Before making an appointment, the governor is expected to obtain approval from the state senator in whose district the prospective appointee resides; failure to obtain such approval will probably cause the Senate to "bust" the appointee.

impeachment
Process in which the Texas House of Representatives, by a simple majority vote, initiates action (brings charges) leading to possible removal of certain judicial and executive officials (e.g., the governor) by the Senate.

Procedure

Enacting a law is not the only way to get things done in Austin. Passing bills and adopting resolutions, however, are the principal means whereby members of the Texas legislature participate in making public policy. The legislature conducts its work according to detailed rules of procedure.

Rules To guide legislators in their work, each chamber adopts its own set of rules at the beginning of every regular session. Usually, few changes are made to the rules of the preceding session. Whether a bill is passed or defeated depends heavily on the skills of sponsors and opponents in using House rules and Senate rules.

The lieutenant governor and the Speaker, who wield the gavel of authority in their respective chambers, decide questions concerning interpretation of rules. Because procedural questions may be complex and decisions must be made quickly, each chamber uses a **parliamentarian** to assist its presiding officer. Positioned on the dais immediately to the left of the lieutenant governor or Speaker, these respective experts on Senate or House rules are ever ready to provide answers to procedural questions.

A Bill Becomes a Law The Texas Constitution calls for regular legislative sessions divided into three periods for distinct purposes. The first 30 days are reserved for the introduction of bills and resolutions, action on emergency appropriations, and the confirmation or rejection of recess appointments (between-session appointments made by the governor). The second 30 days are generally devoted to committee consideration of bills and resolutions. The remainder of the session, which amounts to 80 days because regular sessions always run the full 140 days allowed, is devoted to floor debate and voting on bills and resolutions. Throughout a session, action may be taken at any time on an emergency matter identified by the governor and incorporated into a bill that is introduced by a legislator. Although the full process of turning a bill into a law is complex, certain basic steps are clearly outlined.

The following paragraphs trace these steps from introduction to action by the governor. We will describe the path of a bill that originates in the House.[18] (The step numbers in Figure 7.4 will help you visualize the bill's progress.)

1. Introduction in the House Any House member may introduce a bill by filing nine copies (or 11 copies of every bill related to conservation and reclamation districts) with the chief clerk. This staff person supervises legislative administration in the House. Members and members-elect (newly elected but not yet having taken the oath of office) may prefile bills as early as the first Monday after the November general election before a regular session begins in January, or 30 days before the start of a special session.

It is common practice for an identical bill, known as a **companion bill**, to be introduced in the Senate at the same time the bill is introduced in the House. This action allows simultaneous committee action in the two chambers.

parliamentarian
An expert on rules of order who sits at the left of the presiding officer in the House or Senate and is ever ready to give advice on procedural questions.

companion bill
Filed in one house but identical or similar to a bill filed in the other chamber; speeds passage of a bill because committee consideration may take place simultaneously in both houses.

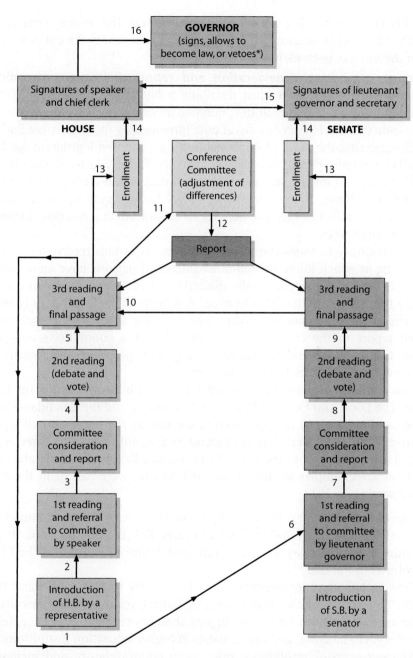

Figure 7.4 Route Followed by a House Bill from Texas Legislature to Governor.

*In case of veto while the legislature is still in session, a bill can be passed over the governor's veto by a two-thirds majority of each house.
Source: Prepared with the assistance of Dr. Beryl E. Pettus.

A senator must sponsor a House bill if it is to receive serious consideration in the Senate. Likewise, a representative must sponsor a Senate bill in the House.

2. First reading (House) and referral to committee After receiving a bill, the chief clerk assigns it a number in order of submission. Then the bill is turned over to the reading clerk for the first reading. The reading clerk reads aloud the caption (a summary of contents) and announces the committee to which the bill has been assigned by the Speaker.

3. House committee consideration and report Before any committee action, the committee staff must distribute a bill analysis that summarizes important provisions of the bill to committee members.[19] The committee chair decides whether the bill needs a fiscal note (provided by the Legislative Budget Board) projecting the costs of implementing the proposed legislation for five years. The committee chair also decides whether the Legislative Budget Board should prepare an impact statement for a bill that would change punishment for a felony offense, change the public school finance system, create certain water districts, affect or create a state fee or tax, or affect a retirement system for public employees.

As a courtesy to sponsoring representatives, most bills receive a committee hearing at which lobbyists and other interested persons have an opportunity to express their views. At the discretion of the committee chair, a bill may go to a subcommittee for a hearing. A subcommittee includes only some members of the full committee. After a hearing, the subcommittee submits a written report to the committee. If a majority of a committee's members decides that a bill should be passed, usually with proposed amendments, a favorable report is referred to the chief clerk.

Two committees determine the order in which bills are cleared for floor action. The Local and Consent Calendars Committee and the Calendars Committee conduct sessions that are open to the public, the press, and all representatives. The Local and Consent Calendars Committee assigns three types of legislative proposals to the Local, Consent, and Resolutions Calendar. The following are examples of these types of bills that were passed in the 82nd regular session in 2011:

- *Local bills* affecting a limited number of localities, districts, counties, or municipalities: H.B. 367 by Representative Rob Orr (R-Burleson), designating State Highway 121 in Tarrant and Johnson counties as the Chisholm Trail Parkway
- *Consent bills* that are uncontested and not likely to face opposition: H.B. 2910 by Representative Dan Branch (R-Dallas), relating to the measure to increase completion rates and support students enrolled in science, technology, engineering, and mathematics at higher-education institutions
- *Noncontroversial resolutions*, other than congratulatory and memorial resolutions: H.C.R. 84 by Representative Erwin Cain (R-Como), designating "42" as the official State Domino Game of Texas

The Calendars Committee places other bills on three daily calendars. The following are examples of these types of bills:

- The *Emergency Calendar*, for bills needing immediate action, as well as all taxing and spending bills: H.B. 15 by Representative Sid Miller (R-Stephenville), relating to informed consent to an abortion (mandatory sonogram before abortion)

- The *Major State Calendar*, for nonemergency bills that change policy in a major field of government activity and that have a major statewide impact: H.B. 9 by Representative Dan Branch (R-Dallas), relating to student success-based funding for and reporting of public higher-education institutions
- The *General State Calendar*, for nonemergency bills having statewide application but limited legal effect and policy impact: H.B. 33 by Representative Dan Branch (R-Dallas), relating to measures to increase the affordability of textbooks used for courses at public or private higher-education institutions

Within 30 days after receiving a bill, a calendars committee must decide by record vote whether to place the bill on a calendar for floor consideration. After this period expires, any representative may introduce a motion on the House floor to place the bill on an appropriate calendar. When seconded by five representatives and adopted by a simple majority vote, the House may schedule the bill for floor action without approval of a calendars committee, though this procedure is seldom attempted.

4. Second reading (House)   Usually, the second reading is limited to caption only. The author of a bill, the committee member reporting on behalf of the committee, or another designated member has the privilege of beginning and ending floor debate with a speech of not more than 20 minutes. Other speakers are limited to not more than 10 minutes each, unless extra time is granted. A computer on each representative's desk provides easy access to the text of amendments proposed during floor debate. After discussion ends and any amendments are added, a vote is taken on "passage to engrossment" (preparation of an officially inscribed copy). A quorum (the minimum number required to do business) is constituted when at least two-thirds of the House members (100 representatives) are present.

Approval of a bill on second reading requires a simple majority vote. Such a House vote marks an important step in the enactment of any proposed bill. A motion may be made to suspend the rules by a four-fifths majority vote of members present and to give the bill an immediate third reading. Thus, an exception can be made to the constitutional rule that all bills must be read on three separate days, though an exception for the third reading is seldom made in the House.

Provisions of the Texas Constitution, statutes, procedural rules, and practices within the respective chambers govern legislative voting. A record vote usually involves an electronic system. Votes are recorded and tallied as each representative presses the button on a desktop voting machine. This action turns on a light (green, yes; red, no; white, present but not voting) beside the representative's name on the two huge tote boards mounted on the wall behind (and to the right and left of) the House Speaker's podium. House and Senate journals list the record votes of members of the respective chambers. Any House member may call for a record vote.

A "division vote" leaves no official record. For several years, newspaper editors and others demanded record votes in the House and Senate. Finally, their demands were heeded by the 80th legislature, and H.J.R. 19 was approved by Texas voters in November 2007. This constitutional amendment stipulates that a record vote must be taken in either chamber on final passage of a bill or of a proposal or ratification of a constitutional amendment or any other nonceremonial resolution. Final passage is defined as a vote on third reading (or second reading if the rule for a third reading has been suspended), on concurrence with amendments of the other house, or on adoption of a conference report. In fact, the most important vote is taken on the second reading rather than on the third reading.

House rules prohibit **ghost voting** (pressing the voting button for another representative, unless [since 2009] a member has given permission for the vote to be cast). Months after an Austin television report on ghost voting aired locally in 2007, it was posted on YouTube. Subsequently, a Travis County grand jury called for enforcement of House rules.[20] Thus, when a representative asks for "strict enforcement," the voting machine of an absent member is locked. During the 81st regular session in 2009, however, "ghosts continued to vote while fingerprint-recognition equipment (which would have helped prevent ghost voting) costing $128,000 remained unused in storage. If installed, this equipment would allow representatives to vote from the members' lounge or elsewhere around the House chamber when not at their desks.

Occasionally (especially at the end of a session) representatives engage in lengthy debates on bills that they do not oppose. Such action is intended to prevent the House from taking up a bill that they do oppose, but that would probably be approved if brought up for a vote. This delaying action is called **chubbing**. In 2009, House Democrats engaged in chubbing by discussing bills on the Local and Consent Calendar for many hours. This tactic prevented action on a Republican-backed voter ID bill that would have required more identification checks before a person could vote, but this legislation was passed in 2011. Chubbing can be ended if 100 members vote to suspend House rules.

To limit legislative logjams and discourage uninformed voting in the final days of a regular session, House rules contain prohibitions against second and third readings for the following bills:

- Nonlocal House bills during the last 17 days
- Local House bills during the last 10 days
- Senate bills during the last five days

Other detailed restrictions apply to House actions on the 126th to 139th days of a regular session. On the 140th, or final, day, House voting is limited to correcting bills that have passed. The Senate has similar end-of-session restrictions on considering legislation.

5. Third reading (House) On the third reading, passage of a bill requires a simple majority vote of members present. Amendments may still be added at this stage, but such action requires a two-thirds majority vote. After the

ghost voting
A prohibited practice whereby one representative presses the voting button of another House member who is absent.

chubbing
A practice whereby supporters of a bill engage in lengthy debate for the purpose of using time and thus preventing floor action on another bill that they oppose.

addition of an amendment, a copy of the amended bill is made, checked over by the chief clerk, and stamped "Engrossed."

6. First reading (Senate) After a bill passes on the third reading in the House, the chief clerk adds a statement certifying passage and transmits the bill to the Senate (where the original House number is retained). In the Senate, the secretary of the Senate reads aloud the House bill's caption and announces the committee to which the bill has been assigned by the lieutenant governor.

7. Senate committee consideration and report Senate procedure differs somewhat from House procedure. A senator may "tag" any bill by filing a request with either the Senate secretary or the committee chair to notify the tagging senator 48 hours before a hearing will be held on the bill. A tag usually kills the bill if done during the last days of a session.

If a majority of the committee members wants a bill to pass, it receives a favorable report. Bills are listed on the Senate's Regular Order of Business in the order in which the secretary of the Senate receives them. Unlike the House, the Senate has no calendar committees to control the flow of bills from standing committees to the Senate floor. At the beginning of each session, however, the Senate Administration Committee "parks" a blocking bill (called a "blocker")—on which floor action is not intended—at the head of the line. Bills arriving later are designated "out of order," and a vote of two-thirds of senators present and voting is required to suspend the regular order (that is, bypass the blocker bill) and bring the "out-of-order" bill to the Senate floor for debate. In 2011, two blockers were used: S.B. 445, establishing a county park beautification and improvement program, and S.J.R. 18, allowing the state to receive gifts of historical value. This **two-thirds rule** enhances the power of a party or a bipartisan group that can control more than one-third of the votes (which would be 11 votes if all 31 senators were voting).[21] In May 2007, Senator Mario Gallegos (D-Houston), who was having liver-transplant problems, rested in a hospital bed near the Senate floor so he could block floor consideration of a voter ID bill.[22]

8. Second reading (Senate) As with second readings in the House, the Senate debates the bill and considers proposed amendments. A computer on the desk of each senator displays the texts of proposed amendments. During the debate, custom permits a senator to speak about a bill as long as physical endurance permits. This delaying tactic is known as **filibustering**. But a filibuster may be stopped if another senator is recognized for the privileged, nondebatable motion to "move the previous question," which means requiring an immediate vote. The motion must be seconded by at least five senators and requires a majority vote of senators present. Another privileged, nondebatable motion that can halt a filibuster is a motion to adjourn or recess. A filibuster is most effective if undertaken toward the end of a session when time is short. In 2011, for example, Senator Wendy Davis killed a school finance bill with a filibuster that forced a special session.

When debate has ended, a roll call vote is called by the secretary of the Senate. Unless a senator holds up two fingers to indicate an intention to

two-thirds rule
A procedural device to control bringing bills to the Senate floor for debate.

filibustering
A delaying tactic whereby a senator may speak, and thus hold the Senate floor, for as long as physical endurance permits, unless one of two possible actions is taken to end the filibuster.

vote no, the presiding officer usually announces that the chamber unanimously approves the bill after only a few names are called. The vote is recorded only if requested by three senators. A computer-controlled board at the front of the chamber shows how each senator has voted. A vote requires a quorum of 21 senators present. A simple majority of "yea" votes of members present is sufficient to pass a bill.

9. *Third reading (Senate)*   If passed on the second reading, a bill can have its third reading immediately, assuming the rules have been suspended. This action is routinely taken in the Senate by the required four-fifths majority vote of members present. Amending a bill on the third reading requires a two-thirds majority vote of members present. A simple majority vote is required for passage.

10. *Return to the House*   After passage by the Senate, a House bill returns to the chief clerk of the House, who supervises preparation of a perfect copy of the bill and delivers it to the Speaker. When an amendment has been added in the Senate (as usually happens), the change must be voted on in the House. If the House is not prepared to accept the amended bill, the ordinary procedure is to request a conference. Otherwise, the bill will die unless one of the chambers reverses its position.

11. *Conference committee*   When the two chambers agree to send the bill to conference, each presiding officer appoints five members to serve on the **conference committee**. Attempts are made to adjust differences and produce a compromise version acceptable to both the House and the Senate. At least three Senate members and three House members must agree before the committee can recommend a course of action in the two houses. The author of the House bill (usually, but not necessarily) serves as the conference committee chair.

12. *Conference committee report*   The conference committee's recommended settlement of questions at issue must be fully accepted or rejected by a simple majority vote in each chamber. Most recommendations are accepted. Both chambers, however, may agree to return the report to the committee, or, on request of the House, the Senate may accept a proposal for a new conference.

13. *Enrollment*   After both chambers have accepted a conference report, the chief clerk of the House prepares a perfect copy of the bill and stamps it "Enrolled." The report is then presented to the House.

14. *Signatures of the chief clerk and Speaker*   When the House receives the enrolled bill and the conference committee report, the bill is identified by chamber of origin and read by number only. Subsequently, it is signed by the chief clerk, who certifies the vote by which it passed. Then the House Speaker signs the bill.

15. *Signatures of the secretary of the Senate and the lieutenant governor*   Next, the chief clerk of the House takes the bill to the Senate, where it is read by number only. After certifying a passing vote, the secretary of the Senate signs the bill. Then the lieutenant governor does likewise.

16. *Action by the governor*   While the legislature remains in session, the governor has three options. The governor can sign the bill; allow it to

conference committee
A committee composed of representatives and senators appointed to reach agreement on a disputed bill and recommend changes acceptable to both chambers.

remain unsigned for 10 days, not including Sundays, after which time it becomes law without the chief executive's signature; or, within the 10-day period, veto the measure by returning it to the House unsigned, with a message giving a reason for the veto (or the Senate if a bill originated there). The Texas Constitution requires a vote of "two-thirds of the membership present" in the first chamber that considers a vetoed bill (in this case, the House of Representatives) and a vote of "two-thirds of the members" in the second chamber (in this case, the Senate) to override the governor's veto.[23]

After a session ends, the governor has 20 days, counting Sundays, in which to veto pending legislation and file the rejected bills with the secretary of state. A bill not vetoed by the governor automatically becomes law at the end of the 20-day period. Because the legislature is no longer in session, the governor's postadjournment veto is of special importance because it cannot be overridden. Usually, relatively few bills are vetoed.

Point/Counterpoint

THE ISSUE In 2007, by a vote of 109 to 29, the House passed H.J.R. 59, authored by Representative Gary Elkins (R-Houston). This constitutional amendment proposal would allow the Texas legislature to override vetoes during a special five-day session at the end of the 20-day postadjournment veto period. A companion measure died in the Senate State Affairs Committee. Again in 2009, by a vote of 131 to 16, the House passed a similar proposal (H.J.R. 29) by Elkins for a special three-day session. It, too, died in the Senate.

Should There Be Special Sessions to Override Vetoes?

Arguments For Override Session

- In 33 other states, either the legislature or the governor can call special sessions.
- Veto override authority would strengthen the lawmaking power of the Texas legislature.
- In 2007, 2009, and 2011, the 80th, 81st, and 82nd legislatures passed more than 80 percent of their bills in the last 10 days of the regular session; the governor vetoed 51 in 2007, 35 in 2009, and 24 in 2011.

"The veto is one of the governor's strongest powers. No one is advocating that he be stripped of that power, but there needs to be a better form of checks and balances."

— *My SA* editorial, posted April 7, 2007

Arguments Against Override Sessions

- Veto override authority for the Texas legislature would further weaken the office of the governor.
- Legislators can discipline themselves to pass bills earlier in a session rather than in the last days.
- The Legislative Budget Board's fiscal notes in 2007 and 2009 estimated that costs associated with a five-day veto-override session would be about $177,500 for publication expenses and legislators' per diem allowances. For a three-day session, the total cost would be about $166,800.

Denouncing supporters of H.J.R. 59, Representative David Swinford (R-Dumas) declared, "I know a lot of people would like to spit in the governor's eye." He added, "I hope you enjoy doing that."

— Quoted by Janet Elliott, "House Votes to Trim Governor's Veto Power," *Houston Chronicle*, March 21, 2007

Learning Check 7.4   (Answers on p. 292)

1. What legislative measure is abbreviated as H.J.R.?
2. True or False: The reading clerk reads aloud the full text of a House bill before it is referred to a committee.

Students in Action

An Internship with the Texas Legislature

"My aspirations in the political sphere are driven by the understanding that elected officials are public servants. The internship allowed me to witness this theory in practice."

—Farrah Najmuddin

How She Became Involved

In 2009, during the 81st regular session of the Texas legislature, Farrah Najmuddin lived in Austin and earned 12 semester hours of credit while participating in Baylor University's Bullock Scholars Program. Course requirements included preparing biographies of legislators, writing a detailed report on major issues of the previous regular session, and submitting weekly reports to the coordinating professor.

What She Did

Farrah also participated in the Texas Legislative Internship Program, founded by Senator Rodney Ellis (D-Houston). She worked in the office of Senator Judith Zaffirini (D-Laredo) as the legislative director's intern. Farrah worked on bills that the senator

(Monkey Business Images/Shutterstock.com)

authored for committees of which she was not a member. Much of Farrah's time and effort was spent on bills about booster seats for children, penalties for illegal parking in a disabled parking spot, protocol for folding the Texas flag, and unemployment insurance. For the last two, she was responsible for work at each step in the legislative process, from drafting the initial proposal to working with office staff of a House member at the conference committee stage. Other responsibilities included creating and editing Senator Zaffirini's daily floor notebook, which covered her activities for the day, as well as any legislation that she would be called upon to bring to the floor.

What She Learned

This internship gave Farrah more responsibility than she had been given previously. At the same time, she was able to see the fruits of her efforts. She learned the legislative process and the proper way to communicate with lobbyists, while also learning that being a public servant means serving your constituents.

Farrah Najmuddin earned a B.A. degree at Baylor University. She graduated in December 2009, with a major in philosophy and a minor in political science. This report is printed with her permission.

Influences Within the Legislative Environment

In theory, elected legislators are influenced primarily, if not exclusively, by their constituents (especially constituents who vote rather than those who make big campaign contributions). In practice, however, many legislators' actions bear little relationship to the needs or interests of the "folks back home." To be sure, Texas senators and representatives are not completely indifferent to voters, but many of them fall far short of being genuinely representative. One problem is that large numbers of citizens are uninterested in most governmental affairs and have no opinions about how the legislature should act in making public policy. Others may have opinions but are inarticulate or unable to communicate with their legislators. Therefore, lawmakers are likely to yield not only to the influence of the presiding officers in the House and Senate but also to pressure from the governor and other powerful political actors (especially lobbyists) seeking to win their voluntary support or force their cooperation.

LO5

The Governor

The threat of executive veto has an important influence on legislative behavior. Even a bill popular with many senators and representatives may not pass because of such a threat. Knowledge that the governor opposes the measure is often sufficient to discourage its introduction. A bill introduced despite the governor's opposition is likely to be buried in a committee, tabled (postponed without commitment to reconsider), or defeated on the House or Senate floor.

Each governor campaigns for office on a platform of promises and then feels compelled to promote certain policies after being elected. Thus, legislators must be influenced to ensure the success of the governor's plans for taxing, spending, building, and educating, among other things. If any doubt arises about what the governor wants, gubernatorial policies are outlined in messages from time to time. Popular support for the chief executive's ideas makes opposition difficult, even though the people in a legislator's district may be adversely affected.[24]

Judges, the Attorney General, and the Comptroller of Public Accounts

An act may be politically expedient and even popular with constituents, but it may conflict with provisions of the Texas Constitution or the U.S. Constitution. Thus, in their lawmaking, all legislators are influenced by what state and federal judges have done or could do about possible legislative action. Usually, senators and representatives wish to avoid spending time or investing political capital in legislative efforts that will be struck down by judicial decisions or opinions of the attorney general. Therefore, while considering a bill, the committee chair may turn to the attorney general for an opinion concerning its constitutionality.

The state comptroller exercises great influence by estimating how much money will be collected under current and projected revenue laws, because the legislature must keep state spending within the limits of anticipated revenue. For example, after an appropriation bill has passed the House and Senate, it goes to the comptroller. If the comptroller determines that Texas will not collect sufficient revenue, the bill does not receive the comptroller's certification and cannot be enacted unless both houses approve it by a four-fifths majority vote.

Lobbyists

Lobbying as an interest group tactic is discussed in Chapter 6,"The Politics of Interest Groups." Opinions vary concerning lobbyists' influence on legislative behavior and public policy. In many minds, lobbying means corrupting legislators with offers of campaign money and other inducements. Others see lobbyists as performing a useful role by supplying information and serving as links with organized groups of constituents living within a legislator's district.[25]

Lobbyists must register with the Texas Ethics Commission and make state-required lobbying reports to that agency. Both lobbyists and political action committees (PACs) contribute directly to the campaign funds that cover legislators' election expenses. These same influence-seekers pay for a wide range of political and officeholder expenses.[26]

Research Organizations

Policymakers need reliable information. Most Texas legislators depend heavily on information provided by their staffs, by administrative agencies, and by lobbyists. In addition, legislators obtain information from three official research bodies:

- The Texas Legislative Council: http://www.tlc.state.tx.us
- The House Research Organization: http://www.hro.house.state.tx.us
- The Senate Research Center: http://www.senate.state.tx.us/src/index.htm

Two of Texas's more important independent providers of public policy research and analysis are the following:

- The Center for Public Policy Priorities: http://www.cppp.org
- The Texas Public Policy Foundation: http://www.texaspolicy.com

The Texas Legislative Council Authorizing special research projects by its staff is one function of the Legislative Council. This council comprises the lieutenant governor (joint chair), the Speaker of the House (joint chair), six senators appointed by the lieutenant governor, the chair of the House Administration Committee, and five representatives appointed by the Speaker. The council's employees provide bill drafting, advice for legislators, legislative research and writing, publishing and document distribution, interim study committee research support, demographic and statistical data compilation and analysis, computer mapping and analysis, and other computer services.

The House Research Organization A bipartisan steering committee of 15 representatives–elected by the House membership for staggered four-year terms–governs the House Research Organization (HRO). In 2012, eight Republicans and seven Democrats served on the steering committee. Although the HRO is an administrative department of the House, it is independent of the House leadership. The HRO's annual operating budget is set by the steering committee and the House Administration Committee. The HRO employed 19 staff personnel during the 82nd regular session in 2011, and about half that number remained during the interim.

The HRO produces reports on a variety of policy issues. Of special importance is its *Daily Floor Report* for each day that the legislature is in session. In this publication, HRO personnel analyze important bills to be considered, providing an objective summary of bill content and presenting arguments for and against each bill. After a regular session, the HRO staff publishes a report on the session's important bills and resolutions, including some that were defeated. (For example, see *Major Issues of the 82nd Legislature*, published on September 30, 2011.) This report may also cover the work of one or more subsequent special sessions. HRO publications are accessible online.

The Senate Research Center Organized under the secretary of the Senate, the Senate Research Center analyzes bills under consideration by the Senate and conducts research on diverse issues. Primarily, it responds to requests from Senate members for research and information. The lieutenant governor, however, as president of the Senate, also calls on the center's information and expertise. The center's periodic publications range from the semimonthly *Clearinghouse Update*, which presents brief accounts of issues facing Texas and the nation, to *Highlights of the ... Legislature*, which summarizes hundreds of bills and joint resolutions for each regular session. Other publications produced by the center include *Interim Digest: A Compilation of Interim Committee Action*; *A Senate Guide to Ethics and Disclosure*; and *Legislative Lexicon*, which defines words, terms, and phrases that form the "legislative lingo" used by legislators and staff.

The Center for Public Policy Priorities Founded in 1985 as an Austin office of the Benedictine Resource Center, the Center for Public Policy Priorities has been operating as an independent nonprofit organization since 1999. Its principal focus is on the problems of low- and moderate-income families in Texas. Legislators and other public officials have used its policy analyses on issues ranging from state taxation and appropriations to public education and health-care access. But some critics, like former House Appropriations Committee chair Rob Junell (D-San Angelo), insist that research by staff of "The Center for Too Many P's" is tainted with liberal bias.

The Texas Public Policy Foundation Established in 1989 in San Antonio, the Texas Public Policy Foundation (TPPF) has been heavily funded and influenced by its founder, Dr. James Leininger, a regular donor to election campaigns of conservative politicians. The foundation focuses its research on issues supporting limited government, free enterprise, private property rights, and individual responsibility. Using policy research and analysis, TPPF seeks to influence Texas government by recommending its findings to legislators and other policymakers, group leaders, media persons, and the general public. An editorial in the liberal *Texas Observer* asserted that "the Texas Public Policy Foundation has become the in-house think tank of the state's current Republican leadership."[27]

The Media

It is difficult to measure (or even estimate) the influence of newspapers, magazines, television, the Internet, and radio on legislative behavior. Legislators are aware that the press (especially the *Austin American-Statesman* and other big-city newspapers in Texas) will publicize some of their activities. In addition, news concerning legislative affairs is posted on websites created by special-interest groups and spread through blogs, radio and television broadcasts, and magazines such as *Texas Monthly* and *The Texas Observer*. A recent entry to Texas journalism is the *Texas Tribune*, a free electronic news source that focuses on Texas politics. In addition, newsletters and other publications produced for subscribers or members of special-interest groups frequently highlight legislators' actions. On some policy issues, lawmakers (as well as voters) may be impressed by reasoned opinions expressed in editorials, persuasive analyses from political columnists and commentators, reporters' news stories, postings by bloggers, and editorial cartoons such as those printed in *Practicing Texas Politics*.[28]

 Learning Check 7.5 (Answers on p. 292)

1. True or False: Under Texas law, lobbyists are encouraged, but not required, to register with the Texas Ethics Commission.
2. True or False: The House Research Organization influences the House through the *Daily Floor Report* that presents arguments for and against each bill.

★ # Conclusion

The framework of the Texas legislature reflects the public demand for representative government. All legislators are chosen in a process featuring primaries and elections. Much of the work of both the House and the Senate is done in committees, but floor debate and votes on bills and resolutions attract more public attention. Through their control of state taxing and spending, legislators have an immediate impact on the state's economy and the well-being of all Texans.

Chapter Summary

- The Texas legislature is composed of 31 senators elected for four-year terms and 150 representatives elected for two-year terms. Biennial regular sessions are limited to 140 days, and special sessions called by the governor are limited to 30 days. New legislative districts are drawn after each federal decennial census.
- Legislators must be U.S. citizens, qualified Texas voters, and residents of their districts for one year. Minimum Texas residence is one year for representatives and two years for senators. Minimum age is 21 for representatives and 26 for senators.
- The lieutenant governor presides over the Senate, and the Speaker presides over the House. Both appoint committee members and name committee chairs and vice chairs for their respective chambers. Senators and representatives form legislative caucuses, which are groups with common interests. There are party caucuses for Democrats and Republicans, racial/ethnic caucuses for African Americans and Mexican Americans, and ideological caucuses for conservatives and liberals.
- Constitutional provisions and rules of the House and Senate control the detailed process whereby a bill is passed in both chambers. The governor may sign a bill, allow it to become law without signing, or veto it. A veto kills a bill, unless the veto is overridden by a two-thirds vote in each chamber.
- Although legislators are popularly elected, they are influenced by the governor and other state officials, lobbyists, research organizations, and the media.

Key Terms

bicameral, p. 251
unicameral, p. 251
regular session, p. 252
special session, p. 252
redistricting, p. 253
gerrymandering, p. 254
single-member district, p. 254
multimember district, p. 254
president of the Senate, p. 267
Speaker of the House, p. 268
substantive committee, p. 270
procedural committee, p. 270
standing committee, p. 270
select committee, p. 270
special interim committee, p. 270

legislative caucus, p. 272
simple resolution, p. 275
concurrent resolution, p. 275
joint resolution, p. 275
bill, p. 276
oversight, p. 276
senatorial courtesy, p. 277
impeachment, p. 277
parliamentarian, p. 278
companion bill, p. 278
ghost voting, p. 282
chubbing, p. 282
two-thirds rule, p. 283
filibustering, p. 283
conference committee, p. 284

Learning Check Answers

7.1

1. A full term for a member of the Texas House of Representatives is two years.
2. False. Usually, gerrymandered districts are oddly shaped rather than compact.

7.2

1. The Texas Constitution specifies 26 years as the minimum age to be a state senator and 21 years as the minimum age to be a state representative.
2. True. Salary increases for legislators must be submitted to the state's voters for approval or disapproval.

7.3

1. False. The Speaker of the House of Representatives can vote on bills or resolutions.
2. True. The president of the Senate determines the Senate committee to which a bill will be sent after introduction.

7.4

1. A House joint resolution is abbreviated H.J.R.
2. False. The reading clerk reads aloud the caption (a summary of the contents) of a House bill before it is referred to a committee.

7.5

1. False. Under Texas law, lobbyists must register with the Texas Ethics Commission.
2. True. The House Research Organization influences the House through the *Daily Floor Report* that provides arguments for and against each bill.

Discussion Questions

1. Do you think that Texas's legislative redistricting process meets the needs of Texans, or do you believe that it should be changed? Explain why or how.
2. Do you believe that the Texas legislature should include equal numbers of men and women and members of different racial or ethnic groups in proportion to their populations? Why or why not?
3. Which state official has the most power to influence legislation, and how is this power used?
4. Which legislative caucus identified in this chapter would probably work for or against legislation that you support or that you would like to see introduced?
5. Which steps in passing a bill are most critical in the legislative process?
6. How should the legislature regulate lobbying activities to ensure that freedoms are preserved while also protecting the public interest?
7. What role do research organizations play in lawmaking?

Internet Resources

Legislative Reference Library of Texas:
http://www.lrl.state.tx.us

National Conference of State Legislatures:
http://www.ncsl.org

Texas Conservative Roundtable:
http:texasconservativeroundtable.com

Texas House of Representatives:
http://www.house.state.tx.us

Texas Legislature Online:
http://www.capitol.state.tx.us

Texas Senate: **http://www.senate.state.tx.us**

Texas Watch: **http://www.texaswatch.org**

Notes

1. Alan Rosenthal, *The Decline of Representative Democracy: Process, Participation, and Power in State Legislatures* (Washington, D.C.: CQ Press, 1998), x.

2. Alan Rosenthal, *Heavy Lifting: The Job of the American Legislature* (Washington, D.C.: CQ Press, 2004), 246–247. See also Alan Rosenthal, *Engines of Democracy: Politics and Policymaking in State Legislatures* (Washington, D.C.: CQ Press, 2009), 8–11.

3. For the experiences of Melissa and Rick Noriega (D-Houston), see Paul Burka, "Duty Calls," *Texas Monthly*, March 2006, 12, 14, 16.

4. For chapters by Gary Keith and six other authorities on redistricting in the Lone Star State, see Gary Keith, ed., Rotten Boroughs, *Political Thickets, and Legislative Donnybrooks: Redistricting in Texas* (Austin: University of Texas Press, 2013).

5. Quoted by Jim Wright in his preface to James W. Riddlesberger Jr. and Anthony Champagne, *Lone Star Leaders: Power and Personality in the Texas Congressional Delegation* (Fort Worth: TCU Press, 2011), xii.

6. See Nancy Baker Jones and Ruth Winegarten, *Capitol Women: Texas Female Legislators, 1923–1999* (Austin: University of Texas Press, 2000), 53; and Sharon A. Navarro, *Latina Legislator Leticia Van der Putte and the Road to Leadership* (College Station: Texas A&M University Press, 2008).

7. Still active in Texas politics, Ben Barnes served as Speaker of the House from 1965 to 1969 and as lieutenant governor from 1969 to 1973. For information on his service as presiding officer in each chamber, see Ben Barnes, with Lisa Dickey, *Barn Burning, Barn Building: Tales of a Political Life, From LBJ to George W. Bush and Beyond* (Albany, Tex.: Bright Sky Press, 2006). Bob Bullock's years as lieutenant governor (1991–1999) are covered in Dave McNeely and Jim Henderson, *Bob Bullock: God Bless Texas* (Austin: University of Texas Press, 2008). Bill Hobby's experiences and observations from 18 years as lieutenant governor (1973–1991) are related in Bill Hobby with Saralee Tiede, *How Things Really Work: Lessons from a Life in Politics* (Austin: Center for American History, University of Texas at Austin, 2010).

8. The changing role of the Speaker since 1876 is described by authors Patrick L. Cox and Michael Phillips in *The House Will Come to Order: How the Texas Speaker Became a Power in State and National Politics* (Austin: University of Texas Press, 2010).

9. For one speaker pro tempore's responses to questions about his role in the 78th and 79th Texas legislatures, see Monica Gutierrez, "Turner on a Tightrope: A Few Questions with Speaker Pro Tempore Sylvester Turner," *The Texas Observer*, June 24, 2005, 10–11, 18.

10. Laylan Copelin, "Judge Tosses Out Spending Restrictions for Speaker Elections," *Austin American-Statesman*, August 26, 2008. See also *Free Market Foundation v. Reisman, 573 F Supp 2d 997* (W.D. Tex. 2008).

11. After casting the only dissenting vote, Representative Lon Burnam (D-Fort Worth) stated that he liked Craddick but explained, "I don't like the way he votes. I don't like his sense of ethics." Quoted by R. A. Dyer, "Lone Dissent Marks Craddick's Swearing In," *Austin American-Statesman*, January 15, 2003.

12. See S. C. Gwynne, "How Did Tom Craddick Become the Most Powerful Speaker Ever and the Most Powerful Texan Today?" *Texas Monthly*, February 2005, 100–103, 186–196.

13. For coverage of 2007 and 2008, see a collection of articles, "The 80th Legislature: Blood on the Floor," in *The Texas Observer*, June 15, 2007, 4–26; and two

articles by Paul Burka, "Animal House," *Texas Monthly*, February 2007, 18, 14, 16, and "The Democraddick Primary," *Texas Monthly*, March 2008, 10, 12, 14. See also Cox and Phillips, *The House Will Come to Order*, 190–192.

14. Emily Ramshaw, "Straus Formally Voted Speaker," *Texas Tribune*, January 11, 2011, accessed March 30, 2012, http://www.texastribune.org/texas-house-of-representatives/2011-house-speakers-race/straus-formally-voted-speaker/.

15. Jay Root, "Conservative Activists Are Backing Straus's Opponent," *Texas Tribune*, March 30, 2012, http://www.politicsinstereo.com/2012/03/30/conservative-activists-are-backing-straus-opponent/.

16. "Tea Party Caucus of Texas Introduced," *Texas Insider*, posted on December 16, 1910, http://www.texasinsider.org/?p-39413.

17. See *Major Issues of the 82nd Legislature: Regular Session*, Focus Report No. 82-7 (Austin: House Research Organization, Texas House of Representatives), September 30, 2011, 5, http://www.hro.house.state.tx.us/pdf/focus/major82.pdf.

18. For a more detailed description of the lawmaking process, see *How a Bill Becomes a Law: 82nd Legislature*, Focus Report No. 82-2 (Austin: House Research Organization, Texas House of Representatives), February 14, 2011, http://www.hro.house.state.tx.us/pdf/focus/hwbill82.pdf.

19. For more information on how committees work, see *House Committee Procedures: 82nd Legislature*, Focus Report No. 82-3 (Austin: House Research Organization, Texas House of Representatives), February 18, 2011, http://www.hro.house.state.tx.us/pdf/focus/compro82.pdf.

20. See Karen Brooks, "Grand Jury Warns Against 'Ghost Voting,'" *Dallas Morning News*, July 27, 2008.

21. For a defense of the two-thirds rule, see Paul Burka, "First, Dew No Harm," *Texas Monthly*, February 2006, 16, 18.

22. Mark Lisheron, "Ill Senator Settles in for Voter ID Fight," *Austin American-Statesman*, May 22, 2007.

23. As one authority explains, this difference in the two-thirds majorities required by Article IV, Section 14, represents "a mysterious error in the present constitution." See George D. Braden, *Citizens' Guide to the Proposed New Texas Constitution* (Austin: Sterling Swift, 1975), 15.

24. For contrasting accounts of relations between Governor Bush and the Texas legislature, see George W. Bush, *A Charge to Keep* (New York: Morrow, 1999), 110–131; and Molly Ivins and Lou Dubose, *Shrub: The Short but Happy Political Life of George W. Bush* (New York: Random House, 2000), 84–106.

25. For a scholarly yet readable description of lobbying in the Lone Star State, see Keith E. Hamm and Charles W. Wiggins, "Texas: The Transformation from Personal to Information Lobbying," in *Interest Group Politics in the Southern States*, ed. Ronald J. Hrebenar and Clive S. Thomas (Tuscaloosa: University of Alabama Press, 1992), 152–180.

26. For a study featuring interviews with 14 former Texas legislators, see Sam Kinch Jr., with Anne Marie Kilday, *Too Much Money Is Not Enough: Big Money and Political Power in Texas* (Austin: Campaigns for People, 2000).

27. Dave Mann and Jake Bernstein, "UndemoCraddick," *The Texas Observer*, February 18, 2005, 3.

28. For a veteran Texas journalist's account of four decades of reporting on the Texas legislature, see Dave McNeely, "A Press Corps on the Lege," *The Texas Observer*, May 27, 2005, 8–11. See also the biography of the late Molly Ivins (1944–2007), a liberal journalist who covered the Texas legislature for many years: Bill Minutaglio and W. Michael Smith, *Molly Ivins: A Rebel Life* (New York: Public Affairs, 2009).

Recent Congressional Redistricting in Texas*

Charles Jerry Wilkins and Lyle C. Brown

Congressional redistricting in the Lone Star State is a responsibility of the state legislature, but litigation invariably results in districts drawn by federal courts. Such has been the case in the twenty-first century. Jeff Wentworth, a Republican lawyer who represented San Antonio districts in the Texas House of Representatives (1989–1993) and Senate (1993–2013), believes that there is a better way.

Legislative and Judicial Actions Since 2001

After redistricting in 2001, Texas Republicans won 88 (59 percent) of the 150 state House seats in 2002 and 19 (61 percent) of the 31 state Senate seats; but GOP candidates won only 15 (47 percent) of the 32 U.S. House seats. Desiring a larger GOP representation in Washington, then-U.S. House majority leader Tom DeLay (R-Sugar Land) pressured the Texas Legislature to draw new districts in its 78th Regular Session in 2003. To prevent this action, 51 Democrats broke a House quorum (100 of 150 members) by fleeing to Ardmore, Oklahoma, where they remained until time ran out for action on a redistricting bill.[1]

In the summer of 2003, Governor Rick Perry called three special sessions. During the first of these sessions, Senate Democrats invoked a two-thirds rule that prevented consideration of a congressional redistricting bill. Then, when they learned that the president of the Senate would not

follow that rule in a second session, 11 of the Senate's 12 Democrats made a quorum-busting flight to Albuquerque, New Mexico, where they remained until Senator John Whitmire caved in and returned to Austin. The passing of a redistricting bill in the third special session brought court challenges, but Republicans were elected to 21 (66 percent) of Texas's 32 congressional seats.[2]

As a result of subsequent elections in the first decade of the 21st century, Texas Republicans elected to the U.S. House totaled 19 (59 percent) in 2006, 20 (63 per cent) in 2008, and 23 (72 percent) in 2010. Only 2 of the Democrats elected in 2010 were Anglos, while 4 were Latinos and 3 were African Americans. Among Republican representatives, 21 were Anglos, 2 were Latinos (or at least had a Spanish surname), and none was an African American.

Because Texas's population grew from nearly 23 million in 2000 to about 25 million in 2010, the Lone Star State gained four seats in the U.S. House of Representatives. Latinos accounted for about 65 percent of the population growth. Consequently, they called for increased representation. For Republicans in control of the Texas Legislature, the problem has been that Latinos tend to vote for Democratic candidates.

In 2011, the legislature failed to pass a congressional redistricting bill during its 82nd Regular Session that ended May 30.[3] On the following day, however, Governor Perry called a special session; and one item on the agenda was congressional redistricting. SB 4, the congressional redistricting bill, was passed on June 20; but Governor Perry did not sign it until July 18. On the following day, as required by the federal Voting Rights Act, Texas's Attorney General Greg Abbott

---

*Charles Jerry Wilkins is adjunct professor of public affairs at San Diego State University. Lyle C. Brown is professor emeritus of political science at Baylor University. This article is based on a paper entitled "Redistricting in Different Directions: California and Texas," which Wilkins and Brown presented at a meeting of the Southwestern Political Science Association in San Diego, California, on April 7, 2012. The article is reprinted by permission of the authors.

"formally" sought preclearance of the Texas congressional district maps (together with district maps for both houses of the Texas Legislature and the State Board of Education) from a three-judge panel of the U.S. District Court for the District of Columbia in Washington. It was anticipated that this court would be more inclined to grant preclearance than the Voting Rights Division of the Democrat-controlled U.S. Department of Justice within the Obama Administration. Nevertheless, Abbott also "informally" submitted the congressional maps to the U.S. Department of Justice.

On September 19, the U.S. Department of Justice announced that it opposed preclearance for Texas's congressional districts. Two months later, on November 8, 2011, the Washington court refused to grant summary judgment for preclearance and announced that a full trial would be required. This court did not rule on the preclearance issue until August 28, 2012. One sticking point was the gerrymandering of Representative Lloyd Doggett's District 25. It contained parts of the City of Austin and Travis County, with their large numbers of Democrats.

As Texas's most liberal congressman, Doggett aroused GOP anger by his effort to prevent Texas from receiving $830 million of federal aid for education unless Governor Perry guaranteed that the money would be used to increase state spending on education rather than replace state funding as happened with $3.35 billion of federal aid in 2009. After nine months of controversy, the "Doggett Amendment" was repealed by Congress in April 2011 while congressional redistricting was being considered in the Texas Legislature. Concerning the repeal, Doggett complained: "Removing all accountability on Governor Perry's use of $830 million of federal aid to education by repealing the 'Save Our Schools' Amendment is one of many unwise concessions made to Republicans to avoid their threatened government shutdown."[4]

In 2003, Republican legislators had sought to destroy Doggett politically by dividing Travis County among three districts. They drew Doggett's district to extend southward from Austin through a largely Latino-populated area, but he was reelected

from 2004 through 2010. In 2011, Republicans went further in their effort to purge Doggett. The congressional redistricting bill that was passed and signed by the governor divided Travis County among five districts. Now it appears that the D.C. court is trying to decide whether Doggett's District 25 comprises a minority-coalition district that should be protected under the Voting Rights Act. Meanwhile, Doggett sought and won the Democratic Party's nomination to represent the newly drawn District 35 that stretches from Austin southward to San Antonio and has a population that is heavily Latino.[5]

Even before the D.C. court began considering the preclearance issue, several groups and individuals filed lawsuits contending that the congressional districts adopted by the Texas Legislature had been drawn to the disadvantage of racial and ethnic groups in violation of Section 5 of the Voting Rights Act. On July 27, 2011, these suits were consolidated for trial by a three-judge panel of the U.S. District Court for the Western District of Texas in San Antonio. The trial was conducted from September 6 through September 17. Deciding that temporary redistricting was needed before the 2012 primaries could be held, the San Antonio court produced interim maps on November 26.[6]

Responding to Republican complaints that these maps favored Latinos and Democrats, Attorney General Abbott petitioned the U.S. Supreme Court to block use of the maps. In a per curiam opinion dated January 20, 2012, that court ruled against the interim maps and directed the district court in San Antonio to use the legislature's maps as a "starting point" for creating new maps.[7]

In response to this directive, the San Antonio court instructed parties to the lawsuit to seek agreement on drawing new congressional districts. Nevertheless, Attorney General Abbott insisted that there could be no compromise concerning District 25 because its population had an Anglo majority and thus is not protected against gerrymandering. Negotiation, however, did produce an agreement between Abbott and the Texas Latino Redistricting Task Force influenced largely by the Mexican American Legal Defense and

Education Fund, Texas LULAC, the Southwest Voter Registration Education Project, and the GI Forum. But the Mexican American Legislative Caucus, the NAACP, the Legislative Black Caucus, and the Texas Democratic Party rejected the agreement. Nevertheless, on February 28, 2012, the San Antonio court produced maps providing opportunities for minority representation in two of the four new congressional districts: District 33 in the Dallas-Fort Worth area and District 35 in the Austin-San Antonio area. May 29 was the date that the court set for the 2012 primaries that should have been conducted on March 6.[8]

On August 28, 2012 (three months after the May primaries), the U.S. District Court for the District of Columbia denied preclearance for all Texas legislative and congressional maps authorized by the Texas Legislature in 2011. Although maps ordered by the U.S. District Court in San Antonio were based on the legislature's maps, on September 19, the U.S. Supreme Court refused to prevent use of the San Antonio court's maps for the general election in November 2012.

Senator Wentworth's Proposal

Frustrated by a redistricting system featuring time-consuming legislative battles, political gerrymandering, and court actions, former Senator Jeff Wentworth proposed redistricting reform in several legislative sessions beginning in 1993. In that year he responded to Democratic gerrymandering in the preceding regular session. His proposals were approved in the Senate in regular sessions in 2005, 2007, and 2011, but did not pass in the House. Wentworth's latest effort was Senate Bill 22, which was passed by the Senate but not the House in the same special session of the 82nd legislature that passed the 2011 congressional redistricting bill.[9]

Wentworth's proposal called for a congressional redistricting commission composed of nine members selected for two-year terms as follows:

- 2 members appointed by a majority vote of representatives belonging to the political party with the most members of the House
- 2 members appointed by a majority vote of representatives belonging to the political

party with the second-highest number of members of House
- 2 members appointed by a majority vote of senators belonging to the political party with the most members of the Senate
- 2 members appointed by a majority vote of senators belonging to the political party with the second-highest number of members of the Senate
- 1 nonvoting member who serves as presiding officer and is appointed by the affirmative vote of at least 5 of the other members

Each member must be a resident of Texas, and at least one member appointed by the Senate and one member appointed by the House must reside in a county not designated as a metropolitan statistical area. Disqualified from serving on the commission are holders of an elective public office, holders of an office in a political party other than that of precinct committee member, persons required to register as a lobbyist, or persons who have served in any of these capacities within the previous two years. A commission member cannot be a candidate for public office or actively participate in or contribute to the campaign of any candidate for state or federal office. A redistricting plan is adopted by a vote of at least five commission members.[10]

While many Texans are less than enthusiastic about establishing a congressional redistricting commission, redistricting failures and resulting delay of party primaries have caused several of Texas's newspaper editors to conclude that Wentworth's proposal or a similar plan, such as the one used in California, for changing the state's redistricting process is overdue.[11] It remains to be seen what the 83rd Legislature will do when it tackles congressional redistricting again in 2013. Wentworth will not be able to introduce another proposal, because he was defeated in a Republican primary runoff in 2012.

What's to Be Done in Texas?

In the aftermath of the census of 2010, the Republican majority in the Texas Legislature (with the blessing of the Republican Governor) re-drew Congressional district boundaries to their own distinct advantage. In California, however, a new Citizens Redistricting Commission significantly re-drew their boundaries in a formally nonpartisan way that was not specifically designed to benefit either a particular political party or a particular incumbent. Both the Texas redistricting plan and the California plan were challenged in the courts. All legal challenges to the California plan were dismissed, but Texas redistricting is still in legal limbo. Although the California process has been criticized, it appears to be supported by a strong majority of California voters and very well may stand the test of time.

In response to the partisan and legal bickering in Texas, there have been suggestions that perhaps that state would do well to follow California's example and turn redistricting over to a commission as Wentworth proposed. Even if there is a popular groundswell of support for this approach, however, it will have to be funneled through the Texas Legislature, since the Lone Star State does not have a direct initiative process available to its voters.

1. Lyle C. Brown and Jerry Wilkins, "Redistricting and Electoral Results in Texas in the Twenty-first Century," in Lyle C. Brown, Joyce A. Langenegger, Sonia Garcia, Ted A. Lewis, and Robert E. Biles, *Practicing Texas Politics*, 13th ed. (Boston: Houghton Mifflin, 2008), 295.
2. See Steve Bickerstaff, *Lines in the Sand: Congressional Redistricting in Texas and the Downfall of Tom DeLay* (Austin: University of Texas Press, 2007); and Tom DeLay, with Stephen Mansfield, *No Retreat, No Surrender* (New York: Sentinel, 2007).
3. For hundreds of posts concerning redistricting politics in Texas since February 11, 2011, see lawyer Michael Li's Texas Redistricting Blog at http://www.txredistricting.org
4. Maria Recio, "Perry Hails Congressional Deal Giving Texas $830 Million in Education Funds That Were Frozen," *Fort Worth Star-Telegram*, April 13, 2011.
5. See Tim Eaton, "Doggett District Could Be Sticking Point in Redistricting Case," *Austin American-Statesman*, February 14, 2012.
6. *Perez v. Perry*, Case 5:11-cv-00360-OLG-JES-XR Document 544 filed 11/26/11.
7. *Perry v. Perez*, 565 U.S. _____ (2012).
8. *Perez v. Perry*, Case 5:11-cv-00360-OLG-JES-XR Document 681 filed 02/28/21.
9. For the text of S.B. 22, see http://www.capitol.state.tx.us/BillLookup/Text.aspx?LegSess=821&Bill=SB22
10. For concise descriptions of Senator Wentworth's proposal, see Brian D. Sweany, "Mappily Ever After," *Texas Monthly*, February 2012, pp. 8 and 10; and Jeff Wentworth, "Time for a Redistricting Commission," *Austin American-Statesman*, September 17, 2012.
11. For examples of these editorials, see "Texas Redistricting's Bumpy Road," *Fort Worth Star-Telegram*, November 10, 2011; "Congressional Remap Confusion Illustrates Need for New System," *San Angelo Standard-Times*, November 29, 2011; "Shift Redistricting to Bipartisan Panel," *Austin American-Statesman*, January 19, 2012; and "Texas' Flawed Redistricting System on Display," *Corpus Christi Caller-Times*, February 8, 2012.

For further resources, please visit **www.cengagebrain.com**.

The Executive

8

(©John Branch/San Antonio Express-News)

Learning Objectives

1. Summarize the role of the governor and the process of governorship.
2. Analyze the governor's informal power.
3. Explain the executive powers of the governor, taking the process of checks and balances into account.
4. Discuss the shared power of the executive and the legislature.
5. Illustrate powers the governor exercises over the judicial branch of state government.
6. Describe the powers of the secretary of state and elected department heads.

I n mid-April 2008, nearly two years before the next Republican primaries, Governor Rick Perry announced that he would seek the GOP nomination in 2010 and win another four-year term. This early announcement did not please some Texans who remembered his veto of an eminent domain bill concerning the taking of privately owned property (especially land) for public use. Furthermore, many Texans believed that he had been governor too long (see John Branch's cartoon). For members of the Texas Senate and House of Representatives, it meant that Perry could, if reelected in November 2010 (which he was), continue to exercise a check on their legislative power until the end of a third four-year term in January 2015. Since the Texas Constitution does not limit the number of terms for which a governor can be elected, there was no guarantee that Perry's gubernatorial service would end in that year. As of late 2012, it was impossible to know whether Perry would seek a fourth term. Running against Perry in 2010, Democrat Bill White called for a constitutional amendment limiting a governor to not more than two four-year terms (as is the case with the president of the United States). A large majority of states have term limits on governors.

Given the level of attention and media coverage the office receives, you might be surprised to learn that, unlike the president of the United States, the Texas governor shares executive power with other elected executive officials. The U.S. president (with Senate approval) appoints and can independently remove members of a cabinet. In Texas, however, Article IV of the Texas Constitution establishes a multiheaded executive branch or plural executive over which the governor has only limited formal powers (see Figure 8.1).

As you learn about the workings of the executive branch of Texas government, consider an observation by Dr. Brian McCall, a former member of the Texas House of Representatives and now chancellor of the Texas State University System. In his book, *The Power of the Texas Governor: Connally to Bush*, McCall states: "It is widely reported that the governorship of Texas is by design a weak office. However, the strength of an individual governor's personality can overcome many of the limitations imposed on the office."[1] As you read this chapter, answer the following questions: Is the current head of Texas's executive branch a strong governor? How much power should other elected officials in this branch have?

Overview of the Governorship

LO1   Several of Texas's political traditions and institutions stem from the state's experiences after the Civil War. Even today, the state's executive structure shows the influence of anti-Reconstruction reactions against Governor E. J. Davis's administration (1870–1874). A large majority of Anglo Texans complained that numerous abuses of power occurred, committed by state officials reporting directly to Governor Davis.[2] This piece of Texas history helps explain why, after more than 140 years, many Texans still distrust the "strong" executive model of state government.

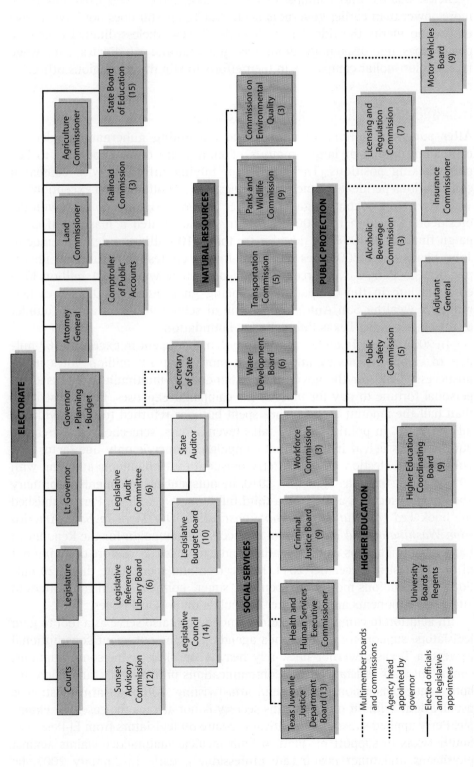

Figure 8.1 The Structure of Texas Government: Important Agencies and Offices (with number of governing body members).

Acts of the Texas legislature and appointment of every leader of state agencies, boards, and commissions since 2001 have given Governor Perry more power than earlier governors held;[3] but Texas still does not have a governor who merits the title "chief executive." Nevertheless, limited executive power does not discourage ambitious gubernatorial candidates who wage multimillion-dollar campaigns in their efforts to win this prestigious office.[4]

Gubernatorial Politics: Money Matters

After pumping millions of dollars into a winning gubernatorial election campaign, donors of large amounts of money are often appointed to key policymaking positions. The practice of buying influence with campaign contributions permeates American politics. Texas politics is no exception.

Even before becoming governor after Governor George W. Bush won the presidential election in 2000, Rick Perry demonstrated a mastery of campaign finance. In 1998, he raised more than $10 million to defeat Democrat John Sharp by 68,700 votes in a hard-fought contest for lieutenant governor. Key to Perry's 1.8 percent margin of victory was a $1.1 million loan obtained late in the campaign after being guaranteed by Dr. James Leininger, a wealthy San Antonio advocate of school vouchers and a founder of the conservative Texas Public Policy Foundation.[5]

In 2002, South Texas Democrat Tony Sanchez spent in excess of $67 million of campaign money and received more than 1.8 million votes in an unsuccessful bid for the governorship. Sanchez, a multimillionaire, used his personal fortune to pay for most of his campaign expenses. Perry raised less than half the amount that Sanchez spent but was returned to office with 2.6 million votes. In politics, money talks (even shouts, screeches, and screams), but Sanchez's defeat indicates that campaign finance is only one factor in a gubernatorial election. In 2006, Perry outspent four opponents and won with 39 percent of the vote. Again, in 2010, he outspent his opponents in primary and general elections as he won a third full term. A year later, Perry published the book *Fed Up! Our Rights, Our Constitution, Our Fight to Save America from Washington* and launched an unsuccessful campaign for the Republican Party's nomination as its presidential candidate in 2012.[6] Before dropping out of this contest in December 2011, he received and spent more than $20 million; many millions more were spent by "super" political action committees to attack his opponents and "educate" the public on political issues.

In addition to campaign donations, money can also serve as a tool to gain legislators' support for a governor's agenda. Lacking sufficient constitutional powers, a Texas governor must rely heavily on skills in personal relations, competent staff assistance from communications professionals, and talent for both gentle persuasion and forceful arm-twisting. Although arm-twisting is usually done without publicity, this secrecy is not always the case. For example, Perry applied substantial political pressure on legislators from El Paso and South Texas to support his plan to limit medical malpractice claims against physicians and other health-care professionals. Early in January 2003, he made public statements about funding a new medical school in El Paso and expanding the Regional Academic Health Center in the Rio Grande Valley. According to a newspaper report, the governor warned that such spending would depend on legislators in those areas supporting his plan to change the state's medical malpractice and liability laws.[7]

Election

Successful gubernatorial candidates must meet constitutional prerequisites, including minimum age (30 years), U.S. citizenship, and Texas residency (for five years immediately preceding the gubernatorial election), plus numerous extralegal restraints. Historically, governors elected after the Reconstruction Era were Democrats with a conservative-moderate political ideology. This mold for successful gubernatorial candidates seemed unbreakable, but William P. ("Bill") Clements Jr. (in 1978 and 1986) and George W. Bush (in 1994 and 1998) partially broke tradition by becoming Texas's first and second Republican governors, respectively, since E. J. Davis. (See the inside back cover of this text for a listing of Texas governors since 1874.) As conservative businesspeople, Clements and Bush resembled most of their Democratic predecessors in the Governor's Office; however, their Republicanism, and the fact that they had not previously held elective public office, represented a dramatic departure from the past.[8]

Republican Rick Perry entered the governor's mansion at the end of 2000 without having won a gubernatorial election. He had served for two years as lieutenant governor before Governor Bush was elected president of the United States. In 2006, four years after defeating Democratic candidate Tony Sanchez for his first full four-year term as governor, Perry was reelected. This time he defeated Democrat Chris Bell, Libertarian James Werner, and independent candidates Carole Keeton Strayhorn and Kinky Friedman.

Although Bell lost the gubernatorial contest, he hit two jackpots after suing the Perry campaign organization and the Republican Governors Association. At issue was a $1 million contribution from Houston builder Bob

How Do We Compare...in Qualifications for the Office of Governor?

Most Populous U.S. States	Minimum Age Required	Length of State Residency Required	U.S. States Bordering Texas	Minimum Age Required	Length of State Residency Required
California	18 years	5 years	Arkansas	30 years	7 years
Florida	30 years	7 years	Louisiana	25 years	5 years
New York	30 years	5 years	New Mexico	30 years	5 years
Texas	**30 years**	**5 years**	Oklahoma	31 years	10 years

Source: The Book of the States: 2012 (Lexington, Ky.: Council of State Governments, 2012), 216.

Perry (not related to the governor) to the association, which passed the money to Rick Perry's campaign shortly before the 2006 general election. The association was not a qualified political committee under Texas law, and Perry's campaign did not report the contribution to the Texas Ethics Commission. In 2010, Perry's campaign settled the suit by paying Bell $426,000.[9] After a trial in Austin, district judge John Dietz ordered the association to pay an additional $2 million to Bell.[10] As of late 2012, Dietz's order was under appeal. Ironically, Mitt Romney chaired the Republican Governors Association when Bob Perry's money was contributed, and Rick Perry chaired the association from 2008 until he resigned in August 2011 to compete against Romney and others for the GOP's presidential nomination.

In December 2008, Perry broke Bill Clements's eight-year record for the longest tenure as Texas's governor. Then in 2010, Perry was reelected governor for another four years, which will give him a tenure of 14 years in the Governor's Office if he serves to the end of that term.

Compensation and Benefits

The biennial state budget for fiscal years 2012–2013 set the governor's salary at $150,000 per year, which is the same as salaries for the state's attorney general and comptroller of public accounts. At the same time, Perry has opted to receive early retirement benefits worth more than $92,000 per year. This amount is based on Perry's length of military and state government service.[11]

State money pays the governor's expenses for official trips but not travel expenses for political campaigning or other nonofficial activities. Nevertheless, the Department of Public Safety provides personnel to protect the governor at all times. According to an Associated Press report, travel expenses and overtime for Perry's security detail during the 160 days he campaigned for the Republican Party's presidential nomination cost the state more than $3.6 million.[12] This information caused some Texans to insist that such expenses be covered by campaign funds.[13] The Texas Supreme Court ruled that the Department of Public Safety is not required to provide a detailed breakdown of how money for the governor's security is spent, because concern for that official's safety can override state law requiring disclosure of public records.[14]

Fringe benefits of the governor's office include staff and maintenance for a personal residence. In October 2007, while the historic governor's mansion near the Capitol was being renovated, Rick and Anita Perry moved into a $10,000-per-month, state-leased estate. They were there when an unknown arsonist set fire to the governor's mansion in the early hours of June 8, 2008. Because the damage was extensive, the Perrys remained in their temporary quarters until extensive repairs and reconstruction were completed in July 2012. The cost of refurbishment of the governor's mansion exceeded $25 million, including about $21.5 million in state money and the balance in private contributions to the Texas Governor's Mansion Restoration Fund. Annual state expenditure for the governor's cooks, housekeepers, and stewards amounts to about $200,000. In addition, many thousands of dollars are contributed each year by the governor's political supporters to cover the costs of luncheons, dinners, receptions, and other social activities at the Perrys' residence and elsewhere.[15]

The Texas Constitution forbids the governor and other executive officers (except the lieutenant governor) from holding any other civil or corporate office, and the governor may receive neither compensation nor the promise of pay for other employment after taking office. Nevertheless, governors do own property and make investments while serving. To avoid the appearance of conflict between their personal economic interests and the public's interest, both Bush and Perry placed their assets in blind trusts (a legal arrangement whereby holdings are administered by others and the elected official does not know which assets are in the trust). This action has not prevented Perry from being accused of benefitting from improper real estate deals while in office.[16] In March 2011, he was fined $1,500 by the Texas Ethics Commission for not reporting rental properties and for failing to file information regarding amounts owed on that property.[17]

Succession

Should a governor die, resign (as did George W. Bush after his 2000 election to the U.S. presidency), or be removed from office, or should a governor-elect refuse to take office or be permanently unable to fill the office, a successor serves for the remainder of the governor's four-year term. The lieutenant governor heads the constitutional order of succession. Next in line is the president pro tempore of the Senate. After these two officials, the legislature has designated the following line of succession: Speaker of the House, attorney general, and chief justices of the 14 courts of appeals in ascending numerical order, beginning with the chief justice of the First

Points to Ponder

Before Republican Rick Perry won election to four-year terms as Texas's first Aggie governor in 2002, 2006, and 2010, he

- graduated from Texas A&M University, where he was an Aggie yell leader;
- served as a U.S. Air Force pilot for five years and then engaged in farming and ranching;
- was elected as a Democrat and served six years in the Texas House of Representatives;
- was elected as a Republican for two terms as commissioner of agriculture; and
- was elected lieutenant governor in 1998 and became the governor when George W. Bush was elected U.S. president in 2000.

Court of Appeals and ending with the chief justice of the Fourteenth Court of Appeals, both of whom have their primary seats in Houston.

If the governor is temporarily unable to serve, is temporarily disqualified, or is impeached (see discussion below), the lieutenant governor exercises the powers of the governor until the governor becomes able or qualified to serve or is acquitted of impeachment charges. The lieutenant governor becomes acting governor while the governor is absent from the state. In the absence of both of these officials, the president pro tempore of the Texas Senate acts as governor. By custom, the Texas governor and lieutenant governor arrange their schedules so that, on at least one occasion during the tenure of a president pro tempore, both are conveniently out-of-state at the same time. In such circumstances, the president pro tempore of the Senate has the honor of becoming acting governor until the governor or lieutenant governor returns. Typically, the president pro tempore will host a day of festivities (largely financed by lobbyists) for supporters while first serving temporarily as governor. If the president pro tempore is absent, too, the Speaker of the House becomes acting governor.

Although the governor receives full pay when away from Texas, an acting governor receives an amount equal to the governor's daily pay (about $410) for each full day served. Because Governor Perry spent many days in other states during his campaign for nomination as the Republican Party's presidential candidate, the state paid Lieutenant Governor David Dewhurst a total of $29,589 between August 13, 2011, and January 19, 2012. For the days when both Perry and Dewhurst were absent from Texas, the president pro tempore of the Senate, Mike Jackson (R-Lake Jackson), received $2,876. Speaker Joe Straus served as acting governor for only parts of two days, so he did not receive compensation for his service.[18]

Removal from Office

Impeachment by the House of Representatives and conviction by the Senate form the only constitutionally prescribed method of forcing a Texas governor from office before the end of a term. Article XV, Section 1, of the Texas Constitution states, "The power of impeachment shall be vested in the House of Representatives." Each article of impeachment (similar to a grand jury's indictment) must be approved by a simple majority vote of the House. To remove the governor, one or more impeachment articles must be approved by a two-thirds majority vote of the senators present.

The penalty for conviction on an impeachment charge is removal from office and disqualification from holding any other appointive or elective office at state or local levels in Texas. But conviction does not bar the person from holding a federal office, such as U.S. senator or representative. After removal, a former governor who has been ousted for violating a criminal law may be tried and convicted in a regular trial. Violation of a civil law may subject the individual to a money judgment. Grounds for removing governors or other officials in the executive branch are not stipulated in the Texas Constitution. Impeachment proceedings are highly charged political affairs with legal overtones.

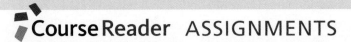

CourseReader ASSIGNMENTS

Log in to www.cengagebrain.com and open CourseReader to access the reading:

Impeachment of Governor Ferguson
Frederic A. Ogg

The impeachment of a governor does not happen very often, and it makes a great story when it does. Texas history is full of great stories, and the impeachment of Governor Ferguson is one of them. This event led to the election of the first female governor of Texas, Miriam Ferguson.

1. True or False: Governor James E. Ferguson was impeached during a regular session of the Texas legislature.

2. Did Governor Ferguson's animosity toward the University of Texas affect his impeachment?

Although all of Texas's state constitutions have provided for impeachment and removal of the governor, only Governor James E. "Pa" Ferguson has been impeached and removed. His troubles stemmed from misuse of state funds and a feud with faculty and administrators of the University of Texas. On September 25, 1917, the Senate convicted Ferguson on 10 articles of impeachment, one of which charged him with official misconduct. The other nine articles involved violations of the state's banking laws and use of state funds for private gain. Although removed from office, Ferguson did not stand trial in a criminal proceeding. Reporting the outrage of University of Texas students and powerful alumni when Ferguson used his veto power on the university's state appropriation, one historian noted: "Soon after Ferguson's 'war' with the University, the Ex-Students' Association voted to remain an independent organization, outside the sphere of state control, where it would be free to defend the University again if needed."[19]

Staff

Even though the Texas governor's hands are often tied when dealing with the state bureaucracy, the chief executive's personal staff continues to function under direct gubernatorial supervision. A governor's success in dealing with lobbyists, legislators, media reporters, and the general public depends largely on staff input and support. The **Governor's Office** staff directs programs mandated by the legislature, such as statewide planning and economic development (see Figure 8.2).

As the state's population grew and governors embellished their roles in the 20th century, staff size burgeoned. Although fiscal belt-tightening has required recent governors to cut back, staff numbers are still substantially

Governor's Office
The administrative organization through which the governor of Texas makes appointments, prepares a biennial budget recommendation, administers federal and state grants for crime prevention and law enforcement, and confers full and conditional pardons on recommendation of the Board of Pardons and Paroles.

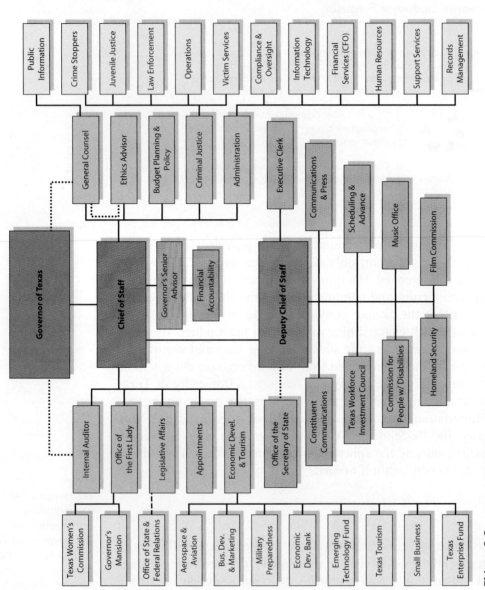

Figure 8.2 The Office of the Governor.

Public Information

Crime Stoppers

Juvenile Justice

Law Enforcement

Operations

Victim Services

Compliance & Oversight

Information Technology

Financial Services (CFO)

Human Resources

Support Services

Records Management

General Counsel

Ethics Advisor

Budget Planning & Policy

Criminal Justice

Administration

Executive Clerk

Communications & Press

Scheduling & Advance

Music Office

Film Commission

Governor of Texas

Chief of Staff

Governor's Senior Advisor

Financial Accountability

Deputy Chief of Staff

Homeland Security

Commission for People w/ Disabilities

Texas Workforce Investment Council

Constituent Communications

Internal Auditor

Office of the First Lady

Legislative Affairs

Appointments

Economic Devel. & Tourism

Office of the Secretary of State

Texas Women's Commission

Governor's Mansion

Office of State & Federal Relations

Aerospace & Aviation

Bus. Dev. & Marketing

Military Preparedness

Economic Dev. Bank

Emerging Technology Fund

Texas Tourism

Small Business

Texas Enterprise Fund

How Do We Compare...in Governor's Compensation and Staff Size?

Most Populous U.S. States	Governor's Annual Salary	Number of People Working in the Governor's Office	U.S. States Bordering Texas	Governor's Annual Salary	Number of People Working in the Governor's Office
California	$173,987	185	Arkansas	$ 86,890	67
Florida	$130,273	325	Louisiana	$130,000	93
New York	$179,000	180	New Mexico	$110,000	39
Texas	**$150,000**	**266**	Oklahoma	$147,000	30

Source: The Book of the States: 2012 (Lexington, Ky.: Council of State Governments, 2012), 217.

greater than in earlier years. From more than 300 on Governor Ann Richards's staff at the end of her term in January 1995, that number had dropped to 266 under Governor Perry 17 years later. But even the size of Perry's staff dwarfs the 68 full-time staff employees who served under Governor John Connally in the 1960s. Staff members are appointed and removed by the governor without legislative approval.

How much the governor's appointed assistants and unofficial advisers influence gubernatorial decisions is open to speculation. Protecting their chief is still a primary function of many staff assistants, particularly the press secretary and the director of appointments. All Texas governors have placed close friends and political associates in staff positions—persons who can be relied on for their loyalty to the chief executive. For example, Mike McKinney, Mike Toomey, and Rick Perry began serving in the House of Representatives in 1985. With two other conservative representatives, they became known as the "Pit Bulls" for their budget-cutting zeal as members of the House Appropriations Committee. After Perry became governor, he appointed McKinney as his first chief of staff. In 2003, Toomey (former chief of staff for Governor Bill Clements) replaced McKinney. Like other top staffers, Toomey and successors Deirdre Delisi (appointed in 2004), Brian Newby (2007), Jay Kimbrough (2008), Ray Sullivan (2009), and Jeff Boyd (2011) received a six-digit state salary and a large salary supplement from the governor's campaign fund.[20]

☑ Learning Check 8.1 (Answers on p. 333)

1. What is the constitutional procedure for removing a governor from office?
2. True or False: All Texas governors have placed close friends and political associates in staff positions.

★ Informal Powers of the Governor

LO2   A governor's ability to sway public opinion and to direct or influence the actions of other government officials depends on more than constitutional powers or powers conferred by the legislature. Informal powers are not based on law; rather, they stem from a governor's popularity with the public and are based on traditions, symbols, and ceremonies. As an Eagle Scout, runner, and bicyclist Governor Perry uses these personal interests to relate to Texans who share his Boy Scout values[21] and who respond to his challenge to "fight the war on fat"[22] by bicycle riding, jogging, and engaging in other physical activities. The governor's bike riding has not been without injury, however. In 2009, he broke his collarbone when he lost control of his mountain bike. Perry demonstrated his political abilities when he subsequently addressed law enforcement personnel and jokingly offered special thanks to bicycle patrol officers because of "the dangerous way they made a living."[23] The fact that Perry is a concealed-weapon licensee appeals to a large number of Texans but repels others. In 2010, while jogging near his temporary residence a few miles south of the Capitol, Perry used his .380 Ruger pistol to kill a coyote believed to be a menace to his daughter's dog.[24] Subsequently, the Connecticut-based gun manufacturer began marketing a "Coyote Special" model of Perry's semi-automatic pistol.[25]

Many of the governor's speeches and public appearances reflect his role as chief of state.[26] Of course, a governor cannot accept all invitations to deliver speeches or participate in dedications, banquets, and other public events. Within the limits of time and priorities, however, every governor does attempt to play the role of chief of state. The breadth and depth of this role cannot be fully measured, but its significance should not be underestimated in determining a governor's success. Effective governors must be able to make impressive speeches, to remain at ease while communicating in interviews with newspaper and television reporters, and to express their views in newspaper articles.[27] In the midst of his GOP primary campaign in 2010, however, Perry opted not to debate opposing candidates.[28] In that same year, he addressed the National Conference of Editorial Writers, but he refused to meet with editorial boards in Texas to answer questions concerning his policies and the campaign. (An editorial board usually is composed of the editorial page editor and editorial writers for a newspaper.) Perry's reasoning was that his time was limited and "it takes a lot of time to do 12 to 15 editorial boards."[29]

Public involvement of family members may be a source of support for a governor. Laura Bush, for example, enhanced her husband's image as a governor committed to improving education. Her First Lady's Family Literacy Initiative Program for Texas was especially designed to improve the reading skills of children from lower-income families living in disadvantaged neighborhoods. A former librarian, she was a founder of the Texas Book Festival, held annually on the grounds of the Capitol since 1995. Anita Perry, with a bachelor's and master's degree in nursing and 17 years of experience in various fields of nursing, often speaks on topics such as Alzheimer's disease, breast cancer awareness, and prevention of family violence. In addition, she has worked with her husband to host the annual Texas Conference for Women, at which women from all parts of Texas, as well as other states, meet to consider a wide range of women's interests, such as health care, personal growth, and professional development. She made history when she began work as a consultant for the Texas Association Against Sexual Assault. No wife of any earlier governor was employed while her husband was in office.[30] In 2011, Anita Perry encouraged her husband to seek the presidency and played an important role in his effort to obtain the GOP nomination.[31]

✓ Learning Check 8.2   (Answers on p. 333)

1. True or False: The governor's informal powers are not based on law.
2. True or False: Public involvement of family members may be a source of support for the governor.

★ Executive Powers of the Governor

The governor of Texas is inaugurated on the third Tuesday in January of every fourth year (January 20, 2015), and always in the odd-numbered year before a presidential election. In the inauguration ceremony, the governor swears "to cause the laws to be faithfully executed."

LO3

The governor's executive powers include nominating individuals to fill appointive offices (subject to approval of the Senate) and exercising limited control over state administration as authorized by the Texas Constitution and by statutes enacted by the Texas legislature. These powers are used for the following:

- Nominate (and in some cases remove) state officials
- Deal with problems caused by civil disorder and natural disasters
- Participate in state budget making and budget management
- Announce policies by issuing executive orders
- Make public proclamations for ceremonial and other purposes
- Promote the economic development of Texas

In some respects, the governor exercises executive powers like those wielded by heads of other large organizations (for example, university presidents, business chief executive officers, union leaders, or the U.S. president), though with obvious differences. Of course, the executive powers of the governor of Texas resemble those of the country's other 49 state governors; however, different state laws and state constitutions give some governors more executive powers and other governors less.

Appointive Power

One of the most significant executive powers of the Texas governor is **appointive power**. The same laws that create administrative agencies allow a governor to nominate friends and political supporters. The governor's ability to nominate citizens for these positions, subject to approval by the Texas Senate, remains both an important political tool and a fundamental management power.

The relationship between campaign contributions and gubernatorial appointments is documented in studies by Texans for Public Justice, an Austin-based, nonprofit organization. According to one study, during his first nine years as governor, Perry appointed nearly 4,000 people to 592 governing bodies or directors for boards, committees, councils, corporations, task forces, compact authorities, teams, groups, and departments. Among the appointees (some of whom received more than one appointment) were 921 individuals who contributed to the governor's political campaigns or who had a spouse who was a contributor. These donor-appointees contributed more than $17 million, which was 20 percent of the $83 million that Perry raised from January 2001 to February 2010. The top 10 average donations per appointee ranged from $48,342 for the Higher Education Incentives Task Force to $118,488 for the Parks and Wildlife Commission. The average donations from regents appointed to the top four university systems were Texas A&M, $113,127; University of Texas, $83,462; Texas Tech, $64,343; and University of Houston, $48,714. The ranking of the Texas A&M System above the University of Texas System is due to the large amount of campaign money transferred to Perry from Phil Gramm when the latter retired from the U.S. Senate. That made Gramm's wife, Wendy, Perry's top donor-appointee after her appointment as a regent of the Texas A&M system and later as a member of the state's Tax Reform Commission.[32]

Department heads appointed by the governor include the secretary of state; the adjutant general, who heads the Texas Military Forces; the executive director of the Office of State-Federal Relations; the executive commissioner of health and human services; commissioners of education, insurance, and firefighters' pensions; and the chief administrative law judge of the State Office of Administrative Hearings (SOAH). House Bill 7, passed by the 78th legislature in 2003 in its third special session, significantly increased the appointive power of the governor. It allows the governor, "notwithstanding other law," to designate and change the chairs of most state boards and commissions. The law also allows the governor to change designation of the chair of a board or commission from one member to another. Not affected by this law are the presiding officers of governing bodies of higher-education institutions and systems, along with those who advise or report to statewide-elected officials other than the governor.

Gubernatorial appointive power is not without certain legal and political limitations. The Texas Constitution requires that all appointees (except personal staff) be confirmed by the Senate with a two-thirds vote of senators present. This practice is known as "advice and consent," and it applies

appointive power
The authority to name a person to a government office. Most gubernatorial appointments require Senate approval by two-thirds of the members present.

to the appointees of U.S. presidents and governors in most other states as well. To avoid rejection by the Senate, the governor respects the tradition of senatorial courtesy by obtaining approval of the state senator representing a prospective appointee's senatorial district before sending that person's name forward for Senate confirmation. Political prudence also demands that the appointments director in the Governor's Office conduct a background check on the appointee to avoid possible embarrassment—as occurred when, for example, Governor Dolph Briscoe appointed a dead man to a state board.

Governors may try to circumvent the Senate by making appointments while the Senate is not in session. The Texas Constitution, however, requires that these **recess appointments** be submitted to the Senate for confirmation within 10 days after it convenes for a regular or special session, though confirmation hearings do not have to occur immediately. Failure of the Senate to confirm a recess appointment prevents the governor from reappointing that person to the same position.

Chairs of governing boards of state agencies are commonly appointed by the governor. Thus, Dr. Don McLeroy (R-Bryan), a long-time member of the popularly elected State Board of Education, was appointed by Governor Perry to chair that board after the Senate adjourned in 2007; but McLeroy was not confirmed by the Senate when it convened in 2009. Perry made another recess appointee, Gail Lowe (R-Lampasas) to chair the board, but she was not confirmed in 2011. Again, Perry waited until after the Senate adjourned that year and then named Barbara Cargill (R-The Woodlands) as chair of the board.[33]

Senate approval is not required for appointment of the nonvoting, student member on the board of regents for each of the state's university systems, such as the Texas A&M University System, which consists of 10 universities and a health science center. In 2011, however, such an appointment did provoke strong criticism of Perry. Section 51.355 of the Texas Education Code stipulates that the student government of each general academic teaching institution and medical and dental unit in a university system shall select five applicants for student regent and send their applications to the chancellor of that system. From these applications, the chancellor picks two or more applicants and forwards their applications to the governor.

Although the governor may ask to review all applications received by a student government, the code does not authorize appointment of someone who applies directly to the governor. Nevertheless, Perry opted to appoint Fernando Treviño, Jr., a conservative activist enrolled at Texas A&M University in College Station, even though he had submitted his application to the Governor's Office rather than to the student government of the university. (For more on Fernando Treviño, Jr., see "Students in Action" in Chapter 4, "Political Parties.") By a vote of nine to five, the Texas A&M student senate adopted a resolution criticizing Perry's appointment, but the governor did not back down. The Education Code does not include penalty provisions that would apply to the governor in this situation.[34]

recess appointment
An appointment made by the governor when the Texas legislature is not in session.

One limitation on the governor's appointive power is that the members of most state boards and commissions serve for six years, with overlapping terms of office. Thus, only one-third of the members finish a term every two years. A first-term governor must work with carryovers from previous administrations, even if such carryovers are not supportive of the new governor. By January 2007, after six years in office, Governor Perry had enhanced his power because he had appointed all members of the state's many appointive boards and commissions. Data provided by the Office of the Governor on gender classification of Perry's 5,043 appointments as of May 2012 (not including the Interstate Oil and Gas Compact Commission and a few others), showed that 76 percent were men and 24 percent were women. Racial/ethnic classification of the appointees was as follows: Anglo, 69 percent; Latino, 17 percent; African American, 11 percent; and Asian or other, 3 percent.

The appointive power of the governor extends to filling vacancies for elected heads of the executive departments, members of the Railroad Commission, members of the State Board of Education, and judges (except those for county, municipal, and justice of the peace courts). These appointees serve until they are elected or replaced at the next general election. In addition, when a U.S. senator from Texas dies, resigns, or is removed from office before his or her term expires, the governor fills the vacancy with an interim appointee. That appointee serves until a successor is elected in a special election called by the governor. A vacancy in either chamber of the Texas legislature or in the Texas delegation to the U.S. House of Representatives does not result in an interim appointment. Instead, the governor calls a special election to fill the position. The winner of the special election serves until after the next regularly scheduled general election.

Removal Power

In creating numerous boards and commissions, the legislature gives the governor extensive appointive power but no independent **removal power** over most state agencies. This limitation restricts gubernatorial control over the state bureaucracy. The legislature limits the governor's independent removal power to members of the governor's staff and three statutory officials whose offices were created by the legislature: the executive director of the Department of Housing and Community Affairs, the executive commissioner of health and human services, and the insurance commissioner.

Elected department heads and their subordinates are not subject to the governor's removal power. Moreover, the governor's hands are tied in directly removing most board and commission officials. The governor may informally pressure an appointee to resign or accept another appointment, but this pressure is not as effective as the power of direct removal. Except for the few positions described previously, governors may not remove someone appointed by a predecessor. They may remove their own appointees with consent of two-thirds of the state senators present; however, this authority still falls short of independent removal power.

removal power
Authority to remove an official from office. In Texas, the governor's removal power is limited to staff members, some agency heads, and his or her appointees with the sent of the Senate.

Military Power

Article 4, Section 7, of the Texas Constitution states that the governor "shall be Commander-in-Chief of the military forces of the State, except when they are called into actual service of the United States." Branches of the Texas Military Forces (with approximate personnel numbers) are the Texas Army National Guard (19,000), the Texas Air National Guard (3,000), and the Texas State Guard (2,000).

The president of the United States can order units of the Army National Guard and Air National Guard to federal service in time of war or national emergency. Pay for National Guard personnel while on active duty and for training periods (usually one weekend each month) is the same as that for regular military personnel of the same rank. Texas State Guard units serve within Texas and support the other two branches of the Texas Military Forces. For the most part, State Guard soldiers are not paid for training activities, but when activated by the governor, they receive full pay.

A race riot in June 1943, when all Texas National Guard personnel were in federal service because of World War II, caused acting governor A. M. Aiken to use Texas State Guard units to impose **martial law** (temporary rule by state military forces and suspension of civil authority) on Beaumont.[35] The action was taken according to the constitutional provision that the governor "shall have power to call forth the militia to execute the laws of the State, to suppress insurrections, and to repel invasions." Until the constitution was amended in 1999, this power extended to "protecting the frontier from hostile incursions by Indians or other predatory bands." As circumstances demand, the governor authorizes the mobilization of Army and Air National Guard personnel to perform relief and rescue service in counties hit by hurricanes, floods, fires, and other natural disasters. In recent years, units of Texas National Guard soldiers have served in Afghanistan, Iraq, and other countries. In March 2010, Governor Perry ordered Texas Air National Guard helicopters to the Rio Grande border area to help law enforcement officers block extension of drug-related violence from Mexico into the state.

Law Enforcement Power

In Texas, law enforcement is primarily a responsibility of city police departments and county sheriffs' departments. Nevertheless, the Texas Department of Public Safety (DPS), headed by the Public Safety Commission, is an important law enforcement agency. The governor appoints the commission's five members, subject to Senate approval. The director of public safety is appointed by the commission and oversees more than 8,000 personnel in the DPS. Included among the department's responsibilities are highway traffic supervision, driver licensing, and criminal law enforcement in cooperation with local and federal agencies.

If circumstances demand swift but limited police action, the governor is empowered to assume command of the Texas Rangers, a division of DPS composed of a small number of highly trained law enforcement personnel operating statewide. Although the Texas legislature has authorized

martial law
Temporary rule by military authorities when civil authorities are unable to handle a riot or other civil disorder.

150 rangers, as of July 2012, membership in this elite group totaled only 123: 121 men (98 Anglo, 16 Latino, seven African American) and two Anglo women.

Budgetary Power

Gubernatorial **budgetary power** is subordinated in part to the legislature's prerogative of controlling the state's purse strings. By statutory requirement, the governor (assisted by personnel in the Budget, Planning, and Policy Division of the Governor's Office) and the Legislative Budget Board should prepare separate budgets for consideration by the legislature. Texas law requires distribution of the governor's budget to each legislator before delivery of the governor's State of the State message. Traditionally, both the House and the Senate have been inclined to give greater respect to the Legislative Budget Board's spending proposals.

The Texas governor's principal control over state spending comes from constitutional power to veto an entire appropriations bill or to use the **line-item veto** to eliminate individual budget items. In June 2011, after the end of a special session, Perry announced 35 line-item vetoes; but 33 were vetoes of **contingency riders** for bills that had not been passed by the legislature. The other two line-item vetoes were for contingency riders for bills that had been passed but were vetoed by the governor.[36] Republican control of the 82nd legislature and Perry's influence on drafting the appropriations bill (H.B. 1) made ordinary line-item vetoes unnecessary.

Executive Orders and Proclamations

Although the Texas Constitution identifies the governor as the "Chief Executive Officer of the State," it does not empower him or her to tell other state officials what they must do unless such action is authorized by the legislature. Nevertheless, governors use executive orders to set policy within the executive branch and to create or abolish task forces, boards, commissions, and councils. Each **executive order** is identified by the governor's initials and is numbered chronologically.

In September 2009, for example, Perry issued his 73rd executive order (RP73), calling for "a comprehensive review of higher education cost efficiency." This order directed the Texas Higher Education Coordinating Board, in cooperation with public colleges and universities, to look at "opportunities for achieving cost efficiencies." Subjects under review were state funding for higher education based on courses completed, faculty workload, distance learning, alternatives to new campuses, energy use, and cost of instructional materials. One of Perry's more recent executive orders was RP75, issued in August 2011. This order relates to the establishment and support of WGU Texas (a partnership with the Western Governors University). WGU Texas is a nonprofit independent university offering "online degrees based on demonstrated competence as opposed to degrees based on credit hours, clock hours or grades."[37]

---

budgetary power
The governor is supposed to submit a state budget to the legislature at the beginning of each regular session. When an appropriation bill is enacted by the legislature and certified by the comptroller of public accounts, the governor may veto the whole document or individual items.

line-item veto
Action by the governor to eliminate an individual budget item while permitting enactment of other parts of an appropriation bill.

contingency rider
Authorization for spending state money to finance provisions of a bill if it passes.

executive order
The governor issues executive orders to set policy within the executive branch and to create task forces, councils, and other bodies.

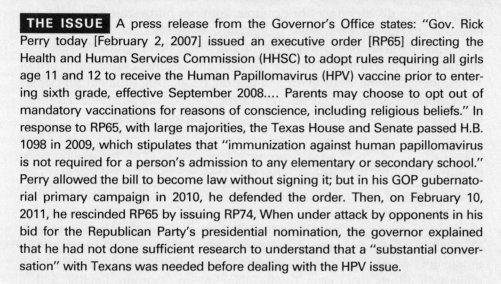

Point/Counterpoint

THE ISSUE A press release from the Governor's Office states: "Gov. Rick Perry today [February 2, 2007] issued an executive order [RP65] directing the Health and Human Services Commission (HHSC) to adopt rules requiring all girls age 11 and 12 to receive the Human Papillomavirus (HPV) vaccine prior to entering sixth grade, effective September 2008.... Parents may choose to opt out of mandatory vaccinations for reasons of conscience, including religious beliefs." In response to RP65, with large majorities, the Texas House and Senate passed H.B. 1098 in 2009, which stipulates that "immunization against human papillomavirus is not required for a person's admission to any elementary or secondary school." Perry allowed the bill to become law without signing it; but in his GOP gubernatorial primary campaign in 2010, he defended the order. Then, on February 10, 2011, he rescinded RP65 by issuing RP74, When under attack by opponents in his bid for the Republican Party's presidential nomination, the governor explained that he had not done sufficient research to understand that a "substantial conversation" with Texans was needed before dealing with the HPV issue.

Should the Governor Direct by Executive Order the Vaccination of Girls Against HPV?

Arguments For RP65

- The three-shot Gardasil vaccine is effective against HPV strains, which cause 70 percent of cervical cancer cases and 90 percent of genital warts cases.
- Approximately one-fourth of all male and female Americans in the 15- to 24-year age group are infected with HPV.
- State spending for vaccinating girls would be much less than the cost of treating HPV-related cervical diseases that annually kill about 400 Texas women.

On May 8, 2007, while speaking to reporters about legislators who voted for H.B. 1098, Governor Perry stated: "They have sent me a bill that will ensure three-quarters of our young women will be susceptible to a virus that not only kills hundreds each year, but causes great discomfort to thousands more."

—"Governor Rick Perry's Remarks on the Decision Regarding House Bill 1098," http://www.statesman.com/blogs/content/shared-gen/blogs/austin/capitolpressreleases/entries/2007/05/08/

Arguments Against RP65

- Creating regulations to protect Texans against diseases is a function of the legislative branch of government, not the executive branch.
- Vaccination would reduce fear of infection and encourage sexual activity.
- Merck, the only company marketing an HPV vaccine in 2007, contributed $6,000 to Governor Perry's campaign fund in 2005; and it employed Mike Toomey, Perry's former chief of staff, as a lobbyist.

In a message to Governor Perry concerning RP65, Nick Funnell of Longview wrote: "Aside from endorsing sexual conduct in young girls, the requirement of this vaccination is an invasion into the people's rights—it's one big step toward big government."

—Quoted by Kelly Shannon in "Thousands Message Perry on HPV Order," *Austin American-Statesman,* March 10, 2007

Another instrument of executive authority is the **proclamation**, an official public announcement often used for ceremonial purposes (for example, proclaiming Cowboy Poetry Week for April 19–25, 2009). Proclaiming a region to be a disaster area (for example, counties hit by Hurricanes Ike and Dolly in 2008), qualifies some individuals, businesses, and local governments for financial assistance). In 2011 and 2012, Perry issued disaster proclamations concerning a statewide drought and wildfires affecting much of Texas, including the Bastrop area in central Texas. Other uses of proclamations include calling special sessions of the legislature and special elections and announcing the ratification of constitutional amendments.

Economic Development

After a series of mismanagement problems within the Texas Department of Economic Development, Perry sought direct control over efforts to attract investment and move businesses to Texas from other states and countries. The 78th legislature abolished the department and placed the state's economic development program within the Governor's Office. Perry intervened directly in efforts to bring a Toyota plant to San Antonio. Finally, with a $133 million incentive package for Toyota and $28.5 million for an 8-mile rail spur and other infrastructure improvements, Toyota Motor Company announced on February 5, 2003, that it would build a pickup truck plant in San Antonio.[38]

At Perry's urging, the 78th legislature established the Texas Enterprise Fund (TEF) by taking $295 million from the state's "rainy day" fund (an account intended to pay for state operations in times of emergency) and using it to attract or retain industry in fiscal years 2004 and 2005. Other multi-million-dollar appropriations for TEF were made in 2005, 2007, 2009, and 2011. To complement this money, Perry established TexasOne, a nonprofit, tax-exempt corporation that operates with directors appointed by the governor. Its primary mission is to attract businesses from other states and countries by marketing economic opportunities in Texas. Perry invited major companies and business-related groups to support the fund for three years with a range of annual tax-deductible contributions.[39] To recruit out-of-state companies, prospective contributors were informed that visiting executives would be given "red carpet treatment throughout: flight into Texas, limousine transportation, four-star hotel accommodations, reception on arrival, evening with local and state leadership, . . . etc."[40]

Under pressure from Governor Perry, the 79th legislature created the Emerging Technology Fund (ETF) in 2005 and appropriated $200 million to cover fiscal years 2006 and 2007. Similar appropriations have been made in subsequent legislative sessions. ETF is designed to help small to midsize companies develop new technology for a wide range of high-tech industries. (For more on ETF, see this chapter's Selected Reading, "The Low Politics of High Tech in the Lone Star State.")

proclamation
A governor's official public announcement (such as calling a special election or declaring a disaster area).

Governor Rick Perry's ceremonial signing of HB 274, the so-called "Loser Pay" Tort Reform Bill, on May 30, 2011, the last day of the 82nd legislature. Standing immediately behind Perry (left to right) are Representative Paul D. Workman (R-Austin), Representative Connie Scott (R-Corpus Christi), and Senator Joan Huffman (R-Houston).

(© Marjorie Kamys Cotera/Daemmrich Photos/The Image Work)

 Learning Check 8.3 (Answers on p. 333)

1. True or False: Most gubernatorial appointments must be approved by a two-thirds vote of the House of Representatives.
2. What constitutional power allows the governor to exercise control over state spending?

★ Legislative Powers of the Governor

LO4

Perhaps the most stringent test of a Texas governor's capacity for leadership involves handling legislative matters. The governor has no direct lawmaking authority, but **legislative power** is exercised through four major functions authorized by the Texas Constitution:

- Delivering messages to the legislature
- Signing bills and concurrent resolutions
- Vetoing bills and concurrent resolutions
- Calling special sessions of the legislature

However, the success of a legislative program depends heavily on a governor's ability to bargain with influential lobbyists and legislative leaders (in particular, the Speaker of the House of Representatives and the lieutenant governor).[41]

legislative power
A power of the governor exercised through messages delivered to the Texas legislature, vetoes of bills and concurrent resolutions, and calls for special sessions of the legislature.

Message Power

Article 4, Section 9, of the Texas Constitution requires the governor to deliver a State of the State address at the "commencement" (beginning) of each regular session of the legislature, but this is not interpreted to mean the first day of the session. On occasion, the governor may also present other messages, either in person or in writing, to the legislature. A governor's success in using **message power** to promote a harmonious relationship with the legislature depends on such variables as the timing of messages concerning volatile issues, the support of the governor's program by the chairs of legislative committees, and the governor's personal popularity with the public.

Bill-Signing Power

While the legislature is in session, the governor indicates approval by signing bills and concurrent resolutions within 10 days (not counting Sundays) after receiving them. But bills and concurrent resolutions that are neither signed nor vetoed by the governor during that period become law anyway. After the legislature adjourns, however, the governor has 20 days (counting Sundays) to veto pending bills and concurrent resolutions.

Most media coverage of signings is the result of "photo ops" staged in Austin or elsewhere weeks or even months after official signings. Defenders of these ceremonial re-signings contend that the events help inform Texans about new laws. But critics insist that the principal objective of the signings is to give favorable publicity to the governor, bill sponsors, and others who wish to be identified with the legislation.[42]

Veto Power

The governor's most direct legislative tool is the power to *block* legislation with a veto. During a legislative session, the governor vetoes a bill by returning it unsigned (with written reasons for not signing) to the chamber in which the bill originated. If the legislature is no longer in session, a vetoed bill is filed with the secretary of state. **Veto power** takes different forms. In addition to general veto authority, the governor has the line-item veto (described earlier in this chapter), which can be used to eliminate one or more specific spending authorizations in an appropriation bill, while permitting enactment of the remainder of the budget. Using the line-item veto power to refuse funding for a specific agency, the governor can effectively eliminate that agency. This line-item veto authority places the governor in a powerful bargaining position with individual legislators in the delicate game of **pork-barrel politics**. That is, the governor may strike a bargain with a senator or representative in which the chief executive promises not to deny funding for a lawmaker's pet project (the pork). In return, the legislator agrees to support a bill favored by the governor.

During a session, the governor's veto can be overriden by a two-thirds majority vote in both houses; but overriding a veto has occurred only once since the administration of Governor W. Lee O'Daniel (1939–1941). In 1979, the House and Senate overrode Governor Clements's veto of a bill giving

message power
The governor's State of the State address at the "commencement" of a legislative session and messages delivered in person or in writing are examples of the gubernatorial exercise of message power to communicate with legislators and the public.

veto power
Authority of the governor to reject a bill or concurrent resolution passed by the legislature.

pork-barrel politics
A legislator's tactic to obtain funding for a pet project, usually designed to be of special benefit for the legislator's district.

Comal County commissioners power to establish hunting and fishing regulations for the county. The strong veto power that the Texas Constitution gives to the governor and the governor's informal power of threatening to veto a bill are formidable weapons for dealing with legislators.

The governor of Texas may also exercise a **postadjournment** veto by rejecting any pending legislation within 20 days after a session has ended. Because most bills pass late in a legislative session, the postadjournment veto allows the governor to veto measures without threat of any challenge. It is therefore almost absolute.

Throughout most of the 77th legislature's regular session in 2001, Governor Perry vetoed only a few bills. But in what some critics termed the "Father's Day Massacre," he exercised 78 postadjournment vetoes at 9 p.m. on the last possible day to do so (June 17). Surpassing Governor Clements's 59 vetoes in 1989, Perry's total of 82 vetoes in 2001 set a record. For the following five regular legislative sessions, his veto totals were 48 (78th, 2003), 19 (79th, 2005), 51 (80th, 2007), 35 (81st, 2009), and 24 (82nd, 2011).[43] One of Perry's most controversial vetoes in 2011 killed H.B. 242, which he condemned as "a government effort to micromanage the behavior of adults." Passed by a House vote of 80–61 and a Senate vote of 28–3, this bill prohibited texting while driving.

Special-Sessions Power

Included among the governor's powers is the authority to call special sessions of the legislature. The Texas Constitution places no restrictions on the number of special sessions a governor may call, but the length of a special session is limited to 30 days. During a special session, the legislature may consider only those matters the governor specifies in the call or subsequently presents to the legislature. The two exceptions to this requirement of gubernatorial approval are confirmation of appointments and impeachment proceedings.

postadjournment veto
Rejection by the governor of a pending bill or concurrent resolution during the 20 days after a legislative session ends.

 Learning Check 8.4 **(Answers on p. 333)**

1. True or False: During a session, the governor's veto can be overridden by a two-thirds majority vote in the House and in the Senate.
2. How can the legislature be convened for a special session?

 # Judicial Powers of the Governor

The governor exercises a few formal judicial powers, including the power to do the following:

LO5

- Fill vacancies on state (but not county or city) courts
- Play a limited but outdated role in removing judges and justices
- Perform acts of clemency to undo or reduce sentences given to some convicted criminals

Appointment and Removal of Judges and Justices

More than half of Texas's state judges and justices first serve on district courts and higher appellate courts through gubernatorial appointment to fill a vacancy caused by a judge's death, resignation, or removal from office. Governors have used this power to diversify the state's judicial system. For example, in 2001, Wallace B. Jefferson became the first African American to serve on the Texas Supreme Court after Governor Perry appointed him to replace Justice Alberto Gonzales. Perry's stamp on that court is reflected by the fact that nearly all his appointees have won subsequent election.[44]

Although most appointees to appellate courts have had previous judicial experience, Governor Perry appointed Don Willett to the Texas Supreme Court in 2005. Willett had never held a judicial position, although he had served as an assistant attorney general and is a close friend of Mike Toomey, Perry's former chief of staff.[45] Texas voters elected Willett to a six-year term on that court in 2006 and reelected him in 2012.

According to Article XV, Section 8, of the Texas Constitution, the governor may remove any jurist "on address of two-thirds of each house of the Legislature for willful neglect of duty, incompetence, habitual drunkenness, oppression in office, or other reasonable cause which shall not be sufficient ground for impeachment." Governors and the legislature have not used this process for many years. Instead, they have left removal of state jurists to other proceedings and to voters. (See Chapter 10, "Laws, Courts, and Justice," for a discussion of the disciplining and removal of judges and justices.)

Acts of Executive Clemency

Until the mid-1930s, Texas governors had extensive powers to undo or lessen punishment for convicted criminals through acts of clemency that set aside or reduced court-imposed penalties. A constitutional amendment adopted in 1936 reduced the clemency powers of the governor and established the Board of Pardons and Paroles, which is now a division of the Texas Department of Criminal Justice.

Release of a prisoner before completion of a sentence on condition of good behavior is called **parole**. The seven-member Board of Pardons and Paroles grants parole without action by the governor. The governor, however, may perform various acts of executive clemency that set aside or reduce a court-imposed penalty through pardon, reprieve, or commutation of sentence. Only if recommended by the Board of Pardons and Paroles can the governor grant a full pardon or a conditional pardon; however, pardons are rare in Texas. In fiscal year 2011, for example, the board considered 190 requests for full pardon and recommended pardon in 36 of these cases. Governor Perry announces pardons around Christmas each year. In 2011, he granted eight.[46]

A **full pardon** releases a person from all consequences of a criminal act and restores the same rights enjoyed by persons who have not been convicted

parole
Supervised release from prison before completion of a sentence; good behavior of the parolee is a condition of release.

full pardon
On recommendation of the Board of Pardons and Paroles, the governor may grant a full pardon. This act of executive clemency releases a convicted person from all consequences of a criminal act and restores the same rights enjoyed by others who have not been convicted of a crime.

of crimes. In 2010, Governor Perry granted a full pardon to Timothy Cole after DNA evidence proved he had been wrongfully imprisoned for more than 13 years. Unfortunately, Cole died in prison nine years before he was cleared by DNA testing and pardoned.[47] Attorney General Greg Abbott subsequently issued an opinion stating that parole could be granted posthumously. Under a **conditional pardon**, the governor may withhold certain rights, such as being licensed to practice a selected occupation or profession. Acting independently, the governor may revoke a conditional pardon if the terms of that pardon are violated.

The governor may also independently grant one 30-day **reprieve** in a death sentence case. A reprieve temporarily suspends execution of a condemned prisoner, but governors seldom grant reprieves. Ann Richards refused nearly all requests for reprieve from the 48 condemned men executed during her four years as governor.

Perry's decision not to grant a reprieve to Cameron Todd Willingham, who was executed in 2004, subjected the governor to substantial criticism when subsequent evidence suggested that Willingham might have been innocent. In the midst of controversy over the Willingham case, former governor Mark White stated in an interview on National Public Radio that it is time for Texas to reconsider use of the death sentence. White had strongly supported capital punishment while he was governor (1983–1987).[48]

If recommended by the Board of Pardons and Paroles, the governor may reduce a penalty through **commutation of sentence** and may remit (return) forfeitures of money or property surrendered as punishment. After having granted only one death-penalty commutation in his administration, in June 2005, Governor Perry commuted the sentences of 28 death row inmates convicted of crimes committed when they were younger than age 18. He took this action after the U.S. Supreme Court ruled in *Roper v. Simmons* 543 U.S. 551 (2005) that people cannot be executed if they were minors at the time of the crime. The court held that execution of these individuals would violate the Eighth Amendment's ban on cruel and unusual punishment.

In 2009, the Board of Pardons and Paroles voted 5 to 2 to recommend that the death sentence for Robert Lee Thompson be commuted to life in prison. Thompson was an accomplice in a fatal robbery and was convicted under the state's "law of parties." Although he did not do the killing, he participated in the robbery. Governor Perry rejected the board's recommendation, and Thompson was executed.[49]

☑ Learning Check 8.5 (Answers on p. 333)

1. True or False: A vacancy on a Texas district court or higher appellate court is filled by gubernatorial appointment.
2. Which Texas official has power to independently grant one 30-day reprieve in a death sentence case?

conditional pardon
On recommendation of the Board of Pardons and Paroles, the governor may grant a conditional pardon. This act of clemency releases a convicted person from the consequences of his or her crime but does not restore all rights, as in the case of a full pardon.

reprieve
An act of executive clemency that temporarily suspends execution of a sentence.

commutation of sentence
On the recommendation of the Board of Pardons and Paroles, the governor may commute (reduce) a sentence.

★ The Plural Executive

LO6 Politically, the governor is Texas's highest-ranking officer; but the governor and the lieutenant governor share executive power with four elected department heads. These department heads (with annual salaries budgeted by the legislature for the biennial period covering fiscal years 2012–2013) are the attorney general ($150,000), comptroller of public accounts ($150,000), commissioner of the General Land Office ($137,500), and commissioner of agriculture ($137,500). The secretary of state is appointed by, and serves at the pleasure of, the governor. The salary for the secretary of state in fiscal years 2012–2013 was $125,880. The positions of governor, lieutenant governor, comptroller of public accounts, and commissioner of the General Land Office are created in Article IV of the Texas Constitution. The commissioner of agriculture holds an office created by statute, now located in the Texas Agriculture Code. These executive officials are referred to collectively as the state's **plural executive**. Also performing executive functions are the three elected members of the Railroad Commission of Texas and the 15 elected members of the State Board of Education. (For information on these two agencies, see Chapter 9, "Public Policy and Administration.")

Elected department heads are largely independent of gubernatorial control. However, should one of these positions become vacant in an official's term of office, with the advice and consent of the Senate, the governor appoints a successor until the next general election.

Points to Ponder

Since 1846, following annexation by the United States in 1845, Texas has had the following numbers of state executive officials (through September 2012):

- 62 governors
- 42 lieutenant governors
- 50 attorneys general
- 26 comptrollers of public accounts
- 28 commissioners of the General Land Office
- 11 commissioners of agriculture (office created by the legislature in 1907)
- 92 secretaries of state

Source: Texas Almanac 2012–2013 (Denton: Texas State Historical Association, 2012), 475–479; Office of the Commissioner of Agriculture; and websites for the executive departments.

plural executive
The governor, elected department heads, and the secretary of state, as provided by the Texas Constitution and statutes.

The Lieutenant Governor

Some observers consider the **lieutenant governor** to be the most powerful Texas official, yet the lieutenant governor functions less in the executive branch than in the legislative branch, where he serves as president of the Senate. The Texas Constitution requires the Senate to convene within 30 days whenever a vacancy occurs in the lieutenant governor's office. Senators then elect one of their members to fill the office as acting lieutenant governor until the next general election. Thus, the Senate chose Senator Bill Ratliff to replace Lieutenant Governor Rick Perry when Perry succeeded Governor George W. Bush following the 2000 presidential election.

The annual state salary for the office of lieutenant governor is only $7,200, the same as that paid to members of the legislature. Like legislators, the lieutenant governor may also hold a paying job in private business or practice a profession. For example, from 1992 to 1998, Lieutenant Governor Bob Bullock was affiliated with the law firm of Scott, Douglass, & McConnico, LLP, in Austin, from which he received a six-figure annual salary.

Many Texas lobbyists and members of the business community supported John Sharp, a Democrat and former comptroller of public accounts, in the 2002 race for lieutenant governor; but multimillionaire Republican David Dewhurst, the state's commissioner of the General Land Office at that time, won the November general election. To finance his campaign, Dewhurst used more than $10 million of his own money plus $13 million that he borrowed. After his victory, Dewhurst recouped some of this money at fundraising events where Sharp's former supporters "caught the late train" by making postelection contributions to Dewhurst.[50] In 2006, Dewhurst won a second term; and he was reelected in 2010. In 2012, Dewhurst continued as lieutenant governor after Ted Cruz defeated him in a run-off primary contest for nomination as GOP candidate for the office of U.S. senator.

The Attorney General

One of Texas's most visible and powerful officeholders is the **attorney general.** Whether joining lawsuits to overturn federal health care reform, arguing affirmative action questions in court, or trying to resolve redistricting disputes, the state's chief lawyer is a major player in making many important public policy decisions. This officer represents the state in civil litigation and issues advisory opinions on legal questions when requested by state and local authorities.

With more than 4,000 employees, the Office of the Attorney General gives advice concerning the constitutionality of many pending bills. The governor, heads of state agencies, and local government officials also request opinions from the attorney general on the scope of an agency's or official's jurisdiction and the interpretation of vaguely worded laws. Although neither judges nor other officials are bound by these opinions, the attorney general's rulings are considered authoritative unless overruled by court decisions or new laws. Another power of the attorney general is to initiate, in a district court, quo warranto proceedings, which challenge an official's right to hold public office.

lieutenant governor
Popularly elected constitutional official who serves as president of the Senate and is first in the line of succession if the office of governor becomes vacant before the end of a term.

attorney general
The constitutional official elected to head the Office of the Attorney General, which represents the state government in lawsuits and provides legal advice to state and local officials.

Such action may lead to removal of an officeholder who lacks a qualification set by law or who is judged guilty of official misconduct. Among its many functions, the Office of the Attorney General enforces child-support orders issued by state courts; and it administers the Crime Victims' Compensation Fund.

San Antonio lawyer John Cornyn, a Republican and former Texas Supreme Court justice, was elected as attorney general in 1998. When Cornyn decided to run for a seat in the U.S. Senate in 2002, the Republican Party nominated Supreme Court Justice Greg Abbott for attorney general. In the November election of that year, Abbott defeated Democrat Kirk Watson, a former Austin mayor. Before Abbott began his elected term in January 2003, Governor Perry appointed him to serve for a few weeks in that office following Cornyn's resignation in November 2002.

Upon his appointment, Abbott declared that he was "philosophically very committed to open government" and that he would enforce the state's open records laws for the benefit of the public and the media. This statement was welcomed by the press and public interest groups that had complained about lack of access to information concerning government operations.[51]

Abbott won a second term in 2006 and was reelected in 2010. Among his many advisory opinions is one that declares that a state representative is not legally required to resign from his or her House seat upon announcing his or her candidacy for governor.[52] A 2009 opinion issued by Abbott disappointed about 250,000 retired educators. He ruled that they could not receive a one-time $500 supplemental payment, because the legislature did not properly appropriate this money.[53] On March 23, 2010, the same day that President Barack Obama signed the controversial health-care reform bill, Abbott joined other state attorneys general in a lawsuit challenging the constitutionality of this sweeping Patient Protection and Affordable Care Act.[54] The U.S. Supreme Court upheld the law's constitutionality in the case of National Federation of Independent Business v. Sebelius, 567 U.S. ___ (2012). In 2011 and 2012, Abbott took a strong stand for the Texas legislature's congressional and legislative redistricting actions, and he fought the U.S. Department of Justice in defense of Texas's Voter ID law. In the course of voter ID litigation, Abbott's office erred by releasing about 6.5 million Social Security numbers to lawyers challenging the Voter ID law. Luckily, the mistake was detected before any identity damage was done.

The Comptroller of Public Accounts

One of the most powerful elected officers in Texas government is the **comptroller of public accounts**, the state's chief accounting officer and tax collector. After a biennial appropriation bill passes by a simple majority vote in the House and Senate, the Texas Constitution requires the comptroller's certification that expected revenue will be collected to cover all of the budgeted expenditures. Otherwise, an appropriation must be approved by a four-fifths majority vote in both houses. One of the comptroller's duties is to designate hundreds of Texas financial institutions (mostly banks, but also a few savings associations and credit unions) to serve as depositories for state-collected funds.

comptroller of public accounts
An elected constitutional officer responsible for collecting taxes, keeping accounts, estimating revenue, and serving as treasurer for the state.

Governor Perry administers oath of office for Comptroller Susan Combs.

(Courtesy of the Texas Comptroller's Office)

Susan Combs, former commissioner of agriculture, was elected as comptroller in 2006. Four years later, she was reelected without a Democratic opponent, although she had angered and disappointed many Texans who were unable to reserve rebates for energy-efficient home appliances. As part of the 2009 federal economic stimulus package, Texas received $23 million to distribute for this purpose. The comptroller then gave an $876,500 contract to a Minnesota company for handling rebate reservations, but the company's telephone lines and website were swamped. All of the rebate money was allocated within a few hours.[55] Then, in April 2011, Combs was the object of much criticism after a security lapse exposed personal data for 3.5 million teachers, state employees, and recipients of unemployment compensation. Responsible employees in Combs's agency resigned or were fired, and there is no proof that these data were misused. Free credit monitoring has been made available for persons affected, but this incident could hurt Combs in any future election campaign.[56] In 2011, conflict arose between Combs and Governor Perry when the comptroller notified online-retailer Amazon.com, Inc., based in Seattle, Washington, that it owed Texas $269 million in sales tax. The amount of the claim was based on the value of digital downloads, books, Kindle e-readers, and other merchandise sold to purchasers in Texas from the company's website. Governor Perry criticized Combs's action, but she did not back down. Although the governor vetoed a bill in 2011 that strengthened Combs' argument for taxes, he ultimately approved similar legislation that was included in the state's biennial budget for 2012-2013. In April 2012, the comptroller negotiated an agreement with Amazon.[57] (For more information on the Amazon affair, see Chapter 11, "Finance and Fiscal Policy.")

As the state's comptroller, Combs supervises about 2,800 employees. She promotes the cause of "transparency in government" by maintaining the

"Window on State Government" website (http://www.window.state.tx.us/finances/). This site allows anyone to see how state tax money is being spent. For example, you can find the amount of money Combs's department has paid to individual vendors for goods or services or to its employees for official travel expenses. Other state agencies post similar information on this website. As directed by the legislature, Combs promotes consistency in accounting methods and standards by all state agencies; she does the same for Texas's counties, cities, and special districts.[58]

The Commissioner of the General Land Office

Although less visible than other elected executives, the **commissioner of the General Land Office** is an important figure in Texas politics. Since the creation of the General Land Office under the Constitution of the Republic of Texas (1836), the commissioner's duties have expanded to include awarding oil, gas, and sulfur leases for lands owned by the state; serving as chair of the Veterans Land Board; and sitting as an ex officio member of other boards responsible for managing state-owned lands. With more than 600 employees, the General Land Office also oversees growth of the Permanent School Fund, which is financed by oil and gas leases, rentals, and royalties and which each year provides hundreds of millions of dollars to benefit the state's public schools. In addition to these responsibilities, the General Land Office maintains an archive of about 35 million documents and historic maps relating to land titles in Texas.

When Democrat Garry Mauro left the land commissioner's post to make an unsuccessful bid for the governorship in 1998, his decision afforded Republicans an opportunity to gain control of the General Land Office. Houston businessman David Dewhurst seized that moment, spending $7 million of his own money in winning his first political office.

After Dewhurst decided to run for lieutenant governor in 2002, lobbyist and former state senator Jerry Patterson became the GOP candidate for land commissioner. Patterson defeated the Democratic candidate, state senator David Bernsen, and then won reelection in 2006 and 2010. He has been a controversial politician since he began service in the legislature, where he sponsored a bill that became Texas's concealed handgun law. Unlike the governor, lieutenant governor, and attorney general, who are protected by bodyguards provided by the Department of Public Safety, Patterson is his own security officer. He carries a .22 Magnum pistol in his left boot and a .380-caliber semiautomatic pistol at the small of his back.[59]

After the British Petroleum oil spill off the coast of Louisiana in 2010, Jerry Patterson assured Texans, as well as the nation, that Texas was unlikely to sustain ecological damage from the spill and that Texas seafood remained safe for consumption. He regularly stressed how well prepared Texas was to deal with a similar disaster off its coast. Because the General Land Office administers vast landholdings for the state, the commissioner is involved in many legal disputes. His enforcement of Texas's Open Beaches Act, separating private land and public land along the Gulf Coast, attracts media attention when controversies arise over construction in the beach

commissioner of the General Land Office
As head of Texas's General Land Office, this elected constitutional officer oversees the state's extensive landholdings and related mineral interests, especially oil and gas leasing, for the benefit of the Permanent School Fund.

Students in Action

The Mickey Leland Environmental Internship Program

What It Is

The Mickey Leland Environmental Internship Program was founded in 1992 at the Texas Water Commission, which was a predecessor to the current Texas Commission on Environmental Quality. While representing Houston districts in the Texas House of Representatives (1973–1979) and the U.S. House of Representatives (1979–1989), Mickey Leland worked to promote a clean and healthy environment, proving to be an effective leader on environmental issues within Texas as well as the entire nation. Congressman Leland was a member of the Subcommittee on Health and Environment and encouraged public awareness in the protection of public health as well as environmental issues. In August 1989, he died in a plane crash while on a mission to visit a camp for Sudanese refugees in Ethiopia. The internship in his honor is designed to continue his work at increasing the awareness of environmental issues, to encourage students to consider careers in the environmental field, and to promote the participation of minorities and the disadvantaged in environmental-related policy development. Learn more at the internship's website (http://www.tceq.texas.gov/adminservices/employ/mickeyleland/index.html).

What You Can Do

Undergraduate students enrolled full-time are eligible to apply for the internship program. Depending on your area of study, the internship has the opportunity to fit a broad range of interests, while providing a hands-on experience within the Texas legislature. Students are involved in the decisions and actions of the legislature, including researching and drafting legislation, as well as attending committee hearings, working on special projects, and assisting in general office operations.

How it Helps

Any internship provides the ever-important real world experience that businesses and professionals look for upon graduation. The Mickey Leland Internship is no exception and encourages careers in law, political science, communications, psychology, and education, among others.

(Monkey Business Images/Shutterstock.com)

area. After the Supreme Court of Texas ruled in *Severence v. Patterson* (2012) that the state's Open Beaches Act does not apply to a beachfront area on Galveston Island, Patterson declared that voters should oust the justices who were responsible for the decision.[60]

The Commissioner of Agriculture

By law, the **commissioner of agriculture** is supposed to be a "practicing farmer." This criterion is vague enough to qualify anyone who owns or rents a piece of agricultural land. Name recognition by the state's voters (most of

commissioner of agriculture
The elected official, whose position is created by statute, who heads Texas's Department of Agriculture, which promotes the sale of agricultural commodities and regulates pesticides, aquaculture, egg quality, weights and measures, and grain warehouses.

whom live in suburbs or central cities) is the principal requirement for winning the office.

In 1998, Susan Combs, a lawyer, former state representative from Austin, and current comptroller of public accounts, became Texas's first woman to be elected agriculture commissioner. This state officer is responsible for enforcing agricultural laws and for providing service programs to Texas farmers, ranchers, and consumers. Control over the use of often-controversial pesticides and herbicides is exercised through the Department of Agriculture's Pesticide Programs Division. This division restricts the use of high-risk chemicals; and it licenses dealers, professional applicators, and private applicators who apply dangerous pesticides and herbicides on their own farms and ranches. Other enforcement actions of the department include inspections to determine the accuracy of commercial scales, pumps, and meters.

Combs won a second term in 2002. Subsequently, she gained widespread publicity with demands that Mexico repay its water debt by releasing more water into the Rio Grande. Other matters that attracted her attention were childhood obesity and diabetes. As the Texas administrator of the National School Lunch and Breakfast programs, Combs used her authority to curb the sale of junk food in Texas schools and to prohibit sodas in elementary schools during the school day, in middle schools before the end of the last lunch period, and in high schools during meal periods. Some school districts set even stricter policies controlling soda sales.[61]

After Combs announced that she would run for the office of comptroller of public accounts in 2006, Senator Todd Staples sought and won nomination as the Republican candidate for commissioner of agriculture. His credentials for the office include a degree from Texas A&M University with a major in agricultural economics, experience as a rancher and real estate broker, and 12 years of service in the Texas legislature. In November 2006, Staples won his first term as commissioner of agriculture. He was reelected in 2010.

In May 2008, Staples led a 24-member trade delegation to Cuba to promote the export of Texas agricultural products to that country.[62] In March 2009, he travelled to Iraq as a guest of Texas A&M University's Norman Borlaug Institute for International Agriculture. While there, he promoted the export of Texas agricultural products to Iraq; and he announced that he had asked President Obama to give a priority to lifting the U.S. trade embargo against Cuba.[63]

Under Staples's direction, the Texas Public School Nutrition Policy has become more restrictive than Combs's original limitations. It now prohibits schools from serving deep-fried food in cafeterias and from selling soft drinks, candy, and other "foods of minimal nutritional value" until the end of a day's last scheduled class. Moreover, Staples has announced that he wants to fight obesity by taking healthy eating habits into children's homes—that is, from "the lunchroom into the living room."[64]

secretary of state
The state's chief elections officer, with other administrative duties, who is appointed by the governor for a term concurrent with that of the governor.

The Secretary of State

The only constitutional executive officer appointed by the governor is the **secretary of state**. This appointment must be confirmed by a two-thirds vote of the Senate. The secretary of state serves a four-year term concurrent with that of the governor. As noted below, however, most secretaries of state serve for only a year or so. The secretary of state oversees a staff of approximately 250 people and is the chief elections officer of Texas. Principal responsibilities of the office include the following:

- Administering state election laws in conjunction with county officials
- Tabulating election returns for state and district offices
- Granting charters to Texas corporations
- Issuing permits to outside corporations to conduct business within Texas
- Processing requests for extradition of criminals to or from other states for trial and punishment

With these diverse duties, the secretary of state is obviously more than just a record keeper. How the office functions is determined largely by the occupant's relations with the governor. As indicated by the following summary of the six appointments to the office within the 12 years before 2013, secretaries of state do not remain in office very long.

After Rick Perry became governor at the end of 2000, he appointed Representative Henry Cuellar (D-Laredo) as his first secretary of state. When Cuellar resigned after two years, Perry named Republican Gwyn Shea to that office in January 2002. She resigned in July 2003 and was replaced by Geoffrey S. Connor. Before his appointment by Perry, Connor served for two years as assistant secretary of state.

During his 15 months as secretary of state, Connor, at Governor Perry's direction, made several international trips to promote Texas products abroad and to attract foreign investment in Texas. Early in 2005, Perry replaced Connor with J. Roger Williams, a businessman and GOP fundraiser. Phil Wilson, Perry's deputy chief of staff, replaced Williams in 2007, but resigned after a year to become senior vice president for public affairs for Luminant, an electric energy company. Then, Perry appointed Esperanza "Hope" Andrade in July 2008.

Andrade was raised in San Antonio and with a partner founded an in-home child-care business, a business for cleaning homes and offices, and two home health-care businesses. After selling her businesses, she raised funds for the Republican Party and was a member of the State Transportation Commission for five years. She then served briefly as interim chair of the commission before being appointed by Governor Perry as secretary of state. Subsequently, Andrade has visited communities throughout Texas in support of Perry's economic development and job-growth policies. In addition, she promotes Texas business abroad and is Perry's liaison on border and Mexican affairs.[65]

In 2010, the governor gave Andrade additional work as the Texas Census Ambassador, with responsibility for coordinating efforts to encourage Texans to complete and submit the short federal census form by the April 1 target date. Completion of these forms is important to a state because many federal grant programs, as well as representation in the U.S. House of Representatives, rely on a state's official population count for allocation of money and seats.[66]

Early in April 2012, Andrade announced a voter education program titled "Make Your Mark on Texas," and she began touring the state to encourage voting in the primaries and general election of the 2012 election cycle.[67] After nearly four years as secretary of state, she is approaching the record set by Zollie Steakley, who served in that office for five years (1957–1962).

 Learning Check 8.6 (Answers on p. 333)

1. True or False: Heads of state agencies may not request opinions from the attorney general concerning the scope of their jurisdiction.
2. What is one important power of the secretary of state for persons desiring to establish a Texas corporation?

★ Conclusion

Texas's constitutionally weak governor has grown stronger in recent years, but the term *chief executive* still does not accurately describe the head of the state's executive branch. Success in Texas politics made Governor Rick Perry a serious contender for the Republican Party's presidential candidate nomination in 2012, for a time. Within Texas, his ability to raise campaign money and to appeal to conservative voters has enabled him to win successive elections. This political success has allowed Perry to influence legislators and to fill thousands of appointive positions throughout state government. Use of executive, legislative, and judicial powers vested in the Texas governor by statutes and the state constitution—when combined with political leadership and informal powers not based on law—enhance the importance of the office.

Chapter Summary

- Since 1876, Texas governors have held a weak constitutional office.
- Principal among the governor's prerogatives are extensive power to appoint members to the state's multiple boards and commissions with approval of the Texas Senate, along with a strong veto power in dealing with the Texas legislature.
- Governor Rick Perry has promoted economic development through incentives financed by the Texas Enterprise Fund and the state's Emerging Technology Fund.
- All governors must share executive power with the lieutenant governor and four elected department heads: the attorney general, state comptroller, land commissioner, and agriculture commissioner. The only appointed executive department head provided for in the Texas Constitution is the secretary of state.

Key Terms

Governor's Office, p. 307
appointive power, p. 312
recess appointment, p. 313
removal power, p. 314
martial law, p. 315
budgetary power, p. 316
line-item veto, p. 316
contingency riders, p. 316
executive order, p. 316
proclamation, p. 318
legislative power, p. 319
message power, p. 320
veto power, p. 320
pork-barrel politics, p. 320
postadjournment veto, p. 321
parole, p. 322
full pardon, p. 322
conditional pardon, p. 323
reprieve, p. 323
commutation of sentence, p. 323
plural executive, p. 324
lieutenant governor, p. 325
attorney general, p. 325
comptroller of public accounts, p. 326
commissioner of the General Land Office, p. 328
commissioner of agriculture, p. 329
secretary of state, p. 330

Learning Check Answers

8.1

1. The Texas Constitution provides for impeachment by a simple majority vote of the House and conviction by a two-thirds majority vote of the Senate.
2. True. All Texas governors have placed close friends and political associates in staff positions.

8.2

1. True. Informal powers of the governor are not based on law.

2. True. Public involvement of family members may be a source of support for the governor.

8.3

1. False. Most gubernatorial appointments must be approved by a two-thirds vote of the Senate.
2. The governor may veto an entire appropriation bill or use the line-item veto to eliminate individual budget items.

8.4

1. True. During a session, the governor's veto can be overridden by a two-thirds majority vote in the House and in the Senate.
2. The governor can call a special session.

8.5

1. True. If recommended by the Board of Pardons and Paroles, the governor can grant a full pardon.
2. The governor can independently grant one 30-day reprieve in a death sentence case.

8.6

1. True. A vacancy on a Texas district court or higher appellate court is filled by gubernatorial appointment.
2. The secretary of state grants charters to Texas corporations.

Discussion Questions

1. Is the governor compensated adequately?
2. Should changes be made in the governor's removal powers?
3. How does the governor exercise influence over legislation?
4. How does the governor exercise influence over judicial matters?
5. Should executive department heads be popularly elected or appointed by the governor?

6. Which executive department head appears to have the greatest potential for affecting your personal life and career?

Internet Resources

Office of the Attorney General:
https://www.oag.state.tx.us

Office of the Comptroller of Public Accounts:
http://www.window.state.tx.us/

Office of the Governor:
http://www.governor.state.tx.us/

Office of the Lieutenant Governor:
http://www.ltgov.state.tx.us/

Office of the Secretary of State:
http://www.sos.state.tx.us/

Texas Department of Agriculture:
http://texasagriculture.gov/

Texas General Land Office:
http://www.glo.texas.gov/

Notes

1. Brian McCall, *The Power of the Texas Governor: Connally to Bush* (Austin: University of Texas Press, 2009), 3.
2. For a revisionist view of Davis and his administration, see Carl H. Moneyhon, *Edmund J. Davis of Texas: Civil War General, Republican Leader, Reconstruction Governor* (Fort Worth: Texas Christian University Press, 2010).
3. Jonathan Weisman, "In Texas, a Weak Office Becomes Stronger," *Wall Street Journal*, September 12, 2011.
4. For former Governor Dolph Briscoe's account of his election campaigns and six years (1973–1979) as governor, see his *Dolph Briscoe: My Life in Ranching and Politics*, as told to Don Carleton (Austin: Center for American History, University of Texas at Austin, 2008), 151–261. A biography that tells Governor Ann Richards' story is Jan Reid, *Let the People In: The Life and Times of Ann Richards* (Austin: University of Texas Press, 2012). For an insider's view of George W. Bush's years as governor, see Karl Rove, "A New Kind of Governor," in *Courage and Consequences: My Life as a Conservative in the Fight* (New York: Threshold Editions, 2010), chap. 6.
5. Robert Bryce, "The Pols He Bought," *Texas Observer*, February 5, 1999, 11. For Dr. Leininger's account of political spending, see his interview by Evan Smith, "Money Talks," *Texas Monthly*, June 2006, 138–141, 268–269.
6. Rick Perry, *Fed Up! Our Rights, Our Constitution, Our Fight to Save America from Washington* (New York: Little, Brown, 2010). Sales of this book benefit the conservative Texas Public Policy Foundation's Center for Tenth Amendment Studies.
7. "Perry Links Funding for Medical Facilities to Reform Legislation," *Houston Chronicle*, January 11, 2003.
8. See Carolyn Barta, *Bill Clements: Texian to His Toenails* (Austin: Eakin Press, 1996); Bill Minutaglio, *First Son: George W. Bush and the Bush Family Dynasty* (New York: Times Books, 1999); and Clarke Rountree, *George W. Bush: A Biography* (Santa Barbara, CA.: Greenwood, 2011).
9. Jason Embry, "Perry Campaign Paid Bell to Settle Suit over '06 Race," *Austin American Statesman*, July 17, 2010.
10. Laylan Copelin, "GOP Governors Group Violated Law, Judge Rules," *Austin American-Statesman*, September 1, 2010.

11. Gary Scharrer and Richard Dunam, "Perry's Retirement, Pay Boost Spark Charges of Hypocrisy," *Houston Chronicle*, December 17, 2011.
12. Will Weissert, "Perry's Presidential Nomination Cost the State $3.6 Million," *Fort Worth Star-Telegram*, March 31, 2012.
13. For example, see Bob Ray Sanders, "Gov. Perry's Campaign Should Reimburse Texas," *Fort Worth Star-Telegram*, April 4, 2012.
14. "The Texas Supreme Court and Legislature Help Perry Cloak Travel Security Expenses," *Houston Chronicle*, July 10, 2011.
15. R. G. Ratcliff, "Perry's a Long Way from the Cotton Farm," *Houston Chronicle*, July 26, 2009; Jay Root, "Despite Budget Woes, State Pays Big Bucks for Perry Home," *Austin American-Statesman*, May 18, 2010; and Kelly Shannon, "Governor's Mansion Restoration Builds Steam," *Dallas Morning News*, July 27, 2011.
16. James Drew, Steve McGonigle, and Ryan McNeil, "Murky Land Deals Mark Perry's Past," *Dallas Morning News*, July 25, 2010; and "Renewed Scrutiny of Blind Trust Law," *Austin American-Statesman*, September 2, 2010.
17. Joe Holiday, "Ethics Panel Fines Perry $1,500 over Rental Property," *Houston Chronicle*, March 24, 2011.
18. Wayne Slater, "Rick Perry Won't Rule Out Another Presidential Bid," *Dallas Morning News*, February 7, 2012; and Peggy Fikac, "Our Travelin' Governor Perry Will Spend Even More Time on the Road," *Houston Chronicle*, September 12, 2011.
19. Jim Nicar, "A Summer of Discontent," *Texas Alcalde*, September/October 1997, 83. For detailed accounts of Jim Ferguson's downfall, which opened the way for Miriam "Ma" Ferguson to be elected governor for two terms, see Bruce Rutherford, *The Impeachment of Jim Ferguson* (Austin: Eakin Press 1983); and Cortez A. M. Ewing, "The Impeachment of James E. Ferguson," *Southwestern Social Science Quarterly* 48 (June 1933): 184–210.
20. These salary supplements are authorized by an opinion of the Texas State Ethics Commission, EAO No. 254 (1995).
21. See Rick Perry, *On My Honor: Why the American Values of the Boy Scouts Are Worth Fighting For* (Macon, Ga.: Stroud and Hall, 2008).
22. William Pack, "Governor Fires 1st Volley in War on Fat," *San Antonio Express-News*, November 21, 2003.
23. Gary Scharer, "Perry Describes Bike Mishap," *San Antonio Express-News*, June 12, 2009.
24. Ana Campoy, "Texas Duels Over Guns," *Wall Street Journal*, February 8, 2010; Jim Vertuno, "Wily Coyote No Match for Governor's Gun," *Austin American-Statesman*, April 28, 2010.
25. Tim Eaton, "Pistol-packing Perry Apparent Inspiration for 'Coyote Special,'" *Austin American-Statesman*, May 25, 2010.
26. A video of Perry's full inaugural address delivered on January 18, 2011, is posted at http://www.texastribune.org/texas-state-agencies/governors-office/video-of-gov-rick-perrys-inauguration-speech/
27. For example, see Governor Rick Perry, "Health Care Plan Is a Deception," *Austin American-Statesman*, April 1, 2010.
28. "Hutchison, White Seek Newspaper Endorsements," *Corpus Christi Caller-Times*, February 21, 2010.
29. Quoted by Theodore Kim in "National Editorial Writers Get Access Perry Denies in Texas," *Dallas Morning News*, September 2, 2010.
30. Ken Herman, "First Lady of Texas Takes a New Job," *Austin American-Statesman*, November 7, 2003. Concerning her salary, see "Anita Perry's Salary

Comes Indirectly from Governor's Backers," *Austin American-Statesman*, September 14, 2011. For Anita Perry's responses to questions about her life in politics, see her interview by Evan Smith, "Anita Perry," *Texas Monthly*, September 2005, 178–180, 182, 184.

31. Christi Hoppe, "Embracing a Role Not Envisioned," *Dallas Morning News*, September 26, 2011; and Melissa Ludwig, "Anita Perry Puts Faith Out Front," *San Antonio Express-News*, October 23, 2011.

32. *Governor Perry's Patronage* (Austin: Texans for Public Justice, 2010), http://info.tpj.org/docs/pdf/perrypatronagereport.pdf. For information on Governor Perry's efforts to control higher education through appointment of university regents, see Paul Burka, "Storming the Ivory Tower," *Texas Monthly*, October 2012, 108–113, 290, 292, 294, 296, 300, and 302.

33. "Politics of Perry's Appointments," *Austin American-Statesman*, July 7, 2011.

34. For more details concerning this appointment, see Vimal Patel, "Perry Skirts A&M Process for Selecting Student Regents," *Bryan Eagle*, May 19, 2011; and Vimal Patel, "A&M Student Senate Chides Governor in Resolution," *Bryan Eagle*, June 29, 2011.

35. See James S. Olson and Sharon Phair, "Anatomy of a Race Riot: Beaumont, Texas, 1943," *Texana* 11, no. 1 (1973): 64–72; James A. Burran, "Violence in an 'Arsenal of Democracy'," *East Texas Historical Journal* 14 (Spring 1976): 39–51; and Valentine Belfiglio, *Honor, Pride, Duty: A History of the Texas State Guard* (Austin: Eakin Press, 1995), 64.

36. Dated June 11, 2011, the text of this announcement is posted at http://governor.state.tx.us/news/veto/16302.

37. Dated August 3, 2011, the full text of RP75 is posted at http://governor.state.tx.us/news/executive-order/16466.

38. See T. A. Badger, "Perry Proposes $15 Million for Rails to Entice Toyota," *Fort Worth Star-Telegram*, December 19, 2002; and L. A. Lorek, "Luring Plant Was a Texas-Size Job," *San Antonio Express-News*, February 9, 2003.

39. See Ken Herman, "Lunch and Hunt with Perry for $150,000," *Austin American-Statesman*, November 5, 2003; Clay Robison, "Perry's Perks Go to Big Spenders," *Houston Chronicle*, November 5, 2003; and W. Gardner Selby, "Critic Pans Perry's Bid for Funds as 'Greedy and Seedy,'" *San Antonio Express-News*, November 5, 2003.

40. Quoted by Wayne Slater, "Perry Criticized for Soliciting Funds," *Dallas Morning News*, November 5, 2003.

41. Details of legislative-executive relations are found in Patrick Cox and Michael Phillips, *This House Will Come to Order: How the Texas Speaker Became a Power in State and National Politics* (Austin: University of Texas Press, 2010); Bill Hobby and Saralee Tiede, *How Things Really Work: Lessons from a Life in Politics* (Austin: Center for American History, University of Texas at Austin, 2010); and Dave McNeely and Jim Henderson, *Bob Bullock: God Bless Texas* (Austin: University of Texas Press, 2008).

42. See Dave Montgomery, "Perry Defends Ceremonial Bill Signings that Hutchison Blasts as 'Phony'," *Fort Worth Star-Telegram*, August 21, 2009.

43. See *Vetoes of Legislation*, 77th, 78th, 79th, 80th, 81st, and 82nd legislatures, Focus Reports No. 77-10, No. 78-11, No. 79-9, No. 80-6, No. 81-7, and No. 82-5 (Austin: House Research Organization, Texas House of Representatives, 2001, 2003, 2005, 2007, 2009, and 2011).

44. Beth Brown, "Supreme Court Is Elected, But Bears Perry's Stamp," *New York Times*, August 12, 2011.

45. "Bad Judgment: Perry Proves Texas Needs New Way to Appoint Judges," *Waco Tribune-Herald*, January 3, 2005.

46. Texas Board of Pardons and Paroles, Annual Report for Fiscal Year 2011 (Austin, 2012), 22; and Governor Rick Perry's press release dated December 22, 2011, "Governor Perry Grants Clemency to Eight," http://governor.state.tx.us/news/press-release/16812/.

47. Angela K. Brown, "Texas Governor Gives Copy of Pardon to Man's Family," *Fort Worth Star-Telegram*, March 20, 2010.

48. Bob Ray Sanders, "Ex-governor's Death Penalty Skepticism a Welcome Step," *Fort Worth Star-Telegram*, October 25, 2009.

49. Michael Graczynk, "Man Executed after Perry Rejects Parole Board's Clemency Recommendations," *Fort Worth Star-Telegram*, November 20, 2009.

50. Michèle Kay and Gary Susswein, "Supporters Gave Millions in 'Late Train' Donations," *Austin American-Statesman*, January 16, 2003.

51. Bob Richter, "AG Vows to Defend Open Records," *San Antonio Express-News*, December 12, 2002.

52. Adam Russell, "Attorney General Says Berman Can Run for Governor While in Office," *Tyler Morning Telegraph*, March 9, 2009.

53. Terrance Stutz, "AG Says Legislature Erred on Pay for Retired Teachers," *Dallas Morning News*, November 24, 2009.

54. Tim Eaton, "Abbott Joins Attorneys General in Suit Opposing Health Care Law," *Austin American-Statesman*, March 24, 2010.

55. Christi Hoppe, "State Seeks Answers to Rebate Fiasco," *Dallas Morning News*, April 9, 2010.

56. Kate Alexander and Barry Harrell, "Combs Accepts Fault for Lapse, Offers Free Help," *Austin American-Statesman*, April 29, 2011.

57. For the comptroller's press release dated April 27, 2012, concerning the agreement, see "Texas-Amazon Announce Agreement to Create Jobs," http://window.state.tx.us/news2012/120427-Amazon.html.

58. Mike Norman, "Government Transparency Is Only for Those Who Want to Look," *Fort Worth Star-Telegram*, September 4, 2009.

59. Mike Ward, "DPS Adds Top Officials to Guard List," *Austin American-Statesman*, January 14, 2011; Ken Herman, "Must You Have a Gun in Your Boot in the Capitol?" *Waco Tribune-Herald*, April 20, 2010; and Manny Fernandez, "Old-Time Texas Politicians, Verbally Quick on the Draw," *New York Times*, June 14, 2012.

60. See Harvey Rice, "Official Wants Judges Ousted for Texas Beach Ruling," *Beaumont Enterprise*, April 4, 2012; and Mark Collette, "In Open Beaches Case, Two Cherished Texas Values Collide," *Corpus Christi Caller-Times*, April 29, 2012.

61. "Texas's Soft Drink Rules," *Austin American-Statesman*, May 4, 2006.

62. W. Gardner Selby, "In Cuba, Delegation to Tout Texas Exports," *Austin American-Statesman*, May 14, 2008.

63. Jim Landers, "Ag Chief: Iraq Ripe for Texas Food," *Dallas Morning News*, March 27, 2009.

64. Michelle De La Rosa, "Junk Food Out as New School Year Starts," *San Antonio Express-News*, August 22, 2009.

65. Tania Lara, "State Diplomat Climbed Ladder by Standing Tall," *Austin American-Statesman*, October 11, 2009.

66. Steve Taylor, "Perry Names Andrade Texas Census Ambassador," *Rio Grande Guardian* (McAllen), March 10, 2010.

67. Steve Taylor, "Andrade Launches Statewide Voter Education Initiative," *Rio Grande Guardian*, April 5, 2012.

The Low Politics of High Tech in the Lone Star State

Jeff Key*

The purpose of the Emerging Technology Fund is to use state government money to promote growth in the high-technology sector of the Texas economy and provide jobs for Texans. Professor Jeff Key examines the politics of this fund, giving special attention to the involvement of Governor Rick Perry.

In 2003, Governor Rick Perry persuaded the state legislature to launch the Texas Enterprise Fund, which offers state-funded incentives to entice businesses in other states (especially California) to relocate to Texas. Two years later, similar legislation established the Emerging Technology Fund to provide venture capital for helping high tech businesses get their products "out of the laboratory and onto the market." Though the Texas Enterprise Fund has been criticized as "corporate welfare" that is not cost effective, greater controversy has been provoked by the state's Emerging Technology Fund (hereafter identified as "ETF" or "the Fund").

Troubling Questions

Governor Perry's role in the operation of ETF came under nationwide scrutiny during his gubernatorial election campaign in 2010 and again at the time of his unsuccessful bid for the 2012 Republican presidential nomination. Labels such as "crony capitalism" and "pay-to-play" were used by both Democrats and Republican opponents as well as journalists reporting for the *Wall Street Journal*, the *New York Times*, and other newspapers nationwide. Therefore, troubling questions about ETF and its management have cast a shadow over the leadership and legacy of the Lone Star State's longest-serving governor.

From the beginning, ETF has drawn public attention because it clearly reflects Perry's budget priorities and his desire to expand gubernatorial power. To create the Fund in 2005, he authorized dipping into the state's Rainy Day Fund just as he had done earlier for creation of the Texas Enterprise Fund. Thus, if Perry had a costly pet project, the Rainy Day Fund was where he went to find money to pay for it. Yet, when Texas faced a massive $27 billion budget deficit in 2011, the governor reluctantly approved use of less than one-third of the $9.4 billion in the Rainy Day Fund as deep budget cuts were made for education and social services. Management of ETF has given Perry great influence over its operations. As originally established, Perry was given power to appoint all members of the Fund's seventeen-member advisory committee, while sharing final grant approval power with the lieutenant governor and speaker of the House of Representatives.

The Convergen Case

Governor Perry's role in overseeing ETF became a major issue when he sought reelection in 2010. Both his principal challenger (Kay Bailey Hutchison) in the Republican primary, and his Democratic opponent (former Houston mayor Bill White) in the general election raised questions about Perry's role in managing the Fund. Reporters for the *Dallas Morning News* found that businesses and firms tied to major contributions to Perry's campaign had received more than $16 million in ETF grants.

....

*Jeffrey Key is professor and department head of the Department of Political Science at Hardin-Simmons University. This article was written especially for *Practicing Texas Politics*, 2013–2014.

His lax oversight of possible conflicts of interest among ETF's advisory committee members and grant recipients also came under scrutiny. Investigations uncovered a troubling pattern of current and former committee members with ties to companies receiving ETF grants.

A $4.5 million cancer-research grant to Convergen LifeScience, Inc., in August 2010, drew particular attention. Perry tried to prevent release of ETF's grant contract with Convergen until after the 2010 election. This company was headed by Perry's friend and long-time campaign donor, David Nance, who was a former advisory committee member.

Controversy over the Convergen grant shed light on all of the problems involving Perry's handling of the Fund. Close ties between Perry and David Nance became even more apparent when it was revealed that a California-based firm operated by Nance's daughter, CJ Nance, was paid almost $70,000 by TexasOne. Founded by Perry in 2003 and affiliated with the governor's Office of Economic Development, TexasOne promotes the Fund. Payment to Verve Public Relations was covered by a donation to TexasOne from Developtech Corporation, a company owned by CJ's father David. Moreover, Verve Public Relations had done work for six companies that received ETF grants while David Nance was a member of the advisory committee.

Perry's ties to David Nance might not have attracted so much attention if Convergen's grant application had been treated like any other ETF application, but the proposal seems to have received preferential treatment. Rules for the grant process provide for review by a regional review board. Life science proposals, like Convergen's application, must be approved also by the Texas Life Science Center. If both approve a grant request, the proposal goes to the ETF's advisory committee. Final action involves signing by the governor, lieutenant governor, and Speaker of the House.

The Central Texas regional review board rejected Convergen's proposal, and it was never submitted to the Texas Life Science Center. Instead, Nance appealed directly to the governor's office. ETF executive director Alan Kirchoff, and ETF advisory committee chair Bob Pearson. Subsequently, Convergen's proposal was approved by the advisory committee; and Governor Perry, Lieutenant Governor David Dewhurst, and Speaker Joe Straus signed off on the grant. Kirchoff, who had been employed by the Fund since its creation and had served as executive director since 2008, resigned on August 11, 2010, just a few days before the grant contract was signed. Then he began promptly to lobby state officials on behalf of Nance-owned companies.

Investigations and House Bill 2457

Finally, the conflicts of interest swirling around ETF became too visible to ignore. The Texas Rangers launched an investigation into financial dealings between Kirchoff and William Morrow, a former chair of ETF's advisory committee. Although Kirchoff became a millionaire while working for the Fund, the investigation did not find sufficient grounds for criminal prosecution. Thus, in early September 2010, the office of the Travis County district attorney announced that charges would not be filed. In the wake of bad publicity connected with the Convergen case, however, the Governor's Office did produce the first written ethics policy for ETF's advisory committee.

Another investigation involved a five-month audit of the Fund by State Auditor John Keel. His findings were issued in April 2011, while the 82nd legislature was in session. Two issues covered by the auditor's report were of particular interest to some legislators. They were concerned about the way that the Fund operates and inconsistency in the grant process. In their opinion, these failings created opportunities for corruption and left the Fund open to charges of favoritism. The Republican-controlled legislature never considered abolishing

ETF, but it attempted to make the Fund more open and accountable.

House Bill 2457, authored by Representative John Davis (R-Houston) was passed by the legislature in May 2011 and signed by Perry in the following month. Under this law, the governor now appoints only 13 members of the Fund's 17-member advisory committee, Two members are appointed by the Speaker and two by the lieutenant governor. The law also requires greater openness in the entire grant process from initial submission of a proposal to final authorization. With these reforms in place, an ETF appropriation of almost $140 million was made for fiscal years 2012–2013. With this action, controversy over ETF appeared to be over until Perry decided to seek nomination as the Republican Party's presidential candidate in 2012.

ETF and Presidential Campaign Politics

Perry's presidential bid focused nationwide attention on his decade-long leadership as governor of the Lone Star State. Both the national media and Republican rivals challenged some of the governor's claims about success in creating Texas jobs. His handling of ETF affairs generated special criticism. The "crony capitalism" label re-emerged, and the *New York Times* referred to ETF as Governor Perry's "cash machine." Ethical questions aside, the Fund's success in creating jobs for Texans generated much criticism. A study by the progressive Texans for Public Justice found that $169 million in Fund grants had produced only 820 jobs! Lingering questions about Perry's leadership and poor debate performances prompted him to withdraw from the Republican presidential primary race in January 2012.

Conclusion

Controversy generated by ETF illustrates important facts about politics and policy in the Lone Star State. Ethical oversight and accountability are usually addressed after a scandal rather than built into government programs at the beginning. Pressures on policy makers in the twenty-first century tend to overwhelm the state's political institutions that were designed in the 19th century. Nowhere is this problem more evident than in the low politics of high tech at the ETF.

Public Policy and Administration

Learning Objectives

1. Describe the role of bureaucracy in making public policy.
2. Analyze the major challenges faced by the Texas education system.
3. Discuss how Texas higher education has taken steps to increase the participation of all Texans.
4. Examine the health and human services programs in Texas and discuss how efforts to address the needs of its citizens have been approached.
5. Compare the role of government to generate economic development with its duty to maintain a safe and clean environment for the state's residents.

One good way to see what is important in public policy is to follow the money. For many years in Texas, the state government has spent the lion's share of the budget on four areas. For example, in the 2012–2013 biennium (two-year budget cycle), the legislature appropriated $173.5 billion as follows:

- Education: 42 percent
- Health and human services: 32 percent
- Business and economic development: 14 percent
- Public safety and criminal justice: 7 percent
- Everything else: 6 percent[1]

Although regulation costs the state government little (0.4 percent of the total in 2012–2013), it has profound cost effects on individuals, companies, and local governments. Regulation commonly shifts costs and benefits from one group to another. For example, poor air hurts the quality of life and increases medical costs for children with respiratory problems such as asthma, as well as for the elderly, but regulations requiring scrubbers to reduce emissions from smokestacks cost businesses money. Similarly, clean water benefits ordinary citizens, but it costs cities money to process sewage and companies money to clean up, or store, the by-products of their production. Not surprisingly, regulatory policy is fraught with controversy.

This chapter examines public policy in Texas through two lenses: (1) the situation and behavior of the agencies and people who implement the policies and (2) the nature of the policies themselves. Covered are the major policy areas of education, health and human services, business and economic development, environment, and homeland security. The other big-ticket item in Texas state government—public safety and criminal justice—is covered in Chapter 10, "Laws, Courts, and Justice," and details on state spending are provided in Chapter 11, "Finance and Fiscal Policy."

State Agencies and State Employees

LO1 State government has a profound effect on the lives of all of us. Services, subsidies, taxes, and regulations affect students from kindergarten through graduate school, the impoverished, the middle class, the wealthy, small businesses, and large corporations. Government policies affect our safety and health; our education; the quality of our air, water, and food; and the profitability of our businesses.

State Agencies and Public Policy

Public policy is the product of a long series of interactions of a variety of groups and institutions. Interest groups generally bring problems to the attention of government and then lobby for solutions that benefit the members of the interest group. Political parties and chief executives often select and combine the proposals of interest groups into a manageable number and push them as part of their program or agenda. The legislature then accepts some of the proposals through the passage of laws, the creation or modification of agencies, and the appropriation of money to carry out the policies. Finally, the executive branch implements the policies. At the national level, the president provides rules and instructions for the agencies that actually carry out the policies. In Texas, the more than 200 agencies have substantial independence from the governor, which means that each agency has more latitude and independence than federal agencies in deciding what was meant by the legislature and in applying the law to unforeseen circumstances. Not surprisingly, a great deal of informal interaction (and lobbying) occurs among interest groups, the political parties, the state's top executives, legislators, and the agencies themselves.

The Institutional Context

The way in which the Texas executive branch is organized has a major effect on public policy. A key reason is that the fragmentation of authority strongly affects who has access to policy decisions, as well as how visible the decision process is to the public. The large number of agencies means they are covered less by the media and, therefore, are less visible to the public. Moreover, relationships with agency personnel have limited influence on the state's agencies. Special interest groups, on the other hand, have strong incentives (profits) to develop cozy relationships with the agency personnel, and most agencies do not have to defend their decisions before a higher authority (such as the governor).

In addition to agencies headed by the elected officials discussed in Chapter 8, "The Executive," more than 200 boards, commissions, and departments implement state laws and programs in Texas. Most boards and commissions are appointed by the governor; however, once citizens are appointed to a board, the governor generally must rely on persuasion and personal or political loyalty to exercise influence. The exceptionally long tenure of Governor Rick Perry has meant that he has appointed all of the members of most boards and has developed a close working relationship with those agencies of special interest to him. For example, Governor Perry has a strong interest in his alma mater, Texas A&M University, and has significantly influenced its direction in recent years through the policies and hiring decisions made by the members of the board of regents of the Texas A&M University system (whom he appoints).

Fragmentation of the state executive into so many largely independent agencies was an intentional move by the framers of the Texas Constitution and later legislatures to avoid centralized power. Administering state programs through boards was also thought to keep partisan politics out of public administration. Unfortunately, this fragmentation simply changes the nature of the politics, making it more difficult to hold the agencies responsible to the public and to coordinate efforts.

Boards heading state agencies are not typically full time; instead, they usually meet quarterly or more frequently. In most cases a full-time, board-appointed executive director oversees day-to-day agency operations. Boards usually make general policy decisions and leave much of the detail to the executive director; however, some boards are much more active and involved (for example, the Texas Commission on Environmental Quality). In recent years, the influence of the governor has increased through the ability to name a powerful executive commissioner to run two major agencies—the Health and Human Services Commission and the Texas Education Agency. Two important boards—the Railroad Commission of Texas (RRC) (which regulates the oil and gas industry) and the State Board of Education—are elected. Members of both tend to be quite active; however, the State Board of Education is limited by its lack of authority over the commissioner of education, who heads the Texas Education Agency and reports to the governor.

Some agencies were created in the Texas Constitution. Others were created by the legislature, either as directed by the state constitution or independent of it. As problems emerge that elected officials believe government must address, they look to existing state agencies or create new ones to provide solutions. Sometimes, citizen complaints force an agency's creation. For example, citizen outrage at rising utility rates resulted in the creation of the Public Utilities Commission (PUC) to review and limit those rates. (Lobbying by special-interest groups and the orientation of gubernatorial appointments over time, however, have changed the direction of the PUC's policies to again draw the ire of consumer advocates.) Lobbying by special-interest groups to protect their own interests is also important in the creation of agencies. The most famous Texas case was lobbying by the oil and gas industry in the early 20th century to have the Railroad Commission create a system of regulation to reduce economic chaos in the fledgling industry. Similarly, in 2003, the legislature created the Texas Residential Construction Commission in response to lobbying by home builders. But complaints by consumer advocates that the agency served primarily to protect builders from homeowner suits over shoddy construction led to its abolition in 2009 through the sunset review process.

The **sunset review process** is an attempt to keep state agencies efficient and responsive to current needs. Each biennium, a group of state agencies is examined by the Sunset Advisory Commission, which recommends to the legislature whether the agency should be abolished, merged, reorganized, or retained. It is the legislature that makes the final decision. At least once every 12 years, each of 150 state agencies must be evaluated. (Universities and courts are not subject to the process.) The Sunset Advisory Commission is composed of 10 legislators (five from each chamber) and two public members. Serving as public members in 2012 were Casandra Ortiz, a San Antonio business lawyer, and Jan Newton, former president of Southwestern Bell Telephone (SBC; now AT&T) and chair of the board of directors for the Electric Reliability Council of Texas. The commission has a staff of 31 employees. In 2012–2013, it reviewed 24 agencies.

A major problem with the sunset review process, according to critics, is that the legislature has little taste for the abolition or major restructuring of big agencies. For example, the Sunset Advisory Commission's staff found

sunset review process
During a cycle of 12 years, each state agency is studied at least once, and then the legislature decides whether to abolish, merge, reorganize, or retain that agency.

that the mission and "byzantine" regulations of the Alcoholic Beverage Commission were hopelessly outdated, and yet the legislature continued the commission with only minor changes. It is not surprising that regulated groups (often enjoying close relationships with friendly administrators and legislators) and state employees fighting for their jobs and turf (the **institution's** size, power, and responsibility) wage vigorous campaigns to preserve agencies and continue business as usual. From the Sunset Advisory Commission's beginning in 1978 through 2011, eighty-one percent of state agencies were retained, 9 percent were abolished, and 10 percent were reorganized in major ways (such as combining two or more agencies). Of those agencies retained, some had changes, such as adding public members (people not from the regulated industry) on governing boards, improving procedures, or changing policies.

The sometimes convoluted sunset process is illustrated by the case of the Texas Youth Commission (TYC), which was responsible for incarcerating juvenile offenders. In the face of child sexual abuse charges, the TYC underwent a full sunset review in 2008. The Sunset Commission recommended that it be consolidated with the Texas Juvenile Probation Commission. However, the legislature chose to leave the two as stand-alone agencies for a two-year probationary period. When the Sunset Commission did a follow-up review in 2010, they found that the agencies had met 96 percent of the reforms mandated by the legislature and recommended that the two be continued for six years. The 2011 legislature voted to abolish the two agencies and transfer their functions to a new agency, the Texas Juvenile Justice Department. More detail on the TYC is provided in the next chapter, "Laws, Courts, and Justice." From 1982 to 2011, the sunset process saved the state $945 million, or approximately $29 for every dollar spent in the sunset review process.[2]

State Employees and Public Policy

For most people, the face of state government is the governor, legislators, and other top officials. Certainly, these people *are* critical decision makers. However, most of the work of Texas state government (called **public administration**) is in the hands of people in agencies headed by elected officials and appointed boards. These **bureaucrats** (public employees), though often the subject of criticism or jokes about inefficiency and "red tape," are responsible for delivering governmental services to the state's residents. The public may see them in action as a clerk taking an application, a supervisor explaining why a request was turned down, or an inspector checking a nursing home. They are the focus of this section.

The nature of bureaucracy is both its strength and its weakness. Large organizations, such as governments and corporations, need many employees doing specialized jobs with sufficient coordination to achieve the organization's goals (profits for a company, service for a government). That means employees must follow set rules and procedures so they can provide relatively uniform results. When a bureaucracy works well, it harnesses many individual efforts to achieve the organization's goals. Along the way, however, "red tape"

public administration
The implementation of public policy by government employees.

bureaucrats
Public employees.

(the rules that bureaucrats must follow) slows the process and prevents employees from making decisions that go against the rules. State rules should mean the same in Dallas as in Muleshoe, but making the decisions may seem slow, and the "street level" bureaucrat may not have the authority to make adjustments for differences in local conditions. Thus, bureaucracies are necessary but sometimes frustrating.

Bureaucracy and Public Policy We often think of public administrators as simply implementing the laws passed by the legislature, but the truth is that they must make many decisions not clearly specified in the law. Not surprisingly, their own views, their bosses' preferences, their agency's culture, and the lobbying they receive make a difference in how they apply laws passed by the legislature. Agencies also want to protect or expand their turf. Lobbyists understand the role of the bureaucracy in making public policy and work just as hard to influence agency decisions as they work to influence legislation.

Public agencies also must build good relations with top state leaders (such as the governor), key legislators, and executive and legislative staff members, because these people determine how much money and authority the agency receives. Dealing with the legislature often involves close cooperation between state agencies and lobbyists for groups that the agencies serve or regulate. For example, the Texas Good Roads/Transportation Association (mostly trucking companies and road contractors) and the Texas Department of Transportation have long worked closely, and relatively successfully, to lobby the legislature for more highway money.

In Texas, three factors are particularly important in determining agencies' success in achieving their policy goals: the vigor and vision of their leadership, their resources, and the extent to which elites influence implementation (called elite access below). Many Texas agencies define their jobs narrowly and make decisions on narrow technical grounds, without considering the broader consequences of their actions. Texas environmental agencies have often taken this passive approach, which is one reason for Texas's many environmental problems. For example, a former Texas Commission on Environmental Quality commissioner complained:

> One [issue] that always floored me was the high mercury level in East Texas lakes.... People were eating fish contaminated with levels of mercury that could only be attributed to pollution from nearby coal-fired power plants. Yet when permit applications for new coal plants came before the board, the majority of commissioners refused to consider the impact on area lakes. They said water issues are not relevant to air permits.... The regulators tasked with cleaning up the lake, meanwhile, considered airborne emissions to be beyond their purview. So the issue never gets addressed.[3]

Other agency heads, however, take a proactive approach. Beginning in 1975, for example, three successive activist comptrollers transformed the Texas Comptroller's Office into a major player in Texas government, a more aggressive collector of state taxes, a problem-solver for other agencies, and, under comptroller Carole Keeton Strayhorn, a focus of controversy. It appears that elected agency heads, such as the comptroller and attorney general, have more clout (and perhaps incentive) to be proactive about their agency's job than do appointed agency heads.

Historically, Texas government agencies have had minimal funds to implement policy. Consider the example of nursing homes, which are big business today and mostly run for profit. In the words of one commentator:

> While costs for nursing homes are going up, there's less money coming in from state Medicaid programs. With state budgets so tight, Medicaid rates have been stagnant. Texas's Medicaid rates for nursing homes rank 49th in the country.... Because the vast majority of nursing home residents rely on Medicaid to pay their way, these trends make it increasingly difficult for nursing homes to make money. The less scrupulous for-profit nursing homes boost earnings by curtailing staff and services.[4]

Nursing home residents are generally weak and unable to leave if the service is bad or threatens their well-being. Therefore, residents depend heavily on government inspectors to ensure that they are treated well. Unfortunately, the number of nursing home inspectors in Texas has been like a rollercoaster—sometimes up, sometimes down. For example, in early 2012, the number of inspectors was reduced, and inspections of assisted-living facilities were expected to be extended from being done annually to taking place every 18–24 months. When the number of inspectors relative to the number of residents decreases, the number of inspections decreases, and abuse tends to increase. Even when there are enough inspectors, connections of nursing home company executives and lobbyists to top agency administrators often ensure that infractions result in a slap on the wrist and a promise to do better. (This is called **elite access**.) Over the years, both the Health and Human Services Commission and the state attorney general have been criticized for their lack of vigor in pursuing nursing home violations.

As the nursing home example illustrates, elite access and lack of resources make policy less effective and abuse more common in Texas nursing homes. At least since the 1990s, Texas has had more severe and repeated violations of federal patient care standards than most other states. Results can include neglect, physical and verbal abuse, injury, and death. For-profit nursing homes tend to have more serious and repeated actions harmful to residents than do government and nonprofit homes.[5]

Number of State Employees Governments are Texas's biggest employers. In 2010, the equivalent of 318,000 Texans drew full-time state paychecks. Put another way, Texas had 126 full-time state employees for every 10,000 citizens. Although this number sounds like a lot, Texas ranked 45th of the 50 states in number of state employees per 10,000 citizens. As you can see in "How Do We Compare ... in Number of State Employees?" Texas is following two national patterns. First, more populated states tend to have fewer employees relative to their population. Second, as populations grow, most states, including Texas, are hiring proportionately fewer employees. From 1993 to 2010, the number of state employees declined relative to the

elite access
The ability of the business elite to deal directly with high-ranking government administrators to avoid full compliance with regulations.

How Do We Compare...in Number of State Employees?

Full-Time Equivalent (FTE) State Employees and Number per 10,000 Population

Most Populous U.S. States	Number of FTE Employees 2010	Number per 10,000 of State Population 1993	2010	U.S. States Bordering Texas	Number of FTE Employees 2010	Number per 10,000 of State Population 1993	2010
California	411,000	110	110	Arkansas	63,000	190	218
Florida	184,000	120	98	Louisiana	89,000	209	196
New York	251,000	146	130	New Mexico	48,000	262	234
Texas	**318,000**	**136**	**126**	Oklahoma	71,000	210	188
All 50 states	4,378,000	150	142				

Source: Calculations based on data from U.S. Census Bureau, 2010 Census; and *2010 Annual Survey of Public Employment and Payroll,* revised January 2012, **http://www.census.gov//govs/apes/historical_data_2010.html.**

population in both Texas and the nation. One reason Texas ranks so low is that the state government passes a great deal of responsibility to local governments. Texas local governments employed 1,134,000 workers, or 451 per 10,000 residents in 2010. That placed them seventh among the 50 states. Moreover, like local governments in other states, local government employment in Texas is increasing faster than the state's population. For more detail, see Chapter 3, "Local Governments."

Competence, Pay, and Retention Although most public administrators do a good job, some are less effective than others. Many observers believe that bureaucratic competence improves with a civil service system and good pay and benefits. In the first century of our nation, many thought that any fool could do a government job, and as a result, many fools worked in government. From local to national levels, government jobs were filled through the **patronage system**, also known as the spoils system. Government officials hired friends and supporters, with little regard for whether they were competent. The idea was that "to the victor belong the spoils." **Merit systems**, on the other hand, require officials to hire, promote, and fire government employees on the basis of objective criteria such as tests, education, experience, and performance. If a merit system works well, it tends to produce a competent bureaucracy. A system that provides too much protection, however, makes it difficult to fire the incompetent and gives little incentive for the competent to excel.

Texas has never had a merit system covering all state employees, and in 1985, the partial state merit system was abolished. What replaced it was a highly centralized compensation and classification system covering most of the

patronage system
Hiring friends and supporters of elected officials as government employees without regard to their abilities.

merit system
Hiring, promoting, and firing on the basis of objective criteria such as tests, degrees, experience, and performance.

executive branch but not the judicial and legislative branches or higher education. The legislature sets salaries, wage scales, and other benefits. Individual agencies are free to develop their own systems for hiring, promotion, and firing (so long as they comply with federal standards, where applicable). Critics worried that the result would be greater turnover and lower competence. A survey of state human resource directors, however, indicates that agencies have developed more flexible personnel policies that provide some protection for most employees. Moreover, patronage appointments have not become a major problem in state administration. In the words of one observer, "It's not uncommon for state agencies to become repositories for campaign staff or former officeholders.... But there are no wholesale purges" when new officials are elected.[6]

In recent years, state government employee turnover has been consistently high: 14 to 17 percent in fiscal years 2003–2010. By comparison, in fiscal year 2004, turnover was 9 percent for Texas's local governments and 10 percent for the nation. In that year, turnover cost the state $345 million, according to the State Auditor's Office. Turnover is highest for workers in social services and criminal justice. Exit surveys (filled out by employees leaving state employment) reveal that the top three reasons for leaving state employment are retirement, the desire for higher pay or better benefits, and the desire for more satisfactory working conditions. Note in "How Do We Compare ... in State Employee Compensation?" that state government salaries in Texas tend to be higher than those of our neighbors but lower than those of other large states. In 2009, the legislature increased the number of state positions with salaries that compare favorably with Texas's private sector from approximately 56 to 83 percent. The higher wages and the recent recession have contributed to holding down turnover.[7]

How Do We Compare...in State Employee Compensation?

Average Monthly Pay per Full-Time-Equivalent (FTE) Employee, 1993 and 2010

Most Populous U.S. States	1993	2010	U.S. States Bordering Texas	1993	2010
California	$3,644	$5,474	Arkansas	$2,261	$3,666
Florida	$2,266	$3,826	Louisiana	$2,242	$4,149
New York	$3,335	$5,416	New Mexico	$2,223	$3,824
Texas	**$2,426**	**$4,178**	Oklahoma	$1,897	$3,765

Source: Calculations based on data from U.S. Census Bureau, 2010 Census, and *2010 Annual Survey of Public Employment and Payroll,* revised January 2012, **http://www.census.gov//govs/apes/historical_data_2010.html**.

Table 9.1 Texas Minorities and Women in State Government Compared with the Total Civilian State Workforce (in percentage)*

Job Category	African American		Hispanic American		Female	
	Govt.	Total Workforce	Govt.	Total Workforce	Govt.	Total Workforce
Official, administrator	10	8	14	21	51	38
Professional	11	10	16	19	56	53
Technical	14	14	22	27	54	54
Administrative support	19	13	29	32	88	67
Skilled craft	8	7	24	46	5	6
Service and maintenance	29	14	25	50	51	39
TOTALS	**17**	**11**	**21**	**35**	**56**	**45**

Note on interpretation: The first cell indicates that 10 percent of Texas government officials and administrators are African American; the next cell shows that 8 percent of the officials and administrators in the state's total economy are African American.

*State Agencies Workforce (including executive agencies and higher education, fiscal year 2010–2011) and Statewide Civilian Workforce (including both private and public workers) for calendar year 2009.

Source: Compiled from Texas Workforce Commission, Civil Rights Division, January 2011, **http://www.twc.state.tx.us/news/eeorptsum110.pdf**.

Other nonfinancial factors help attract state employees. Studies consistently show that large numbers of government employees have a strong sense of service and thus find being a public servant rewarding. Three "perks" also increase the attractiveness of public employment: paid vacations, state holidays, and sick leave.

Another incentive for employment can be equitable treatment. For many years, Texas state government has advertised itself as an "equal opportunity employer," and evidence indicates that it has been, albeit imperfectly. Table 9.1 shows that women make up more than one-half of state employees and are more likely to hold higher positions in government than in the private economy. African American citizens have a greater proportion in public than private employment, whereas Latino Texans are more likely to be employed in the private economy. In relation to their numbers in the state's population, Latinos are underrepresented in the top job categories in both the public and private arenas. Data on newly hired state employees indicate that these patterns will probably continue.

☑ Learning Check 9.1   (Answers on p. 383)

1. Demands for the creation of new state agencies come from what groups?
2. True or False: Public administrators simply implement the laws passed by the legislature without making any changes.
3. What three factors are particularly important in determining how successful agencies are in Texas?

Education

After a legislative hearing on health problems along the Mexican border, Representative Debbie Riddle (R-Tomball) asked an *El Paso Times* reporter, "Where did this idea come from that everybody deserves free education, free medical care, free whatever? It comes from Moscow, from Russia. It comes straight out of the pit of hell."[8] Indeed, education and social services are controversial in Texas.

Public Schools

Texas's commitment to education began with its 1836 constitution, which required government-owned land to be set aside for establishing public schools and "a University of the first class." Later, framers of the 1876 constitution mandated an "efficient system of public free schools." What continues to perplex state policymakers is how to advance public schools' efficiency while seeking equality of funding for students in districts with varying amounts and values of taxable property. (See Chapter 11, "Finance and Fiscal Policy," for a discussion of school finance issues.) Texas schools are also faced with meeting the needs of a changing student body. In the 21st century, students have come increasingly from families that are ethnic minorities or economically disadvantaged. According to Texas Education Agency data, in the 2009–2010 academic year, 49 percent of Texas students were Latino, 33 percent Anglo, 14 percent African American, and 4 percent Asian and others. In addition, 59 percent were economically disadvantaged. Historically, Texas has not served minority and less-affluent students as well as it has Anglo and middle-class students. If this pattern continues, studies project that in the future, Texans' average income will decline, while the expense of welfare, prisons, and lost tax revenues will increase. One indication that the state can do better is that 10 Texas high schools made the *U.S. News and World Report*'s list of the 100 best high schools in the nation; in seven of the schools, a majority of students were ethnic minorities.[9]

Today, 1,237 independent school districts shoulder primary responsibility for delivery of educational services to more than 4.8 million students. (Chapter 3, "Local Governments," discusses the organization and politics of local school districts.) Although local school districts have somewhat more independence today, they are part of a relatively centralized system in which state authorities substantially affect local decisions, from what is taught to how it is financed.

State Board of Education Oversight of Texas education is divided between two bodies: the elected **State Board of Education (SBOE)** and the commissioner of education, who is appointed by the governor to run the Texas Education Agency. Over the years, the sometimes extreme ideological positions taken by many SBOE members have embarrassed the legislature and caused it to whittle away the board's authority. For years, the board was even made appointive rather than elective. Today, the greater power over state education is

LO2

State Board of Education (SBOE)
A popularly elected 15-member body with limited authority over Texas's K–12 education system.

in the hands of the commissioner of education through control of the Texas Education Agency, but the SBOE remains important and highly controversial.

Among the board's most significant powers are curriculum approval for each subject and grade, textbook review for the public schools, approval of State Board for Educator Certification rules, and management of the investments of the Permanent School Fund. Revenue from the $28 billion fund goes to public schools. Among other things, it pays for textbooks and guarantees more than $50 billion in bonds for school districts.

Representing districts with approximately equal population (1.7 million), the 15 elected SBOE members serve without salary for overlapping terms of four years. The governor appoints, with Senate confirmation, a sitting SBOE member as chair for a two-year term.

Deep ideological differences divide the board. The ideological split also follows partisan and ethnic lines. The socially conservative members tend to be Anglo Republicans, whereas the moderate and liberal members are commonly African American and Latino Democrats. Openly hostile debates on subjects such as textbook adoption and public criticism surrounding possible conflict of interest in the selection of investment managers and independent financial consultants for the Permanent School Fund have led some legislators to advocate reforming board procedures and others to call for elimination of the SBOE.

Probably the most contentious issue facing the SBOE is its periodic review of textbooks.[10] Books for the foundation curriculum (English, math, science, and social studies) are reviewed at least once every eight years; other textbooks may have a longer cycle. The SBOE places a book on an accepted or rejected list. To be eligible for adoption, instructional materials must cover at least 50 percent of the elements of the Texas Essential Knowledge and Skills (TEKS) for its subject and grade level. Approved books must also meet the SBOE's physical specifications (for example, quality of binding and paper). Recently, the number of electronic books and instructional materials has been increasing, although traditional paper materials still predominate. Books must be free of factual errors. Critics charge that some board members have interpreted this requirement to mean that ideas that might conflict with their own views are errors. A long-standing source of conflict has been the challenge to the theory of evolution by supporters of creationism and intelligent design. The board's debate over the TEKS social studies standards in 2010 was particularly harsh and was described by some as a "culture war."[11]

Individual school districts make their own textbook adoption decisions. The state, however, will pay 100 percent of the cost if a local school district uses books on the approved lists, but not more than 70 percent for books not on the adoption lists. Because most districts prefer the state to pay the full cost, textbook publishers want their books on one of the adoption lists. Texas is one of 22 states with a state-level approval process. Texas, California, and Florida purchase huge numbers of textbooks. (The Texas Education Agency distributes more than 48 million textbooks each year.) Thus, publishers cater to these markets. Other states complain that their textbook options tend to be limited

Points to Ponder

Education is increasingly important to both individuals and the nation as a whole. Not surprisingly, both leaders and ordinary citizens regularly speak about the importance of education. But how serious are we? Do the numbers below suggest that Texas is seeking or achieving the excellence in education that it could?

Rank Among the 50 States

Texas Public Schools		Texas Public Higher Education	
State and local expenditure per pupil	39th	Expenditure per full-time student	12th in nation
Average teacher salary	33rd	Average faculty salary	27th in nation
High school graduation rate	44th	Average tuition and fees at public universities	27th in nation
Average math score on NAEP* for eighth graders	5 states higher, 34 lower Rest similar	Percent of population with a bachelor's degree or higher	30th
Average reading score on NAEP* for eighth graders	31 states higher 7 lower Rest similar		
Percentage of high school students who play on a sports team	12th		

Source: Legislative Budget Board, *Texas Fact Book, 2012,* **http://www.lbb.state.tx.us**; Texas Higher Education Coordinating Board, *2012 Texas Public Higher Education Almanac,* **http://www.thecb.state.tx.us**; and National Center for Education Statistics, *National Assessment of Educational Progress, 2011,* **http://nces.ed.gov/nationsreportcard/states/**.

*NAEP: National Assessment of Educational Progress, called the Nation's Report Card.

to books published for one or more of the three big "adoption state" markets. Publishers and advocates of electronic books argue that the national impact of Texas's selection process is exaggerated or at least will decline over time.

Texas Education Agency Which level of government should make educational policy? The local level, according to many Texans. Local officials know local needs, and most parents and citizens believe that they should have a say. Many who study education (such as university professors), however, along with many public officials, believe that the broader, more professional perspective found at the state or national level encourages higher educational standards. Texas responds to both of these views. Local school boards and superintendents run the schools, but almost all of their decisions are shaped by state and, to a much smaller extent, federal rules and procedures. The U.S. Department of Education provides some financial assistance, requires nondiscrimination in several areas (including race, sex, and disability), and, under the No Child Left Behind and Race to the Top programs, demands extensive testing.

In the Lone Star State, the **Texas Education Agency (TEA)**, headquartered in Austin, has under 700 employees. Created by the legislature in 1949, the TEA today is headed by the **commissioner of education**, appointed by the governor to a four-year term with Senate confirmation. Under Governor Rick Perry, commissioners have been closely connected and responsive to the governor. The TEA has the following powers:

- Oversees development of the statewide curriculum
- Accredits and rates schools. In 2012, the rating system was under review. Changes may include the rating terms (such as Exemplary and Unacceptable)
- Monitors accreditation (that is, whenever a local school district or school fails to meet state academic or financial standards for consecutive years, TEA has a range of sanctions, including changing its leaders and closure)
- Oversees the testing of elementary and secondary school students
- Serves as a fiscal agent for the distribution of state and federal funds (administers about three-fourths of the Permanent School Fund and supervises the Foundation School Program, which allocates state money to independent school districts)
- Monitors compliance with federal guidelines
- Grants waivers to schools seeking charter status and exemptions from certain state regulations
- Manages the textbook adoption process, assisting the State Board of Education and individual districts
- Administers a data collection system on public school students, staff, and finances and operates research and information programs
- Handles the administrative functions of the State Board for Educator Certification (placed under TEA in 2005 as part of the sunset review process)

Much of what the TEA does goes unnoticed by the general public, but some decisions receive considerable attention and have effects beyond education. The ratings of schools are advertised to draw homebuyers into neighborhoods and subdivisions, and the decision to close a school or school district has profound effects on the community it serves. Thus, TEA has been cautious and taken less drastic steps before closing schools or districts. In the words of one education reporter,

> It's rare for the state to revoke the accreditation of an entire school district. Since 1995, it has only happened four times. The two districts marked for closure [in 2011], Premont ISD in South Texas and North Forest ISD in northeast Houston, challenged the decisions. And for the first time in TEA history, both of the districts ... have received one-year reprieves to make financial and academic turnarounds.[12]

Texas Education Agency (TEA)
Administers the state's public school system of more than 1,200 school districts and charter schools.

commissioner of education
The official who heads the TEA.

Charter Schools In 1995, the legislature authorized the SBOE to issue charters to schools that would be less limited by TEA rules. There was hope that with greater flexibility, these schools could deal more effectively with at-risk students. Compared with students at traditional schools, charter school students are more economically disadvantaged, more are African American, slightly more are Latino, and fewer are Anglo. Although charter schools are public schools, they draw students from across district lines, use a variety of teaching strategies, and are exempt from many rules, such as state teacher certification requirements. Charters are granted to nonprofit corporations that, in turn, create a board to govern the school. The particular organization varies from school to school. Charter schools cannot impose taxes but can now issue bonds for new construction. They receive most of their funding from the state, with the rest coming from federal and private sources. Thus, most charter schools have less revenue per pupil than do traditional schools ($7,578 for charter schools compared to $8,785 for other Texas public schools in 2007).[13] In 2011, Texas had 482 charter school campuses serving 134,000 students (which is less than 3 percent of public school students).

The effectiveness of charter schools in meeting the needs of at-risk students is sharply debated. Some Texas charter schools have "compiled terrific records of propelling minority and low-income kids into college," whereas others have been marked by corruption and academic failure.[14] A study by Stanford University researchers found that results varied by state. In Texas, the researchers compared the progress of students of comparable background in charter and traditional schools and found that Latino and African American students tended to do better in traditional schools, whereas students in poverty (including all ethnicities) tended to fare slightly better in charter schools.[15]

Testing Educators and political leaders are sharply divided about how to assess student progress and determine graduation standards. Nevertheless, testing as a major assessment tool is now federal and state policy. Texas first mandated a standardized test in 1980 and began to rely heavily on testing in 1990. An essential component of the state testing program is the **Texas Essential Knowledge and Skills (TEKS)**, a core curriculum that sets out the knowledge students are expected to gain. This curriculum is required by the legislature and is approved by the State Board of Education.

The current testing program is the **State of Texas Assessment of Academic Readiness (STAAR)**. Mandated by the legislature in 2007 and 2009, STAAR went into effect in the spring of 2012. It includes 12 end-of-course examinations in the four high school core subject areas (math, science, English, and social studies). Members of the class of 2015 will be the first to be required to pass the new end-of-course tests, as well as pass their courses, in order to graduate. For grades 3–8, new tests will assess reading and math for each level, as well as writing, science, and social studies for certain grade levels. The new tests and the accompanying curriculum should be more closely tied to college readiness standards and preparation for the workplace. They are also intended to be more rigorous and to measure both performance

Texas Essential Knowledge and Skills (TEKS)
A core curriculum (a set of courses and knowledge) setting out what students should learn.

State of Texas Assessment of Academic Readiness (STAAR)
A state program of end-of-course examinations in core subjects.

and academic growth. Standards will be gradually raised through 2016. In the first round of STAAR tests, statewide passing rates for freshmen varied from 55 percent for writing to 87 percent for biology. However, if the 2016 standards had been applied, a majority of students would have failed in each subject. Not surprisingly, the results were met with controversy.

One of the most controversial aspects of the testing programs is that test results are used to evaluate teachers, administrators, and schools. This practice is intended to increase "accountability"—that is, to hold teachers and administrators responsible for increasing student learning. Many educators object to their pay and perhaps their job depending on student performance because student success is so affected by students' backgrounds and home environments. The use of test results for accountability will be continued under STAAR; however, the ratings were temporarily suspended in 2012 to allow development of a new system to debut in 2013.

From its beginning, the statewide testing program has drawn cries of protest from many parents and educators. Social conservatives argue that the program tramples on local control of schools, whereas African American and Latino critics charge that the tests are discriminatory. Educational critics complain that "teaching to the test" raises scores on the test but causes neglect of other subjects. Questions are also raised when the federal No Child Left Behind program sometimes produces substantially different evaluations of schools than does the Texas system (because they use different criteria). Supporters of testing argue that it holds schools responsible for increasing student learning and point to the improved test scores of most groups of students since the program began. Because test results are so important to both students and their schools, there has been controversy over how high standards should be. Some parents and advocates for disadvantaged students argue that standards are too high. Other critics argue that the previous test (Texas Assessment of Knowledge and Skills, or TAKS) suffered from grade inflation—that is, scores increased because of low standards, not due to student improvement.[16] In January 2012, education commissioner Robert Scott, who led much of the development of the use of testing, said that testing had become a "perversion." Over the previous decade, he argued, too much reliance had been placed on tests. He wanted test results to be "just one piece of the bottom line, and everything else that happens in a school year is factored into that equation."[17] In August 2012, following Scott's resignation, Governor Perry named former Railroad Commissioner Michael Williams to head the agency.

Some critics believe that national tests such as the National Assessment of Educational Progress (NAEP) are better measures because they are not "taught to." The NAEP shows mixed results for Texas. For example, between 1990 and 2011, the math scores on the NAEP for Texas eighth graders improved significantly for African Americans, Latinos, Anglos, the economically disadvantaged, and the more affluent. The gap in scores between African American and Anglo eighth graders narrowed, as did the gap between the less and more affluent. However, the gap between Latinos and Anglos was not significantly different. On the other hand, on the eighth-grade reading test, the scores over the years were flat, and the score gap did not substantially improve for

African American, Latino, or economically disadvantaged students.[18] Not surprisingly, testing and accountability remain controversial.

Colleges and Universities

Texas has many colleges and universities—104 public and over 40 independent and for-profit institutions of higher education serving almost 1.6 million students annually. The large and growing number of institutions reflects several factors: the early tradition of locating colleges away from the "evils" of large cities, the demand of communities for schools to serve their needs, and the desire to make college education accessible to students. Most potential Texas students live within commuting distance of a campus. The public institutions include 38 universities, nine health-related institutions, 50 community college districts (many with multiple campuses), three two-year state colleges, and four colleges of the Texas State Technical College System. All receive some state funding and, not surprisingly, state regulation.

Texas has three universities widely recognized as being among the prestigious tier-one national research universities: Rice University (private), the University of Texas at Austin (public), and Texas A&M University in College Station (public). Among public schools, the latter two are commonly referred to as the "flagship" universities; they have traditionally been the most prestigious academically and the most powerful politically. Most observers believe that Texas needs more flagship universities to serve the increasing number of highly qualified students and to carry out the research necessary

LO3

CourseReader ASSIGNMENTS

Log in to www.cengagebrain.com and open CourseReader to access the reading:

"All Hat and No Cattle": Separate and Unequal Funding for Higher Education in Texas
Sandra Dahlberg

Higher education in Texas had been in a critical condition even before the state faced a serious budget deficit. With more students entering and charges of not equitably serving minority populations, the system as a whole was facing many difficult questions. Once budget cuts became necessary, however, the situation got worse. This article examines the funding structure in Texas and how difficult funding decisions have been made.

1. Is higher education a *public good* or a *personal benefit*? Or is it some of both? Why? How do Texas policies reflect these two views?

2. Drawing on the article and the discussions in the chapter, how well does public policy promote equality of opportunity in Texas higher education?

to attract new businesses and grow the economy. In 2009, a constitutional amendment gave access to funding through the Texas Research Incentive Program that will allow seven other universities to try to join the list of tier-one universities: the University of Texas at Arlington, Dallas, El Paso, and San Antonio; Texas Tech University; University of Houston; and University of North Texas. In 2012, Texas State University–San Marcos was added to the list of emerging research institutions by the Higher Education Coordinating Board. To achieve tier-one status, each school will have to raise more money and produce more research and successful doctoral graduates.

Most Texas universities are governed by systems. A university system has a board of regents, a chancellor, and other officials who provide governance and services for the universities making up the system. The University of Texas and Texas A&M University have evolved into large systems with multiple campuses spread across the state. Four universities are independent (for example, Texas Woman's University), and the rest are part of four other university systems (for example, the Texas State University System). The website for the Texas Higher Education Coordinating Board (THECB) lists all public schools and indicates their systems.

Boards of Regents Texas's independent public universities, university systems, and the Texas State Technical College System are governed by boards of regents. The regents are appointed by the governor for six-year terms with Senate approval. The board makes general policy, selects each university's president, and provides general supervision of the universities in their system. In the case of systems, the board usually selects a chancellor to handle administration and to provide executive leadership. The president of one of the universities may simultaneously serve as chancellor. Day-to-day operation of the universities is in the hands of the individual school's top officials (commonly the president and the academic vice president, though terminology varies). The governance of community colleges is by local boards, as discussed in Chapter 3 "Local Governments."

Texas Higher Education Coordinating Board The Texas Higher Education Coordinating Board (THECB) is not a super board of regents, but it does provide some semblance of statewide direction for all public (not private) community colleges and universities. The coordinating board must approve new academic programs, degrees, universities, community colleges, and technical colleges. To force greater use of campus facilities (which means more afternoon classes), the THECB has long refused new construction permits to schools with low use of existing classrooms. Students who have problems transferring course credits from one public Texas college or university to another may appeal to the board. The nine members of the board receive no pay and are appointed by the governor to six-year terms with Senate approval. Gubernatorial power also extends to designating two board members as chair and vice chair, with neither appointment requiring Senate confirmation. Governors commonly have a close relationship with the board, which increases their influence over higher education. The board

Texas Higher Education Coordinating Board (THECB)
An agency that provides some direction for the state's public community colleges and universities.

Students in Action

Booze and Ballots: A Tale of Two Different Times

"We involved a lot of students in the public sphere for the first time, and some continued to be involved. We saved some lives and had a lot of fun."

—Anonymous

Texas law allows citizens of almost any political entity to vote their area wet (the sale of alcohol is allowed) or dry (the sale of alcohol is prohibited). Walker County, home of Huntsville and Sam Houston State University (Sam), voted dry in 1914 and remained so until 1971. That year, Citizens for a Progressive Huntsville, composed mainly of Sam students and led by two students, circulated a petition for an election to permit alcohol sales within the city. Most of the 916 who signed the petition were thought to be Sam students or faculty. Townspeople were reluctant to sign the petition, because others could see their names on the list. When the vote was held by secret ballot, however, all four voting boxes favored a wet community, which won with 62 percent of the votes. An estimated 800 students voted (out of 3,118 total votes).

In 2008, a Sam student ran unsuccessfully for the Huntsville City Council. Although it was not part of his public message, he told fellow students that his major concern was to extend bar hours from 12 midnight to 2 a.m. Even so, he couldn't get his own fraternity brothers out to the polls.

In 1971, in the wet issue, campus activists found a concern that could pull together students of widely varying views. Nearly 40 years later, the presidential election of 2008 produced a larger-than-usual student vote, but there was no student-led movement to capitalize on the bar hours issue.

What's the Advice to Students?

"Sometimes it takes an issue like booze to get people interested enough to act on other, more important matters."

(Monkey Business Images/Shutterstock.com)

Souces: Interviews and archives of the Walker County Clerk, City of Huntsville, and the Huntsville Public Library.

appoints (and can remove) the commissioner of higher education, who runs the agency on a day-to-day basis and who usually plays a substantial role in higher education policy.

The feeling by many community college leaders that the Coordinating Board tends to give priority to senior colleges led to a $350,000 appropriation by the 2011 legislature to fund a study looking at the possibility of creating a separate administrative structure for community colleges. The release of the report in 2012 created a furor in the Coordinating Board (which was not interested in a reduction in its authority) and an issue for the 2013 legislature.

Higher Education Issues Two sets of issues have challenged Texas higher education in recent years: funding and affirmative action. Funding and the sharp increase in tuition rates are discussed in Chapter 11, "Finance and Fiscal Policy," but we address affirmative action in the following paragraphs.

Improving the educational opportunities of Texas's ethnic minorities and the economically disadvantaged is an important but controversial issue, and one with a long history in the state. A 1946 denial of admission to the University of Texas law school on the grounds of race led to the "landmark case, *Sweatt v. Painter*, that helped break the back of racism in college admissions" throughout the country.[19] Texas's long history of official and private discrimination still has consequences today. Although many Latinos and African Americans have made it into the middle class since the civil rights changes of the 1960s and 1970s, both groups remain overrepresented in the working class and the ranks of the poor but underrepresented in Texas higher education. To overcome this problem, the THECB adopted an ambitious program, called Closing the Gaps, to increase enrollment and graduation rates for all groups by 2015. The program has been relatively successful. By 2011, African American and Latino enrollment in higher education was more than 10 percent above target levels, whereas Anglo enrollment had increased but was somewhat below target levels. For all three ethnic groups, women were enrolled at higher rates than men. Graduation rates increased for all three ethnic groups, but African Americans and Latinos were somewhat below target levels.[20] A study financed by the Bill and Melinda Gates Foundation concluded that if the goals of Closing the Gaps are achieved, "When all public [state and local] and private costs are considered, the annual economic returns per $1 of expenditures by 2030 are estimated to be $24.15 in total spending, $9.60 in gross state product, and $6.01 in personal income."[21]

Texas colleges and universities commonly describe themselves as equal opportunity/affirmative action institutions. **Equal opportunity** simply means that the school takes care that its policies and actions do not produce prohibited discrimination, such as on the basis of race and sex. (Schools do discriminate on the basis of such things as grades and qualifications.) **Affirmative action** means that the school takes positive steps to attract women and minorities. For most schools, this means such noncontroversial steps as making sure that the school catalog has pictures of all groups— Anglos and minorities, men and women—and recruiting in predominantly minority high schools, not just Anglo schools. However, some selective-admission schools have actively considered race in admissions and aid, and other schools have had scholarships for minorities. This side of affirmative action has created controversy.

Some Anglo applicants denied admission or scholarship benefits challenged these affirmative action programs in the courts. In the case of *University of California v. Bakke* (1978), the U.S. Supreme Court ruled that race could be considered as one factor, along with other criteria, to achieve diversity in higher education enrollment; however, setting aside a specific number of slots for one race was not acceptable.[22] Relying on the *Bakke* decision, the University of Texas Law School created separate admission pools based on race and ethnicity, a practice the U.S. Fifth Circuit Court of

equal opportunity
Ensures that policies and actions do not discriminate on factors such as race, gender, ethnicity, religion, or national origin.

affirmative action
Takes positive steps to attract women and members of racial and ethnic minority groups; may include using race in admission or hiring decisions.

Appeals declared unconstitutional in *Hopwood v. Texas* (1996).[23] Subsequently the U.S. Supreme Court issued two rulings on affirmative action in 2003. In the Michigan case of *Grutter v. Bollinger,* the court ruled that race could constitute one factor in an admissions policy designed to achieve student body diversity;[24] then, in another Michigan case, *Gratz and Harnacher v. Bollinger,* the court condemned the practice of giving a portion of the points needed to guarantee admission to every underrepresented minority seeking admittance.[25]

After the *Hopwood* ruling, Texas schools looked for ways to maintain minority enrollment. In 1997, Texas legislators mandated the **top 10 percent rule**, which provides that the top 10 percent of every accredited public or private Texas high school graduating class could be admitted to tax-supported colleges and universities of their choosing, regardless of admission test scores. Thus, the students with the best grades at Texas's high schools, including those that are heavily minority, economically disadvantaged, or in small towns, can gain admission. The top 10 percent rule has helped all three groups. For students not admitted on the basis of class standing, the University of Texas at Austin uses a "holistic review" of all academic and personal achievements, which may take into consideration family income, race, and ethnicity (with no specific weight and no quotas). The use of race in the holistic review produced another court challenge (*Fisher v. University of Texas*), which was heard before the U.S. Supreme Court during the fall of 2012.[26]

In fall 2010 and again in fall 2011, Anglos were a minority of incoming University of Texas at Austin (UT-Austin) freshmen—48 percent—although they remained a majority for the university as a whole. In 2004, Texas A&M University announced that it would not use race in admissions decisions but would increase minority recruiting and provide more scholarships for first-generation, low-income students. (First-generation students are the first in their immediate family to attend college.) In fall 2011, fifty-nine percent of A&M's new undergraduates were Anglos. All Texas institutions of higher education are under mandate from the Higher Education Coordinating Board to actively recruit and retain minority students under its Closing the Gaps initiative.

The top 10 percent rule is controversial, especially among applicants from competitive high schools denied admission to the state's flagship institutions—the University of Texas at Austin and Texas A&M University. Moreover, in fall 2009, 86 percent of students offered admission to the University of Texas at Austin qualified by the top 10 percent rule, a situation that leaves little room for students to be admitted on the basis of high scores or other talents (such as music or leadership). According to the university's president, even football might have had to be abolished. In any event, the 2009 legislature modified the rule so that UT-Austin would not have to admit more than 75 percent of its students on the basis of class standing. The class standing that the university chose for admission varied by year: top 8 percent for fall 2011 and 2013, but top 9 percent for fall 2012. The 75 percent cap is in effect only through the 2015 school year, unless it is renewed by the legislature.

top 10 percent rule
Texas law gives automatic admission into any Texas public college or university to those graduating in the top 10 percent of their Texas high school class with limitations for the University of Texas at Austin.

Point/Counterpoint

THE ISSUE To promote diversity in Texas colleges and universities without using race as an admission criterion, the state legislature in 1997 passed a law guaranteeing admission to any public college or university in the state to Texas students who graduate in the top 10 percent of their high school class. The law sought to promote greater geographic, socioeconomic, and racial/ethnic diversity. The law applies to all public colleges and universities in the state, but it has had its greatest effect on the two flagship universities—the University of Texas at Austin and Texas A&M University—prestigious schools with more qualified applicants than they can admit. The rule has increased minority representation at both schools but more so at the University of Texas. In 2009, the legislature capped automatic admission to the University of Texas at Austin at 75 percent.

Should Texas Continue to Use the "Top 10 Percent Rule"?

Arguments For the Top 10 Percent Rule

- It is doing what it was designed to do—increase diversity among highly qualified students.
- Virtually all top 20 percent students from competitive high schools who choose UT–Austin or Texas A&M actually succeed in enrolling there.
- The problem is not that Texas has too many students entering schools under automatic admission. Rather, there are too few flagship universities to accommodate the number of qualified students.

Arguments Against the Top 10 Percent Rule

- It unfairly puts students who attend high schools with rigorous standards at a disadvantage. Thus, they are tempted to take lighter loads or attend less-demanding high schools.
- So many students are admitted under this one criterion that the universities have too little discretion, and students with other talents (such as music and the arts) are left out.
- The rule is creating a brain drain; many top students are leaving Texas to attend college in other states, where they often remain after graduation.

For more information, see *Should Texas Change the Top 10 Percent Law?* Focus Report No. 79-7 (Austin: House Research Organization, Texas House of Representatives, February 25, 2005), **http://www.hro. house.state.tx.us/ frame4.htm#fac**; and House Research Organization, "UT-Austin Implements New Top 10 Percent Rules for Freshman Admissions," *Interim News,* December 16, 2009, **http://www.hro.house. state.tx.us/frame4.htm#int**.

✓ Learning Check 9.2   (Answers on p. 383)

1. Which two state government entities are most important for public schools?
2. True or False: Almost all observers consider Texas's testing program a success.
3. What is the "top 10 percent rule" in Texas higher education?

Health and Human Services

Most people think of Texas as a wealthy state, and indeed there are many   **LO4**
wealthy Texans and a large middle class. Texas, however, also has long been
among the states with the largest proportion of its population in poverty.
Texas's 2010 poverty rate was the ninth highest in the nation at 17.9 percent. From 1980 to 2010, Texas's poverty rate varied from 15 to 19 percent.
Poverty is particularly high for children and ethnic minorities, as can be
seen in detail in Table 9.2. Even more Texans are low income, meaning they
earn an income above the poverty line but insufficient income for many
"extras," such as health insurance. (A common measure of low income is an
income up to twice the poverty level. In 2010, more than one in five Texans
fell into this category—that is, between 101 and 200 percent of the poverty
level.)

Access to health care is a national issue that is even more acute in Texas.
In a 2007 editorial, the *Fort Worth Star-Telegram* stated that

> The Commonwealth Fund, a well respected foundation ... ranks Texas
> near the bottom of the nation after evaluating 32 measures of
> [health-care] quality. Only Mississippi and Oklahoma rank lower.... So
> what gives? Two words: health insurance. If you have it, Texas is one
> of the best places on Earth for care. If you don't, it can be an unfor-
> giving address. The state's low-cost safety net has too little depth or
> breadth.[27]

The Commonwealth Fund's 2007 and 2009 state-by-state comparisons of
health system performance, as well as the 2011 comparison of child health
system performance, and the 2012 scorecard for local health system
performance all ranked Texas in the bottom quarter of the 50 states.[28] Texas
has led the nation in the proportion of people without health insurance
since at least 1988—about one in four Texans has no health insurance, as
compared with one in six in the nation. It also leads in the proportion of
uninsured children.

The passage of the controversial national health insurance program,
the Patient Protection and Affordable Care Act, (popularly known as
"Obamacare") in 2010 was aimed at significantly improving this situation. Although most provisions of the act do not come into effect until
2014, by 2012, several provisions had been implemented. For example,
young adults up to age 26 could be on their parents' insurance, preexist-
ing conditions were covered in many cases, and the caps on lifetime
benefits were lifted. In June 2012, the U.S. Supreme Court upheld most
of the act in a suit brought by Texas and 25 other states (*National
Federation of Independent Business v. Sebelius* 567 U.S. ___ [2012]). The
major part of the act not approved will be discussed below in the section
on Medicaid. By 2014, most individuals who can afford it will be required
to purchase a basic health insurance policy or pay a fee. Insurance

Table 9.2 Who's in Poverty in Texas and the United States? (2010)

	Texas		U.S.
	Number (million)	%	%
Individuals	4.4	18	15
Anglos	1.0	9	10
Hispanics	2.5	27	27
African Americans	0.7	25	27
Children younger than 18	1.8	26	22
Age 65 and older	0.3	11	9

Note: Poverty level varies by family size. In 2011, the poverty level for a family of three was an annual income of $18,530; for a family of four, it was $22,350.

Sources: U.S. Census Bureau, **http://www.census.gov/hhes/www/poverty/**, and Center for Public Policy Priorities, "Poverty 101," November 2011, **http://www.cppp.org/research.php?aid=96**.

exchanges will be available for those who cannot obtain insurance through their employer.

Since the Great Depression of the 1930s, state and national governments have gradually increased efforts to address the needs of the poor, the elderly, and those who cannot afford adequate medical care. In the 20th century, social welfare became an important part of the federal relationship (see Chapter 2, "Federalism and the Texas Constitution" and Chapter 3, "Local Governments"). Over time, the national government has taken responsibility for relatively popular social welfare programs, such as Social Security, Medicare, and aid to the blind and disabled. The states, on the other hand, have responsibility for less popular programs with less effective lobbying behind them, such as Medicaid, Supplemental Nutrition Assistance Program (SNAP, formerly food stamps), and Temporary Assistance for Needy Families (TANF). The federal government pays a significant part of the cost of state social welfare programs, but within federal guidelines the states administer them, make eligibility rules, and pay part of the tab.

Health and human services programs are at a disadvantage in Texas for two reasons. First, the state's political culture values individualism and self-reliance; thus, anything smacking of welfare is difficult to fund at more than the most minimal level. In addition, the neediest Texans lack the organization and resources to compete with the special-interest groups representing the business elite and the middle class. Thus, the Lone Star State provides assistance for millions of needy Texans, but at relatively low benefit levels. And many are left out.

The Texas Health and Human Services Commission (HHSC) coordinates social service policy. Sweeping changes were launched in 2003 when the 78th legislature consolidated functions of 12 social service agencies under the **executive commissioner of the Health and Human Services Commission**. The legislation also began a process of privatizing service delivery, creating more administrative barriers to services, and slowing the growth of expenditures.

The executive commissioner of the HHSC is appointed by the governor for a two-year term and confirmed by the Senate. The executive commissioner controls the agency directly and is not under the direction of a board; instead, commissioners tend to be responsive to the governor. The executive commissioner appoints, with the approval of the governor, commissioners to head the four departments of the HHSC: Department of State Health Services, Department of Aging and Disability Services, Department of Assistive and Rehabilitative Services, and Department of Family and Protective Services. See Figure 9.1 for the commission's organization chart and major tasks of the departments. The HHSC, itself, handles centralized administrative support services, develops policies, and makes rules for its agencies. In addition, the commission determines eligibility for TANF, SNAP, the Children's Health Insurance Program (CHIP), Medicaid, and long-term care services. For 2012–2013, the legislature authorized 57,000 employees for HHSC and its four departments.

The legislature not only consolidated agencies under HHSC in 2003, but it also mandated major changes in the state's approach to social services. A change that created widespread problems involved replacing local offices and caseworkers with call centers operated by private contractors rather than staffed by state employees. Applicants for social services were encouraged to use the telephone and Internet to establish eligibility for most social services. A similar but much smaller privatized system had worked reasonably well in 2000. However, this new, large system performed poorly. After 2003, the number of children covered by insurance dropped sharply, and eligible people faced long waits and lost paperwork. In response to these problems, the offshore private contractor was replaced, many state employees were brought back, and attempts were made to bring children back into the system. Yet, in 2010, a federal official complained about Texas's "five-year slide" to last place among the states in the speed and accuracy of handling food stamp applications after privatization. Promised savings and better service had yet to appear. State officials say the problem is that privatization is still a work in progress and that there is no turning back. Critics argue that profit incentives and social services are inherently in conflict.[29]

Human Services

The Health and Human Services Commission administers a variety of programs, three of which have long received a great deal of attention and controversy: Temporary Assistance for Needy Families, Supplemental Nutritional Assistance Program (food stamps), and Medicaid. All three are administered by the executive commissioner within federal guidelines and are paid for by the federal government and to a lesser extent by the state. In the words of budget analyst Eva DeLuna Castro, eligibility for these and other "public

executive commissioner of the Health and Human Services Commission Appointed by the governor with Senate approval, this executive commissioner administers the HHSC, develops policies, makes rules, and appoints (with approval by the governor) commissioners to head the commission's four departments.

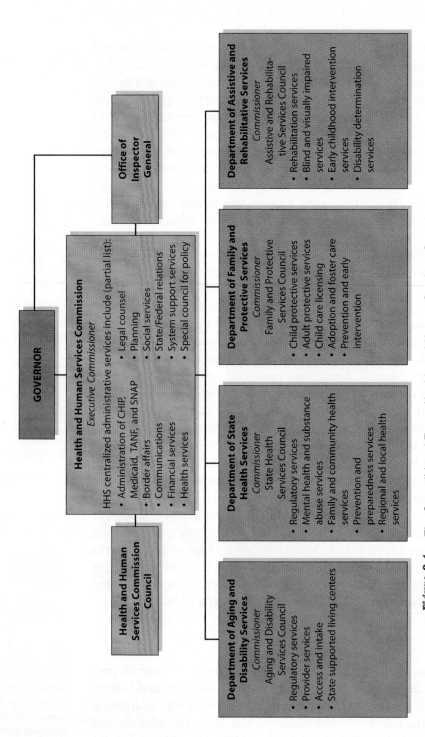

Figure 9.1 The Consolidated Texas Health and Human Services System.

Source: Based on Texas Health and Human Services Commission, February 2012, **http://www.hhsc.state.tx.us**

assistance programs in Texas is very restrictive compared to other states, the benefits are lower, and health benefits for poor adults are more limited. As a result, a smaller share of the poor in Texas receives any public assistance."[30] In addition, all three programs suffered financially from the budget cutbacks carried out by the 2011 legislature.

The executive commissioner has direct responsibility for the **Temporary Assistance for Needy Families (TANF)** program. In Texas, this program provides limited support for extremely poor families. For a family of three in 2012, the poverty level was $19,090. To receive TANF, the family could earn no more than $2,300 a year (just over 12 percent of the poverty level). Caretakers must be U.S. citizens or legal residents and agree to work or to enroll in a job-training program. According to HHSC, the "most common" TANF caretaker is a woman about 30 years old with one or two children younger than age 11. She is unemployed, has no other income, and receives a TANF grant of $208 or less per month for fewer than 12 months. In addition to the small amount of cash provided directly to clients by TANF, recipients may receive benefits from other programs, such as SNAP and Medicaid.

A second federal-state program administered by the executive commissioner is the **Supplemental Nutritional Assistance Program (SNAP)**, formerly called food stamps. It makes food available to elderly or disabled people, families, and single adults who qualify because of low income up to 130 percent of the poverty level. Approximately 80 percent of those who benefit from SNAP receive no TANF support. Benefits vary, depending on income and the number of people in a household. In 2012, for example, a qualified Texas household composed of three people could obtain groceries costing up to $526 each month. To reduce fraud, the program has replaced paper stamps used for purchases with a plastic Lone Star Card, which functions like a debit card. For more information on these and other benefits, log on to Your Texas Benefits at **http://www.yourtexasbenefits.com/**.

Health and Mental Health Services

The third major federal-state program administered by the executive commissioner is **Medicaid**. Part of President Lyndon B. Johnson's Great Society initiatives in the 1960s, Medicaid is designed to provide medical care for persons whose income falls below the poverty line. Resources not counted against the poverty-level limit are a home, personal possessions, and a low-value motor vehicle. Not to be confused with Medicaid is **Medicare**, another Great Society initiative. A federal program providing medical assistance to qualifying applicants age 65 and older, Medicare is administered by the U.S. Department of Health and Human Services without use of state funds. Because Medicaid is considered welfare and serves the poor, it has much less political clout than Medicare, which serves a more middle-class clientele. Medicaid has much more difficulty gaining funding, and benefits for clients and reimbursements for service providers tend to be lower. Benefits are so low that the majority of Texas doctors now refuse new Medicaid patients, and nursing homes have trouble covering their costs.

Temporary Assistance for Needy Families (TANF)
Provides financial assistance to the poor in an attempt to help them move from welfare to the workforce.

Supplemental Nutritional Assistance Program (SNAP)
Joint federal-state program administered by the state to provide food to low-income people.

Medicaid
Funded in larger part by federal grants and in part by state appropriations, Medicaid is administered by the state. It provides medical care for persons whose incomes fall below the poverty line.

Medicare
Funded entirely by the federal government and administered by the U.S. Department of Health and Human Services, Medicare provides medical assistance to qualified applicants age 65 and older.

Under the 2010 federal health-care reform, the states were required to expand Medicaid coverage to virtually all non-elderly adults earning up to 133 percent of the poverty line by 2014. States that did not provide the expanded coverage could lose their existing federal Medicaid funds. However, the U.S. Supreme Court held that the federal government could not use the threat of withholding the existing funding to coerce expansion of Medicaid. Thus, states have the option of participating in the expansion or keeping their existing program. Editorials in most of the major newspapers in the state supported the expansion; however, in July 2012, Governor Perry wrote to federal authorities that Texas would not participate in the expansion of Medicaid. Most states that initially rejected expansion are expected to eventually accept the expansion, but it is unclear whether Texas will join them. For those states participating, the federal government will pay the entire cost of the expansion for the first three years and at least 90 percent beyond that. Payments for primary care physicians will also be raised to Medicare levels.

An additional controversy arose when the 2011 Texas legislature excluded Planned Parenthood from receiving funding under Medicaid's Women's Health Program, which provides routine exams, contraception, and preventive health services. Planned Parenthood, which treated almost half the patients under Texas's Medicaid Women's Health Program, was excluded because some of its clinics provide abortions (which cannot be paid for by state or federal money). Implementation of the program in 2012 led to conflicts over cutting off federal funds to the program and attempts by the state to find funding.

The Department of State Health Services performs a wide variety of functions, including public health planning and enforcement of state health laws. As with public assistance, state health policies are closely tied to several federal programs. One example is the Special Supplemental Nutrition Program for Women, Infants, and Children (WIC), a delivery system for food packages, nutritional counseling, and health-care screening.

Because diseases are a constant threat to human life and a drain on the economy, the Department of State Health Services is responsible for educating Texans about infectious diseases. Acquired immunodeficiency syndrome (AIDS) is caused by the human immunodeficiency virus (HIV) and commonly transmitted by sexual contact (both homosexual and heterosexual) and contaminated needles used by drug addicts. AIDS is an international epidemic but more stable in Texas. According to the department's comprehensive 2010 report on AIDS/HIV:

> Since 2004, the number of persons living with HIV (PLWH) in Texas has increased steadily, by about 5 percent each year ... In Texas, the number of new HIV diagnoses and deaths among PLWH has remained largely stable in the past seven years, averaging around 4,180 new diagnoses and 1,470 deaths per year ... The increase ... in PLWH over time reflects continued survival due to better treatment, not an increase in new diagnoses. In an environment of increasing numbers of PLWH, the fact that new diagnoses have remained level speaks to successful prevention and treatment efforts, but more must be done in order to actually reduce the number of new HIV diagnoses.[31]

Among the more than 65,000 Texans living with HIV in 2010, 80 percent were male, 34 percent Anglo, 38 percent African American, and 27 percent Latino. HIV is the state's fifth leading cause of death among both men and women ages 35–44.

A related problem is the continuing increase in the number of cases of sexually transmitted diseases (STDs) other than HIV/AIDS reported in Texas each year. This number reached almost 158,000 in 2010. Persons between 15 and 24 years of age account for about two-thirds of this total. The actual STD numbers are probably higher, because not all STDs must be reported, and many cases go unreported.

The Department of State Health Services is also responsible for disseminating information under the Women's Right to Know Act of 2003, which is aimed at reducing the number of abortions. Controversy and court action arose over an amendment to the act passed by the 2011 legislature requiring that women seeking an abortion must undergo a sonogram and hear a detailed description of the fetus at least 24 hours before the abortion. The woman can decide whether to view the sonogram or to hear the fetal heartbeat.

The Texas departments of State Health Services and Aging and Disability Services provide public mental health programs for persons unable to afford private therapy for emotional problems. However, Texas's per capita funding for mental health programs ranks 50th among the 50 states (in fiscal year 2009, $38, compared to the national average of $123).[32] As a result, the state serves only a fraction of those needing assistance. Thousands are on waiting lists for care, and an unknown number of the mentally ill are detained in jails or living on the streets.

Like most states, Texas relies heavily on community outpatient services for mental health treatment, which is the cheaper and medically preferred option for most patients. The number of patients receiving community mental health services has been relatively flat, fluctuating from 62,000 to 68,000 during the 2007–2013 period. Annually, approximately 2,400 patients are in state mental-health hospitals, and 4,000 are in state-supported living centers. In addition to a long-standing debate about whether these large facilities are appropriate for all patients, reports of abuse in the living centers brought an agreement in 2009 between the U.S. Justice Department and Texas to increase the number of workers and federal inspections. Since then, the number of workers has increased, but the failure to increase wages for direct care workers has contributed to continuing high rates of neglect.

Employment

Texas's state employment services cut across three areas of policy: human services, education, and economic development. The agency receives appropriations from the legislature in the category of business and economic development, which probably works to its advantage because of the legislature's more friendly view of business and development. The **Texas Workforce Commission (TWC)** serves both employers and workers. For

Texas Workforce Commission (TWC)
A state agency headed by three salaried commissioners who oversee job training and unemployment compensation programs.

employers, TWC offers recruiting, retention, training and retraining, out-placement services, and information on labor law and labor market statis-tics. For job seekers, TWC offers career development information, job search resources, training programs, and unemployment benefits. As part of this effort, the TWC matches unemployed workers with employers offering jobs. The TWC also collects an employee payroll tax paid by employers, which funds weekly benefit payments to unemployed workers covered by the Texas Unemployment Compensation Act. The amount paid depends on wages earned in an earlier quarter (three months). In 2012, the maximum weekly compensation was $426, and the minimum was $61. The Great Recession increased unemployment and claims, although Texas unemployment ran below the national average. In 2009, Governor Perry rejected $555 million in federal stimulus funds for the unemployed. To cover increased costs, the tax paid by Texas employers to finance unemployment insurance was raised in 2010 to the highest level in 20 years. (The average tax rate went from 0.99 percent of the first $9,000 of an employee's salary in 2009 to 1.83 per-cent in 2010. In 2012, it was 1.96 percent.) The agency is directed by three salaried commissioners appointed by the governor, with consent of the Sen-ate, for overlapping six-year terms. One member represents employers, one represents labor, and one is intended to represent the general public.

 Learning Check 9.3   **(Answers on p. 383)**

1. Compared with other states, is poverty high or low in Texas?
2. Why are health and human services programs at a disadvantage in Texas?
3. What program provides limited cash benefits to poor families?
4. Which program is better funded, Medicaid or Medicare?

★ Economic, Environmental, and Homeland Security Policies

LO5   Education, health, and human services are three-fourths of Texas state government expenditure. Business, economic development, and regulation together account for 14 percent of the budget, but they have a substantial and often direct effect on the lives of Texans. The state tries to generate economic development that, when successful, produces jobs and profits. Regulations affect the prices we pay for electricity and insurance, as well as the quality of the air we breathe. Historically, regulation was supported as a means to protect the individual, the weak, and the general public against the economically powerful and the special interests. In practice, this protection has been difficult to achieve because the benefits of regulation tend to be diffuse and the costs specific. For example, cleaner air benefits a broad range of the public, but few can put a dollar amount on their own benefit. On the other hand, companies that must pay to clean up their air emissions see a specific (and sometimes large) cost. Thus, they may have more incentive to spend money to fight regulation than do those who benefit from it. Moreover, businesses are better organized and have more connections to policymakers than does the public. For most of Texas's history, economic and regulatory policies have tilted toward business. The Republican ascendancy in recent years has enhanced this tendency, although consumer, environmental, and labor advocates are increasingly heard.

Economic Regulatory Policy

Have you ever complained about a high telephone bill, a big automobile insurance premium, or the cost of a license to practice a trade or profession for which you have been trained? Welcome to the Lone Star State's regulatory politics. For businesses seeking to boost profits or professional groups trying to strengthen their licensing requirements, obtaining or avoiding changes in regulations can be costly but rewarding. Less-organized consumers and workers often believe they are left to pick up the tab for higher bills and fees and, on occasion, inferior service.

Railroad Commissioner David Porter

(Courtesy Texas State Railroad Commission)

Business Regulation The **Railroad Commission of Texas (RRC)** and the state's Public Utility Commission are among Texas's most publicized agencies. This attention is because the former regulates the oil and gas industry, which is experiencing a resurgence in its influence on the Texas economy, while the latter affects the telephone and electric power bills paid by millions of Texans.

The three **Railroad Commission (RRC)** members function in several capacities, most of which have nothing to do with railroads. Today, the commission no longer "busts" railroad monopolies; rather, the RRC is primarily involved in granting permits for drilling oil and gas wells and performing other regulatory duties designated by the legislature. For example, the RRC regulates natural gas rates in rural areas and hears appeals of municipally set gas rates for residential and business customers. Other important functions of this agency include preventing waste of valuable petroleum resources, ensuring pipeline safety, and overseeing the plugging of depleted or abandoned oil and gas wells.

Textbooks often cite the RRC as the classic case of "agency capture," a situation in which the regulated industry exerts excessive influence over the agency intended to regulate it. Despite legislation requiring protection of consumers and the environment, the RRC has long seen its major function as maintaining the profitability of the state's oil and gas industry. The industry's earlier decline and the state's greater economic diversity have

Railroad Commission of Texas (RRC)
A popularly elected, three-member commission primarily engaged in regulating natural gas and petroleum production.

**Railroad Commissioner
Barry T. Smitherman**

*(Courtesy Texas State Railroad
Commission)*

reduced industry dominance somewhat. Under law, the three commissioners are elected to six-year terms with one commissioner seeking election every two years. However, the RRC is often considered a way-station in the career of rising politicians. Only a minority stay six years, so many commissioners take office as a result of gubernatorial appointment. A high proportion come to office with much of their career in the oil and gas industry. The commissioners are full-time and earn $137,500 a year. At the time of this book's publication, the commissioners are David Porter, Barry Smitherman, and newly-elected Christi Craddick.

In 2009–2010, drilling for natural gas in the Barnett Shale put more than 1,000 wells within Fort Worth's city limits, creating a variety of public concerns—environmental pollution, pipeline rights-of-way, drilling near homes, and even earthquakes. The outcry contributed to the defeat of RRC Chair Victor Carrillo in the 2010 Republican primary—an unusual occurrence. (Carrillo complained that his Spanish surname also played a role in his defeat.)

Another related controversy facing the RRC is fracking, which involves injecting large amounts of water, sand, and chemicals underground at high pressure to break up shale formations, allowing oil or gas to flow up the wellbore. The process is contributing to the rebirth of the oil and gas industry in the state and elsewhere, but it raises major questions about fracking's effect on the environment, including the underground water supply and the contaminated water that returns to the surface.

Regulation of Public Utilities State regulation of Texas's utility companies did not begin until 1975 with the creation of the **Public Utility Commission (PUC)**. Its three members are appointed by the governor, with Senate approval, to overlapping six-year terms. They work full-time and earn $150,000 a year.

The PUC's responsibility for overseeing telecommunications within Texas is limited by national policies. Federal law allows the Federal Communications Commission (FCC) to preempt state regulation of telephone companies. Ultimately, determining whose regulations apply is a matter for courts to decide.

Today, PUC operations exemplify recent trends in regulatory policies nationwide. Business practices formerly controlled by government agency rules are now governed more by market conditions. The objective of this industry-backed policy, known as **deregulation**, is to free businesses from governmental restraints and to depend largely on competition to protect the public interest.

During the past decade, the Texas legislature has caused the PUC to shift from setting rates that telephone and electric power companies may charge to a policy of deregulation that emphasizes competition. Allowing consumers to choose their telephone service supplier was expected to result in reasonable telephone bills and reliable service from companies that must compete for customers. With the growth of competition from cell phones, this system has arguably worked. According to critics, however, deregulation of most suppliers of Texas electricity has made Texas rates among the highest in the nation—a reversal of two decades of lower-than-average rates under state regulation. In 2010, Texans paid more for electricity than consumers in neighboring states or Texans served by regulated entities (such as municipal power companies).[33] In 2012, the PUC was facing major concerns over the reliability of the flow of electricity. To avoid blackouts during periods of high usage, such as the summer air conditioning season, the commission was considering raising rates substantially to encourage the construction of additional generating plants.[34]

Insurance Regulation The commissioner of insurance heads the Texas Department of Insurance, which regulates to some degree the $50 billion insurance industry in the Lone Star State. The commissioner is appointed by the governor for a two-year term and earns $164,000 a year. The Office of Public Insurance Counsel represents consumers in rate disputes.

At the beginning of 2003, Texans who owned homes and automobiles paid the highest insurance rates in the country. Rates were unregulated and rising rapidly. In response to the public outcry, the 2003 legislature gave the commissioner of insurance authority to regulate all home insurers doing business in Texas. The following year, Texas began a largely deregulated "file and use" system for auto and homeowners insurance. Insurers are free to set their rates, but the commissioner of insurance is authorized to order reductions and refunds if rates are determined to be excessive. Advocates of this system expected it to produce reasonable rates by promoting competition among insurance companies; however, as of 2010, Texans were paying 52–76 percent more than the national average for homeowners insurance. In the more competitive car insurance industry, Texas was near the middle of the 50 states in average cost in 2010 and 2011 (and within $70 of the national averages) but $220 over the average in 2012.

Because of natural disasters such as hurricanes, hail, and mold, insurance rates in Texas tend to be high. But are they higher than necessary, as consumer groups argue they are? The "loss ratio," which is considered the best measure of insurance company profitability, is what a company pays in benefits as a percentage of the premium money it receives. From 1992 to 2009, the average loss ratio for Texas insurance companies was 68 percent—greater than the 60 percent the industry prefers and lower than consumer advocates would prefer.[35]

Business Promotion

Some cynical observers contend that the business of Texas government is business. Others argue that boosting business strengthens the Texas

Public Utility Commission (PUC)
A three-member appointed body with regulatory power over the electric and telephone companies.

deregulation
The elimination of government restrictions to allow free-market competition to determine or limit the actions of individuals and corporations.

commissioner of insurance
Appointed by the governor, the commissioner heads the Texas Department of Insurance, which is responsible for ensuring the industry's financial soundness and for protecting policy holders. It affects insurance rates.

economy and creates jobs that benefit the lives of all Texans. Certainly, Texas's political culture and the strength of business lobbyists make most of Texas government highly responsive to business. In 2011, Texas was ranked third among the 50 states in "Policy Environment" for entrepreneurship, behind South Dakota and Nevada and far ahead of neighboring states.[36] State agencies in at least three policy areas—transportation, tourism, and licensing—are administered to promote and protect economic interests.

Highways The Texas Department of Transportation (TxDOT) has constructed and maintains more than 80,000 miles of roads and highways. This agency is headed by a five-member commission appointed by the governor, with Senate concurrence, to six-year overlapping terms. Drawing no state salary, each commissioner must be a "public" member without financial ties to any company contracting with the state for highway-related business. Commission appointees must reflect Texas's diverse population groups and regions and include at least one commissioner who resides in a rural area. For the 2012–2013 biennium, TxDOT was authorized more than 12,000 full-time-equivalent employees and a $19.8 billion budget. In 2009, the legislature created the Department of Motor Vehicles and transferred to it vehicle titling and registration, motor carrier registration and enforcement, and motor vehicle dealer regulation.

Texans' love affair with their cars has led to growing traffic congestion and increased accidents. In 2010, Texans spent an average of 25 minutes commuting to work (one way), just at the national average. Most experts agree that Texas needs billions of dollars of improvements to existing roads and bridges, as well as new roads and more public transit. Which projects get priority, however, and how should they be paid for? In 2003, the

Points to Ponder

- In 1935, 16.6 people in Texas died in car crashes for every 100 million miles driven.
- In 2009, 1.34 people in Texas died in car crashes for every 100 million miles driven, the lowest rate since records were first kept.
- In 2011, traffic deaths dropped nationally but remained flat in Texas and surrounding states.

Observers credit safer roads and cars, more seatbelt use, less drunken driving, and better law enforcement for the improvements. Excessive speed and alcohol remain the largest factors in highway deaths. According to some observers, Texas's recent deviation from the national downward trend may be attributable to the influx of oil and gas workers into Texas, while much of the rest of the nation was just recovering from the recession.

Texas Department of Transportation (TxDOT)
Headed by a three-member appointed commission, the department maintains almost 80,000 miles of roads and highways and promotes highway safety.

legislature enacted Governor Perry's Trans Texas Corridor (TTC) plan to build a 4,000-mile network of roads, toll roads, and rail. This plan ignited a firestorm of opposition that made its full implementation unlikely. In 2009, the executive director of TxDOT declared TTC dead, but indicated that the agency would pursue individual projects that had once been lumped together as part of the TTC. Under the influence of TTC, and facing a shortage of public funds, TxDOT had moved to create 80 new toll roads, many of them to be financed and run by private companies. The 2007 legislature responded with a loophole-laden bill that has slowed the movement toward private toll roads, though public toll roads continue to expand. The TTC experience and the move toward toll roads show the attractiveness to many Texas officials of privatization and charging fees for government services, but there are difficulties in selling these ideas to the public.

Compared with highways, public transportation has less public and official support. Only a few Texas cities (such as Austin's Capital MetroRail) have light rail for public transportation. In Texas, 95 percent of public transportation is by bus. In 2010, Texas had eight large urban transit agencies serving areas with 200,000 or more residents. These agencies provide 90 percent of Texans' public transit trips. The most common organizational form is a metropolitan transit authority (MTA), which is a local regional government that can service the central city and the surrounding suburbs and impose taxes. TxDOT has little role in the planning, finance, or operation of MTAs. In 2010, there were also 30 urban transit agencies and 39 rural transit systems serving smaller communities, as well as more than 135 operators providing transportation services to the elderly and to individuals with disabilities under varying arrangements.[37]

Tourism Responsibility for preserving Texas's natural habitats and managing public recreational areas lies with the **Texas Parks and Wildlife Department**. The nine members of its governing commission are appointed by the governor with senatorial approval. The governor also designates the chair of the commission from among the members. The commission sets fees for fishing and hunting licenses and entrance fees for state parks. The department's game wardens enforce state laws and departmental regulations that apply to hunting, fishing, and boating; the Texas Penal Code; and certain laws affecting clean air and water, hazardous materials, and human health.

Tourism is the third-largest industry in the Lone Star State. The state park system attracts seven to 10 million visitors a year (both Texans and out-of-state tourists) and generates $1.2 billion for the economy. With Texas ranked 49th in state money spent on parks in the first years of this century, however, state parks were suffering deterioration in quality and services. Fewer parks and park amenities hurt business and were a loss to middle- and working-class Texans, many of whom depend on public parks for recreation. In 2007, Parks and Wildlife leaders orchestrated a publicity campaign that convinced the legislature to boost the budget from $439 million to $665 million. The 2009 legislature kept the increased level

Texas Parks and Wildlife Department
Texas agency that runs state parks and regulates hunting, fishing, and boating.

of funding. Although this amount was not as much as park and wildlife advocates felt was needed, it did help maintain the system. In the revenue-strapped 2011 legislative session, however, the budget was cut by $153 million, which has left the state parks struggling once again. (For further information on this topic, see the Chapter 11 Selected Reading, "Texas Parks and Wildlife.")

Certification of Trades and Professions Citizens in more than 40 occupations—half of which are health related—are certified (licensed) to practice their profession by state boards. Each licensing board has at least one "public" member (not from the regulated occupation). All members are appointed to six-year terms by the governor with approval of the Senate. In addition to ensuring that practitioners qualify to enter a profession (giving them a license to practice), the boards are responsible for ensuring that licensees continue to meet professional standards. For example, the Texas Board of Nursing (formerly called the Board of Nurse Examiners) licenses nurses to practice. According to investigative reporter, Yamil Berard, it "is perhaps the most aggressive healthcare regulator in Texas, taking patient safety to heart."[38] Because of a shortage of legal staff, this board has been criticized for having a backlog of cases. Ironically, it and the Texas Medical Board, which regulates doctors, receive criticism from legislators and medical practitioners for being too tough, while simultaneously receiving public criticism for not being tough enough.

Environmental Regulation

Among Texas's many public policy concerns, none draws sharper disagreements than how to maintain a clean and safe environment while advancing business development that will provide jobs and profits. Because of the nature of its industry and Texans' love for driving, Texas has been among the most polluted states for years. Texas industries, for example, produce more toxic contaminants (chemical waste) than do those of any other state. This grim reality confronts local, state, and national policymakers, and the decisions of all three affect the quality of our air and water.

Since the early 1970s, federal policies have driven state and local environmental efforts, with Texas state and local officials generally trying to resist or slow the impact of federal policies. Mandates come from the national level through the U.S. Environmental Protection Agency (EPA) and congressional directives in the Clean Air and Clean Water Acts. Under the Obama administration, the EPA became more vigorous, and the number of conflicts with Texas officials increased. Responses by Texas officials have included public complaints, legislation introduced by the state's representatives in Congress, requests for waivers, and lawsuits filed by the state. Concern about climate change and Texas's substantial greenhouse gas emissions have also increased federal-state conflict.

Texas business people usually support state policies designed to forestall federal regulations. Tracking corporate Texas's every step, however, is a growing army of public "watchdogs" (such as the Sierra Club), who do much to inform the public concerning environmental problems. Early in the recent Great Recession, however, many of the environmental groups had to lay off employees and reduce their efforts.

Air and Water The Texas Commission on Environmental Quality (TCEQ), commonly called "T-sec," coordinates the Lone Star State's environmental policies. Three full-time commission members earning $150,000 per year, an executive director earning $145,000 a year, and about 2,700 employees oversee environmental regulation in Texas. The commissioners are named by the governor for six-year staggered terms. The governor designates one of the commissioners as chair, and the commissioners choose the executive director. As with actions of other regulatory bodies, TCEQ's decisions can be appealed to state courts. In the 2012–2013 biennium, the agency received an appropriation of $692 million, which was a reduction of $260 million from the previous biennium.

State policymakers must balance federal directives and state law with pressures from businesses and environmentalists, which is a tough challenge. In recent years, TCEQ has pushed the state's metropolitan areas to meet federal air standards, with moderate success. However, in 2010, the EPA proposed tougher smog standards and rejected a Texas program that let thousands of companies bypass rigorous reviews under the Clean Air Act. Another recent issue is how to generate more electrical power—through coal-burning plants, nuclear plants, or wind and solar power. Even "green" solutions can produce conflict. In 1999, the legislature mandated the development of renewable energy. Within seven years, Texas had become the leading producer of wind power in the nation. When the Public Utility Commission created a $5 billion project to build transmission lines from the West Texas windfields to Dallas–Fort Worth and Houston, however, opposition arose over increased electrical rates to pay for the lines and the acquisition of rights-of-way across private land.

Water is another important issue in a state that is largely arid. Texas's growing population, industry, and irrigation-based agriculture face serious water shortages; in addition, drought and flooding are regular problems for many areas. The TCEQ, working with local prosecutors, deals with contamination of waterways. Major sources of water pollution include industry (through both air emissions and improper disposal of toxic waste), agriculture (particularly from fertilizer, manure, and pesticide runoff), and poorly

Cracks in the dry bed of Lake Lavon, northeast of Dallas, December 2005. Texas's alternating periods of drought and flooding, together with the highly unequal distribution of rainfall from one region to another, make water policy a critical element of the state's development.

(AP Photo/Matt Slocum)

Texas Commission on Environmental Quality (TCEQ)

The state agency that coordinates Texas's environmental protection efforts.

treated sewage. The six-member Texas Water Development Board (TWDB) and its staff develop strategies, collect data, and administer grants and loans to support water supply, wastewater treatment, and flood control projects. Three sets of interconnected issues have run through the water supply debate:

- Conflicts over who controls the water: Under Texas law, surface water (in lakes and rivers) belongs to the state, but citizens and other entities may be granted rights to it. Water is overappropriated—that is, if every entity actually received the amount it has been allocated by the state, lakes and rivers would be dry. Underground water (called ground water) has almost no regulation. Under the legal concept of the Rule of Capture, landowners own the water below their property. But problems arise when upstream landowners pump so much water that downstream land-owners' wells and springs dry up.

- The desire of metropolitan areas and drier Central and Western Texas to build lakes and pipelines to capture and move water from wetter areas, such as East Texas: Many communities want to keep their water. Others object to loss of land to lakes and damage to rivers and wetlands. Closely related are the conflicts between the users of water—agriculture, cities, industry, and environmentalists—over who gets priority over water.

- Maintenance of the quality and quantity of underground water, such as the Ogallala and Edwards aquifers, on which many cities, farms, and rivers depend.

Flooding in Corpus Christi, 2010. While experiencing periodic drought, the Corpus Christi area also suffered flooding in seven of twelve years, from 2001–2012.

(Todd Yates/Black Star/Newscom)

One thing on which most sides of the water disputes agree is that Texas has not developed an effective water plan. With the continued growth of population and the needs of agriculture and industry, the water fights will continue to grow in importance.[39] The issue of water supply is driven home by Texas's periodic droughts, which are often followed by flooding. The 1950–1957 drought cost Texas agriculture $22 billion (in 2011 dollars), while the 2010–2011 drought cost at least $8 billion and saw fires char four million acres. Since 1945, the state has experienced six periods of severe drought and two of extreme drought.[40] Water problems are also discussed in Chapter 1, "The Environment of Texas Politics," while financial implications are covered in Chapter 11, "Finance and Fiscal Policy."

Hazardous Waste Hazardous waste is a fact of modern life. From the use of low-level radioactive materials in hospitals to diagnose disease to industrial production of plastics and chemicals on which we depend, we generate large quantities of dangerous waste. This waste ranges in danger from high-level radioactive material with potential toxicity for thousands of years to nonradioactive hazardous waste. Those who produce hazardous materials want to get rid of them as cheaply as possible, and they have the money and incentive to succeed in doing so. Although environmental groups in Texas have grown in power and political skill, they generally can only delay and modify actions favored by pollution producers. For its part, much of the public simply says "Not in my backyard."

In the case of low-level radioactive waste, the result has been a series of political skirmishes stretching back to at least the 1970s, a lack of a coordinated plan, and a growing amount of waste. By 2009, a private radioactive waste dumpsite had been built in sparsely populated Andrews County and a license was issued to bury radioactive waste from Texas and Vermont. Eventually, low-level radioactive waste from 38 or more states may be deposited at the site. By 2012, permission from the TCEQ had been granted, and the first loads of waste had arrived. The substantial campaign contributions and lobbying by the company Waste Control Specialists and its owner, Harold Simmons, led to charges of crony capitalism (government officials favoring and subsidizing their friends in the private sector who have helped them).[41] The Selected Reading for this chapter, "Cronies at the Capitol," provides details of one scandal in this saga. The demand for dumpsites is likely to grow in the years to come.

Generated largely by Texas's petrochemical industry, nonradioactive hazardous waste stored in landfills presents another environmental dilemma. Poorly stored materials may leak into the water table or nearby waterways or contaminate the dirt above them. Housing and commercial land developers covet landfill sites for their building projects, for which TCEQ has tended to approve less restrictive guidelines. As the state's population increases in the years ahead, even greater demands will be placed on the quality of its air, water, and land.[42]

Homeland Security After the September 11, 2001, terrorist attacks on New York City and the Pentagon, federal, state, and local officials began giving more attention to preparations for preventing or coping with terrorism. Likewise, Texas's experience with tornados and hurricanes such as Katrina, Dolly, and Ike heightened awareness of the need for preparation and for a coordinated effort to deal with natural disasters. In Texas, the Governor's Office provides strategic planning, emergency response resources, and information concerning disaster preparedness; the Texas Department of Public Safety has a counterterrorism and intelligence unit; the departments of State Health Services and of Agriculture compile relevant information; a state health and medical operations center has been established; and many cities and counties have developed plans and cooperative arrangements with neighboring communities. (Chapter 11, "Finance and Fiscal Policy," addresses financial implications of disaster preparedness.)

With the heightened debate about illegal immigration, the state has also increased cooperation with federal authorities and put limited amounts of money into border security. The construction of a major fence or wall along parts of the border with Mexico by the federal government has generated considerable opposition in South Texas. Additional security issues include protecting the large number of refineries and petrochemical plants on the upper Gulf Coast that are potential terrorist targets, developing storm evacuation plans, hardening (improving the survivability) of the electrical grid to prevent outages during storms, and finding adequate funding for fire and other emergency services outside of cities. The fires that ravaged many parts of Texas in 2011 brought home the extent to which Texas relies on volunteers for fighting fires and the need for training, coordination, and resources.

Texas missed a major environmental disaster on April 20, 2010, when the offshore oil drilling rig *Deepwater Horizon* exploded, killing 11 workers, rupturing the wellhead 5,000 feet beneath the Gulf of Mexico, and spilling millions of gallons of crude oil into the Gulf of Mexico. The drilling rig was leased by BP, one of the world's largest oil companies, which has its American headquarters in Houston. Because of the pattern of Gulf currents, Texas's coastline was spared, and the Texas tourism and fishing industries picked up business lost by Louisiana and other Gulf states. The cleanup efforts produced a great deal of both conflict and cooperation among BP; the individuals affected; and national, state, and local governments. By mid-2012, Gulf Coast fishing and tourism were substantially recovered, but environmental worries and disputes over indemnification continued. Concerns intensified when oil from the spill showed up on beaches after Hurricane Isaac in August 2012.

✓ Learning Check 9.4   (Answers on p. 383)

1. True or False: Business regulation in Texas tends to be tough on businesses.
2. Is the movement in Texas toward more regulation or deregulation?
3. How does Texas compare with other states on levels of pollution?
4. What are some demands that state environmental policymakers must balance?
5. What are the major issues involved in homeland security in Texas?

★ Conclusion

Public policymaking is a dynamic process in which bureaucracy plays a vital role in helping to shape the nature of policy. Texas's political culture and political process shape public policies that are responsive to business and government elites but that provide less of a social safety net than can be found in the majority of other states. The Texas education system faces challenges created by serving large numbers of disadvantaged students, coupled with a reluctance to devote sufficient state resources to education. Texas has a large proportion of poor and working-class citizens in need of help in health and human services; this segment of the population has little political power to effectively satisfy their needs. In the areas of economic development and regulation, public policy has often tended to serve the interests of business over those of consumers.

Chapter Summary

- Most of the state's budget is spent on four areas: education, health and human services, business and economic development, and public safety and corrections.
- The sunset review process requires periodic review of state agencies by the legislature. While producing few major changes in state government, it has had positive effects.
- The state's large number of agencies provide a variety of services to Texans, including public and higher education, social services, and business regulation and promotion.
- State agencies and their employees (bureaucrats or public administrators) carry out laws passed by the legislature, but add their influence through interpreting and applying the laws to specific situations.
- The success of agencies in Texas is influenced by the vigor of their leaders, the lack of resources for most agencies, and elite access.
- State employees are Texas's largest work group.
- Texas state government has done better than the private sector in providing access to employment for women and African Americans, but the access for Latinos has been more mixed.
- Whether in public school districts, institutions of higher education, or the legislature, policymakers face the challenge of achieving educational excellence at a price that Texas taxpayers can pay and that voters will support.
- Texas schools face the challenge of a changing student body—more ethnically diverse and from less affluent families. Failure to respond to the challenge is likely to damage the state's economy.
- The State Board of Education is weak and highly controversial. The greater state role in education is handled by the commissioner of education, who heads the Texas Education Agency.
- Testing remains a major tool for trying to improve education in the state. It is also a source of great controversy.
- The Texas Higher Education Coordinating Board oversees all institutions of higher education; boards of regents govern universities; and local boards make policy for community colleges.
- Affirmative action and the top 10 percent rule have been major issues in college admission.
- State responsibility for many public assistance programs and the state's high poverty rate will continue to place demands on Texas's

social service agencies to provide financial help for needy families and to assist impoverished people who are physically or mentally ill or who are aged or disabled.

- Health and human services programs in Texas are politically weak and poorly funded.
- Health and human services programs are coordinated by the Health and Human Services Commission.
- Privatization of service delivery has a mixed record in Texas, with some major failures.
- It remains to be seen whether deregulation (the current direction of regulators) will be more effective than regulation in protecting the public interest; meanwhile, Texas consumers demand low-cost utilities, safe and plentiful drinking water, and cleaner air.
- Texas regulators tend to be protective of the industries they are charged to regulate.
- The deterioration of state parks because of funding shortages may cause Texas to lose tourist dollars.
- Texas has long had major pollution problems and public policies that have done little to improve the environment. Challenges to polluters are increasing, but change is slow.
- Texas has responded to the threat of terrorism and natural disasters by seeking grants of federal money for homeland security, compiling information, and seeking more coordination and planning.

Key Terms

sunset review process, p. 344
public administration, p. 345
bureaucrats, p. 345
elite access, p. 347
patronage system, p. 348
merit system, p. 348
State Board of Education (SBOE), p. 351
Texas Education Agency (TEA), p. 354
commissioner of education, p. 354
Texas Essential Knowledge and Skills (TEKS), p. 355
State of Texas Assessment of Academic Readiness (STAAR), p. 355
Texas Higher Education Coordinating Board (THECB), p. 358
equal opportunity, p. 360
affirmative action, p. 360
top 10 percent rule, p. 361

executive commissioner of the Health and Human Services Commission, p. 365
Temporary Assistance for Needy Families (TANF), p. 367
Supplemental Nutritional Assistance Program (SNAP), p. 367
Medicaid, p. 367
Medicare, p. 367
Texas Workforce Commission (TWC), p. 369
Railroad Commission of Texas (RRC), p. 371
Public Utility Commission (PUC), p. 372
deregulation, p. 372
commissioner of insurance, p. 373
Texas Department of Transportation (TxDOT), p. 374
Texas Parks and Wildlife Department, p. 375
Texas Commission on Environmental Quality (TCEQ), p. 377

Learning Check Answers

9.1

1. Demands for the creation of new state agencies come from citizens, lobbyists, and occasionally state leaders.
2. False. Public administrators must make many decisions not clearly specified in the law. Their own views, their bosses' preferences, and their agency culture all make a difference in how they apply laws passed by the legislature.
3. The vigor of agency leaders, resources, and elite access are particularly important in determining how successful agencies are in Texas.

9.2

1. The State Board of Education and the commissioner of education (who runs the Texas Education Agency) are the most important state entities for public schools.
2. False. Texas's testing program is highly controversial, supported by some and opposed by others.
3. According to the top 10 percent rule, Texas students graduating in the top 10 percent of their high school class must be admitted to the public college or university of their choice.

9.3

1. Compared with other states, poverty in Texas is high.
2. Health and human services programs are at a disadvantage in Texas because of the state's political culture and the lack of resources and organization of those needing the services.
3. Texas Assistance for Needy Families (TANF) provides provides limited cash benefits to poor families.
4. Medicare is better funded than Medicaid.

9.4

1. False. Regulation of business in Texas tends not to be tough on businesses (consider the Railroad Commission, for example).
2. The movement in Texas is toward deregulation (consider the Public Utility Commission and the commissioner of insurance, for example).
3. Texas is one of the country's most polluted states.
4. State environmental policymakers must balance federal directives, business pressures, and demands from environmental groups.
5. Terrorist attacks against such targets as refineries, border security, and preparedness for natural disasters are major homeland security issues.

Discussion Questions

1. What services should Texas's government provide to the state's residents?
2. Does Texas need its State Board of Education? Why has the board faced criticism and controversy?
3. Is Texas's emphasis on testing students a good thing? Why or why not?
4. Discuss the impact of *Hopwood v. Texas* on Texas colleges and universities, and explain why you support or oppose affirmative action programs in institutions of higher education. Is the top 10 percent rule a good solution?
5. Why are some health and human services programs better supported than others?
6. State regulators seem to be moving toward deregulation. Which agencies are doing this, and is it a good idea? Who benefits and who loses from deregulation?
7. What are Texas's principal environmental problems? Which government agencies deal with these problems, and what do they do?

Internet Resources

Center for Public Policy Priorities (liberal orientation): **http://www.cppp.org**

Department of Public Safety of the State of Texas: **http://www.txdps.state.tx.us**

Employees Retirement System: **http://www.ers.state.tx.us**

Finding Help in Texas: **http://www.211texas.org/211**

National Center for Education Statistics: **http://nces.ed.gov/**

Office of Public Utility Counsel: **http://www.opc.state.tx.us**

Public Utility Commission of Texas: **http://www.puc.state.tx.us**

Railroad Commission of Texas: **http://www.rrc.state.tx.us**

State Board of Education: **http://www.tea.state.tx.us/index4.aspx?id=1156**

State Board of Educator Certification: **http://www.tea.state.tx.us/portals.aspx?id=2147484909**

Sunset Advisory Commission: **http://www.sunset.state.tx.us**

Texas Commission on Environmental Quality: **http://www.tceq.state.tx.us**

Texas Comptroller of Public Accounts: **http://www.window.state.tx.us**

Texas Department of Insurance: **http://www.tdi.state.tx.us**

Texas Department of Transportation: **http://www.dot.state.tx.us**

Texas Education Agency: **http://www.tea.state.tx.us**

Texas Health and Human Services Commission: **http://www.hhs.state.tx.us**

Texas Higher Education Coordinating Board: **http://www.thecb.state.tx.us**

Texas Parks and Wildlife Department: **http://www.tpwd.state.tx.us**

Texas Public Policy Foundation (conservative orientation): **http://www.texaspolicy.com**

Texas Water Development Board: **http://www.twdb.state.tx.us**

Texas Workforce Commission: **http://www.twc.state.tx.us**

U.S. Census Bureau: **http://www.census.gov**

Notes

1. General Appropriations Act for the 2012–2013 Biennium, 82nd Texas Legislature, October 27, 2011, http://www.lbb.state.tx.us/Bill_82/GAA.pdf.
2. Sunset Advisory Commission, *Sunset in Texas*, January 2012, http://www.sunset.state.tx.us/suntx.pdf; and Mark Lisheron, "Its Own Ideals May Condemn Watchdog," *Austin American-Statesman*, September 23, 2007.
3. Commissioner Larry Soward, a Republican appointed by Governor Perry, quoted in Nate Blakeslee, "Up in the Air," *Texas Monthly*, December 2011, 207.
4. Dave Mann, "A Death in McAllen," *The Texas Observer*, September 23, 2005, 6, http://www.texasobserver.org. Texas continued to rank 49th in 2010. Because the Great Recession (officially 2007–2009, but with lingering effects in 2012)

reduced revenue to the states, Medicaid reimbursements were negatively affected in most states, including Texas.

5. Larry Wheeler and Robert Benincasa, "Analysis Finds Clusters of Nursing Home Violations by State, Ownership," *Gannett News Service*, 2003, http:// content.gannettonline.com/gns/nursinghomes/story1.html; U.S. House of Representatives, *Nursing Home Conditions in Texas*, October 28, 2002, http:// www.house.gov; Robert T. Garrett, "Texas Steps Back from Stiffest Punishment of Lax Nursing Homes," *DallasNews.Com*, November 12, 2011, http:// www.dallasnews.com/news/state/headlines/20111112-texas-steps-back-from-stiffest-punishment-of-lax-nursing-homes.ece?ssimg=376326#ssStory376334 (part of a series based on an investigation by the *Dallas Morning News*).

6. Harvey Kronberg, quoted in Jonathan Walters, "Life after Civil Service Reform," Human Capital Series, IBM Endowment for The Business of Government, October 2002, 20, http://www.businessofgovernment.org/report/life-after-civil-service-reform-texas-georgia-and-florida-experiences.

7. Texas State Auditor's Office, "Classified Employee Turnover for Fiscal Year 2009," December 2009, and "An Annual Report on Classified Employee Turnover for Fiscal Year 2010," December 2010, http://www.sao.state.tx.us; and Donald P. Moynihan and Noel Landuyt, "Explaining Turnover Intention in State Government," *Review of Public Personnel Administration* 28 (June 2008): 120–143.

8. Gary Scharrer, "Legislator Questions Border Health," *El Paso Times*, March 6, 2003.

9. *Snapshot 2010: State Totals, Texas Education Agency* (latest available in May 2012), http://ritter.tea.state.tx.us/perfreport/snapshot/index.html; Gary Scharrer, "Report: Poverty, Dropout Rate Bode Grim Texas Future," *Houston Chronicle*, June 21, 2010; Brian J. Gottlob, "The High Cost of Failing to Reform Public Education in Texas," Milton and Rose D. Friedman Foundation, revised January 2008, http://www.edchoice.org/Research/Reports/The-High-Cost-of-Failing-to-Reform-Public-Education-in-Texas–revised-January–08-.aspx; and Brian Burnsed, "Schools Populated with Minorities Are Among Nation's Best High Schools," USNews.com, June 8, 2010, http://usnews.com. The seminal work on demographic change in Texas in the 21st century and the consequences of not meeting the needs of Texas minorities is Murdock, Steve H., and Others, *The New Texas Challenge: Population Change and the Future of Texas* (College Station, Texas: Texas A&M University Press, 2003).

10. For background and details, see Dana Jepson, *Fact or Fiction: The SBOE's Role in Textbook Adoption*, Focus Report No. 77-17 (Austin: House Research Organization, Texas House of Representatives, February 22, 2002). For a careful analysis of Texas education, including the SBOE, see Cal Jillson, *Lone Star Tarnished* (New York: Routledge, 2012), pp. 103–27.

11. A sampling of commentary includes James C. McKinley Jr., "Texas Conservatives Win Curriculum Change," *New York Times*, March 15, 2010; Stephanie Simon, "Education Board in Texas Faces Curbs," *Wall Street Journal*, April 13, 2009; and Traci Shurley, "State Board of Education Members Get Authors Mixed Up," *Fort Worth Star-Telegram*, January 22, 2009.

12. Morgan Smith, "Texas School Closings Rare, But Should They Be?" *The Texas Tribune*, April 5, 2012, http://www.texastribune.org/texas-education/public-education/school-district-closures-rare-should-they-be/.

13. Debra S. Haas examines 2005 to 2007 data in "An Analysis of Gaps in Funding for Charter Schools and Traditional Districts," Institute for Public School Initiative, The University of Texas System, http://utsystem.edu/ipsi. An analysis

paid for by the Texas Charter School Association had similar conclusions for 2005-2009. See R.C. Wood & Associates, "Comparative Analyses of Revenues Generated from the Texas Foundation school Program for Independent School Districts and Charter School Districts, February 2011, http://www.txcharterschools.org/sites/default/files/resources/Funding%20Inequity%20Rolle%20Study%202%203%2011%20final.pdf.

14. "Charter Schools No Cure-All for Black Students, Says Study," April 11, 2012, http://www.utexas.edu/news/2012/04/11/charter_vasquez_heilig/; "Failure Is an Option," *Houston Chronicle*, January 31, 2010; and Jennifer Radcliffe, "Study Supports KIPP Success," *Houston Chronicle*, June 22, 2010, Bl.

15. Center for Research on Education Outcomes, "Multiple Choice: Charter School Performance in 16 States," 2009, http://Credo.Stanford.edu; and Debra S. Haas, "An Analysis of Gaps in Funding for Charter Schools and Traditional Districts," Institute for Public School Initiatives, University of Texas Systems, March 2009, http://www.ipsi.utexas.edu/docs/pubs/brief_05_charter_funding_analysis_v8.pdf.

16. Rick Casey, "TAKS Grade Inflation is Nothing New" and "Lies, Damn Lies and Magic Statistics," *Houston Chronicle*, June 13 and June 20, 2010.

17. Mike Norman, "Testing Has Become a 'Perversion,' Texas Education Chief Robert Scott Says,"*Star-Telegram*, February 2, 2012, http://www.star-telegram.com/2012/02/02/3708173/testing-has-become-a-perversion.html.

18. National Center for Education Statistics, *National Assessment of Educational Progress*, 2011, http://nces.ed.gov/nationsreportcard/states/. The TEA website (http://www.tea.state.tx.us/) has substantial information on testing. For a critique of testing, see Diane Ravitch, *The Death and Life of the Great American School System: How Testing and Choice Are Undermining Education* (New York: Basic Books, 2010).

19. Paul Burka, "General Admission," *Texas Monthly*, April 2012, http://mobile.texasmonthly.com/id/16332/Law/#part1; *Sweatt v. Painter*, 339 U.S. 629 (1950).

20. "Closing the Gaps Progress Report, 2011," Higher Education Coordinating Board, June 2011, http://www.thecb.state.tx.us/reports/PDF/2357.PDF?CFID=7562420&CFTOKEN=51730738.

21. The Perryman Group, "A Tale of Two States—And One Million Jobs," March 2007, http://www.thecb.state.tx.us/reports/PDF/1345.PDF?CFID=7562420&CFTOKEN=51730738.

22. *University of California Regents v. Bakke*, 438 U.S. 265 (1978).

23. *Hopwood v. Texas*, 78 F.3d 932 (1996).

24. *Grutter v. Bollinger*, 539 U.S. 306 (2003).

25. *Gratz v. Bollinger*, 539 U.S. 244 (2003).

26. Tamar Lewin, "At the University of Texas, Admissions as a Mystery," *New York Times*, April 1, 2012, http://www.nytimes.com/2012/04/02/education/university-of-texas-mysterious-admissions-process.html.

27. "A Red Flag," *Fort Worth Star-Telegram*, June 15, 2007. A similar argument is made by two health policy specialists from the University of Virginia, Arthur Garson, Jr., and Carolyn Long Engelhard, "Texas Has Top Medical Centers but Provides Poor Health Care," *Houston Chronicle*, September 17, 2011, http://www.chron.com/opinion/outlook/article/Texas-has-top-medicalcenters-but-provides-poor-2174885.php.

28. The Commonwealth Fund, "Featured Scorecards," http://www.commonwealthfund.org/Publications/Health-System-Scorecards.aspx. Another study, "Code Red," financed by Rice University, reached similar

conclusions: Ruth Campbell, "Texas Health Care in Critical Condition," *Midland Reporter-Telegram*, April 1, 2007. The U.S. Census Bureau provides data on both poverty and insurance coverage. For insurance coverage, see U.S. Census Bureau, CPS ASEC: 2010 (P 60–239), http://www.census.gov/prod/2011pubs/p60-239.pdf.

29. Robert T. Garrett, "Texas Faulted on Food Stamps," *Dallas Morning News*, January 13, 2010; and Editorial Board, "Privatization Failure Is Taxpayers' Burden," *Austin American-Statesman*, March 26, 2008.

30. Eva DeLuna Castro, Center for Public Policy Priorities, *Poverty 101*, November 2011, http://www.cppp.org/files/8/2011_11_Poverty101.pdf.

31. Department of State Health Services, *2010 Texas Integrated Epidemiologic Profile for HIV/AIDS Prevention and Services Planning*, revised January 31, 2012, http://www.dshs.state.tx.us/hivstd/reports/.

32. Texas's ranking is for 2009, the latest data available in June 2012 from National Alliance on Mental Illness, "State Mental Health Cuts: The Continuing Crisis," November 2011, http://www.nami.org/ContentManagement/ContentDisplay.cfm?ContentFileID=147763, and the National Association of State Mental Health Program Directors, at http://www.nri-inc.org/projects/Profiles/RevExp2009/FY09Presentation.pdf. In 2005, the state served only 27 percent of those needing assistance. Information on mental health services comes from Legislative Budget Board, *Fiscal Size-Up, 2012–13 Biennium*, January 2012.

33. Mose Buchele, "Electric Deregulation Turns Ten in Texas," StateImpact, January 25, 2012, http://stateimpact.npr.org/texas/2012/01/25/electric-deregulation-turns-ten-in-texas/; and Jay Doegey, "Electricity," *Fort Worth Star-Telegram*, March 4, 2009. But see M. Ray Perryman, "Power Competition Has Benefited Texas," *Fort Worth Star-Telegram*, April 16, 2006.

34. Loren Steffy, "A Summer of Darkness Looms Under Deregulation," *Houston Chronicle*, June 20, 2012, p. D1.

35. House Research Organization, "Focus Report: Regulating Homeowners Insurance in Texas," October 18, 2010, http://www.hro.house.state.tx.us/pdf/focus/HOI81-14.pdf; Jennifer LaFleur and Ed Timms, "Coverage at What Cost?" *Dallas Morning News*, February 15, 2009; and Laura Elder, "Dolly, Ike Ended Feast Years for Insurers," *Galveston County Daily News*, March 24, 2009.

36. Small Business and Entrepreneurship Council, *Small Business Survival Index 2011*, November 2011, http://www.sbecouncil.org/resources/publications/survivalindex2011/.

37. Texas Department of Transportation, *Texas Transit Statistics*, September 2011, https://ftp.dot.state.tx.us/pub/txdot-info/ptn/transit_stats/2010.pdf.

38. Yamil Berard, "Nursing Board Sets High Standards," and "Inadequate Doctors Still Slip by System," *Fort Worth Star-Telegram*, June 13 and June 10, 2007.

39. *The Texas Observer*, June 25, 2010, and *Texas Monthly*, July 2012, each have a series of articles on water. For an environmentalist perspective, see http://www.texaswatermatters.org/; for a business perspective, see http://www.texaspolicy.com/publications.php?cat_level=87; and for the Texas Water Development Board's perspective, see http://www.twdb.state.tx.us/home/index.asp.

40. Stuart Staniford, "Drought History in Texas," April 20, 2011, http://earlywarn.blogspot.com/2011/04/drought-history-in-texas.html. Note the link to the National Climatic Data Center for the relevant data.

41. Christopher Helman, "Texas Billionaire Builds Giant Nuclear Waste Dump," *Forbes*, April 1, 2011, http://www.forbes.com/sites/christopherhelman/2011/04/01/

texas-billionaire-builds-giant-nuclear-waste-dump/; Julie Bykowicz, "Republican
Donor Simmons Seeks Rule to Fill Texas Dump." *Bloomberg News*, April 5, 2012,
http://www.businessweek.com/news/2012-04-04/republican-donor-simmons-seeks-
rule-to-fill-texas-dump#p1; and Kate Galbraith and Jay Root, "Texas Billionaire
Nears Radioactive Waste Dump Victory, *Texas Tribune*, May 17, 2011, http://
www.texastribune.org/texas-environmental-news/environmental-problems-and-
policies/texas-billionaire-nears-radioactive-waste-dump-vic/.

42. For more information on the Texas environment, see the websites of the
Texas Commission on Environmental Quality at http://www.tceq.state.tx.us,
the federal Environmental Protection Agency at http://www.epa.gov, the
Texas Public Policy Foundation (from a business perspective) at
http://www.texaspolicy.com/publications.php?cat_level=84, and the Center
for Public Policy Studies (from an environmentalist perspective) at
http://www.texascenter.org.

Cronies at the Capitol: Connecting the Dots at TCEQ*

Eliot Shapleigh

Most (not all) Texas government regulatory agencies have a close relationship with those they are intended to regulate. Many, like the Railroad Commission (which regulates the oil and gas industry), are examples of agency capture; that is, they act as if they are controlled by the industry they were created to regulate. Senator Eliot Shapleigh (D-El Paso, 1997-2011) argues that this is the case for the Texas Commission on Environmental Quality (TCEQ), the state's major agency for protecting the environment. Although the extent has varied over time, TCEQ consistently tends to favor business interests over those of the environment. Mr. Shapleigh uses two long-standing cases to explain why.

AUSTIN, Feb. 7 [2010] - Texans want to leave a cleaner, healthier state for their children and grandchildren to enjoy. Despite this, Texas' air and water are amongst some of the dirtiest in the nation. Texas is first in the nation in air pollution emissions, the amount of cancer-causing carcinogens released into the air, and the amount of carbon dioxide emissions. It's second in the amount of hazardous waste generated and seventh in the amount of carcinogens released into the water. We have a governor and environmental agency that prides itself in opposing increased air standards that would save both lives and money. So where is the disconnect? Where does the public pressure to clean our soil, waterways, and skies get lost in Austin? Let's connect the dots.

Much of the blame lies with the state's environmental agency, the Texas Commission on Environmental Quality (TCEQ), which has been captured and corrupted by polluters—especially in the permitting process. Polluters have been able to work the system so well that their needs and goals are addressed far in advance of the average Texan's. Two recent examples connect the dots: the ASARCO smelter in El Paso and the Waste Control Specialists (WCS) permit in the Panhandle.

ASARCO's Record

For over a century, ASARCO's El Paso smelter released thousands of tons of contaminants into the bi-national airshed of El Paso and Ciudad Juarez. One hundred twenty years of pollution and environmental degradation has left our community with soil full of arsenic, lead, cadmium, mercury, and other heavy metals. Years of ASARCO's arsenic have created a 233 million cubic foot plume of toxic water in aquifers right near the Rio Grande. The actual smelter site is even covered with a shell of slag an astounding 75 feet thick.

Further, there are contaminants that the community still cannot identify. A smoking gun memo obtained from the Environmental Protection Agency (EPA) through a Freedom of Information Act request and the Federal Department of Justice shows that 5,000 tons of hazardous waste, including 300 tons of residues from the Rocky Mountain Arsenal, were illegally burned by the smelter. What exactly was burned—be it nerve gas or other chemical weapons—has never been disclosed to our community.

Beyond El Paso, ASARCO is well-known throughout the United States for having contaminated communities across the country. In fact, it recently went through the largest environmental

*From Eliot Shapleigh, *Owner's Box* (El Paso, 2009), 30–33. Printed by permission. Eliot Shapleigh practices law in El Paso, which he represented as a Democrat in the state Senate from 1997 to 2011. He chose not to run for reelection in 2010.

bankruptcy in U.S. history. The bankruptcy proved to be a test case for polluters across the country: could a privately held company declare bankruptcy in order to shed environmental liabilities, thus forcing taxpayers to foot the bill? As Sen. Maria Cantwell (D-WA) said, "[ASARCO's parent company] tried to use a bankruptcy court to avoid ASARCO's cleanup responsibilities, and they almost got away with it."

Renewal of an Air Permit

With that as the backdrop, in 2002, ASARCO began the application process at TCEQ to have their air permit renewed. Since the permit would have allowed ASARCO to emit annually over 7,000 tons of pollutants, the affected communities united behind the goal of never again having the company poison their air, water, and soil. During the process, TCEQ commissioners referred the matter to two administrative law judges who conducted a ten day hearing in El Paso. After careful consideration, both judges found that ASARCO had failed to meet their burden of proof and recommended denial of the permit renewal.

Yet despite public outcry and against the recommendations of the administrative law judges, TCEQ's executive director Glenn Shankle supported the permit's issuance. On February 13, 2008, the TCEQ commissioners voted 3-0 to grant ASARCO the controversial operating permit. The decision followed six years of litigation, a contested case hearing, and well-publicized opposition from organizations and governments in Texas, New Mexico, and Chihuahua, Mexico. On February 14 and 18, 2008, our office submitted two public information requests to TCEQ, requesting various communications between TCEQ commissioners, ASARCO, and ASARCO's legal representatives, including personal cell phone and email records that relate to the transaction of official business. The requests were made under the "legislative purpose" statute, which allows legislators to gain access to otherwise confidential information provided that it is for a legislative use.

TCEQ Fights Public Information Requests

TCEQ immediately began fighting our request, delivering an 18-page brief to the Office of the Texas Attorney General (OAG) arguing that the records are confidential and should not be made available to our office. Citing executive privilege and a violation of separation of powers, TCEQ argues that the statute is unconstitutional—that legislators and the public they represent have no right to documents in the possession of agencies created by that very same legislature. As such, they are effectively arguing that the imposition of one statute—the legislative purpose exception—makes it harder to follow a second statute—their air permitting responsibilities—and thus it is the court's responsibility to remove that burden. The OAG disagreed, ruling that we are entitled, by state law, to the agency's records.

What TCEQ Attempted to Hide

It soon became clear what TCEQ was attempting to hide. A few months after our request, billing records from ASARCO's law firm, Baker Botts LLP, became public in ASARCO's bankruptcy and showed repeated illegal ex parte communications between the firm and TCEQ staff and commissioners. The ex parte communications occurred prior to and leading up to the ASARCO permitting decision in February. In other words, ASARCO had an inside track to the commissioners without affording the same opportunity to the other parties to the contested permit.

The ex parte communications at issue took place between an ASARCO lobbyist employed by Baker Botts and then-Chairman, Commissioner Buddy Garcia. Garcia was hand-picked by Gov. Rick Perry to lead the agency despite having no prior environmental experience whatsoever. During his confirmation hearing before the Senate Nominations Committee, I questioned Garcia regarding the troubling lack of faith El Paso and other areas of the state have in the agency. In response, he promised to "get to the bottom" of issues that lead to "even a minute suggestion of criminal wrongdoing." Clearly this standard was not followed and certainly not applied to Garcia himself. After all, any evidence of illegal communications between Garcia and lobbyists would merely show the agency for what it is: corrupted and captured by the state's polluters.

The Legal Process

As the open records request continued through the legal process, it has become more clear that TCEQ has no solid legal argument. After the OAG ruled against the agency, TCEQ filed suit in Travis County, still arguing that the legislative purpose statute was unconstitutional. The District Court also ruled against TCEQ and in our favor. TCEQ appealed this decision, resulting in oral arguments that took place before the 3rd Court of Appeals just last week.**

TCEQ attempting to hide evidence of ex parte communications is standard operating procedure for an agency that values supporting polluters over protecting the public. TCEQ's mission statement is "to protect our state's human and natural resources consistent with sustainable economic development. Our goal is clean air, clean water, and the safe management of waste." But they have lost sight of those values. By arguing executive privilege, the agency aims to conceal the network of influence and contacts that make money off of the ability to pollute. The public's interest, however, has been piqued, resulting in calls to release the records and public outcry over the state's air permitting process.

The Waste Control Specialty Scandal

In addition to the ASARCO air permit, the WCS permit scandal raises serious concerns as to what's happening at the highest levels of TCEQ. Discussed by our office recently, WCS is a hazardous waste disposal company that is burying train loads of New York's toxic waste in the Texas panhandle.

In 2005, WCS received a TCEQ permit to accept and bury poisonous sludge despite even TCEQ's own scientists expressing serious concerns that the site is too close to water aquifers and that waste stored at the site could potentially leak into groundwater. After TCEQ executive director Glenn Shankle supported the issuance of the permit over staff recommendations, three TCEQ employees left the agency due to frustration with the licensing process. WCS eventually did receive the permit and, as of January 26, 2010, had received 16 full trainloads of New York's toxic waste so far with a total weight of approximately 248,359,000 pounds.

Not Very Circumspect

After doing his part to ensure that WCS received their permit, Shankle left the agency in June 2008. Only six months later, he signed on to lobby for the very polluter he was just regulating: WCS. Apparently appearance of quid pro quo did not shy Shankle away from getting paid between $100,000 and $150,000 by the company, according to the Texas Ethics Commission. When told of Shankle's new gig, one of the staffers who quit in protest of the WCS permit replied, "[e]ven the Mafia was more circumspect than this."

Indeed, Shankle's departure to industry is not anything new. Pam Giblin, the lead Baker Botts attorney working on the ASARCO air permit, is another former TCEQ employee who left the agency to work for polluters. Representing oil, chemical, and power industries, she is now happy to bill $675 an hour to fight against Texas' air, water, and soil. Giblin and other Baker Botts attorneys were also happy to help host a reception for the newest TCEQ commissioner, Bryan Shaw. I questioned Shaw about this very event during his Senate confirmation hearing.

Sunlight Needed

As former U.S. Supreme Court Justice Louis Brandeis stated, "sunlight is the best disinfectant." Until these and other backroom deals and revolving-door practices are discussed openly, reported on by the press, and investigated by national and state committees with oversight on clean air and water, Texas' environmental agency will continue to value polluters' pocketbooks over the public interest.

Help connect the dots – then tell Austin that our skies are not for sale.

....

**Senator Shapleigh won the appeal in April 2010.

For further resources, please visit **www.cengagebrain.com**.

10 Laws, Courts, and Justice

(© Nick Anderson of the Houston Chronicle, dist. by The Washington Post Writers Group. Reprinted with Permission.)

Learning Objectives

1. Identify the sources of Texas law.
2. Explain the structure and jurisdiction of Texas courts.
3. Compare the functions of all participants in the justice system.
4. Describe the judicial procedure for the adjudication of civil and criminal lawsuits.
5. Explain the four-pronged mission of the Texas Department of Criminal Justice.
6. Evaluate the fairness of Texas's justice system.

n the early morning hours of August 13, 1986, Christine Morton was bludgeoned to death in her Williamson County home, near Austin. Her three-year-old son was unharmed. Michael Morton, her husband, assured authorities she had been alive when he left for work at 5:30 that morning. Seven months later, a jury sentenced him to life in prison for murdering his wife. For 25 years, Morton fought to establish his innocence, beginning with his statement upon conviction, "Your honor, I didn't do this. That's all I can say. I didn't do this."

The evidence against Morton was compelling to jurors: a marriage that included loud arguments; a medical examiner's report that the level of Christine Morton's food digestion indicated her death occurred around 1:30 a.m.; a note Morton left the morning of the murder stating he felt "hurt and unwanted" when his wife turned him down for sex; and a billy club that had gone missing from his truck. The district attorney, Ken Anderson (now a state district judge), concluded his version of events by telling jurors that after murdering his wife, the defendant defiled her. It took the jury less than an hour to find Morton guilty.

Defense attorneys argued that an unknown assailant committed the crime. They noted a footprint in the Mortons' backyard and unidentified fingerprints on a sliding glass door and in the couple's bedroom. A bloodied blue bandana was discovered near the victim's home. Morton's attorneys suspected that prosecutors had information to support this version of the facts. Prior to trial they asked the presiding judge to determine whether the district attorney's file contained any exculpatory evidence. Under the U.S. Supreme Court's decision in *Brady v. Maryland*, 373 U.S. 83 (1963), prosecutors must disclose evidence that could be favorable to an accused.

The district attorney delivered some of the contents of his files, but not all. He failed to include a statement by the Mortons' three-year-old son to his grandmother that "a monster" had killed his mother when his father was not present. In addition, the district attorney did not disclose evidence that Christine Morton's credit card was used in San Antonio two days after her death; a report that a check made payable to her was cashed nine days after her death; or neighbors' descriptions of a suspicious van with a driver who appeared to be staking out the Morton home. This information was discovered by Morton's appellate attorneys in 2011, after years of attempting to gain access to the district attorney's files.

In 2004, Morton's attorneys asked then Williamson County district attorney John Bradley to agree to postconviction DNA testing of the blue bandana, arguing that advances in DNA technology now made the process viable. For the next seven years, Bradley fought this request. Tests were eventually conducted in 2011, and the results confirmed the presence of Christine Morton's blood on the bandana, along with that of an individual later identified as Mark Alan Norwood. His DNA was also linked to a similar murder that occurred in Austin in 1988, more than a year after Michael Morton began serving his life sentence.

As a result of these findings, Morton was fully exonerated on December 19, 2011. When he delivered the exoneration, District Judge Sid

Harle stepped down from the bench and said, "I think you've probably had enough of judges looking down on you."[1] In addition, on the recommendation of Judge Harle, the Texas Supreme Court convened a court of inquiry to review the legality of Ken Anderson's actions. In May 2012, John Bradley lost the Republican nomination for district attorney.

In his opinion in *Brady v. Maryland*, U.S. Supreme Court Justice William O. Douglas observed, "Society wins not only when the guilty are convicted but when criminal trials are fair; our system of the administration of justice suffers when any accused is treated unfairly." Fairness becomes even more critical in cases that involve the death penalty. Cases such as Michael Morton's remind us that unlike the proviso in the cartoon that opens this chapter, we must continue to ask if anyone convicted of a felony might be innocent. As you learn about Texas's justice system, consider what the state does to make the system fair and what practices might interfere with that goal.

LO1

State Law in Texas

Texans have given substantial power to their justice system. The Texas Constitution and state statutes grant government the authority, under appropriate circumstances, to take a person's life, liberty, or property. It is the role of the state's judges to interpret and apply state constitutional provisions, statutory laws, and agency regulations. Through these interpretations, judges are involved in the policymaking process. Yet, judges attract less public attention than state legislative and executive officials, even though their decisions affect Texans every day. It is therefore important that the state's residents understand the purpose and workings of the judicial branch.

With more than 3,300 justices and judges, and almost that many courts, Texas has one of the largest judicial systems in the country. Including traffic violations handled in lower courts, millions of cases are processed each year. Texas courts deal with cases involving **civil law** (for example, disputes concerning business contracts, divorces and other family issues, and personal injury claims). They also hear cases involving **criminal law** (proceedings against persons charged with committing a **misdemeanor**, such as using false identification to purchase liquor, which is punishable by a fine and jail sentence; or a **felony**, such as armed robbery, which is punishable by a prison sentence and a fine). A court's authority to hear a particular case is its **jurisdiction**.

Sources of Law

Regardless of their jurisdiction, Texas courts interpret and apply state law.[2] These laws include the provisions of the Texas Constitution, statutes enacted by the legislature, regulations adopted by state agencies, and judge-made common law based on custom and tradition dating back to medieval England. A court may apply a statute, constitutional provision, regulation, and common law all in the same case. Procedures for filing a

civil law
The body of law concerning noncriminal matters, such as business contracts and personal injury.

criminal law
The body of law concerning felony and misdemeanor offenses by individuals against other persons and property, or in violation of laws or ordinances.

misdemeanor
Classified as A, B, or C, a misdemeanor may be punished by fine and/or jail sentence.

felony
A serious crime punished by fine and prison confinement.

jurisdiction
A court's authority to hear a particular case.

case, conducting a trial, and appealing a judgment depend on whether the case is civil or criminal.

The Texas Constitution and statutes are available on the Internet at http://www.statutes.legis.state.tx.us. In addition, Thomson Reuters Westlaw publishes the same information in *Vernon's Texas Statutes and Codes Annotated.* Newly enacted laws passed in each legislative session are compiled and made available on the website of the Statutory Documents section of the Office of the Secretary of State at http://www.sos.state.tx.us/statdoc/bills/index.shtml. Agency regulations are codified in the *Texas Administrative Code.*

Code Revision

In 1963, the legislature charged the Texas Legislative Council with the responsibility of reorganizing Texas laws related to specific topics (such as education or taxes) into a systematic and comprehensive arrangement of legal codes. More than 50 years later, the council continues to work on this project. In addition to piecemeal changes resulting from routine legislation, the legislature also sometimes undertakes extensive revision of an entire legal code. Current efforts include compiling all statutes related to local governments into the Special District Local Laws Code, as authorized by the 78th legislature in 2003. Subsequent legislative sessions have approved ongoing revisions.

Points to Ponder

Laws enacted in 2011 made the following changes to state law:

- "Sexting" by underage offenders became a misdemeanor offense; offenders and their parents are required to attend educational classes on the dangers (SB 407)
- Separate speed limits for day and night driving were eliminated (HB 1353)
- "Noodling," allowing fishermen to catch catfish by using "hands only without any other fishing device" became legal (HB 2189)

✔ Learning Check 10.1   (Answers on p. 436)

1. True or False: Civil law cases involve misdemeanors and felonies.
2. True or False: Texas state law includes judge-made common law based on custom and tradition.

Courts, Judges, Lawyers, and Juries

LO2
LO3

Article V of the Texas Constitution is titled "Judicial Department." This article provides that all state judicial power "shall be vested in one Supreme Court, in one Court of Criminal Appeals, in Courts of Appeals, in District Courts, in County Courts, in Commissioners Courts (which have no judicial authority, as discussed in Chapter 3, "Local Governments"), in Courts of Justice of the Peace and in such other courts as may be provided by law." In exercising its constitutional power to create other courts, the Texas legislature has established municipal courts, county courts-at-law, and probate courts (all of which are described in this chapter). These courts are referred to as statutory courts.[3]

The legislature has also authorized the creation of a number of specialized courts to meet specific needs of the state's residents. Among these specialized courts are "cluster courts," which are traveling courts that adjudicate only Children's Protective Services cases; drug courts, which focus on treatment options rather than incarceration for substance abusers; and veterans courts, which deal with offenders who have suffered some type of mental disorder related to their military service experiences.[4]

Trial and Appellate Courts

Texas's judicial system is complex. (See the structure of the current judicial system presented in Figure 10.1.) The law creating a particular court fixes the court's jurisdiction, which may be civil, criminal, or both. In addition, some courts have **original jurisdiction** only, meaning they are limited to trying cases being heard for the first time. Other courts are restricted to hearing appeals from lower courts and thus have only **appellate jurisdiction**. Still other courts exercise both original and appellate jurisdiction. A court may have both exclusive and concurrent jurisdiction. A court that has **exclusive jurisdiction** is the only court with the authority to decide a particular type of case. **Concurrent jurisdiction** means that more than one court has authority to try a specific dispute. In that instance, a plaintiff selects the court in which to file the case. Further distinctions are made regarding whether a court resolves criminal matters, civil disputes, or both. Qualifications and compensation for judges vary among the different courts, as shown in Table 10.1.

Local Trial Courts The courts with which Texans are most familiar are municipal courts and justice of the peace courts. Together, these local trial courts handle, among other types of cases, charges involving Class C misdemeanors, which are the least serious category of criminal offenses. Both municipal judges and justices of the peace, like other Texas justices and judges, may perform marriages. They also serve as magistrates of the state. In this latter capacity, these officials issue warrants for the arrest of suspects and conduct hearings to determine whether a person charged with a criminal act will be released on bail or jailed pending further court action.

original jurisdiction
The power of a court to hear a case first.

appellate jurisdiction
The power of a court to review cases after they have been tried elsewhere.

exclusive jurisdiction
The authority of only one court to hear a particular type of case.

concurrent jurisdiction
The authority of more than one court to try a case (for example, a civil dispute involving more than $500 but less than $10,000 may be heard in either a justice of the peace court, a county court, or a district court).

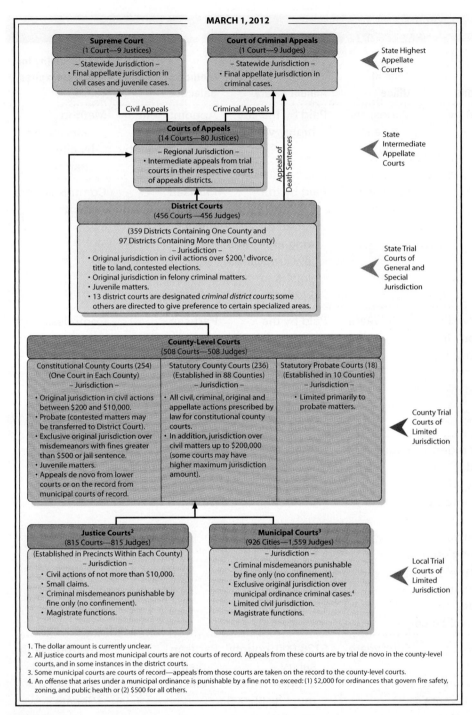

MARCH 1, 2012

Supreme Court
(1 Court—9 Justices)
– Statewide Jurisdiction –
• Final appellate jurisdiction in civil cases and juvenile cases.

Court of Criminal Appeals
(1 Court—9 Judges)
– Statewide Jurisdiction –
• Final appellate jurisdiction in criminal cases.

State Highest Appellate Courts

Civil Appeals   Criminal Appeals

Courts of Appeals
(14 Courts—80 Justices)
– Regional Jurisdiction –
• Intermediate appeals from trial courts in their respective courts of appeals districts.

State Intermediate Appellate Courts

Appeals of Death Sentences

District Courts
(456 Courts—456 Judges)
(359 Districts Containing One County and 97 Districts Containing More than One County)
– Jurisdiction –
• Original jurisdiction in civil actions over $200,[1] divorce, title to land, contested elections.
• Original jurisdiction in felony criminal matters.
• Juvenile matters.
• 13 district courts are designated *criminal district courts;* some others are directed to give preference to certain specialized areas.

State Trial Courts of General and Special Jurisdiction

County-Level Courts
(508 Courts—508 Judges)

Constitutional County Courts (254) (One Court in Each County) – Jurisdiction –	Statutory County Courts (236) (Established in 88 Counties) – Jurisdiction –	Statutory Probate Courts (18) (Established in 10 Counties) – Jurisdiction –
• Original jurisdiction in civil actions between $200 and $10,000. • Probate (contested matters may be transferred to District Court). • Exclusive original jurisdiction over misdemeanors with fines greater than $500 or jail sentence. • Juvenile matters. • Appeals de novo from lower courts or on the record from municipal courts of record.	• All civil, criminal, original and appellate actions prescribed by law for constitutional county courts. • In addition, jurisdiction over civil matters up to $200,000 (some courts may have higher maximum jurisdiction amount).	• Limited primarily to probate matters.

County Trial Courts of Limited Jurisdiction

Justice Courts[2]
(815 Courts—815 Judges)
(Established in Precincts Within Each County)
– Jurisdiction –
• Civil actions of not more than $10,000.
• Small claims.
• Criminal misdemeanors punishable by fine only (no confinement).
• Magistrate functions.

Municipal Courts[3]
(926 Cities—1,559 Judges)
– Jurisdiction –
• Criminal misdemeanors punishable by fine only (no confinement).
• Exclusive original jurisdiction over municipal ordinance criminal cases.[4]
• Limited civil jurisdiction.
• Magistrate functions.

Local Trial Courts of Limited Jurisdiction

1. The dollar amount is currently unclear.
2. All justice courts and most municipal courts are not courts of record. Appeals from these courts are by trial de novo in the county-level courts, and in some instances in the district courts.
3. Some municipal courts are courts of record—appeals from those courts are taken on the record to the county-level courts.
4. An offense that arises under a municipal ordinance is punishable by a fine not to exceed: (1) $2,000 for ordinances that govern fire safety, zoning, and public health or (2) $500 for all others.

Figure 10.1   Court Structure of Texas

Source: Office of Court Administration, 2012, available at **www.courts.state.tx.us**.

Table 10.1	Texas Judges and Justices				
Court	**Judicial Qualifications**	**Term of Office**	**Annual Salary**	**Method of Selection**	**Responsibility for Filling Unexpired Terms**
Local Courts Municipal Courts	Varies; set by each city	Varies; set by each city	Paid by the city; highly variable	Appointment or election, as determined by city charter	Method determined by city charter
Justice of the Peace Courts	None	Four years	Paid by the county; highly variable, ranging from a few thousand dollars to $120,000	Partisan precinctwide elections	Commissioners court
County Courts Constitutional County Courts	Must be "well informed" in Texas law; law degree not required	Four years	Paid by the county; highly variable, ranging from a few thousand dollars to more than $150,000	Partisan countywide elections	Commissioners court
Statutory County Courts (courts-at-law and probate courts)	Age 25 or older; licensed attorney with at least four to five years' experience, depending on statutory requirements; two years' county residence	Four years	Paid by the state and county; somewhat variable	Partisan countywide elections	Commissioners court
State Courts District Courts	Ages 25–74; licensed attorney with at least four years' experience; two years' county residence	Four years	$125,000; county salary supplements; must be $5,000 less than court of appeals justices' salaries	Partisan districtwide elections	Governor, with advice and consent of Senate

Court	Judicial Qualifications	Term of Office	Annual Salary	Method of Selection	Responsibility for Filling Unexpired Terms
Courts of Appeals	Ages 35–74; licensed attorney with at least 10 years' experience	Six years	$137,500 (justices); $140,000 (chief justices); county salary supplements; must be $5,000 less than Texas Supreme Court justices' salaries	Partisan districtwide elections	Governor, with advice and consent of Senate
Court of Criminal Appeals	Ages 35–74; licensed attorney with at least 10 years' experience	Six years	$150,000 (judges); $152,500 (presiding judge)	Partisan statewide elections	Governor, with advice and consent of Senate
Supreme Court	Ages 35–74; licensed attorney with at least 10 years' experience	Six years	$150,000 (justices); $152,500 (chief justice)	Partisan statewide elections	Governor, with advice and consent of Senate

Table 10.1 Continued

Sources: Compiled from Office of Court Administration, *Report on Judicial Salaries and Turnover for Fiscal Years 2010 and 2011,* http://www.courts.state.tx.us/oca/pdf/judicial_turnover_rpt-fy10-fy11.pdf; Texas Legislature Online, http://www.capitol.state.tx.us.

Judicial bodies in more than 900 incorporated cities, towns, and villages in Texas are known as **municipal courts**. Although mayors of a general-law city have the authority to serve as municipal judges (unless the city council provides for the election or appointment of someone to perform this function), only 2 percent of municipal judges are mayors. Usually, municipal court judges of home-rule cities are named by city councils for two-year terms. State law does not require these citizens to be licensed attorneys, unless they preside over a municipal court of record (as is discussed below). City councils, however, set professional qualifications, as well as determine the number of judges and judicial salaries for their municipalities.

Municipal courts have limited civil jurisdiction in cases involving owners of dangerous dogs. These courts have no appellate jurisdiction. Their original and exclusive criminal jurisdiction extends to all violations of city ordinances, and they have criminal jurisdiction concurrent with justice of

municipal court
City-run courts with jurisdiction primarily over Class C misdemeanors committed within a city's boundaries.

the peace courts over Class C misdemeanors committed within city limits. If an individual is dissatisfied with the result of a municipal court ruling, the case can be appealed to the county court or a county court-at-law. Appeals are filed in less than 0.5 percent of municipal court cases.

If a city has a municipal **court of record** (a court with a court reporter or electronic device to record the testimony and proceedings), a transcript of the municipal trial is made, and any appeal at the county level is based on that record of the case. Otherwise, appealed cases receive a trial de novo (a completely new trial). Although incorporated cities are authorized to maintain municipal courts of record, few do so because of the expense.

A **justice of the peace**, often called the JP, is elected by voters residing in a precinct with boundaries created by the county commissioners court. The Texas Constitution mandates the number of precincts per county (one to eight) according to population. The number of JPs (one or two) per precinct is also directed, in part, by that same document. The position requires neither previous legal training nor experience. Approximately 10 percent of Texas's JPs (usually in large cities) are lawyers who may engage in private legal practice while serving as a justice of the peace. Within a year after election, a justice of the peace who is not a lawyer must, by law, complete an 80-hour course in performing the duties of that office. Thereafter, the JP is supposed to receive 20 hours of instruction annually. Because failure to complete the training is a violation of a JP's duties under the law, arguably a noncomplying JP could be removed from office for official misconduct. However, such removal is highly unlikely; though the State Commission on Judicial Conduct, a state agency that has the authority to recommend removal, frequently orders justices who do not comply to complete the mandatory education.

In urban areas, being a justice of the peace is a full-time job, whereas justices in many rural precincts hear few cases. In addition to presiding over the justice court, a justice of the peace serves as an ex officio notary public. A JP also functions as a coroner, determining cause of death when the county commissioners court has not named a county medical examiner. Justice of the peace courts have both criminal and civil jurisdiction. In all cases, their jurisdiction is original. In criminal matters, these local courts try Class C misdemeanors; however, any conviction may be appealed to the county court or a county court-at-law for a new trial.

Exclusive civil jurisdiction of JP courts is limited to cases in which the amount in controversy is $200 or less, not including interest. Concurrent civil jurisdiction is shared with county courts and district courts (discussed later) if the amount in controversy exceeds $200, but is not more than $10,000. Appeals from JP courts of cases involving $250 or more are taken to the county level, where cases are tried de novo. For cases involving less than $250, the JP court is the court of last resort—that is, the highest state court that can render a judgment in the matter.

Did the cleaners damage your sweater and then refuse to replace it? Did you work last week and now your boss is withholding your wages? **Small-claims court**, also administered by the JP, is where you should seek justice.

court of record
A court that has a court reporter or electronic device to record testimony and proceedings.

justice of the peace
A judge elected from a justice of the peace precinct who handles minor civil and criminal cases, including small claims court.

small-claims court
A court presided over by a justice of the peace that offers an informal and inexpensive procedure for handling damage claims of $10,000 or less.

Presided over by the justice of the peace, a small-claims court can hear almost any civil dispute in which the damages claimed are for $10,000 or less, except for divorces, slander, or suits affecting title to land. Plaintiffs must pay a fee of approximately $100 to bring a case against one individual. Additional amounts will likely be charged if the case has more than one defendant. Because these proceedings are informal, parties to the suits often represent themselves. When the amount in controversy exceeds $250, the losing party may appeal to a county-level court.[5]

County Trial Courts Each of Texas's 254 counties has a county court, as prescribed by the state constitution. More than 80 counties have one or more additional county-level courts created by statute. All are courts of record. Judges of constitutional county courts need not be attorneys. Statutory county court judges must be experienced attorneys.

Every county has a county judge. If these officials perform judicial functions, they must take Texas Supreme Court–approved courses in court administration, procedure, and evidence, along with judges of county courts-at-law, district courts, and appellate courts. Less than 15 percent of Texas's constitutional county court judges are licensed attorneys.

Most constitutional county courts have original and appellate jurisdiction, as well as probate, civil, and criminal jurisdiction. In some instances, however, the legislature has created county courts-at-law to exercise such jurisdiction. Although **probate** matters relate specifically to the estates of decedents, primarily establishing the validity of wills, courts with probate jurisdiction also handle guardianship proceedings and mental competency determinations. Original civil jurisdiction is limited to cases involving between $200 and $5,000 (if the court has concurrent jurisdiction with district courts) or $10,000 (if the court has concurrent jurisdiction with justice courts). Original criminal jurisdiction includes all Class A and Class B misdemeanors.

Appellate criminal jurisdiction extends to cases originating in JP courts and municipal courts. A constitutional county court's appellate jurisdiction is final with regard to criminal cases involving fines of $100 or less. For cases in which greater fines are imposed, the plaintiff may appeal to a court of appeals. Civil cases are heard on appeal from JP courts. County court decisions are final if the amount in controversy does not exceed $250.

In counties with large populations, the burden of presiding over the county commissioners court and handling many administrative responsibilities has left the judges of constitutional county courts with little or no time to try civil, criminal, and probate cases. Thus, to relieve constitutional county court judges of some or all courtroom duties, the legislature has authorized more than 200 statutory courts, most commonly called county courts-at-law. With few exceptions, the criminal jurisdiction of county courts-at-law is limited to misdemeanors. Civil jurisdiction of most county courts-at-law is limited to controversies involving amounts of $200 to $100,000.

In 10 counties throughout the state, the legislature has created statutory county courts to handle guardianship and competency proceedings, as well as the admission of wills to probate. These courts are located in six of Texas's

probate
Proceedings that involve the estates of decedents. Additionally, courts with probate jurisdiction (county courts, county courts-at-law, and probate courts) handle guardianship and mental competency matters.

most populous metropolitan areas. In the authorizing statutes creating each probate court, the legislature restricts their jurisdiction to hearing these types of cases only.

State Trial Courts Texas's principal trial courts are composed of district-level courts of general and special jurisdiction. Most state trial courts are designated simply as district courts, but a few are called criminal district courts. Each district-level court has jurisdiction over one or more counties. Heavily populated counties may have several district courts with countywide jurisdiction.

Most district court judges are authorized to try both criminal and civil cases, though a statute creating a court may specify that the court give preference to one or the other. All criminal cases are matters of original jurisdiction. Misdemeanor jurisdiction is limited to cases transferred from constitutional county courts, cases specifically authorized by the state legislature, and offenses involving misconduct by government officials while acting in an official capacity. Felony jurisdiction extends to all types of felonies. Appeal after a capital felony conviction is taken directly to the Court of Criminal Appeals. Other criminal convictions are appealed to an intermediate appellate court.

District courts have exclusive original jurisdiction over civil cases involving divorce, land titles, contested elections, contested wills, slander, and defamation of character. They have original civil jurisdiction in controversies involving $200 or more (however, one court of appeals in Texas held the minimum amount to be $500). Thus, concurrent jurisdiction with lower courts begins at this level; above the maximum "dollar amount" jurisdiction of those courts, district courts exercise exclusive civil jurisdiction. Appeals of civil cases go to courts of appeals.

Appellate Courts The Lone Star State's appellate courts consist of courts of appeals, the Court of Criminal Appeals, and the Supreme Court of Texas. Each of these courts has three or more judges or justices. The judges' six-year terms are staggered so that one-third of the members are elected or reelected every two years. This arrangement helps ensure that at any given time—barring death, resignation, or removal from office—each appellate court will have two or more judges with experience on that court. Decisions are reached by majority vote of the assigned judges after they examine the written record of the case, review briefs (written arguments) prepared by the parties' attorneys, and hear oral arguments by the attorneys. The Supreme Court of Texas and the Court of Criminal Appeals are authorized to answer questions about Texas law asked by federal appellate courts (for example, the U.S. Fifth Circuit Court of Appeals or the U.S. Supreme Court). In 2011, the U.S. Fifth Circuit Court of Appeals asked the Texas Supreme Court to determine whether the state's "rolling easement" on beachfront property violated the state's constitution. The court found that rolling easements violated the constitution. This case is discussed in the CourseReader selection for this chapter.

CourseReader ASSIGNMENTS

Log in to www.cengagebrain.com and open CourseReader to access the reading:

Out of Beach? Coastal Access Is Pretty Much the Only Area of Property Rights in Texas Where the Public Interest Has Always Trumped the Private Interest. That May Finally Be Eroding.
Paul Burka

With nature constantly reshaping coastlines of states that border the ocean, public easements must be constantly reevaluated for beach access. Historically in Texas, these public rights have trumped private ownership of beachfront property and structures. This article explores a new case addressing the legal questions related to public easements in Texas and formulates an opinion on the outcome of the case. In March 2012, the Texas Supreme Court determined that public easements do not shift with beach shorelines.

1. What is a rolling easement?

2. To what portion of Texas's state beaches did the public have access under the state's public easement?

The legislature has divided Texas into 14 state court of appeals districts and has established a court of appeals in every district. Each of these intermediate appellate courts is composed of a chief justice and from two to 12 justices. These courts hear appeals of civil and criminal cases from district courts and county courts (but not those involving capital punishment or DNA-forensic testing appeals for individuals sentenced to death).

How Do We Compare...in Salaries of Highest Court Justices and Judges?

Annual Salaries of Highest Court Justices and Judges (in dollars as of 2011)

Most Populous U.S. States	Chief Justice/ Judge	Associate Justice/Judge	U.S. States Bordering Texas	Chief Justice/Judge Associate Justice/Judge	
California	$228,856	$218,237	Arkansas	$156,864	$145,204
Florida	$157,976	$157,976	Louisiana	$157,050	$149,572
New York	$156,000*	$151,200*	New Mexico	$125,691	$123,691
Texas	**$152,500**	**$150,000**	Oklahoma	$147,000	$137,655

*Salaries for New York's appellate judges increased to $182,600 and $177,000, respectively, in April 2012.
Source: Judicial Salary Resource Center (July 2011), **http://www.ncsc.org**.

Final jurisdiction includes cases involving divorce, slander, boundary disputes, and elections held for purposes other than choosing government officials (for example, bond elections). Courts must hear appeals in panels of at least three justices. A decision requires a majority vote of a panel of justices.

Texas and Oklahoma are the only states in the Union that have **bifurcated** (divided) court systems for dealing with criminal and civil appeals. In Texas, the highest tribunal with criminal jurisdiction is the Court of Criminal Appeals. This nine-judge court hears criminal appeals exclusively. Texans continue to resist the creation of a unified judicial system, which would have a single appellate court of last resort for both criminal felony cases and complex civil cases.[6]

Members of the Court of Criminal Appeals, including one whom voters elect as presiding judge, are chosen in partisan elections on a statewide basis for six-year terms. Sharon Keller became the first woman to head the Texas Court of Criminal Appeals in 2000. As of 2012, four of the other eight judges were women. Judge Elsa Alcala became the first Latina judge on the court when she was appointed in 2011. She was elected to a full term in 2012. In that same year, no African Americans were on the Court of Criminal Appeals, and all members of the court were Republicans.

Supreme Court Officially titled the Supreme Court of Texas, the state's highest court with civil jurisdiction has nine members elected statewide on a partisan basis: one chief justice and eight justices. No Democrats have served on the Texas Supreme Court since 1998. Through September 2012, two African American justices served on the court. As of late 2012, Chief Justice Wallace Jefferson was the only African American on the court. Latinos held two other positions. Two of the nine justices were women. All of the justices were Republican.

Without criminal jurisdiction, this high court is supreme only in cases involving civil law. Because it has severely limited original jurisdiction (for example, issuing writs and hearing cases involving denial of a place on an election ballot), nearly all of the court's docket involves appeals of cases that it determines must be heard. Much of the supreme court's work involves handling petitions for review, which can be requested by a party who argues that a court of appeals made a mistake on a question of law. If as many as four justices favor granting an initial review, the case is scheduled for argument in open court. In 2011, the Texas Supreme Court granted an initial review for approximately 13 percent of the almost 800 petitions that were filed. Justices do not make public their votes to accept or deny a petition for review.

The supreme court performs other important functions as well. It is responsible for formulating the rules of civil procedure, which set out the manner in which civil cases are to be handled by the state's trial courts and appellate courts. The supreme court also has the authority to transfer cases for the purpose of equalizing workloads (cases pending on the dockets) of courts of appeals. The chief justice can temporarily assign district judges outside their administrative judicial regions and assign retired appellate

bifurcated
A divided court system in which different courts handle civil and criminal cases. In Texas, the highest-level appeals courts are bifurcated.

justices (with their consent) to temporary duty on courts of appeals. In 2009, the Texas Supreme Court created the Texas Court Records Preservation Task Force, comprised of attorneys, judges, district clerks, and professors who work to determine how best to preserve historical court documents. The Selected Reading at the end of this chapter is a result of this effort.

Early in each regular session of the Texas legislature, the chief justice is required by law to deliver a State of the Judiciary message, either orally or in written form, to the legislature. In his 2011 address, Chief Justice Jefferson urged the legislature to provide funding for both civil and criminal legal representation of the indigent (defendants a court determines are too poor to hire a lawyer) and to reform criminal justice procedures to limit incarceration of the innocent. He also continued his plea for limiting the effect of partisan election of judges in Texas.[7]

Selecting Judges Texas, along with Alabama, Louisiana, and West Virginia, chooses all judges (except municipal judges) in partisan elections. Many commentators, political scientists, and judges (including the last three chief justices of the Texas Supreme Court) oppose this practice. In discussing "the peculiar [American] institution" of electing judges, Harvard Law professor Jed Handelsman Shugerman observed that although a number of foreign countries have adopted the American legal system, few have chosen to follow the practice of popular election of judges.[8]

Texas Supreme Court Justice Wallace Jefferson delivers his biennial State of the Judiciary address to a joint session of the Texas Senate and House of Representatives.

(AP Photo/LM Otero)

The ways that other states select judges is far from uniform. Legal scholar Roy Schotland identified at least 15 different selection processes for judges.[9] Some opponents of the popular election of judges argue that Texas should consider some version of the merit selection process initiated by the state of Missouri in 1940. The **Missouri Plan** features a nominating commission that recommends a panel of names to the governor whenever a judicial vacancy is to be filled. The appointee then serves for a year or so before the voters decide, based on his or her judicial performance record, whether to give the new judge a full term or to allow the nominating commission and governor to make another appointment on a similar trial basis.

Missouri Plan
A judicial selection process in which a commission recommends a panel of names to the governor, followed by a one-year or so appointment of a judge before voters determine whether the appointee will be retained for a full term.

Others favor an **appointment–retention system** for all courts of record. In this system, the governor appoints a judge and the voters determine whether to retain the appointee. Reform proposals have consistently failed in the Texas legislature. As noted earlier, in his 2011 State of the Judiciary speech, Chief Justice Jefferson urged legislators to propose a full reform of the system with a constitutional amendment that would replace popular partisan election of judges. Noting that "a justice system built on some notion of Democratic judging or Republican judging is a system that cannot be trusted," he asked legislators to at least establish nonpartisan election of judges. Neither request resulted in action.

Disciplining and Removing Judges and Justices

Each year, a few of Texas's judges and justices commit acts that warrant discipline or removal. These judges can be removed by the voters at the next election; by trial by jury; or if they are state court judges, by legislative address or impeachment. The State Commission on Judicial Conduct, however, plays the most important role in disciplining the state's judiciary. This 13-member commission is composed of six judges, each from a different level court; two attorneys; and five private citizens, who are neither attorneys nor judges.

In 2011, the commission resolved almost 1,200 complaints. Eight judges resigned to avoid disciplinary action. Seven public and 27 private reprimands were issued to 34 judges. The remaining complaints were dismissed. Summaries of sanctions are available on the commission's website at http://www.scjc.state.tx.us/actions.asp. Table 10.2 provides an overview of the number of complaints and disciplinary actions by court type. Parties to a lawsuit—either a litigant or a criminal defendant—file most complaints (for

appointment-retention system
A merit plan for judicial selection, whereby the governor appoints to fill a court vacancy for an interim period after which the judge must win a full term in an uncontested popular election.

Table 10.2 Disposition of Cases by Judge Type, 2011

Judge Type	Number of Judges	Number of Complaints	Portion of Total Complaints	Number of Disciplinary Actions	Portion of Total Actions
Municipal	1,531	98	9%	10	24%
Justice of the Peace	819	218	19%	23	55%
Constitutional county court	254	33	3%	4	10%
Statutory county court	251	99	9%	1	2%
District court	456	492	44%	3	7%
Appellate court	98	36	5%	0	0%
Senior or retired	302	87	8%	1	2%
Associate*	189	56	5%	0	0%
Total	3,900	1,119	102%**	42	100%

*Full- or part-time judges appointed as masters, magistrates, or referees to assist with specific types of cases.
**Totals of more than 100 percent are due to rounding.

Source: State Commission on Judicial Conduct, *Fiscal Year 2011 Annual Report,* **http://www.scjc.state.tx.us/pdf/rpts/AR-FY11.pdf**.

example, 66 percent of all complaints in 2011 were filed by parties to a lawsuit). Complaints against justices of the peace are the most likely to result in disciplinary action.

The commission's jurisdiction extends to judges and justices at all levels of the court system. In 2009, the commission issued a finding that the presiding judge of the Court of Criminal Appeals, Sharon Keller, brought "public discredit" to the judicial branch for her refusal to delay the closing of the court's offices to accept a last-minute appeal from a death row inmate. The condemned man, who likely would have been granted a brief stay of execution, was put to death later the same evening. Other than the public nature of these proceedings, no action was taken against Judge Keller.[10]

A justice of the peace in Brazos County (College Station) was less fortunate in 2011. He received a public reprimand for violating the requirement "to perform judicial duties without bias or prejudice."[11] During a proceeding to set bond for a student at nearby Blinn College who was accused of tossing a Texas A&M student's Aggie ring into the grass and losing it, the JP pointed to his own Aggie ring and then suggested that the accused consider attending college outside the College Station area. The JP set bond at $50,000 (10 times more than the standard bond for the offense for which the student was charged). The accused was released after someone else admitted guilt.[12]

Any judge given a public or private reprimand or ordered to take additional training may request the chief justice of the Texas Supreme Court to appoint a Special Court of Review (a three-judge panel of appellate judges) to hear an appeal. The commission has the authority to recommend removal of a judge. Such a recommendation is considered by a seven-member tribunal appointed by the Texas Supreme Court. If the tribunal votes to remove the judge, the decision may be appealed to the Texas Supreme Court.

The State Commission on Judicial Conduct also oversees an employee assistance program called Amicus Curiae. The program locates service providers for judges suffering from substance abuse or mental or emotional disorders. Judges receiving services through Amicus Curiae may do so through a self-referral or be referred by the commission. In all instances, participation is voluntary.

Lawyers

Both the Texas Supreme Court and the State Bar of Texas play roles in regulating the state's 78,000-plus attorneys, as well as an additional 10,000 attorneys who do not reside in Texas. The supreme court is involved with issues relating to the training and licensing of lawyers. Although accreditation of law schools is largely a responsibility of the American Bar Association, the supreme court appoints the eight-member Board of Law Examiners. That board supervises administration of the bar examination for individuals seeking to become licensed attorneys, and it certifies the names of successful applicants to the court. The State Bar of Texas oversees the state's lawyers.

State Bar of Texas To practice, a licensed attorney must be a member of the State Bar of Texas and pay dues for its support. Although the state bar is well known for its high-pressure lobbying activities, the organization also promotes high standards of ethical conduct for Texas lawyers and conducts an extensive program of continuing legal education. As an administrative agency of the state, it is authorized to discipline, suspend, and disbar attorneys. One of the primary purposes of the state bar is to maintain public confidence in the integrity of lawyers in the Lone Star State.

It is possible to research an attorney's qualifications. Many lawyers are rated by their fellow attorneys in the areas of legal ability and ethics in the *Martindale-Hubbell Legal Directory.* Information about an attorney's professional disciplinary record is also available from the Find-A-Lawyer link on the state bar's website.

Points to Ponder

In 2011, according to the State Bar of Texas, the state's attorneys included the following:

- A membership that was 67 percent male and 33 percent female.*
- A racial composition that was 83 percent Anglo Caucasian, 8 percent Latino, and 5 percent African American.*
- Membership in the Texas Young Lawyers Association (TYLA), the section of the State Bar of Texas to which all young and recently licensed attorneys belong, that was 54 percent male and 46 percent female. The racial composition of TYLA was 74 percent Anglo Caucasian, 11 percent Latino, and 6 percent African American.**

Sources: State Bar of Texas Department of Research and Analysis. *State Bar of Texas Membership: Attorney Statistical Profile (2010–2011), and **Texas Young Lawyers Association Members: Attorney Statistical Profile (2010–2011).

Legal Services for the Poor Under the Bill of Rights in the Texas Constitution and the Sixth Amendment to the U.S. Constitution, individuals who are accused of a crime are entitled to representation by an attorney. Courts must appoint attorneys for criminal defendants who establish that they are indigent. No assistance is available for cases brought by prisoners who challenge the constitutionality of their incarceration (habeas corpus proceedings), unless the defendant has been sentenced to death. In that instance, the Office of Capital Writs manages habeas corpus appeals. Programs such as the American Bar Association's Death Penalty Representation Project recruit attorneys from large civil law firms to assist a limited number of death row inmates. If these same individuals were seeking legal help for a civil matter, little or no free assistance would be available.

A person whose claim arises from a physical injury may be able to hire an attorney on a **contingency fee** basis, in which the lawyer is paid from any money recovered in a lawsuit. Representation in legal matters such as divorce, child custody, or contract disputes, however, requires the client to make direct payment to the attorney before or at the time services are performed. Despite an abundance of lawyers, nationally, less than 20 percent of the civil legal matters of the poor actually receive attention from an attorney.[13] When legal assistance is available, it is often through an attorney with the Legal Services Corporation, more commonly referred to as Legal Aid. According to Legal Services Corporation officials, nationally, no more than 50 percent of eligible individuals who seek assistance from legal aid programs actually receive services, creating a "justice gap" for the poor. Texas's ratio of poor people per legal aid attorney is twice as high as the national average. One of the primary funding sources for legal aid services is from interest paid on bank accounts that lawyers hold in trust for their clients. However, the dramatic reductions in bank interest rates that began in 2008 have had a devastating effect on these accounts. This income source declined from $20 million in 2007 to $4 million in 2011. As a result, legal aid attorneys have served even fewer Texans. In an effort to supplement funding for the state's legal aid programs, the 82nd legislature appropriated more than $17 million. Approximately 80 banks also agreed to pay interest on lawyer trust accounts at rates higher than those offered to the general public.

Many attorneys and judges agree with former U.S. Supreme Court justice Lewis Powell that "[e]qual justice under law is ... one of the ends for which our entire legal system exists.... [I]t is fundamental that justice should be the same, in substance and availability, without regard to economic status."[14] The Texas Access to Justice Commission, created by the Texas Supreme Court, works to coordinate and increase delivery of legal services to the state's poor. The 15-member commission includes judges, lawyers, and private citizens. The State Bar of Texas and the Texas Access to Justice Foundation support and collaborate with these efforts. The foundation maintains a website (http://www.texaslawhelp.org) that provides information, forms, and links to low- and no-cost legal services providers.

Attorney volunteers fill some of the representation gap. Special programs, such as Texas Lawyers for Texas Veterans, target particular populations for legal services provided by these private attorneys. State bar officials recommend that lawyers donate 50 hours per year assisting needy clients. According to a 2009 survey, more than 50 percent of Texas attorneys provided an estimated 2.5 million hours of free legal service to the poor.[15]

Computerized Assistance For-profit companies are also in the business of furnishing self-help legal materials. Some of the sites include lawyer referrals in the event purchasers decide they want assistance. It is also possible to purchase interactive software and legal self-help books that allow a person to write a will, obtain a divorce, or create a corporation. Legal documents that would cost hundreds, and sometimes thousands, of dollars if prepared by an attorney can be completed at little or no cost with self-help products. In addition, many attorneys now maintain virtual offices online.

contingency fee
A lawyer's compensation paid from money recovered in a lawsuit.

Juries

A jury system lets citizens participate directly in the administration of justice. Texas has two types of juries: grand juries and trial juries. The state's Bill of Rights guarantees that individuals may be charged with a felony only by grand jury indictment. It also provides that anyone charged with either a felony or a misdemeanor has the right to trial by jury. If requested by either party, jury trials are required in civil cases.

Grand Jury Composed of 12 citizens, a **grand jury** may be either chosen at random or, in a method known as the "key-man system," selected by a judge from a list of 15 to 40 county residents recommended by a judge-appointed grand jury commission. Most states and the federal government only use random selection to choose grand jurors. Members of a grand jury must have the qualifications of trial jurors (see the following "Trial Jury" section). County commissioners determine the pay for grand jurors. The district judge appoints one juror to serve as presiding juror or foreman of the jury panel. A grand jury's life lasts for a district court's term, which varies from three to six months, though a district judge may extend a grand jury's term. During this period, grand juries have the authority to inquire into all criminal actions but devote most of their time to felony matters.

A grand jury works in secrecy. Jurors and witnesses are sworn to keep secret all they hear in grand jury sessions. If, after investigation and deliberation (often lasting only a few minutes), at least nine grand jurors decide there is sufficient evidence to warrant a trial, an indictment is prepared with the aid of the prosecuting attorney. The indictment is a written statement accusing some person or persons of a particular crime (for example, burglary of a home). An indictment is referred to as a true bill; failure to indict constitutes a no bill. Grand jury indictments are authorized but not required for misdemeanor prosecutions. On the basis of a complaint, the district or county attorney may prepare an information, which is a document that formally charges the accused with a misdemeanor offense.

Trial Jury Although relatively few Texans ever serve on a grand jury, almost everyone can expect to be summoned from time to time for duty on a trial jury (**petit jury**). Official qualifications for jurors are not high, and thousands of jury trials are held in the Lone Star State every year. To ensure that jurors are properly informed concerning their work, the court gives them brief printed instructions (in English and Spanish) that describe their duties and explain basic legal terms and trial procedures. In urban counties, these instructions are often shown as a video in English and other languages common to segments of the county's population, such as Spanish or Vietnamese.

Qualifications, Selection, and Compensation of Jurors A qualified Texas juror must be

- a citizen of the United States and of the state of Texas;
- 18 years of age or older;

grand jury
Composed of 12 persons with the qualifications of trial jurors, a grand jury serves from three to six months while it determines whether sufficient evidence exists to indict persons accused of committing crimes.

petit jury
A trial jury of six or 12 members.

- of sound mind;
- able to read and write (with no restriction on language), unless literate jurors are unavailable; and
- neither convicted of a felony nor under indictment or other legal accusation of theft or any felony.

Qualified persons have a legal responsibility to serve when called, unless exempted or excused. Exemptions include

- being age 70 or older;
- having legal custody of a child or children younger than age 10;
- being enrolled in and attending a university, college, or secondary school;
- being the primary caregiver for an invalid;
- being employed by the legislative branch of state government;
- having served as a petit juror within the preceding two years in counties with populations of at least 200,000 or the preceding three years in counties with populations of more than 250,000; and
- being on active military duty outside the county.

Judges retain the prerogative to excuse others from jury duty in special circumstances. A person who is legally exempt from jury duty may avoid reporting to the court as summoned by filing a signed statement with the court clerk at any time before the scheduled date of appearance. In many counties, prospective jurors can complete necessary exemption forms on the Internet. In addition, anyone summoned for jury duty is entitled to reschedule the reporting date one time (at least twice in large, urban counties), as long as the new date is within six months of the original. Subsequent rescheduling requires an emergency that could not have been previously anticipated, such as illness or a death in the family. A failure to report for jury duty or falsely claiming an exemption is punishable as contempt of court, and a guilty individual can be fined up to $1,000.

A **venire** (panel of prospective jurors) is chosen by random selection from a list provided by either the secretary of state or another governmental agency or a private contractor selected by the county commissioners court. The list includes the county's registered voters, licensed drivers, and persons with identification cards issued by the Department of Public Safety. A trial jury is composed of six or 12 citizens, one of whom serves as foreman or presiding juror: six serve in a justice of the peace court, municipal court, or county court, whereas 12 serve in a district court. A jury panel generally includes more than the minimum number of jurors.

Attorneys question jurors through a procedure called **voir dire** (which means "to speak the truth") to identify any potential jurors who cannot be fair and impartial. An attorney may challenge for cause any venire member suspected of bias. If the judge agrees with the attorney, the prospective juror is excused from serving. Some individuals try to avoid jury duty by answering voir dire questions in a way that makes them appear biased.

An attorney challenges prospective jurors either by peremptory challenge (up to 15 per side, depending on the type of case, without having to

venire
A panel of prospective jurors drawn by random selection. These prospective jurors are called *veniremen.*

voir dire
Courtroom procedure whereby attorneys question prospective jurors to identify any who cannot be fair and impartial.

give a reason for excluding the venire members) or by challenge for cause (an unlimited number). Jurors may not be eliminated on the basis of race or ethnicity. For a district court, a trial jury is made up of the first 12 venire members who are neither excused by the district judge nor challenged peremptorily by a party in the case. For lower courts, the first six venire members accepted form a jury.

When jurors are impaneled, a district judge may direct the selection of four alternates, and a county judge may require the selection of two alternates. If for some reason a juror cannot finish a trial for either a civil or a criminal case, an alternate juror may be seated as a replacement. Even if no alternate has been selected and a juror cannot complete service, the Texas Court of Criminal Appeals has ruled that in criminal cases, once a jury has been impaneled, it can proceed to trial and judgment with only 11 members.

Although daily pay for venire members and jurors varies from county to county, minimum pay for juror service is $6 for all or part of the first day of jury duty and is supposed to be $40 for each subsequent day. Under state law, counties fund the first $6 per juror each day, and the state reimburses the counties up to $34 per juror for each subsequent day of service. The financial constraints that faced the state in 2011 resulted in the 82nd legislature's reducing juror pay for fiscal years 2012 and 2013. (The state's fiscal year begins on September 1 and ends on August 31 of the following year. The 2012-2013 biennium began on September 1, 2011, and will end on August 31, 2013.) For that period, the legislature authorized only $28 for state-funded juror pay and allowed counties to eliminate their contributions for all days but the first day of service. The state obligation only extended to the availability of funds during each fiscal year. Employers are not required to pay wages to an employee summoned or selected for jury duty; however, they are prohibited by law from discharging permanent employees for such service.

 Learning Check 10.2   (Answers on p. 436)

1. A court must have jurisdiction to hear a case. What does this mean?
2. Does Chief Justice Wallace Jefferson favor the current method of selecting judges in Texas?
3. True or False: It is the responsibility of the grand jury to determine whether a defendant is guilty.

★ Judicial Procedures

LO4 Many Texas residents, as well as people from outside the state, appear in court as litigants or witnesses. As a litigant, for example, a person may become a party to a civil case arising from an automobile accident or a divorce. A person would become a party in a criminal case when accused of a crime such as theft. Witnesses may be summoned to testify in any type of case brought before the trial courts of Texas, but a court pays each witness only $10 per day for court attendance. In still another capacity, a citizen (even someone without legal training) may be elected to the office of county judge or justice of the peace. For these reasons, Texans should understand what happens in the state's courtrooms.

Civil Justice System

The term *civil law* generally refers to matters not covered by criminal law. The following are important subjects of civil law: **torts** (for example, unintended injury to another person or a vehicle in a traffic accident); contracts (for example, agreements to deliver property of a specified quality at a certain price); and domestic relations or family law (such as marriage, divorce, and parental custody of children). Civil law disputes usually involve individuals or corporations. In criminal cases, a person is prosecuted by the state. It is possible for a single incident to result in a civil suit for personal damages and prosecution on a criminal charge.

The state legislature frequently changes both criminal and civil law. In recent years, recoveries in tort cases have been greatly limited by state lawmakers, through changes in statutes, and by the people of Texas, as the result of constitutional amendments.[16] In civil cases, plaintiffs may be eligible to recover for three different types of damages:

- Economic damages, which include lost wages and actual expenses (for example, hospital bills)
- Noneconomic damages, which include a loss in quality of life, such as disfigurement, mental anguish, and emotional distress
- Exemplary or punitive damages, which are intended to punish the defendant

The law originally allowed juries to determine the maximum amount of money judgments. Over time, however, the legislature has exercised more control over recovery amounts.

A major justification for limiting recoveries in tort cases is that individuals and businesses must pay high liability insurance premiums for protection against the risk of lawsuit judgments. After limitations were placed on recoveries in medical malpractice cases, many insurers reduced their malpractice insurance rates, and the number of physicians relocating to Texas increased.[17] Skeptics suggest, however, that the only beneficiaries of tort reform have been insurance companies, whose malpractice payouts declined by 67 percent, and physicians, whose malpractice premiums were reduced by 27 percent. The skeptics cite evidence that since the inception of tort reform, the cost of health care and health insurance premiums for consumers has continued to rise, while physician availability in rural areas has declined.[18]

Civil Trial Procedure The Supreme Court of Texas makes rules of civil procedure for all courts with civil jurisdiction. These rules, however, cannot conflict with any general law of the state. Rules of civil procedure are enacted unless they are rejected by the legislature.

tort
An injury to a person or an individual's property resulting from the wrongful act of another.

Civil cases normally begin when the **plaintiff** (injured party) files a petition, or a written document containing the plaintiff's complaints against the **defendant** and the remedy sought—usually money damages. This petition is filed with the clerk of the court in which the lawsuit is contemplated, and the clerk issues a citation. The citation is delivered to the defendant, directing that person to answer the charges. If the defendant wants to contest the suit, he or she must file a written answer to the plaintiff's charges. The answer explains why the plaintiff is not entitled to the remedy sought and asks that the plaintiff be required to prove every charge made in the petition.

Before the judge sets a trial date (which may be many months or even years after the petition is filed), all interested parties should have had an opportunity to file their petitions, answers, or other pleas with the court. These written instruments constitute the pleadings in the case and form the basis of the trial. Prior to the trial, the parties also have the opportunity to gather information related to the pending case from each other. This process is known as discovery and includes examining documents, obtaining written and oral answers to questions, inspecting property under the control of the other party, and similar activities.

Either party has the option to have a jury determine the facts. Over the past 20 years, the number of cases decided by a jury has declined.[19] Less than 0.5 percent of civil lawsuits are tried to a jury. When a jury determines the facts after receiving instructions from the judge, the judge's only duty is to apply the law to the jury's version of the facts. If no one demands a jury, the trial judge decides all facts and applies the law. Approximately one-third of all filed lawsuits are tried by the judge. The remaining cases are settled by an agreement between the plaintiff and defendant, or they are dismissed.

Trial and Appeal of a Civil Case As a trial begins, lawyers for each party make brief opening statements. The plaintiff's case is presented first. The defendant has the opportunity to contest all evidence introduced and may cross-examine the plaintiff's witnesses. After the plaintiff's case has been presented, it is the defendant's turn to offer evidence and the testimony of witnesses. The plaintiff may challenge this evidence and testimony. The judge is the final authority as to what evidence and testimony may be introduced by all parties, though objections to the judge's rulings can be used as grounds for appeal.

In a jury trial, after all parties have concluded, the judge writes a charge to the jury, submits it to the parties for their approval, makes any necessary changes they suggest, and reads the charge to the jury. In the charge, the judge instructs the jury on the rules governing their deliberations and defines various terms. After the charge is read, attorneys make their closing arguments to the jurors, after which the jury retires to elect one of its members to serve as the presiding juror (commonly referred to as foreman) and to deliberate.

The jury will not be asked directly whether the plaintiff or the defendant should win. Instead, the jury must answer a series of questions that will establish the facts of the case. These questions are called **special issues**. The judgment will be based on jurors' answers to these special issues. To decide a case in

plaintiff
The injured party who initiates a civil suit or the state in a criminal proceeding.

defendant
The person sued in a civil proceeding or prosecuted in a criminal proceeding.

special issues
Questions a judge gives a trial jury to answer to establish facts in a civil case.

a district court, at least 10 jurors must agree on answers to all of the special issues; in a county court or JP court, five must agree. If the required number of jurors cannot reach agreement, the presiding juror (foreman) reports a hung jury. If the judge agrees with this report, the jury is discharged. Either party to the case may then request a new trial, which will be scheduled unless the case is dismissed. If the judge disagrees with the foreman's report, jurors continue to deliberate.

A jury's decision is known as a **verdict.** If there is no jury, the judge arrives at a verdict. In either case, the judge prepares a written decision, known as the **judgment** or decree of the court. Either party may then file a motion for a new trial based on the reason or reasons the party believes the trial was not fair. If the judge agrees, a new trial will be ordered; if not, the case may be appealed to a higher court. In each appeal, a complete written record of the trial is sent to the appellate court. The usual route of appeals is from a county or district court to a court of appeals and then, in some instances, to the Texas Supreme Court.

Criminal Justice System

The State of Texas has identified approximately 2,600 crimes as felonies.[20] Less serious offenses are classified as misdemeanors. Features of the Texas Penal Code include **graded penalties** for noncapital offenses and harsher penalties for repeat offenders. First-, second-, and third-degree felonies may involve imprisonment and fines in cases involving the most serious noncapital crimes. Some lesser offenses (especially those involving alcohol and drug abuse) are defined as state-jail felonies (so-called fourth-degree felonies) and are punishable by fines and confinement in jails operated by the state. The three classes of misdemeanors (A, B, and C) may involve county jail sentences and/or fines. (See Table 10.3 for categories of noncapital offenses and ranges of penalties.) People who engage in organized criminal activity, repeat offenders, and those who commit hate crimes (anyone motivated by bias against a person's race, ethnicity, religion, age, gender, disability, or sexual preference) are punished as though they had committed the next higher degree of felony. This practice is called *enhanced punishment.*

The Texas Penal Code describes the required two-step procedure for establishing whether a crime punishable by death (a **capital felony**) has been committed and, if so, whether a death sentence should be ordered. The issue of capital punishment remains controversial.[21] During the past three decades, no state has executed more capital felons than Texas (482 men and three women from January 1982 through September 2012). In addition to questions regarding the possible innocence of some of these individuals, concerns about the method used to impose the death penalty keep this matter before the public. Texas prison officials use a lethal injection of pentobarbital, the same drug used to euthanize animals. Through July 2012, the state used a three-drug process that first rendered a prisoner unconscious, then induced paralysis, and finally stopped the heart. State officials stockpiled pentobarbital (sold under the trade name Nembutal) when European pharmaceutical manufacturers announced they would no longer produce the drug for use in human executions.[22]

verdict
A jury's decision about a court case.

judgment
A judge's written opinion based on a verdict.

graded penalties
Depending on the nature of the crime, felonies are graded as first, second, third degree, and state jail; misdemeanors are graded as A, B, and C.

capital felony
A crime punishable by death or life imprisonment.

Table 10.3   Selected Texas Noncapital Offenses, Penalties for First Offenders, and Courts Having Original Jurisdiction

Selected Offenses	Offense Category	Punishment	Court
Murder Theft of property valued at $200,000 or more	First-degree felony	Confinement for 5–99 years or life Maximum fine of $10,000	District court
Theft of property valued at $100,000 or more but less than $200,000 Aggravated assault, including of a spouse	Second-degree felony	Confinement for 2–20 years Maximum fine of $10,000	District court
Theft of property valued at $20,000 or more but less than $100,000 Unlawfully taking a weapon to school	Third-degree felony	Confinement for 2–10 years Maximum fine of $10,000	District court
Theft of property valued at $15,000 or more but less than $20,000 Possession of 4 ounces to 1 pound of marijuana	State-jail felony	Confinement for 180 days to 2 years Maximum fine of $10,000	District court
Theft of property valued at $500 or more but less than $1,500 Manufacture, sale, or possession of a counterfeit disabled parking placard	Class A misdemeanor	Confinement for 1 year Maximum fine of $4,000	Constitutional county court and county court-at-law
Theft of property valued at $20 or more but less than $500 Engaging in computer-assisted hunting if the animal is in Texas	Class B misdemeanor	Confinement for 180 days Maximum fine of $2,000	Constitutional county court and county court-at-law
Theft of property valued at less than $20 Advertising, preparing, or selling term papers and reports used by others	Class C misdemeanor	No confinement Maximum fine of $500	Justice of the peace court and municipal court (if offense committed within city limits)

© Cengage Learning

Under the Texas Penal Code, a person commits murder if there is evidence of intent to kill or cause serious bodily harm to the victim. The presence of additional circumstances makes the crime a capital felony, for which the death penalty may be applied. Murder becomes a capital felony if the victim was younger than 10, a police officer, a firefighter, or a prison employee. In addition, murders become capital felonies when they occur during the commission of another felony or a prison escape or are retaliation against a judge. Murder for hire, serial murders (including killing an unborn child), or inmate-on-inmate murder are also capital felonies. After a jury has found a defendant guilty of a capital offense, jurors must unanimously determine whether the accused represents a continuing threat to society and whether circumstances in the defendant's life warrant life imprisonment rather than death. The minimum sentence for a capital felony is life imprisonment without parole. If the state seeks the death penalty, all jurors must agree to the sentence. The death certificate of someone who has been executed reflects the cause of death as "Death caused by judicially ordered execution."

Assessment of the death penalty has declined across the United States and in Texas in recent years. Commentators suggest at least three reasons for this reduction:

- *Concerns about the execution of innocent people*: Between 1973 and 2012, 140 people were released from the nation's death rows based on evidence of their innocence; 12 of these were from Texas. Some Texans share State Representative Lon Burnam's (D-Ft. Worth) concerns that the death penalty is "both imperfect and irreversible."
- *The passage of punishment laws that provide for life without parole*: The number of death penalty sentences has steadily declined since this punishment option became available. In 2011, juries across the Lone Star State sentenced only eight individuals to death, compared with 48 in 1999.
- *The cost of prosecuting death penalty cases*: Some officials estimate that a capital punishment case costs as much as $3 million. By comparison, both the trial and incarceration of a life-without-parole sentence costs approximately $500,000.[23]

Some states have placed a moratorium on the death penalty.[24] Although the American Bar Association has encouraged other states with death penalty laws to do the same, Texas legislators have consistently rejected such a moratorium. One factor that supports continued use of the death penalty is deterrence. A 2009 study of the relationship between executions in Texas and subsequent homicides suggested reductions occur in murders for a short time after an execution.[25] These findings have been challenged, however, as not establishing a causal relationship between executions and deterrence.[26]

Some capital defendants are exempt from the death penalty. As the result of U.S. Supreme Court decisions and state law, for example, the death penalty cannot be used as punishment for anyone who was younger than 18 when committing a capital crime (*Roper v. Simmons*, 543 U.S. 551 [2005]) or anyone who is "mentally retarded" (now classified as intellectually disabled; *Atkins v. Virginia*, 536 U.S. 304 [2002]). The death penalty cannot be assessed if a defendant is found to have been mentally incompetent at the time of committing a capital crime. In addition, the death penalty cannot be carried out on a convicted individual who is mentally ill.

Criminal Trial Procedure Rules of criminal procedure are made by the legislature. The Texas Code of Criminal Procedure is written to comply with U.S. Supreme Court rulings regarding confessions, arrests, searches, and seizures. Additional rules of procedure have been adopted to promote fairness and efficiency in handling criminal cases.

It is likely that millions of illegal acts are committed daily in Texas. For example, many people drive faster than official speed limits allow or drive while under the influence of alcohol. After an arrest and before questioning, police must advise suspects of their constitutional rights to remain silent and have an attorney present (a procedure commonly known as a Miranda warning). When a prosecuting attorney files charges, a suspect must appear before a judicial officer (usually a justice of the peace), who names the offense or offenses charged and provides information concerning the suspect's legal rights. A person charged with a noncapital offense may be released on personal recognizance (promising to report for trial at a later date), released on bail by posting personal money or money provided for a charge by a bail bond service, or denied bail and jailed.

People who cannot afford to hire a lawyer must be provided with the services of an attorney in any felony or misdemeanor case in which conviction may result in a prison or jail sentence. The 13-member Texas Indigent Defense Commission, comprised of judges, attorneys, and legislators, oversees the development of statewide policies and procedures for the representation of indigent defendants. In addition, it monitors county compliance and coordinates state monetary assistance for these programs. County taxpayers, however, bear the major burden of this expense. In 2011, these defense costs totaled approximately $200 million, of which $33 million was funded by the state and the balance by local governments.

Private attorneys, appointed by judges, provide most of the defense for indigent defendants, and an increasing number of counties maintain public defenders' offices to meet some of the representation needs of the poor. Although the 19 public defenders' offices (as of February 2012) appear to be more cost effective than the appointment of private attorneys and, some argue, provide better-quality services to indigent defendants, private criminal defense attorneys often oppose the creation of public defenders' offices.[27] The Texas Fair Defense Act requires counties to devise standards for appointed counsel and establishes minimum attorney qualifications for the appointment of counsel for indigent defendants charged with capital crimes.

Under Texas law, the right to trial by jury is guaranteed in all criminal cases. Except in death penalty cases, defendants may waive jury trial (if the prosecuting attorney agrees), regardless of the plea—guilty, not guilty, or nolo contendere (no contest). To expedite procedures, prosecuting and defense attorneys may engage in plea bargaining, in which the accused pleads guilty in return for a promise that the prosecutor will seek a lighter sentence or will recommend community supervision. Usually, a judge will accept a plea bargain. If the defendant waives a trial by jury and is found guilty by a judge, that judge also determines punishment.

Trial of a Criminal Case After the trial jury has been selected, the prosecuting attorney reads an information (misdemeanor) or an indictment (felony) to inform the jury of the basic allegations of the state's case. The defendant then enters a plea.

As plaintiff, the state begins by calling its witnesses and introducing any evidence supporting the information or the indictment. The defense may then challenge the evidence and cross-examine witnesses. Next, the defense may present its case, calling witnesses and submitting evidence that, in turn, is subject to attack by the prosecution. After all evidence and testimony have been presented, the judge charges the jury by instructing the jury on the rules governing their deliberations and explaining the law applicable to the case. Both prosecuting and defense attorneys then address final arguments to the jury before it retires to reach a verdict.

Verdict, Sentence, and Appeal The jury must reach a unanimous decision to return a verdict of guilty or not guilty. If jurors are hopelessly split, the result is a hung jury. In that event, the judge declares a mistrial and discharges the jurors. When requested by the prosecuting attorney, the judge orders a new trial with another jury.

If a jury brings a verdict before a court, the judge may choose to disregard it and order a new trial on the grounds that the jury failed to arrive at a verdict that achieves substantial justice. In a jury trial, the jury may fix the sentence if the convicted person so requests; otherwise, the judge determines the sentence. A separate hearing on the penalty is held, at which time the person's prior criminal or juvenile record, general reputation, and other relevant factors may be introduced, such as facts concerning the convicted person's background and lifestyle as determined by a presentence investigation.

A convicted defendant has the right to appeal on the grounds that an error in trial procedure occurred. All appeals (except for capital punishment cases) are heard first by the court of appeals in the district in which the trial was held. A few of these appeals are ultimately reviewed by the Texas Court of Criminal Appeals. Death penalty appeals are made directly to the Texas Court of Criminal Appeals.

☑ Learning Check 10.3   (Answers on p. 436)

1. What are the parties to a civil lawsuit called?
2. True or False: In a civil jury trial, jurors will be asked to decide which party should win.
3. A capital felony for which the defendant received the death penalty is appealed to which court?

Correction and Rehabilitation

Confinement in a prison (either a penitentiary or a state jail) or a county or municipal jail is designed to punish lawbreakers, deter others from committing similar crimes, and isolate offenders from society, thus protecting the lives and property of citizens who might otherwise become victims of criminals.[28] Ideally, while serving a sentence behind bars, a lawbreaker will be rehabilitated and, after release, will obey all laws, find employment, and make positive contributions to society. In practice, approximately 25 percent of convicted adult criminals violate the conditions of their release or commit other crimes after being released, for which they are resentenced to prison. Juvenile justice systems, which actually conduct their proceedings as civil cases and are, therefore, outside the criminal justice system, have a similar design but with a greater emphasis on rehabilitation rather than punishment. Descriptions of the criminal justice system in this section relate to adults, and references to the juvenile justice system include individuals between the ages of 10 and 16.

The number of adult Texans either imprisoned or supervised by local and state criminal justice authorities is larger than in any other state. In 2010, approximately 700,000 Texans were incarcerated, on parole, or under community supervision (formerly known as probation). In response to high crime rates at the end of the 20th century, the Texas legislature lengthened prison sentences. In addition, the Texas Board of Pardons and Paroles and the legislature tightened the procedures and circumstances of parole. In addition, the legislature increased the minimum number of years of incarceration prisoners must serve before qualifying for parole. In the closing years of the last decade, prison populations began to stabilize.

The Texas Department of Criminal Justice

LO5   The principal criminal justice agencies of the state are organized within the Texas Department of Criminal Justice (TDCJ). The agency has a four-part mission:

- To provide public safety
- To promote positive behavioral changes
- To reintegrate offenders into the general society
- To assist crime victims

The organizational structure of TDCJ includes governance by the nine-member nonsalaried Texas Board of Criminal Justice; a full-time executive director hired by the board; and directors of the department's divisions, who are selected by the executive director. Each division director is responsible for hiring division personnel. Almost 40,000 Texans worked for TDCJ in 2012. These employees are responsible for a prison population of approximately 155,000 inmates and more than 100,000 parolees. They also oversee local community supervision programs that monitor an additional 415,000 offenders on probation.

How Do We Compare...in Prison Incarceration Rates?

Number of Prisoners per 100,000 State Residents (as of December 2010)

Most Populous U.S. States	Number of Prisoners per 100,000 Residents	U.S. States Bordering Texas	Number of Prisoners per 100,000 Residents
California	458	Arkansas	522
Florida	559	Louisiana	881
New York	298	New Mexico	316
Texas	**648**	Oklahoma	657

Source: Paul Guerino, Paige M. Harrison, and William J. Sabol, *Bureau of Justice Statistics Bulletin: Prisoners in 2010* (Washington, D.C.: U.S. Department of Justice, December 2011), **http://www.ojp.usdoj.gov**.

Providing Public Safety For many years, the primary focus of the Texas legislature, and therefore the TDCJ, was on providing public safety. Legislators classified an increasing number of actions as felonies, lengthened sentences for all types of crimes, funded construction of additional prison units, and balanced the state's budget by reducing drug treatment programs and other interventions intended to alter an individual's behavior. From the early 1980s through most of the first decade of the 21st century, the state's prison population increased. As recently as 2007, state officials predicted continued growth.[29] In that year, Governor Rick Perry urged the 80th legislature to authorize funding for the construction of two new prisons. A bipartisan legislative effort redirected funding efforts to expand treatment and counseling services. Reversing a decades-long trend, Texas's prison population declined in 2009 and remained stable in 2010. For the first time in its history, Texas closed a prison in 2011—the Central Unit in Sugar Land. With a $27 billion shortfall facing the Lone Star State for the 2012–2013 biennium, some lawmakers predicted a likely cost-saving measure would be a reduction in treatment programs. The majority of legislators, however, chose to maintain funding levels for all treatment programs except those available to individuals under community supervision.

The sector of TDCJ responsible for ensuring public safety is the Correctional Institutions Division. Staff members in this division supervise the operation and management of state prisons, state jails, and other specialized facilities. Older prison units are largely in East Texas, while more recently constructed units have been located throughout Texas. State jail facilities, located across the state, are designed for nonviolent offenders. Private contractors operate seven prisons, five state jails, and various prerelease, work, substance abuse, and intermediate sanctions facilities. Figure 10.2 shows the location of prison and state jail units in Texas.

Maintaining a trained work force to provide security has been an ongoing problem for the Correctional Institutions Division. Historically,

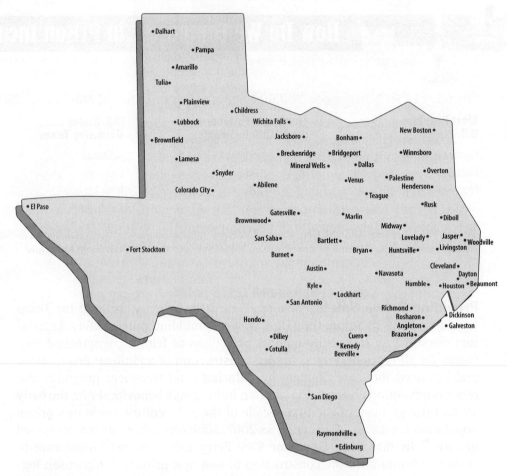

Figure 10.2   Facilities of the Texas Department of Criminal Justice, 2012.

Source: Texas Department of Criminal Justice.

difficult working conditions and low pay produced correctional officer annual turnover rates of more than 25 percent. Salary increases, signing bonuses, and a depressed economy, temporarily improved staff retention. By 2012, increased job opportunities in the oil and gas industry reversed the trend.

The Lone Star State's prisons face other problems. Some staff members supplement low wages by smuggling in contraband for prisoners.[30] An aging prison population adds to the cost of incarceration because of extra health-care expenses. In a post–September 11, 2001, world, the state's correctional officers are also now engaged in the war on terrorism. Prison officials remain on alert to terrorist recruitment efforts among inmates. Staff members monitor inmate behavior and correspondence (especially letters written in Arabic, Farsi, and other Middle Eastern languages). In addition, several gangs exist within the prison system. More than 8,700 violent inmates and gang members (identified as "security threat groups" by prison officials) are held in administrative segregation cells. Here, they have little or no contact with anyone other than corrections officers.

General characteristics of the inmate population highlight some common issues, including poor education levels and substance abuse. Approximately 45 percent of Texas prisoners have less than a high school education and one-third are functionally illiterate. The number of inmates with a serious mental illness is also high. The National Institute of Mental Health estimates that 5 percent of the general population has a serious mental illness. Studies of jail and prison populations reflect that 16 percent of prisoners have been similarly diagnosed. In Texas, based on the availability of psychiatric facilities, an individual with a serious mental illness is eight times as likely to be incarcerated as to receive treatment.[31] The profile of Texas prisoners in Table 10.4 identifies some characteristics of the state's incarcerated population.

Promoting Positive Behavioral Changes Several departments and divisions of TDCJ focus on correcting or modifying the behavior of incarcerated felons. Training and instructional programs are used to rehabilitate inmates and equip them with a means for self-support after release. Discipline and education are the primary means of combating **recidivism** (criminal behavior resulting in reimprisonment after release). Every prisoner must be given a job but may elect not to work. Prisoners' labor saves money for the state and for local governments and, in some instances, generates revenue for the state. Prisoners repair engines, perform all types of agricultural labor and manufacture furniture, including dorm room furnishings and mattresses in the school's colors for several state universities. They even make the wooden gavels used by the presiding officers of the Texas legislature.

Table 10.4 Some Characteristics of Texas's Prison Population (2011)

Characteristic	Measurement (%)
Gender	
Male	92
Female	8
Race	
African American	36
Anglo	31
Hispanic	33
Type of Offense Leading to Incarceration	
Violent	51
Property	17
Drugs	17
Other	15
IQ	
Average	90.6

Source: Texas Department of Criminal Justice, *Fiscal Year 2011 Statistical Report*, http://www.tdcj.state.tx.us/documents/Statistical_Report_2011.pdf.

recidivism
Criminal behavior that results in reincarceration after a person has been released from confinement for a prior offense.

Lee College Huntsville Center graduates celebrate their accomplishment with family and friends. The degrees they earn while incarcerated prepare them for a productive life after release.

(Photo Courtesy of Lee College)

More than one-half of Texas prisoners are enrolled in vocational and academic classes offered through the prison system's Windham School District. In addition, some prisoners take community college and university courses. In 2011, approximately 1,600 prisoners completed workforce training through community colleges. Almost 500 inmates graduated with degrees ranging from associates to masters. Although the state pays tuition costs for vocational training, once released, the former inmate must reimburse the state these amounts. Tuition for academic courses must be paid by the individual prisoner. The state encourages postsecondary education by prisoners and parolees by shortening sentences and length of incarceration for those who enroll in and complete academic and vocational training courses.

As a result of legislative reforms adopted in 2007, officials at TDCJ now offer more substance abuse and therapy programs. Increased funding for these programs expanded services to 3,000-plus inmates. In 2012, the Rehabilitation Programs Division of TDCJ coordinated 12 treatment options. Of the eight programs studied to determine recidivism rates, all but one, the Pre-Release Substance Abuse Program, lowered the likelihood of reimprisonment for participants.

Renewed funding also aided the state's 18 state felony jails. Nonviolent offenders housed in state jails serve "up-front" time, during which they receive substance abuse treatment and participate in other support programs. Treatment options are now favored by both liberals, who maintain that treatment rehabilitates the individual prisoner, and conservatives, who defend the cost-effectiveness of such programs.[32]

Reintegrating Offenders State Representative Jerry Madden (R-Richardson) provided the rationale for the state's shift to treatment options: to "return [inmates] to society as productive citizens." A major goal of treatment and education programs is to equip prisoners with the skills to succeed upon release. After the 81st legislature (2009) directed TDCJ to prepare comprehensive reentry plans for released prisoners, the agency created the Reentry and Integration Division to provide extensive support to released offenders. Headed by a director, the division has more than 60 reentry counselors located throughout the state to assist released inmates.

Two agencies are responsible for convicted criminals who serve all or a part of their sentences in the community: the Community Justice Assistance Division and the Parole Division. The Community Justice Assistance Division establishes minimum standards for county programs involving community supervision and community corrections facilities (such as a boot camp or a restitution center). In cases involving adult first-time offenders convicted of misdemeanors and lesser felonies, jail and prison sentences are commonly commuted to community supervision (formally called adult probation). These convicted persons are not confined if they fulfill certain court-imposed conditions.

Through specialty courts, judges have also become directly involved in community supervision. Designed to meet the needs of particular classes of offenses, such as prostitution, or specific categories of offenders, such as military veterans, judges frequently order those convicted to receive treatment for substance abuse problems and other psychological therapy. To address the needs of mentally impaired individuals, several urban counties have established mental health courts to coordinate treatment for those who act from diminished mental capacity rather than from intent to harm a victim. Probationers in specialty-court programs return to court regularly to meet with other offenders and the judge. Participating military veterans can have convictions removed from their records.

The Parole Division manages Texas's statewide parole and mandatory supervision system for convicted felons. The seven-member Board of Pardons and Paroles recommends acts of clemency (such as pardons) to the governor and grants or revokes paroles. The board's presiding officer employs and supervises 12 commissioners. A three-member panel comprised of at least one parole board member, along with commissioner(s), reviews inmate applications and decides whether to grant or deny parole. The board may impose restrictions that it deems necessary to protect the community. If a parolee violates any conditions of release, a board panel determines whether to revoke parole.

Prisoners who have served some portion of their sentences may be eligible for parole. A matrix is developed for each inmate, identifying the likelihood of the individual's successfully completing parole. Factors reviewed include static factors that cannot change, such as the prisoner's original offense, and dynamic factors, such as education and training programs completed while incarcerated. Felons who commit serious, violent crimes, such as rape or murder, must serve 30 to 40 years of "flat time" (without the possibility of having prison time reduced for good behavior). Other offenders may apply for parole after serving one-fourth of a sentence or 15 years, whichever is less (minus good-time credit).

Successful reintegration of offenders is complicated by a number of barriers to reentry. Not only do those convicted of felonies lose many civil rights, such as the right to serve on juries and administer estates, they, along with those convicted of misdemeanors, also encounter lifetime impediments to employment.

Assisting Victims The fourth-prong of TDCJ's mission directs attention to crime victims and their close relatives. The Victim Services Division provides information to crime victims about any change in the offender's status within the TDCJ system, as well as notification of pending parole hearings. Upon a finding of guilt, and before sentencing, victims may deliver victim impact statements in open court. They may also complete written statements that remain available to prison and parole officials. When an inmate is executed, up to five family members and close friends of the victim may witness the execution. Victim Services Division staff members facilitate dialogues between offenders and their victims, if both parties agree.

Information on other programs designed to assist crime victims is available on the division's website. For example, the State of Texas maintains a Crime Victims' Compensation Fund that provides up to $50,000 to victims and their families for expenses related to a crime ($125,000 in the event of a total disability). Covered costs include medical treatment, counseling, and burial expenses. The program is funded by court costs, fees, and fines collected from convicted offenders. Because of less revenue from court costs and the diversion of some collected funds to other programs, however, Attorney General Greg Abbott projected that the fund might not have sufficient money to pay all eligible claims in fiscal year 2013.[33]

Local Government Jails

In addition to prisons and state jails operated by the Texas Department of Criminal Justice, counties and cities across the state operate jails. These facilities are financed largely by county and municipal governments, respectively. Like penal institutions of the TDCJ, however, local government jails are used to control lawbreakers by placing them behind bars.

All but 19 Texas counties maintain a jail. Some counties have contracted with commercial firms to provide "privatized" jails, but most counties maintain public jails operated under the direction of the county sheriff. Originally established to detain persons awaiting trial and to hold individuals serving sentences for misdemeanor offenses, county jail facilities vary in quality and, except in some urban areas, do not offer rehabilitation programs. The Texas Commission on Jail Standards has oversight responsibility for county jails. The commission determines appropriate population and staffing levels, and issues remedial orders to enforce its standards. In the case of an ongoing failure to comply with commission rules, a jail may be closed, or the commission, represented by the attorney general, may take court action against the county.

Texas also has approximately 350 municipal jails. Some are used primarily as "drunk tanks" to detain people for a few hours after they have been arrested for public intoxication. In large cities, these facilities often house hundreds of inmates who have been arrested for a variety of offenses ranging from Class C misdemeanors to capital murder. Those charged with more serious crimes are usually held temporarily until they can be transferred to a more secure county jail. The quality of municipal jail facilities varies greatly. A city jail is not subject to regulation by the Texas Commission on Jail Standards, unless it is managed by a private vendor or houses out-of-state prisoners. Some commentators have suggested that all municipal jails should be under state supervision. The Texas Municipal League, a special-interest group representing towns and cities, argues that compliance with state regulations would increase the cost of operating facilities and that local supervision is sufficient.

Private Prisons

Both state and local governments have contracted with private companies to construct and operate prisons and direct prerelease programs. Texas now has more privately operated facilities than any other state. Approximately 11 percent of Texas's inmates are housed in private prisons. These facilities are under the supervision of the Private Facility Contract Monitoring/Oversight Division of the TDCJ. The Texas Juvenile Justice Department oversees community-based private contract juvenile facilities. In addition to prisons and jails, private contractors also provide substance abuse treatment programs and halfway houses, where state and county prisoners are incarcerated in privately operated units. Some also house out-of-state convicts and federal offenders. Controversy surrounds having private corporations provide a government service like incarceration, as discussed in the Point/Counterpoint feature that follows.

Juvenile Justice

Texas's juvenile justice system clearly distinguishes between youthful pranks and violent, predatory behavior. In general, young Texans at least 10 years of age but younger than 17 are treated as "delinquent children" when they commit acts that would be classified as felonies or misdemeanors if committed by adults. Children are designated as "status offenders" if they commit noncriminal acts such as running away from home, failing to attend school, or violating a curfew established by a city or county. From 1957 to 2011, the Texas Youth Commission (TYC) was the agency responsible for the rehabilitation and training of delinquent youth. After several years of scandal highlighting deficiencies in the agency, the 82nd legislature (2011) abolished the TYC. The Texas Juvenile Probation Commission, the agency that oversaw county juvenile probation departments, was abolished at the same time. As a part of the sunset review process (see Chapter 9, "Public Policy and Administration"), the legislature created the Texas Juvenile Justice Department (TJJD) to assume the responsibilities of the abolished agencies. The 11-member board of TJJD, appointed by the governor with the consent of the Senate, is charged with unifying juvenile justice services from an individual's entry into the system through departure.

Point/Counterpoint

THE ISSUE Across the United States, approximately 130,000 inmates are incarcerated in prison facilities operated by private corporations. The percentage of Texas prisoners held in private prisons is almost twice the national average: 11 percent in Texas versus 6 percent for all states. A number of questions surround governments' contracting with private companies to incarcerate people. Considered a panacea to the prison population explosion that began in the 1980s, this same practice is undergoing renewed scrutiny as the source of revenue (inmates) continues to decline.

Should Governments Contract with Private Corporations to Operate Prisons?

Arguments For Using Private Contractors

- Contracting with private companies allows for greater flexibility. When prison populations climb rapidly, the private sector offers an immediate solution without requiring substantial, long-term investments by government in the construction of facilities. As inmate populations decline, these contracts can be renegotiated or canceled.

- Contracts are awarded to those who offer the most cost-efficient proposal; thus, the per prisoner cost of incarceration will decline.

- Private contractors will be more innovative and responsive than government in responding to and resolving problems. Competition with other service providers will force innovation and responsiveness.

  [T]he existence of competition, even potential competition, will make the public less tolerant of facilities that are crowded, costly, dirty, dangerous, inhumane, ineffective, and prone to riots and lawsuits. Indeed, the fact that these conditions have existed for so long in monopolistic state prisons is a big part of what makes private prisons seem attractive.

  —Charles H. Logan, *Private Prisons: Cons and Pros* (New York: Oxford, 1990).

Arguments Against Using Private Contractors

- Private contractors enjoy the benefits when business is good and step away when business is bad because the inmate population has declined. In recent years, private contractors have abandoned several privately managed, but publicly financed, jails in Texas. Without sufficient numbers of prisoners to continue profitable operations, private contractors cancelled their contracts to manage the facilities. Local taxpayers, however, were left to repay any money borrowed to build or maintain the facilities.

- Private prisons provide no cost savings to state governments, as suggested by recent studies. Further, their executives are criticized for influencing policymakers to increase incarceration.

- Contracting for incarceration services is an improper delegation of government's power. Physical freedom is one of our most cherished liberties. Allowing private contractors to enforce that loss of liberty violates our fundamental rights.

  When private prison companies are successful at the game of political influence, their profits rise, benefitting their stockholders and top management.... [T]he biggest losers in this political game are the people who are taken away from their families and communities due to the policies private prison companies promote to increase the number of people going into prisons and the length of time they spend behind bars.

  —Paul Ashton, *Gaming the System: How the Political Strategies of Private Prison Companies Promote Ineffective Incarceration Policies* (Washington, D.C.: Justice Policy Institute, June 2011)

State and Local Agencies Each county has a juvenile probation board that designates one or more juvenile judges, appoints a chief juvenile probation officer, and makes policies carried out by a juvenile probation department. The TJJD board provides policy direction, allocates state funds to county juvenile boards, trains and certifies juvenile probation officers, and sets standards for local detention and probation facilities. When youth must be incarcerated, the responsibility also rests with the TJJD. Here, the goal has shifted from sending juveniles to facilities far from their families to keeping them within their local areas. If children must be removed from family settings, the law reflects a preference for group homes over correctional facilities. Treatment options are subject to ongoing research to identify those that are most effective.

In mid-2012, an increase in youth-on-youth and youth-on-staff violence focused attention on security within TJJD facilities. The executive director resigned and was replaced by Jay Kimbrough, a former chief of staff for Governor Rick Perry. A new program to isolate the most aggressive inmates in a separate facility was announced. Youth advocates claimed this practice represented a return to unsuccessful methods used in the previous decade. Legislators and some juvenile detention officials argued that inadequate security substantially reduced the success of treatment programs. In September 2012, Mike Griffiths, an experienced juvenile corrections official was hired to lead the agency.

Procedures Although juvenile offenders are arrested by the same law enforcement officers who deal with adult criminals, they are detained in separate facilities. Some, along with their parents, are merely warned by police officers not to engage in delinquent behavior. Others are held in short-term residential detention facilities until they are released to their families or the case against them is resolved.

Counseling and probation are the most widely used procedures for dealing with juvenile offenders, although probation, residential treatment, and commitment to TJJD facilities remain options. An arresting officer has the discretion to release a child or refer the case to a local juvenile probation department. Other referrals come from public schools, victims, and parents. Approximately 100,000 Texas youths entered the state's juvenile justice system annually.

Trials in juvenile courts are termed **adjudication hearings**. Juvenile courts are civil rather than criminal courts; therefore, any appeal of a court's ruling will be made to the appropriate court of appeals. Ultimately a few cases are appealed to the Texas Supreme Court.

A juvenile determinate sentencing law covers more than 20 serious offenses. Under this sentencing provision, juveniles who commit offenses such as capital murder and aggravated sexual assault can be transferred to adult prisons when they reach age 19 and can be held there for as long as 40 years. In addition, approximately 1 percent of juveniles charged with serious crimes stand trial and are punished as adults. Prior to a determination of guilt, these young offenders remain in juvenile facilities "separated by sight and sound" from adult offenders; but once found guilty, convicted youths are transferred to the adult prison system. In 2012, the TDCJ reported that the adult prison population included 15 inmates between the ages of 14 and 16.

adjudication hearing
A trial in a juvenile court.

Learning Check 10.4   (Answers on p. 436)

1. True or False: In recent years the prison population in Texas has increased.
2. What is the reasoning used to justify Texas's shift to treatment options in its prison system?
3. The court of last resort for juvenile proceedings is the Texas Supreme Court. Is the juvenile justice system governed by civil or criminal law?

★
Problems and Reforms: Implications for Public Policy

LO6   Throughout the late 20ᵗʰ century, Texas's justice system experienced an increased number of civil and criminal cases requiring courts to resolve the disputes. The legislature responded (often slowly) with authorizations for more courts and judges and alternative means to resolve lawsuits. Legislators must also deal with the 21ˢᵗ-century issues of technology and changing demographics and respond to these issues in ways that assure fairness for all within the judicial system.

Coping with Crowded Dockets

The state has adopted several methods to encourage litigants to resolve their disputes without going to trial. To reduce workloads, speed the handling of civil disputes, and cut legal costs, each county is authorized to set up a system for **alternative dispute resolution (ADR)**. Two frequently used ADR procedures are mediation (in which an impartial mediator facilitates communication between the parties in a conference designed to allow them to resolve their dispute) and arbitration (in which impartial arbiters hear both sides and make an award that is binding or nonbinding, depending on the parties' previous agreement). In the past 25 years, studies report a sharp decline in the number of jury trials across the nation, including Texas. Consistently, commentators identify ADR as a contributing factor to the "vanishing jury trial."[34]

Collaborative divorce is another nonadversarial method for resolving disputes outside the courtroom. If either spouse elects to litigate after the process begins, both attorneys must resign. The 82ⁿᵈ legislature codified the collaborative law process in 2011 by adding the Collaborative Family Law Act to the Texas Family Code. The law encourages the use of collaborative procedures, especially in divorces involving children. If family violence is involved, however, the use of this procedure is discouraged. Thus, attorneys are required to inquire about family violence issues. If such a history exists, the abuse victim must expressly request continuing the collaborative

alternative dispute resolution (ADR)
Use of mediation, conciliation, or arbitration to resolve disputes among individuals without resorting to a regular court trial.

process, and the lawyer is required to work with the client to devise procedures to limit the possibility of further violence.

Technology

From Internet divorces to video cameras at stoplights, technology now touches every aspect of the civil and criminal justice systems. Evidence found only in science fiction a few years ago is now commonplace in Texas courtrooms. One subject that has gained significant attention in recent years is DNA evidence. The advent of DNA testing, developed by geneticist Alec Jeffreys, transformed courtrooms.[35] This biological evidence is used to identify suspects, as well as exonerate the innocent. The state maintains a DNA database. Both TDCJ and TJJD collect DNA samples of all inmates convicted of a felony. Convicted felons who receive community supervision must provide DNA samples, as do juveniles released on probation who committed the most serious felonies (murder, rape, aggravated robbery, and similar violent crimes) or who used a weapon to commit their offenses. Crime scene evidence can then be tested against the state's database samples. Postconviction analysis is available for certain inmates tried and convicted before the development or refinement of DNA testing. As noted in Michael Morton's case, discussed in the opening to this chapter, DNA evidence not only establishes innocence, it may also aid in identifying the guilty. The delays that Morton experienced in having evidence submitted for testing are no longer possible due to laws passed by the 82nd legislature.

Although DNA evidence has proved almost conclusive in establishing the guilt or innocence of accused criminals, high levels of police and juror confidence in the accuracy of biological test results can be devastating if that trust is misplaced. State law requires all public crime labs to be accredited and DNA evidence to be held for retesting. As further protection against the miscarriages of justice caused by crime lab deficiencies, the Texas Forensic Science Commission investigates charges of negligence and misconduct. The 11-member commission, appointed by the governor, lieutenant governor, and attorney general, includes attorneys, scientists, and professors from across the state. Confidence in the judicial system depends on evidence that can be relied on to convict the guilty and exonerate the innocent.

Exoneration Issues

The Fourteenth Amendment to the U.S. Constitution guarantees that no state can "deprive any person of life, liberty, or property without due process of law." The many rules and procedures that must be followed in criminal cases are specifically designed to protect people from losing their lives, liberty, or property from arbitrary acts by the government. And yet, despite all of these protections, as discussed in the opening to this chapter, innocent people continue to lose their liberty, their property, and perhaps even their lives. According to the Innocence Project at New York's Cardozo Law School, almost 300 inmates across the nation were exonerated between 1989 and

2012 after DNA analysis proved their innocence. Forty-six of those individuals were from Texas. One was on death row.

Although DNA test results have contributed to the release of innocent prisoners, this evidence is not the panacea that will eliminate all wrongful imprisonment. In fact, 35 individuals who were released from prison between 1992 and 2012 had no DNA evidence to exonerate them. For example, Claude Simmons and Christopher Scott, whose case is highlighted in the Students in Action feature, were exonerated without DNA evidence. They, like more than 75 percent of exonerees across the nation, were victims of mistaken eyewitness identification, another form of evidence jurors consider highly reliable. Research now indicates several flaws in this type of evidence, including overlooking facial features of people of different races, transference to an individual encountered in a different setting, and poor recall due to the stress of being a crime victim or witness.[36] In response to these concerns, the 82nd legislature revised state law in 2011 to require police departments and other agencies to develop written procedures on the ways in which law enforcement officers conduct photo and live line-ups. The Blackwood Institute at Sam Houston State University is responsible for developing evidence-based procedures for local law enforcement agencies to follow.

Although most people convicted of a crime are guilty, the probability of exoneration is remote, even for the innocent. The political reality is that to obtain a pardon and be fully exonerated requires the agreement of district attorneys, judges, the Board of Pardons and Paroles, and the governor. Based on an attorney general's opinion issued in 2010, the state is allowed to grant posthumous pardons, should someone be exonerated after his or her death. The state of Texas compensates individuals wrongfully

(From left) Dallas County Public Defender Michelle Moore, Chris Scott, University of Texas at Arlington student Natalie Ellis (the student featured in this chapter's "Students in Action"), and Claude Simmons celebrate Scott's and Simmons's exoneration in October 2009.

(© Lara Solt/Dallas Morning News/Corbis)

Students in Action

Innocence Network

"You don't just help an innocent person get released from prison; you've also given back a father to his children, a grandfather to his grandchildren, a brother to his family."

Natalie Ellis

On her second day as a volunteer with the Innocence Network at the University of Texas at Arlington, Natalie Ellis began to read the state's opening for Claude Simmons's trial. Both Simmons and a second man, Christopher Scott, were serving life sentences for the capital murder of Alfonso Aguilar. Within the first two pages, Natalie began to question what she was reading. Although the victim had died from a single gunshot wound and no other evidence indicated additional bullets had been fired, the state claimed both Scott and Simmons were the "shooters." When she asked about this discrepancy, she was told, "Just keep reading. Maybe there's information somewhere else in the file that will clear it up."

Natalie kept reading. She read the entire file. What she found led her to another inmate who ultimately reconfirmed his earlier confession. Natalie continued to work on the case while attending school. Through the combined efforts of volunteer law students from the University of Texas at Austin and undergraduate students at the Innocence Network, the Dallas Police Department reopened its investigation of the murder.

On October 23, 2009, Simmons and Scott were released on a personal recognizance bond. At the same time, the judge forwarded his recommendation to the Texas Court of Criminal Appeals that the two men be fully exonerated. They had been in prison for 12 years.

When Natalie Ellis, a 32-year-old high school dropout, enrolled at the University of Texas at Arlington, she knew she wanted to become a lawyer. In her first semester, her political science and history professors recommended she get involved with the Innocence Network, an organization devoted to obtaining the release of people wrongfully convicted of crimes they did not commit. She attended a meeting and decided to follow her professors' suggestion. What is Natalie's advice to students? "If you see an area in life that you feel strongly about, step out there. You never know what might happen."

Sources: Interview with Natalie Ellis, December 10, 2009; Linda Stewart Ball, "Dallas County Frees Two Men Convicted of Murder," *Dallas Morning News,* October 23, 2009; Herb Booth, "UT Arlington Innocence Network Helps Free Two Wrongfully Convicted Men," UTA News Center, October 21, 2009, **http://www.uta.edu/news/releases/2009/10/stickels-ellis-featured.php.**

(Monkey Business Images/Shutterstock.com)

incarcerated. Someone found innocent after being imprisoned is entitled to $80,000 for each year he or she was wrongly incarcerated, $25,000 for each year on parole or required registration on a sex-offender registry, tuition for training or college, a lifetime annuity, assistance in accessing social service providers, and health insurance. Since 1992, the state has paid more than $42 million to 74 exonerated individuals. Lump sum payments can be made to the heirs of those exonerated after their deaths. Even though the state funds innocence projects at its public law schools, the legislature has consistently rejected establishing an innocence commission to examine the causes of wrongful convictions.

Racial and Ethnic Diversity

Changes in the state's demography have begun to affect its justice system. The underrepresentation of African Americans and Latinos in elected and appointed leadership positions is matched by their overrepresentation in the criminal justice system.[37] If the race or ethnicity of those enforcing the law is consistently different from those against whom the law is enforced, the system has less credibility and may be viewed as unfair.

Studies in the early part of the past decade provided evidence that more than two-thirds of Texas law enforcement agencies targeted members of historical minority groups for stops and searches. More recent studies reflect a reduction in the disparity between consent searches of minorities and Anglos. Perhaps, a contributing factor to this reduction is the requirement that law enforcement agencies provide annual racial profiling reports to their governing bodies and to the Texas Commission on Law Enforcement Standards and Education. These reports make public the number of traffic stops by race, gender, and age, as well as subsequent action, such as searches and arrests, that resulted from the stops. Instances of racial and ethnic bias are the subject of growing concern as Texas has evolved into a state in which two historical minority groups, African Americans and Latinos, make up the majority population, and the state's Latino population continues movement toward becoming the majority.

☑ Learning Check 10.5   (Answers on p. 436)

1. True or False: Legal scholars suggest that alternative dispute resolution proceedings have decreased the number of jury trials.
2. Most individuals who have been exonerated were sent to prison based on what type of evidence?
3. Each year, law enforcement agencies in Texas must report the number of traffic stops and subsequent actions based on those stops. What problem is this required reporting attempting to limit?

 # Conclusion

The Texas legal system is indeed confusing. From sorting out overlapping court jurisdictions to decide which court should hear a case to identifying elected judges and justices—the system appears to be shrouded in mystery and anonymity. Often understood only by those who use the system daily—Texas lawyers—decisions of criminal and civil court judges affect every Texan. It is therefore critical that Texans understand this complex system. Issues of fairness and efficiency remain paramount in ensuring that residents accept the legitimacy, or authority, of the courts and criminal justice system over them. In recent years, the shift in Texas from punishment to rehabilitation appears to have made the state a leader in reducing the number of prisoners and lowering the cost of the criminal justice system. The legal system, however, is not error-free. Only by understanding the system can citizens and lawmakers develop effective solutions.

Chapter Summary

- Ensuring that the judicial system treats all individuals fairly is critical to its legitimacy.
- Texas state law includes both civil law and criminal law. Texas courts and judges apply and interpret the state's constitution, its statutes, and the common law.
- Both constitutional and statutory laws have been used to create the state's court system. Courts may have original or appellate jurisdiction, or both. Texas has local, county, trial, and appellate courts. Judges and lawyers are subject to regulation and discipline.
- Texas is one of only four states that select all judges (except municipal judges) through popular, partisan elections.
- There are two types of juries: grand juries (which determine if adequate cause exists to bring a defendant to trial in a criminal case) and petit juries (which determine the facts in criminal and civil cases).
- The civil justice system includes contract cases, tort cases, family law matters, and juvenile justice cases. The Texas legislature has limited the amount of punitive and noneconomic damages in tort cases.
- Criminal law regulates many types of behavior. Less severe crimes are classified as Class A, B, or C misdemeanors and result in fines or detention in a county jail. More severe crimes include state-jail felonies; first-, second-, and third-degree felonies; and capital felonies.
- Approximately 700,000 Texans were under the supervision of a state judicial or correctional officer in 2010. Recent changes in state laws have emphasized the rehabilitative role of incarceration.
- The juvenile justice system is administered through the Texas Family Code. Youths between the ages of 10 and 16 are subject to its provisions. Years of scandal at Texas Youth Commission (TYC) facilities resulted in the abolition of the TYC and the Texas Juvenile Probation Commission. The Texas Juvenile Justice Department replaced these agencies in 2011.
- Issues that remain problematic for the Texas justice system include crowded court dockets; technological and scientific advances; the probable innocence of some inmates; and possible racial and ethnic bias in the justice system.

Key Terms

civil law, p. 394
criminal law, p. 394
misdemeanor, p. 394
felony, p. 394
jurisdiction, p. 394
original jurisdiction, p. 396
appellate jurisdiction, p. 396
exclusive jurisdiction, p. 396
concurrent jurisdiction, p. 396
municipal court, p. 399
court of record, p. 400
justice of the peace, p. 400
small-claims court, p. 400
probate, p. 401
bifurcated, p. 404
Missouri Plan, p. 405
appointment-retention system, p. 406
contingency fee, p. 409
grand jury, p. 410
petit jury, p. 410
venire, p. 411
voir dire, p. 411
tort, p. 413
plaintiff, p. 414
defendant, p. 414
special issues, p. 414
verdict, p. 415
judgment, p. 415
graded penalties, p. 415
capital felony, p. 415
recidivism, p. 423
adjudication hearing, p. 429
alternative dispute resolution (ADR), p. 430

Learning Check Answers

10.1

1. False. Misdemeanors and felonies are considered criminal law cases and are heard in criminal law courts.
2. True. Texas courts interpret and apply state laws that include the provisions of the Texas Constitution, statutes enacted by the legislature, regulations adopted by state agencies, and judge-made common law based on custom and tradition dating back to medieval England.

10.2

1. Jurisdiction means that the court must have the authority to hear a particular kind of case. Jurisdiction may be granted in the Texas Constitution or in the statute creating a court.
2. No. Chief Justice Jefferson has encouraged state legislators to reform the judicial selection process to eliminate the popular, partisan election of judges.
3. False. A grand jury only determines if there is enough evidence to go to trial in a criminal case. A petit jury determines if a defendant is guilty.

10.3

1. The parties to a civil lawsuit are the plaintiff, who is the injured party bringing the lawsuit, and the defendant, who is the person being sued.
2. False. In a civil jury, trial jurors answer special issues, or a series of questions about the facts in the case. The judge then applies the law to the answers to the special issues and renders a judgment establishing who won the case.
3. A capital felony for which the defendant received the death penalty is appealed to the Court of Criminal Appeals.

10.4

1. False. After reforms enacted by the 80th legislature (2007) that placed more emphasis on treatment, rehabilitation, and reintegration of prisoners, the number of prisoners in Texas has declined.
2. According to State Representative Jerry Madden (R-Richardson) explained the goal of shifting more state money into treatment programs when he explained that the goal was "to return [inmates] to society as productive citizens."
3. The juvenile justice system is governed by civil law.

10.5

1. True. Many scholars suggest that fewer jury trials can be directly attributed to the use of alternative dispute resolution methods because they are more cost efficient and can be completed more quickly.
2. More than 75 percent of convicted felons who have been exonerated in the United States were convicted in part because of mistaken eyewitness identification.
3. The annual reports are attempting to limit the possibility of racial profiling by law enforcement agencies.

Discussion Questions

1. Is Texas's justice system fair?
2. What are the advantages and disadvantages of electing judges?
3. What are the advantages and disadvantages of Texas's court system?
4. What can be done to make the legal system accessible to more Texans?
5. What are the advantages and disadvantages of the death penalty?
6. What are the appropriate purposes of a prison system?

Internet Resources

Death Penalty Information Center:
http://www.deathpenaltyinfo.org

Innocence Project:
http://www.innocenceproject.org

State Bar of Texas:
http://www.texasbar.com

State Commission on Judicial Conduct:
http://www.scjc.state.tx.us

Texans for Public Justice:
http://www.tpj.org

Texas Courts Online:
http://www.courts.state.tx.us

Texas Department of Criminal Justice:
http://www.tdcj.state.tx.us

Texas Department of Public Safety:
http://www.txdps.state.tx.us

Texas Juvenile Justice Department:
http://www.tjjd.texas.gov

Texas Law Help:
http://www.texaslawhelp.org

Notes

1. An excellent discussion of this case can be found at Andrew McLemore, "Until Proven Innocent: Parts 1–3," *Williamson County Sun*, October 9, 16 and 23 2011, http://wilcosun.com/pages/morton-10-16trial.php. McLemore won the Livingston Award for this series.
2. An easy-to-understand book that explains Texas law is Richard Alderman, *Know Your Rights: Answers to Texans' Everyday Legal Questions*, 8th ed. (Dallas: Taylor, 2010). In addition, Professor Alderman hosts The People's Lawyer website at http://www.peopleslawyer.net.
3. Annual statistics and other information on the Texas judicial system are available from the Texas Judicial Council and the Office of Court Administration, http://www.courts.state.tx.us.
4. For a discussion of specialized courts for veterans, see Judy L. Marchman, "Veterans Courts in Texas," *Texas Bar Journal*, 75, no. 8 (September 2012): 616–618.
5. The State Bar of Texas's website includes a how-to manual for prosecuting a claim in small-claims court, titled *How to Sue in Small Claims Court*, which is

available at http://www.texasbar.com/Content/NavigationMenu/ForThePublic/
FreeLegalInformation/ConsumerTenantRights/HowToSueinSmallClaimsCourt.
pdf.

6. For an excellent discussion of the development and adoption of the
constitutional amendment granting courts of civil appeals criminal appellate
jurisdiction, see former Chief Justice Joe R. Greenhill, "The Constitutional
Amendment Giving Criminal Jurisdiction to the Texas Courts of Civil Appeals
and Recognizing the Inherent Power of the Texas Supreme Court," *Texas Tech
Law Review* 33, no. 2 (2002): 377–404.

7. Chief Justice Wallace B. Jefferson, "State of the Judiciary," February 23, 2011,
http://www.supreme.courts.state.tx.us/advisories/pdf/SOJ.pdf.

8. Jeb Handelsman Shugerman, *The People's Courts: Pursuing Judicial
Independence in America* (Cambridge, MA: Harvard University Press, 2012).

9. Roy A. Schotland, "New Challenges to State's Judicial Selection," *Georgetown
Law Journal* 95 (2007): 1077–1105.

10. A discussion of this proceeding is available in Dave Montgomery, "Judge
Who Refused to Keep Office Open in Death Row Case Shouldn't Be
Removed, Ruling Says," *Fort Worth Star-Telegram,* January 21, 2010. The
Special Master's findings in this case can be accessed at
http://www.scjc.state.tx.us/pdf/skeller/ MastersFindings.pdf.

11. Texas Code of Judicial Conduct, Canon 3 B. 5 (2002).

12. State Commission on Judicial Conduct, "Public Sanctions, FY2011,"
http://www.scjc.state.tx.us/pdf/actions/FY2011-PUBSANC.pdf.

13. Legal Services Corporation, 2010 Annual Report (Washington, D.C.: Legal
Services Corporation, July 2011), http://www.lsc.gov/about/annual-report.

14. Lewis Powell, Address to the ABA Legal Services Program, American Bar
Association Annual Meeting, August 10, 1976.

15. D'Arlene Ver Duin and Paul Ruggeire, *State Bar of Texas Survey of 2009
Pro Bono* (Austin: State Bar of Texas, 2010), http://www.texasbar.com/
AM/Template.cfm?Section=Research_and_Analysis&Template=/CM/
ContentDisplay.cfm&ContentID=11247.

16. For a discussion of the history of tort reform in Texas, see Mimi Swartz, "Hurt?
Injured? Need a Lawyer? Too Bad!" *Texas Monthly*, November 2005, 164–169,
218–234, 254–258.

17. Bryn Nelson, "Texas Sized Tort Reform," *The Hospitalist* (March 2010), http://
www.the-hospitalist.org/details/article/574165/Texas-Sized_Tort_Reform.html.

18. David Arkush, Peter Gosselar, Christine Hines and Taylor Lincoln, "Liability
Limits in Texas Fail to Curb Medical Costs," December 2009,
http://www.citizen.org/documents/Texas_Liability_Limits.pdf.

19. David W. Elrod and Worthy Walker, "Fact or Fiction: Are There Less Jury Trials
and Lawyers? If So, What Do We Do about It?" *Litigation Commentary &
Review* 53 (June/July 2010), http://www.elrodtrial.com/docs/publications/good-
reads-david-elrod.pdf.

20. The Texas Board of Pardons and Paroles (BPP) provides a list and severity
ranking for every felony offense. This listing can be accessed at http://
www.tdcj.state.tx.us/bpp/.

21. Bruce Jackson and Diane Christian, *In This Timeless Time: Living and Dying on
Death Row in America* (Chapel Hill: University of North Carolina Press, 2012).
This book includes images of and interviews with Texas death row inmates.
For a full discussion of the possible execution of an innocent man, see James

Liebman, Shawn Crowley, Andrew Markquart, Lauren Rosenberg, Lauren Gallo White, and Daniel Zharkovsky, "Los Tocayos Carlos," *Columbia Human Rights Law Review* 43, no. 3 (2012): 711–1152.

22. For a discussion of the Danish manufacturer's response to the use of Nembutal as a part of the execution process, see Ed Pilkington, "Florida Execution: Drug Firm Protests to Governor over Lethal Injection," *The Guardian*, September 27, 2011, http://www.guardian.co.uk/world/2011/sep/27/death-penalty-florida-pentobarbital-lethal-injection. For details about Texas's purchase of the drug, see Mike Ward, "Records: Texas Bought Execution Drugs Before Supply Dwindled," *Austin American Statesman*, June 20, 2012, http://www.statesman.com/news/texas/records-texas-bought-execution-drugs-before-supply-dwindled-2402079.html?cxtype=rss_ece_frontpage.

23. Pete Kendall, "Judge Favors Sentence Other Than Death," *Cleburne Times-Review*, April 13, 2009.

24. For a list of those states in which a moratorium is in force, see "Death Penalty in Flux," Death Penalty Information Center, http://www.deathpenaltyinfo.org/death-penalty-flux.

25. Kenneth C. Land, Raymond H. C. Teske Jr., and Hui Zheng, "The Short-term Effects of Executions on Homicides: Deterrence, Displacement, or Both?" *Criminology* 47, no. 4 (2009): 1009–1043.

26. Kerwin Kofi Charles and Steven N. Durlauf, "Pitfalls in the Use of Time Series Methods to Study Deterrence and Capital Punishment," *Journal of Quantitative Criminology* (February 2012), doi: 10.1007/s10940-012-9169-7.

27. Jeremy Roebuck and Jared Janes, "The Price of Justice—Three Day Indigent Defense Series," *The McAllen Monitor*, December 20–22, 2009. This series of articles provides an in-depth review of the indigent defense program in Hidalgo County.

28. For a discussion of the history of the Texas prison system, see Robert Perkinson, *Texas Tough: The Rise of America's Prison Empire* (New York: Metropolitan, 2010). This book has been faulted by some reviewers for not reflecting improvements in the Texas prison system in recent years.

29. *Adult and Juvenile Correctional Population Projections: Fiscal Years 2007–2012* (Austin: Legislative Budget Board, January 2007). By January 2008, based on the additional diversion and treatment services available due to the decisions of the 80th legislature, the LBB lowered the projected incarceration population for 2012 by 10,000 inmates.

30. An investigation at one prison unit disclosed drug and money-laundering activities that allegedly involved both prisoners and prison staff members. In a recorded phone call between a prisoner and his father, the inmate observed that prison guards would continue to smuggle contraband "as long as there was money to be made." Mike Ward, "Prison Smuggling Detailed," *Austin American-Statesman,* May 6, 2010.

31. E. Fuller Torrey, Erran Kennard, Don Eslinger, Richard Lamb, and James Pavle, "More Mentally Ill Persons Are in Jails and Prisons Than Hospitals: A Survey of the States," Treatment Advocacy Center and National Sheriff's Association, May 2010, http://www.treatmentadvocacycenter.org/storage/documents/final_jails_v_hospitals_study.pdf.

32. Marc Levin, "Breaking Addiction without Breaking the Bank," Texas Public Policy Foundation, April 2011, http://www.texaspolicy.com/pdf/2011-04-PP05-SubstanceAbuse-mlevin.pdf.

33. Office of the Attorney General, "Appreciation for Dedication: Annual Report, 2011," https://www.oag.state.tx.us/AG_Publications/pdfs/cvs_annual2011.pdf.

34. Elrod and Walker, "Fact or Fiction."

35. Howard Safir and Peter Reinharz, "DNA Testing: The Next Big Crime-Busting Breakthrough," *City Journal* 10, no. 1 (Winter 2000): 49–57, http://www.city-journal.org/html/10_1_dna_testing.html.

36. Colin G. Tredoux, Christian A. Meisner, Roy S. Malpass, and Laura A. Zimmerman, "Eyewitness Identification," *Encyclopedia of Applied Psychology*, vol. 1, ed. C. D. Spielberg (New York: Elsevier Academic Press, 2004), 875–887.

37. For a discussion of the criminal justice system's disparate impact on African Americans, see Michelle Alexander, *The New Jim Crow: Mass Incarceration in the Age of Colorblindness* (New York: New Press, 2010).

Jack County Minute Book A (1870s): The Trial of Satanta and Big Tree

"The history of our courts is the history of Texas," according to State District Judge Mark Davidson. The Texas Court Records Preservation Task Force is working to preserve the history of Texas by protecting historical court records. In the March 2012 issue of the Texas Bar Journal, *several lawyers, professors, and judges used these documents to tell a part of the history of Texas. In the selection that follows, attorney Bill Kroger, chair of the task force, recounts the events of Kiowa Chief Satanta's trial and imprisonment.*

—Bill Kroger*

On May 18, 1871, a wagon train led by Henry Warren was traveling down the Jacksboro-Belknap Road when it encountered a large group of Kiowa and Comanche warriors. The wagon train shifted into a ring formation, with all the mules put into the center of the ring. The warriors killed and mutilated seven of the waggoners. Five men managed to escape.

A few months later, three of the leaders involved in the massacre, Satanta, Satank, and Addo-Etta (Big Tree), were arrested at Fort Sill after Satanta foolishly bragged about his involvement in the incident. Gen. William Tecumseh Sherman, who was visiting at the base, ordered that the chiefs be delivered to Jacksboro in Jack County, where they had been indicted in the district court for these killings. During the journey, Satank tried to escape and was shot and killed.

District Court Judge Charles Soward appointed two lawyers, Thomas Ball and Joseph Woolfolk, to represent the two surviving Kiowa

chiefs. Despite able representation by their counsel, the war chiefs were formally indicted on July 1, 1871; their trial began on July 5; and three days later they were convicted of seven counts of first-degree murder. The jury sentenced them to death.

The transcripts and other records of the trial were lost shortly after the trial, and it was thought that no records existed of the proceedings.[1] However, with the help of the Jack County District Clerk Tracie Pippin, the Texas Court Records Preservation Task Force found the minute book that contains the records of the indictment, trial, jury verdict, and post-trial proceedings.

The minute book reflects that after the verdict, the court ordered that Satanta "be taken by the Sheriff of Jack County and hanged until he is dead, dead, dead and God have mercy on his soul."[2] A similar order was entered for Big Tree. The records also show that the chiefs' lawyers made real efforts to defend them—both lawyers moved for new trials for their clients.[3] Most important, despite the court's pronouncements, Judge Soward showed concern about the trial's outcome. To buy time, he set the hangings for Sept. 1, two months after the convictions, at "some convenient place near the courthouse at the town of Jacksboro." Then, he wrote Gov. Edmund J. Davis, encouraging him to commute the sentence to life in prison.[4]

Gov. Davis agreed. The minute book contains the Aug. 2, 1871, commutation. The governor thought that a "commutation of said sentence to imprisonment for life will be more likely to operate as a restraint upon others of the tribe to which these Indians belong" and that "the killing for which these Indians were sentenced can hardly be considered on a just consideration of the amicus, as coming within the technical crimes of murder

*Bill Kroger is a partner in the Houston office of Baker Botts, L. L. P. He is the chair of the Supreme Court's Texas Court Records Preservation Task Force. This article first appeared in the *Texas Bar Journal* 73, no. 9 (March 2012).

under the statute of the State, but rather as an act of Savage Warfare."[5]

The Jack County District Court honored the commutation, and the two chiefs were delivered to Huntsville. Somewhat surprisingly, Texas authorities released Satanta and Big Tree on parole in 1873, also on the assumption that this would help pacify the Kiowas. However, a year after their release, Satanta was arrested for parole violations due to his participation in the attack on Adobe Walls. One night, he crawled through a high window of the Huntsville facility and leaped to his death on the bricks of the prison yard. This scene later became fictionalized in the account of the death of Chief Blue Duck in the book *Lonesome Dove*.

Notes

1. Smythe, Historical Sketch of Parker County and Weatherford, Texas, p. 274 (1877). This remarkable volume contains what may be the closest thing to a transcript of the trial, although some newspaper accounts may be found. The author states that "every effort" was made to obtain copies of court records from the trial, but the district clerk wrote that "the papers in the Satanta case have been lost and cannot be found."
2. Jack County Minute Book at 237–238.
3. This observation is consistent with Smythe's account: "The prisoners were ably represented by Messrs. Ball and Woolfolk, both of whom were faithful to their clients. They took advantage of every legal technicality, and conducted their defense with excellent judgment and decided impressiveness." Id. at 266.
4. The letter is reproduced in whole in Smythe's book. Judge Soward explained that he agreed with the Indian Agent Lowrie Tatem that the verdict would hinder efforts to get the Indians to come to the reservations. Judge Soward explained that he would have petitioned the governor to commute the sentences himself, "were it not that I know a great majority of the people on the frontier demand their execution." Id. at 276.
5. Jack County Minute Book at 243.

For further resources, please visit **www.cengagebrain.com**.

Finance and Fiscal Policy

(Sargent © 2008 Austin American-Statesman. Reprinted with permission of Universal Uclick. All rights reserved.)

Learning Objectives

1. Assess the fairness of Texas's budgeting and taxing policies.
2. Describe the sources of Texas's state revenue.
3. Describe the procedure for developing and approving a state budget.
4. Evaluate the effectiveness of the financing of education by the state of Texas.
5. Describe the uses of Texas's state revenue.

I n January 2011, Texas legislators arrived in Austin for the 82nd legislative session. A principal responsibility of these elected officials was the adoption of a biennial budget to fund state government activities and services for the next two years. The 82nd legislature faced a formidable task. Although the Great Recession that began in 2007 officially ended in June 2009, job losses and a slow economic recovery resulted in lower state revenue at a time when people were becoming more reliant on government services.[1] State Comptroller Susan Combs estimated that the fiscal year (FY) 2011 budget would require an additional $5.1 billion in funding. Actual expenditures from the 2010–2011 budget exceeded $187 billion. The state had $172 billion available for appropriation for fiscal years 2012 and 2013, which was approximately $15 billion less than officials spent in the previous biennium.[2]

At the same time, the number of Texas residents was increasing. The state comptroller reported an annual population growth of approximately 500,000. Therefore, the reality for the legislature and the governor was a decrease in available revenue and an increase in demand for services, thus creating a shortfall. As suggested in the opening cartoon for this chapter, the "Shortfall Monster" did not go away during the 82nd legislature. In fact, the difference between needs and resources grew to $27 billion by the time the budget was adopted. Because the Texas Constitution prohibits the legislature's passing a budget that results in a deficit, the difference had to be resolved.

In this environment, the legislature completed its work of preparing and approving a biennial budget for the state of Texas. Legislators attempted to equalize what Texans expect of their government with what they are willing to pay. This chapter examines the balance between costs and services; it provides an overview of the Lone Star State's fiscal policies, budgeting processes, and most costly public policy areas. Taxing, public spending, and governmental policy priorities will continue to have significant impacts on 21st-century Texans.

Fiscal Policies

LO1

During the 82nd legislative session in 2011, Texas's traditional, low-tax approach to **fiscal policy** (public policy that concerns taxes, government spending, public debt, and management of government money) faced key challenges. To resolve a similar dilemma in 2009, the 81st legislature had relied heavily on federal government support to meet the needs of the Lone Star State.

The American Recovery and Reinvestment Act of 2009 provided a one-time stimulus package designed to help state governments meet their fiscal needs and create jobs. As of August 2011, the state comptroller reported that Texas had spent $14.3 billion of stimulus funding. An additional $1 billion was given by the federal government to local governments. The state legislature and Governor Rick Perry used more than 90 percent of the stimulus

fiscal policy
Public policy that concerns taxing, government spending, public debt, and management of government money.

funds to balance Texas's budget (the highest percentage of the 25 states that researchers at the Pew Trust studied).

Because stimulus funds from the federal government were no longer available for the 2012–2013 biennium, officials used a combination of state taxes, nontax revenue, and accounting devices to create a balanced state budget. Tax revenue includes state sales taxes, as well as taxes on specific items such as cigarettes, motor vehicles, and gross receipts from businesses. Income from sources other than taxes comes from items like oil and gas royalties, land sales, and federal grants-in-aid. In addition, the 82nd legislature used a number of accounting maneuvers, such as delaying some mandatory payments beyond August 31, 2013 (the end of the biennial budget period), encouraging early payment of taxes to speed up revenue collection, and intentionally underfunding high-cost items such as Medicaid, to achieve a balanced budget.[3] Spending was reduced for public education, higher education, health-care programs, children's protective services, and all other areas of the budget, except natural resources and economic development. As a result, hundreds of thousands of Texans endured a loss or reduction of government benefits and services. In some instances the state's residents paid more for the services they received.

The state's economic condition began to improve in late 2011. State tax collections for FY2011 were $5 billion greater than the comptroller's original estimates. Increases in oil prices and escalation in oil and gas production brought both revenue and jobs to the Lone Star State. In April 2012, the governor reported that all of the jobs lost during the Great Recession had been restored. Unemployment, however, remained at 6.9 percent, because so many employment-aged people had migrated to Texas.

In 2012, state agencies were directed to reduce by 10 percent their upcoming budget requests to the 83rd legislature. Despite complaints about reduced government services, Governor Perry called on Texas's elected officials to join him in supporting the "Texas Budget Compact." This compact required legislators and candidates to sign a pledge to oppose any new taxes; to restrict spending from the **"rainy day" fund** (a special fund similar to a savings account) to one-time emergencies; to further reduce expenditures and programs; and to eliminate accounting devices to achieve a technically balanced budget.[4] The proposal incorporated Texas's individualistic and traditionalistic political culture in its call for personal self-reliance and benefits for business. Embedded in the compact was the assumption that Texans remained committed to pay-as-you-go spending and low taxes.

The Lone Star State's history and the voting behavior of the electorate support these views. The state's fiscal policy has not deviated from its 19th-century origins. Today, the notion of a balanced budget, achieved by low tax rates and low-to-moderate government spending levels, continues to dominate state fiscal policy. Consequently, state government, its employees, and its taxpayers face the daily challenge of meeting higher demands for services with fewer resources.

The state's elected officials appear to adopt the view expressed by economist and Nobel Prize winner Milton Friedman (1912–2006) that "the

"rainy day" fund
A fund used like a savings account for stabilizing state finance and helping the state meet economic emergencies when revenue is insufficient to cover state-supported programs.

preservation of freedom requires limiting narrowly the role of government and placing primary reliance on private property, free markets, and voluntary arrangements."[5] Texas legislators and other state leaders have repeatedly demonstrated a willingness to reduce services, outsource governmental work to decrease the number of employees on the state's payroll, and maintain or lower tax rates as solutions to the state's fiscal problems. A comparison of per capita taxing and spending rates (see "How Do We Compare ... in Taxes and Spending?") illustrates these policies.

Taxing Policy

tax
A mandatory assessment exacted by a government for a public purpose.

Texans have traditionally opposed mandatory assessments for public purposes, or **taxes.** Residents have pressured their state government to maintain low taxes. When additional revenues have been needed, Texans have indicated in poll after poll their preference for **regressive taxes,** which favor the rich and fall most heavily on the poor ("the less you make, the more government takes"). Under such taxes, the burden decreases as personal income increases. Figure 11.1 illustrates the impact of regressive taxes on different levels of income. Under the current tax structure, the poorest 20 percent of Texans pay more than three times as much of their income for taxes as the wealthiest 20 percent.

regressive tax
A tax in which the effective tax rate falls as the tax base (for example, individual income, corporate profits) increases.

Texas lawmakers have developed one of the most regressive tax structures in the nation. A general sales tax and selective sales taxes have been especially popular. **Progressive taxes** (taxes in which the impact increases as income rises—"the more you make, the more government takes") have been unpopular. Texas officials and citizens so oppose state income taxes that the state constitution requires a popular referendum before an income

progressive tax
A tax in which the effective tax rate increases as the tax base (for example, individual income, corporate profits) increases.

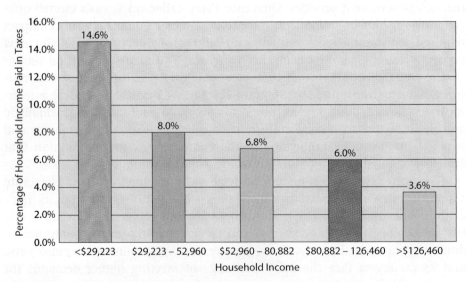

Figure 11.1   Percent of Average Annual Family Income Paid in Local and State Taxes in Texas (FY2011).

Source: Chandra King Villanueva, "Who Pays Texas Taxes?" Austin: Center for Public Policy Priorities" September 25, 2012.

How Do We Compare...in Taxes and Spending?

Per Capita Taxes and Spending for FY2010

Most Populous U.S. States	Per Capita State Taxes	Per Capita State Expenditures	U.S. States Bordering Texas	Per Capita State Taxes	Per Capita State Expenditures
California	$2,814	$5,532	Arkansas	$2,496	$6,832
Florida	$1,675	$3,300	Louisiana	$1,932	$6,427
New York	$3,278	$6,654	New Mexico	$2,144	$7,404
Texas	**$1,567**	**$3,703**	Oklahoma	$1,887	$5,760

Source: The Henry J. Kaiser Family Foundation, "Fifty State Comparisons," **http://www.statehealthfacts.org/comparecat.jsp?cat=1&rgn=6&rgn=1**.

tax can be levied. Newspaper columnists often observe that any elected official who proposes a state income tax commits political suicide.

To finance services, Texas government depends heavily on sales taxes, which rank among the highest in the nation. In addition, the Lone Star State has a dizzying array of other taxes. The Texas state comptroller's office collects more than 60 separate taxes, fees, and assessments on behalf of the state and local governments.[6] Yet the sales tax remains the most important source of state revenue.

Many observers have criticized the regressive characteristics of Texas's tax system as being unfair. An additional concern is that the state primarily operates with a 19th-century land- and product-based tax system that is no longer appropriate to the knowledge- and service-based economy of the 21st century. Local governments rely heavily on real estate taxes for their revenue. More than half of the state's general revenue tax collections are sales and use taxes. Until 2006, business activities of **service-sector** employers (including those in trade, finance, and the professions) remain tax-free. In that year, however, the state altered the franchise tax law to subject most Texas businesses to a tax calculated on their profit margins. This extension of the franchise tax subjected many service-sector entities to taxation.

Texas is recognized as one of the "top performers" in the nation in its ability to respond to shifts in the economy.[7] Even so, a comparison of sales and use tax collections ($41.1 billion) and franchise tax collections ($7.7 billion) for the 2010–2011 biennium reflects the extent to which the Lone Star State persists in relying on sales tax revenue. Changes in Texas's economy, without corresponding changes in its tax system, are projected to continue to erode the tax base. Under the current structure, the part of the economy generating the greatest amount of revenue frequently pays the least amount in taxes.

service-sector
Businesses that provide services, such as finance, health care, food service, data processing, or consulting.

Points to Ponder

Few items in Texas avoid some form of taxes, fees, or assessments. Some of the more unusual taxes and fees that the Office of State Comptroller is authorized to collect include the following:

- A 2 percent tax on the sale of fireworks
- A $5 fee on each entry by each customer to a sexually oriented business
- A $1 fee on each 300-pound barrel of oysters removed from Texas waters
- A $3.50 tax on each gram of marijuana that a dealer acquires and a $200 per gram tax on all other controlled substances, along with a fee of $2,000 per dosage unit

In addition, the state funds many activities through special fees and assessments that are not called taxes, but that represent money the state's residents pay to government. Texas legislators, reluctant to raise taxes, have often assessed these fees and surcharges. Is a **fee**, defined as a charge "imposed by an agency upon those subject to its regulation"[8] different from a tax? Some argue that these assessments represent an artful use of words, not a refusal to raise taxes, and that these charges meet the definition of a tax if the proceeds benefit the general public. For example, every year attorneys pay an attorney occupation tax (required since 1991) and a legal services fee (required since 2003), in addition to their mandatory dues to the State Bar of Texas (an administrative agency and their professional organization, discussed in Chapter 10, "Law, Courts, and Justice"). The legal services fee is used to pay for legal defense for the poor. Attorneys must pay each of these amounts in order to maintain the right to practice law in the state. Whether assessments are called dues, taxes, or fees, they represent money that an attorney must pay to finance government.

Budget Policy

Hostility to public debt is demonstrated in constitutional and statutory provisions that are designed to force the state to operate with a pay-as-you-go **balanced budget**. The Texas Constitution prohibits the state from spending more than its anticipated revenue "[e]xcept in the case of emergency and imperative public necessity and with a four-fifths vote of the total membership of each House."[9] In addition, the cost of debt service limits the state's borrowing power. This cost cannot exceed 5 percent of the average balance of general revenue funds for the preceding three years.

fee
A charge imposed by an agency upon those subject to its regulation.

balanced budget
A budget in which total revenues and expenditures are equal, producing no deficit.

To ensure a balanced budget, the comptroller of public accounts must submit to the legislature in advance of each regular session a sworn statement of cash on hand and revenue anticipated for the succeeding two years. Appropriation bills enacted at that particular session, and at any subsequent special session, are limited to not more than the amount certified, unless a four-fifths majority in both houses votes to ignore the comptroller's predictions or the legislature provides new revenue sources.

Despite these constitutional provisions, casual deficits (unplanned shortages) occur periodically. These deficits usually arise in the **General Revenue Fund** (the fund available to the legislature for general appropriations). Although it is only one of more than 400 funds in the state treasury, the General Revenue Fund is the critical fund in that maze of accounts. Like a thermometer, this fund measures the state's fiscal health. If the fund shows a surplus, fiscal health is good; if a deficit occurs (as in FYs 2012–2013 and as projected for FYs 2014–2015), then fiscal health is poor. Less than one-half of the state's expenditures come from the General Revenue Fund; the remainder comes from other funds that state law designates for use for specific purposes. Because of restrictions on use, these accounts are defined as **dedicated funds**. In most cases, the funds can only be used for their designated purposes, though in some instances money can be diverted to the state's general fund. For a discussion of the effects of this practice with regard to the Texas Parks and Wildlife Department, see the Selected Reading at the end of this chapter.

Even amounts that can only be spent for a designated purpose may be manipulated to satisfy the mandate for a balanced budget. As long as the account is consolidated with the General Revenue Fund, as is the case for more than 200 dedicated funds, the legislature can incorporate any unspent balances into its budget calculations. In the 82nd legislative session, the legislature refused to appropriate more than $5 billion in dedicated funds in order to give the appearance of a balanced budget. Among the frozen accounts was the System Benefit Fund. Most Texans' electricity bills include a monthly surcharge that consumers must pay to provide funding for a discount to low-income customers during the summer months. After the Public Utility Commission reduced the available discount by 40 percent in 2011, the state legislature used the remaining unspent funds of $851 million to balance the budget. State lawmakers justify these actions by noting that the high costs of programs such as Medicaid force them to freeze these balances. State Representative Sylvester Turner, who had originally proposed the creation of the System Benefit Fund, characterized this decision somewhat differently. He described the practice as "dishonest governing,"[10] because it is an accounting trick that makes money appear available on paper that in fact is not available.

Spending Policy

Historically, Texans have shown little enthusiasm for state spending. In addition to requiring a balanced budget, the Texas Constitution restricts

General Revenue Fund
An unrestricted state fund that is available for general appropriations.

dedicated fund
A restricted state fund that can only be appropriated for its designated purpose. If the fund is consolidated within the general revenue fund, it usually must be spent for its intended purpose. Any unappropriated amounts can be included in the calculations to balance the state budget.

increases in spending that exceed the rate of growth of the state's economy and limits welfare spending in any fiscal year to no more than 1 percent of total state expenditures. Consequently, public expenditures have remained low relative to those of other state governments. Texas has consistently ranked between 48th and 50th in state spending per capita. Furthermore, although the state's voters have indicated moderate willingness to spend for highways, roads, and other public improvements, they have demonstrated much less support for welfare programs, recreational facilities, and similar social services.

The continuation of the global economic downturn challenged Texans to consider government's role in providing assistance to people in need. As mentioned earlier, Governor Perry urged his fellow Texas politicians to adopt his view of less spending and lower taxes through his Texas Budget Compact. In addition, elected officials encountered a conflict between their desire to obtain funds from the national government and the "price," in terms of federal control, exacted for the use of that money. Continued economic turmoil, with some economists predicting that the state would not return to pre-recession employment and income levels for at least 20 years, suggests Texans will debate these issues for decades to come.

☑ Learning Check 11.1   (Answers on p. 484)

1. What are three characteristics of Texas's fiscal policy?
2. The state of Texas has one of the highest sales tax rates in the nation. It does not have a state income tax. Is Texas's tax structure an example of a regressive or a progressive tax system?
3. True or False: Dedicated funds must be fully spent each year for the purposes for which they were created.

★ Revenue Sources

LO2

Funding for government services primarily comes from those who pay taxes. In addition, the state derives revenue from fees for licenses, sales of assets, investment income, gambling, borrowing, and federal grants. When revenue to the state declines, elected officials have only two choices: increase taxes or other sources of revenue or decrease services. When faced with budget shortfalls, the legislature's first response has often been to decrease services.

The Politics of Taxation

According to generally accepted standards, each tax levied and the total tax structure should be just and equitable. Of course, notions vary widely about what kinds of taxes and what types of structures meet these standards. Conflicts became most apparent as state officials struggled to lower real estate taxes for the state's property owners between 2003 and 2006. Because these property taxes funded public schools, any reduction in revenue had to be replaced by the state to comply with the constitutional mandate to provide "an efficient system of public free schools." Pressure from special-interest groups made the imposition of taxes on those in the professions or businesses difficult. Proposed increases in the sales tax brought criticism from groups that advocate for poor Texans. Although some legislators and several public policy groups called for the imposition of an income tax, elected officials consistently refused to consider this issue, allowing any proposed legislation to languish in the House Ways and Means Committee and never reach the full House for a vote.

In 2006, despite resistance from several large law firms, the 79th legislature modified and expanded the franchise tax (discussed below). It also imposed an additional $1 tax on cigarettes, increased taxes on other tobacco products (except cigars), and required buyers to pay a tax on used cars at their presumptive value as determined by publications such as *Kelley Blue Book*. In response to pressure from small business owners, the 81st legislature in 2009 reduced the number of businesses subject to the franchise tax and increased taxes on tobacco products. Although the exemption of most businesses was to be temporary, the 82nd legislature left all exemptions in place. Governor Perry argued that these exemptions should be made permanent through his Texas Budget Compact. These modifications reflected both the political strength of business owners and the ease of raising taxes on items that some people might deem unhealthy or morally questionable.

Sales Taxes By far, the most important single source of tax revenue in Texas is sales taxation. (See Figure 11.2 for the sources of state revenue.) Altogether, sales taxes accounted for more than 55 percent of state tax revenue and 22 percent of all revenue in fiscal years 2010–2011. These sales taxes function as a regressive tax, and the burden they impose on individual taxpayers varies with spending patterns and income levels.

For more than 50 years, the state has levied and collected two kinds of sales taxes: a general sales tax and several selective sales taxes. First imposed in 1961, the limited sales, excise, and use tax (commonly referred to as the **general sales tax**) has become the foundation of the Texas tax system. The current (2012) statewide rate of 6.25 percent is one of the nation's highest (ranking as the 12th-highest rate among the 45 states that imposed a sales tax as of midyear 2012). Local governments have the option of levying additional sales taxes for a combined total of state and local taxes of 8.25 percent (see Chapter 3, "Local Governments"). The base of the tax is the sale price of "all tangible personal property" and "the storage, use, or other consumption of tangible personal property purchased, leased, or rented." Among exempted tangible property are the following: receipts from water, telephone, and telegraph services; sales of goods otherwise taxed (for

general sales tax
At the rate of 6.25 percent of a sale, the general sales tax is Texas's largest source of tax revenue. It is applied largely to the sale price of tangible personal property and "the storage, use, or other consumption of tangible personal property purchased, leased, or rented."

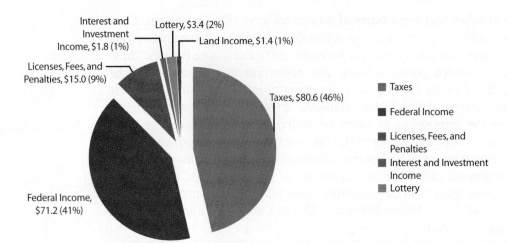

Figure 11.2 Projected Sources of State Revenue, Fiscal Years 2012–2013.

Note: Amounts are in billions of dollars.
Source: Calculated from Susan Combs, Texas Comptroller of Public Accounts, *The 2012–2013 Certification Revenue Estimate,* December 2011.

example, automobiles and motor fuels); food and food products (but not restaurant meals); medical supplies sold by prescription; nonprescription drugs; animals and supplies used in agricultural production; and sales by university and college clubs and organizations (as long as the group has no more than one fundraising activity per month).

Two other important items exempt from the general sales tax are goods sold via the Internet and most professional and business services. According to U.S. Supreme Court decisions, a state cannot require businesses with no facilities in the state to collect sales taxes for it because the practice interferes with interstate commerce. Therefore, when a student buys a textbook from an online seller with no facilities in the state, no sales tax is collected. The book is, however, subject to a use tax, which requires the purchaser to file a form with the comptroller's office and pay taxes on items purchased out-of-state for use in Texas. Because the cost of enforcing such a provision on individual consumers is prohibitive, these transactions remain largely untaxed.

Some online merchants, such as kitchen retailer Williams-Sonoma, Inc., voluntarily collect sales taxes for the states. Other sellers argue that multiple rates and definitions of products subject to state sales taxes create a collection nightmare. Through the Streamlined Sales Tax Project 24 states, not including Texas, are devising a uniform tax system that would overcome these arguments. If the U.S. Congress were to grant states that adopt these uniform policies the authority to force out-of-state retailers to collect sales taxes on their behalf, Texas could only benefit if the state's leaders joined the Streamlined Sales Tax Project. According to the state comptroller, if Texas did adopt these policies, the state would receive approximately $600 million annually in additional revenue.

In 2010, State Comptroller Susan Combs attempted to collect $269 million (including unpaid sales tax, penalties, and interest) from the online bookseller Amazon. The company owned an interest in a distribution center in Irving (near Dallas). According to the comptroller, the distribution center created "a nexus" in the state of Texas sufficient to permit taxation. Amazon responded with a lawsuit in which it asked that the state produce records to justify the amount of its tax claim. The company also threatened to close its Texas facility if the state did not relent. Subsequently, reversing this tactic, the retailer offered to build additional distribution centers in Texas if the state withheld tax collection efforts for several years. The 82nd legislature joined the fray by passing a law that strengthened the comptroller's position. Governor Perry vetoed the bill, stating he had "serious concerns about its impact and appropriateness."[11] When the legislature included the provisions of the bill in the state's budget, Perry approved the legislation. The Legislative Budget Board estimated that the new law would increase tax collections by $16 million over the 2012–2013 biennium. In April 2012, the comptroller and Amazon settled their disputes. The comptroller agreed to release claims for past due sales taxes, and Amazon agreed to collect sales taxes on goods sold to Texans after July 2012. In addition, the retailer agreed to invest more than $200 million in the state and create an additional 2,500 jobs. Additional controversy surrounded this settlement when some legal experts argued that the Texas Constitution prohibited the comptroller's forgiving unpaid taxes. Other attorneys and tax specialists countered that the comptroller had great latitude in resolving tax disputes.

Because the general sales tax primarily applies to tangible personal property, many services are untaxed. A sales tax is charged for dry cleaning, football tickets, and parking; however, accountants, architects, and consultants provide their services tax-free. Because professional service providers and businesses represent some of the most powerful and well-organized interests in the Lone Star State, proposals that would require these groups to collect a sales tax have faced strong resistance. (See Chapter 6, "The Politics of Interest Groups.") Although the comptroller estimates that eliminating sales tax exclusions for professional services would generate approximately $6 billion in additional revenue, even in the recent economic downturn, legislators made no effort to change the law.[12]

Since 1931, when the legislature first imposed a sales tax on cigarettes, many items have been singled out for **selective sales taxes**. For convenience of analysis, these items may be grouped into three categories: highway user taxes, sin taxes, and miscellaneous sales taxes. Highway user taxes include taxes on fuels for motor vehicles that use public roads and registration fees for the privilege of operating those vehicles. The principal **sin taxes** are those on cigarettes and other tobacco products, alcoholic beverages, mixed drinks, and admission fees to so-called "gentlemen's clubs." Additional items subject to selective sales taxes include hotel and motel room rentals (also called a "bed tax") and retail sales of boats and boat motors.

selective sales tax
A tax charged on specific products and services.

sin tax
A selective sales tax on items such as cigarettes, other forms of tobacco, alcoholic beverages, and admissions fees to sex-oriented businesses.

Business Taxes As with sales taxes, Texas imposes both general and selective business taxes. A general business tax is assessed against a wide range of business operations. Selective business taxes are those levied on businesses engaged in specific or selected types of commercial activities.

Commercial enterprises operating in Texas have historically paid three general business taxes:

- Sales taxes, because businesses are consumers
- Franchise taxes, because many businesses operate in a form that attempts to limit personal liability of owners (that is, corporations, limited liability partnerships, and similar structures)
- Unemployment compensation payroll taxes, because most businesses are also employers

The **franchise tax**, which has existed for almost 100 years, is imposed on businesses for the privilege of doing business in Texas. As a part of the restructuring of the state's school finance system, the legislature expanded the franchise tax to include all businesses operating in a format that limited the personal liability of owners. Sole proprietorships, general partnerships wholly owned by natural persons, passive investment entities (such as real estate investment trusts or REITs), and businesses that make $1,000,000 or less in annual income ($600,000 or less after 2013) or that owe less than $1,000 in franchise taxes are exempt. The tax is levied on a business's taxable margin, which is its total income less either (1) the cost of goods sold or (2) compensation paid to employees, not to exceed $300,000 per employee. To gain support from the Texas Medical Association for the tax, the law allows health-care providers to deduct amounts collected from government-sponsored programs, such as Medicaid and Medicare, and the cost of uncompensated medical care.

Although proponents estimated that this tax would produce about $6 billion in state revenue each fiscal year, actual collections have been far less. In FY2011, franchise tax collections were $3.9 billion. For the two-year period covering the 2012–2013 biennium, the comptroller projected total collections of $8.2 billion (or approximately $4.1 billion per fiscal year). Collections for FY2012 exceeded the comptroller's original estimate for that fiscal year by $500 million (totaling $4.6 billion in receipts). Even so, collections were below the amounts predicted by the tax's original proponents. Several reasons have been cited for this shortfall in collections, including a weak economy, the increase in the exemption from tax liability to include businesses earning less than $1,000,000, and a definition of "cost of goods sold" to include deductions not available under federal law. The tax is highly unpopular among small business owners, who continue to seek its repeal.[13]

All states have unemployment insurance systems supported by **payroll taxes**. The payroll tax is levied against a portion of the wages and salaries paid to individuals to insure employees against unemployment. These amounts are paid into the Unemployment Trust Fund in the U.S. Treasury. Benefits are distributed to qualified workers who lose their jobs.

franchise tax
A tax levied on the annual receipts of businesses that are organized to limit the personal liability of owners for the privilege of conducting business in the state.

payroll tax
A tax levied against a portion of the wages and salaries of employees to provide funds for payment of unemployment insurance benefits to these people when they lose their jobs.

The most significant of the state's selective business taxes are levied on the following:

- Oil and gas production
- Insurance company gross premiums
- Public utilities gross receipts

Selective business taxes accounted for approximately 15 percent of the state's tax revenue in FY2008, when the economy was strong and oil and gas prices and production were high. When the economy floundered and oil and gas prices and production declined, these taxes amounted to only 10 percent of tax collections for the 2010–2011 biennium, confirming their sensitivity to market conditions.

One of the more important selective business taxes is the severance tax. Texas has depended far more than other states on **severance taxes,** which are levied on a natural resource, such as oil or natural gas, when it is removed from the earth. Texas severance taxes are based on the quantity of minerals produced or on the value of the resource when removed. The Texas crude oil production tax and the gas-gathering tax were designed with two objectives in mind: to raise substantial revenue and to regulate the amount of natural resources mined or otherwise recovered. Each of these taxes is highly volatile, reflecting dramatic increases and decreases as the price and demand for natural resources fluctuate. Current production in Texas relies heavily on hydraulic fracture stimulation to recover oil and gas reserves. This recovery method uses substantial amounts of water. In 2011, the comptroller expressed concerns that the ongoing Texas drought would limit oil and gas recovery (see Chapter 1 "The Environment of Texas Politics"). Additional controversies about the environmental impact of this recovery method on groundwater and on underground stability could also reduce production and, therefore, revenue to the Lone Star State.[14]

Death Tax Because of changes to federal law, no death tax is collected on the estates of individuals dying on or after January 1, 2005. Some states have enacted laws imposing a tax on estates. It is unlikely that Texas will do so.

Tax Burden The U.S. Census Bureau places Texas well below the national average for the state tax burden imposed on its residents. In 2010 (the most recent year for which information was available at the time of publication), when state taxes alone were considered, the Lone Star State ranked 48th among the 50 states. A candidate's "no new taxes" pledge remains an important consideration for many Texas voters and will likely result in state officials' continuing to choose fewer services over higher taxes to balance the state budget.

Tax Collection As Texas's chief tax collector, the comptroller of public accounts collects more than 90 percent of state taxes, including those on motor fuel sales, oil and gas production, cigarette and tobacco sales, and franchises. Amounts assessed by the comptroller's office can be challenged

severance tax
An excise tax levied on a natural resource (such as oil or natural gas) when it is severed (removed) from the earth.

through an administrative proceeding conducted by that office. Taxpayers dissatisfied with the results of their hearings can appeal the decision to a state district court. (See Chapter 10, "Laws, Courts, and Justice.")

Retailers and others who prepay their sales tax collections receive an incentive for doing so. In an effort to increase tax revenue, the 82nd legislature authorized temporary changes to the state's tax collection laws. These changes included "speed up" provisions to force early tax payments before the end of FY2013 and a tax amnesty program to encourage tax scofflaws to pay past-due taxes. Retailers were also mandated to prepay by August 31, 2013, a portion of sales taxes, motor fuel taxes, and alcoholic beverage taxes that would have otherwise been due in September 2013. These prepayments were expected to generate an additional $231 million in revenue for the 2012–2013 biennium. Correspondingly, available revenue for the 2014–2015 biennium was reduced by this amount. Amnesty laws allowed taxpayers who owed money to the state to pay amounts due without penalty or interest. The comptroller anticipated additional collections of $75 million from this program.

Other agencies also collect taxes on behalf of the state. The Department of Motor Vehicles, created by the 81st Legislature in 2009, collects motor vehicle registration and certificate-of-title fees through county tax collectors' offices; the State Board of Insurance collects insurance taxes and fees; and the Department of Public Safety collects driver's license, motor vehicle inspection, and similar fees. The Texas Alcoholic Beverage Commission collects state taxes on beer, wine, and other alcoholic beverages. Although taxes represent the largest source of state revenue, Texas has other funding means.

Revenue from Gambling

Texas receives revenue from three types of gambling (called "gaming" by supporters) operations: horse racing and dog racing, a state-managed lottery, and bingo. Owners of horse racing operations have lobbied politicians for legalization of slot machines at their tracks. In addition, the state's three Native American tribes (the Kickapoo nation near Eagle Pass, the Alabama-Coushatta in East Texas, and the Tigua near El Paso) continue to argue for the right to operate Las Vegas–style casinos. Opposition from both social conservatives and many Democrats remains strong. Seventeen bills supporting the expansion of gambling operations in the state were introduced in the 82nd legislature in 2011. Supporters argued that these proposals would mean billions of dollars in revenue that was being spent by Texans in casinos in Oklahoma and Louisiana. Despite the difficult economic conditions of the state, however, the legislature passed none of the proposed bills.

Racing Pari-mutuel wagers on horse races and dog races are taxed. This levy has never brought Texas significant revenue. Proceeds from uncashed mutuel tickets, less the cost of drug testing the animals at the racing facility, revert to the state. In most years, the Racing Commission collects far less revenue than its operating expenses. Texas has four types of horse racing permits, ranging from Class 1 (with no limit on the number of race days per year) to Class 4 (limited to five race days annually). As of 2012, the Lone Star State had 10 permitted horse racing tracks (five that were active and five that were inactive) and three dog tracks providing live and simulcast racing events on which people could wager legal bets.

Lottery Texas operates one of 43 state-run lotteries. Chances for winning the jackpot are 1 in 26 million. Major competitors for lottery players' money are the multistate lotteries Mega Millions and Powerball. Texas is one of 41 states participating in both Mega Millions and Powerball. The largest prize money in U.S. history was offered by Mega Millions in April 2012, when winners shared a jackpot of $656 million. None were from Texas, though the Texas Lottery Commission noted that Texans had won more than $723 million from the Mega Millions lottery between 2003 and 2012. Chances for winning are 1 in 176 million. Powerball odds are even more daunting: 1 in 195 million.

The global economic crisis had a negative impact on lottery ticket sales. To bolster sales, lottery officials became increasingly creative in their offerings. Officials created a new game in which people who had not won a money prize from certain scratch-off games were given a "second chance" to win drawings for football tickets, motorcycles, and sport-utility vehicles. In addition, the lottery began selling $20 and $50 scratch-off tickets for multimillion-dollar instant-winner games.

The Texas Lottery Commission administers the state's lottery. Among its functions are determining the amounts of prizes, overseeing the printing of tickets, advertising ticket sales, and awarding prizes. Because this three-member commission also oversees bingo operations, one member must have experience in the bingo industry.

All profits from the lottery are dedicated to public education spending, rather than to the General Revenue Fund. In 2011, approximately $1 billion went to the Texas Foundation School Fund. This amount constituted a small portion of the state's budgeted expenditure of more than $26 billion on public education in that same year. Unclaimed prizes from the Texas lottery revert to the state 180 days after a drawing. These funds are transferred to hospitals across the state to provide partial reimbursement for unfunded indigent medical care. In addition, in 2009, the legislature authorized a Veteran's Cash scratch-off game. Some of the proceeds from the sale of these tickets benefit the Veterans' Assistance Fund.

Bingo State law allows bingo operations to benefit charities (for example, churches, veterans' organizations, and service clubs). The 5 percent tax on bingo prizes is divided 50-50 between the state and local governments. State revenue from bingo taxes remains low. Local charities do benefit from the portion of the proceeds that is distributed to them. In 2011, these donations were approximately $29 million. In that same year, the Texas Lottery Commission reported that gross receipts from charitable bingo games were $705 million, exceeding all previous years. This increase in gross revenue was not reflected in donations, however. The amount was used to increase winners' prizes.

Nontax Revenues

Less than 45 percent of all Texas state revenue comes from taxes and gambling operations; therefore, other nontax revenues are important sources of funds. The largest portion of these revenues (more than two-thirds in the 2012–2013 biennium) comes from federal grants. The graph shown as Figure 11.3 reflects the growth of this funding source from FY2001 through FY2011. State business operations (such as sales of goods by one government agency to another government agency) and borrowing also are significant sources of revenue. In addition, the state has billions of dollars invested in interest-bearing accounts and securities.

Federal Grants-in-Aid Gifts of money, goods, or services from one government to another are defined as **grants-in-aid**. Federal grants-in-aid contribute more revenue to Texas than any single tax levied by the state. More than 95 percent of federal funds are directed to three programs: health and human services, business and economic development (especially highway construction), and education. For the 2012–2013 biennium, federal funds, including grants, were expected to account for more than $71 billion in revenue. This amount, however, is less than the $75.3 billion received in the 2010–2011 biennium.

State participation in federal grant programs is voluntary. States choosing to participate must (1) contribute a portion of program costs (varying from as little as 10 percent to as much as 90 percent) and (2) meet performance specifications established by federal mandate. Funds are usually allocated to states on the basis of a formula. Factors commonly used in deriving a formula include lump sums (made up of identical amounts to all states

grant-in-aid
Money, goods, or services given by one government to another (for example, federal grants-in-aid to states for financing public assistance programs).

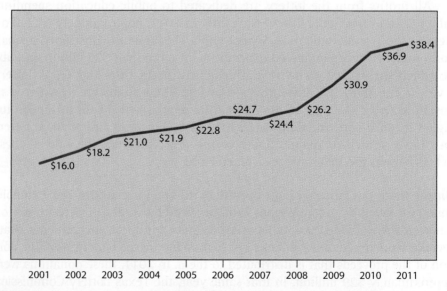

Figure 11.3   Annual Federal Grants to Texas (FY2001–FY2013) (in billions).

Source: Developed from information available from State Comptroller, "Texas Net Revenue by Source, 1973–2010" and "Texas Net Revenue by Source, 2011," available at **http://www.window.state.tx.us/finances/morefinancial.html**.

receiving funds) and uniform sums (based on items that vary from state to state, such as population, area, highway mileage, need and fiscal ability, cost of service, administrative discretion, and special state needs).

In response to the economic crisis in the United States, on February 17, 2009, President Barack Obama signed the $787 billion American Reinvestment and Recovery Act into law. The stated purpose of this act was to create jobs and stimulate the recovery of the U.S. economy. Through April 2012, the state of Texas, including its colleges and universities, had received more than $22.9 billion under this program.[15] The total amount of this one-time funding and its impact on the state's economy will not be known for several years.

Land Revenues Texas state government receives substantial nontax revenue from public land sales, rentals, and royalties. Sales of land, sand, shell, and gravel, combined with rentals on grazing lands and prospecting permits, accounted for approximately 0.7 percent of the state's budget in the 2012–2013 biennium. A substantial portion of revenue from state lands is received from oil and natural gas leases and from royalties derived from mineral production. The volatility of oil and natural gas prices causes wide fluctuations in the amount the state receives from these mineral leases. Projected collections for 2012–2013 represented almost a billion dollar decline from 2010–2011 land revenues. A new source of revenue is anticipated from commercial offshore wind turbines. The General Land Office, the agency responsible for managing the more than 20 million acres of land surface and mineral rights that the state owns, also leases offshore sites for wind power. Officials with this office note that Texas's ownership of its tidelands, which extend 10.3 miles into the Gulf of Mexico, allows turbine operators to avoid much "federal entanglement."[16] As of mid-2012, the General Land Office had entered seven leases with wind power operators.

The Tobacco Suit Windfall Early in 1998, the American tobacco industry settled a lawsuit filed by the state of Texas. During a period of 25 years, cigarette makers will pay the Lone Star State $18 billion in damages for public health costs incurred by the state as a result of residents' tobacco-related illnesses. These funds support a variety of health-care programs, including the Children's Health Insurance Program (CHIP), Medicaid, tobacco-education projects, and endowments for health-related institutions of higher education. Payments averaged approximately $500 million per year through 2011. Because of increases in taxes that have reduced consumption in Texas and other states, revenue from the sale of tobacco products has declined in recent years. As a result, the comptroller predicted that settlement payments from the tobacco lawsuit would decline by $20 million in the 2012–2013 biennium. An additional $2.3 billion is administered as a trust by the state comptroller to help reimburse local governments (cities, counties, and hospital districts) for unreimbursed health-care costs. In 2011, these political subdivisions received $51 million from this fund. In that same year, the much larger total in unreimbursed health-care expenditures for these recipients was $2.6 billion. Providers were advised to anticipate even lower reimbursement rates in 2012–2013 due to low investment returns on the trust fund.

Miscellaneous Sources Fees, permits, and income from investments are major miscellaneous nontax sources of revenue. Fee sources include those for motor vehicle inspections, college tuition, student services, state hospital care, and certificates-of-title for motor vehicles. The most significant sources of revenue from permits are those for trucks and automobiles; the sale of liquor, wine, and beer; and cigarette tax stamps. During the 2012–2013 biennium, income from these sources continued to decline due to Texas's economic problems.

At any given moment, Texas actually has billions of dollars on hand, invested in securities or on deposit in interest-bearing accounts. Trust funds constitute the bulk of the money invested by the state (for example, the Texas Teacher Retirement Fund, the State Employee Retirement Fund, the Permanent School Fund, and the Permanent University Fund). Investment returns closely track fluctuations in the stock market. The chaos in the financial markets that began in September 2008 had a direct effect on this revenue source. Interest and investment income for the 2012–2013 biennium was less than half of amounts collected during fiscal years 2008 and 2009. The Texas state comptroller is responsible for overseeing the investment of most of the state's surplus funds. Restrictive money-management laws limit investments to interest-bearing negotiable order withdrawal (NOW) accounts, treasury bills (promissory notes in denominations of $1,000 to $1 million) from the U.S. Treasury, and repurchase agreements (arrangements that allow the state to buy back assets such as state bonds) from banks. Interest and investment income was expected to provide approximately 1 percent of state revenue in 2012–2013.

The University of Texas Investment Management Company (UTIMCO) invests the Permanent University Fund and other endowments for the University of Texas and the Texas A&M University systems. Its investment authority extends to participating in venture capital partnerships that fund new businesses. Board members for UTIMCO include the chancellor and three regents from the University of Texas system, two individuals selected by the Board of Regents of the Texas A&M University System, and three outside investment professionals. This nonprofit corporation was the first such investment company in the nation affiliated with a public university.

The Public Debt

When expenditures exceed income, governments finance shortfalls through public borrowing. Such deficit financing is essential to meet short- and long-term crises and to pay for major projects involving large amounts of money. Most state constitutions, including the Texas Constitution, severely limit the authority of state governments to incur indebtedness.

For more than 70 years, Texans have sought, through constitutional provisions and public pressure, to force the state to operate on a pay-as-you-go basis. Despite those efforts, the state is allowed to borrow money by issuing **general obligation bonds** (borrowed amounts repaid from the General Revenue Fund) and **revenue bonds** (borrowed amounts repaid from a specific revenue source, such as college student loan bonds repaid by students who received the funds). Commercial paper (unsecured short-term business loans) and promissory notes also cover the state's cash flow shortages. Whereas general obligation bonds and commercial paper borrowings must have voter approval, other forms of borrowing do not require voter approval. Bonded debt that is outstanding must be repaid from the General Revenue Fund was approximately $36.2 billion as of FY2011. In November 2011, the Lone Star State's voters authorized an additional $6 billion in borrowing by the Texas Water Development Board to assist local governments with the construction of water projects. Many Texas voters approve both a balanced budget and bond amendments that authorize the state to increase its debt by borrowing money.

Bond Review Specific projects to be financed with bond money require legislative approval. Bond issues also must be approved by the Texas Bond Review Board. The four members of this board are the governor, lieutenant governor, Speaker of the House, and comptroller of public accounts. It approves all borrowings by the state or its public universities with a term in excess of five years or an amount in excess of $250,000.[17]

Economic Stabilization Fund The state's Economic Stabilization Fund (popularly called the "rainy day" fund) operates like an individual's savings account. It is intended for use when the state faces an economic crisis and is used primarily to prevent or eliminate temporary cash deficiencies in the General Revenue Fund. The "rainy day" fund is financed with one-half of any excess money remaining in the General Revenue Fund at the end of a biennium and with oil and natural gas taxes that exceed 1987 collections (approximately $1.3 billion in that year). This fund has provided temporary support for public education, Medicaid, and the criminal justice system, as well as financing for the Texas Enterprise Fund, which is designed to attract new businesses to the state. The Emerging Technology Fund, also financed in part with money from the "rainy day" fund, is intended for use by companies engaging in work with new technologies that are likely to produce medical or scientific breakthroughs. The effects of a weak economy are revealed in collections by the "rainy day" fund. In August 2008, the state transferred more than $3.1 billion into the "rainy day" fund, including a budget surplus of approximately $1 billion. The 2011 transfer included no budget surplus, and the total amount deposited in the fund equaled $1 billion, or one-third the revenue transferred in 2008. Improvements in the Texas economy resulted in an increase in the fund's balance to $8.1 billion by November 2012.

Responding to Governor Perry's threat to veto any attempt to use the "rainy day" fund to balance the state's 2012–2013 biennial budget, the legislature knowingly underfunded estimated Medicaid costs by $4.8 billion. The solution to this problem remained an issue to be addressed by the 83rd

general obligation bond
Amount borrowed by the state that is repaid from the General Revenue Fund.

revenue bond
Amount borrowed by the state that is repaid from a specific revenue source.

legislature in 2013. Because the federal government funds approximately 60 percent of Medicaid expenditures, the state is required to appropriate sufficient amounts to cover its share of costs. Legislators in the 82nd legislature were hopeful that these funds would come from increased state revenue; however, if sufficient amounts failed to materialize, the state match would have to come from the "rainy day" fund.

 Learning Check 11.2   (Answers on p. 484)

1. What is the largest source of tax revenue for the state of Texas?
2. On what government service must lottery profits be spent?
3. What is the stated purpose of the "rainy day" fund?

LO3

★ Budgeting and Fiscal Management

The state's fiscal management process begins with a statewide vision for Texas government and ends with an audit.[18] Other phases of this four-year process include development of agency strategic plans, legislative approval of an appropriations bill, and implementation of the budget. Each activity is important if the state is to derive maximum benefit from the billions of dollars it handles each year.

Budgeting Procedure

A plan of financial operation is usually referred to as a **budget**. In modern state government, budgets serve a variety of functions, each important in its own right. A budget outlines a plan for spending that shows a government's financial condition at the close of one budget period and the anticipated condition at the end of the next budget cycle. It also makes spending recommendations for the coming budget period. In Texas, the budget period covers two fiscal years. Each fiscal year begins on September 1 and ends on August 31 of the following year. The fiscal year is identified by the initials FY (for "fiscal year") preceding the number for the ending year. For example, FY2013 began on September 1, 2012, and ended on August 31, 2013.

Texas is one of only four states that have biennial (every two years) legislative sessions and budget periods. Many political observers argue that today's economy fluctuates too rapidly for this system to be efficient. Voters, however, have consistently rejected proposed constitutional amendments requiring annual state appropriations. See the Point/Counterpoint feature for arguments for and against annual budgeting.

Legislative Budget Board By statute, the **Legislative Budget Board (LBB)** is a 10-member joint body of the Texas House of Representatives and the Texas Senate. Its membership includes as joint chairs the lieutenant

budget
A plan of financial operation indicating how much revenue a government expects to collect during a period (usually one or two fiscal years) and how much spending is authorized for agencies and programs.

Legislative Budget Board (LBB)
A 10-member body cochaired by the lieutenant governor and the Speaker of the House. This board and its staff prepare a biennial current-services budget. In addition, it assists with the preparation of a general appropriation bill at the beginning of a regular legislative session. If requested, staff members prepare fiscal notes that assess the economic impact of a proposed bill or resolution.

Point/Counterpoint

THE ISSUE Four states use biennial budgeting and have biennial legislative sessions: Montana, Nevada, North Dakota, and Texas. The other three states are much less populous than Texas and have substantially smaller budgets. The trend for states over the past 70 years has been toward annual budgeting. Four states used annual budgeting in 1940. Today, 31 states rely on annual budgeting, and 15 states have annual legislative sessions and biennial budgets. Several states have returned to biennial budgeting after officials became dissatisfied with annual budgets, and a few states have moved between the two approaches over the years.

Should Texas Adopt Annual Budgeting?

Arguments For Annual Budgets

- State budgets are too complex to be developed only every other year. Multiple sources of revenue, convoluted federal government programs, and multibillion-dollar budgets are complicated and require careful monitoring.
- State revenue sources, such as a sales tax, are too volatile to allow for accurate predictions. Research suggests that errors in estimates of revenue and spending in states with biennial budgets is twice that of states with annual budgets.
- Biennial budgets require frequent revisions. A study conducted at Texas A&M University suggests that annual budgets require fewer supplemental appropriations by legislatures than do biennial budgets.

Two-year budgets are a historical accident— at one time the Legislature didn't meet every year. And no other entity the state deals with—federal, county, municipal, or business—uses the biennial format. Scrap it.

—Newspaper columnist Douglas Brooks, arguing for an annual budget in Maine

Arguments For Biennial Budgets

- Biennial budgets save time for all parties because they are only developed every other year. Although some research supports that less time is spent on budgeting by the executive branch when a biennial system is used, results are mixed with regard to the legislative branch.
- Biennial budgets force long-term planning. Results are inconclusive on whether biennial budgeting improves long-term planning. No clear evidence exists that the budgeting system has any correlation to a state's frugality.
- Biennial budgets allow sufficient time for legislators to evaluate the effects of their decisions. Weak evidence exists to suggest that legislators give more attention to evaluation of program outcomes in states that use biennial budgeting.

The present system [of annual budgeting] does not allow enough time to review expenditures in depth. Those preparing the budget finish one year and then immediately plunge into the next year's budget.

—[Connecticut] Commission to Study the Management of State Government

Ronald K. Snell, *State Experiences with Annual and Biennial Budgeting* (Washington, D.C.: National Council of State Legislatures, 2011).

governor and the Speaker of the House of Representatives. Assisted by its director and staff, the LBB prepares a biennial (two fiscal years) current services–based budget. This type of budget projects the cost of meeting anticipated service needs of Texans over the next biennium. The comptroller of public accounts furnishes the board with an estimate of the growth of the Texas economy from the current biennium to the next biennium. Legislative appropriations from tax revenue not dedicated by the Texas Constitution cannot exceed that rate of growth. Based on the comptroller's projections, the LBB capped the growth of appropriations from undedicated revenue at slightly less than 9 percent for the 2012–2013 biennium.

The board's staff also helps draft the general appropriation bill for introduction at each regular session of the legislature. Furthermore, if requested by a legislative committee chair, staff personnel prepare fiscal notes that assess the potential economic impact of a bill or resolution. Employees of the LBB also assist agencies in developing performance evaluation measures and audits, and they conduct performance reviews to determine how effectively and efficiently agencies are functioning.

Governor's Office of Budget, Planning, and Policy Headed by an executive budget officer who works under the supervision of the governor, the Governor's Office of Budget, Planning, and Policy (GOBPP) is required by statute to prepare and present a biennial budget to the legislature. Traditionally, the governor's plan is policy based. It presents objectives to be attained and a plan for achieving them. As a result of this dual arrangement, two budgets, one legislative in origin and the other executive, should be prepared every two years. Although Governor Perry submitted a separate budget for the first four biennia of his administration (2001–2007), in 2009, he proposed the same budget as the LBB. His base budget recommendations for the 2012–2013 biennium varied only minimally from that proposed by the LBB. Early in the legislative session, Governor Perry expressed his opposition to any tax increases or attempts to use money from the "rainy day" fund to balance the budget. The 82nd legislature responded by balancing the budget without raising taxes or dipping into the "rainy day" fund.

Budget Preparation Compilation of each budget begins with the development of a mission statement for Texas by the governor in cooperation with the LBB. That vision for the 2014–2015 biennia urged agency personnel to "continue to critically examine the role of state government by identifying core programs and activities necessary for the long-term economic health of our state."[19] Every even-numbered year, each operating agency requesting appropriated funds must submit a five-year strategic operating plan to the GOBPP and to the LBB. These plans must incorporate the state's mission and philosophy of government, along with quantifiable and measurable performance goals. Texas uses performance-based budgeting; thus, strategic plans provide a way for legislators to determine how well an agency is meeting its objectives.

Legislative Appropriation Request forms and instructions are prepared by the LBB. (See Figure 11.4 for a diagram of the budgeting process.) These

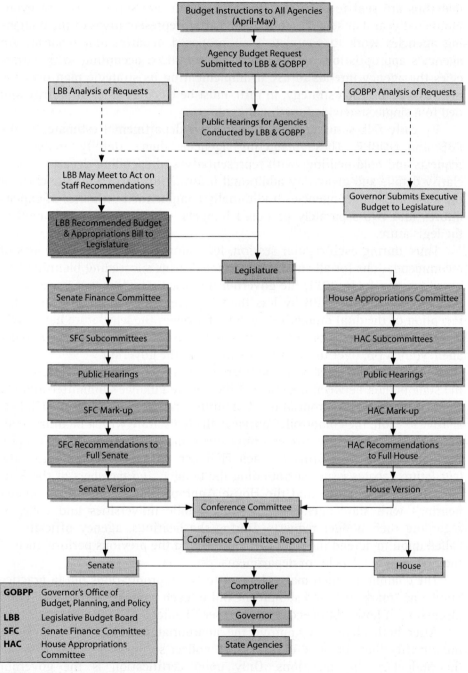

Figure 11.4 Texas Biennial Budget Cycle

Source: Senate Research Center, Budget 101: A Guide to the Budget Process in Texas (Austin: Senate Research Center, January 2011), **http://www.senate.state.tx.us/src/pdf/Budget_101-2011.pdf**.

materials are sent to each spending agency in late spring in every even-numbered year. For several months thereafter, representatives of the budgeting agencies work to complete their proposed departmental requests. An agency's appropriations request must be organized according to the strategies the agency intends to use in implementing its strategic plan over the next two years. Each strategy, in turn, must be listed in order of priority and tied to a single statewide functional goal.

By early fall, state agencies submit their departmental estimates to the LBB and GOBPP. These budgeting agencies then carefully analyze all requests and hold hearings with representatives of spending departments to clarify details and glean any additional information needed. At the close of the hearings, budget agencies traditionally compile their estimates of expenditures into two separately proposed budgets, which are then delivered to the legislature.

Thus, during each regular session, legislators normally face two sets of recommendations for all state expenditures for the succeeding biennium. As noted previously, in 2011, the governor proposed a budget that varied from that proposed by the LBB by less than 2 percent (or $3 billion). Since the inception of the **dual budgeting system**, however, the legislature has shown a marked preference for the recommendations of its own budget-making agency, the LBB, over those of the GOBPP and the governor.

By custom, the legislative chambers rotate responsibility for introducing the state budget between the chair of the Senate Finance Committee and the chair of the House Appropriations Committee. At the beginning of each legislative session, the comptroller provides the legislature with a biennial revenue estimate. The legislature can only spend in excess of this amount upon the approval of four-fifths of each chamber. In subsequent months, the legislature debates issues surrounding the budget, and members of the Senate Finance Committee and the House Appropriations Committee conduct hearings with state agencies, including public universities and colleges, regarding their budget requests. During the hearings, agency officials are called upon to defend their budget requests and the previous performance of their respective agencies or departments.

The committees then make changes to the appropriations bill (a practice known as "mark-up") and submit the bill to each chamber for a vote. (For a discussion of how a bill becomes a law, see Chapter 7, "The Legislature.")

After both chambers approve the appropriations bill, the comptroller must certify that the state of Texas will collect sufficient revenue to cover the budgetary appropriations. Only upon certification is the governor authorized to sign the budget. The governor has the power to veto any spending provision in the budget through the line-item veto (that is, rejecting only a particular expenditure in the budget). (See Chapter 8, "The Executive," for a discussion of the governor's line-item veto power.)

Budget approval does not guarantee that funds will remain available to an agency, including public colleges and universities. For example, in January 2010, Governor Perry, Lieutenant Governor David Dewhurst, and House Speaker Joe Straus jointly requested all state-funded entities to identify ways

dual budgeting system
The compilation of separate budgets by the legislative branch and the executive branch.

to reduce by 5 percent their portion of the FY2010 and FY2011 budgets funded by the state. Approximately $1.2 billion in reductions were approved (cuts amounting to 1.4 percent of state funding). Because the state's revenue collections exceeded expectations for FY2012, no such requests were made of state agencies; however, agencies were directed to reduce their initial requests for FY2014–2015 by 10 percent from the prior biennium's funding.

Budget Expenditures

Analysts of a government's fiscal policy classify expenditures in two ways: functional and objective. The services being purchased by government represent the state's functional budget. An objective analysis is used to report how money was spent. Figure 11.5 illustrates Texas's proposed functional expenditures for fiscal years 2012 and 2013. For more than five decades, functional expenditures have centered on three principal functions: public education, human services, and highway construction and maintenance (incorporated under business and economic development). The 2012–2013 biennial budget reflected the same priorities.

Budget Execution

In most state governments, the Governor's Office or an executive agency responsible to the governor supervises **budget execution** (the process by which a central authority in government oversees implementation of a spending plan approved by the legislative body). The governor of Texas and the Legislative Budget Board have limited power to prevent an agency from spending part of its appropriations, to transfer money from one agency to another, or to change the purpose for which an appropriation was made. Any modification the governor proposes must be made public, after which the LBB may ratify it, reject it, or recommend changes. If the board recommends changes

budget execution
The process whereby the governor and the Legislative Budget Board oversee (and, in some instances, modify) implementation of the spending plan authorized by the Texas legislature.

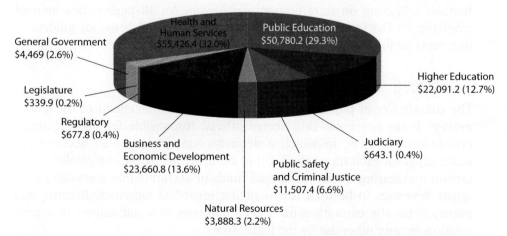

Figure 11.5 All Texas State Funds Appropriations by Function for Fiscal Years 2012–2013 (in millions).

Source: House Research Organization, Texas Budget Highlights: Fiscal 2012–13, State Finance Report No. 82-5 (Austin: House Research Organization, December 2011), **http://www.hro.house.state.tx.us/pdf/focus/highlights82.pdf**.

in the governor's proposals, the chief executive may accept or reject the board's suggestions.

The proper functioning of Texas's budget execution system requires a coordinated effort among the state's political leadership. The board met once in 2010. It held no meetings in 2011, though board members did receive updates of revenue collections from the comptroller's office. In August 2012, the board held a public meeting to review the financial condition of the state in compliance with a law passed by the 82nd legislature.

Purchasing

Agencies of state government must make purchases through or under the supervision of the Texas Procurement and Support Services, a division of the Office of the Comptroller of Public Accounts. Depending on the cost of an item, agency personnel may be required to obtain competitive bids. This division places greater emphasis on serving state agencies for which it purchases goods than on controlling what they purchase. It also provides agencies with administrative support services, such as mail distribution and messenger services. In addition, the division negotiates contracts with airlines, rental car agencies, and hotels to obtain lower prices for personnel traveling on state business. These services are also available to participating local governments. The seven-member Council on Competitive Government, chaired by the governor, is required to determine exactly what kinds of services each agency currently provides that might be supplied at less cost by private industry or another state agency.

Facilities

A seven-member appointed board oversees the Texas Facilities Commission. This agency provides property management services for state facilities, including the Texas State Cemetery. In addition, agency personnel manage football tailgating on state property in Austin. An 18-page policy manual available on the Internet describes the procedures and behavior guidelines that must be followed in tailgating on state property.

Accounting

The comptroller of public accounts oversees the management of the state's money. Texas law holds this elected official responsible for maintaining a double-entry system, in which a debit account and a credit account are maintained for each transaction. Other statutes narrow the comptroller's discretion by creating numerous special funds or accounts that essentially designate revenues to be used for financing identified activities. Because this money is usually earmarked for special purposes, it is not subject to appropriation for any other use by the legislature.

Major accounting tasks of the Comptroller's Office include preparing warrants (checks) used to pay state obligations, acknowledging receipts from various state revenue sources, and recording information concerning receipts and expenditures in ledgers and other account books. Contrary to usual business practice, state accounts are set up on a cash basis rather than an accrual basis. In cash accounting, expenditures are entered when the money is actually paid rather than when the obligation is incurred. In times of fiscal crisis, such as the 2012–2013 biennium, the practice of creating obligations in one fiscal year and paying them in the next allows a budget to appear balanced. Unfortunately, it complicates the task of fiscal planning by failing to reflect an accurate picture of current finances at any given moment. The comptroller issues monthly and annual reports that include general statements of revenues and expenditures. These reports allocate spending based on the object of expenditures that are the goods, supplies, and services used to provide government programs. Salaries, wages, and employment benefits for state employees consistently lead all objective expenditures.

Auditing

State accounts are audited (examined) under direct supervision of the state auditor. This official is appointed by and serves at the will of the Legislative Audit Committee, a six-member committee comprised of the Lieutenant Governor; the Speaker of the House of Representatives; one appointed member of the Senate; and the chairs of the Senate Finance Committee, the House Appropriations Committee, and the House Ways and Means Committee. The auditor may be removed by the committee at any time without the privilege of a hearing.

With the assistance of approximately 200 staff members, the auditor provides random checks of financial records and transactions after expenditures. Auditing involves reviewing the records and accounts of disbursing officers and custodians of all state funds. Another important duty of the auditor is to examine the activities of each state agency to evaluate the quality of its services, determine whether duplication of effort exists, and recommend changes. The State Auditor's Office is also responsible for reviewing performance measures that agencies include in their strategic plans to ensure that accurate reporting procedures are in place. The agency conducts audits in order of priority by reviewing activities most subject to potential or perceived abuse first. Its stated mission is to provide elected officials with information to improve accountability in state government.

☑ Learning Check 11.3 (Answers on p. 484)

1. What is a fiscal year?
2. Texas has a dual budgeting system. What does this mean?
3. Who has the authority to transfer money from one agency to another after a budget has been approved?

★ Future Demands

LO4
LO5

Elected officials have worked to keep taxing levels low. As a result, Texas has also kept its per capita spending levels among the lowest in the nation. Some observers believe that this limited funding is merely deferring problems in the areas of education, social services, and the state's infrastructure. In addition, public safety concerns and homeland security demands strain the state's human and fiscal resources. A growing population, additional social service needs, an outdated infrastructure, changing views of the role of government, federal mandates, and a weakening economy are problems facing Texans, their government, and its agencies in the 21st century.

Public Education

The state, together with local school districts, is responsible for providing a basic education for all Texas school-age children. Public education accounted for almost 29 percent of the state's projected expenditures (approximately $25 billion per year) for the 2012–2013 biennium. That amount of state funding reportedly accounted for less than 50 percent of the actual cost of public education. School district officials expected to cover the remaining balance with local taxes and federal grants.

This hybrid arrangement may explain some of the difficulties in operating and financing Texas's schools. Is public education a national issue

Points to Ponder

- In 2010–2011, Texas ranked 31st in the nation in average teacher salaries—$48,638 per year (Texas) versus $55,623 (national average).*
- In 2010–2011, Texas ranked 42nd in public school student per capita expenditures—$8,751 (Texas) versus $10,770 (national average).*
- Slightly more than 1 in 5 (21.9 percent) Texas students who were in the eighth grade from 1996–1998 held a postsecondary certificate or degree 11 years later. Nationally, more than 1 in 4 (29.3 percent) students earned a postsecondary degree or certificate 11 years after entering eighth grade.**

Sources: *National Education Association; *Rankings and Estimates,* **http:// www.nea.org/assets/docs/NEA_Rankings_And_Estimates_FINAL_20120209.pdf.**
** National Center for Higher Education Management Systems, "A New Measure of Educational Success in Texas: Tracking the Success of 8th Graders into and through College" (Houston: Houston Endowment, 2012), **http://www.houstonendowment .org/Assets/PublicWebsite/Documents/News/measureofsuccess.pdf.**

deserving of federal funding, attention, and standards, similar to the inter-state highway system, in which the federal government pays for a road system that connects all parts of the nation? Or should education be a state function, similar to the state's role in building and maintaining state highways so that all Texans are entitled to drive on the same quality of paved roads? Or is public education a local responsibility, more akin to city streets so that towns with more money have better-quality streets than their poorer neighbors? Although education appears to integrate all three levels of government—national, state, and local—into one system, confusion and conflict surround the fiscal responsibility and role of each in the state's educational system. When the Texas legislature created the Property Tax Relief Fund in 2006, state leaders predicted that by 2008, state funding would provide at least 50 percent of public school funding. Through 2013, however, the state's share of funding for public schools remained at less than 50 percent.

Sources of Public School Funding Texas state government has struggled with financing public education for more than 40 years. Table 11.1 provides a history of relevant court decisions, state constitutional provisions, and legislative responses that have established funding sources and shaped the ways in which those sources are administered. In promoting public education, Texas state government has usually confined its activity to establishing minimum standards and providing basic levels of financial support. School districts and state government share the cost of three elements—salaries, transportation, and operating expenses. Local funding of school systems relies primarily on the market value of taxable real estate within the school district, because local schools raise their share primarily through property taxes. Average daily attendance of pupils in the district, types of students (for example, elementary, secondary, or disabled), and local economic conditions determine the state's share.

In 1949, the Texas legislature passed the Gilmer-Aiken Law, intended to provide a minimum level of state support for every public school student in Texas. This law established the Minimum Foundation Program (now called the Foundation School Program). School districts also raise local revenue through property taxes to fund programs beyond the minimum level of services financed by the Foundation School Program. (For a discussion of school district taxing procedures, see Chapter 3, "Local Government.")

Money to finance the Foundation School Program is allocated to each school system from the Foundation School Fund. This fund receives its money from four sources:

- the Available School Fund (revenue received from a variety of state taxes and income from the Permanent School Fund)
- the School Taxing Ability Protection Fund (money appropriated by the legislature to offset revenue reduction incurred by rural school districts)
- the Texas Lottery
- the General Revenue Fund

In 2006, the legislature created the Property Tax Relief Fund. At the same time, the legislature changed the law to increase the businesses to

Table 11.1 History of Texas Public School Finance in the Courts

Case	Year	Question	Decision	Legislative Response
Rodriguez v. San Antonio	1971	Does Texas's school funding system violate the Equal Protection Clause?	No, because education is not a federally protected right.	None
Edgewood v. Kirby	1989	Is Texas's school funding system "efficient" as required by the Texas constitution?	No, a 9-to-1 difference in per-student funding is inefficient. An efficient system must produce "similar revenue for similar effort."	Decided to study the issue
Edgewood v. Kirby	1991	Is Texas's school funding system "efficient"?	No	Authorized county education districts
Carrollton-Farmers Branch v. Edgewood	1992	Do countywide education districts create a statewide property tax, a practice prohibited by the Texas Constitution?	Yes	Established a program to recapture wealth from property-rich districts to redistribute to property-poor districts (also known as the "Robin Hood" plan)
Edgewood v. Meno	1995	Is a recapture program constitutional?	Yes, because it provides funding for a "general diffusion of knowledge."	None
West Orange-Cove v. Neeley	2005	Does the need for most districts to tax at the maximum allowable tax rate create a statewide property tax?	Yes	Lowered the property tax by establishing the Property Tax Relief Fund at the state level
Multiple cases involving more than 500 school districts, parents, the Texas Association of Business, and the Texas Charter School Association.	2012	Is Texas's school funding system "efficient"? Does the need for most districts to tax at the maximum allowable tax rate create a statewide property tax? Is the Texas public school system efficient?	Not yet determined	Joint interim committee appointed to study school finance

Sources: Compiled from Albert H. Kauffman, "The Texas School Finance Litigation Saga: Great Progress, Then Near Death by a Thousand Cuts," *St. Mary's Law Review* 40, (2008): 511–579; Morgan Smith, "A Guide to the Texas School Finance Lawsuits," *Texas Tribune*, February 29, 2012, **http://www.texastribune.org/texas-education/public-education/how-navigate-texas-school-finance-lawsuits/**.

which the franchise tax applies and the way in which the tax is calculated. This new account receives that portion of the franchise tax that exceeds what would have been collected under the previous law. Legislators also increased the tobacco sales tax. That increase, plus a portion of the sales tax increase on tobacco products passed by the 81st legislature in 2009, also provides money for the Property Tax Relief Fund. In addition, taxes paid on the presumptive market value of used vehicles provide some revenue. Amounts in the fund must be used to reduce school district property taxes and to equalize funding among school districts.

Funding Equalization As Table 11.1 indicates, a continuing controversy surrounding public school finance in Texas has been court-mandated funding equalization. The legislatively enacted wealth equalization plan, labeled the **"Robin Hood" plan** by its critics, requires wealthier districts (those with a tax base equal to $319,500 or more per student) to transfer money to poorer school districts. These wealthier school districts are known as "Chapter 41 districts," in reference to the Education Code chapter that designates them. Despite court challenges, the "Robin Hood" plan has been found to be constitutional. One-third of the state-administered Property Tax Relief Fund may be used to equalize funding among districts and, thus, reduce funding demands on "Chapter 41 districts."

At the heart of the dispute regarding how to achieve equalized funding is whether all students in the state are entitled to receive the same quality of education. The Texas Education Agency created a system to measure educational quality by reviewing characteristics such as test score results, dropout rates, and completion rates. Districts that consistently fail to meet acceptable levels of performance risk losing accreditation and funding. State accreditation standards require districts to meet academic and financial accountability performance standards. Loss of accreditation results in a loss of state funding and closure. In addition, individual campuses that are rated academically unacceptable must achieve an academically acceptable rating within four years. Failure to do so results in the school's being closed or being transferred to a nonprofit organization or another school district.

Although court decisions have granted Texas students the right to equal educational opportunities, not all students enter school equally prepared to succeed. Frequently, the parents of economically disadvantaged students have been unable to offer their children the same learning opportunities as those provided by more affluent parents. To make up for this difference in preparation, both the state and federal governments provide additional funding to help school districts equalize learning outcomes for impoverished students. The number of economically disadvantaged students enrolled in Texas's public schools, however, continues to increase. In 2011, the Texas Education Agency reported that approximately 60 percent of all public school students in the Lone Star State were eligible for free or reduced-price lunches, which is the measurement used to determine whether children are poor. According to the Center for Public Policy Priorities, in some school districts, the percentage of economically disadvantaged students was in excess of 90 percent.

"Robin Hood" plan
A plan for equalizing financial support for school districts by transferring tax money from rich districts to poor districts.

Many public officials and education experts have expressed concern that educating an increasing number of economically disadvantaged students increases the cost of public education. Yet, the 82nd legislature reduced state funding of public education by more than $5.4 billion for the 2012–2013 biennium, despite predictions that school enrollments would increase by 160,000 students during the same period. Since the inception of the Foundation School Program, no legislature had failed to fund student growth. In March 2012, the Texas Education Agency reported that more than 25,000 school personnel had lost their jobs as a result of budget cuts, including almost 11,000 teachers. Parents, teachers, and sympathetic legislators joined in several demonstrations at the Capitol to protest the state funding reductions. Although providing a forum for people to express their dissatisfaction, the demonstrations did not result in any changes to the budgetary decisions.

Public Higher Education

The state's public higher-education institutions also faced reduced state funding for the 2012–2013 biennium. Like the public schools, the public higher-education system endures the dual pressures of increasing enrollment and declining state support. The Texas Higher Education Coordinating Board's Closing the Gaps initiative requires all public institutions to participate actively in increasing the number of Texas college students by 630,000 over year 2000 enrollment levels by the year 2015. At a time when Texas legislators, as well as other state legislatures across the nation, work to balance state budgets by reducing funding to higher education, the Closing the Gaps initiative, if successful, will place additional demands on colleges and universities for faculty, staff, and facilities. Furthermore, the success of this effort depends on more economically disadvantaged students enrolling in institutions of higher education.

Points to Ponder

- Students at public universities who attempt more than 30 credit hours above those required for a baccalaureate degree in their major (typically 120 credit hours) can be charged out-of-state tuition rates (on average, a difference of approximately $8,000 per year). Hours attempted include any courses in which a student remains enrolled after the 12th class day.
- Students who earn a baccalaureate degree within four years of enrollment (five years for some programs like architecture and engineering) and attempt no more than three credit hours beyond the number required for the degree are eligible for a $1,000 tuition rebate upon graduation.
- To encourage students to graduate in a timely way, HB 3025, passed by the 82nd legislature, requires students seeking an associate or baccalaureate degree to file a degree plan upon the completion of 45 credit hours.

State financial aid, which is already insufficient to meet demand, was reduced further by the 82nd legislature. To solve some of these problems, the state has developed financial rewards and punishments, rewarding those who move quickly through their academic programs and punishing those who dawdle. Even these initiatives sustained budget reductions in 2011. Increasing enrollments and low levels of state funding have meant that students are bearing more of the cost of their educations by paying higher tuition and taking out more and larger loans.

In recent years, the governor, the legislature, and the Texas Higher Education Coordinating Board have argued for a change in the method of calculating state funding of colleges and universities. Rather than basing state appropriations on the number of students enrolled on the 12th class day of each semester, outcomes-based funding plans link the amount of state funding to the number of students who successfully complete courses and the number of students an institution graduates (and, if a community college, transfers to a university). Governor Perry addressed the issue in his State of the State speech to the 82nd legislature. He called on legislators to shift most funding to outcomes-based budgeting because "Texans deserve college graduation for their hard-earned tax dollars, not just college enrollment."[20] The 82nd legislature complied by passing HB 9, requiring the Texas Higher Education Coordinating Board to develop an outcomes-based formula for funding the state's public universities and colleges. Proponents maintain that the emphasis on successful outcomes will improve higher education. Opponents argue that such a funding structure will reduce the amount of financial support institutions receive and will have a negative effect on students who need the most assistance.[21] Outcomes-based funding is consistent with Governor Rick Perry's view that higher education should more closely follow business models, as discussed in the CourseReader Assignment.

CourseReader ASSIGNMENTS

Log in to www.cengagebrain.com and open CourseReader to access the reading:

Texas Governor Thinks of Colleges as Businesses; Regents Promote His Agenda, to Faculty Members' Chagrin
Katherine Mangan

Governor Rick Perry has operated under the assumption that colleges can be viewed as businesses. In this sense, at times he has aimed more to make money than to educate students. Efficiency takes precedence over other worthy goals, and academic stars receive competitive salaries. This article examines Perry's mind-set and considers possible ramifications.

1. What are examples of Governor Perry's recommended reforms that make universities and colleges more transparent to students?

2. To what aspects of Governor Perry's proposals do professors object?

The 82nd legislature, meeting in 2011, reduced state appropriations to universities and community colleges by more than 9 percent from their original funding levels for the 2010–2011 biennium. Student financial aid benefits were reduced by an even larger percentage of approximately 15 percent. Table 11.2 provides an analysis of these funding decisions and their effect on Texas students. Reductions in financial aid occurred as the state decreased state funding to higher-education institutions. Many colleges and universities offset a portion of these reductions with increases in student tuition.

Community College Funding State financing of public community or junior colleges is currently based on a "contact hour of instruction" rate for vocational-technical and academic courses. This rate is determined by calculating the hours of contact between an instructor and students. In addition, these two-year institutions use local property tax revenues, tuition, fees, gifts, and state and federal grants to finance their operations. Contact-hour funding for community colleges remains significantly below 1998 funding levels. Since that year, however, costs have increased. This gap in funding has been financed

Table 11.2 Effect of Budget Reductions by the 82nd Legislature on State-funded Student Financial Aid Programs

Grant	Funding 2010–2011	Students Served	Funding 2012–2013	Students Served	Students Affected
Texas Armed Services Scholarship	$ 1.75 million	80	$ 1.75 million	80	No change
Texas Education Opportunity Grant	$ 24 million	9,900	$ 24 million	9,900	No change
Work Study	$ 15 million	4,400	$ 15 million	4,400	No change
TEXAS Grants	$ 622 million	106,000	$559.5 million	77,000	Decrease 29,000
Texas Equalization Grant	$211.8 million	30,375*	$168.8 million	24,300	Decrease 6,075
B-on-Time Interest-free Loans	$157.1 million	12,960*	$111.9 million	9,200	Decrease 3,760
Top 10 Percent Scholarship	$ 51.5 million	21,040*	$ 39.6 million	16,200	Decrease 4,840

*Estimate based on percentage in program reduction in dollars.

Source: Compiled from Office of External Affairs, Texas Higher Education Coordinating Board, *Summary of Higher Education Legislation: 82nd Texas Legislature,* (Austin: Texas Higher Education Coordinating Board, July 2011), **http://www.tfaonline.net/Legislative SummaryReport82ndFINAL.pdf**.

by students and local taxpayers. Reductions in state support have been so severe that the president of Vernon College (near Wichita Falls) reported that he was identifying ways to fund college operations without any state revenue.

University Funding Texas's state universities and the Texas State Technical College System obtain basic financing from legislated biennial appropriations from the General Revenue Fund. They also obtain money from fees other than tuition, such as student service and computer use fees (which are deposited in the General Revenue Fund), auxiliary services income (for example, rent for campus housing and food service fees), grants, gifts, and special building funds. The University of Texas and the Texas A&M University systems share revenue from the Permanent University Fund (PUF) investments (approximately $575 million in 2011), with the University of Texas System receiving two-thirds of the money and the Texas A&M University System receiving one-third.

Tuition Deregulation In late 2002, the University of Texas System led an effort to eliminate legislative caps on tuition and fees. According to university officials, funding limitations threatened the University of Texas at Austin's ability to remain a premier research institution. Despite fears that escalating tuition and fees would limit access to higher education for Texas's lower-income students, the proposal became law in 2003.

Public community colleges and universities quickly moved to raise tuition. Both the dollar increase in tuition and the rate of increase have been dramatic. By the fall of 2011, universities had raised tuition rates and fees approximately 90 percent above their 2003 levels. In addition, state support of universities and community colleges declined during that same period. Students' concerns about rising tuition and the ways some students are addressing the issue are discussed in the "Students in Action" feature.

Texas Tomorrow Funds The Texas Guaranteed Tuition Plan and Tomorrow's College Investment Plan comprise the Texas Tomorrow Funds. The Tuition Plan provides a way for parents to save for their children's education and to lock in the cost of tuition and fees at the state's public colleges and universities. Tuition increases have also affected these programs. The Texas Tomorrow Fund is backed by the full faith and credit of the state of Texas. According to the fund's provisions, approximately 90,000 students must be educated at an anticipated expense to the state of $2.1 billion. As of 2010 (the last year for which public information is available), the fund had an unfunded liability of $600 million, an amount the state would be required to finance from general revenue. Actuarial projections, an analysis that estimates annual revenue versus cost, indicate the state will be forced to supplement the fund as early as 2015. Because of rapid tuition increases, the state closed the fund to new participants in 2003. The fund reopened as the Texas Tuition Promise Fund in 2008, though at much higher rates. Most important, the Texas Tuition Promise Fund is not guaranteed by the full faith and credit of the state of Texas. College living costs can still be covered by investment in Tomorrow's College Investment Plan.

How Do We Compare...in Tuition and Fees?

Average Tuition and Fees for Academic Year 2011–2012

Most Populous U.S. States	Private University	Public University	Public Community College	U.S. States Bordering Texas	Private University	Public University	Public Community College
California	$35,766	$9,022	$1,119	Arkansas	$18,250	$6,646	$2,661
Florida	$26,494	$5,626	$3,006	Louisiana	$30,024	$5,123	$2,452
New York	$33,151	$6,213	$4,253	New Mexico	$36,156	$5,457	$1,498
Texas	**$26,828**	**$8,078**	**$2,049**	Oklahoma	$22,415	$6,059	$3,043

Source: Compiled from information available through "Joe Biden Claims College Tuition Rose 300 Percent over 20 Years," *PolitiFact Check Florida,* **http://www.politifact.com/florida/statements/2012/feb/09/joe-biden/joe-biden-college-tuition-rose-300-percent-over/**.
Note: Tuition rates are for in-state students at public universities and community colleges.

State Grants Rather than give money directly to colleges and universities, legislators across the country have preferred to give students the funding and allow them to select the institution at which the funds will be spent. The **TEXAS Grants Program** (Toward Excellence, Access, and Success) provides grant funding to eligible students to pay all tuition and fees at any public college or university in the state. To qualify, a student must be a Texas resident, enroll in college within 16 months of high school graduation, show financial need, and have no convictions for a crime involving a controlled substance. The student must maintain a 2.5 grade point average in college to continue to qualify. At state 2012–2013 biennium funding levels, only 30 percent of eligible students received grants. The Teach for Texas program provides loan repayment assistance for eligible teachers. The 82nd legislature also reduced funding for this program in 2011. Information about both of these programs is available from the Texas Higher Education Coordinating Board.

Public Assistance

Enrolling more students in higher education is one way in which Texas's political leaders hope to address the issue of poverty. Income disparity between the wealthiest 20 percent of Texans and the poorest 20 percent widened throughout the first decade of the 21st century. A higher percentage of Texans lack health insurance than residents of any other state. The number of children without coverage also ranks as the highest in the nation, in both percentage and sheer numbers. Poverty levels remain above the national average (18.4 percent for Texas versus 15.1 percent for the nation as a whole) and are even more pronounced for young children (27

TEXAS Grants Program "Toward Excellence, Access, and Success" is a college financial assistance program that provides funding for qualifying students.

Students in Action

"Wealth should never determine what university you go to. It should be the work you do."
— *Ryan Lofton Payne*

Education has always been a part of Ryan Payne's life. The son of high school teachers, he never doubted the importance of a college diploma. Once he enrolled in college, however, he watched the price of his education increase every year. Some of his friends struggled with paying higher tuition rates, and others dropped out because they could no longer afford the cost of school. To Ryan, the image of the state's public universities as institutions of higher education was being replaced by an image of the universities as five-star resorts— "places where you fly in, stay as long as you can afford to, and then go earn some more money

until you can afford to return." On April 15, 2009, Ryan Payne had the opportunity to share his views when he testified to the House Higher Education Committee in support of the tuition regulation bill proposed by Representative Patrick Rose (D-Dripping Springs). The bill did not pass.

Ryan advises students, "Don't be afraid to get involved. In the end, politics is just people talking."

Source: Interview with Ryan Payne, January 18, 2010.

(Monkey Business Images/Shutterstock.com)

percent for Texas versus 22 percent for the nation as a whole). According to the Center for Public Policy Priorities, an advocacy group for low- and moderate-income people, access to public assistance benefits is more restricted in Texas than in most other states because of eligibility requirements and lower levels of support.[22]

Increasing health-care costs present significant challenges to state government. The percentage of the total state budget dedicated to health and human services (32 percent in FY2012–FY2013) is below the amount of state funding available to education (42 percent in FY2012–FY2013). In 2014, the provisions of the Patient Protection and Affordable Care Act (the federal health-care reform law) will further expand the number of people eligible for Medicaid benefits. State officials argue that this additional burden will prove catastrophic to state finance. The U.S. Supreme Court agreed in the case of *National Federation of Independent Business v. Sebelius*, 567 U.S. _____(2012). Noting that federal Medicaid funding constituted more than 20 percent of most states' budgets, Chief Justice John Roberts described the federal government's attempt to withhold funding for states that did not expand coverage as "a gun to the head." The court found this level of coercion to be unconstitutional. Whether Texas will expand Medicaid coverage had not been determined at the time of publication. The cost of Medicaid and the **Children's Health Insurance Program (CHIP)** (an insurance program with minimal premiums for children from low-income families) frequently exceed budget allocations, even though many eligible individuals are not included. Coverage for children remains a concern for lawmakers. Although almost three million children were enrolled in one of these two programs in 2011, another 1.2 million young Texans remained uninsured. Some observers suggest that up to one-half of uninsured children qualify for Medicaid or CHIP.

Denying benefits to eligible children lowers the state's obligation to pay for benefits, but at what cost? The federal government funds almost 60 cents of every dollar paid for Medicaid services. In addition, the federal portion of CHIP expenditures is approximately 72 cents of every dollar paid for medical services. One study found that only 58 percent of uninsured children could be classified as healthy, whereas 69 percent of those with some sort of public insurance coverage met a healthy standard. It appears likely that these unhealthy children will continue to have health issues as adults.

In an attempt to provide at least minimal insurance coverage to more children, in 2009, the 81st legislature created a third program targeting uninsured young Texans. **ChildLINK**, administered by the Attorney General's Child Support Program, purchases insurance coverage with money paid by noncustodial parents who have been ordered to pay medical support for their children. Proponents argued that this program will ultimately provide insurance for an additional 200,000 children. Opponents maintained that the coverage had fewer benefits than Medicaid or CHIP.

Much of the cost and care burden for uninsured residents, both children and adults, has shifted to local governments, hospitals, and the insured. Counties and hospitals must subsidize unreimbursed costs for treating the uninsured by charging higher rates to the insured, which translates into higher insurance premiums, as well as higher county property taxes. Analysts project a continuing increase in indigent health-care costs in the years to come. The ability of local entities to meet the social service needs of the state's low-income residents is one of the key challenges of the 21st century.

Other Needs

In addition to demands for education, health, and human services, Texans look to state government to meet other needs. The state of Texas has a responsibility to provide an infrastructure for its residents, including both highway and water systems. Public safety concerns are important to those who live here. Furthermore, federal mandates regarding homeland security and the obligations of a state with a 1,248-mile long border with Mexico require both human and financial resources.

Transportation Consistent with Texas's pay-as-you-go budget system is its pay-as-you-ride system of financing construction and maintenance of roads and highways. Historically, Texas roads have been financed through a combination of motor fuel taxes, motor vehicle registration fees, and the Federal Highway Trust Fund, to which certain federal highway user taxes

Children's Health Insurance Program (CHIP)
A program that provides medical insurance for minimal premiums to children from low-income families.

ChildLINK
A program administered by the Texas Attorney General's Child Support Program in which medical support payments paid by noncustodial parents are used to provide insurance for the parent's children.

are allocated. A 2011 study by the Center for Transportation Research reported that the state would require more than $315 billion to meet its roadway needs through 2031. Authors of the same study noted that only $160 billion was available under current funding strategies.[23]

As increases in construction costs have exceeded funding, much of this expense has been transferred to users in the form of tolls. The reality of financing new highway construction with tolls was perhaps best expressed by former Texas Transportation Commission chair Ric Williamson, when he described the policy as, "It's the no road, the toll road, or the slow road."[24] Increasing costs have required borrowing concessions, as authorized by Texas voters by constitutional amendment. The Texas Mobility Fund allows the state to issue bonds and use the proceeds for road construction. Proponents argued that the bonds would be repaid from tolls collected for roadway usage. Unfortunately, another victim of the state's declining economic condition was toll road revenues. Projections of toll road revenues exceeded actual collections by more than $100 million from 2009 to 2011; as a result, Texas taxpayers, many of whom did not use toll roads, subsidized these roadways with taxpayer dollars. In 2011, the Lone Star State spent more to service outstanding debt than it did for the construction of new roads.

Water The Texas drought that began in 2007 and relented only briefly in 2010 has highlighted the state's water needs. In 2012, the Texas Water Development Board issued its state water plan. Six years in development, the plan had dire predictions for the state if efforts were not made to increase the state's water supply in the coming years. The projected cost to provide adequate water supplies for anticipated population growth was $53 billion. If the state took no action, in the event of a significant drought, the report estimated annual losses of $12 billion in income and 115,000 jobs.[25]

Public Safety Programs Historically, responsibility for protecting persons and property and providing other public safety programs was delegated to local governments. Today, various state agencies share the responsibility. The Department of Public Safety, for example, furnishes routine highway patrol functions, assists local law enforcement authorities in handling major crimes, and coordinates statewide efforts against lawlessness. For confinement of convicted felons, the Texas Department of Criminal Justice operates a system of prison units and state felony jails. (See Chapter 10, "Laws, Courts, and Justice.")

After years of increasing the number of prison beds and passing laws that lengthened prison sentences, the legislature recognized the economic realities of these policies in the 21st century. State legislators now closely review the economic impact of proposed legislation to define new crimes or enhance punishment for existing felonies. An economic analysis convinced a majority of legislators that in many situations, the cost of housing a felon for a longer term exceeded any potential benefit. With limited resources, prioritization became critical. In addition, the legislature increased resources for programs designed to reduce recidivism. These efforts included providing greater access to substance-abuse treatment programs and making counselors available to assist released inmates with reentry into their local communities. The programs have reduced the recidivism rate.

Homeland Security Since September 11, 2001, federal, state, and local officials throughout the United States have given more attention to preparations for preventing or coping with terrorist actions. Most of the impetus for homeland security derives from the federal government. Yet, the states bear much of the cost and must perform and finance these unfunded mandates. In addition to securing the Texas–Mexico border against potential terrorist threats, Texas law enforcement officials have responded to escalating violence in the area, much of it attributed to warring Mexican drug cartels. The 2012–2013 biennium budget included approximately $220 million for border security. As the United States continues to operate in an environment of heightened threat and as illegal drug use in this country continues to provide a market for drug traffickers, Texans can anticipate increasing demands on their state budget for protection.

Natural disasters, such as hurricanes and the wildfires that ravaged the state in 2011, will also add cost. Because of pressure on the national government to reduce its debt, residents of the Lone Star State will continue to receive less monetary support from the federal government to cover these expenses.

☑ Learning Check 11.4   (Answers on p. 484)

1. True or False: Since its inception, the Property Tax Relief Fund has been adequate to meet funding needs for public education.
2. True or False: Tuition deregulation resulted in lower tuition at the state's public colleges and universities.
3. What three programs provide health insurance for Texas children?

★ Conclusion

Economists suggest that a full recovery from the global economic crisis that erupted in 2008 may take as long as 20 years. (Even though the Great Recession officially ended in June 2009, this shift only marked the beginning of an economic recovery.) Before the state achieves a full recovery, Texas's governmental agencies will be forced to respond to the competing stresses of increasing demand and decreasing revenue. Doing more with less will be critical. In addition, taxpayers want better (at least from a business perspective) results for their money. This view is reflected in Governor Rick Perry's 2012 announcement of his Texas Budget Compact, when he observed: "[W]hether tax receipts are coming in higher than expected or lower than expected, we must always look to cut expenses first. We must always do everything we can to get the most possible out of every single dollar we get from the taxpayers." He concluded, "I believe we can continue to be a beacon to those seeking the freedom and liberty to follow their dreams and find success." Whether the Lone Star State can sustain this image in the years ahead remains to be seen.

Chapter Summary

- Because of the effect of the global economic recession and population growth, elected officials have struggled to balance the state's budget in recent years.
- Texas has one of the most regressive state tax systems in the United States because the Lone Star State relies so heavily on the sales tax and has no state income tax. Inability to tax most Internet purchases and failure to tax many services cost the state significant revenue.
- Rather than raise taxes, Texas's elected officials often increase fees, fines, and other assessments.
- Texas operates with a pay-as-you-go budget.
- Each biennium, the Legislative Budget Board and the Governor's Office of Budget, Planning, and Policy are required to prepare proposed budgets. Tax collection, investment of the state's surplus funds, and overseeing management of the state's money are responsibilities of the comptroller of public accounts. The state auditor is responsible for examining all state accounts to ensure honesty and efficiency in agency spending of state funds.
- State revenue pays for services to Texas's residents. Most state money pays for public education (including higher education) and public assistance.
- Higher numbers of economically disadvantaged students enrolled in the state's public schools will likely increase the cost of public education.
- Texans who use services such as higher education and roads now must provide a greater portion of their funding.
- Unfunded mandates and reduced federal funding have increased spending at the state level.

Key Terms

fiscal policy, p. 444
"rainy day" fund, p. 445
tax, p. 446
regressive tax, p. 446
progressive tax, p. 446
service-sector, p. 447
fee, p. 448
balanced budget, p. 448

General Revenue Fund, p. 449
dedicated fund, p. 449
general sales tax, p. 451
selective sales tax, p. 453
sin tax, p. 453
franchise tax, p. 454
payroll tax, p. 454
severance tax, p. 455

grant-in-aid, p. 458
general obligation bond, p. 461
revenue bond, p. 461
budget, p. 462
Legislative Budget Board (LBB), p. 462
dual budgeting system, p. 466
budget execution, p. 467
"Robin Hood" plan, p. 473
TEXAS Grants Program, p. 478
Children's Health Insurance Program (CHIP),
  p. 479
ChildLINK, p. 480

Learning Check Answers

11.1

1. Texas requires a balanced budget, favors low taxes, and spends at low-to-moderate levels.
2. Texas has a regressive tax system, which means that poor people pay a higher percentage of their incomes in taxes than do wealthier residents.
3. False. Dedicated funds may be held in the state treasury to give the appearance of a balanced budget.

11.2

1. The general sales tax is the state's largest source of tax revenue.
2. Lottery profits must be spent on public education.
3. The "rainy day" fund is to be used when the state faces an economic crisis.

11.3

1. A fiscal year is a budget year. In Texas, it begins on September 1 and ends on August 31 of the following calendar year.
2. A state with a dual budgeting system requires both the executive branch and the legislative branch to prepare and submit proposed budgets to the legislature. In Texas, both the governor and the Legislative Budget Board submit proposed budgets.
3. The governor must request a transfer from one agency to another. That transfer must be approved by the Legislative Budget Board.

11.4

1. False. The Property Tax Relief Fund has consistently underperformed and has not yet provided adequate funding for public education.
2. False. Since tuition deregulation, student tuition has risen an average of 90 percent over 2003 levels at public colleges and universities.
3. Health insurance is provided to Texas children through Medicaid, CHIP, and Child-LINK.

Discussion Questions

1. What services should Texas's government provide to the state's residents?
2. What are the advantages and disadvantages of a pay-as-you-go balanced budget requirement?
3. Should goods sold on the Internet be taxed?
4. What is the procedure for developing and approving a state budget?
5. What are some benefits and some disadvantages of the "Robin Hood" plan for public schools?
6. Who should pay more for higher education—the state's taxpayers or students?

Internet Resources

Center for Public Policy Priorities:
http://www.cppp.org

Legislative Budget Board:
http://www.lbb.state.tx.us

Office of the Texas Comptroller of Public Accounts: **http://www.window.state.tx.us**

Texas Education Agency:
http://www.tea.state.tx.us

Texas Higher Education Coordinating Board:
http://www.thecb.state.tx.us

Texas Public Policy Foundation:
http://www.texaspolicy.com

Texas Lottery Commission:
http://www.txlottery.org

Texas State Auditor's Office:
http://www.sao.state.tx.us

Notes

1. United States Department of Labor, "Regional and State Unemployment (Annual) News Release," February 27, 2009, http://www.bls.gov/news.release/srgune.htm.
2. Susan Combs, *Biennial Revenue Estimate: 2012–2013 Biennium* (Austin: Office of the Comptroller of Public Accounts, January 2011), http://www.window.state.tx.us/taxbud/bre2012/96-402_BRE_2012-13.pdf.
3. House Research Organization, *Texas Budget Highlights: Fiscal 2012–13*, State Finance Report No. 82-5 (Austin: House Research Organization, December 2011), http://www.hro.house.state.tx.us/pdf/focus/highlights82.pdf.
4. Rick Perry, "An Opportunity to Strengthen the Texas Budget Process," April 24, 2012, http://governor.state.tx.us/news/editorial/17190/.
5. Milton Friedman, *Dollars and Deficits: Inflation, Monetary Policy, and Balance of Payments* (Saddle Brook, N.J.: Prentice-Hall, 1968), 7.
6. For a complete list of taxes and descriptions of each, see Texas Comptroller of Public Accounts, "Overview of Texas Taxes," http://www.window.state.tx.us/taxes/.
7. Katherine Barrett and Richard Greene, "Growth and Taxes," *Governing* (January 2008), 20–26.
8. *San Juan Cellular Telephone Company v. Public Service Corporation of Puerto Rico* (First Cir.), 967 F 2d 683 (1992).
9. Art. III, Sec. 49a, Texas Constitution (1942, amended 1999).
10. Rodney Ellis and Sylvester Turner, "Short-sighted Cuts Costly to Poor," *Houston Chronicle*, August 29, 2011.
11. Office of the Governor, "Gov. Perry Vetoes HB 2403," May 31, 2011, http://governor.state.tx.us/news/veto/16213/.
12. Susan Combs, *Tax Exemptions and Tax Incidence* (Austin: Office of the Comptroller of Public Accounts, February 2011), http://www.window.state.tx.us/taxinfo/incidence/96-463TaxIncidence02-11.pdf.
13. Joseph Henchman, "Texas Margin Tax Experiment Failing Due to Collection Shortfalls, Perceived Unfairness for Taxing Unprofitable and Small Businesses, and Confusing Rules" (Washington, D.C.: Tax Research Foundation), http://www.taxfoundation.org/news/show/27544.html; Laylan Copelin, "Smaller Companies to Lawmakers: Margins Tax Creates Unlevel Playing Field," *Austin American Statesman*, June 6, 2012.
14. StateImpact: Texas-Reporting on Power, Policy, and the Planet, "How Does Hydraulic Fracturing 'Fracking' Work?" http://stateimpact.npr.org/texas/tag/fracking/.
15. For lists of all recipients of funding under the American Reinvestment and Recovery Act of 2009, see Office of the Comptroller, "Texas Stimulus Tracking," http://www.window.state.tx.us/recovery/.

16. General Land Office of Texas, "Texas Offshore Wind Energy," http://www.glo
.texas.gov/glo_news/hot_topics/articles/offshore-wind-energy.html.

17. For discussions and updates regarding the process for issuing bonds in Texas,
see various references on the Texas Bond Review Board website at http://
www.brb.state.tx.us, including "Debt Primer" and the posted *Annual Reports.*

18. For excellent descriptions of the Texas budgeting process, see *Budget 101: A
Guide to the Budget Process in Texas* (Austin: Senate Research Center, January
2011) and *Writing the State Budget: 82nd Legislature*, State Finance Report No.
82-1 (Austin: House Research Organization, February 2011).

19. Governor's Office of Budget, Planning, and Policy, and Legislative Budget
Board, *Instructions for Preparing and Submitting Agency Strategic Plans for
Fiscal Years 2011–2015* (March 2012), http://governor.state.tx.us/files/bpp/
StrategicPlanFY_2011-2015.pdf.

20. Rick Perry, "State of the State Address, 2011," February 8, 2011, http://
governor.state.tx.us/news/speech/15673/.

21. Thomas L. Harnisch, *Performance-based Funding: A Re-emerging Strategy in
Public Higher Education Financing* (Washington, D.C.: American Association of
State Colleges and Universities, June 2011), http://www.aascu.org/policy/.

22. Eva de Luna Castro, *Texas Poverty 101* (Austin: Center for Public Policy Priorities, November 2011), 3.

23. Nolan Hicks, "Texas Highway System Nearly Running on Empty," *Houston
Chronicle*, March 8, 2011.

24. Patrick Driscoll, "Gas Taxes Can't Fuel All Road Projects," *San Antonio
Express-News*, December 4, 2005.

25. Texas Water Development Board, *Water for Texas: 2012 State Water Plan*
(Austin: Texas Water Development Board, January 2012), http://www.twdb
.state.tx.us/publications/state_water_plan/2012/00.pdf.

Texas Parks and Wildlife Department

In recent legislative sessions, legislators have used funds intended for the Texas Parks and Wildlife Department to balance the state's biennial budgets. Reduced funding, coupled with damage from wildfires and drought in 2011, placed an unprecedented burden on this agency. The response by agency officials was also considered unprecedented by some. Austin American-Statesman *columnist Ken Herman offers his reaction. State Representative Jessica Farrar (D-Houston) explains what happened to the state funds intended for this agency.*

Government Goes Begging
Ken Herman

As far back as anyone can remember (or at least as far back as I can remember, and I'm just this side of geezerdom), government has had limited options for gathering the money needed to do the important things (and the other things) government does.

Here's the list of what government folks call "revenue streams": taxes, fines, fees, civil penalties, change found in sofa cushions at the Capitol. That's pretty much it, I think. We hate taxes and fees, don't like to pay fines and civil penalties and can't figure out how the change wound up in the sofas. But the system has worked.

On [December 6, 2011], in 11 news conferences in state parks, we added a new way for government to raise money. It's not new to humankind, just new to governmentkind. You see the method in action on street corners among folks down on their luck. (Best sign I've seen recently: "I'd say some change would do me good.")

It's begging. A major state agency, facing a budget crisis, now is begging. "We need to raise $4.6 million to keep state parks operating, and we can't do it without you," it says on the Texas Parks and Wildlife Department website.

"I'm here for one simple reason," the department's Executive Director Carter Smith says on a video backing up the begging. "Your state parks need our help now more than ever. Record drought, devastating wildfires, associated declines in park visitation and revenue have created a real sense of urgency in a time of critical need for your state parks." The department calls it the "triple whammy."

"If we're going to keep these special treasures open for all Texans to use and enjoy, we need to raise $4.6 million," Smith said.

Our state parks long have depended on tax allocations, park entrance fees and contributions to a Parks and Wildlife-related foundation. That's not cutting it any more. At a news conference at McKinney Falls State Park in Austin, Smith detailed the problem at our 94 state parks and historical sites. It costs about $69 million a year to run them. For a long time, about half that money has come from fee-paying visitors. It seems like a good model, but, thanks to the triple whammy of drought, heat and wildfires, the model is broken.

And that means the department is en route to additional job cuts. Park services and hours also could face trimming. This summer, Parks and Wildlife whacked 230 jobs and enacted some cuts in hours and services. That was caused by a 21 percent spending cut ordered by lawmakers.

There's also the Legislature's history of not giving the department the full share of the sales tax on sporting goods, which is supposed to go to parks. Legislative Budget Board figures show that tax was projected to generate $236 million in the current two-year budget cycle. But the budget sent only $82 million of it to Parks and Wildlife.

The state's general fund got the rest as lawmakers struggled to write a two-year budget without raising taxes. They succeeded. And now the department, which always has sought donations to its foundation, is into unprecedented begging. Amazing. And let's see if this new revenue stream catches on with other cash-strapped state agencies. "Please act now to help keep our state parks open for all Texans to enjoy, because our state parks won't be the same without you," Smith said on the video.

Here's a thought: If begging fails, maybe Parks and Wildlife will have to make a tough decision between parks and wildlife. Maybe we can't afford both.

Source: This article appeared in the *Austin American-Statesman,* December 9, 2011.

Stop Diverting Park Money to Unrelated State Purposes
State Rep. Jessica Farrar (D-Houston)

A few weeks ago, I wrote Gov. [Rick] Perry a letter in which I confessed that I am a fiscal conservative. I explained to the governor that I believe government is supposed to be a wise steward of tax dollars. If the government must spend money, it should do so only for essential public services, like education, infrastructure, health services for the young and elderly, and disaster relief. Tax dollars do not belong to the government or elected officials; tax dollars belong to taxpayers.

I mention my letter because being a fiscal conservative also means providing full financial transparency.

If state budget writers divert millions of dollars away from a fund dedicated to pay for state parks, that diversion should be openly disclosed. Diverting funds is precisely what state budget writers did last session, which led to the crisis the Texas Parks and Wildlife Department (TPWD) currently faces.

Because I am a fiscal conservative, I am going to tell taxpayers the truth: The state's coffers are not empty and the state could fully fund every state park under the care of TPWD. The state does not need more tax dollars or donations to keep state parks open. As far as I'm concerned, the state of Texas owes money to the generous people who recently donated more than $1.14 million to help keep state parks open.

Some quick background: In 1993, the Legislature created the Sporting Goods Sales Tax, a portion of which is supposed to fund Texas state parks. Last session, as in previous sessions, rather than using money from the Sporting Goods Sales Tax for state parks, as taxpayers were told would be the case, budget writers chose to divert $154 million away from TPWD, leading to park closures, layoffs and deteriorating park infrastructure.

The practice of diverting so-called dedicated funds away from their intended purpose is nothing new. Texas legislators and governors have shuffled dedicated funds around for decades; but that doesn't make it right. Diverting dedicated funds is nothing more than a game of deception in which budget writers rob one government service to pay for another.

So where's the money? Some of it is sitting in Fund 64, one of many state accounts maintained by the Texas comptroller. As of earlier this month, Fund 64 had a balance of $34,270,883.67. The rest of the $154 million that was supposed to help support TPWD was diverted to other accounts for other services. Bait and switch is the name of the game.

Although diverting dedicated funds is an old practice, what is new is the Legislature asking citizens to pay more for a service that should already be funded. The Legislature authorized the Department of Motor Vehicles to solicit donations for TPWD from drivers when they renew their annual vehicle registrations. Additionally, TPWD officials are being forced to consider raising park visitors' fees, again. Budget writers have even duped a group of conservative bloggers into helping the state raise donations: "Help SAVE Texas State Parks: Donate Now or Visit a Park Soon" the headline reads. The money is already in state coffers.

Over the years, several budget writers have advocated ending the practice of diverting dedicated funds, yet the practice continues. This is partly because the governor and comptroller like these accounting tricks. Being able to shuffle money around allows them to gloat about balancing the budget.

In 2007, when asked about the idea of fully funding TPWD with the sporting goods tax, Gov. Perry's response was that state parks would not be able to effectively spend that much money if it were "dump[ed] overnight on the Texas Parks and Wildlife Department." Having recently visited fire-ravaged Bastrop State Park, I can guarantee they would know just how to spend that money.

Over the next 18 months, TPWD needs an additional $4.6 million to keep facilities operating and another $10 million to recover from last years' wildfires. Fortunately, the governor has options to fund TPWD. He can order a special session and call on the Legislature to appropriate money to TPWD. Or, using interim budget execution authority, the governor and Legislative Budget Board can authorize the agency to spend from their 2013 appropriation; then, during the next regular or special session, the Legislature could provide supplemental appropriations to TPWD.

Diverting money from dedicated accounts is wrong. The practice belies the governor's and Legislature's duty to provide full transparency and accountability. Taxpayers deserve to know why they are paying tax dollars, who is not paying their fair share, and where their money is going after it reaches state coffers. Being a true fiscal conservative takes more than lip service; it takes action.

Source: This editorial appeared in the *Houston Chronicle,* February 25, 2012.

For further resources, please visit **www.cengagebrain.com**.

Glossary

Numbers in parentheses indicate the chapter in which the term is found.

adjudication hearing A trial in a juvenile court. (10)

affirmative action Takes positive steps to attract women and members of racial and ethnic minority groups; may include using race in admission or hiring decisions. (9)

affirmative racial gerrymandering Drawing districts designed to affect representation of a racial group previously discriminated against (e.g., African Americans) in a legislative chamber, city council, commissioners court, or other representative body. (5)

African American A racial classification indicating African ancestry. (1)

alien A person who is neither a national nor a citizen of the country where he or she is living. (1)

alternative dispute resolution (ADR) Use of mediation, conciliation, or arbitration to resolve disputes among individuals without resorting to a regular court trial. (10)

Anglo A term commonly used in Texas to identify non–Latino white people. (1)

annex To make an outlying area part of a city. Within a city's extraterritorial jurisdiction, the city can annex unincorporated areas without a vote by those who live there. (3)

appellate jurisdiction The power of a court to review cases after they have been tried elsewhere. (10)

appointive power The authority to name a person to a government office. Most gubernatorial appointments require Senate approval by two-thirds of the members present. (8)

appointment-retention system A merit plan for judicial selection, whereby the governor appoints to fill a court vacancy for a trial period after which the judge must win a full term in an uncontested popular election. (10)

Asian American A term used to identify people of Asian ancestry (such as, Chinese, Japanese, Korean). (1)

at-large election Members of a policymaking body, such as some city councils, are elected on a citywide basis rather than from single-member districts. (3)

at-large majority district A district that elects two or more representatives. (5)

attorney general The constitutional official elected to head the Office of the Attorney General, which represents the state government in lawsuits and provides legal advice to state and local officials. (8)

balanced budget A budget in which total revenues and expenditures are equal, producing no deficit. (11)

Basin and Range Province An arid region in West Texas that includes the Davis Mountains, Big Bend National Park, and El Paso. (1)

bicameral A legislature with two houses or chambers, such as Texas's House of Representatives and Senate. (7)

bifurcated A divided court system in which different courts handle civil and criminal cases. In Texas, the highest-level appeals courts are bifurcated. (10)

bill A proposed law or statute. (7)

Bill of Rights Composed of 30 sections in Article I of the Texas Constitution, it guarantees protections for people and their property against arbitrary actions by state and local governments. Included among these rights are freedom of speech, press, religion, assembly, and petition. The Texas Bill of Rights is similar to the one found in the U.S. Constitution. (2)

block grant Congressional grant of money that allows the state considerable flexibility in spending for a program, such as providing welfare services. (2)

bond A certificate of indebtedness issued by a borrower to a lender that constitutes a legal obligation to repay the principal of a loan plus accrued interest. In Texas, both state and local governments issue bonds under restrictions imposed by state law. (3)

budget A plan of financial operation indicating how much revenue a government expects to collect during a period (usually one or two fiscal years) and how much spending is authorized for agencies and programs. (11)

budget execution The process whereby the governor and the Legislative Budget Board oversee (and in some instances modify) implementation of the spending plan authorized by the Texas legislature. (11)

budgetary power The governor is supposed to submit a state budget to the legislature at the beginning of each regular session. When an appropriation bill is enacted by the legislature and certified by the comptroller of public accounts, the governor may veto the whole document or individual items. (8)

bureaucrat Public employee. (9)

business organization An economic interest group, such as a trade association (e.g., Texas Association of Builders) that lobbies for policies favoring Texas business. (6)

Campaign Reform Act Enacted by the U.S. Congress and signed by President George W. Bush in 2002, this law restricts donations of "soft money" and "hard money" for election campaigns, but its effect has been limited by federal court decisions. (5)

canvass To scrutinize the results of an election and then confirm and certify the vote tally for each candidate. (5)

capital felony A crime punishable by death or life imprisonment. (10)

caucus A meeting at which members of a political party assemble to select delegates and make other policy recommendations at the precinct, county or state senatorial district, and state levels. (4)

ChildLINK A program administered by the Texas Attorney General's Child Support Program in which medical support payments paid by noncustodial parents are used to provide insurance for the parent's children. (11)

Children's Health Insurance Program (CHIP) A program that provides medical insurance for minimal premiums to children from low-income families. (11)

chubbing A practice whereby supporters of a bill engage in lengthy debate for the purpose of using time and thus preventing floor action on another bill that they oppose. (7)

civil law The body of law concerning noncriminal matters, such as business contracts and personal injury. (10)

closed primary A primary in which voters must declare their support for the party before they are permitted to participate in the selection of its candidates. (5)

colonia A low-income community, typically located in South Texas and especially in counties bordering Mexico, that lacks running water, sewer lines, and other essentials. (3)

combined statistical area (CSA) A geographic entity consisting of two or more adjacent core-based statistical areas. (1)

commission form A type of municipal government in which each elected commissioner is a member of the city's policymaking body, but also heads an administrative department (e.g., public safety with police and fire divisions). (3)

commissioner of agriculture The elected official, whose position is created by statute, who heads Texas's Department of Agriculture, which promotes the sale of agricultural commodities and regulates pesticides, aquaculture, egg quality, weights and measures, and grain warehouses. (8)

commissioner of education The official who heads the Texas Education Agency (TEA). (9)

commissioner of insurance Appointed by the governor, the commissioner heads the Texas Department of Insurance, which is responsible for ensuring the industry's financial soundness and for protecting policy holders. It affects insurance rates. (9)

commissioner of the General Land Office As head of Texas's General Land Office, this elected constitutional officer oversees the state's extensive landholdings and related mineral interests, especially oil and gas leasing for the benefit of the Permanent School Fund. (8)

commissioners court A Texas county's policymaking body, with five members: the county judge, who presides, and four commissioners representing single-member precincts. (3)

commutation of sentence On the recommendation of the Board of Pardons and Paroles, the governor may commute (reduce) a sentence. (8)

companion bill Filed in one house but identical or similar to a bill filed in the other chamber; speeds passage of a bill because committee consideration may take place simultaneously in both houses. (7)

comptroller of public accounts An elected constitutional officer responsible for collecting taxes, keeping accounts, estimating revenue, and serving as treasurer for the state. (8)

concurrent jurisdiction The authority of more than one court to try a case (for example, a civil dispute involving more than $500 but less than $10,000 may be heard in either a justice of the peace court, a county court, or a district court). (10)

concurrent resolution A resolution adopted by House and Senate majorities and then approved by the governor (for example, a request for action by Congress or authorization for someone to sue the state). (7)

conditional pardon On recommendation of the Board of Pardons and Paroles, the governor may grant a conditional pardon. This act of clemency releases a convicted person from the consequences of his or her crime but does not restore all rights, as in the case of a full pardon. (8)

conference committee A committee composed of representatives and senators appointed to reach agreement on a disputed bill and recommend changes acceptable to both chambers. (7)

conservative A person who advocates minimal intervention by government in social and economic matters and who gives a high priority to reducing taxes and curbing public spending. (4)

constable A citizen elected to assist the justice of the peace by serving papers and in some cases carrying out security and investigative responsibilities. (3)

constitutional amendment election Takes place in a regular election in even-numbered years or in a special election. Voters must approve proposed constitutional amendments with a simple majority. (2)

constitutional amendment process Article XVII, Section 1, of the Texas Constitution stipulates that an amendment must be proposed by a two-thirds vote of members in each chamber of the legislature and approved by a simple majority of voters in a general or special election. (2)

constitutional guarantees Included among the U.S. Constitution's guarantees to members of the Union are protection against invasion and domestic violence, territorial integrity, a republican form of government, representation by two senators and at least one representative in the U.S. Congress, and equitable participation in the constitutional amendment process. (2)

constitutional history of Texas Texas's constitutional history began with promulgation of the Constitution of Coahuila y Tejas within the Mexican federal system in 1827 and the Constitution of the Texas Republic in 1836. Texas has since been governed under its state constitutions of 1845, 1861, 1866, 1869, and 1876. (2)

constitutional revision Extensive or complete rewriting of a constitution. (2)

constitutional revision convention A body of delegates who meet to make extensive changes in a constitution or to draft a new constitution. (2)

contingency fee A lawyer's compensation paid from money recovered in a lawsuit. (10)

contingency rider Authorization for spending state money to finance provisions of a bill if it passes. (8)

council-manager form A system of municipal government in which an elected city council hires a manager to coordinate budgetary matters and supervise administrative departments. (3)

council of government (COG) A regional planning body composed of governmental units (e.g., cities, counties, special districts); functions include review and comment on proposals by local governments for obtaining state and federal grants. (3)

county Texas is divided into 254 counties that serve as an administrative arm of the state and that provide important services at the local level, especially within rural areas. (3)

county attorney A citizen elected to represent the county in civil and criminal cases, unless a resident district attorney performs these functions. (3)

county auditor A person appointed by the district judge or judges to check the financial books and records of other officials who handle county money. (3)

county chair Elected by county party members in the primaries, this key party official heads the county executive committee. (4)

county clerk A citizen elected to perform clerical chores for the county court and commissioners court, keep public records, maintain vital statistics, and administer public elections, if the county does not have an administrator of elections. (3)

county convention A party meeting of precinct delegates held on the second Saturday after precinct conventions; it elects delegates and alternates to the state convention. (4)

county executive committee Composed of a party's precinct chairs and the elected county chair, the county executive committee conducts primaries and makes arrangements for holding county conventions. (4)

county judge A citizen popularly elected to preside over the county commissioners court and, in smaller counties, to hear civil and criminal cases. (3)

county sheriff A citizen popularly elected as the county's chief law enforcement officer; the sheriff is also responsible for maintaining the county jail. (3)

county tax appraisal district The district appraises all real estate and commercial property for taxation by units of local government within a county. (3)

county tax assessor-collector This elected official no longer assesses property for taxation but does collect taxes and fees and commonly handles voter registration. (3)

county treasurer An elected official who receives and pays out county money as directed by the commissioners court. (3)

court of record A court that has a court reporter or electronic device to record testimony and proceedings. (10)

criminal law The body of law concerning felony and misdemeanor offenses by individuals against other persons and property, or in violation of laws or ordinances. (10)

crossover voting A practice whereby a person participates in the primary of one party, then votes for one or more candidates of another party in the general election. (5)

cumulative voting When multiple seats are contested in an at-large election, voters cast one or more of the specified number of votes for one or more candidates in any combination. It is designed to increase representation of historically underrepresented ethnic minority groups. (3)

dealignment Occurs when citizens have no allegiance to a political party and become independent voters. (4)

decentralized government Decentralization is achieved by dividing power between national and state governments and separating legislative, executive, and judicial branches at both levels. (6)

dedicated fund A restricted state fund that can only be appropriated for its designated purpose. If the fund is consolidated within the general revenue fund, it usually must be spent for its intended purpose. Any unappropriated amounts can be included in the calculations to balance the state budget. (11)

defendant The person sued in a civil proceeding or prosecuted in a criminal proceeding. (10)

delegated powers Specific powers entrusted to the national government by Article I, Section 8, of the U.S. Constitution (e.g., regulate interstate commerce, borrow money, and declare war). (2)

deregulation The elimination of government restrictions to allow free-market competition to determine or limit the actions of individuals and corporations. (9)

Dillon's Rule A legal principle that local governments have only those powers granted by their state government. Still followed in the majority of states, including Texas. (3)

direct primary A nominating system that allows voters to participate directly in the selection of candidates for public office. (5)

district attorney A citizen elected to serve one or more counties who prosecutes criminal cases, gives advisory opinions, and represents the county in civil cases. (3)

district convention Held on the second Saturday after the first primary in counties that have more than one state senatorial district. Participants elect delegates to the party's state convention. (4)

district court clerk A citizen elected to maintain records for the county and district courts. (3)

district executive committee Composed of county chairs within a district that elects a state senator, U.S. or state representative, or district judge, this body fills a vacancy created by the death, resignation, or disqualification of a nominated candidate. (4)

dual budgeting system The compilation of separate budgets by the legislative branch and the executive branch. (11)

early voting Conducted at the county courthouse and selected polling places before the designated primary, special, or general election day. (5)

economic interest group Trade associations and labor unions are classified as economic interest groups because they are organized to promote policies that will maximize profits and wages. (6)

election judge Appointed by the county commissioners court to administer an election in a voting precinct. (5)

electioneering Active campaigning by an interest group in support of, or opposition to, a candidate; actions urging the public to act on an issue. (6)

elections administrator Person appointed to supervise voter registration and voting. (5)

elite access The ability of the business elite to deal directly with high-ranking government administrators to avoid full compliance with regulations. (9)

equal opportunity Ensures that policies and actions do not discriminate on factors such as race, gender, ethnicity, religion, or national origin. (9)

exclusive jurisdiction The authority of only one court to hear a particular type of case. (10)

executive commissioner of the Health and Human Services Commission Appointed by the governor with Senate approval, this executive commissioner administers the HHSC, develops policies, makes rules, and appoints (with approval by the governor) commissioners to head the commission's four departments. (9)

executive order The governor issues executive orders to set policy within the executive branch and to create task forces, councils, and other bodies. (8)

extraterritorial jurisdiction (ETJ) The limited authority a city has outside its boundaries. The larger the city's population size, the larger the reach of its ETJ. (3)

federal grant-in-aid Money appropriated by the U.S. Congress to help states and local governments provide needed facilities and services. (2)

fee A charge imposed by an agency upon those subject to its regulation. (11)

felony A serious crime punished by fine and prison confinement. (10)

filibustering A delaying tactic whereby a senator may speak, and thus hold the Senate floor, for as long as physical endurance permits. (7)

fiscal policy Public policy that concerns taxing, government spending, public debt, and management of government money. (11)

franchise tax A tax levied on the annual receipts of businesses that are organized to limit the personal liability of owners for the privilege of conducting business in the state. (11)

frontier experience Coping with danger, physical hardships, and economic challenges tested the endurance of 19th-century Texans and contributed to the development of individualism. (1)

full faith and credit clause Most government actions of another state must be officially recognized by public officials in Texas. (2)

full pardon On recommendation of the Board of Pardons and Paroles, the governor may grant a full pardon. This act of executive clemency releases a convicted person from all consequences of a criminal act and restores the same rights enjoyed by others who have not been convicted of a crime. (8)

general election Held in November of even-numbered years to elect county and state officials from among candidates nominated in primaries or (for small parties) in nominating conventions. (5)

general-law city A municipality with a charter prescribed by the legislature. (3)

general obligation bond Amount borrowed by the state that is repaid from the General Revenue Fund. (11)

General Revenue Fund An unrestricted state fund that is available for general appropriations. (11)

general sales tax At the rate of 6.25 percent of a sale, the general sales tax is Texas's largest source of tax revenue. It is applied largely to the sale price of tangible personal property and "the storage, use, or other consumption of tangible personal property purchased, leased, or rented." (11)

gerrymandering Drawing the boundaries of a district, such as a state senatorial or representative district, to include or exclude certain groups of voters and thus affect election outcomes. (7)

ghost voting A prohibited practice whereby one representative presses the voting button of another House member who is absent. (7)

government A public institution with authority to allocate values by formulating, adopting, and implementing public policies. (1)

Governor's Office The administrative organization through which the governor of Texas makes appointments, prepares a biennial budget recommendation, administers federal and state grants for crime prevention and law enforcement, and confers full and conditional pardons on recommendation of the Board of Pardons and Paroles. (8)

graded penalties Depending on the nature of the crime, felonies are graded as first, second, third degree, and state jail; misdemeanors are graded as A, B, and C. (10)

grand jury Composed of 12 persons with the qualifications of trial jurors, a grand jury serves from three to six months while it determines whether sufficient evidence exists to indict persons accused of committing crimes. (10)

grandfather clause Although not used in Texas, exempted people from educational, property, or tax requirements for voting if they were qualified to vote before 1867 or were descendents of such persons. (5)

grant-in-aid Money, goods, or services given by one government to another (for example, federal grants-in-aid to states for financing public assistance programs). (11)

grassroots Local (as in grassroots government or grassroots politics). (3)

Great Plains A large area in West Texas extending from Oklahoma to Mexico, this region is an extension of the Great High Plains of the United States. (1)

group leadership Individuals who guide the decisions of interest groups. Leaders of groups tend to have financial resources that permit them to contribute money and devote time to group affairs. (6)

Gulf Coastal Plains Stretching from the Louisiana border to the Rio Grande, this area is an extension of the Gulf Coastal Plains of the United States. (1)

hard money Campaign money donated directly to candidates or political parties and restricted in amount by federal law. (5)

high technology Technology that applies to research, development, manufacturing, and marketing of computers and other electronic products. (1)

home-rule city A municipality with a locally drafted charter. (3)

impeachment Process in which the Texas House of Representatives, by a simple majority vote, initiates action (brings charges) leading to possible removal of certain judicial and executive officials (e.g., the governor) by the Senate. (7)

implied powers Powers inferred by the constitutional authority of the U.S. Congress "to make all laws which shall be necessary and proper for carrying into execution the foregoing [delegated] powers, and all other powers vested by this Constitution in the government of the United States, or in any department or officer thereof." (2)

independent candidate A candidate who runs in a general election without party endorsement or selection. (4,5)

independent school district (ISD) Created by the legislature, an independent school district raises tax revenue to support its public schools. Voters within the district elect a board that hires a superintendent, determines salary schedules, selects textbooks, and sets the district's property tax rate. (3)

individualistic culture This culture looks to government to maintain a stable society, but with minimum intervention in the lives of the people. (1)

initiative A citizen-drafted measure proposed by a specific number or percentage of qualified voters, which becomes law if approved by popular vote. In Texas, this process occurs only at the local level, not at the state level. (2, 3)

interest group An organization that seeks to influence government officials and their policies on behalf of members sharing common views and objectives (e.g., labor union or trade association). (6)

interest group technique An action such as lobbying, personal communication, favors and gifts, grassroots activities, electioneering, campaign financing by political action committees, and, in extreme instances, bribery and unethical practices intended to influence government decisions. (6)

intergovernmental relations Relationships between and among different governments that are on the same or different levels. (3)

Interior Lowlands This region covers the North Central Plains of Texas extending from the Dallas–Fort Worth metroplex westward to the Abilene area and northward to the Wichita Falls area. (1)

Jim Crow "Jim Crow" laws were ethnically discriminatory laws that segregated African Americans and denied them access to public services for many decades after the Civil War. (1)

joint resolution A resolution that must pass by a majority vote in each house when used to ratify an amendment to the U.S. Constitution. As a proposal for an amendment to the Texas Constitution, a joint resolution requires a two-thirds majority vote in each house. (7)

judgment A judge's written opinion based on a verdict. (10)

jungle primary A nominating process whereby voters indicate their preferences by using a single ballot on which are printed the names and respective party labels of all persons seeking nomination. California and Louisiana conduct a jungle primary in which candidates from all parties compete in a single election. A candidate who receives 50 percent or more of the vote is elected; otherwise, a runoff between the top two candidates must be held. (5)

junior college or community college district Establishes one or more two-year colleges that offer both academic and vocational programs. (3)

jurisdiction A court's authority to hear a particular case. (10)

justice of the peace A judge elected from a justice of the peace precinct who handles minor civil and criminal cases, including civil disputes in a small claims court. (3, 10)

labor organization A union that supports public policies designed to increase wages, obtain adequate health insurance coverage, provide unemployment insurance, promote safe working conditions, and otherwise protect the interests of workers. (6)

Latino This is an ethnic classification of Mexican Americans and others of Latin American origin. When applied to females, the term is *Latina*. (1)

Legislative Budget Board (LBB) A 10-member body cochaired by the lieutenant governor and the Speaker of the House. This board and its staff prepare a biennial current-services budget. In addition, it assists with the preparation of a general appropriation bill at the beginning of a regular legislative session. If requested, staff members prepare fiscal notes that assess the economic impact of a proposed bill or resolution. (11)

legislative caucus An organization of legislators who seek to maximize their influence over issues in which they have a special interest. (7)

legislative power A power of the governor exercised through messages delivered to the Texas legislature, vetoes of bills and concurrent resolutions, and calls for special sessions of the legislature. (8)

liberal A person who advocates for government support in social and economic matters and who favors political reforms that extend democracy, achieve a more equitable distribution of wealth, and protect individual freedoms and rights. (4)

lieutenant governor Popularly elected constitutional official who serves as president of the Senate and is first in the line of succession if the office of governor becomes vacant before the end of a term. (8)

line-item veto Action by the governor to delete a line item while permitting enactment of other parts of an appropriation bill. (8)

literacy test Although not used in Texas as a prerequisite for voter registration, this test was designed and administered in ways intended to prevent African Americans and Latinos from voting. (5)

lobbying Communicating with legislators or other government officials on behalf of an interest group or a corporation for the purpose of influencing decision makers. (6)

local government The Texas Constitution authorizes these units of local government: counties, municipalities, school districts, and other special districts. These "grassroots governments" provide a wide range of services that include rural roads, protection of persons and property, city streets, and public education. (2)

maquiladora An assembly plant that uses cheap labor and is located on the Mexican side of the U.S.–Mexican border. (1)

martial law Temporary rule by military authorities when civil authorities are unable to handle a riot or other civil disorder. (8)

Medicaid Funded in larger part by federal grants and in part by state appropriations, Medicaid is administered by the state. It provides medical care for persons whose incomes fall below the poverty line. (9) (11)

Medicare Funded entirely by the federal government and administered by the U.S. Department of Health and Human Services, Medicare provides medical assistance to qualified applicants age 65 and older. (9) (11)

merit system Hiring, promoting, and firing on the basis of objective criteria such as tests, degrees, experience, and performance. (9)

message power The governor's State of the State address at the "commencement" of a legislative session and messages delivered in person or in writing are examples of the gubernatorial exercise of message power to communicate with legislators and the public. (8)

metro government Consolidation of units of local government within an urban area under a single authority. (3)

metropolitan division County or group of counties within a core-based statistical area that contains a core with a population of at least 2.5 million. (1)

metropolitan statistical area (MSA) A freestanding urban area with a minimum total population of 50,000. (1)

metropolitanization Concentration of people in urban centers that become linked. (1)

micropolitan statistical area (mSA) An area that has at least one urban cluster with a population of at least 10,000, but less than 50,000. (1)

middle class Social scientists identify the middle class as those people from white-collar occupations (such as professionals and small business workers), and the working class, composed of people with blue-collar (manual) occupations.

misdemeanor Classified as A, B, or C, a misdemeanor may be punished by fine and/or jail sentence. (10)

Missouri Plan A judicial selection process in which a commission recommends a panel of names to the governor, followed by a one-year or so appointment of a judge before voters determine whether the appointee will be retained for a full term. (10)

moralistic culture This culture influences people to view political participation as their duty and to expect that government will be used to advance the public good. (1)

motor-voter law Legislation requiring certain government offices (e.g., motor vehicle licensing agencies) to offer voter registration applications to clients. (5)

multimember district A district in which all voters participate in the election of two or more representatives to a policymaking body, such as a city council, a state House, or a state Senate. (7)

municipal bond A mechanism by which cities borrow money. General obligation bonds (redeemed from city tax revenue) and

revenue bonds (redeemed from revenue obtained from the property or activity financed by the sale of the bonds) are authorized under Texas law. (3)

municipal court City-run courts with jurisdiction primarily over Class C misdemeanors committed within a city's boundaries. (10)

municipal (city) government A local government for an incorporated community established by law as a city. (3)

national supremacy clause Article VI of the U.S. Constitution states, "This Constitution, and the Laws of the United States which shall be made in Pursuance thereof; and all Treaties made, or which shall be made, under the Authority of the United States, shall be the supreme Law of the Land." (2)

Native American A descendent of the first Americans, who were called *indios* by Spanish explorers and Indians by Anglo settlers who arrived later. (1)

neoconservatism A political ideology that reflects fiscal conservatism, but accepts a limited governmental role in solving social problems. (4)

neoliberal A political ideology that advocates less government regulation of business, but supports more governmental involvement in social matters. (4)

noneducation special districts Special districts other than school districts or community college districts, such as fire prevention or water districts, that are units of local government and may cover part of a county, a whole county, or areas in two or more counties. (3)

nonpartisan election An election in which candidates are not identified on the ballot by party label. (3)

North American Free Trade Agreement (NAFTA) An agreement among the United States, Mexico, and Canada designed to expand trade among the three countries by reducing and then eliminating tariffs over a 15-year period. (1)

off-year or midterm election A general election held in the even-numbered year following a presidential election. (5)

open primary A primary in which voters are not required to declare party identification. (5)

ordinance A local law enacted by a city council or approved by popular vote in a referendum election. (3)

organizational pattern The structure of a special interest group. Some interest groups have a decentralized pattern of organization (e.g., the AFL-CIO, with many local unions). Others are centralized (e.g., the National Rifle Association, which is a national body without affiliated local or regional units). (6)

original jurisdiction The power of a court to hear a case first. (10)

oversight A legislative function that requires reports from state agencies concerning their operations; the state auditor provides information on agencies' use of state funds. (7)

parliamentarian An expert on rules of order who sits at the left of the presiding officer in the House or Senate and is ever ready to give advice on procedural questions. (7)

parole Supervised release from prison before completion of a sentence; good behavior of the parolee is a condition of release. (8)

patrón system A type of boss rule that has dominated areas of South Texas. (1)

patronage system Hiring friends and supporters of elected officials as government employees without regard to their abilities. (9)

payroll tax A tax levied against a portion of the wages and salaries of employees to provide funds for payment of unemployment insurance benefits to these people when they lose their jobs. (11)

permanent party organization In Texas, the precinct chairs, county and district executive committees, and the state executive committee form the permanent organization of a political party. (4)

petit jury A trial jury of six or 12 members. (10)

physical region An area identified by unique geographic features, such as, the Gulf Coastal Plains and the Great Plains. (1)

plaintiff The injured party who initiates a civil suit or the state in a criminal proceeding. (10)

platform A document that sets forth a political party's position on issues such as income tax, school vouchers, or public utility regulation. (4)

plural executive The governor, elected department heads, and the secretary of state as provided by the Texas Constitution and statutes. (8)

political action committee (PAC) An organizational device used by corporations, labor unions, and other organizations to raise money for campaign contributions. (5, 6)

political culture Attitudes, habits, and general behavior patterns that develop over time and affect the political life of a state or region. (1)

political inefficacy The inability to influence the nomination and election of candidates and the decision making of governing bodies. In Texas, this has been a major problem for minorities and low-income groups. (1)

political influence of interest groups A highly variable factor that depends largely on the size of a group's membership, financial resources, quality of leadership, and degree of unity to measure its effectiveness. (6)

political party An organization influenced by political ideology whose primary interest is to gain control of government by winning elections. (4)

politics The process of policymaking that involves conflict between political parties and other groups that seek to elect government officials or to influence those officials when they make public policy, such as enacting and interpreting laws. (1)

poll tax A tax levied in Texas from 1902 until a similar Virginia tax was declared unconstitutional in 1962; failure to pay the annual tax (usually $1.75) made a citizen ineligible to vote in party primaries or in special and general elections. (5)

population shift Within Texas, changes in population density have featured demographic movements from rural to urban areas and from large cities to suburbs and back. (1)

pork-barrel politics A legislator's tactic to obtain funding for a pet project, usually designed to be of special benefit for the legislator's district. (8)

postadjournment veto Rejection by the governor of a pending bill or concurrent resolution during the 20 days after a legislative session ends. (8)

power group An effective interest group strongly linked with legislators and bureaucrats for the purpose of influencing decision making and having a continuing presence in Austin as a "repeat player" from session to session. (6)

precinct chair The party official responsible for the interests and activities of a political party in a voting district; typical duties include encouraging voter registration, distributing campaign literature, operating phone banks, and getting out the vote on Election Day. (4)

precinct convention At the lowest level of political party organization, voters convene in March of even-numbered years to adopt resolutions and to name delegates to a county or district convention. (4)

president of the Senate Title of the lieutenant governor in his or her role as presiding officer for the Texas Senate. (7)

presidential preference primary A primary in which the voters indicate their preference for a person seeking nomination as the party's presidential candidate. (4)

primary A preliminary election conducted within the party to select candidates who will run for public office in a subsequent general election. (5)

privileges and immunities Article IV of the U.S. Constitution guarantees that "citizens of each state shall be entitled to the privileges and immunities of citizens of the several states."

According to the U.S. Supreme Court, this means that citizens are guaranteed protection by government, enjoyment of life and liberty, the right to acquire and possess property, the right to leave and enter any state, and the right to use state courts. (2)

probate Proceedings that involve the estates of decedents. Additionally, courts with probate jurisdiction (county courts, county courts-at-law, and probate courts) handle guardianship and mental competency matters. (10)

procedural committee These House committees (such as the Calendars Committee and House Administration Committee) consider bills and resolutions relating primarily to procedural legislative matters. (7)

proclamation A governor's official public announcement (such as calling a special election or declaring a disaster area). (8)

professional group An organization of physicians, lawyers, accountants, or other professional people that lobbies for policies beneficial to members. (6)

progressive tax A tax in which the effective tax rate increases as the tax base (for example, individual income, corporate profits) increases. (11)

property tax A tax that property owners pay according to the value of their homes and businesses. At the local level, property owners pay this tax to the city, the county, the school district, and often other special districts. (3)

public administration The implementation of public policy by government employees. (9)

public interest group An organization claiming to represent a broad public interest (environmental, consumer, civil rights) rather than a narrow private interest. (6)

public officer and employee group An organization of city managers, county judges, or other public employees or officials that lobbies for public policies that protect group interests. (6)

public policy Government action designed to meet a public need or goal as determined by a legislative body or other authorized officials. (1)

Public Utility Commission (PUC) A three-member appointed body with regulatory power over the electric and telephone companies. (9)

racial and ethnic groups Organizations that seek to influence governmental decisions that affect a particular racial or ethnic group, such as the National Association for the Advancement of Colored People (NAACP) and the League of United Latin American Citizens (LULAC), which seek to influence government decisions affecting African Americans and Latinos, respectively. (6)

Railroad Commission of Texas (RRC) A popularly elected, three-member commission primarily engaged in regulating natural gas and petroleum production. (1, 9)

"rainy day" fund A fund used like a savings account for stabilizing state finance and helping the state meet economic emergencies when revenue is insufficient to cover state-supported programs. (11)

realignment Occurs when members of one party shift their affiliation to another party. (4)

recall A process for removing elected officials through a popular vote. In Texas, this power is available only at the local level, not at the state level. (3)

recess appointment An appointment made by the governor when the Texas legislature is not in session. (8)

recidivism Criminal behavior that results in reincarceration after a person has been released from confinement for a prior offense. (10)

redistricting Redrawing of boundaries after the federal decennial census to create districts with approximately equal population (e.g., legislative, congressional, commissioners court, and city council districts in Texas). (3, 7)

referendum A process by which issues are referred to the voters to accept or reject. Voters may also petition for a vote to repeal an existing ordinance. In Texas, this process occurs at the local level in home rule cities. At the state level, bonds secured by taxes and state constitutional amendments must be approved by the voters. (3)

regressive tax A tax in which the effective tax rate falls as the tax base (for example, individual income, corporate profits) increases. (11)

regular session A session of the Texas legislature that begins on the second Tuesday in January of odd- numbered years and lasts for a maximum of 140 days. (7)

religious-based group An interest group such as the Texas Faith Network that lobbies for policies promoting its religious interests. (6)

removal power Authority to remove an official from office. In Texas, the governor's removal power is limited to staff members, some agency heads, and his or her appointees with the consent of the Senate. (8)

reprieve An act of executive clemency that temporarily suspends execution of a sentence. (8)

reserved powers Reserved powers are derived from the Tenth Amendment of the U.S. Constitution. Although not spelled out in the U.S. Constitution, powers reserved to the states include police power, taxing power, proprietary power, and power of eminent domain. (2)

revenue bond Amount borrowed by the state that is repaid from a specific revenue source. (11)

right of association The U.S. Supreme Court has ruled that this right is part of the right of assembly guaranteed by the First Amendment of the U.S. Constitution and that it protects the right of people to organize into groups for political purposes. (6)

"Robin Hood" plan A plan for equalizing financial support for school districts by transferring tax money from rich districts to poor districts. (11)

runoff primary Held a month after the first primary to allow party members to choose a candidate from the first primary's top two vote-getters. (5)

secretary of state The state's chief elections officer, with other administrative duties, who is appointed by the governor for a term concurrent with that of the governor. (8)

select committee This committee, created independently by the House Speaker, may consider legislation that crosses committee jurisdictional lines or may conduct special studies. (7)

selective sales tax A tax charged on specific products and services. (11)

senatorial courtesy Before making an appointment, the governor is expected to obtain approval from the state senator in whose district the prospective appointee resides; failure to obtain such approval will probably cause the Senate to "bust" the appointee. (7)

separation of powers The assignment of lawmaking, law-enforcing, and law-interpreting functions to separate branches of government. (2)

service sector Businesses that provide services such as finance, health care, food service, data processing, or consulting. (11)

severance tax An excise tax levied on a natural resource (such as oil or natural gas) when it is severed (removed) from the earth. (11)

simple resolution A resolution that requires action by one legislative chamber only and is not acted on by the governor. (7)

sin tax A selective sales tax on items such as cigarettes, other forms of tobacco, alcoholic beverages, and admissions fees to sex-oriented businesses. (11)

single-member district An area that elects only one representative to serve on a policymaking body such as city council, county commissioners court, state House or state Senate. (7)

single-member district election Voters in an area (commonly called a district, ward, or precinct) elect one representative to serve on a policymaking body (e.g., city council, county commissioners court, state House and Senate). (3)

small-claims court A court presided over by a justice of the peace that offers an informal and inexpensive procedure for handling damage claims of $10,000 or less. (10)

social interest group Included among groups concerned primarily with social issues are organizations devoted to civil rights, racial and ethnic matters, religion, and public interest protection. (6)

soft money Campaign money that is used for independent expenditures and therefore is unrestricted in amount by federal law. (5)

sound bite A brief statement of a candidate's theme communicated by radio or television in a few seconds. (5)

Speaker of the House The state representative elected by House members to serve as the presiding officer for that chamber. (7)

special district A unit of local government that performs a particular service, such as providing schools, hospitals, or housing, for a particular geographic area. (3)

special election An election called by the governor to fill a vacancy (e.g., U.S. congressional or state legislative office) or to vote on a proposed state constitutional amendment or local bond issue. (5)

special interim committee A Senate committee appointed by the lieutenant governor to study an important policy issue between regular sessions. (7)

special issues Questions a judge gives a trial jury to answer to establish facts in a civil case. (10)

special session A legislative session called by the governor and limited to not more than 30 days. (7)

Spindletop Field Located near Beaumont, this oil field sparked a boom in 1901 that made Texas a leading petroleum producer. (1)

standing committee A Senate committee appointed by the lieutenant governor for the purpose of considering proposed bills and resolutions before possible floor debate and voting by senators. (7)

State Board of Education (SBOE) A popularly elected 15-member body with limited authority over Texas's K-12 education system. (9)

state convention Convenes every even-numbered year to make rules for a political party, adopt a party platform and resolutions, and select members of the state executive committee; in a presidential election year, it elects delegates to the national convention, names members to serve on the national committee, and elects potential electors to vote if the party's presidential candidate receives the plurality of the popular vote in the general election. (4)

state executive committee Composed of a chair, vice chair, and two members from each senatorial district, this body is part of a party's permanent organization. (4)

State of Texas Assessment of Academic Readiness (STAAR) A state program of end-of-course examinations in core subjects. (9)

statutory county court A court created by the legislature at the request of a county; may have civil or criminal jurisdiction or both depending on the legislation creating it. (3)

straight-ticket voting Voting for all the candidates of one party. (4)

stratarchy A political system wherein power is diffused among and within levels of party organization. (4)

strong mayor-council form A type of municipal government with a separately elected legislative body (council) and an executive head (mayor) elected in a citywide election with veto, appointment, and removal powers. (3)

substantive committee Appointed by the House Speaker, this committee considers bills and resolutions related to the subject identified by its name (such as the House Agriculture

Committee) and may recommend passage of proposed legislation to the appropriate calendars committee. (7)

suburbanization Growth of relatively small towns and cities, usually incorporated but outside the corporate limits of a central city. (1)

suffrage The right to vote. (2)

sunset review process During a cycle of 12 years, each state agency is studied at least once, and then the legislature decides whether to abolish, merge, reorganize, or retain that agency. (9)

super PAC Independent expenditure-only committees that may raise unlimited sums of money from corporations, unions, nonprofit organizations, and individuals . (5)

superdelegate An unpledged party official or elected official who serves as a delegate to a party's national convention. (4)

Supplemental Nutritional Assistance Program (SNAP) Joint federal-state program administered by the state to provide food to low-income people. (9)

tax A mandatory assessment exacted by a government for a public purpose. (11)

tax reinvestment zone (TRZ) An area in which municipal tax incentives are offered to encourage businesses to locate in and contribute to the development of a blighted urban area. Commercial and residential property taxes may be frozen. (3)

Temporary Assistance for Needy Families (TANF) Provides financial assistance to the poor in an attempt to help poor people move from welfare to the workforce. (9)

temporary party organization Primaries and conventions that function briefly to nominate candidates, pass resolutions, adopt a party platform, and select delegates to party conventions at higher levels. (4)

Tenth Amendment The Tenth Amendment of the U.S. Constitution declares that "the powers not delegated by the Constitution, nor prohibited by it to the States, are reserved to the States, respectively, or to the people." (2)

term limit A restriction on the number of terms officials can serve in a public office. (3)

Texas Commission on Environmental Quality (TCEQ) The state agency that coordinates Texas's environmental protection efforts. (9)

Texas Constitution of 1876 Texas's lengthy, much-amended constitution is a product of the post-Reconstruction era. (2)

Texas Department of Transportation (TxDOT) Headed by a three-member appointed commission, the department maintains almost 80,000 miles of roads and highways and promotes highway safety. (9)

Texas Education Agency (TEA) Administers the state's public school system of more than 1,200 school districts and charter schools. (9)

Texas Election Code The body of state law concerning parties, primaries, and elections. (5)

Texas Equal Legal Rights Amendment (ELRA) Added to Article I, Section 3, of the Texas Constitution, it guarantees that "equality under the law shall not be denied or abridged because of sex, race, color, creed, or national origin." (2)

Texas Essential Knowledge and Skills (TEKS) A core curriculum (a set of courses and knowledge) setting out what students should learn. (9)

Texas Ethics Commission A state agency that enforces state standards for lobbyists and public officials, including registration of lobbyists and reporting of political campaign contributions. (5, 6)

Texas Grange Known as the Patrons of Husbandry, this farmers' organization was well represented in the constitutional convention that produced the Constitution of 1876. (2)

TEXAS Grants Program "Toward Excellence, Access, and Success" is a college financial assistance program that provides funding for qualifying students. (11)

Texas Higher Education Coordinating Board (THECB) An agency that provides some direction for the state's public community colleges and universities. (9)

Texas Parks and Wildlife Department Texas agency that runs state parks and regulates hunting, fishing, and boating. (9)

Texas Water Development Board (TWDB) A board that conducts statewide water planning as mandated by state law. (1)

Texas Workforce Commission (TWC) A state agency headed by three salaried commissioners who oversee job training and unemployment compensation programs. (9)

third party A party other than the Democratic Party or the Republican Party. Sometimes called a "minor party" because of limited membership and voter support. (4)

top 10 percent rule Texas law gives automatic admission into any Texas public college or university to those graduating in the top 10 percent of their Texas high school class with limitations for the University of Texas at Austin. (9)

tort An injury to a person or an individual's property resulting from the wrongful act of another. (10)

traditionalistic culture A product of the Old South, this culture uses government as a means of preserving the status quo and its leadership. (1)

two-thirds rule A procedural device to control bringing bills to the Senate floor for debate. (7)

undocumented alien A person who enters the United States in violation of federal immigration laws. (1)

unicameral A one-house legislature, such as the Nebraska legislature. (7)

universal suffrage Voting is open for virtually all persons 18 years of age or older. (5)

urbanization Migration of people from rural areas to cities. (1)

venire A panel of prospective jurors drawn by random selection. These prospective jurors are called *veniremen*. (10)

verdict A jury's decision about a court case. (10)

veto power Authority of the governor to reject a bill or concurrent resolution passed by the legislature. (8)

voir dire Courtroom procedure whereby attorneys question prospective jurors to identify any who cannot be fair and impartial. (10)

voter registration A qualified voter must register with the county voting registrar, who compiles lists of qualified voters residing in each voting precinct. (5)

voter turnout The percentage of the voting-age population casting ballots in an election. (5)

voting precinct The basic geographic area for conducting primaries and elections; Texas is divided into more than 8,500 voting precincts. (5)

weak mayor-council form A type of municipal government with a separately elected mayor and council, but the mayor shares appointive and removal powers with the council, which can override the mayor's veto. (3)

white primary A nominating system designed to prevent African Americans and some Mexican Americans from participating in Democratic primaries from 1923 to 1944. (5)

women's organization A women's group, such as the League of Women Voters, that engages in lobbying and educational activities to promote greater political participation by women and others. (6)

working class Social scientists identify the working class as those people with blue-collar (manual) occupations. (3)

Index

A

Abbott, Greg, 255, 257, 295–296, 323, 326
Abortion, 146
Adams, Cathie, 142
Addo-Etta, 441–442
Adjudication hearing, 429
ADR. *See* Alternative dispute resolution
Affirmative action, 360, 381
Affirmative racial gerrymandering, 184
AFL-CIO. *See* American Federation of Labor-Congress of Industrial Organizations
African Americans, 7, 15, 38, 46, 256
  candidates, 254, 263
  math scores, 356
  public employment, 350
  public services and, 93
  racial and ethnic group, 20–21
  racial and ethnic politics, 180–181
  students, 351
  Texas Supreme Court justices, 404–405
Agriculture, 27–28
Aguilar, Alfonso, 433
Aguilar, Julián, 46–47
Aiken, A. M., 315
Air pollution, 15
Alcala, Elsa, 178, 404
Alcoholic Beverage Code, 188
Alien, 3
Alternative dispute resolution (ADR), 430
Alternative energy, 25
Amazon, 453
American Bar Association, 417
American Federation of Labor-Congress of Industrial Organizations (AFL-CIO), 214, 216, 218
American Recovery and Reinvestment Act of 2009, 444, 459
"The American Tradition of Language Rights: The Forgotten Right to Government in a 'Known Tongue'", 86–89
Amicus Curiae, 407
Anderson, Ken, 393–394
Anderson, Nick, 90, 134, 170, 250, 392
Andrade, Esperanza ("Hope"), 178, 331
Anglos, 15, 38, 46
  candidates, 177
  immigrants, 86–87
  math scores, 356
  public services and, 93
  racial and ethnic group, 18–19
  students, 351
Annex, 125–126
Annual budget, 463
Anwar, Javaid, 176

Appeal, 419
Appellate courts, 402–404
Appellate jurisdiction, 75, 396
Appointive power, 312–314
Appointment-retention system, 406
Appointments
  Bush, G. W., 180
  judges, 322
  justices, 322
  Perry, R., 151, 178, 180, 312–314, 322, 331, 356, 390
  recess, 313
  Texas Constitution on, 312
  Texas Supreme Court, 178
Apportionment formulas, 254
ASARCO, 389–391
Ashton, Paul, 328
Asian Americans, 21, 38
Atkins v. Virginia, 417
At-large election, 102
At-large majority district, 185
Attorney General, 287–288, 325–326
Austin, Stephen F., 6, 87
Avery v. Midland County, 113
Avison, April, 125

B

Bachmann, Michele, 166
Bailey, Kay, 68
Balanced budget, 448
Ball, Linda Stewart, 433
Ball, Thomas, 441
Barnes, Ben, 293
Barr, Rita, 194
Basin and Range Province, 11
Bell, Chris, 153, 303
Bentsen, Lloyd, 149
Berard, Yamil, 376
Bicameral legislature, 251
Biennial budget, 463
Bifurcated courts, 404
Bills, 276
  bill-signing power, 320
  chief clerk and Speaker signatures, 284
  companion, 278
  conference committee, 284
  consent, 280
  enrollment, 284
  governor action, 284–285
  House committee consideration and report, 280–281
  House first reading, 279–280
  House second reading, 281–282
  House third reading, 282–283

  introduction in House, 278–279
  local, 280
  return to House, 284
  route, 279
  Senate committee consideration and report, 283
  Senate first reading, 283
  Senate second reading, 283–284
  Senate secretary and lieutenant governor signatures, 284
  Senate third reading, 284
Bingo, 457–458
Biotechnology, 26
Birdwell, Brian, 273
Black, Debra, 34
Blakeslee, Nate, 166–168
Blocker, 283
Block grants, 57
Blogging, 172
Blue laws, 7
Boards of regents, 358
Bonds, 116
Bonilla, Ruben, 178
Book of States, 71
Border counties, 117–118
Border Patrol, 30–31
Boyd, Jeff, 309
Bradley, John, 393–394
Brady v. Maryland, 393–394
Branch, Dan, 280–281
Branch, John, 299–300
Bribery, 233–234
Briscoe, Dolph, 72, 313
Brooks, Douglas, 463
Brooks, Karen, 229
Brown, Lyle C., 295–298
Brownsville, 118
Bryant, Megan, 105
Budgets
  accounting, 468–469
  annual compared to biennial, 463
  appropriations, 467
  auditing, 469
  balanced, 448
  budgetary power, 316
  cycle, 465
  defined, 462
  execution, 467–468
  expenditures, 467
  facilities, 468
  pay-as-you-go, 448, 480, 483
  Perry, R., and, 466–467
  policies, 448–449
  preparation, 464, 466–467
  procedure, 462–467

purchasing, 468
   Texas Budget Compact, 445
Bullock, Bob, 325
Bureaucracy, 345–347
Bureaucrats, 345
Bureau of Labor Statistics, U.S., 216
Burklund, Adam, 329
Burnam, Lon, 293
Bush, George H. W., 3
Bush, George W., 3, 31, 53, 56, 303, 325
   appointments, 180
   blind trust, 305
   conservative, 143
   devolution and, 57
   elected governor, 7, 149
   neoconservative, 144
   presidential election, 152–153
   reelection, 187
Bush, Laura, 310–311
Business, 326, 479
   organizations, 211, 215–216
   Perry, R., and, 318
   promotion, 373–376
   taxes, 454–455
Buzbee, Tony, 176

C

Cain, Becky, 103
Cain, Erwin, 280
Calderón, Felipe, 29
Calhoun, John C., 145
Campaign Reform Act, 175
Campaigns, 166–168. See also Voting
   Campaign Legal Center, 173
   eliminating negative, 173
   Federal Election Campaign Act, 175
   finance, 174–177, 230–233
   media in, 170–172, 173–174
   mudslide, 172
   Occupy Wall Street, 168
   Perry, R., 150
   reform, 173–174
   Texas Campaign on the Environment, 25
   in 21st century, 170–173
Canales, J. T., 245
Cantwell, Maria, 390
Canvass, 201
Capital felony, 415
Capital punishment, 146–147
Car crashes, 374
Cargill, Barbara, 313
Carrillo, Victor, 157, 178, 372
Carrizales, Martha, 246–248
Cartels, 29
Casares, Kathy, 32
Castañeda, Carlos, 245
Castro, Eva DeLuna, 365
Castro, Julián, 100, 104
Cattle, 12
Caucuses, 139, 214
   ideological, 273–274
   legislative, 272–274
   party, 272
   racial and ethnic, 272–273
CBP. See Customs and Border Protection
CBSA. See Core-based statistical area

Center for Innovation in Advanced
   Development and Manufacturing, 26
Center for Public Integrity, 238
Center for Public Policy Priorities, 289
Century Council, 152
Certification, 376
Charter schools, 355
Chavez, César, 247–248
ChildLink, 480
Children's Health Insurance Program (CHIP),
   57, 217, 221, 365, 459, 479
Christian Coalition, 143, 150
Chubbing, 282
Cigler, Allan, 211
Cisneros, Henry, 100
Citizens United v. Federal Election
   Commission, 175, 237
Civil justice system, 413–415, 435
Civil law, 394, 413, 435
Civil War, 7, 19, 49, 58
Clark, Tom C., 3
Clayton, Billy, 233, 272
Clean Air Act, 376–377
Clean Water Act, 376
Clements, Bill, 149, 253, 303, 309, 320–321
Clinton, Bill, 53, 149
Closed primary, 198–199
Closing the Gaps, 360
COGs. See Councils of government
Coke, Richard, 64
Colbert, Stephen, 176
Colleges and universities, 357–362
Colonia, 118
Combined Law Enforcement Association, 218
Combined statistical area (CSA), 17
Combs, Susan, 327–328, 330, 444, 453
Commissioner of agriculture, 329–330
Commissioner of education, 354
Commissioner of insurance, 373
Commissioner of the General Land Office,
   328–329
Commissioners court, 113–114
Commission form, 99–100
Committee system, 270–272
Common Cause Texas, 176, 214, 222
Commonwealth Fund, 363
Communication Workers of America, 217
Communities Organized for Public Service
   (COPS), 221
Community colleges, 476
Commutation of sentence, 323
Companion bill, 278
Comptroller of Public Accounts, 287–288
Comptroller of public accounts, 326–328
Concurrent jurisdiction, 396
Concurrent resolution, 275
Conditional pardon, 323
Conference committee, 284
Connally, John, 309
ConocoPhillips, 24
Consent bills, 280
Conservatives, 143–144
Constable, 115
Constitution, Texas, 134
   amendment elections, 69
   amendment process, 68–75
   apportionment formulas, 254
   articles, 80–81

Bill of Rights, 73, 76–78
Coahuila y Tegas of 1827, 60
conclusion, 80–81
constitutional revision, 71–74
Constitution of 1836, 61
Constitution of 1845, 62
Constitution of 1861, 62
Constitution of 1866, 62
Constitution of 1869, 62
Constitution of 1876, 64–65, 70–71, 239
current amendments, 65–67
explanatory statements, 71
framers, 351
historical developments, 59–65
length, 59
local governments, 79–80
piecemeal revision, 74–75
preamble, 59
provisions, 4
re-writing, 74
rights in, 250
separation of powers, 78–79
suffrage, 79
summary, 75–76
Constitution, U.S., 134, 276
   full faith and credit clause, 53
   guarantees, 50–51
   interstate relations, 53–54
   limitations, 51
   powers, 50
   state immunity, 53–54
Constitutional amendment elections, 69
Constitutional amendment process, 68
Constitutional guarantees, 50–51
Constitutional history of Texas, 60
Constitutional revision, 71–74
Constitutional revision convention, 72
Constitutional rights against arbitrary
   governmental actions, 76
Contingency fee, 409
Contingency rider, 316
Conventions, 72, 136–140
Cooley Doctrine, 92
COPS. See Communities Organized for Public
   Service
Core-based statistical area (CBSA), 17
Cornyn, John, 29, 326
Correctional officers, 422, 435
Correction and rehabilitation
   juvenile justice, 427–430
   local government jails, 426–427
   number of prisoners, 421
   private prisons, 427–428
   TDCJ, 420–426
Cotton, 12–13
Council-manager form, 96, 98, 99
Councils of government (COGs), 124–125
County attorney, 114
County auditor, 115
County chair, 141
County clerk, 115
County conventions, 138
County executive committees, 141
County finance, 115
   bonds, 116
   bottom line, 116
   expenditures, 117
   non-tax sources, 116

subsidies, 116
taxation, 116
County government
 border counties, 117–118
 commissioners court, 113–114
 constable, 115
 district attorney, 114
 district court clerk, 114
 expenditures, 109
 finance, 115–117
 Harris County Government, 111
 justice of the peace, 115
 Loving County Government, 112
 reform, 117
 statutory county courts, 114
 structure and operation, 110–115
County judge, 114, 218
County sheriff, 114
County tax appraisal district, 115
County tax assessor, 115
County treasurer, 115
County trial courts, 401–402
Courts. *See also* Judicial procedures; Juries;
 Justices; Supreme Court, Texas; Supreme
 Court, U.S.
 appellate, 402–404
 bifurcated, 404
 conclusion, 434–435
 county trial courts, 401–402
 crowded dockets, 430–431
 DNA evidence, 431
 exoneration issues, 431–434
 judges, 398–399
 justices, 398–399
 lawyers, 407–409
 legislature and, 396
 local trial, 396, 399–401
 municipal, 399
 original jurisdiction, 416
 problems and reforms, 430–434
 public school finance in, 472
 racial and ethnic diversity, 434
 of record, 400
 small claims, 400–401
 state trial, 402
 structure, 397
 technology and, 431
Craddick, Tom, 233–234, 269, 272
Creighton, Brandon, 58
Criminal justice system, 415–419
Criminal law, 394, 435
"Cronies at the Capitol: Connecting the Dots at
 TCEQ," 389–391
Crony capitalism, 338, 340, 389–391
Crossover voting, 199
Crouch, Barry A., 63
Cruz, Ted, 144
CSA. *See* Combined statistical area
Cuba, 29
Cuellar, Henry, 178, 331
Cumulative voting, 102
Customs and Border Protection (CBP), 31

D

Dahlberg, Sandra, 357
Daily Floor Report, 289

Dallas Cowboys, 55
Davidson, Mark, 441
Davis, E. J., 63–64, 145, 300, 303
Davis, Wendy, 257, 283
Dealignment, 156
Death penalty, 394, 417
Death tax, 455
Decentralized government, 211
Dedicated funds, 449
Deepwater Horizon explosion and oil spill, 15,
 380
Defendant, 414
DeLay, Tom, 3, 153, 184, 230, 233–234
 redistricting and, 295
Delegated powers, 50
Delegate selection, 134, 139–140
Democratic Party, 138. *See also* Texas
 Democratic Party
 delegate selection, 139–140
 Jackson Democrats, 145
 SDEC, 136
 Texas Two-Step, 134, 139
Demographic features, 16–18
Deregulation, 372
Devolution, 57
Dewhurst, David, 144, 306, 325, 328, 339, 466
Dietz, John, 78
Dillon's Rule, 92
Direct primary, 197–199
Direct-Record Electronic (DRE), 194–195
Dishonest governing, 449
Distribution of powers, 49–52
District attorney, 114
District conventions, 138
District court clerk, 114
District executive committees, 141
Districting
 multi-member districts, 254
 single-member districts, 254
 state legislative districts, 253–257
 U.S. Congressional districts, 257
Division vote, 282
DNA evidence, 431
Dobie, J. Frank, 12
Doggett, Lloyd, 296
Doggett Amendment, 296
Dole, Bob, 150
Douglas, William O., 394
DRE. *See* Direct-Record Electronic
Driver, Joe, 250, 265
Drought, 34–35
dual budgeting system, 466

E

Early voting, 190–191
Economic development, 25, 36–37, 106–107,
 318
Economic directions, 23
 agriculture, 27–28
 biotechnology, 26
 energy, 24–25
 high technology, 25–26
 services, 26–27
 trade, 28–29
Economic geography, 12–15
Economic interest groups, 215–217

Economic regulatory policy, 371–373
Economic Stabilization Fund, 461
Education, 146, 185, 220. *See also* Schools
 boards of regents, 358
 charter schools, 355
 colleges and universities, 357–362
 commissioner of, 354
 community colleges, 476
 fiscal policies, 474–478
 funding, 476
 issues, 359–361
 legislators, 263–264
 NAEP, 356
 noneducation special districts, 122–123
 policy issues, 36–37
 public schools, 119–120, 351–357, 381,
  472
 rankings, 353
 SBOE, 351–353
 Southwest Voter Registration Education
  Project, 185
 TEA, 344, 353–354, 381
 testing, 355–357
 Texas Democratic Party and, 146
 Texas for Real Efficiency and Equity in
  Education, 211
 Texas Republican Party and, 146
 THECB, 358–359, 381
 top 10 percent rule, 361–362
 tuition deregulation, 476
 voting and, 188
 wet and dry areas, 359
Eighth Amendment, 323
Eisenhower, Dwight D., 149
Elazar, Daniel, 4–6, 8
Electioneering, 228–230, 240
Election judge, 194
Elections. *See also* Primaries
 administering, 189–197
 amendment, 69
 at-large, 102
 Bush, G. W., 7, 149, 152–153, 187
 constitutional amendment, 69
 emergency, 188
 Federal Election Campaign Act, 175
 general, 197–198, 201–202
 governors, 303–304
 legislature, 251–252
 nonpartisan, 100
 Obama, 154, 187, 289
 officials, 192–193
 off-year or midterm, 201
 Perry, R., 149, 153–155, 160, 303
 recall, 94–95, 188
 runoff, 188
 sample ballot, 196
 single-member district, 102
 special, 201–202
 tax levy, 188
 Texas Election Code, 135, 138, 159–160,
  189, 195
Elections administrator, 193
Electoral trends, 156–157
 independents, 159–161
 third parties, 157–159
Electoral votes, 139
Eleventh Amendment, 54
Elite access, 347

Elkins, Gary, 285
Elliott, Janet, 285
Ellis, Natalie, 432–433
Ellis, Rodney, 286
El Paso, 118
ELRA. *See* Texas Equal Legal Rights
    Amendment
Emergency calendar, 280
Emergency elections, 188
Emerging Technology Fund (ETF), 318, 332, 338–
    340
Eminent domain, 68
Employment, 369–370
Energy, 24–25, 146–147
Enhanced Border Security and Visa Entry
    Reform Act of 2002, 31
Enron Corporation, 24
Environmental protection, 35
Environmental Protection Agency (EPA), 25,
    35, 376, 389
Environmental regulation, 376–380
EPA. *See* Environmental Protection Agency
Equal opportunity, 360
ETF. *See* Emerging Technology Fund
ETJ. *See* Extraterritorial jurisdiction
Exclusive jurisdiction, 396
Executive clemency, 322–323
Executive commissioner of the Health and
    Human Services Commission, 365
Executive orders, 316–317
Exoneration issues, 431–434
Expenditures
    county finance, 117
    county government, 109
    municipal (city) government, 109
    school districts, 109
    special district government, 109
    state government, 109
Expense allowance, 265
Explanatory statements, 71
Extraterritorial jurisdiction (ETJ), 125–126
ExxonMobil, 24

F

Facebook, 170, 174, 265
Fagre, Danielle, 103
Farenthold, Frances ("Sissy"), 262
Fayette County Courthouse, 113
FCC. *See* Federal Communications Commission
Federal Communications Commission (FCC),
    372
Federal Election Campaign Act, 175
Federal grants-in-aid, 56
Federalism, 92
Federal-state relations, 56–59
Federal structure, 49, 81
    constitutional guarantees, 50–51
    constitutional limitations, 51
    constitutional powers, 50
    distribution of powers, 49–52
    federal-state relations, 56–59
    privileges and immunity, 53–54
    state powers, 54–56
Federal Voting Rights Act, 101–102
*Fed Up! Our Fight to Save America from
    Washington* (Perry), 58, 155, 167, 303

Fees, 107, 448, 460
Felony, 394
Ferguson, James E. ("Pa"), 307
Ferguson, Miriam A. ("Ma"), 181, 307
Fifteenth Amendment, 183, 184, 186
Fifth Amendment, 55
File and use system, 373
Filibustering, 283
Finance. *See also* County finance; Fiscal
    policies
    campaign, 174–177, 230–233
    Immigration Control and Financial
        Responsibility Act of 1996, 31
    Johnson, L. B., on, 174
    primaries, 201
    public school, 472
    school, 77–78
Fincke, Michael, 192
First Amendment, 76
Fiscal policies. *See also* Budgets; Revenues
    budget, 448–449
    conclusion, 482–483
    defined, 444
    homeland security, 482
    overview, 444–446
    pay-as-you-go, 445, 460
    public assistance, 478–480
    public education, 470–474
    public higher education, 474–478
    public safety, 481–482
    spending, 449–450
    taxing, 446–448
    transportation, 480–481
    tuition deregulation, 476
    water, 481
Fisher v. University of Texas, 361
Flooding, 378
Flowers, Kolby, 198
Fortune 500 companies, 23–24
Fourteenth Amendment, 51, 183, 184
Fox, Vincente, 29
Fracking, 24, 33–34, 372
Fragmentation, 343
Franchise tax, 454
Freedmantowns, 20
Freedom of Information Act, 389
Friedman, Milton, 445
Friedman, Richard S. ("Kinky"), 154, 160, 161,
    173, 303
Frontier experience, 6
Frost, Rebecca, 20
Full faith and credit clause, 53
Full pardon, 322–323
Funnell, Nick, 317
Furgeson, Will, 24

G

Gallegos, Mario, 283
Gambling revenues, 7, 456–457
Garcia, Buddy, 373, 390
Garcia, Gus, 245
Garner, John Nance, 3
Garza, Ben, 245
Garza, Edward, 100
Garza, Tony, 178
General elections, 197–198, 201–202

General Land Office, 328–329
General-law cities, 94
General obligation bonds, 461
General Revenue Fund, 449, 457, 461
General sales tax, 451–454
General state calendar, 281
Gerry, Elbridge, 254
Gerrymandering, 184–185, 254, 258, 296
Ghost voting, 282
Gilbert, Hank, 161
Gingrich, Newt, 167
Glass, Kathie, 164
GMOs, 26
GOBPP. *See* Governor's Office of Budget,
    Planning, and Policy
Gonzales v. Raich, 55–56
Gonzalez, Alberto, 178
González, M. C., 245
Gonzalez, Raul, 20, 150, 178
Gonzalez, Rueben, Jr., 157
Goodwyn, Wade, 207–208
Gore, Al, 152
Government, 86–89, 112. *See also* County
    government; Local governments; Metro
    government; Municipal (city) government;
    Special district government; State
    government
    COGs, 124–125
    decentralized, 211
    defined, 2
    political behavior patterns, 2–4
    structure of Texas, 301
Governor-restricted removal power, 75
Governors. *See also specific governors*
    appointive power, 312–314
    bill-signing power, 320
    budgetary power, 316
    compensation and benefits, 304–305, 309
    conclusion, 332
    economic development, 318
    election, 303–304
    executive clemency, 322–323
    executive orders and proclamations,
        316–318
    executive powers, 311–319
    governorship overview, 300–309
    influence, 287
    informal powers, 310–311
    judges and justices and, 322
    judicial powers, 321–324
    law enforcement power, 315–316
    legislative power, 319–321
    message power, 320
    military power, 315
    office, 307–309
    politics, 302–303
    removal from office, 306–307
    removal power, 314
    security, 304
    special-sessions power, 321
    succession, 305–306
    veto power, 320–321
Governor's Office of Budget, Planning, and
    Policy (GOBPP), 464, 466
Graded Penalties, 415
Grandfather clause, 183
Grand jury, 410, 435
Grant, Ulysses S., 64

Grants-in-aid, 458–459
Grassroots, 91–93
Great Depression, 49, 364
Great Plains, 11
Great Recession, 120–121, 444–445
Great Society, 57, 367
Green, Robert, 132
Greenback Party, 159
Green Party, 152, 159
Groce, Jared, 13
Group leadership, 214
Grutter v. Bollinger, 361
Guerino, Paul, 421
Guinn v. United States, 183
Gulf Coastal Plains, 10
Guns, 6, 250
Gutiérrez, José Ángel, 246–247
Guzman, Eva, 178

H

Hall, Ralph, 172
Hard money, 175
Harle, Sid, 394
Harper v. Virginia State Board of Elections, 183
Harris County Government, 111
Harrison, Paige M., 421
Hazardous waste, 378–379
HCR. *See* House Concurrent Resolution
Health and human services
    HHSC, 364–365, 367, 382
    overview, 363–365
    programs, 365, 367–369
    system, 366
Health and Human Services Commission
    (HHSC), 364–365, 367, 382
Health care, 147, 217
Heflin, Talmadge, 21
Herman, Ken, 487–489
Hernandez, Alfred J., 246
Herrera, Veronica, 52
HHSC. *See* Health and Human Services
    Commission
High technology, 25–26
Hinojosa, Gilberto, 142
Hispanic Women's Network of Texas, 220
HIV/AIDS, 368–369
Hobby, Bill, 72–73
Hogg, James S., 252
Homeland security, 379–380, 482
Home-rule cities, 94, 96, 102
Hopson, Chuck, 263
Hopwood v. Texas, 361
Horwitz, Sari, 194
House Concurrent Resolution (HCR), 58
House Research Organization (HRO), 289
Houston, 15, 190
    diverse political system, 104
    municipal government, 97
    voters, 101
Houston, Sam, 61, 145, 252
Houston Chronicle, 190
Houston Dynamos, 91
HPV. *See* Human Papillomavirus
HPV vaccine, 317
HRO. *See* House Research Organization
Hudson, Darren, 13

Huffman, Joan, 319
Human Papillomavirus (HPV), 317
Hurricane Dolly, 318
Hurricane Ike, 92, 318
Hurricane Katrina, 92
Hurricane Rita, 92
Hutchinson, Kay Bailey, 149, 152, 154–155
    cha-ching ad, 172
    votes received, 181–182

I

ICE. *See* Immigration and Customs
    Enforcement
ICRT. *See* Independent Conservative
    Republicans of Texas
Ideological caucus, 273–274
Immigration, 30–33
Immigration and Customs Enforcement (ICE), 31
Immigration Control and Financial
    Responsibility Act of 1996, 31
Immigration Reform and Control Act of 1986, 30
Immunity, 53–54, 275–277
Impeachment, 277, 306–307
Implied powers, 50
Incorporation theory, 51
Independent candidates, 159–161, 197
Independent Conservative Republicans of
    Texas (ICRT), 273
Independent republic, 5
Independent school districts (ISDs), 119
Individualistic culture, 5
Initiative, 71, 94–95
Institutional Revolutionary Party (PRI), 29
Insurance regulation, 373. *See also* Children's
    Health Insurance Program
Interest groups
    bribery, 233–234
    characteristics, 213–215
    conclusion, 239–240
    defined, 210–211
    economic, 215–217
    electioneering, 228–230
    lobbying, 224–228, 240
    PAC campaign financing, 230–233
    political influence, 238–239
    political power, 239
    power groups, 222–224
    professional groups, 217–219
    public interest groups, 222
    reasons for, 211–212
    regulation, 235–238
    social groups, 219–222
    techniques, 224, 240
Intergovernmental relations, 92
Interior Lowlands, 11
Internet, 172
Interstate relations, 53–54
Investments, 460
ISDs. *See* Independent school districts
Ivins, Molly, 237

J

"Jack County Minute Book A (1870s): The
    Trial of Satanta and Big Tree," 441–442
Jackson, Mike, 306

Jackson, Sheila, 21
Jackson Democrats, 145
Jails, 426–427. *See also* Correction and
    rehabilitation; Prisoners; Prisons
Jefferson, Wallace Bernard, 180, 322, 404–406
Jim Crow laws, 7
Johnson, Alan A., 52
Johnson, Lyndon B., 3, 149
    on finance, 174
    Great Society, 57, 367
Joint resolution, 275
Jones, Anson, 61
Jordan, Barbara, 262
Juarez, José Roberto, 86–89
Judge-made common law, 395
Judges, 395. *See also* Justices
    appointments, 322
    county, 114, 218
    court, 398–399
    disciplining and removing, 406–407
    disposition of cases, 406
    election, 194
    governors and, 322
    influence, 287–288
    salaries, 403
    selection, 404–405
Judgment, 415
Judicial powers, 321–324
Judicial procedures, 412–413
    civil justice system, 413–415, 435
    conclusion, 435
    criminal justice system, 415–419
    special issues, 414–415
    trials, 413–415, 418–419
Junell, Rob, 73, 75, 289
Jungle primary, 199
Junior or community college districts, 120–122
Juries
    grand, 410, 435
    petit, 410, 435
    qualifications, selection, compensation,
        410–412
    trial, 410
    venire, 411–412
    voir dire, 411
Jurisdiction, 394
    appellate, 75, 396
    concurrent, 396
    ETJ, 125–126
    exclusive, 396
    original, 396, 416
Justice gap, 409
Justice of the peace, 115, 400–401
Justices, 115, 400–401
    court, 398–399
    disciplining and removing, 406–407
    governor appointing and removing, 322
    salaries, 403
    Texas Supreme Court, 404–405
Juvenile justice, 427
    agencies, 429
    procedures, 429–430

K

Keller, Sharon, 404, 407
Kelo v. New London, 68

Kenedy, Mifflin, 12
Kerry, John, 153, 207
Key, Jeff, 26, 338–340
Kilday, Anne Marie, 237
Kilgarlin v. Martin, 254
Kimbrough, Jay, 309
Kinch, Sam, 237
King, Martin Luther, Jr., 247
King, Richard, 12
King James Bible, 251
King Ranch, 12
Kirchoff, Alan, 339
Kirk, Ron, 21, 104, 152, 180
KKK. *See* Ku Klux Klan
Kroger, Bill, 441–442
Ku Klux Klan (KKK), 183

L

Labor organizations, 216–217
Land
    area in square miles, 8
    economic geography, 12–15
    physical regions, 10–11
    politics of geography, 9–11
    revenues, 459
Landslides, 171
Laney, Pete, 175, 272
"Laredo's Modest Advocate," 132
Latinos, 15, 38, 46, 256–257
    candidates, 254, 263
    Latino opportunity districts, 102
    math scores, 356
    private employment, 350
    public services and, 93
    racial and ethnic group, 19–20
    racial and ethnic politics, 177–180
    students, 351
Law enforcement power, 315–316
Lawrence v. Texas, 101
Laws. *See also* State law; *specific laws and acts*
    blue, 7
    civil, 394, 413, 435
    criminal, 394, 435
    Jim Crow, 7
    judge-made common, 395
    martial law, 315
    motor-voter law, 186, 190
Lawyers
    computerized assistance, 409
    legal aid for poor, 408–409
    State Bar of Texas and, 407–408
LBB. *See* Legislative Budget Board
League of United Latin American Citizens
    (LULAC), 177–178, 185, 219, 223, 257
    influence, 297–298
    Perales as father of, 245–248
League of Women's Voters of Texas, 220
Lee, Thomas J., 262
Legal Aid, 409
Legal services, 408–409
Legislative Budget Board (LBB), 462–467
Legislative power, 319–321
Legislators
    compensation, 265–266
    education and occupation, 263–264

experience, 264
gender and ethnic classifications, 262
political parties, 263
qualifications and characteristics,
    259–264
religion, 264
retirement pension, 266
women, 262
work of, 250
Legislature
    bicameral, 251
    caucus system, 272–274
    committee system, 270–272
    conclusion, 290
    courts and, 396
    districting, 253–258
    election and terms of office, 251–252
    framework, 250–259
    influences, 287–290
    internships, 286
    lingo, 289
    operations, 274–286
    powers and immunities, 275–277
    presiding officers, 267–270
    procedure, 278–286
    regular session, 252–253
    seats, 253
    special sessions, 252–253
    unicameral, 251
Leininger, James, 289
Lewis, Gib, 233, 272
Liberals, 144
Libertarian Party, 152, 158–159, 164, 172
Lieutenant governor, 284, 291, 325
Line-item veto, 316
Literacy tests, 183
Lobbying, 240, 297
    defined, 224
    favors and gifts, 228
    full and part-time, 225
    grassroots activities, 228
    personal communication, 226–227
Lobbyists, 288, 297
Local bills, 280
Local governments, 79–80
    challenges, 92–93
    comparing with Texas state, 73
    conclusion, 126–127
    federalism and, 92
    jails, 426–427
    overview, 90–91
Logan, Charles H., 328
Logjams, 282
Longhorns, 12
Loomis, Burnett, 211
Loser Pay Tort, 319
Loss ratio, 373
"Lots of GOP Money Flowing from the Texas
    Two," 207–208
Lottery, 7, 457
Loving County Government, 112
"The Low Politics of High Tech in the Lone
    Star State," 338–340
Lozano, Jose, 263
LULAC. *See* League of United Latin American
    Citizens
LULAC v. Perry, 220

M

Madden, Jerry, 424
Major state calendar, 281
MALDEF. *See* Mexican American Legal
    Defense and Education Fund
Manifest Destiny, 86
Maquiladoras, 28
Markle Commission on Media and Electorate,
    173
Marriage Act, 53
Martial law, 315
Martindale-Hubbell Legal Directory, 408
Mattox, Jim, 172
Mauro, Gerry, 328
McCain, John, 154, 187, 207
McCall, Brian, 300
McConnell v. FEC, 175
McDonald, Craig, 208, 230
McKinney, Mike, 309
McLeroy, Don, 313
Media
    in campaigns, 170–172, 173–174
    increasing free, 173–174
    influence, 290
Medicaid, 56, 363, 367–368, 454, 462
Medicare, 364, 367–368, 454
Medina, David, 178
Medina, Debra, 155, 232
Merit system, 338
Message power, 320
Metro Alliance, 221
Metro government, 123
    COGs, 124–125
    municipal annexation, 125–126
Metropolitan division, 17
Metropolitanization, 17
Metropolitan statistical area (MSA), 17
Mexican American Legal Defense and
    Education Fund (MALDEF), 185, 220
Mexican Americans, 7, 185
Micromanagement, 99
Micropolitan statistical area (MSA), 17–18
Middle class, 99
Middle of the ballot candidates, 171
La Migra, 30–31
Military power, 315
Miller, Sid, 280
"Minorities Drove Texas Growth, Census
    Figures Show," 46–47
Minority opportunity district, 130
Misdemeanor, 394
Missouri Plan, 405
Moneyhon Carl H., 63
Monsanto, 26
Montford, John, 73
Moore, Michelle, 432
Morales, Dan, 178, 179
Moralistic culture, 4–5
Moreno, Paul, 266
Morgan, Katherine, 475
Morrow, William, 339
Morton, Christine, 393
Morton, Michael, 393–394, 431
Motor-voter law, 186, 190
MSA. *See* Metropolitan statistical area;
    Micropolitan statistical area

Mudslide campaigns, 172
Multi-member districts, 254
Munguia, Ruben, 246
Municipal annexation, 125–126
Municipal bonds, 107
Municipal courts, 399
Municipal (city) government
    commission, 99–100
    council-manager, 96, 98, 99
    economic development, 106–107
    expenditures, 109
    forms of, 95–100
    Houston, 97
    internships, 105
    legal status, 94–95
    micromanagement, 99
    politics, 100–104
    revenues, 106–108
    San Antonio, 98
    services, 104–105
    socioeconomic changes, 103–104
    strong mayor-council, 95–97
    weak mayor-council, 96
    zoning, 104–105
Municipal revenues
    bottom line, 108
    fees, 107
    municipal bonds, 107
    municipal (city) government, 106–108
    property tax, 106–107
    tax exemptions, 107–108
Munisteri, Steve, 142
Murdock, Steve, 46
Murphy, Ryan, 46–47
Mutscher, Gus, 233
MySpace, 174

N

NAACP. *See* National Association for the
    Advancement of Colored People
NAACP v. Alabama, 211
NAEP. *See* National Assessment of Education
    Progress
NAFTA. *See* North American Free Trade
    Agreement
Najmuddin, Farrah, 286
Nance, C. J., 339
Nance, David, 339
National Assessment of Education Progress
    (NAEP), 356
National Association for the Advancement of
    Colored People (NAACP), 7, 185, 219
National Conference of State Legislatures,
    53, 229
National Education Association, 57
National Federation of Independent Business v.
    Sebelius, 326, 479
National Research University Fund, 66
National Rifle Association (NRA), 214
National supremacy clause, 50
National Voter Registration Act of 1993, 186.
    See also Motor-voter law
National Women's Political Caucus, 214
Native Americans, 6, 22–23, 38
Navarro, Jose Antonio, 61
Nelson, WIllie, 161, 173

Neoconservative, 144
Neoliberals, 144
Newby, Brian, 309
Newton, Jan, 344
Nieto, Enrique Pena, 29
Nineteenth Amendment, 186
No Child Left Behind, 57, 356
Noncapital offenses, 416
Noncontroversial resolutions, 280
Noneducation special districts, 122–123
Nonpartisan elections, 100
Nontax revenues, 458–460
Noodling, 395
North American Free Trade Agreement
    (NAFTA), 28–29, 117–118
Norwood, Mark Alan, 393
NRA. *See* National Rifle Association
Nugent, Ted, 173

O

Obama, Barack, 57, 140, 207, 256, 376, 459
    election race, 187
    iPhone application, 174
    Patient Protection and Affordable Care
        Act, 326
    presidential election, 154, 289
    State of the Union address, 176
Occupy Wall Street campaign, 168
O'Conner, Karen J., 2
O'Daniel, W. Lee ("Pappy"), 170–171, 173, 320
Off-year or midterm election, 201
Ogg, Frederic A., 307
Oil, 14–15, 23, 214, 380
One-person, one-vote, 113
Open primary, 199
Optical scan, 194–195
Ordinances, 94–95
Organizational patterns, 214
Original jurisdiction, 396, 416
Orr, Rob, 280
Ortiz, Casandra, 344
Ortiz, Solomon, 132, 151
Oversight, 276

P

PACs. *See* Political action committees
Panhandle region, 9, 255
Parker, Annise, 101, 181
Parliamentarian, 278
Parole, 322, 425
Party caucus, 272
Party line, 263
Patient Protection and Affordable Care Act of
    2010, 56, 326, 363
Patrick, Dan, 273
Patronage system, 348
Patrón system, 7
Patterson, Jerry, 328–329
Paul, Ron, 159, 166–168
Pay-as-you-go, 445, 448, 460, 480, 483
Payne, Ryan Lofton, 479
Payroll taxes, 454
Pay-to-play, 338
Peña, Aaron, 156

People, 15
    demographic features, 16–18
    population estimates, 2011, 16
    population shifts, 16
    racial and ethnic groups, 18–23
Perales, Alonso, S., 245–248
Perales, Mary, 246
Per diem allowance, 265
Perla, Albert, 245
Permanent party organization, 135
    county and district executive committees, 141
    defined, 140
    precinct chair, 140–141
    state executive committee, 141–142
Permits, 460
Perot, Ross, 158
Perry, Anita, 304
Perry, Bob, 207–208, 303–304
Perry, Rick, 7, 25–26, 33, 35, 37, 132
    Aggie governor, 305
    appointments, 151, 178, 180, 312–314,
        322, 331, 356, 390
    bailout commercial, 172
    bill signing, 176, 255
    blind trust, 305
    budgets and, 466–467
    business and, 318
    campaigning, 150
    Century Council, 152
    Combs and, 327
    commissioners, 354
    debates, 159, 166–167
    elected governor, 149, 153–155, 160, 303
    endorsements for, 229
    ETF and, 338–340
    executive orders, 317
    full pardon by, 323
    fundraising, 232, 302–303
    lobby day, 225
    long tenure, 343
    Loser Pay Tort, 319
    Medicaid and, 368
    military service, 304
    PAC created by, 237
    personal interests, 310
    presidential nomination sought by, 173,
        300, 304, 306
    primaries and, 173
    rainy day fund and, 461, 464
    redistricting, 257
    special sessions, 252, 295
    spending, 174, 450
    staff, 309
    State of the State address, 252, 475
    states' rights and, 58
    Tea Party movement and, 144
    Texas Budget Compact, 445
    Texas constitutional amendments and, 65
    TTC, 375
    on tuition, 179
    vetoes, 316, 321, 453
Petit jury, 410, 435
Physical regions, 10–11
Pickens, T. Boone, 122
Pilgrim, Lonnie ("Bo"), 175
Pippin, Tracie, 441
Pit Bulls, 309

Pitts, Jim, 269
Plaintiff, 414, 419
Planned Parenthood, 58, 274, 368
Platform, 136
Plural executive, 324
Pluralist, 103
Police power, 54
Policy issues
    economic development, 36–37
    education, 36–37
    environmental protection, 35
    immigration, 30–33
    poverty, 37
    social problems, 37
    water, 33–35
Political action committees (PACs), 175–177,
    288. *See also specific PACs*
    campaign financing, 230–233
    defined, 230
    Perry, R., creating, 237
Political behavior patterns, 2–5
Political culture, 4–5
Political ideology, 142–143, 211
Political inefficacy, 5
Political influence
    governors, 287
    interest groups, 238–239
    judges, 287–288
    legislature, 287–290
    LULAC, 297–298
    media, 290
Political parties. *See also* Democratic Party
    conclusion, 162
    conservatism, 143–144
    controlling statehouses, 160
    defined, 134
    delegate selection, 134
    electoral trends, 156–161
    ideology, 142–143
    legislators, 263
    liberalism, 144
    one-party dominant system, 148–149
    party caucus, 272
    permanent party organization, 135, 140–142
    selection of national convention delegates,
        139–140
    strength of system, 211
    structure, 134–141
    temporary party organization, 135–139
    Texas origins, 145–148
    two-party system, 149–151
Politics. *See also* Racial and ethnic politics
    behavior patterns, 2–4
    defined, 2
    of geography, 9–11
    governors, 302–303
    municipal (city) government, 100–104
    pork-barrel, 320
    taxation, 450–455
    women in, 181–182
Poll tax, 183
Pollution, 376, 382
Population, 2. *See also* People
    distribution, 16
    shifts, 16
Populist Party, 148–149, 158
Pork-barrel politics, 320

Porter, David, 371
Positive behavioral changes, 423–424
Postadjournment veto, 321
Poverty, 37, 363–364
Powell, Lewis, 409
Power groups, 222–224
Power of eminent domain, 54–55
The Power of the Texas Governor (McCall), 300
Precinct chair, 140–141
Precinct conventions, 137–138
Presidential preference primary, 139
President of the Senate, 267–268
PRI. *See* Institutional Revolutionary Party
Primaries, 136
    administering, 200–201
    closed, 198–199
    conducting, 197–201
    defined, 197
    direct, 197–199
    financing, 201
    jungle, 199
    open, 199
    Perry, R., and, 173
    presidential preference, 139
    runoff, 198
    Texas, 199–200
    types, 200
    white, 183–184
Prindle, Jim, 172
Prisoners, 421
    characteristics, 423
    reintegration, 424–426
Prisons, 427–428, 439
Private prisons, 427–428
Privileges, 53–54
Probate, 401
Procedural committees, 270–271
Proclamations, 316–318
Professional groups, 217–219
Progressive Party, 159
Progressive taxes, 446
Prohibition Party, 159
Property tax, 75, 106–107
Proprietary power, 54
Public administration, 345
Public assistance, 478–480
Public Citizen, 176–177
Public debt, 460–462
Public easement, 403
Public interest groups, 222
Public officer and employee group, 218
Public policy. *See also* Education; Health and
    human services
    boards for, 343–345
    bureaucracy and, 345–347
    business promotion, 373–376
    conclusion, 380–381
    court problems and reforms, 430–434
    defined, 3
    economic regulatory policy, 371–373
    elite access and, 347
    employment, 369–370
    environmental regulation, 376–380
    fragmentation and, 343
    homeland security, 379–380
    institutional context for, 343–345
    political behavior patterns, 2–4

    state agencies and, 342–350, 381
    state employees and, 342–350, 381
    sunset review process, 344–345, 381
Public safety, 421–423
Public schools, 351–357, 381
    districts, 119–120
    finance, 472
Public services, 93
Public Utilities Commission (PUC), 344, 372–
    373, 377
Punch-card ballots, 195
Puritanism, 4

R

Racial and ethnic groups, 219
    African Americans, 20–21
    Anglos, 18–19
    Asian Americans, 21
    Latinos, 19–20
    Native Americans, 22–23
Racial and ethnic politics
    African Americans, 180–181
    caucuses, 272–273
    Latinos, 177–180
    legislators, 262
Racial gerrymandering, 184–185
Racing, 456–457
Railroad Commission of Texas (RRC), 14, 150,
    180, 344, 371–372
Rainy day fund, 445, 461, 464
Ramsdell, Charles William, 63
Ramsey, Ross, 46–47, 208
Raney, John, 202
Ratcliff, R. G., 225
Ratliff, Bill, 73, 325
Rayburn, Sam, 3, 257
Raza Unida Party, 178, 246
Reagan, Ronald, 167
Realignment, 156
Recall elections, 94–95, 188
"Recent Congressional Redistricting in Texas,"
    295–298
Recess appointments, 313
Recidivism, 323
Reconstruction, 63–64, 78, 145, 184
Redistricting, 100–101, 153, 253
    DeLay and, 295
    Perry, R., and, 257
Referendum, 94–95
Reform Party, 158
Regressive taxes, 446
Regular session, 252–253
Religion
    legislators, 264
    religious-based groups, 221
    religious freedom, 76
Removal power, 75, 314, 322
Reprieve, 323
Republican Party, 134. *See also* Texas
    Republican Party
    delegate selection, 140
    nonbinding resolutions, 137
    rules, 138
    SREC, 136–138
Research organizations, 288–290
Reserved powers, 54

Revenue bond, 461
Revenues. *See also* Municipal revenues
   fees, permits, investments, 460
   gambling, 7, 456–458
   grants-in-aid, 458–459
   land, 459
   nontax, 458–460
   projected sources, 452
   public debt and, 460–462
   taxation politics, 450–455
   tobacco suit, 459–460
Reyna, Israel, 132
Reynolds v. Sims, 254
Richards, Ann, 149, 155, 172, 174
Richards, Cécile, 221
Rights, 79, 86–89, 101–102. *See also* Texas Bill
   of Rights; Voting Rights Act of 1965
   against arbitrary governmental actions, 76
   of association, 211
   civil, 245–248
   of criminals and victims, 77
   ELRA, 77
   equal rights for women, 77
   states, 58
   in Texas Constitution, 250
   to-work, 72
   Women's Right to Know Act of 2003, 369
Ritter, Allan, 156, 263
Robin Hood plan, 473
Romney, Mitt, 140, 166, 176, 207, 304
Roosevelt, Franklin D., 57
Roosevelt, Theodore, 161
Roper v. Simmons, 323, 417
Rosenthal, Alan, 250
Rove, Karl, 207
RRC. *See* Railroad Commission of Texas
Ruiz, Francisco, 61
Runoff elections, 188
Runoff primary, 198
Ryan, Brint, 176
Rylander, Carole Keeton, 181–182

S

Sabol, William J., 421
Sáenz, Jose Luz, 245
Saldaña, Hector, 245–248
Same-sex marriage, 65–66
San Antonio, 98, 106
Sánchez, George, 245
Sanchez, Tony, 152, 174, 179, 303
Sanctuary Cities bill, 33
Sanford, Terry, 49
San Jacinto battle flag, 251–252
Santa Anna, Antonio Lopez de, 61
Santorum, Rick, 166, 176, 207
Sargent, Ben, 443
Satank, 441–442
Satanta, 441–442
SBOE. *See* State Board of Education
Schools. *See also* Public schools
   charter, 355
   districts, 109
   finance, 77–78
   ISDs, 119
   prayer, 143
   vouchers, 147–148

Schotland, Roy, 405
Scott, Chris, 432–433
Scott v. Painter, 360
SDEC. *See* State Democratic Executive
   Committee
Secretary of State, 330–332
Secure Fence Act, 31
SEED. *See* Sustainable Energy and Economic
   Development
Seguin, Juan N., 61
Select committees, 270–271
Selective sales taxes, 453
Senate Research Center, 289
Senatorial courtesy, 277
Sentence, 419
Separation of powers, 78–79
September 11 terrorist attacks, 31, 379
Services, 26–27
Service-sector, 447
Severance taxes, 455
Severence v. Patterson, 329
Sexting, 395
Sexually transmitted diseases (STDs), 369
Shale, Barnett, 372
Shankle, Glenn, 391
Shannon, Kelly, 317
Shapleigh, Eliot, 389–391
Sharp, John, 152, 303, 325
Sharpstown Bank scandal, 233
Shaw v. Reno, 184
Shea, Gwyn, 331
Shivers, Alan, 149, 150
Sierra Club, 3, 25
Simmons, Annette, 207
Simmons, Claude, 432–433
Simmons, Gene, 173
Simmons, Harold, 176, 207–208
Simple resolution, 275
Sinclair, Nick, 168
Single-member district election, 102
Single-member districts, 102, 254
Sin taxes, 453
Sixth Amendment, 408
Small claims court, 400–401
Smith, Carter, 487–488
Smith, Tom ("Smitty"), 177
Smitherman, Barry T., 372
Smith v. Allwright, 184
SNAP. *See* Supplemental Nutrition Assistance
   Program
Snell, Ronald K., 463
SOAH. *See* State Office of Administrative
   Hearings
Social conservatives, 356
Social interest groups, 219–222
Social problems, 37
Social Security, 147–148, 364
Socioeconomic changes, 103–104
Soft money, 175
Sound bites, 171–172
Southwest Voter Registration Education
   Project, 185
Soward, Charles, 441
Spam, 172
Speaker of the House, 268–270, 272, 274, 291
   bill signature, 284
   succession, 306

Special district, 119
Special district government
   expenditures, 109
   junior or community college districts,
      120–122
   noneducation special districts, 122–123
   public school, 119–120
Special elections, 201–202
Special interim committees, 270
Special issues, 414–415
Special sessions, 252–253, 285, 295, 321
Special Supplemental Nutrition Program for
   Women, Infants, and Children (WIC), 368
*SpeechNow.org v. Federal Election
   Commission*, 176
Speed limits, 395
Spending policies, 174, 449–450
SREC. *See* State Republican Executive
   Committee
Standing committees, 270–271
Staples, Todd, 29
STARR. *See* State of Texas Assessment of
   Academic Readiness
State agencies, 342–350, 381
State Bar of Texas, 217, 407–408
State Board of Education (SBOE), 351–353
State conventions, 138–139
State Democratic Executive Committee
   (SDEC), 136
State employees, 381
   competence, pay, retention, 348–350
   incentives, 350
   numbers of, 347–348
   public policy and, 342–350
State executive committee, 141–142
State government
   comparing with Texas local, 73
   expenditures, 109
State immunity, 53–54
State law
   civil, 394
   code revision, 395
   criminal, 394
   judge-made common law, 395
   sources, 394–395
State Office of Administrative Hearings
   (SOAH), 312
State of Texas Assessment of Academic
   Readiness (STAAR), 355–356
State powers, 54–56
State Republican Executive Committee (SREC),
   136–138
State trial courts, 402
Statutory county courts, 114
STDs. *See* Sexually transmitted diseases
Steakley, Zollie, 332
Stiles, Matt, 46–47, 226
Straight-ticket voting, 157
Stratarchy, 134
Straus, Joe, 269, 272, 306, 339, 466
Strauss, Annette, 181
Strayhorn, Carole Keeton, 154, 160, 303
Streamlined Sales Tax Project, 452
Strong mayor-council form, 95–97
Subsidies, 116
Substantive committees, 270–271
Suburbanization, 17

Suffrage, 79
Sullivan, Ray, 309
Sunset review process, 344–345, 381
Superdelegate, 139–140
SuperPAC, 176, 207
Supplemental Nutrition Assistance Program
    (SNAP), 364–365, 367
Supreme Court, Texas
    appointments to, 178
    Constitutional Revision Commission
        established, 72
    on executive officers, 305
    on governor's security, 304
    justices, 404–405
    on school finance, 77–78
    structure and sessions, 404–405
Supreme Court, U.S., 51, 176, 363. *See also*
    specific cases
    on eminent domain, 68
    one-person, one-vote, 113
    on power of eminent domain, 55
    on privileges and immunities, 53–54
    on tax collection, 452
Sustainable Energy and Economic
    Development (SEED), 25
"The Swan Song of Ron: Searching for
    Meaning in What Is Likely to Be the Last
    Campaign Ron Paul Ever Runs," 166–168
Swinford, David, 285
System Benefit Fund, 449

T

TAB. *See* Texas Association of Business
TAKS. *See* Texas Assessment of Knowledge
    and Skills
TANF. *See* Temporary Assistance for Needy
    Families
Taxes
    amnesty, 456
    burden, 455
    business, 454–455
    collection, 455–456
    county finance, 116
    death, 455
    exemptions, 107–108
    franchise, 454
    general sales tax, 451–454
    incentives, 116
    levy elections, 188
    payroll, 454
    per capita, 447
    progressive, 446
    property, 75, 106–107
    regressive, 446
    selective sales, 453
    severance, 455
    sin, 453
    Streamlined Sales Tax Project, 452
    taxation politics, 450–455
    taxing policy, 446–448
    unusual, 448
    U.S. Supreme Court on collection, 452
Tax reinvestment zones (TRZs), 109
TCEQ. *See* Texas Commission on
    Environmental Quality

TDJC. *See* Texas Department of Criminal Justice
TEA. *See* Texas Education Agency
Tea Party movement, 144, 155, 168, 208,
    270, 273
Tea Party Patriots, 144
TEF. *See* Texas Enterprise Fund
TEG. *See* Texas Equalization Grants
TEKS. *See* Texas Essential Knowledge and Skills
Temporary Assistance for Needy Families
    (TANF), 364–365, 367
Temporary party organization, 135–139
    components, 136
    county and district conventions, 138
    precinct conventions, 137–138
    state conventions, 138–139
Tenth Amendment, 49–50, 56, 58
Term limits, 102–103
Terrorism, 29, 31
Texans for Public Justice, 235–237
Texas Almanac, 75–76
Texas Assessment of Knowledge and Skills
    (TAKS), 356
Texas Association of Builders, 216
Texas Association of Business (TAB), 211,
    215–216
Texas Association of College Teachers, 217
Texas Bill of Rights, 73, 76–78
Texas Budget Compact, 445
Texas Campaign on the Environment, 25
Texas Capitol, 80
Texas Coalition to Abolish the Death
    Penalty, 210
Texas Code of Criminal Procedure, 418
Texas Commission on Environmental Quality
    (TCEQ), 35, 377, 379, 389–391
Texas Community College Teachers
    Association, 217
Texas Declaration of Independence, 88–89, 250
Texas Democratic Party
    abortion and, 146
    capital punishment and, 146
    education and, 146
    energy and, 146–147
    environment and, 147
    health care and, 147
    school vouchers and, 147
    social security and, 147–148
    strength of, 148–149
    voter registration and, 148
Texas Department of Criminal Justice (TDCJ)
    correctional officers, 422, 435
    facilities, 422
    mission, 420
    offenders reintegrated by, 424–426
    positive behavioral changes promoted by,
        423–424
    prisoner characteristics, 423
    public safety provided by, 421–423
    victim assistance, 426
Texas Department of Transportation
    (TxDOT), 374
Texas Education Agency (TEA), 344,
    353–354, 381
Texas Election Code, 135, 138, 159–160,
    189, 195
    violations, 236
Texas Emerging Technology Fund, 26

Texas Enterprise Fund (TEF), 318, 332
Texas Equalization Grants (TEG), 67, 210
Texas Equal Legal Rights Amendment
    (ELRA), 77
Texas Essential Knowledge and Skills (TEKS),
    352, 355
Texas Ethics Commission, 175–177, 225, 231
    authorization, 236
    charge of, 240
    creation, 235
    lobbyists registering, 288
    review of, 238
Texas Fair Defense Act, 418
Texas Family Code, 430, 435
Texas Federation of Teachers, 217
Texas for a Republican Majority (TRMPAC),
    233–234
Texas for Lawsuit Reform, 216
Texas for Public Justice, 222
Texas for Real Efficiency and Equity in
    Education, 211
Texas Freedom Network, 221
Texas Gaming Association, 216
Texas Grange, 64
TEXAS Grants Program, 67, 478
Texas Guaranteed Tuition Plan and
    Tomorrow's College Investment Plan, 477
Texas Health Care Association, 217
Texas Higher Education Coordinating Board
    (THECB), 358–359, 381
Texas individualism, 5–7
Texas Industrial Areas Foundation, 221
Texas Lawyers for Texas Veterans, 409
Texas Legislative Council, 288–289
Texas Lobby Watch, 237
Texas Medical Association (TMA), 217–218, 223
Texas Mid-Continent Oil and Gas
    Association, 214
Texas Monthly, 290
Texas Municipal Police Association, 218
Texas Observer, 290
Texas Parks and Wildlife Department, 375–
    376, 487–489
Texas Penal Code, 415, 416
Texas political culture
    changing, 8
    frontier experience, 6
    independent republic, 5
    Texas individualism, 5–7
    Texas traditionalism, 7–8
Texas political history
    1840s to 1870s, 145–148
    1870s to 1970s, 148–149
    1970s to 1990s, 149–151
    2000 to 2012, 151–156
Texas Public Employees Association, 218
Texas Public Policy Foundation (TPPF),
    289–290
Texas Rangers, 315–316, 339
Texas Republican Party
    abortion and, 146
    capital punishment and, 146–147
    dominance, 151–156
    education and, 146
    energy and, 147
    environment and, 147
    health care and, 147

officeholders, 153
school vouchers and, 147–148
social security and, 148
strength of, 149
voter registration and, 148
Texas Residential Construction Commission, 344
Texas Salary Commission, 75
Texas Society of Certified Public
    Accountants, 217
Texas State Employees Union, 217
Texas State Teachers Association (TSTA),
    217–218, 228
Texas Sunset Advisory Commission, 238
Texas traditionalism, 7–8
Texas Trial Lawyers Association, 211
Texas Two-Step, 134, 139
Texas Unemployment Compensation Act, 370
Texas v. Whit, 51
Texas Water Development Board (TWDB),
    33, 378
Texas Workforce Commission (TWC), 27,
    369–370
Texas Young Lawyers Association (TYLA), 408
Texas Youth Commission (TYC), 345, 427, 435
Textbooks, 352–353, 371
THECB. See Texas Higher Education
    Coordinating Board
Third parties, 157–159
Thomason, Robert E., 52
Thompson, Robert Lee, 323
Throw one's hat into the ring, 161
Timber, 13–14
TMA. See Texas Medical Association
Tobacco suit, 459–460
Toomey, Mike, 176, 317
Top 10 percent rule, 361–362
Tort, 413
Tourism, 375–376
Tower, John, 149
TPPF. See Texas Public Policy Foundation
Trade, 28–29
Traditionalistic culture, 5
Transportation, 480–481
Trans Texas Corridor (TTC), 375
Treaty of Guadalupe Hidalgo, 62
Trevino, Fernando, Jr., 151, 313
Trial jury, 410
TRMPAC. See Texas for a Republican Majority
Trump, Donald, 167
TRZs. See Tax reinvestment zones
TSTA. See Texas State Teachers Association
TTC. See Trans Texas Corridor
Tuition deregulation, 476
Turner, Sylvester, 449
TWC. See Texas Workforce Commission
TWDB. See Texas Water Development Board
Twenty-First Amendment, 51, 276
Twenty-Fourth Amendment, 183, 186
Twenty-Sixth Amendment, 186
Twitter, 170, 173, 174, 265
Two-thirds rule, 194, 283
TxDOT. See Texas Department of Transportation
TYC. See Texas Youth Commission
TYLA. See Texas Young Lawyers Association

Undocumented aliens, 30
Unicameral legislature, 251
United States v. Lopez, 55
Universal suffrage, 182
University of California v. Bakke, 360
"Unsung Hero of Civil Rights: 'Father
    of LULAC' a Fading Memory,"
    245–248
Urbanization, 17
U.S. News and World Report, 351

Valdez, Avelardo, 247
Valero, 24
Valley Interfaith, 221
Van de Putte, Leticia, 274
Van Ryzin, Jeanne Claire, 171
Vaughn, Edward, 34
Vela, Jose, 132
Venire, 411–412
Verdict, 415, 419
Vernon's Texas Statues and Codes
    Annotated, 395
Vetoes, 287
    of Clements, 320–321
    line-item, 316
    overriding, 285
    of Perry, R., 316, 321, 453
    postadjournment, 321
    power, 320–321
Victim assistance, 426
Vietnam War, 211
Virginia Tech shootings, 250
Vo, Hubert, 21–22
Voir dire, 411
Voters
    registration, 148, 183
    turnout, 187–189
Voting. See also Elections
    conclusion, 202
    crossover, 199
    democratization of ballot, 185–187
    division vote, 282
    early, 190–191
    education and, 188
    ghost, 282
    Hutchinson votes received, 181–182
    obstacles to, 182–185
    Photo ID for, 193–194
    precinct, 192
    qualifications for, 189–190
    from space, 191–192
    systems, 194–197
    trends, 186–187
    voter registrations, 183
    voter turnout, 187–189
Voting Rights Act of 1965, 79, 185–186, 220,
    255–257
    requirements, 295
    violations, 296

Wainwright, Dale, 180
Walker, David, 49
Walthall, Roy, 73
Ward, Mike, 194
Warren, Henry, 441
Warren, Kelcy, 176
Waste Control Specialists (WCS), 389, 391
Watchdogs, 376
Water, 33–35, 481
Watson, Kirk, 326
WCS. See Waste Control Specialists
Weak mayor-council form, 96
Weddington, Susan, 150
Wentworth, Jeff, 250, 295, 297–298
Werner, James, 303
Wet and dry areas, 359
White, Bill, 102–103, 155, 229, 232
White, Hattie, 21
White, Thelma, 52
White primary, 183–184
WIC. See Special Supplemental Nutrition
    Program for Women, Infants, and Children
Wildfires, 2
Wilkins, Charles Jerry, 295–298
Willett, Don, 322
Williams, Clayton, 174
Williams, J. Roger, 331
Williams, Michael, 180, 356
Williams, Patrick G., 63
Williams-Sonoma Inc., 452
Wills, Bob, 173
Wilson, Phil, 331
Wilson, Reid, 158
Women, 220, 369
    equal rights for, 77
    legislators, 262
    National Women's Political Caucus, 214
    organizations, 220
    in politics, 181–182
    Texas Supreme Court justices, 404–405
    WIC, 368
Women's Right to Know Act of 2003, 369
Woolfolk, Joseph, 441
Working class, 99
Workman, Paul D., 319
World War II, 19
Wright, Jim, 3

Yancey, Bob, 202
Yawn, R. Mike, 105
YouTube, 265, 282

Zamora, Emilio, 246–247
Zapata, 227
Zavala, Lorenzo de, 61
Zoning, 104–105